Praise for

The Shakespeare Wars

"*The Shakespeare Wars*: a conversation, a debate, a polemic, a memoir, a seduction, an ecstasy! . . . Electrifying. A spectacular book."

—Cynthia Ozick

"Everyone seriously interested in Shakespeare *must* read [it], and anyone even mildly interested *should.* Mr. Rosenbaum possesses . . . a restlessly inquiring mind, a vivid style, a welcome sense of humor, and an impressive knowledge of not only Shakespeareana but also much else besides."

—John Simon, *The New York Sun*

"In his besotted, passionate new book about contemporary Shakespeare studies . . . Ron Rosenbaum sets out to . . . transmit a sense of ravishment, 'unbearably pleasurable,' brought forth by the 'bottomlessness' of Shakespeare's writings. . . . His search . . . turns his book into a sort of romantic detective story. . . . Informative, diverting . . . Rosenbaum reminds us that scholarship . . . can be a freewheeling battle royal. . . . To be tired of Shakespeare, for Rosenbaum, is to be tired of life, while to be excited about him—in every inky nuance and detail—is to live a deeper, wider life."

—Walter Kirn, *The New York Times Book Review*

"Dizzying, idiosyncratic, entertaining, and illuminating."

—Maureen Corrigan, NPR's *Fresh Air*

"Mr. Rosenbaum pursues his quarry with energy and flair. He brings to life the personalities of the scholars and theater directors whom he interviews. . . . His gift for clear exposition is matched by a lively wit. . . . It is hard to imagine another commentator doing more to convey to general readers the fascination, and the importance, of scholarly topics. . . . Mr. Rosenbaum shows exceptional sensitivity to Shakespeare's language."

—JOHN GROSS, *The Wall Street Journal*

"A superb overview of contemporary Shakespeare scholarship . . . genuinely passionate, insight-filled . . . Anyone who cares for Shakespeare . . . will learn an enormous amount. . . . The investigations of real scholars and theatrical professionals . . . make the book invaluable."

—MICHAEL DIRDA, *The Washington Post*

"Rosenbaum's rewarding book bears witness to Shakespeare's unrivaled appeal [and leads readers] even more deeply into the amazing complexities of his art."

—WILLIAM E. CAIN, *Boston Sunday Globe*

"Rosenbaum's title . . . is spot on. . . . He is the Christiane Amanpour of Shakespeare studies. . . . His book is timely not least for the economy and clarity with which he outlines the casus belli. . . . Rosenbaum's reportage is enlightening. . . . We now have a better sense of what the fuss is about."

—JOHN SUTHERLAND, *The Financial Times*

"Rosenbaum [is] upfront, ecstatic, . . . complex—a streetwise Ancient Mariner."

—*The Economist*

"In . . . brightly written, playful, argumentative and intelligent prose—even the bibliographic notes are good reads—he makes some of the more arcane literary battles over Shakespeare seem lively, fascinating, important and even sexy. Partly, it's his skill in bringing the scenes and participants to life. Partly, it's his at times self-deprecating humor, heavily garnished, almost to a Shakespearean degree, with puns and other forms of wordplay. Above all, it's Rosenbaum's ability to fill his pages with the passion that underlies his intellectual quest. . . . The best thing about *Wars* is Rosenbaum's ability to make scholarship almost as exciting as a first-rate performance, and to make reading about well-performed Shakespeare almost as rewarding as a great night in the theater."

—ROBERT HURWITT, *San Francisco Chronicle*

"[I've been] a lifelong admirer of [Rosenbaum's] work. . . . A joyous appreciation . . . a fine piece of reportage on the scholarly infighting behind the scenes in Shakespeare studies." —STEPHEN METCALF, *Slate*

"What is lovely about this book . . . is its exaltation of the vastness of Shakespearean riches—a vastness proven by the endless intensity of the very debates that Rosenbaum writes about. . . . And then there's Rosenbaum's passion for his subject. It's genuine and highly infectious."

—MARJORIE KEHE, *The Christian Science Monitor*

"Penetrating and deeply felt . . . engrossing, emotionally charged and highly moving." —MARK OLSHAKER, *The Washington Times*

"Fascinating and passionate . . . He engages the reader with his own eagerness, deep reading and lively good sense."

—JEROME WEEKS, *The Dallas Morning News*

"Once upon a time Rosenbaum was a graduate student in English at Yale. But he left that behind to become the most sui generis of investigative reporters. The English department's loss was literature's gain."

—SCOTT MCLEMEE, *Newsday*

"Rosenbaum (*Explaining Hitler*) is one of our best most omnivorously curious journalists. These scholarly wars aren't over who 'really' wrote the plays, but over the actual language: what it reveals and conceals. Is there an encoded orgasm in the speeches of *Romeo and Juliet*? That is the question."

—*Newsweek*

"Rosenbaum . . . brings the style he has perfected over the years—the style of the journalist engaged in indefatigable search of answers to various knotty questions. . . . Engaged in these intellectual quests, Rosenbaum has displayed unfailing intelligence, doggedness, a genuine willingness to entertain different points of view, [and] a relaxed and highly readable prose style. You can see the journalist in Rosenbaum even when he's dealing with brilliant Shakespeare scholars." —PHILIP MARCHAND, *Toronto Star*

"Rosenbaum has now done for Shakespeare studies what he did for Hitler studies. . . . [His analysis of *The Merchant of Venice*] is as nice a summary definition of Shakespeare's uncanny genius as one could desire."

—THOMAS L. JEFFERS, *Commentary*

"Thrilling . . . *The Shakespeare Wars* is too packed with brilliance to ignore. . . . [Rosenbaum] compel[s] us to reach for Shakespeare and begin reading with a new and more nuanced appreciation."

—JOSEPH BEDNARIK, *The Sunday Oregonian*

"Throughout its 600 pages, he manages to transmit genuine sparks of bedazzlement and wonder. . . . It accomplishes something extraordinary: it sweeps the dust off academic discourse and proves that centuries-old language can produce palpable exhilaration."

—JENNIE ROTHENBERG, *The Atlantic Online*

"I've always hoped for a book on Shakespeare . . . by a passionate, brilliant reader steeped in her own reading of the Bard and in the debates by contemporary scholars. . . . But even I couldn't have anticipated how lucky I would get. To have Ron Rosenbaum, the most original and interesting cultural journalist working today, wade through the depths and heights of Shakespeare is more than an embarrassment of riches. It is the very thing itself: like Shakespeare reading Shakespeare to us."

—PRADEEP SEBASTIAN, *The Hindu*, India's national newspaper

"In-depth critical analysis handled with a light touch and unfailing respect for the reader's intelligence: cultural journalism of the highest order."

—*Kirkus Reviews*

"One of the best books of the year."

—*Los Angeles Times, The Christian Science Monitor,* NPR, *The Kansas City Star*

"Just when you thought nothing more could be said on the subject, Ron Rosenbaum comes up with a wholly fresh approach—a thrilling personal confrontation with the inexhaustibility of the work, the frightening bottomlessness of Shakespeare's genius. *The Shakespeare Wars* comes to us in waves of new revelations." —BILLY COLLINS, former U.S. poet laureate

ALSO BY RON ROSENBAUM

Explaining Hitler

The Secret Parts of Fortune

Those Who Forget the Past (editor)

The Shakespeare Wars

the Shakespeare WARS

CLASHING SCHOLARS, PUBLIC FIASCOES, PALACE COUPS

Ron Rosenbaum

RANDOM HOUSE TRADE PAPERBACKS
New York

2008 Random House Trade Paperback Edition

Published in the United States by Random House Trade Paperbacks, an imprint of The Random House Publishing Group, a division of Random House, Inc., New York.

RANDOM HOUSE TRADE PAPERBACKS and colophon are trademarks of Random House, Inc.

Originally published in hardcover in the United States by Random House, an imprint of The Random House Publishing Group, a division of Random House, Inc., in 2006.

ISBN 978-0-8129-7836-0

Printed in the United States of America

www.atrandom.com

2 4 6 8 9 7 5 3 1

Book design by Casey Hampton

To Peter Brook and the cast of his Dream.
For changing my life forever.

Contents

Preface

Why?

WHY IS THIS SHAKESPEARE BOOK DIFFERENT?

First, permit me to protest: it's not another book "on Shakespeare," the shadowy historical figure. It's not a biographical study. I don't propose to tell you whether Shakespeare poached a deer, slept with men, or contracted syphilis from the Dark Lady of the Sonnets, and what any of that might tell us about his work, his language, his plays and poems. It's always seemed to me that the work is what is most worth caring about and that Shakespearean biography, with its few indisputable facts, its suppositions, its conjectures, its maybes, does more to distort than to illuminate the work.

I have nothing against literary biography in general, but I suspect most serious literary biographers must be a bit dismayed at the fantasies spun out by Shakespearean biographers on the basis of such fragmentary evidence. Just as in the old story of the man who persists in searching for his keys under a streetlamp (even though they're not there) "because that's where the only light was," Shakespearean biography, especially the obsessive—often circular—attempts to make inferences about the work on the basis of the few known facts and anecdotes about the life, can be a distraction from the true mystery and excitement, the true source of illumination, the place the hidden keys can *actually* be found: the astonishing language. (Look how little we know about Homer and how little it matters.)

Thus most efforts to forge, fabricate or flesh out the life (as opposed to placing the work in its cultural context) have ended up doing a disservice to the work because they lead inevitably to a reductive biographical perspective on the work and use the work to "prove" suppositions about the life.

Someone once wrote that Shakespearean biographers at their best are like the great old jazz musicians who can spin dizzying riffs out of a few notes of an old standard. But at their worst Shakespearean biographers are like cardsharps, piling suspect suppositions upon shaky conjectures into rickety houses of cards.

Even worse is the tendency to use the suppositional conjectures, and the conjectural suppositions—what Shakespeare supposedly thought of sex, marriage, death, religion—in order to craft a blurry lens through which to look at the attitudes of the plays and poems.

So this is not a biographical study; it is less concerned with Shakespeare the man than with the figure the thoughtful textual scholar Edward Pechter has called "Shakespeare the Writer"—the voice, the mind we can find in the work. What is "Shakespearean" rather than who was Shakespeare. Here, by contrast with the poverty of biography, rich resources are available for this task: thirty-eight or so plays (depending on whether you include collaborations), two long narrative poems, one mystical ode, 154 sonnets. This book is concerned with the clashes over how best to experience the work of Shakespeare the writer, the thrilling esthetic intelligence, more deeply. I want to bring you closer to some of the genuinely exciting contentions over the work, how best to read, speak and act it.

I'M HESITANT TO SAY THAT THE SUDDEN RIVER OF SHAKESPEAREAN biographies is merely a symptom of celebrity culture, but one could trace the origin of the plethora of biographies to the moment in 1998 when Shakespeare became a contemporary celebrity, a movie star, in *Shakespeare in Love.*

Yes, he'd been renowned in elite and popular opinion for four centuries, but suddenly in 1998 he was in bed with Gwyneth Paltrow on the big screen, writing *Romeo and Juliet* while making sweet, sweet love, and his "bio-pic" went on to win the Best Picture Oscar. The same year Harold Bloom in effect pronounced him God—"inventor of the human." God, the ultimate celeb in a faith-obsessed age.

So many biographies followed, with so many speculations, so little besides unproven conspiracy theories and secret codes to add. I'm not saying this is true of *all* the new wave of biographies (I particularly like the contrarian skepticism in *Ungentle Shakespeare* by Oxford's Katherine Duncan-Jones and the focus on the work in Jonathan Bate's *The Genius of Shakespeare*).

But I tend, like Stephen Booth, the great scholar of the Sonnets, to distrust the reading of Shakespeare's work through the lens of biography—or vice versa. As Booth put it: "William Shakespeare was almost certainly homosexual, bisexual, or heterosexual. The Sonnets provide no evidence on that matter."

But there is a price to be paid for the biographical focus. Just before receiving the first galleys of this book, I was alerted by the valuable *Arts & Letters Daily* website (aldaily.com) to a short, sharp critique of the Shakespearean biographical fad by Daniel Swift, a scholar at Columbia, an essay that originally appeared in *The Nation.* In it he argued that, in the obsessive and largely futile focus on the life, "Shakespeare's imagination becomes no more than a mechanism for reproducing biographical experience. . . . If there is a lesson to be learned," Swift suggests, "it is that we must clear a space for wonder."

A space for wonder: Yes! That is what the contentions herein are about: how best to reawaken that sense of wonder.

If there is a virtual river of biographies of the man, they're at least *read,* and perhaps encourage some to read or reread the plays. The same cannot be said for the veritable *ocean* of scholarly papers and books on Shakespeare. So many are really about vindication of their own methodology and the ways in which Shakespeare can be subordinated to fit into Larger Theories that they encourage little but further theorizing or a habit of inattention among readers. Others are written in impenetrable jargon that rarely sends one racing to read the plays.

But while this can be true of some scholarly work, it obscures the fact, the surprisingly pleasurable discovery I made in the seven years I've spent writing this book, that there *are* white whales, so to speak, out in that ocean. Extremely important issues, immensely exciting and unresolved questions that defy easy harpooning (Shake-spearing?). White whales often pursued with Ahab-like intensity, if not madness (although this has happened), by brilliant scholars and directors who have devoted themselves to finding a way to make Shakespeare the writer come alive.

Brilliant scholars (and directors) writing, thinking, clashing over these questions, with illuminating clarity. There are fierce struggles, indeed virtual civil wars going on, not over the Theory of Shakespeare but over the language of Shakespeare. Many of these struggles are lost to the world, or to the realm of "civilian" Shakespeare readers and audiences, invisible behind the curtain of academia, obscured by the forbidding squid's ink of opaque theorizing.

It was a realization that began to dawn on me after I began to meet and correspond with Shakespearean textual scholars in the course of writing a piece for *The New Yorker* on the *Hamlet*-text controversy—the question of which of the three earliest texts of *Hamlet* is most "Shakespearean," and what it means to say so.

"Textual scholarship": it doesn't exactly *sound* seductive, but I found myself seduced. One hope I have for this book is that it will make the seductions of Shakespearean textual scholarship apparent. The best among textual scholars are not pedants, self-exiled to arcana, but quite often lively and acute intellects at the forefront of one of the most provocative and significant debates in all literature: the question of what Shakespeare actually wrote. More often, which *version* of what he wrote is more truly "Shakespearean." Whether the two versions we have of a line or a passage—or a whole play—represent Shakespeare's first and second drafts, his original or his final intentions, whether we can recapture his "considered second thoughts" on a line or a passage—or whether the differences were the result of errors in transcription, actors' interpolations, clumsy compositors' errors.

Small changes can make large differences in meaning, and numerous differences can mean . . . ? Two versions of the same play? Two differing works of art? The question of whether we have two *Lear*s and three *Hamlet*s has provoked a veritable civil war among Shakespeare scholars over the past three decades, the resolution—or irresolution—of which can mean all the difference in the world to how we view two of the foundational works of Western culture.

In some ways both sides of the celebrated "culture wars" over literature in academia have, for different reasons, spent little time dwelling on the genuine scholarship that persists and survives in the academy. For the bearers of the New Truths of Theory (in which, for instance, the author has been replaced by an "author function") the idea of "genuine scholarship" is suspect if not illusory (as is everything else) in a determinist, power-inflected value system. While for those who believe the academy has been invaded by a clone army of Theorists, the persistence of genuine scholarship amid all the cloning around, so to speak, is not generally played up because it tends to contradict sweeping condemnations.

And so what I believe are absolutely absorbing and consequential developments in Shakespearean scholarship have not been made well known to the general public. This is one modest aim of this book.

For instance, most well-educated people I've spoken to outside the academy were unaware that there may be two *Lear*s, much less three *Ham-*

lets. And that the differing versions raise serious questions for all who care about those plays. This is only one of a number of genuinely important, even urgent questions, debates, arguments, century-long *wars,* that have been going on that deserve your attention if you feel Shakespeare is worth caring about. Even the question of why you think Shakespeare's work is worth caring about is the subject of an interesting debate. For his "themes"? For the beauty and pleasure of his language—or are beauty and pleasure no longer legitimate categories of value? And what makes "Shakespearean" beauty and pleasure different—if it is?

Another realization I made in the course of writing this book is that great directors are, in their own way, great scholars of Shakespeare. Often able to discover, to open up, thrilling abysses of possibility on the page that one could not imagine, or had not imagined, before directors "put them on their feet," onstage.

So what I've been doing for the past seven years has been, more than anything, *reporting* on such matters. In a way this book is a tribute not just to the scholars and directors I've singled out, but to so many more so well deserving of a greater hearing for the excitement of their engagement with Shakespeare. Listening to great directors' and scholars' impassioned arguments has been thrilling and I hope to communicate some of that thrill to you. Hearing Sir Peter Hall pound his fists in fury over the vital importance of a pause at the close of a pentameter line, for instance—wonderful! Whatever side one comes down on in these often bitter clashes, the process of thinking through the arguments takes you deeper into the Shakespearean experience. The point, as the fine Shakespearean actor Henry Goodman has said, "is not to decide what to think, but what to think *about.*"

And I suppose if there's a unifying thread to the contentions I report on, and invite you to think about herein, it may have to do with how we decide what we mean when we say something is "Shakespearean." How does one define—if one can—what is the most truly "Shakespearean" way of speaking the iambic pentameter line, say? How do we choose which of the two versions of the last words of King Lear is more "Shakespearean"? How do we decide whether a clunkily written "Funeral Elegy" is Shakespearean? (Is there a Shakespearean way of writing *badly*?)

Recent biographical studies have declared their intention to tell us "what made Shakespeare Shakespeare." I have focused on what makes Shakespeare "Shakespearean."

It's the kind of question in its various guises that I still find myself caring about deeply in an intellectual and visceral way. It's the kind of question I don't find answered by the biographers or by Harold Bloom's thematic globalizations. It's the kind of question I want you to care about.

I want you to care as much as I care about the way the superb director Peter Brook changed the way Shakespeare has been played in the past half-century with a single transformative production.

I want to make you care about Peter Hall's obsession with the pause (or as he now calls it, the "slight sensory break") at the end of the pentameter line. Hall was, after all, founder of the Royal Shakespeare Company. There must be a pause—a certain *kind* of pause, Hall insists—or all is lost. Why the obsession with the pause?

I want you to care as much as Shakespeare scholar John Andrews cares about what is lost from the spell of Shakespeare's language when we "modernize" Shakespeare's spelling. Whether you spell "Tomorrow and tomorrow . . ." as originally printed, "To morrow and to morrow . . ."

I want you to care as much as I care about the bitter dispute over the variations in *Hamlet* and *Lear* and whether Shakespeare may have changed his mind in subtle ways about his greatest works. If we can know for sure they *were* his changes.

I want to convince you that some of the greatest Shakespeare you will ever see is close at hand, on film, at your video store now. That film in certain, yes, anachronistic ways can sometimes offer more intense "Shakespearean" experiences than the stage. And if you won't go *that* far, I want to convince you not to miss or dismiss the four greatest works of Shakespearean cinema because of misplaced snobbery about film versus stage's superiority.

I want you to care about questions of "attribution," not just the "Funeral Elegy" fiasco, which saw much of the Shakespeare profession in the United States, or certainly its publishing arm, accept a terminally tedious, and interminably pious six-hundred-line poem as "Shakespearean" for some seven years, before it was discredited as a misattribution. But I want you to care as well about the lesser known "Hand D" controversy, and what they both tell us about the debate over how we define "Shakespearean."

I want you to care as much as I care about the controversy over Shakespeare's "late language" and all the fascinating attendant controversies. Must what some refer to as Shakespeare's *lapses* be accounted *failures,* bad poetry, bad prose, as Frank Kermode believes? Or are they rather "holes" in the text that lead to larger *wholes,* as Stephen Booth believes? Or is the baroque complexity of the late language a reflection of Shakespeare's growing "preoccupation with the feminine," as Russ McDonald suggests in one of the single most illuminating scholarly essays I've come upon? I don't want to compel you to accept any given position but, rather, to understand why they're worth caring about.

Finally, I want you to care about the argument over pleasure in Shakespeare and my conjecture about the way the unbearable pleasures of Shakespeare have shaped and distorted the way we read and see him.

Why do I care that you care? I want you to share in the pleasures I had in talking and arguing with some of the best scholars and directors about what may be the greatest achievement of the human imagination.

Why do I care that you care? Let me begin by describing why *I* care.

I

The Bottom of Shakespeare's Secrets

Chapter One

The *Dream* Induction

ON THE LAST EVENING OF THE SUMMER OF 1970 IN THE VILlage of Stratford-on-Avon, birthplace of Shakespeare, I had an experience that changed my life and has haunted me ever since. One that left me, ever after, with a question I've been trying to answer: What was *that* about?

An improbable chain of circumstances had resulted in my witnessing one of the first performances of a now-legendary production of *A Midsummer Night's Dream,* one that I subsequently learned changed more lives than mine: it changed the lives of an entire generation of Shakespearean players and directors, changed the way Shakespeare has been played ever since.

But for me, that *Dream*—a Royal Shakespeare Company production directed by Peter Brook—was a kind of initiation into a new realm, a realm I've sought with mixed success to return to ever after. It was the experience that, for me, gave a lifelong urgency to the conflicts over Shakespearean questions examined in the ensuing chapters.

Perhaps I should introduce the conflicted, divided person I was back then when I piloted my rented Austin Mini into Stratford by introducing the forbidden question that led me to flee graduate school, and indirectly set me on the path to that life-changing experience at Stratford.

Just two years before that I had begun what seemed like a promising academic career at Yale Graduate School's Department of English Literature. As an undergraduate at Yale, I had studied primarily pre-seventeenth-century literature and had been granted a Carnegie Teaching Fellowship to Yale Graduate School, a fellowship designed to spur those undecided about an academic career to spend a year tasting the supposed fruits of such a career without many onerous responsibilities. I was only required to take one graduate seminar and teach one undergraduate class per semester, in return for which I was given an official-sounding appointment to the Yale faculty and named a Junior Fellow of Jonathan Edwards (residential) College.

The latter made me briefly a colleague of Stephen Greenblatt, also a Junior Fellow there that year. Greenblatt would go on to found the most influential new school of Shakespeare scholarship in America—New Historicism—and like many original thinkers develop a cultlike following. He would of course end up as star of the Harvard English department and the author of a best-selling Shakespeare biography. I'll never forget an argument Greenblatt and I had that year about the Black Panthers and historical truth, which oddly foreshadowed, in transposed form, our subsequent positions on New Historicism and Shakespeare. (I discuss it further in chapter 4.)

At first things went swimmingly: I was thrilled to find I'd been admitted to a select seminar with Richard Ellmann, the acclaimed biographer of Yeats and Joyce, masterminds of modernism, and felt quite vain when Ellmann singled out a paper I'd read at the seminar, a critique of the determinism of Yeats's muddleheaded mystical cosmology.

But sometime in the second semester, although enjoying a Shakespeare seminar with Howard Felperin, I lost heart, or maybe it was more that my heart was broken. In point of fact, my heart was broken by a question I asked—and an answer I got—about love.

The occasion was a special, ad hoc, invitation-only seminar I'd been asked to, a presentation by one of the English department's favorite wunderkind scholars. A paper on Chaucer's lesser-known love-vision poems, including the *Book of the Duchess* and *The Parliament of Fowles.*

Unlike the wild digressive fabliaux of *The Canterbury Tales,* Chaucer's love-vision poems are exquisite and mysterious shorter works, and I was looking forward to the occasion, although by this time my disillusion with graduate school life had already begun to undermine the pleasure I felt from the study of literature. The faculty sherry parties had a lot to do with it: watching my fellow graduate students assiduously sucking up to Harold Bloom and other stars of the department, their sherry-flushed faces perspiring from the damp mothball-mildew warmth of their tweeds. While the world outside—it was 1968!—was exploding with fearful, thrilling events.

I'd gotten a taste of the adrenaline-fueled rush of reporting when I'd gotten press credentials to cover the 1968 Chicago Democratic Convention for a local daily newspaper. And to return from that history-changing riot to the shallow cynicism of graduate school culture was intensely dismaying.

What was wrong with these people? I asked at first. Then: What was wrong with *me*? Why was I staying there?

The love-vision seminar moment crystallized my doubts. It wasn't Chaucer who was the problem. Nor was it the wunderkind scholar himself, whose paper I recall to be an intelligent if somewhat overwrought examination of the way in which the narrators of Chaucer's dream visions consciously re-envision their visions as poetry. Something like that.

No, it was his response to a question about love. It was a question I asked in the discussion period after his presentation. A question about the vision of love in the love-vision poems. I forget exactly what the offending question I asked was, something along the lines of whether love was more than human delusion in Chaucer's work.

A shocked silence ensued among the other grad students and faculty, and I realized I had committed a terrible solecism, a faux pas of Richter-scale proportions, in asking such a naïve question. I had expressed interest in the ostensible subject matter of the poem!

With a wan, disdainful smile and dismissive wave of his nicotine-stained fingers, the wunderkind scholar informed me that "Love is such an *uninteresting* question." The truly interesting questions raised by the love-vision poems, he said, were not about love but about "the making of poetry." This meta-poetical question, newly fashionable at the time, was far more significant than something as trivial as the nature of love.

All the other acolytes nodded and chuckled. Of course! How naïve! The making of poetry, yes!

"Sez who?" I muttered to myself—one of my father's favorite Brooklynisms—as I slunk off.

What am I *doing* here, I thought to myself as I drove back out to the house on the Sound I'd rented with some friends. That night I stayed up late, desperately searching the classified job sections of the papers for something, anything, even a traveling salesman job that would get me out of the sherry parties and on the road.

Two years later, through a couple of lucky breaks, which began with reading the classified ads that night, I *was* on the road, heading for Stratford-on-Avon. I'd become not a traveling salesman but something analogous: a journalist. A journalist who wanted to write about cops and criminals, underworld and undercover types. I wanted to live life among Falstaffian rogues rather than read about them. But I was still under the spell of literature, a spell graduate school had not broken. So in September 1970 I found myself driving through the English Midlands having decided to undertake a reverse pilgrimage, a pilgrimage *from* Chaucer's Canterbury to some of the icons of my academic literary past, my abandoned academic self.

I headed north toward my first stop, Winchester, where I went to some effort to locate the ridge in the rolling countryside where Keats stood on September 19, 1819, and gazed at the sunset vista on the penultimate day of summer, a vista that gave rise to the haunting and lovely ode "To Autumn."

I arrived there that same day, September 19, and found the landscape had not been altered: that one could still see *exactly what Keats saw*. I could understand for the first time the line "While barred clouds bloom the soft-dying day, / And touch the stubble-plains with rosy hue." I saw those stubble fields! I felt the "soft-dying" end-of-summer melancholy Keats evoked with its intimation of mortality, of the autumnal harvest and the more final harvest of death to come.

AN ORDINARY ECSTASY IN NEW HAVEN

And with that cheerful iconic vista under my belt, I headed farther north to Stratford, to the birthplace of William Shakespeare. I should say I was not a Shakespearean obsessive at that point. I had taken a graduate seminar on Shakespeare at Yale with Howard Felperin, a seminar that focused on the relationship between Shakespeare's Tragedies and his Late Romances. Felperin would later become an avatar of stringent Derrida deconstructionism, although he still made sense to me at the time (and later renounced his deconstructionist perspective). But I hadn't even read all the plays, I can't recall whether I'd seen more than a few productions, I didn't carry around copies of the plays the way I did the works of Keats and Donne, say. I'm not even sure if, when heading up the motorway toward Stratford, I knew that one of the most influential productions of the twentieth century, Peter Brook's *Midsummer Night's Dream,* had just opened. Frankly, I'm not even sure if I knew they put on plays there. The only thing that I was sure of was that it was the birthplace of Shakespeare, and I felt a pilgrimage might in some way help me connect with what I'd been missing.

It's true I *had* had one extraordinary, puzzling, almost mystical experience of Shakespeare before then. It happened during the seminar on literature I was teaching at Yale. I had assigned my class Shakespeare's Sonnets. They were not particular favorites of mine at the time; when it came to love poems, I preferred the more knotty and overtly intellectual lyrics of John Donne and the other seventeenth-century Metaphysical poets to the Sonnets.

But there had been a moment when . . . Well, I recall standing at the blackboard in the seminar room. I had written out one of the Sonnets on the blackboard and was leading the class through its flickering ambiguities. I think it could have been either Sonnet 44 or 45, both of which play upon the themes of absence and presence: how two united as one in love can both be, and not be, apart (can both "two be" and *not* "two" be). In Sonnet 45 the speaker tells an absent loved one how his thought and desire are "present-absent."

How he's *there,* one with the distant lover and thus absent from himself; but to be absent *from* himself is to be two selves, one there and one *not* there, although the one *not* there actually *is* there—one with the absent lover—so really it's one self at two different places. Is that all clear?

He's not split into two so much as flickering in and out of being one and two selves. Not just back and forth from being *at one with*—to *being*—the loved one, but "with swift motion sliding," shifting back to being *himself.* He's not just being in two places at once, he's two *beings* in alternation. Two be *and* not two be.

In any case, I recall standing at the blackboard in that seminar room on Prospect Street in New Haven attempting to unfold for my students this shifting, this flickering-back-and-forth effect, this dual prospect, conjured up not just by this Sonnet but by so many others. In which embracing one aspect of a verbal ambiguity and then shifting back to its counterpart involves something more than a shift in *meaning* in the poem, but a shift in the reader's *being.* In effect you are not merely reading alternative meanings into the poem, the poem is reading alternative meanings, alternative identities, into you.

But suddenly that day this became more than an abstract insight. I recall banging the chalk in my hand on the blackboard, back and forth from "present" to "absent" in the phrase "These present-absent with swift motion slide"—and suddenly experiencing something strange. In some peculiar but pronounced and dramatic way, *my* self, my identity seemed to be shifting, sliding back and forth from presence to absence, from being there in that classroom to being somewhere absent, looking *back* on my presence, and then "with swift motion sliding" back to where I was standing again. I was no longer reading alternative meanings into the Sonnet, I felt like the Sonnet was shifting me back and forth between alternative selves, almost physically. I was standing inside and outside myself.

It wasn't an intellectual experience, or it was disturbingly, mysteriously more than an intellectual experience. An ecstatic experience in the original meaning of the word "ecstatic": standing outside oneself. It was almost an out-of-body experience, or an in-and-out-of-body experience. I came to think that at least in part this flickering-back-and-forth effect is one thing the Sonnets are *about:* the attempt to *induce* this state, which as Stephen Booth points out, is not unrelated to the shifting, flickering state of being in love.

I've subsequently also come to believe that this ecstatic experience of identity change and exchange, of what might be called an alternating current of two-ness and oneness, can be found recurrently throughout Shakespeare's plays and poems. It is embodied most explicitly in his often overlooked mystical love-vision ode, "The Phoenix and Turtle." A poem that seems to express directly some powerful visionary sexual and metaphysical experience of oneness and two-ness that is echoed elsewhere in his work.

In any case, that moment of transport, or transposition, one might say, was unlike anything I'd experienced before, certainly not reading poetry. And I never experienced anything like it again—until that night in Stratford-on-Avon.

As I said, I had no such expectation as I drove into Stratford. I was unaware how lucky I was to get tickets to both productions playing at the Shakespeare Memorial Theatre that weekend: Trevor Nunn's staging of *Hamlet* and Peter Brook's of *A Midsummer Night's Dream.*

The *Hamlet* was memorable, one of the very best I've ever seen. But it was the *Dream* that changed my life. I count it one of the greatest blessings of that life to have been there for that moment. I'd never experienced anything of such radiant clarity. To say it was "electrifying" does not capture the effect; it was more like being struck by lightning. I felt "transported" in the literal sense of being physically as well as metaphysically lifted from the muddy vesture of the earth to some higher realm.

It was a lifelong love potion. It was a lens through which I could not help see all Shakespeare, indeed all literary art, ever after. It was: "Oh, *that's* what the fuss is about."

It was more than merely the shock of a "first time." It was more than the fact of its being my first experience of Shakespeare played by great Shakespeareans because in the decades that followed I've never seen Shakespeare to equal it. I've seen great Shakespearean moments, great Shakespearean performances, unforgettable scenes; I've had illuminations reading passages in Shakespeare, some in other writers. But nothing like the total experience of that *Dream.* Ever after I've sought in vain for something to equal it. I've rarely found it in art, I've rarely found it in *life.* There's nothing like it, the initial falling-in-love business, is there? But it doesn't last, alas, nothing like that does. This *Dream* did.

When I say it changed my life let me elaborate a little bit. For one thing it changed the way I came to experience Shakespeare. Suddenly it changed on the page; the words became charged with that electricity I'd felt transmitted to me by that *Dream* experience. I began to read, I began to *hear* Shakespeare when reading, in a way I never had before. I began a cycle of reading and rereading all of the plays, sometimes in rough chronological order, sometimes all histories, then all comedies, then all tragedies, sometimes whatever emerged on top of a collapsing pile of editions. Sometimes I'd read through the slender, elegant, sparsely annotated Penguins and Pelicans, sometimes the substantial footnote-fattened Ardens, later the often-exciting new Oxford and Cambridge editions, the Facsimile of the First Folio, the ever trustworthy Folger, Riverside and Bevington Complete Works. And every edition of the *Dream,* which I'd read over and over with an ever deepening sense of wonder: What happened that night?

FAST FORWARD FROM THAT NIGHT—FROM ALL THOSE READINGS and rereadings, from all that futile searching in theater after theater for something to match the sustained experience of Brook's *Dream*—to a few years ago at a Mexican restaurant on Lower Fifth Avenue, where I was having a lunch meeting with Nicholas Hytner, the talented British director who had put on a number of acclaimed productions with the Royal Shakespeare Company at Stratford in the eighties and nineties and later as artistic director of the Royal National Theatre.

Hytner had asked to meet because he was interested in acquiring the film rights to my just-published book, *Explaining Hitler.* (Nothing came of it.) So we talked about Hitler, but I wanted to talk about Shakespeare, and something I needed explained. I started telling him hesitantly about the way my life had been changed by seeing Peter Brook's *Midsummer Night's Dream* at Stratford. How I'd spent the years since trying to recapture or at least explain to myself why that night was so transformative. I felt almost a bit embarrassed at making that kind of statement. Perhaps he'd think me naïve or impressionable, maybe I was overreacting to my first exposure to a Royal Shakespeare Company production after seeing only a few American companies do Shakespeare.

Was I crazy in reacting so strongly? I asked Hytner, a veteran of decades of directing Shakespeare.

"It changed my life too," Hytner said, matter-of-factly, "not just my life but my entire generation of Shakespearean actors and directors. It changed the way everyone did Shakespeare in the U.K."

"Thank you," I said. It was somehow immensely important to me to have someone of his stature and experience confirm that I was not alone in feeling life-changing effects from that performance. It was Hytner as well who alerted me to the conflict over Peter Hall's "pause" and verse-speaking theory within the Royal Shakespeare Company (see chapter 7)—and thus gave me a sense of how fascinating the controversies over what the true "Shakespearean" way of doing Shakespeare were. Gave me the impetus to investigate them that was one motive for writing this book.

It's somehow important to mention Hytner's validation of my *Dream* experience before returning to describing that night, and its impact on me. Yes, there are dissenters, but time after time when I find myself in excited discussions of Shakespeare with people in and out of the theater, it will emerge that they *too* had their life changed by seeing Brook's *Dream* either in Stratford or on its American tour. It has grown to near-mythic status now, widely recognized as one of the most influential productions of Shakespeare in the past century.

So what was it? What made it such a life-changing experience for so many? It's easier to begin by telling you some of the things it *wasn't:* it wasn't the gleaming satin Chinese circus costumes Brook modeled on the Peking Opera Circus he'd seen in Paris. It wasn't the trapezes, the juggling, the stilts, the whirring plates spinning on poles, the whirling light sticks. Some subsequent criticism of the production has focused in a *completely* misleading way on these suits and trappings, the trapezes of innovation—on what made the production on the surface seem radically *new.* This is a red herring, but one you most often hear from those who only read about the production, never saw it. (Unfortunately the RSC didn't begin videotaping its performances until the following year, so aside from a ten-second clip there's no record—believe me: I've tracked down rumors of Japanese bootlegs.)

I've come to believe, on the contrary, that what made it so thrilling was not the way in which Brook's *Dream* was new but rather the way it was radically *old.* The way in which it seemed to capture what one imagines was the excitement of the moment the play was first produced four centuries ago. The moment when its lines were first uttered, when its language burst from the lips of its actors in a kind of spontaneous combustion, as if the words were not *recited* so much as thought up and uttered, freshly minted, for the first time.

Part of it was the, well, charismatic aphrodisiac effect of the production. Many scholars believe the *Dream* was a kind of epithalamium—a poetic tribute offered to a newly married couple, on their wedding night, in the interval between the ceremony and the consummation. An interlude designed to prolong and heighten the sense of anticipation—the play as love potion—just as the final wedding night act within the *Dream* does with *its* epithalamium play-within-the-play, the one presented by Bottom's troupe of comic "Mechanicals," *Pyramus and Thisby.*

So there's that, it's a play about, upon, sexual tension. It was there in the first appearance of the four young lovers. All four of them just spilled out onto the stage with an electrifying burst of erotic energy. In the past when I'd read the play, I'd found the jog-trot rhythm and rhyme of the young lovers' verse off-puttingly stilted. But suddenly here were these hot-blooded *firecrackers* going at each other, turning the couplets into virtual *couplings* on stage.

But it had more to do with the language, with the "verse speaking," as Shakespeareans call it. With a company that had so totally mastered the technical and emotional nuances of the verse that it sounded less like recitation than utterances *torn* from them. Each line fluid, lightning-like, *inevitable.* It never seemed, as it does in so many mediocre productions, like *emoting.* The speech bubbled up, burst out, and then sparkled like uncorked champagne. And it had something of a champagne-like effect on me; I felt as if I were imbibing the pure distilled essence of exhilaration. For me it was like the night they *invented* champagne. It *was* like a love potion.

And I did fall in love that night. In the *Dream* the love potion is called "Love in Idleness" and when dropped into a sleeper's eyes, its spell causes the sleeper to fall in love with the very next being he or she sees upon waking. That night, in effect, I awoke from the *Dream* and fell madly, tragically, in love with the experience of Shakespeare played at this dreamlike level.

SPONTANEOUS COMBUSTION

And if that were not enough, the experience was reawakened, born again, you might say, four months later when the Peter Brook *Dream* played New York and something extraordinary happened.

What happened—it seems more than an accident in retrospect, a metaphor as well—was that the production burst into flame. Literally: in the fifth act, during the wedding scene when all the divided lovers were brought together into a ceremony of consummation, celebrated by Bottom's play, one of the torchbearers accidentally set one of the stage curtains ablaze with his torch. Fire in a crowded theater!

It was hard not to take it as spontaneous combustion: some kind of metaphor for Shakespeare's incandescence. For a production so incandescent it virtually burst into flame. In any case, it ignited something in me, a lifelong desire to investigate the origins, the chemistry, so to speak, of that Shakespearean fire.

And it set me on a course of incessant cycles of rereading the plays, watching them played. With each new round of rereading I found, time after time, with play after play, a quantum leap, well, more like a visceral *jolt,* to a new level or new depth of apprehension. Each subsequent round of rereading—and listening to great audiotapes—created a kind of critical mass that set off further revelations like chain lightning, illuminating a realm where I felt my own consciousness tuned to a higher pitch. Each new cycle yielded further tantalizing flashes, glimpses through a text darkly, of ultimate enigmas, further echoes of the music of the spheres, or in any case, the music of the Shake-spheres, one might say.

I began to wonder: How long could this go on? At a certain point with other poets and writers (except, perhaps, Nabokov), rereading had always begun to bring forth diminishing returns. Not here. Which *is* perhaps the ultimate Shakespearean mystery: the exponentially increasing returns of rereading. The question of bottomlessness.

To return to that first experience of the *Dream,* to that initial spell, the trance I've never fully awakened from: it was a state of mind perhaps at best expressed by the most human character in the *Dream,* Bottom the weaver. I say most human because on the one hand there are all these semi-mythological nobles in the Athenian court of Theseus and Hippolyta and the ingenue lovers. And then you have the fully supernatural characters Oberon, Titania, Puck and the fairies. And then you have "the Mechanicals," ordinary humans, ostensibly Athenian workers, but really Elizabethan, sounding like Shakespeare's contemporaries, perhaps modeled on his Stratford neighbors: Peter Quince, Flute the bellows-mender and the like. Of whom Bottom the weaver is the most fully realized. Bottom is the only one in the play to be transported back and forth, between bottom and top of the hierarchy of realms, from simple weaver to an ass who ascends to union with a veritable goddess, Titania, Queen of the Fairies.

And then back again. In any case, when Puck transforms Bottom back from being an ass to Bottom again, the awakened weaver tries to express the radiant dream he's experienced. His "induction" one might say, to use a term from the opening of *The Taming of the Shrew.* His sense of wonder is deeply affecting:

"I have had a most rare vision. I have had a dream, past the wit of man to say what dream it was. Man is but an ass, if he go about t' expound this dream. Methought I was—there is no man can tell what. Methought I was, and methought I had—but man is but a patch'd fool, if he will offer to say what methought I had. The eye of man hath not heard, the ear of man hath not seen, man's hand is not able to taste, his tongue to conceive, nor his heart to report, what my dream was. I will get Peter Quince to write a ballet of this dream. It shall be called 'Bottom's Dream,' because it hath no bottom. . . ."

The loveliness of these lines still breaks my heart. And that night in Stratford I felt like Bottom. I felt I was waking up from a "most rare vision," from a "dream, past the wit of man to say what dream it was." A dream I have spent the rest of my life trying to "expound," to myself and others—trying to recover, trying to relive and repeat. The kind of experience I have just not had from any other dream or drama or dramatist. In fact, from any other literature.

In a sense this book is an attempt to recapture, define, "expound" as Bottom says, the questions raised by that initial experience, that "rare vision," that dream—and by three decades of subsequent engagement with Shakespeare. What made that rare vision so rare, what made it so unique and visionary? Can one get to the bottom of Bottom's Dream—or to the bottom of its bottomlessness? In the seven years or so I've spent writing this book, when people have asked me what it's about, the short answer I've found most applicable is some variation of this: One night in Stratford, England, something strange happened to me watching Peter Brook's *Dream.* Something I haven't recovered from. Ever since then I've been trying to recapture it, to explain what it was and this book, in effect, involves me seeking out those who can help "expound" it for me.

Seeking out those who are most illuminating on the question of what Stephen Booth, the great scholar of the Sonnets, argues should be the great question about Shakespeare: "What's all the fuss about?" Other artists have written great tragedies and comedies, expounded upon *themes* to be found in Shakespeare, but it is not for the themes, for the themes *alone,* we value him. Why do we feel—those of us who do—that there is something in Shakespeare beyond what we find in other literature? What's all the fuss about? Why is Shakespeare, as Booth puts it, still "our most underrated poet"? What is "Shakespearean" about Shakespeare and how best to find and define it: this is the subject of contention at the heart of all the struggles herein.

BOTTOMLESSNESS: A FOOTNOTE

In the course of reconsidering what happened to me in Stratford and my subsequent lifelong fascination with this question, I came to think a clue to "what's all the fuss about" can be found in Bottom's Dream.

There's much more to Bottom's Dream than meets the eye; it deserves deeper consideration than its comic context suggests. It is one of those nodes, one of those knots in the grain of Shakespeare's work, that discloses a glimpse, a more palpable sense of what is meant by "Shakespearean," what is exceptional about the Shakespearean experience. And one of those moments where one rediscovers the value of genuine Shakespearean scholarship.

There are actually two aspects of Bottom's Dream that make it the rare vision it is: its synesthesia and its bottomlessness. Synesthesia is the unusual but well-documented (see *Scientific American Mind,* vol. 16, no. 3) experience of the fusion or the confusion of senses, most commonly when people report the sensation of "seeing" music or "hearing" colors. In his autobiography, *Speak, Memory,* Vladimir Nabokov reported that he could "see" sounds: the letter *k,* for instance, was something he'd experience as the color of huckleberry. Bottom actually describes a confused negative synesthesia, one might say, "The eye of man hath *not* heard, the ear of man hath *not* seen."*

But then he goes on to describe a deeper, rarer kind of synesthesia, a transposition involving the tongue and the heart (or language and soul respectively). Man's tongue is not able "to conceive, nor his heart to report, what [his] dream was." In most poetry the tongue reports what the heart conceives. In Bottom's synesthesia the tongue *can't* conceive what the heart reports or speaks—it's beyond speech. What the heart reports is so ecstatic, so visionary, it's beyond what poetry can express. In this deeper level of synesthesia the heart gives birth to language, while language—the tongue—"conceives," gives birth to life.

I'm not sure my experience that night in Stratford at Peter Brook's *Dream* went as deep as that, but I did feel my heart "report" something it never reported before. And ever since I became a reporter, alongside or perhaps beneath all the other stories I was reporting on, I was investigating *that* report.

And as my reporting came full circle—as I found myself focussing on scholarly disputations in the academic world I'd fled, I kept finding more to report on in Shakespeare—deeper levels to the bottomlessness Bottom speaks of. As I was writing this section, for instance, I had occasion to consult the Oxford single-volume edition of the *Dream,* the one edited by Peter Holland, then director of the Shakespeare Institute at Stratford, now at Notre Dame. And I found there, appended to that passage—the one in which Bottom tries to "expound" his dream—a remarkable footnote. In fact, in a lifetime of searching and finding unexpected revelations in footnotes, it's one of the most remarkable I've come upon.

It's a footnote on the source of Bottom's *name.* For centuries it has been supposed that, while it may have been a fruitful source of bawdy puns, the name "Bottom" as in "Bottom the weaver" had a more prosaic than profane origin: in his craft. A "bottom" was the name given to the large spool at the base of a handloom that spun out the thread to be woven. While that in itself has a lovely resonance for the weaver of plays who spun out the name, the footnote suggests there may be an even more provocative and resonant source of the name Bottom.

* More evidence of this preoccupation can be found in Sonnet 23: "O, learn to read what silent love hath writ: / To hear with eyes belongs to love's fine wit."

Peter Holland's footnote begins by tracing the source of Bottom's lines—"The eye of man hath not heard, the ear of man hath not seen"—to First Corinthians in the New Testament, where the line runs, more logically, "The eye hath not seen, and the ear hath not heard, neither have entered into the heart of man, the things which God hath prepared for them that love him."

Bottom's line, then, does more than just comically invert the eye-ear language of Corinthians, it refers to a passage that speaks of an unimaginable, literally inconceivable experience—the experience of "the things which God hath prepared for them that love him," the experience of ecstatic communion with the divine.

Other scholars have noted the origins of Bottom's language about eye and ear in those lines in Corinthians. But the remarkable disclosure in Peter Holland's footnote comes when he takes us just a little bit further into the New Testament passage than the language about eye and ear that Bottom transposes.

Holland carefully prepares the ground for this by examining the versions of that passage in Corinthians that would have been available to Shakespeare when he wrote *A Midsummer Night's Dream,* sometime around 1595 (two decades before the King James Bible appeared).

In the 1568 Bishops' Bible, the line about the heart of man not yet realizing "the things which God hath prepared for them that love him" is followed by these words: "For the spirit searcheth all things, yea, the deep things of God."

But—and here's the revelation—in the 1557 Geneva Bible, the one more likely to have been the Shakespeare family Bible (since he was born in 1564, before the publication of the Bishops' Bible) and the one he paraphrases elsewhere—that last phrase about "the deep things of God" is translated as "For the spirit searcheth all things, yea, *the bottom of God's secrets*" (my italics).

The bottom of God's secrets! Fascinating: Peter Holland goes on to report in this invaluable footnote on a scholarly dispute that has broken out over "the bottom of God's secrets" and whether it was the source of Bottom's name. Was Shakespeare thinking only of weavers' spools and butts and asses in naming one of his greatest characters Bottom? Or is there an allusion as well to the deepest, most bottomless mysteries of creation, "the bottom of God's secrets"?

Peter Holland and Thomas B. Stroup, the original author of the "Bottom of God's Secrets" conjecture in a 1979 *Shakespeare Quarterly* paper (a conjecture Holland does not endorse), are not alone in linking Bottom's Dream to that passage in Corinthians. Holland's virtually bottomless footnote referred as well to an essay by Frank Kermode, a critic both scrupulous and incisive about Shakespeare and not given to overstatement, in which Kermode speaks of Bottom's dream as a kind of religious vision, one that illuminates the nature of love, both carnal and spiritual, the extrasensory beauty and grace of "blind love."

In the conventional notion of "blind love," Kermode points out, man is the fool, the toy of willful (Puckish) Cupid and treacherous Venus, blinded in a bad way by love. A different notion of blind love is conjured up by Bottom's garbled version of Corinthians, Kermode says:

"This exaltation of blindness was both Christian and Orphic . . . Bottom is there to tell us that the blindness of love, the dominance of the mind over the eye, can be interpreted as a means to grace as well as irrational animalism. That the two aspects are perhaps inseparable."

Blind love, the experience of grace: when I had the opportunity to interview Kermode, now Sir Frank, toward the close of our conversation, I ventured to read to him the other line from the Geneva Bible translation of Corinthians that Peter Holland's footnote called attention to: the one about "the bottom of God's secrets."

I don't want to exaggerate but in his reserved way, I think Sir Frank was taken aback by that.

"What translation is that?" he asked. And when I told him it was the Geneva, he said, "Read it again to me." And after I did: "I wasn't aware of that language, no, but it's quite interesting, yes."

I'm fond of that footnote because it's an instance of something I've pursued in this book—the way that certain passages in Shakespeare open up like the rabbit hole in *Alice in Wonderland* to ever-unfolding ramifications. I'm fond of it as well because, as with Nicholas Hytner, Kermode's reaction validated something inchoate I'd felt so long ago in the playhouse at Stratford, my own Bottom-like experience of the *Dream:* that there was more to Bottom, more to the *Dream* than meets the eye (or the ear).

Of course we can never know with certainty what Shakespeare had in mind, but Holland's footnote—and Stroup's underlying conjecture on Bottom's name and God's secrets—is an instance of the fact that literary scholarship, at its best, still can give us a lot to think about.

One of the things I wanted to attempt in this book was to be a kind of guide—leading the reader, like Virgil in Dante, down into the scholarly inferno, hoping to illuminate some of the genuine intellectual—and visceral—delights, the tormenting conflicts, the unbearable pleasures to be found therein.

When I say visceral, I mean, for instance, that I actually got goose bumps when I read that line about "the bottom of God's secrets." It just seemed to chime on some deep goose bump–generating level with some intimation we have about the *uncanny* power of Shakespeare. (In *Pale Fire,* in the poem of that name, Nabokov speaks of a similar physical reaction.)

I've *gotten* goose bumps from that reference to "the bottom of God's secrets," and I've *given* them too.

I will not claim I gave Frank Kermode goose bumps, but he did sit up and take notice when I told him. And then there was the moment just a few days after I'd met with Kermode, when I was introduced at a party to a well-known actress who was then the girlfriend of a writer I knew. The three of us got into a conversation about Shakespeare and I found myself giving them an account of Holland's footnote about "the bottom of God's secrets."

"Oh my god," said the actress, grabbing my arm. "You're giving me goose bumps."

"How do you know Shakespeare was reading *that* version of the Bible?" her boyfriend said, sounding at least a *bit* jealous. Not of me, I'm sure, but of Shakespeare's still potent physiological effect.

DANGEROUS RADIANCE

But I'm not finished with Bottom's Dream, I haven't gotten to the bottom, so to speak, of its importance, to the real question my experience that night in Stratford, my experience over the subsequent three decades of obsession with Shakespeare, raises: the question of Shakespearean bottomlessness. The question is at the heart of the heart, the knot in the wood, the pearl in the eye, of what is most mysterious about Shakespeare, one of those things that define the "Shakespearean."

There is something threatening about the notion of bottomlessness. When I was growing up on Long Island, the legend about one of the local lakes, Lake Ronkonkoma, was that it was the only lake in the world that *had no bottom.* I've subsequently heard this said of a number of lakes elsewhere in the world, each of which is believed by locals to be the only one in the world to have "no bottom." It's something people seem to want to believe in, although it inspires dread as well as fascination.

Similarly with Shakespeare's bottomlessness. It is my Theory about Theory—the Foucault, Derrida, Lacanian postmodernist fashions that have captured two generations of scholars—that close reading of Shakespeare is at least in part responsible for the flight into the abstractions of Theory. Because close reading opened up something both unbearably pleasurable, beautiful and—in its own way—terrifying. The vision of bottomlessness: of the threatening abyss. Theory was a scaffolding that distanced and protected one from a direct encounter with the abyss: no, you don't have to gaze upon it, at the radiant literary work itself, you just have to look down upon the foolish or venal reasons some people want you to believe it's important.

The close reading of Shakespeare which reached a peak of fecundity in the years from the 1920s to the 1960s brought scholars and readers almost too close to the destabilizing bottomlessness of Shakespeare for comfort. Close reading suggested an *inexhaustible* depth which would inevitably exhaust if not dissolve the identity of the reader in its depths.

Recently in an introduction to Frank Kermode's lecture *Pleasure and Change,* the literary critic Robert Alter speaks of "the horror of the abyss that is opened up by the concept of pleasure," a horror occasioned by a "response so intense that it shatters identity . . ." Or, as it's elsewhere been called, "the terror of pleasure."

Recoiling from this threat, from the identity-shattering bottomless abyss of pleasure that close reading opened up—and readers such as Stephen Booth made dangerously apparent—many felt the need to find distance and the illusion of mastery over this threat by using the leaden jargon of Theory to shield themselves from the virtually radioactive danger of bottomless pleasure.

Thus did bottomlessness—"the horror of the abyss"—give rise to a more comfortable (however complex-seeming) theoretical "contextualizing." A contextualizing that was a form of containment.

Shakespeare himself seems drawn to the experience of bottomlessness. In *Troilus and Cressida* he conjures up "the incomprehensive deep." In *Hamlet* Horatio warns Hamlet against following the ghost because it might tempt him toward

. . . the dreadful summit of the cliff . . .
And draw you into madness[.] *Think of it.*
The very place puts toys of desperation,

Without more motive, into every brain
That looks so many fadoms to the sea. . . .

There's a strikingly similar moment in *Lear* in which Edgar, the good son, conjures up a dizzying vista of bottomlessness in the mind of his blinded father Gloucester as they stand near the top of the Dover cliff. Here bottomlessness becomes not a "toy of desperation" but an instrument of redemption. In *Henry IV* the elusive secrets of the future are "the bottom of the after-time." In *The Tempest* "the dark backward and abysm of time" conjures up the temporal dimension of bottomlessness, the bottomless pit of the past. There is no Tempest more destructive than Tempus, the ravages of time.

And when Bottom the weaver decides that he shall write a ballad about his dream and have it set to music by Peter Quince, he declares, "It shall be called 'Bottom's Dream,' because it hath no bottom."

It hath no bottom because, although Bottom knows he was *in* the dream, he also knows he wasn't really *himself* in the dream: it "hath no Bottom" in that sense. The Bottom drops *out* from his identity, and perhaps that giddy sense of loss of self is what is appealing about contemplating all those alleged bottomless lakes, those unique holes in the world, those sonnets on the blackboard.

But it "hath no Bottom" also in the sense that it's fathomless. That it can't be *sounded,* that there's no end to its depths. This to me is one of the wonders and enigmas: is there no end, no bottom to Shakespearean resonances? It is like Rosalind's declaration of her fathomless affection in *As You Like It:* it "hath an unknown bottom like the Bay of Portugal"—another of those mythic bottomless bodies of water?

For a useful definition of what bottomlessness means in terms of Shakespeare, I would turn to something Christopher Ricks once said to me about value in art. Ricks is the brilliant exegetical scholar, now Oxford professor of poetry, author of acclaimed studies of Milton, Keats and T. S. Eliot, a onetime colleague—and, I'd argue, an inheritor of the mantle—of William Empson, one of the past century's great thinkers about literature.

We had been talking in Ricks's Cambridge, Massachusetts, sitting room (which was presided over by a portrait of Empson in his distinctive neck beard) about the criteria for greatness in literature. A notion that has been scorned and disparaged by most postmodern schools of literary theory which disdain the notion of literary "value." For whom texts are interesting mainly for the way in which they reflect the political and historical forces that "produced" them—the "death of the author" making the *apparent* writer just a mouthpiece for the "power relations of the hegemony," the spirit of the zeitgeist that presses through his language and embeds itself in his art.

There is, by this reasoning, no reason to "privilege" a text such as *Macbeth* over some contemporaneous screed by a religious nut denouncing witches. Most people intuitively feel this is wrong, but the attempt to define what makes Shakespeare "better" than other texts runs into real problems in defining value. Ricks, quite deftly I believe, sidesteps the mountainous accumulation of contorted reasoning on the question of esthetic value with an offhand remark that the test of value in a work of art is "whether or not it continues to repay attention."

It's a deceptively simple formula (in what currency does it repay: pleasure? wisdom? intensity?) but what it does, in a subtle way I think, is introduce the notion of time and *deepening,* a deepening unto bottomlessness. The key word in Ricks's definition is "*continues* to repay attention": that one judges value in literature not from a first or second exposure but from returning again and again, going back to the well, so to speak, and seeing whether the well runs dry or whether the well appears to be bottomless.

Whether each time one returns to it, one returns not to a repeat performance, to a puzzle solved, but to a mystery deepened, compounded, one that continues to give back, repay attentiveness. Pays it back, so to speak, with *interest* in both senses of the word. With compound interest.

Compound in the sense that the more times one returns and rereads, the more *disproportionate* is the return. A third cycle of rereading does not increase one's apprehension (in every sense of the word) by a third—it's more like to the third *power.* This has comported with my experience of Shakespeare where the fourth reading of a play takes one to depths (or heights) one couldn't have *predicted* from the increase from the second to the third reading. Each new level sends back signals and echoes from previously *unimaginable* depths. Will this go on forever? How far has it gone and are the returns diminishing or—is it possible?—still increasing?

Let me try another echo-down-the-well metaphor for the phenomenon of bottomlessness, one suggested by Orson Welles. It came up in a conversation I had with Keith Baxter, the actor who played Prince Hal to Welles's Falstaff and John Gielgud's Henry IV in Welles's amazing and, to me, so-far-bottomless 1966 film fusion of the *Henry IV* plays, *Chimes at Midnight.*

Baxter told some wonderful tales about Welles's Falstaffian filmmaking.

But when I asked him about specific acting directions Welles had given, Baxter told me, "Orson didn't give suggestions, but the one thing he did say, the night before we started shooting, was, 'We want to call down the corridors of time with this.' "

Call down the endless corridors of time. Call down the bottomless *wells* of time, one might say. Welles's echoing metaphor expresses a longing for immortality in the form of undying timeless reverberations that continue to ramify, growing ever more thrilling in their unfolding, compounding complexity.

Does Shakespeare do this in a way that other literature does not? This is the essence of what's known as "the exceptionalist question" in Shakespeare studies. Another meta-contention you might say. Perhaps the best way of defining the exceptionalist question is to put it in the context in which I first encountered it, in the realm of Hitler studies. It's a question that recurred in different forms throughout the dozen years I spent talking with historians, philosophers, theologians, and literary figures in the course of writing *Explaining Hitler.* And perhaps the best way of framing the exceptionalist question was the way the philosopher and theologian Emil Fackenheim expressed it to me when I met with him in his Jerusalem apartment.

"Is Hitler on the same continuum of human nature as us?" Fackenheim asked. Was he someone on the extreme end of that continuum, a very, very, very bad man, but still explicable by the methods which we use—psychology, biology, biography—to explain the psyche of *other* evildoers on the continuum? By the same methods we use to explain *all* human beings on the continuum, including ourselves? Or did Hitler's evil represent a phenomenon beyond any previously known, a "radical evil" as Fackenheim called it using Hannah Arendt's phrase—off the grid, beyond the continuum? A phenomenon that can be explained not psychologically but—if at all—only theologically. At bottom, a mystery, one of God's secrets, you might say.

When it comes to Shakespeare, the exceptionalist question asks: Is he on the continuum of other great writers, Dante, Tolstoy, Goethe and the like—very, very great, but great in a way we understand other writers to be great? Or is his greatness bottomless—fathomless in a *different* way from the others, off the grid, beyond the continuum? Why is this writer different from all other writers, if he *is*? Does his work occupy some realm of its own, does it *create* a realm of its own above and beyond other literature? The question then is: When we call down the corridors of Shakespeare, do we continue to hear back deepening, ramifying echoes, or at some point will we have heard all there is to hear? Can we get to the bottom of Shakespeare or is he in some unique way bottomless?

There is one other comparison between the two realms of scholarship—Hitler and Shakespeare and the exceptionalist dispute about them. In each there is a forbidden or deeply unfashionable word. It was there in the reluctance I found among so many Hitler scholars to use the word "evil" in relation to Hitler. It's not an easy question defining what we mean by that word of course. But the substitutes, the "explanations" substituted for "evil" were no better. There was a tendency for explanation to become excuse: Hitler suffered from a mental aberration, he was a "psychopath," a victim of "unconscious drives" that psychoanalysis could have healed, or of organic brain disease, "low self-esteem." Or he was "merely" a product—a puppet—of his time, of historical and cultural forces, rather than their author (another "death of the author" phenomenon).

In whatever form it took there was a pronounced reluctance to accord to Hitler personal moral choice, personal "agency" as they call it in academia. In part, all this, I argued, stemmed from a reluctance to confront an unbearable alternative: that human nature is capable of committing such a crime as a conscious choice. That Hitler was morally responsible for his acts, that is, evil.

Similar to the flight from the word "evil" in Hitler studies (not in all respects, but in some) there is a reluctance to use the word "Beauty" in relationship to Shakespeare's works. There is similar difficulty in defining the word, and (as Alter and Kermode argue) a similar terror—of pleasure this time—a bottomless "dismay" as Kermode puts it, a horror of the abyss one dissolves into in giving in to bottomless Beauty. The consequences of such a surrender are ones I'll examine in the final sequence of the book. But they're there.

CATULLUS, FOR GOD'S SAKE!

I came to admire those scholars and directors who had the courage not to deny the dismay they felt in facing this abyss. This is not the only question of interest, but the exceptionalist question is the one—just from the fact we're prompted to ask it—that gives the other questions I investigate in this book their special significance. Makes even spurious theories about Shakespeare worth examining the way unreliable legends about Hitler are: because they often reveal hidden agendas; the longings, fantasies that we project on Shakespeare tell us something revealing about ourselves.

Consider the persistence of unprovable theories about Shakespearean authorship—the someone-else-wrote-Shakespeare cult, the way they so often focus on aristocratic candidates—the Earl of Oxford, Walter Raleigh, Francis Bacon. And the way so many of those who propound those theories suffer from aristocratic pretensions themselves. In a snobby way, they can't believe that a middle-class glover's boy without a university education (like theirs) could possibly write Shakespeare's witty and erudite verse. It's an affront somehow to their self-image, so they must imagine instead a hidden aristocratic progenitor, someone more like *them.* It's the Family Romance of the Shakespeare deniers, much as the unfounded belief that Hitler had a wealthy Jew (a Rothschild in one version) in his family tree is the Family Romance of the Hitler explainers. (One could also speculate that the fact that a surprising number of actors are "anti-Stratfordians" is due to actorish self-loathing: the inability to believe one of their own—Shakespeare was an actor after all—was capable of rising to Shakespearean heights.)

Consider as well Harold Bloom's overblown, and yet rarely challenged (on this side of the Atlantic at least) claim that Shakespeare "invented the human"—mainly by creating Bloom's two favorite characters, Hamlet and Falstaff. Shakespeare, in other words, is the Family Romance secret father of all of *us.* A claim that dismisses all the brilliant comic and tragic, lyric, self-aware and introspective characters of Greek and Roman literature—*Catullus* for god's sake—as irrelevant. One that, taken literally—as Bloom seems to wish us to take it—seems to dismiss all human beings before 1600 or so as being somehow less than human. Not yet "invented." When you come down to it, it's really a claim that Shakespeare invented *Bloom*—a composite character with the brain of Hamlet and the body of Falstaff—it's Bloom's Family Romance, too. Shakespeare is his secret father.

THE GREAT "SHAKESPEARE DISCOVERY" FIASCO

In any case, for a quarter century or so after I awoke from—or was awakened by—that *Dream* in Stratford, I'd continued to call down the corridors of Shakespeare, so to speak. But it was a Shakespearean pretender that prompted me to begin in 1996 to investigate and write about Shakespeare questions in a more systematic way.

The pretender, the one the media hailed as a "major new work" by Shakespeare, was the "Funeral Elegy" by "W.S."

On the surface the story had all the elements of great drama: obscure American professor finds overlooked six-hundred-line poem moldering away in an Oxford library, a poem long ignored by British scholars, and with the use of a super-duper, extra-special computer database, a genie in a software program he calls SHAXICON, he "proves" that the cryptic byline "W.S." signified William Shakespeare.

What resulted was a rush to judgment without careful examination of the sources and methods behind the claim made by Professor Donald Foster, the scholar who went on to media stardom for successfully identifying the anonymous author of *Primary Colors,* a triumph that somehow precluded any further serious examination, in the mainstream American media at least, of the shakiness of his Shakespeare claim.

The more I investigated and wrote critically about Foster's claim, the more I became convinced of its inadequacy, the flawed assumptions of the computer database evidence, all the doubts I enumerate and explore in a subsequent chapter. What makes the argument important was not my personal embattlement but the question the Elegy dispute raised: What do we mean when we say something is or isn't "Shakespearean"? A question that is raised by almost every controversy in subsequent chapters.

But to return to the Shakespeare exceptionalist question, it does not, I believe (as you might have gathered), have anything to do with Shakespeare's "invention of the human," as Bloom puts it. A claim so silly it amounts to being a greater misconception than the claim for the "Funeral Elegy." Bloom's phrase is so rarely challenged it could be said to be the Emperor's New Clothes of Literary Claims. But if he didn't invent "the human" I came to wonder if it might be said that Shakespeare invented something *alive,* created a kind of intelligent *life* that survived him, a body of work so bottomlessly self-referential it almost seems self-aware. One that will outlive any one of *us* because a lifetime of rereading will not exhaust what is there to be found and compounded.

IT'S POSSIBLE I'M WRONG; IT'S POSSIBLE THAT THIS PROCESS OF ramifying, refracting and reflecting isn't endless, bottomless, that at a certain point, the levels of resonance will cease deepening on each rereading.

One reason I wanted to devote myself to deeper investigation of Shakespearean enigmas and the conflicts over them is to find out if and when it *would* cease. It hasn't yet. And I'm not alone in invoking the boundary between physics and metaphysics in trying to characterize this strange experience of deepening into bottomlessness. Recently I came across the published transcript of a lecture delivered at Berlin University by a prominent Shakespearean figure. He was speaking about Shakespeare's language, its "inexhaustibility."

He spoke of the way one could take some apparently anomalous phrase in Shakespeare and find, in seeking to probe that anomaly, that node, that one opens up a universe of rich and strange resonances (such as those expounded upon in Peter Holland's footnote to Bottom's Dream). The example given in the Berlin lecture was a phrase in *The Tempest,* from Prospero's farewell in the Epilogue. Perhaps the last words Shakespeare wrote, his prayerful farewell to his audience: a prayer he describes as one "Which pierces so, that it assaults / Mercy itself . . ." Why "assault" mercy, the lecturer asked? Why does Shakespeare use the language of violence to praise an act of mercy? He doesn't exactly answer the question but he goes on to produce a dazzling array of deepening conjectures, exploring the apparently bottomless depths, liberating the untold levels of resonance compressed within that single phrase.

What it tells us, the speaker says, is that actors and directors can do what they want with staging, with delivery, with dramaturgy; critics can impose theories from above; but no one should ever neglect the power at the source, the power *of* the source—the critical mass waiting to be tapped *within* the words themselves.

"Each line of Shakespeare is an atom," the speaker said. "The energy that can be released is infinite—if we can split it open."

Oh, yes: The speaker was Peter Brook.

II

Civil Wars among the Textual Scholars

Chapter Two

One *Hamlet* or Three?

IN 1997, WHEN HAROLD JENKINS, FORMER REGIUS PROFESSOR AT the University of Edinburgh and editor of a leading scholarly edition of Shakespeare's plays, went to see Kenneth Branagh's film version of *Hamlet,* he was both excited and nervous. Sitting in his home two years later, the ninety-year-old scholar became animated as he described to me the anticipation he felt as the play reached the seventh scene, in the fourth act, when Laertes, huddling with Claudius, reacts to the news that Hamlet is back in Denmark.

It's a moment in which Jenkins had made a crucial single-word change in his influential, encyclopedic Arden edition of *Hamlet,* and he wondered whether Branagh would adopt his emendation. "I listened to see what was coming," Jenkins told me. "What would [Laertes] *say*?"

On screen the actor playing Laertes turned to the King and told him, apropos Hamlet (who had killed his father): "It warms the very sickness in my heart / That I shall live and tell him to his teeth / 'Thus diest thou . . .' "

" 'Thus *diest* thou'! Yes!" the dapper, mild-mannered Jenkins exclaimed with all the fervor of a soccer fan celebrating a goal. "He got it right. And of course it is *so* much more effective."

Effective or not, Jenkins believes he's not "improving" Shakespeare but restoring to us Shakespeare's own long-lost word choice. In the two most substantial early texts of *Hamlet* that have come down to us from his time—the 1604 Quarto and the 1623 Folio versions—Laertes doesn't say "Thus diest thou." He says "Thus didst thou" in one and "Thus didest thou" in the other.

But Jenkins believes that what he has done is recover the word Shakespeare originally wrote with his own hand and quill—before it was corrupted through carelessness in the printing house or the playhouse. Jenkins believes that he has given us the word—"diest"—that Shakespeare *intended.*

THE SIGNATURE DRAMA OF THE DIVIDED SOUL: SOON TO BE SUBDIVIDED

Most people who have read *Hamlet* at some point in the past are unaware that what they're reading is usually a version that Shakespeare never wrote, and that his players never played. What most of us have read is, rather, an artificial "conflation" or superimposition of conflicting printed texts from his time and immediately afterward. (There is of course no manuscript in Shakespeare's hand.) Such conflations obscure marked differences between the competing versions. The conflated play is, in effect, a patchwork quilt composed of fabric from the various versions threaded through with conjectures, guesses, and emendations from editors such as Jenkins.

The uncertainties *Hamlet* editors grapple with make crucial differences in the way *Hamlet* is printed, read and played. "Everyone who wants to understand *Hamlet,*" argues Philip Edwards, editor of the New Cambridge *Hamlet,* "as reader, actor or director, needs to understand the nature of the play's textual questions and to have his or her own view of the questions in order to approach the ambiguities in the meaning."

AMONG LITERARY SCHOLARS, THOSE LIKE JENKINS WHO DEVOTE their lives to the maddening intricacies of Shakespearean textual editing are accorded a mixture of awe and pity for the labor they bestow on crucial but seemingly unresolvable problems. And *Hamlet* editors in particular are a special breed: tasked with the responsibility for the transmission of the closest thing there is to a sacred text in a secular culture. For centuries, to be an editor of *Hamlet* has often meant to enter a bewildering labyrinth, a garden of forking paths; for some, it has meant sacrificing a good part of their lives to an ordeal of close focus on maddeningly elusive enigmas. Jenkins himself spent twenty-eight years constructing his Arden edition. The demands of this calling have driven editors to tragedies of their own—drink, despair, obsession, an early grave for at least one.

But for the past century, while there were bitter disagreements over which path to take, there was a reigning consensus on what the final destination was supposed to be: a reconstruction, from the differing texts, of a Lost Archetype, the *Hamlet* Shakespeare "originally" wrote before it was corrupted in the printing house and the playhouse. There's a lovely, haunting phrase coined by Fredson Bowers, one of the preeminent figures of twentieth-century Shakespeare textual editing: "the veil of print." Bowers and his fellow scholars believed that editors could and should attempt to discern, beneath that error-riddled veil of the printed texts, the true hidden face of Shakespeare. To divine, from the fragmentary evidence, the nature of "Shakespeare's intentions."

That consensus has now been shattered. And replaced by a bitter scholarly civil war. One influential faction of scholars has been arguing since the 1980s that the two versions we have of some of Shakespeare's major works, especially *Lear* and *Hamlet,* don't represent two variations from a single Lost Archetype, but rather first and second *drafts,* reflecting Shakespeare's revisions, rewrites, and second thoughts. Drafts that need to be treated as separate works of art, or different stages of the same work.

And they have been winning converts. In 1986, the Oxford *Complete Works* edition of Shakespeare printed two versions of *King Lear* on this theory. The Oxford version was highly controversial ("the Oxford editors should be *hanged*!" Harold Bloom once exclaimed), but a dozen years later, *The Norton Shakespeare,* a leading American Complete Works edition, edited by Harvard's Stephen Greenblatt, followed suit and published not two but *three Lear*s (the two versions adopted from the Oxford edition plus a third, traditional, conflated version).

After dividing *Lear,* the Reviser faction set its sights on *Hamlet.* The coeditor of *The Oxford Shakespeare,* Gary Taylor, told me that he would have liked to have published two versions of *Hamlet* as well as two *Lear*s in the Oxford edition back in 1986, but he feared the notion was too radical back then, and might have undermined the credibility of the case for splitting *Lear.*

But now *Hamlet*'s time has come. In 1995 the editors and publishers of the Arden edition of Shakespeare made a decision that caused the equivalent of an earthquake in textual scholarship. One that will force many in the general public who are as yet unaware that there may be two *Lear*s to confront three *Hamlet*s. The new Arden edition, the one that will supplant Harold Jenkins's conflated version, will be a radically divided *Hamlet,* presenting three differing versions of the play printed one after the other. While the new Arden edition does not endorse the Reviser hypothesis, it will continue what has become a heated debate over what kind of artist Shakespeare was and what kind of play *Hamlet* is, what the differences in the three versions suggest about the play and the playwright.

The fact that the Arden division is the product of scrupulous bibliographic scholarship, and not a deconstructionist conceit, will not diminish the sure-to-be-disturbing, even scandalous fact that scholars seem to be giving up on the effort to judge what belongs in *Hamlet* and what doesn't. As a result, the signature drama of the divided soul in Western civilization is now to be subdivided.

THE NEW, NEW PARADIGM

The source of the split can be found in the uncertainty surrounding the origins of *Hamlet.* It seems to have been written sometime around 1600, but we don't even know when it was first performed, or whether Shakespeare was the first to dramatize the prose predecessor story (there are three reports of a lost predecessor play subsequently known as "the ur-*Hamlet*"). One could say there are two testaments of *Hamlet:* the so-called Good Quarto, which was first published in 1604, a few years after it was first staged (with Shakespeare playing the Ghost, according to legend). This is the version that Harold Jenkins believes is closest to Shakespeare's lost handwritten manuscript. And the First Folio version, published in 1623, seven years after Shakespeare's death, in a compendium of his plays assembled by his theatrical company's owners. ("Quarto" and "Folio" both refer to the size of the paper they were printed on, a quarto being the size of a contemporary paperback, the folio more on the order of an encyclopedia volume.)

Some of the differences are dramatic and obvious: the Quarto gives Hamlet a final, fourth-act soliloquy, the embittered meditation spoken as he watches the armies of Fortinbras prepare to slaughter and be slaughtered "for an egg-shell." It's the soliloquy that begins, "How all occasions do inform against me, / And spur my dull revenge! What is a man . . ." But it's absent from the 1623 Folio.

To lose (or add) thirty-five of Hamlet's most self-lacerating lines—about "thinking too precisely," the end point of his introspection, a self-consciousness *about* self-consciousness—is not inconsiderable. It eliminates a dimension of Hamlet's—and *Hamlet*'s—complexity. In all, there are some 230 lines in the Quarto that are absent from the Folio, including sixteen sustained passages, and some 70 lines in the Folio that are absent from the Quarto. Some of *Hamlet*'s most famous lines and phrases—that entire final soliloquy, "the pales and forts of reason," "the mote it is to trouble the mind's eye," "the sheeted dead that did squeak and gibber in the Roman streets," "stars with trains of fire and dews of blood," "the vicious mole of nature," "the monster custom," "the engineer hoist with his own petard," "Denmark's a prison" and "nothing either good or bad, but thinking makes it so"—are in one, but not the other, version of *Hamlet.* To choose the Quarto, for instance, is to gain "the pales and forts of reason," but to lose the Folio's "Denmark's a prison."

But the catalog of those dropped and added lines does not include—or begin to capture—the subtle and distinctive effect of the hundreds of one- and two-word variations within lines that are present in both versions. For instance, does Hamlet accuse his mother of questioning with "an idle tongue" or "a wicked tongue"? The difference is more than a typo.

Further complicating matters is the existence of a third, highly problematic, much argued over, *Hamlet* text, the so-called Bad Quarto. It's been dubbed "Bad" because it appears to be a truncated and garbled version of the play—a sort of seventeenth-century bootleg edition. It first appeared in 1603, a year before the Good Quarto. While the Good Quarto has some 3,700 lines, the Bad Quarto has just 2,200 lines, many of them sounding like bad imitations of Shakespeare. The "To be or not to be" soliloquy, for instance, begins

To be or not to be; ay, there's the point
To die, to sleep, is that all? Ay all.
No, to sleep, to dream; ay marry there it goes . . .

Many scholars, including Jenkins, believe that the Bad Quarto is a "memorial reconstruction," composed not from any Shakespearean manuscript, but from a recollection of a performance of *Hamlet,* perhaps done with the help of one or more bit players. The likeliest suspect, some say, is the actor who played Marcellus (the soldier who sees the Ghost with Horatio and Hamlet)—since the Bad Quarto is allegedly more faithful to the longer *Hamlet* texts in the scenes in which Marcellus is on stage. But recently, other scholars have tried to make the case that the Bad Quarto was not so much bad as very *early*—Shakespeare's youthful first draft, perhaps even a version of the "ur-*Hamlet*" itself, the lost predecessor play there are reports of in 1589, 1594 and 1596 but often attributed to Thomas Kyd, not Shakespeare. And, alas, there is almost no hard evidence remaining to support any side of the question.

Still the Bad Quarto has its uses: to some scholars it can sometimes suggest an alternative to variants in the other two. Harold Jenkins resolved the conflicting versions of Laertes's speech by triangulating the two "good" texts with the "bad" one. In the 1604 Good Quarto, Laertes declares defiantly of Hamlet, "I shall live and tell him to this teeth / 'Thus didst thou.' " In the 1623 Folio it's "Thus didest thou"—which merely corrects the iambic pentameter by making "didst" two syllables. The Bad Quarto is off on its own, with "thus he dies." Jenkins thinks that they're *all* wrong, and that the correct line is "Thus diest thou." That the Bad Quarto may be a reconstruction of something *heard* (in a performance of *Hamlet*) and reconstructed from memory serves Jenkins's case. If the line is one heard (or slightly misheard), he argues, it's more likely one remembers "Thus diest thou" as "Thus he dies," rather than as "Thus didest" or "Thus didst."

Jenkins believes Shakespeare actually wrote "Thus diest thou" for Laertes (a stronger imprecation than "Thus didst thou"—not just an indictment, but a death sentence), but that, because *e* and *d* are often confused in Elizabethan handwriting, a transcriber of Shakespeare's manuscript or a print shop compositor misread Shakespeare's "diest" as "didst."

Jenkins insists it's not just a matter of *Jenkins* liking "diest" better or thinking Shakespeare ought to have written "diest," but of Jenkins restoring Shakespeare's "original intentions."

But the didest/diest question is important in another respect, Jenkins believes. It is a reproof to, if not refutation of, the new belief that Shakespeare revised *Hamlet.* If Shakespeare had been looking over what most scholars regard as the earlier 1604 Good Quarto version of *Hamlet,* and had seen "Thus didst thou" printed there when he knew he wanted "Thus diest thou," he wouldn't have merely changed "didst" to "didest" in the Folio, he would have changed it to "diest." But he didn't.

"No," Jenkins told me, if Shakespeare had been going over the earlier version to revise it, "Shakespeare would have known that 'didst' was an *error* for 'diest' "—and made the change Jenkins made on his behalf.

Sometimes the art of *Hamlet* editing comes down to that: "Shakespeare would have known," the attempt to read Shakespeare's mind. And so, inevitably, different theories of the variations in the *Hamlet* texts envision not just different *Hamlets* but different Shakespeares, different notions of what is Shakespearean.

Differences, in particular, in the way he approached his dramatic art. There was the Shakespeare characterized by his colleagues as a playwright who never blotted a line—raced through a manuscript for the theater without looking back or revising (although Ben Jonson cattily responded, "would he *had* blotted a thousand").

Harold Jenkins puts a more reverential spin on this view by calling Shakespeare "the supreme poet who saw no *call* to revise *Hamlet*" or any of his other works.

Then there is the Shakespeare of the Oxford University Press editors who see him as a man of the stage rather than a man of the page, one who was happy to cut and rewrite to make his lines more effective on stage. It's not his "original intentions" that count, the Oxford editors argue, but his "final intentions" for the acting version. And there is still another Shakespeare—that of Lukas Erne, author of an influential recent study, *Shakespeare as a Literary Artist,* who concedes that Shakespeare may well have revised for the stage for the convenience of the theater managers' time constraints, but that doesn't mean these revisions represented his *final* intentions. Erne believes Shakespeare's truest, *literary* intentions were expressed rather in the longer, more wordy Good Quarto version.

All these variant Shakespeare personae are blended into a blur in conflated versions, the new Arden *Hamlet* editors Ann Thompson and Neil Taylor argue. By disentangling the linguistic DNA of the texts, they argue, the reader gets to experience not just the different versions of *Hamlet* each text may represent, but the different Shakespeares they represent as well: the different stages of his thinking process perhaps, his second thoughts, or the differing purposes—stage or page—of each variant.

The new Arden *Hamlet* represents the latest in what Barbara Mowat of the Folger Shakespeare Library, and a *Hamlet* editor in her own right (she and textual scholar Paul Werstine are editing the Folger Shakespeare edition), described to me as a series of "paradigm shifts" in the approach to the problem created by the existence of more than one version of several of Shakespeare's plays—including *Lear, Othello, Troilus and Cressida* and *Romeo and Juliet* in addition to *Hamlet.*

The initial paradigm was established by Shakespeare's first editors, John Heminge and Henry Condell, two of the participants in Shakespeare's theater company, who put together the 1623 Folio, which contains thirty-six plays. Heminge and Condell condemned the previously published single-play Quarto editions of the plays as "stolen . . . surreptitious . . . maimed and deformed."

Needless to say, there was some commercial self-interest at work in their defining their edition as the authentic one, and in the late eighteenth century, this paradigm was overturned when scholars discovered that Heminge and Condell had relied on—lifted, really—the texts of many of these allegedly "maimed and deformed" Quartos for use in their Folios. This prompted a return to the Quartos—on grounds they were closer to Shakespeare's "original intentions."

Then in the early twentieth century, Mowat continued, a newer paradigm emerged that divided the Quartos themselves into "Good" and "Bad" and restored some respect to certain of the Folio versions. And launched an entire generation of the best and brightest Shakespearean scholars into the vast, exacting and exhausting quest of "scientific bibliography," the effort to decide which variant of word or phrase in the Quarto and Folio versions represented the reading from the imagined "Lost Archetype," the purported "Shakespearean" original.

Often this involved a mind-numbing focus on the work of the compositors in the printing houses that produced the earliest texts of Shakespeare's plays. For one thing it was important to discover which of the variations between two versions of a play might be due to compositors' errors (as Jenkins argues in the "didst"/"diest" case) and which due to Shakespeare's own revisions.

So in an effort to lift the "veil of print," Shakespearean textual scholars abandoned the playhouses for the printing houses for nearly a century. In the printing houses they discovered (or created) an entire shadow cast of characters for Shakespeare's plays: certain variations were "scientifically" determined to be the result of Compositor E's inexperience or Compositor B's scrupulousness in correcting Compositor C's errors. The results were then "conflated" into hybrid Quarto-Folio combinations. In the past century, in the case of *Hamlet,* particularly in Jenkins's edition, preference was usually given to the longer 1604 Quarto.

And then in the 1980s, a group of scholars—among them Michael Warren at Berkeley, Steven Urkowitz at City College, Gary Taylor at Oxford and the independent scholar Eric Sams—began insisting on a new paradigm that would privilege the Folio versions as Shakespeare's "final intention," his revision for the stage. Their Shakespeare, the man of the theater, was attacked by scholars such as Harold Bloom and Harry Berger (and later, Lukas Erne) who insisted Shakespeare's plays are better read as poetry than seen as drama, that he is a man of the page rather than the stage, a dramatic poet rather than a poetic dramatist.

The new model of Shakespeare the "Reviser" faction imagines is distant from the devil-may-care figure of tradition (and *Shakespeare in Love*) who dashed off scripts before rushing off to the tavern, or to write his next play. In the new vision, Shakespeare is a rather more serious and self-conscious artist, a serial reviser of his great works. The Reviser faction argues that examining the changes from Quarto to Folio versions of *Hamlet, Lear, Othello,* among others, we can get a unique glimpse into Shakespeare's mind at work, rethinking and reconsidering his greatest achievements.

What's significant about the new three-text Arden, Mowat believes, is that it may represent the emergence of a *new*-new paradigm. A very Hamlet-like paradigm, a refusal to choose or decide between alternatives, one that gives respect to each of the different versions because four centuries of paradigm shifts have still left Shakespeare's "intentions," original or final, theatrical or literary, veiled beyond recovery with any degree of certainty.

Barbara Mowat even believes that the key axiom of the Revisers' School—that the Folio version of *Hamlet* is Shakespeare's revision of the Quarto for the theater—may lack foundation because it can't be proved for certain that the Folio version wasn't written *first* (and published later), in which case the Quarto would represent Shakespeare's later revision and *expansion* of *Hamlet.*

These unresolved conflicts leave a real problem for actors and directors. Consider the question of Hamlet's last words. As the play comes to an end, Hamlet's been stuck by a poisoned sword in his duel with Laertes. Dying, he tells Horatio he's had a terrifying vision. "O, I could tell you—" he begins. Did he have a glimpse of the afterlife? But there's no time and it's too awful, so instead he begs Horatio to tell the story behind the pile of bodies in the throne room, and gives the approaching Norwegian prince, Fortinbras, his "dying voice," his nod for the succession to the throne of Denmark.

And then he concludes: "The rest is silence." And so it is—at least in the Good Quarto.

But in the Folio, the line is written thus:

". . . The rest is silence. O, o, o, o."

We don't know for certain whether Shakespeare himself added these hammy-looking "O-groans"—as they're known in the literature (the term was coined by the scholar Maurice Charney)—or whether they were the interpolation of some actor who wanted to prolong his dying scene. How do we decide? The stakes are not inconsiderable: the last words of perhaps the most influential character in Western literature. Unfortunately, there's no direct evidence, no manuscript in Shakespeare's hand, no reminiscence by Richard Burbage, the actor who first played Hamlet, of conferring with the playwright, no witness to Shakespeare inking in the O-groans.

G. R. Hibbard, the Oxford University Press editor, who argues that the Folio version is a text closer to Shakespeare's final intentions as "a man of the theater," still balks at the unsophisticated-looking O-groans in the Folio, and substitutes a stage direction *he* composed: *"He gives a long sigh and dies"*—words Shakespeare never wrote.

Suppose, however, that Shakespeare wanted Hamlet to utter those final four O's? After all, he gives four O-groans to King Lear in the 1608 Quarto. If Shakespeare favored four final O-groans for Lear in 1608, why deny them to Hamlet?

It's also true that actors have played the O-groans beautifully in the past (although most leave them out). They can be transmuted from hollow-looking O's on the page to a tragic aria of grief, each O registering a deeper apprehension of death and terror: in a way, Hamlet's final, wordless, four-syllable soliloquy of grief. (In his 1999 *Hamlet* at the reconstructed Globe in London, Mark Rylance played them that way.) The addition of O-groans could reflect the way Shakespeare changed as a dramatic artist, even if some don't approve of the change.

They can also be seen as a final embodiment of the play's tragic irony. Hamlet decrees "the rest is silence" but instead of silence, those final four O's are torn from him by a sorrow and pain beyond his conscious command. Just as his attempt to stage-manage his revenge was subverted by the "divinity that shapes [his] ends," by Fate, here it costs him his control over his last utterances.

So, to groan or not to groan? The O-groans, like the other thematic variants, are like a Rorschach: theories projected on those inky O's reflect the Theorists' vision of who they think Hamlet (and Shakespeare) *should* be.

THE PALACE COUP

When I met with Gary Taylor down in Tuscaloosa, Alabama, where he's now director of the University of Alabama's Strode Center for Renaissance Studies, he had a chilling phrase to describe the behind-the-scenes triumph of the Revisers, one that has left Harold Jenkins's *Hamlet* edition looking obsolescent to some: palace coup.

"It's like there's been a palace coup," he told me in the Krispy Kreme doughnut shop in a Tuscaloosa strip mall, "but the rest of the country hasn't found out about it yet. And I think that maybe the new Arden, the three-text *Hamlet* will have the effect of making the rest of the world awake to the fact that the coup has happened."

It's unlikely anyone in the Krispy Kreme is aware they are in the presence of one of the chief plotters of the palace coup, the one whose efforts have led *Lear* to be divided and *Hamlet* subdivided. When Gary Taylor, who edited the Oxford *Complete Works* versions of both *Hamlet* and *Lear,* says the rest of the country hasn't found out about the palace coup in the realm of Shakespeare studies, what he means is that most well-educated general readers aren't yet aware there are two *Lear*s—and now they will be told, in effect, by the new Arden edition that there are three *Hamlet*s. That they've been reading the wrong *Hamlet* their entire life; they've been reading a *Hamlet* Shakespeare never wrote or staged in *his* entire life. Two *Lear*s! Three *Hamlet*s? Could it be? What to make of it?

Palace coup: it has a *Hamlet*-like ring to it. *Hamlet* itself, of course, is a play about a palace coup the rest of the country doesn't learn about until it's too late, the one Claudius executed when he murdered Hamlet's father and seized the throne at Elsinore. In fact, a more appropriate analogous figure to Gary Taylor might be not Claudius, but Fortinbras. Unlike Claudius, hoist with his own petard, Fortinbras, who has been executing maneuvers, marching all over the outskirts of Elsinore throughout the play, walks in to take command when the parties within the palace have slaughtered each other. He's a *winner.* And unlike the Machiavellian bedroom intriguer Claudius, he is a military man, and Gary Taylor, scholarly wunderkind, is nothing if not a martial spirit. Military images and talk of tactics, strategies, flanking attacks and the like crop up in his conversation when he speaks of his campaign to divide *Lear* and *Hamlet.*

Perhaps it has something to do with the fact that he's an army brat; his father was an air force officer and he grew up on military bases in the South. It sounds like he's studied the campaigns of Caesar and, in fact, his campaign to divide *Lear* and *Hamlet* may leave a more lasting mark than Caesar's campaigns in Gaul: it is in no small part due to Gary Taylor's crusade that all *Hamlet* will soon be divided into three parts.

It's a sleepy summer Sunday in July and the Krispy Kreme seems an incongruous setting for a discussion of an assault on the citadels of Shakespearean orthodoxy. Gary Taylor presents a somewhat incongruous-looking figure for a Shakespearean scholar as well. He has the long hair, T-shirt and drawl of a roadie for a seventies southern rock band—Lynyrd Skynyrd say, before the tragic air crash. Listening to him discuss Shakespearean revisionism in this slow backwater of the Old Confederacy (home of the legendary Dreamland Barbecue shack), one could hardly imagine the havoc he has wrought in the august precincts of Renaissance scholarship until you begin to think of his resemblance to that striking cover picture of seventies icon Richard Brautigan, looking dandyish in an antiquated gray battle tunic posing for the cover of *A Confederate General from Big Sur.* Gary Taylor is a Confederate general from Oxford University Press, you might say, one who's come close to succeeding in dividing the Union of Shakespeare texts. An act of secession, one might say, as the 1604 Quarto withdraws from its entangled conflation with the Folio version like two strands of a chromosome separating.

He's been telling me how his engagement in the war over the texts of *King Lear* began with a study of the war *in King Lear:* "When I arrived at Cambridge for graduate study, the topic announced for the prize essay that year was 'War and Shakespeare,' and I did mine on the battle scenes in Shakespeare's plays, and what that meant was I had to look at the different stage directions, and the differences in those stage directions led to my essay on 'The War in Lear.' "

In that essay he argued that Shakespeare—or someone—had systematically altered the 1608 Quarto of *King Lear* to make it seem, in the 1623 Folio version, that the war in the final two acts waged by Lear's daughter Cordelia was less an invasion by a foreign power than a civil war. He postulated the changes were designed to make Cordelia's revolt more politically acceptable. Cordelia, you'll recall, had gone off to marry the King of France after Lear had cut her out of the division of his kingdom for refusing to take part in his who-loves-Daddy-best contest with her two sisters. Later, when those two sisters, Goneril and Regan, cast Lear out into the cold, Cordelia returns from France at the head of an army to attempt to rescue her father. The changes from the earlier 1608 Quarto to the 1623 Folio, Taylor argued, made it seem that "Cordelia seems to lead not an invasion but a rebellion, like Bolingbroke or Richmond's" (Henry IV and Henry VII). In the Folio, Taylor argues, Cordelia is made to seem less a French queen than a loyal British daughter. Others would contest this interpretation, but it won adherents.

He went on from his analysis of the alterations in the depiction of the war to make a frontal assault on the long-held Lost Archetype theory about the differences between the 1608 Quarto and the 1623 Folio versions of *Lear*—differences that ranged from the omission from the Folio *Lear* of the mad-scene mock-trial of Lear's daughters, to the addition of a fourth and fifth "never" in Lear's heartbreaking response to Cordelia's dying. It's "Never, never, never, never, never" in the Folio instead of "Never, never, never" in the Quarto. And there's a difference in Lear's last words far greater than the difference in Hamlet's, a difference I'll address in detail in chapter 4.

The Lost Archetype theory argues that the differences in the two versions of *Lear* came not from Shakespeare's revision of a first draft, but from the fact that they both are imperfectly transcribed or recorded versions of the *same* lost Shakespearean original. That Shakespeare didn't revise *Lear,* but scribes, theatrical prompt-book keepers, printers and compositors managed to produce two different imperfect versions of a lost Shakespeare manuscript, the Lost Archetype.

Gary Taylor was not the first to make the counterargument that Shakespeare revised *Lear.* (It was Berkeley's Michael Warren who argued the case in an influential 1976 paper at a Shakespeare Association of America convention, which rekindled the *Lear* text debate. And it was legendary textual scholar Peter Blayney whose book on the printing of the 1608 *Lear* restored the Quarto to the status of a text—however badly printed—based on a Shakespearean manuscript, not on a "memorial reconstruction by actors." Blayney's 1982 work laid the basis for the claim that Shakespeare both wrote and revised the 1608 version.) But Taylor was the one who forged an informal alliance of *Lear* text dissidents into a formidable scholarly phalanx that overwhelmed the opposition, an alliance it's hard to resist calling the Raiders of the Lost Archetype.

IT WAS MORE THAN GARY TAYLOR'S PRIZE-WINNING ESSAY AND HIS position on the cutting edge of the *Lear* revision rebellion that brought him to the attention of Stanley Wells, the scholar mandarin, then undertaking the Herculean task of producing the new edition of the Oxford *Complete Works of Shakespeare* in the early eighties. It was also his dazzling facility at the insanely arcane and complex art of "compositor studies," the hideously labor-intensive attempt to find the truth about the variants in Shakespeare texts based on the analysis of the characteristics of the work of the typesetting compositors in the print shops that inked the plays on quarto- and folio-size pages.

Few have the combination of mental acuity and stamina to excel in this immersion in typographical minutiae. One of the avatars of the art, Charlton Hinman, even invented a kind of special Shakespeare collating machine, a contraption that employed flashing lights and mirrors to scan the seventeenth-century texts to track tiny variants not just among the three substantive *Hamlet* texts, say, but the changes often made, the errors often but not always corrected, during the print run of each of the texts—"on-press variants." Variations that made almost every one of the surviving copies of the early *Hamlet* texts its own idiosyncratic variant of the play.

But Taylor was one of the first, early in the eighties, to bring computer power to bear on Shakespearean bibliography. He combined it with a facility for teasing subtextual dramas and characters out of the typographical minutiae. An ability to find, in the cast of characters of the compositors in the print shop, clues to the cast of characters of Shakespeare in the playhouse. Consider Taylor's influential 1985 study "The Folio Copy for *Hamlet, King Lear,* and *Othello*" in which he advances a heretical new hypothesis about the relationship between the two *Hamlet* texts. To get a flavor of the kind of microscopic attention Shakespearean textual editing devotes to elucidating clarity from the ink-smudged Rorschach of the typographical evidence, let me quote a little from Gary Taylor's argument in that paper.

First he tips his hat in a politic way to his predecessors: he wants to signal he's building on their methods, not dismantling their legacy:

> Not the least of Charlton Hinman's many contributions to bibliographical scholarship was his discovery of an apprentice compositor, "E," at work in the Tragedies section of the First Folio, a discovery subsequently secured and sophisticated by the patient labors of T. H. Howard-Hill, who has developed and applied a whole range of tests to solidify the distinction between E and the compositor he most often worked alongside, B. Both Hinman and Howard-Hill have approached these compositor identifications in a spirit of disinterested research—not as a brief flanking attack on a larger target with more obvious editorial implications . . .

Note the use of military metaphors—the "flanking attack on a larger target"—which, of course, is exactly what Gary Taylor engaged in:

> In the case of Compositor E, happily, the stamina of such bibliographers has now brought us to a position where we can finally resolve one of the major editorial problems in the study of Shakespeare . . .

Taylor then introduces us to "Compositor E," one of those ink-stained wretches who, he says, can help us resolve a mystery of *Hamlet* studies:

> Hinman himself observed that Compositor E was demonstrably very much more influenced by previously typeset copy than either A or B was . . . The extent of E's conservatism can be quickly demonstrated by an analysis of the Folio punctuation of the plays he has known to have set from printed copy . . . The very first page that Compositor E is agreed to have set in the Folio, *pp 4* of *Titus,* he retained Q3 punctuation 77 times and altered only 12 times, on the next page he retained punctuation 126 times and altered it 36 times . . .

Taylor then argues that this habitual caution, this aversion to alteration of printed texts, of Compositor E offers a clue to the revision of *Hamlet.* For years bibliographers have argued that the 1623 Folio text of *Hamlet* was typeset from a cut, printed version of the earlier 1604 Good Quarto. All wrong, Gary Taylor claims to have proved, on the basis of a radical change in Compositor E's punctuation-alteration ratios in the two pages of the Folio edition of *Hamlet* which our man E is said to have set:

"The two pages that E is agreed to have set in *Hamlet* . . . dramatically depart from this pattern." In these pages "the proportion of retained to altered punctuation [from the Quarto to the Folio version] is 53/82 and 65/99. In other words, for these two pages, the ratio of retention to variation is 2–3, whereas the pages from the three plays where Compositor E is known to have set from printed copy, it ranges from 3–1 to 6–1."

Follow that? E's uncharacteristic departure here from his habitual conformity to the punctuation in the printed texts he set *proves* the Folio must have been typeset from a more irregularly punctuated *handwritten* manuscript which in turn suggests a more far-reaching authorial revision:

> The evidence . . . in these two pages demonstrates that E cannot have been setting *Hamlet* from printed copy. And if E was not using printed copy, we have no reason to suspect that any of the other Folio compositors are either: indeed if any compositor were to have been supplied printed copy, it surely would have been the apprentice E.

That latter statement seems more supposition than proof, but more important is the unstated purpose of this flanking attack: to advance the case that the Folio was extensively and personally revised, perhaps rewritten, by hand, by Shakespeare.

SEEING SHAKESPEARE ACROSS THE ROOM

The problem with theories of *Hamlet* texts is the tentative, hypothetical, almost destabilizingly complex nature of their arguments, their dependence on dotted-line rather than solid connections between entities such as "second transcripts" that have never been seen.

The evidence of things unseen: Gary Taylor's ability to grapple with the typesetting minutiae, and the statistical comparisons—and the power of the arguments he derived from them—made his rise within the Oxford Shakespeare hierarchy remarkably rapid. After appointing Taylor an assistant editor in 1978, Stanley Wells made him a full coeditor of *The Oxford Shakespeare* in 1984.

But his facility led him to a deeper level of disillusion—about the ability to ever retrieve, from the texts we have, some true encounter with Shakespeare.

"Paying attention to compositors," Taylor told me, "you become aware of the fact that there's always someone standing between you and Shakespeare. And that's the basis of a lot of my subsequent meditative theorizing about editing, how the mediator is always there. And that came out of paying a lot of attention to identifying these particular mediators, the compositors actually who set the First Folio in type. You become aware in a very concrete way of somebody who is affecting what you see and what you read. And even then—there are some cases where you can quite literally say, well, compositor 'A' always spells that *this* way, or compositor 'I' that I identified in *Henry VIII* always does certain things with suffixes. But that doesn't necessarily tell you anything about what *Shakespeare's* spelling was. You may not be able to see through the compositor and figure out how Shakespeare did spell something, you become aware that there's a limit to what you can know.

"There's always somebody standing between you and him. It's like being at a cocktail party and there may be one person in the room that really interests you the most, but there's other people around, and so it's like seeing Shakespeare across the room at a party. There's always going to be parts of him you can't see, and which parts you do see is partly accidental. . . ."

And yet, he tells me, it was his communion with the inky traces of the compositors and typographers that led him to see, through an ink-smudged glass, darkly, a vision of Shakespeare as a reviser.

It was a reaction to what he calls the "demonization" of the compositors by the partisans of the Lost Archetype who try to blame the variations between the two *Hamlet*s on the inattention, the "eye skip," the carelessness, the willfulness and wandering eyes of an array of compositors. On the contrary, Taylor believes, "You need only one agent to account for all those variations and that's the agent who's present in all of these cases: Shakespeare."

Note that he says you only *need* "one agent" to account for the changes—that's not the same as saying only one agent *is* responsible. But Taylor puts his case in historical context: "The existence of these intermediaries has been used since the eighteenth century as the justification for creating an idealized image of Shakespeare because anything you do not like in Shakespeare could be blamed on other people, these *other* people corrupted him. But when you actually begin seriously investigating these agents of transmission not as demonic figures being used to create a sainted divine figure, if you begin investigating them as actual human beings who had certain identities and practices which you could trace in their other work aside from Shakespeare, it becomes impossible to demonize them, make them responsible for everything bad, everything you don't like.

"And," he adds, "to the extent that these other people become real, then Shakespeare can certainly become more real too. Because he's not a divine figure, he's not a figure you construct in the sort of religious terms that Harold Bloom does."

There are those who believe that in making Shakespeare "more real" as he puts it, Taylor has made him *too* real or too fallible. Some claimed Taylor himself was even a secret *enemy* of Shakespeare. That's the spin some opponents put on Taylor's controversial decision in 1985 to announce to the world (and to put the imprimatur of Oxford University Press upon) an important new "discovery"—attribution really—to Shakespeare of a previously little-known doggerel verse moldering away in Oxford's Bodleian Library, the one that began "Shall I die? / Shall I fly." Only an enemy of Shakespeare would accuse the Bard of having written such awful stuff, some were heard to mutter.

Mutter loudly enough that, without prompting, Gary Taylor tells me at the Krispy Kreme, "Despite what some people say, it's just not true that I *hate* Shakespeare." Although it's clear he does hate the myth of unique Shakespearean genius and transcendence.

But even among his erstwhile scholar allies in the war over *Lear,* there has been, it seems, hatred and strife. Taylor was telling me about the way he teamed up with other Doubters of the Lost Archetype such as Michael Warren, Steven Urkowitz and Peter Blayney, to challenge the tradition of conflating the texts of *Lear.* "I was very much influenced by Peter [Blayney] who was at Cambridge with me," Taylor told me at the Krispy Kreme, "and we were good friends at the time, although he hates me now. We spent huge amounts of time talking together."

"He hates me now. . . ." Casually injected into his conversation, it's a token of the kinds of passions the struggle over Shakespearean texts has engendered. (When I tried to reach Blayney to talk to him about *Lear* texts, he left a phone message telling me I must be mistaken: he had no interest in Shakespeare anymore—only in printing shops of the time.)

Taylor is a bit vague about the reasons for the imputed hatred, but suggests it might have something to do with a "very Perry Mason–like moment," the moment when the rebels, the Beraters of the Lost Archetype, you might say, had their first victory. He depicts it as a dramatic capitulation by the Old Order. The scene of the confrontation was a seminar room at a Shakespeare Association of America convocation in 1980. In his contrarian study of bardolatry though the ages, *Re-Inventing Shakespeare,* Taylor describes the moment when he and three other heretics (not including Peter Blayney, who wasn't present) argued the case for separating the texts of *King Lear* into an early and a later, revised, draft rather than conflating the texts as centuries of editors had done:

> The chairman of the seminar, G. B. Evans of Harvard, editor of the Riverside edition, asks three respected senior scholars to comment on the work of these upstart revisionists: Hunter from Yale, Wells from Oxford and . . . George Walton Williams from Duke. Both Wells and

Williams announce their conversions to the revisionist cause. So does another participant, Thomas Clayton, of the University of Minnesota. Hunter, champion of an orthodoxy that has lasted for centuries, finds himself suddenly surrounded and embattled.

"Surrounded and embattled": yes. It's war, after all. "The revisionist position," Taylor goes on, heady with martial triumph, "immediately acquires the intellectual glamour that David achieved by slaying Goliath. Its new academic credibility results from a classic moment of theatrical recognition . . . the revisionists recognized their own strength. . . ."

Taylor implies Peter Blayney's absence from this primal blooding-by-combat, this transformative battlefield victory, is the reason Blayney "hates me." In any case, the Perry Mason moment was but the first of a number of dramatic victories for the Revisers/Dividers of *Lear.* The decision of Stanley Wells to accede to Gary Taylor's urging and print not one but two *King Lear*s in the 1986 Oxford *Complete Works* edition had the most impact. The 1997 decision to print not two but *three King Lear*s in the American Norton edition—the Quarto and Folio adopted from the Oxford edition plus a third traditional, conflated edition—had a further somewhat confusing but consolidating effect on the division of *Lear.*

The shock, the veritable earthquake reverberations (within the profession, anyway) caused by the Oxford division of *Lear* cracked the foundation of several other two-text plays previously conflated together. *Othello, Henry V, Richard III, Romeo and Juliet* began to be looked upon as candidates for disentangling, as instances of Shakespearean revision. But there was always trepidation about *Hamlet.*

"I thought we *should* have divided Hamlet in the Oxford edition," Taylor tells me, but strategy prevailed over tactics: "To have done an edition that divided both *Hamlet* and *Lear* would have undercut the credibility the Oxford name conferred on the division of *Lear,* made it seem the product of a more radical revolution. So I didn't press it with Stanley."

Stanley Wells himself, writing in 1991, five years after *The Oxford Shakespeare* split *Lear,* spoke of the notion of splitting *Hamlet* with some of the same trepidation early twentieth-century scientists spoke of splitting the atom: "Someday in the future editors will have the courage to do for *Hamlet* what we did with *Lear.*"

The future is now and Stanley Wells was still not sure, when I spoke to him, that the time is right to divide *Hamlet.* One afternoon in London over tea in Mayfair he told me he felt that the multiplication of multiple-text editions "might be misleading" to a bewildered public.

But it's happening, and Gary Taylor thinks the Arden decision a vindication of his position, a signal of the victory of the "palace coup." "It's a revolution that has already happened, fully in place and institutionalized within the intellectual community, but one that hadn't yet reached the wider world in terms of what it's changed."

HIS TRIUMPHALISM MAY BE PREMATURE. THE WAR MAY NOT BE over. The partisans of the Lost Archetype are not ready to surrender. Frank Kermode, for one, is not. In a powerfully argued attack on the theory delivered to the British Academy in 1994 entitled "Disintegration Once Again," Kermode, perhaps the preeminent British Shakespeare critic (his edition of the Arden *Tempest* is considered a classic and he recently published his reflections on the evolution of Shakespeare's verbal style in *Shakespeare's Language*), links the Dividers and Revisers of today to the "disintegrators," the earlier twentieth-century movement in Shakespeare scholarship which professed to find different "hands," ever-multiplying collaborators in many of Shakespeare's plays. (A position that has acquired more selective and credible support in Brian Vickers's 2005 *Shakespeare: Co-Author.*)

To "the new disintegrators," as Kermode called Taylor and his allies, "the disintegration of the texts is part of a larger effort to disintegrate their author, or at any rate to demolish the idolatrous image that over the past couple of hundred years—so it is claimed—has been erected by editors and critics alike in place of a Shakespeare they can see no reason to think worthy of such an apotheosis."

For Kermode then, the Dividers are motivated by the theoretical ideologies of postmodernism, but his argument against them does not depend on a disdain for their theory but rather a refutation of their evidence and argument. He gets deeply into the matrix and texture of the variants in the *Lear* texts to argue that close reading confirms the strength of the case for a Lost Archetype.

He cites several passages in act 1, scene 1 of *Lear,* for instance, that indicate, he believes, that each version was based on a Lost Archetype and suggests that "the collapsed archetype [theory should be] shored up" once again.

Few came forward to shore up Kermode's argument until six years later when a powerful case against Gary Taylor's original thesis on "The War in *King Lear*" appeared in the *International Shakespeare Yearbook.* It was by Richard Knowles, editor of the forthcoming Modern Language Association's variorum edition of *Lear.* Knowles calls Gary Taylor's "War in *King Lear*" essay "a manifesto and a salvo," picking up on its martial spirit, but then salvoes back with a remarkably stark counterblast: "The confident claim of radical differences between Quarto and Folio in [Taylor's] much cited essay, when they are seen against the total evidence of those texts, proves in virtually every instance to be without substance."

Knowles doesn't just disagree, then, he wants to blow Taylor's argument off the map: Taylor's arguments for a revised *Lear,* he says, "depend on over-literal interpretation of some variant stage directions . . . and in some cases these claims even invoke false, non-existent or invented evidence."

A declaration of war! An attempted coup against the "palace coup."

When I faxed Knowles's blast to Kermode, he faxed me back to express great pleasure that someone had taken up the Lost Archetype cause, and added, "The Taylorites still must reply to my evidence from Act I, Scene 1." Approaching Lear's age Frank Kermode is, far more vigorously than the aging king, trying to hold Lear's kingdom together.

In America Richard Knowles has been counterattacking since 1985, earning a counter-counterattack from Taylor as an exemplum of "The Rhetoric of Reaction."

The warlike fractiousness of the scholars and the sometimes personal tone it takes should not obscure, however, the issue at stake in the war over the texts of *Lear* and *Hamlet:* In what ways do the differences make the two variations different works of art? And how much did Shakespeare himself *want* to make them different works of art? To some the question is even more fraught with significance for *Hamlet* than for *Lear.*

As Paul Werstine, one of the most stringently skeptical scholarly observers of the textual wars, has argued, "Those who object to the argument for the revision of *Lear* on the grounds that Shakespeare wouldn't have revised his play merely to change the nature of some secondary characters, need to recognize that the change between the Quarto and Folio *Hamlet* is a change in the role of the main character, Hamlet himself." I would, and will in chapter 4, argue that the variation in Lear's last words in the two texts is as great a change, as great an issue "in the role of the main character" as any change in *Hamlet* with perhaps one exception—Hamlet's last soliloquy, the "How all occasions do inform against me . . ." soliloquy, present in the Quarto but cut from the Folio.

Gary Taylor stresses that the omission of Hamlet's final soliloquy from the fourth act makes the Folio a different play. The soliloquies define *Hamlet* after all, and they are at the very heart of the grandiose claims Harold Bloom has made for *Hamlet:* that it is in these soliloquies that Shakespeare "invented" a new kind of consciousness in Western culture, a meditative, reflective *self* consciousness. And it is in that final soliloquy (at least in the Good Quarto) that Hamlet has his last chance to reflect on the questions of revenge, delay, on the question of self-consciousness itself (the phrase "some craven scruple / Of thinking too precisely on th' event" which appears in that soliloquy might be an instance not of self-consciousness but of something more complex: self-*conscious* self-consciousness, *meta* self-consciousness).

The placement of that fourth-act soliloquy has aroused much debate about its significance. Recall that it takes place during the time Hamlet is being dragged off to the ship that is supposed to take him to enforced exile (and planned murder) in England. As he crosses the darkling coastal plains, he sees Fortinbras's troops, led by the ever-decisive, ever-on-the-move Norwegian prince, here leading his ignorant army in transit across Denmark to attack Poland.

It's a spectacle, the prospect of someone cheerfully risking thousands of deaths in quarrel "for an egg-shell," that causes Hamlet to reconsider his own self-loathing indecisiveness, his failure to revenge his father's death on Claudius, whom he could have slain at prayer after he'd caught "the conscience of the King" in the *Mousetrap* play.

"How all occasions do inform against me . . ." Hamlet begins, seeing the bold Fortinbras as a reproach to his own "thinking too precisely."

"Rightly to be great," he says, "Is not to stir without great argument, / But greatly to find quarrel in a straw . . ."

He already *has* great argument, his father's murder, he insists to himself, and so "from this time forth, / My thoughts be bloody, or be nothing worth!"

There has been bitter division over the function and necessity of this soliloquy. Some argue that it *deserved* to be cut from the Quarto because it's repetition: Hamlet going over the same old self-reproachful ground, while others have maintained that the very fact that Hamlet obsessively returns to "thinking too precisely" about "thinking too precisely" is precisely why it's important as the final instance of Hamlet's self-definition. That his return to the revenge/delay dynamic raises it to a defining moment of his character and the play.

"More than most of Shakespeare's plays," Gary Taylor tells me, "*Hamlet* is dominated by a single theme. And therefore, the question of whether or not he has that soliloquy in the fourth act *does* make a considerable difference to your interpretation of the role and therefore the play. I mean Branagh's *Hamlet* would have been *much* better if he'd cut that." It's very much in fashion among the more fervid of the revisionists to insist not only that all revisions were by Shakespeare but that all revisions (such as cutting the last soliloquy) were brilliant "Shakespearean" decisions (rather than those of a theater manager). John Jones argues that case in *Shakespeare at Work* in 1995 and James Shapiro argues it again in his book *1599*, published in 2005).

As many times as it's made, reiteration of this assertion on various grounds is no substitute for proof. Taylor has a more subtle analysis of the differences: another *level* of difference between the two *Hamlet*s and the conflated text, he argues, has to do with pacing and time:

"One's experience of a work of art is different depending upon how it manipulates time. And therefore what people dismissively refer to as 'theatrical cutting' [in the shorter Folio version] very often is, it seems to me, about the manipulation of time. And that is something people in the theater know experientially, intuitively and practically—from seeing what works and what doesn't work in front of audiences. And Shakespeare's very good at this, knowing when your audience is going to start to get restless, it doesn't matter how beautiful the poetry is. Timing, Timing, Timing. Knowing how to shape time is a crucial part of the art. Whether it makes a difference to the meaning of *Hamlet,* it makes a difference to the experience of *Hamlet* as temporal art form.

"The whole thing of time and the control of time is important. And then you can make an argument about time being important to the *story* that *Hamlet* has to tell, as well. *Hamlet* is the longest play in the Shakespeare canon; it's one of the longest plays in the Western canon, and it takes all that length of time for Hamlet to do it, so what's the justification for this extraordinary long-windedness on Shakespeare's part? Well, the justification for it must be it's a play *about* somebody who can't finish something, instead of a play about Shakespeare not being able to finish something, or not being able to shut up. And the duration becomes an issue. It makes a difference how long something is."

While Taylor feels the Arden decision to do a divided *Hamlet* is a vindication of his anti-conflationist approach, he claims to have withdrawn from the *Hamlet* wars. Moved on to another battle front where, I later learned, he is preparing another surprise flanking attack, actually more of a wholesale invasion and seizure of the Shakespeare canon. Word of this rather shocking new development, not then known to the world, reached me when I was interviewing a scholar at Merton College, Oxford, named Tiffany Stern, author of *Rehearsal from Shakespeare to Sheridan,* which offers an important new critique of the "memorial reconstruction" theory of the Bad Quarto, the third text in the forthcoming Arden tripartite *Hamlet.* Ms. Stern confided to me, in an amusedly scandalized tone, that she'd heard that Gary Taylor was planning a grand raid on the Shakespeare canon on behalf of Thomas Middleton, a dramatist contemporary of Shakespeare best known for *The Revenger's Tragedy* and *The Changeling.* Taylor has been engaged in producing an edition of the complete works of Middleton, and he's argued in the *Times Literary Supplement* that Middleton is, at the very least, Shakespeare's equal as a dramatist, neglected only because Shakespeare happened to be the one chosen by the ruling hegemony of British culture as an icon of its imperial ideology.

But now he's gone further than that. Someone in the know at the Merton College Fellows high table confirmed to Ms. Stern and me this latest dispatch from the battlefield: Gary Taylor had decided to include in his complete edition of Middleton four plays usually attributed to Shakespeare: *Macbeth, Measure for Measure, Timon of Athens,* and *Troilus and Cressida.* While in the past some have argued that Middleton may have collaborated in some of them (the Hecate song in *Macbeth* appears in a Middleton play as well), including them in the Middleton canon will certainly be seen as a deliberate provocation, another front in Gary Taylor's war against . . .

Against what? Not Shakespeare, he insists, but what he regards as Shakespeare's overblown mythic and transcendent reputation.

It made me recall again Gary Taylor's insistence to me that he doesn't "*hate* Shakespeare." It made me recall something else he said to me, specifically about *Hamlet.* He'd been telling me about various productions of *Hamlet* he'd seen over the years. His favorite was the furiously eccentric Steven Berkoff production, in London, "that was most notorious for the bedroom scene in which Hamlet fucked Gertrude. When you speak of it in those terms," he added, "it sounds wild and crazy but in context it seemed perfectly natural." But at another point he casually let drop that "it almost doesn't matter what production, I always cry at the end of *Hamlet.*"

Every *Hamlet*?

"I always find myself choking up," he said, adding, "I cry easily, I get this from my mother."

It could be said without too much exaggeration that if Gary Taylor cries at every *Hamlet,* there are a number of *Hamlet* scholars who cry at the mention of Gary Taylor. Certainly Harold Jenkins, the editor of the Arden *Hamlet,* the last Grand Unification *Hamlet,* the one about to be split in three by his own publisher, is one of them. He was on the verge of tears when he spoke to me about the coming disintegration of his life work.

HAROLD JENKINS: DEATH BEFORE DISINTEGRATION

Harold Jenkins was nearing ninety and physically a bit frail when I met with him at his shipshape little cottage in Finchley in London. Emotionally a bit frail as well; he'd just returned that week from his brother's funeral.

And as it turned out, it was just a year before his own death. But he could still summon vigor, passion and a touch of bitterness when it came to defending the integrity of his life's work, the second Arden edition of *Hamlet,* the one he'd devoted nearly thirty years to compiling. A labor of a lifetime, a labor of love he fears will soon be lost when it will be superseded by the new *Hamlet* his own publisher is replacing his with. The new *Hamlet* that will pull apart, disentangle, disintegrate the fabric he'd labored to weave together. The fabric—the fabrication his critics would say—of a unified *Hamlet,* the conflated Lost Archetype *Hamlet.*

I'm not sure if Jenkins was yet aware—few were—when I spoke to him of the radical surgery the new Arden *Hamlet* was about to perform on Jenkins's conflated *Hamlet.* It wasn't until a few days later I learned about it from the editors of that new *Hamlet,* Ann Thompson and Neil Taylor. They had just made the decision themselves, and I'm not sure anyone had the heart to tell Harold Jenkins before he died.

Still, despite disclaimers of having left the battle behind, Jenkins was still acutely aware of the polemics and counterpolemics that followed in the wake of the 1982 publication of his Arden edition of *Hamlet.* "I've been savagely attacked," he said, his opponents have often been "venomous." But he remained confident his achievement would last. And he was not alone in his belief.

Thomas Pendleton, the judicious coeditor of *The Shakespeare Newsletter,* has suggested "it will remain a classic work, an astounding achievement that will serve readers for years to come." Jenkins took much pleasure in pointing out to me that Harold Bloom, hanging judge of the Oxford *Hamlet,* had conspicuously chosen Jenkins's Arden for all his citations from *Hamlet* in his best-selling Shakespeare book.

A LOSS OF STARS

Harold Jenkins's lifelong closeness to Shakespeare began, he told me, with the fact they both grew up close to the trees and the stars.

"I'm a country boy, Buckinghamshire, in the Midlands. And it was an essential part of my education in Shakespeare. When I think of the language with the buttercups and the lady's-smocks and the marsh marigolds, these are things I was very familiar with as a child. I never see them now in London," he lamented.

He was a country boy, of course, made of sterner stuff than marsh marigolds. Like Shakespeare, he became a success in the metropolis: he was a country boy who rose to a position of unique preeminence at the apex of the demanding and exclusive profession of British literary scholarship, successor to J. Dover Wilson, one of the giants of twentieth-century Shakespeare scholarship, in the University of Edinburgh's Chair of Rhetoric and English Literature, later to become general editor of the entire Arden edition of Shakespeare and editor of its centerpiece, the Arden *Hamlet.* Nonetheless, he said as he fixed tea, dapper in a suit and bow tie, he still missed the landscape of marsh marigolds.

"I don't know when I've last seen the stars and when I've last heard the cuckoo. Whereas if you lived in the country, you were terribly aware of the stars."

Terribly aware of the stars. Terribly aware of their loss. It makes one think of how prominent a role stars play in Shakespeare, angry stars, fortune's stars, the stars Juliet wants to cut Romeo up into and hang upon the night sky. The glowing carpet of stars Jessica and Lorenzo gaze at in the strange fifth act of *The Merchant of Venice.*

Jenkins's lament at the loss of stars evokes the characteristic elegiac gentility that inflects Harold Jenkins's tone, an echo of loss. His friends say he never quite recovered from the loss of his wife of fifty years, struck by a motorbike shortly after his monumental lifework, his 608-page edition of *Hamlet,* was published in 1982. And now he knows his *Hamlet* itself, in effect, has been given a death sentence, its successor already in the works.

Perhaps the best way of capturing Harold Jenkins's achievement is to describe his life work as the Last Grand Unification *Hamlet.* The last heroic attempt to solve the problem of *Hamlet* texts, the problem of Shakespeare's intentions for *Hamlet,* the problem of the score of large and hundreds of small but significant variations in the two major texts, by giving us a single *Hamlet,* a *Hamlet* that presents itself as the one true *Hamlet,* the closest it's humanly possible to get to Shakespeare's intended *Hamlet.*

And perhaps the best way to capture Harold Jenkins's despair at what is about to happen to his *Hamlet* is to record an exchange I had with him about that forthcoming successor edition.

"I suspect I won't like it," he said. "I suspect it will take an anti-Jenkins position. But it doesn't much matter. I'm ninety now, I don't imagine I shall live to see it. And that I shall not regret."

"That I shall not regret": in other words, in his gentle, understated way, he hoped to *die* rather than see his *Hamlet* superseded.

In a sense he was wrong to say that it will be "anti-Jenkins." The coeditor of the new Arden *Hamlet,* Ann Thompson, whom I met the following day, had nothing but respectful things to say to me about Jenkins; her admiration, I believe, was genuine for Jenkins's Sisyphean labor. Her stance, the stance of the *Hamlet* she is splitting in the new Arden, is not anti-Jenkins or pro-Taylor so much as skepticism about conflation.

But Jenkins was convinced on the basis of a casual aside Ms. Thompson had made in a lecture in regard to Ophelia's virginity that she had it in for him on feminist grounds, and that her Arden would be "anti-Jenkins." (Jenkins had intimated it was especially sad Ophelia died a virgin; Ann Thompson suggested that was a peculiarly male editor's response.)

However accurate his apprehension was, Harold Jenkins got his wish. He died less than a year after I spoke to him. His remarks to me were his last attempt to defend the crumbling edifice of a century-long editorial tradition, the "scientific bibliography" which had done so much to clarify what was and what wasn't Shakespearean in the Shakespearean canon. And to rescue Shakespeare's true intention from textual error.

THE *HAMLET* TRANCE

It was reading Jenkins's *Hamlet,* and perhaps a prior affection for Nabokov's *Pale Fire* (though Jenkins was far more tragically rational than Nabokov's mad annotator Kinbote), that inaugurated my abiding admiration for textual scholars and editors. Reading Jenkins's *Hamlet* edition one undertakes a kind of odyssey through the oceans of the past four centuries of previous commentators on *Hamlet.* And talking to Jenkins in person, one begins to get a sense of the almost monastic, even priestlike vocation editing Shakespeare, editing *Hamlet* in particular, becomes: that pressure, the responsibility for the transmission of a sacred text of the culture.

Jenkins's predecessor at Edinburgh, the legendary *Hamlet* scholar J. Dover Wilson, was particularly influential on directors and actors. It was he who convinced John Gielgud that Hamlet *overhears* Ophelia being instructed by Polonius to draw him out—and that *this* explains his sudden "get thee to a nunnery" railing at Ophelia and women in general. (One of Harold Jenkins's departures from his predecessor, Wilson, was to cast doubt on the long-held belief that a "nunnery" would have had a double meaning as brothel at the time Shakespeare wrote *Hamlet.* So many ironic readings of that line would be—if Jenkins is correct—retroactively imposed, non-Shakespearean, strictly speaking.)

I once came across a serious, if somewhat obsessive scholarly paper, asserting that there was "an unbroken chain of Hamlets" that stretched from the original who played the part, Richard Burbage, to Laurence Olivier. An argument that each successor to Burbage had seen a Hamlet who'd seen a Hamlet who'd seen a Hamlet who'd seen, ultimately, Burbage's original Hamlet.

You could probably establish a similar apostolic succession for the *editors* of *Hamlet* beginning with Heminge and Condell, the colleagues who first chose which plays to include in the Folio, the first Complete Works edition of Shakespeare, to the grand literary pontiffs who edited Shakespeare in the eighteenth century, Alexander Pope and Samuel Johnson, to the age of obsessed gentlemen scholars such as Lewis Theobald and Edmond Malone, to the exacting scholar mandarins who were Jenkins's twentieth-century predecessors—inventors of "scientific bibliography," men like W. W. Greg, A. W. Pollard and J. Dover Wilson.

Talking to Jenkins, I had a sense of speaking to the last leaf on an ancient tree, the last defender of the dream of the Lost Archetype. He'd told me of an encounter with Dover Wilson, and how Wilson kept prodding him to bring Jenkins's thirty-year-long march through *Hamlet* texts to a close: "Publish at last!" Wilson told Jenkins. "Prove me wrong!" Look upon it as "a splendid adventure."

Jenkins *said* it was a splendid adventure but he seemed a bit more delicate and thin-skinned sort than Dover Wilson, someone for whom it was, at times, a harrowing—and in the end, to some extent, disappointing—adventure.

As Gary Taylor (who professes much genuine respect for Jenkins's scholarly achievements) put it, "If Jenkins had not been so exacting and published sooner, its reception would have been very different from the one it got when it came out in the eighties." By then some saw it as obsolete—not least in rejecting the Reviser hypothesis that was conquering scholarly convocations the very moment Jenkins's anti-Reviser edition came out. There's a haunting phrase Gary Taylor used to refer to the inability of a couple of Jenkins's predecessors to complete editions of plays they'd devoted their lives to: "the sorrows of McKerrow and Walker." The more the new "scientific bibliography" allowed them to delve into the nuances of typographical minutiae, the further completion receded from them, the deeper the "sorrows."

The sorrows of the poet John Berryman began with his career in literature as a Shakespeare scholar; he began editing an edition of *King Lear* in the late 1930s; worked on it the rest of his life; even after he became an acclaimed poet with *The Dream Songs* one of the sorrows that afflicted him until his suicide in the 1970s was the accumulated frustration of the textual problems of *Lear* that he'd continued to work on without success.* The universally respected *Lear*-text scholar Peter Blayney has abandoned the long-awaited second volume of his promised two-volume study of the *Lear* texts.

Textual scholarship tends to become at the very least a consuming passion, sometimes a life-consuming obsession. It happened to Dover Wilson. While he commended it as a "splendid adventure" to Jenkins, Dover Wilson's description of the sudden onset of his *Hamlet* obsession sounds like the onset of a lifelong fever.

For Dover Wilson it began when he was an obscure bureaucrat in the World War I British Bureau of Munitions, traveling on a slow train to the

* John Haffenden's *Berryman's Shakespeare* offers an affecting complete account.

Midlands to settle a labor dispute at an ammunition plant. He found himself passing the time reading the October 1917 issue of a periodical called the *Modern Language Review,* and fell into a kind of spell, a *Hamlet* trance.

"A spell which changed the whole tenor of my existence and still dominates it," he wrote in a letter to W. W. Greg, one of the other giants of twentieth-century Shakespeare editing—and the man responsible for the spell. It was Greg's piece in the *Modern Language Review* which precipitated it. A piece entitled, aptly enough, "Hamlet's Hallucination," a piece that made the eccentric argument that the Ghost was a figment of Hamlet's paranoid imagination, a hallucination engendered in his vulnerable and distracted mind by reading the play *The Murder of Gonzago,* the one he uses to "catch the conscience of the King."

"For sheer audacity, close knit reasoning and specious paralogism," Dover Wilson wrote in his letter to its author, Greg, "it was unique in the history of Shakespeare criticism." Yet, from the moment he read it on the train and began to grapple with Greg's "hallucination," he fell into a *Hamlet*-spell himself: he found himself "in a state of considerable excitement . . . *filled with some sort of insanity* for weeks afterward" (my italics). *Hamlet* madness.*

The weeks turned into years, decades, a lifetime pursuing elusive *Hamlet* questions. Dover Wilson's attempt to resolve the enigma of Hamlet's madness (feigned? real? both at the same, or different times?) turned into a kind of madness itself: *Hamlet* Editor Syndrome you might call it. He began by attempting to plumb the depths of the problem of the dumb show, the silent prelude to *The Murder of Gonzago.*

He spent the next two years researching a four-part series of scholarly polemics on dumb-show questions. But disputing the Ghost-as-hallucination theory left him troubled by the nature of the Ghost's "reality" as it might be perceived by Shakespeare and his audience: Was the Ghost truly Hamlet's father, or "a spirit damned" tempting Hamlet to the un-Christian act of revenge, as some have argued? "I began to take a course of reading in Elizabethan spiritualism," Dover Wilson tells us. And then it's ten more years before he's ready to publish his conclusions. And he begins to get the feeling that "the digression threatened to last a lifetime . . . the further I went in

* All this is recounted in Wilson's delightful, eccentrically (or ironically) titled *What Happens in Hamlet.*

my investigations, the more the country seemed to open up," he says, choosing (consciously?) a rather curious locution for a *Hamlet* scholar who must be familiar with Hamlet's obscene pun on "country matters" in the dumb-show sequence. Implicitly trying to penetrate *Hamlet*'s inner mysteries becomes a "country matter" in the sense that it's like trying to penetrate "the secret parts of fortune"—to penetrate to a forbidden and unreachable realm, the "undiscovered country from whose bourn no traveller returns."

It is at this point, lost in the labyrinth of *Hamlet* thematic problems, that Dover Wilson turns to the problem of—the ongoing centuries-old war over—*Hamlet* texts. Maybe the answer, some answer, to the maddening questions left by *Hamlet* can be found *there.* It doesn't take him long to decide that "the textual criticism of *Hamlet* was as unsatisfactory as the esthetic, and that until the textual problems were solved [by him, of course] there could be no security for dramatic interpretation."

In other words, one couldn't even *enter* the inner temple of thematic interpretation until one had mortified the flesh intellectually in the thorny encounter with the thicket of textual problems that guard the entrance to the question of meaning.

So Dover Wilson spent the next decade preparing his landmark work, *The Texts of Shakespeare's Hamlet,* which was published in 1934. It was in that monumental two-volume work that Wilson, using the newly developed principles of "scientific bibliography," proved to just about everyone's satisfaction—*at the time*—that the Good Quarto of 1604 was a text printed from Shakespeare's handwritten manuscript. Still, two decades later, by the time Harold Jenkins embarked on his three-decade-long task of producing a new Arden edition of *Hamlet,* very little else in *Hamlet* studies had been settled to anyone's satisfaction.

Consider the fact that Jenkins requires a *six-page-long* footnote (in a two-hundred-page section of "Longer Notes" that follows his already heavily footnoted *Hamlet* text) just to touch on the continuing controversies over the meaning, significance and placement of the "To be or not to be" soliloquy. (In the 1603 "Bad Quarto" the "To be or not to be" soliloquy comes earlier, suggesting to some that this is how it was played on stage.)

Harold Jenkins's *Hamlet* is known for its leviathan-like bulk, six hundred pages, of which the first two hundred are commentary, the second two hundred heavily footnoted text, and the final two hundred, the Longer Notes, Jenkins's structural innovation, footnotes that have grown beyond the footnote form to mega-footnotes.

Jenkins's edition is known for the depth of its textual excavations, but as Jenkins reminded me more than once in the course of our conversation, he has made a contribution to the thematic debate as well.

"I don't think people have appreciated that," he told me. "I don't think they appreciated the way I brought out the duality of Hamlet's role: he is an avenger of a murder but he is also a murderer sought by an avenger, by Laertes."

Jenkins was among the first to stress, in this regard, the duality of Pyrrhus, the bloody slaughterer of Priam in the bombastic poem Hamlet asks the First Player to recite. Many have found the moment Pyrrhus hesitates before slaughtering old King Priam a foreshadowing of Hamlet's hesitation over killing Claudius. But as the murderer of old King Priam, Pyrrhus is *also* an emblem of Claudius as the murderer of old King Hamlet. Jenkins deepens the multiple resonances of Pyrrhus by pointing out that he is *also* (like Hamlet and Laertes) an avenging son—the son of Achilles—avenging the murder of *his* father by Priam's son, Paris.

THE "PRECIOUS INSTANCE"

Laertes figures in Jenkins's approach to a lesser-known textual enigma, one that illustrates both his characteristic loving attentiveness to the language of *Hamlet,* and the adamancy of his opposition to the new revisionist view of Shakespeare, to a Shakespeare who, at the very least, revised *Hamlet.* It's an example, as well, of the way different choices in textual dilemmas give us subtly different *Hamlets*.

It's a moment in act 4 when Laertes storms into the throne room at Elsinore raging at Claudius over the death of his father, Polonius, and—in mid-rant—encounters his sister Ophelia. Sees her grief-addled madness for the first time.

Laertes reacts with a speech that starts out as stentorian posturing:

O heat, dry up my brains! tears seven times salt
Burn out the sense and virtue of mine eye!

And concludes with a bitter

O heavens, is't possible a young maid's wits
Should be as mortal as an old man's life?

At which point—in the Quarto—Ophelia interrupts with her song of grief: "They bore him barefac'd on the bier . . ."

But in the Folio edition, before Ophelia breaks into song, Laertes goes on to add:

Nature is fine in love and where 'tis fine
It sends some precious instance of itself after
The thing it loves.

It is a passage whose ethereal delicacy, almost spiritual tendresse, is deeply moving. "Nature is fine in love" . . . and "precious instance of itself"—the phrases are lovely and loving in a hushed way. It represents an abrupt shift from the bloody-minded rant Laertes had begun with. It's almost as if the passage begins with the kind of rhetoric one finds in Shakespeare's earliest tragedy, *Titus Andronicus* ("O tears dry up my brain"), or in the stagy Pyrrhus speech Hamlet requests from the Players. And then shifts with almost no transition to lines that sound as if they're from one of Shakespeare's Late Romances, in the reconciliatory mode of *The Winter's Tale* with its evocation of "great creating Nature": "Nature is fine in love . . ."

It is almost as if, with the addition of those lines about a "precious instance," we see a Laertes transformed by the heartbreaking, flower-strewing delicacy of his sister Ophelia's grief. A Laertes transported to a mode of thought beyond revenge, one rich and strange in that elegiac, almost musical way of the Late Romances when they speak of nature, love, grief and forgiveness. One could go further and extrapolate a change not just in Laertes, but in Shakespeare himself: between the poet who composed Laertes's rant and the one who made the conjectured addition of these elegiac lines. A change in his sensibility. A change in "Shakespearean" tone and register.

But were they an addition/revision? The "precious instance" passage is itself a particularly salient instance of the whole debate over whether Shakespeare revised *Hamlet*. Recall the numbers: the most obvious difference between the Quarto and the Folio is that some 230 lines in the Quarto have been cut from the Folio. But the more problematic difference is that some 70 lines have been *added* to the Folio. Cuts are far easier to explain or explain away than additions. Anyone can make a cut, and (to be fair to editors) a cut can be made more or less skillfully, with just deletion marks. But composing an addition, composing an addition that sounds and reads as "Shakespearean" as the "precious instance" passage seems to, is different.

It's more difficult for those who refuse to believe Shakespeare revised *Hamlet* to explain the addition of a passage like the "precious instance" lines because the passage certainly suggests that Shakespeare went back to the Laertes speech at a later stage of his evolution and added something more contemplative, more elegiac, more evocative of the mood of the Late Romances, plays he wrote nearly a decade after *Hamlet.*

Precedent for this was suggested to me a few days after my talk with Jenkins by Richard Proudfoot, one of Jenkins's colleagues, formerly one of the three general editors of the Arden Shakespeare, and a specialist in questions of Shakespearean apocrypha—plays sometimes dubiously ascribed to Shakespeare. It's a specialty that requires Proudfoot to be attuned to questions of what is and isn't "Shakespearean."

Proudfoot pointed out to me a somewhat anomalous passage in *Henry VI, Part 2,* one of the very earliest plays attributed to Shakespeare, a passage that Proudfoot suggests may well have been added, "precious instance" fashion, by a more mature Shakespeare returning to improve upon his earliest work. It's a passage in which a character known as "Young Clifford" comes upon the body of his father slain in battle and starts speaking in a somewhat stilted early-Shakespearean mode.

"I'll see if I can do the switch for you," Proudfoot tells me, searching for his edition of *Henry VI, Part 2*, and he flips it open to the fifth act and begins to read the bombastic lines, "O war, thou son of Hell . . ."

"So far early Shakespeare," Proudfoot says, "But then he shifts to 'O, let the vile world end, / And the premised flames of the last day / Knit earth and heaven together! . . . Wast thou ordain'd, dear father, / To lose thy youth in peace, and to achieve / The silver livery of advised age . . . thus / To die in ruffian battle?'

"It's a different voice," Proudfoot insists. "And after a while he modulates back into the insult stuff, but it's irresistible once you've seen it."

"A different voice": it sounds right, but it also sounds inevitably like a highly subjective judgment. Still, the shift is even more pronounced in the "precious instance" passage. From ruffian bombast to the silver livery of reflectiveness.

Jenkins will have none of it. He, too, finds beauty in the "precious instance" passage but *not* revision. Even though it appears only in the Folio, he likes it so much, he seems to have wanted to rescue it for his Quarto-based conflated edition, so he adopted what some might call a far-fetched hypothesis: he argues that the "precious instance" lines were there from the beginning in Shakespeare's "foul papers," his original manuscript for the Quarto, but *mistakenly* omitted by a transcriber or by the printing-shop compositor who set the Quarto into type. Mistakenly omitted because the passage might have been added in a margin on the Quarto manuscript and overlooked by the typesetter. Or there may have been an incidental line on the Quarto manuscript next to the "precious instance" passage that might have been mistaken for a deletion mark. But it's *not* a revision added later to the Folio, Jenkins insists.

Far-fetched to some, but Jenkins's commentary on the "precious instance" passage transcends the textual issue: he's rescued the "precious instance" passage from the disparagement of previous editors by offering a precious instance of his own tender attentiveness to Shakespeare at its best. For two centuries the passage suffered from the disapprobation of that sacred monster of the Shakespeare editing tradition, Samuel Johnson. The "precious instance" passage should be "omitted," Johnson declared, because the lines "are obscure and affected."

Nonetheless, Dr. Johnson claimed to be able to decipher them: "Love (says Laertes) is the passion by which nature is most exalted and refined and as substances refined and subtilised [a term from alchemy for purifying] easily obey any impulse or follow any attractions, some part of nature so purified and refined flies off after the attracting object, after the thing that it loves."

This is a fascinating and rather polemical way of interpreting the "precious instance" passage. A way that seems to disparage the apparent surface sentiment or tone of the passage. Johnson emphasizes how indiscriminate the operation of the emotions is: love is like a substance that easily obeys "any" impulses, follows "any" attractions, implicitly *indiscriminately,* regardless of the value of the attractor. Love, in other words, is so light it's a virtual personified airhead, easily manipulated by alchemy in the same way it was by an herbal potion in *A Midsummer Night's Dream,* where the juice of the flower "Love in Idleness" compels a person to follow the next visual "attraction" that happens to wander by.

But Harold Jenkins sees something more, and *his* footnote on the passage is an implicit reproof to Dr. Johnson. Here is how Jenkins explicates the "precious instance" passage:

"Human nature, when in love, is exquisitely sensitive and being so, it sends a precious part of itself as a token to follow the object of its love. Thus the fineness of Ophelia's love is demonstrated when, after the loved one has gone, her mind goes too . . ." The precious instance then is Ophelia's mind; she's not an airhead but a sensitive soul, whose mind is sent by her exquisitely loving nature after the departing shade of her dead father.

I know: it has a hint of an antiquarian air, but the passage has "the silver livery" of antiquity to it. There is here none of Dr. Johnson's disparagement of the flightiness of human nature and love; Jenkins reads into the lines a quiet tragedy of love and grief leading to madness (a compression one might say of *Hamlet* itself). Although Jenkins might be mortified at the idea, his meditation on the "precious instance" passage could be read as Jenkins's meditation on his own lifelong love of *Hamlet:* his exquisite sensitivity, a precious part of himself, has been transmitted in his edition "as a token to follow the object of its love."

In a slightly different sense a "precious instance" is an image, a reproduction of the thing beloved, almost a kind of twin (twins being precious instances of each other). And here in the "precious instance" passage one almost hears an echo of Shakespeare's own tragic personal experience of twinship: the death of his son Hamnet, one of a pair of twins (the other a daughter, Judith). I have sought to avoid the temptations of biographical inference. But as we know, James Joyce devoted some fifty pages of *Ulysses* to an eccentric (but not utterly as implausible as once thought) theory about the relationship between Shakespeare's tragic hero Hamlet and the tragic death of his son Hamnet. Joyce does not mention it, but the powerful elegiac tone of the "precious instance" passage almost suggests it might have been written or inspired by the death of Hamnet, and the "precious instance" of himself Hamnet left behind in his surviving twin, Judith.

SUCH ARE THE SEDUCTIONS OF A SINGLE CONTROVERSIAL TEXTUAL variation and an instance of the way apparently unpoetic textual debates can illuminate the poetic language and raise suggestive questions about what lies beneath the "veil of print."

But Jenkins resists the seductions of this sort of speculation. Or certain of its implications anyway: while lovingly attentive to the "precious instance" passage, he denies that it is an instance of Shakespeare's revising hand.

"Well, of course, all of the latest people think, 'Poor Jenkins, he's passé.' But I'm very skeptical about this. I'm quite sure the idea of Shakespeare as reviser has been much too readily accepted. The Folio has lots of little things which are to do with adjusting *Hamlet* for performance. In the Quarto when Hamlet's on his way to see Gertrude after the play scene, Polonius says to the Queen, 'Oh I hear him coming.' And in the Folio, he says, 'Mother, mother, mother.' That's just staging: you have someone directing who says, 'We better hear him coming, you know.' But you don't really need this. But then they say, 'Well, if it was prepared for performance, Shakespeare was a member of the company, and he was there, so of course, *he* must have done it!' Well, it seems to me just as likely that Shakespeare, at the height of his imagination, he writes the play and he writes too much, and in the end it's too long, and he knows it's too long, and he says it's too long, just cut it. And even if he did do the cutting, it doesn't follow that therefore Shakespeare *preferred* it. There are plenty of instances of dramatists who are forced to cut, but it doesn't follow that this is how he would have *wanted* it."

He returned to the subject again later in our conversation as he poured more tea for us.

"As for the evidence that the Folio *Hamlet* is Shakespeare's revision, I don't think there *is* any real evidence. It's quite tenuous. I think it comes back to *King Lear,* it all started with *King Lear* and then it was accepted by the Oxford people [that the two *Lear*s were first and second drafts] and everyone was excited about it. But people just *said* this, and we were all waiting for the evidence. And when *The Division of the Kingdoms* [the book of revisionist essays on the *Lear* question edited by Gary Taylor and Michael Warren] appeared, I didn't see they gave evidence at all. They all accepted that it was so, and I am still waiting for this to be proved. There are passages, especially one soliloquy, one speech in *Lear,* where there seemed to be alternate versions, and so one is taken to be a revision of the other. But you know the Folio of *King Lear* is a cut text. And whether or not Shakespeare cut it, they say he wanted to change the characters of Albany and Edgar. I don't believe that for a moment. If he wanted to change the characters, would he do it by simply cutting out speeches and taking one speech and giving it to another chap? So I think a lot of the evidence depends on the transfer of speeches from one to another. But we know Shakespeare is rather casual about indicating the speaker and sometimes speech headings are misinterpreted, and then the same speech is given to somebody in the Quarto and somebody else in the Folio. Well, I think that is very, very rarely to be a case of revision."

Still, at the close of our conversation, he did concede at least a shadow of a doubt. It came in the context of a fanciful question I'd asked about Jenkins meeting Shakespeare. What would the editor of *Hamlet,* who'd given his life to deciphering the ambiguities and uncertainties that have been hidden beneath "the veil of print," want to ask the author if he came face to face with him in the afterlife?

"I wonder what he would think of some of my interpretations," Jenkins mused. "I do think he would agree that the important thing, the central thing in *Hamlet,* is that Hamlet is both the avenger and the object of revenge."

"The duality?"

"Yes, because I think the whole play is structured around that."

"What else would you ask Shakespeare?"

"Well, I think I would ask him one or two things about the 'To be or not to be' soliloquy. 'Whether 'tis nobler in the mind . . .' No, I feel I've got *that* right. Still, I think it's all a little *wrong.* It doesn't seem to relate to the immediate context. I'd quite like to hear his view on it," he says with a mischievous look.

"And, of course, his view on ghosts. Did he believe in ghosts? Did he believe in ghosts?" he repeats. "And also," he adds, in a remarkable final concession of doubt, "I would like to ask him whether he *did* revise it."

A VISIT WITH AN AVENGING ANGEL

One begins to feel the fear and loathing Eric Sams inspired in his academic foes long before one meets him. The much feared name came up in a discussion I had with Harold Jenkins about his stance on the "ur-*Hamlet,*" the legendary lost "original" *Hamlet,* the *Hamlet* referred to, mocked by, a rival playwright as early as 1589, at least ten years before the *Hamlet* we now know was first staged at the Globe. Who wrote this lost first *Hamlet*? Until Sams began his assault, centuries of argument over the question had evolved into fairly stable consensus that the original *Hamlet* must have been written by some older, lesser revenge tragedian, most likely Thomas Kyd, author of *The Spanish Tragedy,* which bears some resemblances to *Hamlet* (feigned madness, for example)—and that Shakespeare took Kyd's melodramatic plot and transformed it with his genius.

This was Jenkins's view, and "This is what initiated my correspondence with the notorious Eric Sams," Jenkins told me, practically wincing at the memory. Sams (who died in 2004) was one of the rare "independent scholars" whose work changes the academic consensus from outside. Sams told me he'd been a World War II cryptologist stationed at the legendary Bletchley Park code-breaking station, home of the Enigma machine, where he said he worked with the team that cracked the Japanese code called MAGIC. In the early eighties, after establishing a formidable reputation as editor, translator and commentator on German music (Penguin published his translations of the songs of Schumann), Sams turned his attention to Shakespeare scholarship—to decrypting the enigma of Shakespeare's MAGIC, one might say—where he soon became the scourge of consensus wisdom, academic reputations and long-established assumptions about Shakespeare's career. Finding a forum for his views in the *TLS* and in a 1995 Yale University Press polemical work called *The Real Shakespeare,* Sams became known for his fierce limpet-like correspondence with his academic opponents and the lack of customary academic decorum in the characterization of their views, often using invective of the "fools and idiots" variety.

In a note to me, for instance, after pointing out that Harold Bloom had recently come around to Sams's position on the ur-*Hamlet*—that it was Shakespeare and not someone else who wrote the lost early version of the play by that name—Sams couldn't resist characterizing another eminent Shakespearean (who shall remain nameless here) as "suffering from senile dementia" for failing to see the light on some point of textual dispute. Here's a sampling from his polemics in the *TLS, Hamlet Studies* (edited in New Delhi, until it shut its doors in 2002, it was then the only peer-reviewed scholarly publication in the world devoted to a single work of art) and *The Real Shakespeare:*

The legendary Dover Wilson, mentor of Harold Jenkins, "initiated a half-century of corruption in *Hamlet* scholarship"; the field suffers from "catastrophic confusion," "baseless invention," "asinine hypotheses," "shameless nonsense," "spuriously presented arguments" that are "corrupt and venal." In sum, "the whole tragical history of twentieth century *Hamlet* criticism will have to be re-written" when Sams's views demolish the conventional wisdom. My favorite is his relatively subdued but eloquently Latinate aside after one assertion: "*pace,* the entire profession."

One of the chief objects of Sams's wrathful polemics has been Harold Jenkins and Jenkins's conclusions about the ur-*Hamlet* and the Bad Quarto in Jenkins's Arden edition. Sams is particularly exercised over Jenkins's adoption of the theory of "memorial reconstruction" (that the Bad Quarto was produced from the bad memories of bit players trying to reconstruct, without the text before them, a performance of a *Hamlet* they'd played in). Sams believes that the Bad Quarto could well have been written by Shakespeare himself, an earlier draft of the play we now know; that the Bad Quarto might even be a version of the legendary lost ur-*Hamlet* itself, hiding in plain sight.

It is part of Sams's radical challenge to consensus notions of Shakespeare's entire career as a dramatist. A challenge that has become conventional wisdom to some like biographer Peter Ackroyd. Sams believes Shakespeare was not the "late starter" who only began writing for the London stage in the 1590s, but rather someone who, as eighteenth-century tradition has it, came to London as early as 1582, and after serving as horse handler and actor at the theater, began writing the early drafts of some of his famous plays. Early drafts that are preserved in the much despised Bad Quartos, early drafts that include the ur-*Hamlet,* a play Sams insists Shakespeare didn't just rewrite from another's play but composed himself (from prose sources). Sams's quarrel with Jenkins about the ur-*Hamlet* is then a quarrel about the entire trajectory of Shakespeare's dramatic career, and the nature of the imagination that created *Hamlet.*

"Sams insists the ur-*Hamlet* was originally by Shakespeare," Jenkins told me, speaking of his attempts to disentangle himself from continuing a contentious correspondence with Sams on the question. "He's the sort of person who always has the last word so you might as well let him have it at the beginning as well as the end. I don't write to him anymore. But, of course, he will attack me in his next book. He told me that I escaped fairly well in the first one. He has, of course, in his bibliography, a star against the people whom he disagrees with. Some of us were kind of amused to share in the stars."

This donnish chuckle is not quite sufficient, though, to dismiss Sams from his mind.

"Eric Sams?" says Jenkins, speaking the name as if he were holding up its possessor like a specimen in a pair of tweezers. "Well, I disbelieve most of what he says. What he wrote in the *TLS* [about Jenkins's view of "memorial reconstruction"] was a complete *travesty* of anything I've thought and said, and so I had to write and say, 'No, not at *all.*' And this reopened the correspondence," he says with a sigh as if discussing the attentions of a stalker.

"He's an avenging-angel type?" I asked Jenkins.

"When he's in his own family, I have no idea what he's like, but he's rather nasty in controversy and he likes to . . ." Jenkins rubs his hands together in an imitation of nasty glee. " 'Heh, heh, heh.' There's a certain spitefulness about it."

Who was this man so many in the Shakespeare scholar establishment feared and loathed?

"I'm a civil servant," Eric Sams likes to say by way of introducing himself. And he was a civil servant in the most literal sense of the word, a civil servant in the Department of Employment for many years, he explained over lunch at our first meeting at his club, the dignified if not posh Civil Service Club in London.

But he's not merely a civil servant, he's a certain *kind* of civil servant, the implacable inspector-general, relentless investigator kind. The hound-of-hell kind.

And, he adds, he's a civil servant who believes in Ockham's razor, the famous injunction by William of Ockham, the medieval logician, that "entities should not be multiplied beyond necessity." That is, one shouldn't invent complex explanations (like "memorial reconstruction") without due cause or evidence.

He was a civil servant who applied his inspector-general zeal to the Shakespeare scholar bureaucracy, one who wielded Ockham's razor like a slasher. He was in the midst of a war over the Bad Quarto when I visited him in his home in Surrey.

Surrey, Sams reminds me, when we'd settled into his spare living room, was the home county of the village of Ockham, home to William of Ockham, clearly Sams's intellectual hero.

"I think there's a kind of advantage to being a latecomer to Shakespeare studies," Sams tells me. Sams was a vigorous seventy-three when I saw him, a compact figure whose most distinctive features were bristling dark gray eyebrows which seemed to reflect and express his fierce views on the state of Shakespearean scholarship and *Hamlet* editors in particular. "What I noticed immediately when I took it up was that people were just making things up! Absolutely nonstop! Beginning with Harold Jenkins! And what you use in bibliography as in science is the notion that you mustn't make things up. Ockham's razor."

To Sams, "memorial reconstruction" multiplies entities *way* beyond necessity, when it requires adherents to conjure up a company of traveling players, including former bit players at the Globe, botching together a maimed version of *Hamlet,* the Bad Quarto, while on tour in the provinces. There is no surviving record or testimony to the existence of such an entity. In fact, Sams believes the number of entities required to explain the Bad Quarto is just one: William Shakespeare. Sams believes the Bad Quarto was not memorially reconstructed but was one of Shakespeare's early drafts of *Hamlet;* perhaps, in fact, a version of the legendary long-lost ur-*Hamlet.*

The ur-*Hamlet:* it's the specter that haunts and stalks *Hamlet* editors the way the ghost of Hamlet's father haunts Hamlet. Sams is its most powerful contemporary champion, virtually its editor in absentia. It's a powerful and disturbing invisible presence despite the fact that all we have to attest to its existence are ghostly echoes. And echoes of ridicule at that.

In 1589 when Shakespeare is but twenty-five, Thomas Nashe, one of the "university wits" who sneered at the more plebeian playwrights in London, is making fun in a pamphlet of a rival he derides as "English Seneca" for allegedly lifting his style from the Roman playwright's tragic dramas. Of "English Seneca" Nashe says, "If you entreat him faire on a frostie morning he will afford whole Hamlets, I should say handfuls, of tragic speeches." This is ten years at least before most scholars believe Shakespeare wrote the *Hamlet* we have. So what *Hamlet* is Nashe referring to in the labored Hamlets/handfuls wordplay? There is a record of a play by that name being performed in 1594. Is it the same *Hamlet* alluded to in 1596, when another university wit, Thomas Lodge, ridicules a *Hamlet* by referring to some "poor devil looking as pale as the vizard of the ghost which cries so miserably like an oyster wife at the theatre, '*Hamlet, revenge!*' "

Most agree Lodge is probably ridiculing the same work of "English Seneca" playing in 1589, a play that by 1596 seems to have become a cliché of hammy melodrama, and not Shakespeare's *Hamlet,* in any case not the version we know.

For one thing, the phrase "Hamlet, revenge!" just doesn't appear in any of the three *Hamlet* texts that have survived. And the consensus has it that the ur-*Hamlet* of "Hamlet, revenge!" could not have been written by Shakespeare but rather by some older, cruder playwright, whom the consensus, epitomized by Harold Jenkins, supposes to be Thomas Kyd.

But Eric Sams will not have it. Whacking away with Ockham's razor, Sams asks, "Why invent another playwright to have written the ur-*Hamlet*?" Why not suppose it was Shakespeare's own early draft, one he later revised? Why not suppose it might not be lost at all but rather preserved in some form in the Bad Quarto?

But the most fascinating aspect of Sams's case for Shakespeare as the early starter and author of the ur-*Hamlet* is the way he puts the case in the context of what he calls "the war against Shakespeare," the little-noted, barely remembered campaign against the fledgling Bard by his early rivals, the university wits, a group of Oxford- and Cambridge-educated poets and dramatists including Christopher Marlowe, Robert Greene, Thomas Lodge, Thomas Nashe and George Peele. The university wits sneered at Shakespeare as "an upstart crowe plumed in our feathers" (as Greene put it), a late-arriving plagiarist who cribbed his style and plots from his university-educated betters.

The university wits of today, Sams believes, the elite academics, are denigrating Shakespeare in essentially the same way: by saying Shakespeare didn't conceive the character of Hamlet, he only punched up someone else's old play. The same with *Lear, Henry V, Pericles:* all old plays he punched up. The history plays, give or take a Falstaff—all old chronicles or old chronicle plays he punched up. The attitude, taken to the extreme, is at the heart of the so-called anti-Stratfordian theories of Shakespeare: no middle-class glover's boy from Stratford without a university education could have dreamt up any of Shakespeare's plays on his own. It had to be an aristocrat, a university wit like the Earl of Oxford, Bacon or Marlowe.

It occurred to me to ask Sams whether his own war against the academic Shakespeare establishment—the university wits of today—recapitulates the war between Shakespeare and the university wits of his day.

"Well, it is true," Sams tells me, "that I did quite well at Cambridge [in modern languages] and I was disappointed I was not asked to stay on."

"To teach?"

"Yes, well, and so I became a civil servant, and I think my later work benefited. Civil servants think differently from [academic] dons in that they realize what you think about, what you decide, actually *matters.* As a don, nobody gets richer or poorer, sicker or better, depending on your opinion. Nobody's life changes. In addition, while civil servants hate to be wrong, unlike dons they *are* able to admit they've made mistakes."

In point of fact, I never heard Sams admit to making a mistake about Shakespeare. But he'd probably have said that it's not from any unwillingness to do so—it's just that it hadn't happened yet. But he does admit there *are* instances of dons who can admit mistakes. In fact, he tells me, one reason he admired Ann Thompson, the editor of the Arden 3 *Hamlet,* is that after he wrote a scathing review of a paper she'd written about *The Taming of the Shrew,* she wrote a note to Sams admitting he was right on some point—at least that's how he tells it. So clearly, Sams does appreciate a don who can admit error; he just rarely succumbs to it himself.

Sams can be charmingly self-aware of his own obsessiveness. He goes off into a digression on a recent vindication he received in a decades-old controversy in German musicology, a field he'd left in the early eighties to take up Shakespeare controversies. He'd long contended, Sams tells me, from examination of Schubert's scores and fragmentary biographical evidence, that the great German composer was syphilitic. "And only recently records have been found in a German archive of Schubert's stay in a sanitarium that show diagnosis and treatment of him as *'syphilitische.'* And now everyone acknowledges it. My fate is for half my life to be called an idiot, and then when everyone agrees, to be called unoriginal."

He runs through a litany of recent vindications or claimed vindications in Shakespearean controversies.

"It's now at least become acceptable to mention the name Eric Sams in scholarly publications," he says. He cites the new Arden edition of *Pericles* which gives Sams—and others—credit for being among the first to argue that Shakespeare wrote an early draft of *Pericles*—long considered a 1609 "Late Romance"—some twenty years earlier, as one of his earliest works. It's something the poet Dryden had first suggested in the seventeenth century, though, *pace* Sams, it is still not widely accepted.

He cites the remarkable tide of opinion among North American scholars (as opposed to "the entrenched English establishment") that has come to question the evidence (or actually, the lack of it) for the "memorial reconstruction" hypothesis. And he calls attention to the work of the gifted dramaturgical scholar Steven Urkowitz of New York's City College, who has made a persistent case for the esthetic and dramatic merit of the long-disparaged Bad Quarto of *Hamlet.* Urkowitz—who was a principal ally in Gary Taylor's war to split *Lear* into original and revised versions—argues that one can see a consistent three-stage pattern of Shakespearean revision in the progression from the 1603 Bad Quarto to the 1604 Good Quarto to the 1623 Folio version of *Hamlet.*

And Sams is particularly pleased that he "won" a debate with Donald Foster, the "Funeral Elegy" promoter.

Sams debated Foster at the University of Virginia over the question of *Edmund Ironside,* an item of Shakespearean apocrypha that Sams believes is a genuine early play of Shakespeare, one which Foster and his computer database reject.

When Sams says he "won," he means he won the vote of the audience that day: the academic consensus has so far resisted Sams's hammering on the *Ironside* question. Although he is now getting credit for his obsessive championing of another play in the Shakespearean apocrypha, *Edward III,* which is now included in respected Complete Works editions such as *The Riverside Shakespeare* as having "at least some" scenes written by Shakespeare.

It occurred to me that what Sams's various crusades have in common is the impulse to restore to Shakespeare's credit works that academics believe are "beneath" the Bard such as the ur-*Hamlet,* the Bad Quarto *Hamlet,* the Bad Quartos of his history plays and less artful apocryphal works such as *Edward III* and *Edmund Ironside.* The academic/university wits' version of Shakespeare tends to see him as at once more sophisticated and less original. More sophisticated in the sense that he cannot be associated with the clumsiness of the Bad Quartos; his talent scarcely seemed to evolve from such crude origins, but rather burst full blown upon the scene. On the other hand, less original because his sophistication depends on the artful transformation of *other* playwrights' earlier versions of *Hamlet,* the history plays, *Pericles,* etc. *They*—other playwrights—wrote his first drafts, so to speak.

I thought of Sams's remark about himself: half his life called an idiot, and then unoriginal. The university wits similarly disparaged Shakespeare for his lack of originality.

In one of our last conversations, I'd asked Sams whether there was something more to the relationship between the "war over Shakespeare" in the 1590s and his own battle with the university wits in the 1990s. It's easy to see he identifies his own enemies in academia with the university wits who looked down their noses at Shakespeare as an outsider, a mere actor who became a playwright by punching up others' old plots. But did Sams also feel a kind of emotional identification with Shakespeare beyond their common enemies?

"I hadn't thought of it that way," he says, "until now. I won't deny it's possible. The difference may be that *his* opponents back then, the university wits, were undeniably intelligent in their own right." Always with the barb.

Originality, of course, is not, in itself, an unequivocal virtue, and is often an overrated one. Does it make a difference to our notion of Shakespeare as an artist if he did or didn't write the ur-*Hamlet*? It doesn't necessarily make him a better artist if he did, but the question is not academic, so to speak; at the very least, it would be an indication that he was a different *kind* of artist, and we might divine something of the fathomless mysteries of *Hamlet* by examining the changes if it *was* Shakespeare rewriting his own work.

I am unpersuaded by Sams's belief that the Bad Quarto is an early Shakespearean draft. Yes, there is little evidence for the memorial reconstruction hypothesis, but reading the Bad Quarto, the early-draft hypothesis feels wrong. And Ockham's razor doesn't (as many mistake it to do) always mandate the *simplest* solution. When it says "entities should not be multiplied beyond necessity," that doesn't identify necessity as simplicity; there are times when necessity (the way things happen to be) requires complexity. But Sams's case for Shakespeare as author of the ur-*Hamlet* seems stronger than his Bad Quarto arguments and has begun to gain support even within the academy he loathes.

Two days after my visit to Sams in Ockham's Surrey, I was surprised to find Ann Thompson, coeditor of the new Arden *Hamlet,* a scholar firmly ensconced in the mainstream of Shakespeare studies, make a remarkable acknowledgment of the force of Sams's case.

"I can't figure out quite why people are so determined to say it's by someone else," Professor Thompson says of the ur-*Hamlet* in her office at King's College, London, a stone's throw away from the Thames, "or why it *can't* be by Shakespeare as Eric Sams says in his book with that modest title, *The Real Shakespeare,*" she says with an indulgent chuckle over Sams's immodest title claim.

"But nobody else is saying that. At the moment I don't see why Shakespeare couldn't have authored a version of *Hamlet* earlier than in 1599 and I don't see why everyone is determined to say it's impossible."

She doesn't go as far as Sams to say that the Bad Quarto is therefore necessarily a version of the ur-*Hamlet,* but her willingness to entertain a case

Sams has been pressing virtually alone for so long is an indication of the unusual equanimity Ms. Thompson displays in navigating the entrenchments of the *Hamlet* battlefield: a lack of investment in excluding dissent, a lack of determination to be seen as always having the right answer at all times in matters where the evidence may be insufficient for the typically masculine need to assert possession of correct answers.

It raises a question about *Hamlet* editors that struck me in the aftermath of my encounters with Ann Thompson, whose Arden edition might be called the *Hamlet* of the near future, and with Bernice Kliman, editor in chief of the Modern Language Association's new *Variorum Hamlet,* which might be called the *Hamlet* of the distant future. In many ways the future shape of *Hamlet* is in the hands of these two women, and in certain ways the play and the prince might be the better for it.

CORDELIA'S PLUNGE AND OPHELIA'S FLAMES

Ann Thompson has a haunting, lovely memory of her first transformative experience of Shakespeare. It was not something she volunteered. Despite the powerful voice she now has in Shakespeare studies, she is extraordinarily soft-spoken and self-effacing in person, constitutionally shy it seems. Someone who frequently seems to want to erase whatever statement she ventures with a charming but self-deprecating chuckle.

When I told her I'd been asking a number of Shakespeare scholars and directors to tell me what their first transformative experience of Shakespeare had been, she did recall a moment that may have set her on the path that would place in her hands the shape of the *Hamlet* of the new millennium.

"As a teenager we had been taken as part of a school trip to an outdoor performance of *Lear* on the Cornish coast," she said. A locale that evokes *Lear*'s Dover cliffs, site of one of the most deeply moving scenes in all Shakespeare: the scene in *Lear* in which the blinded Gloucester, desperately seeking solace in suicide, asks his disguised son and guide Edgar to lead him to the cliff's edge so he can hurl himself to his death. In one of the most spectacularly showy passages in all Shakespeare, Edgar tricks his father into thinking he is on the very edge of the Dover precipice by conjuring up a dazzling fictive description of the dizzying prospect of the drop to the shore below. And it was there at Dover that the befuddled Gloucester, after the "miracle" of his recovery from the imagined cliff leap, encounters the flower-bedecked figure of the deposed King Lear, recovering from the madness on the heath.

But what struck Ann Thompson most powerfully about seeing *Lear* staged in that setting, she told me that afternoon in London, was the disappearance of Cordelia. "I'm not sure why, but I was fascinated to see the actress playing Cordelia, after she came off stage in the first act; it was outdoors in the round so you could observe the actors before and after their entrances and exits. Now you know Cordelia has nothing to do between that exit in the first act and her reappearance two hours or so later at the end of the fourth act. And so I watched her emerge from the backstage in a bathing suit, go down to the shore and plunge into the water for a swim before returning to put on Cordelia's royal robes for her entry in act four. That fascinated me, I don't know why, but it did."

She's not sure why the memory stayed with her but it's possible to speculate: it's almost an allegory of her own subsequent career in Shakespeare studies. In the first act of *Lear* Cordelia is a figure of a kind of principled shyness in her defiant refusal to give lip service to the ritual love test her father demands before he divides the kingdom among his daughters. Exiled for her silence she leaves the play, goes off across the Channel to plunge into a new life as the bride of the French king.

In Ann Thompson's first encounter with *Lear,* the actress playing Cordelia steps out of her role as the silent/silenced young girl, plunges into the ocean and reemerges as a powerful, healing woman when she steps back into the play.

Similarly one might say, in her own career, Ann Thompson began as a shy young scholar who has plunged into the ocean, the turbulent "sea of troubles" that is *Hamlet* studies after four centuries. A "site of contestation" as the Theorists like to say, a place where "ignorant armies clash by night." Here "arrogant armies" might be more appropriate—all those armies of (mainly) men, each of whom insists that his theory of *Hamlet* and "Shakespeare's intentions" for *Hamlet* is the only correct approach.

Ann Thompson signaled her characteristically more open-minded and tentative approach to these rigidities with her willingness to entertain Eric Sams's heretical conjectures on Shakespeare's authorship of the ur-*Hamlet*—and her countervailing unwillingness to accept Sams's *certainty* on that point, nor his corollary, that the Bad Quarto was the lost ur-*Hamlet.*

Her characteristic attitude emerged even more explicitly in her discussion of Hamlet's last soliloquy, Hamlet's last words and the issue of the "O-groans."

"It's not always true that a revision is going to be for the better," she was saying apropos the Shakespeare-as-Reviser partisans. Many of whom, she believes, feel compelled to argue not just that Shakespeare revised *Hamlet* from the Quarto to the Folio but that the later version in almost every way is the *better* version.

"Once the Oxford editors decided they wanted to base their *Hamlet* on the Folio rather than the Quarto on the theory that the Folio is Shakespeare's revision, you see them arguing of *course* it was the correct decision to cut the 'How all occasions do inform against me . . .' soliloquy. They find all sorts of reasons why it doesn't belong, why the play is better without it."

In other words, they're smuggling in, beneath the cloak of their cutting-edge Shakespeare-the-Reviser theories, old-fashioned bardolatry: the Bard can do no wrong, he always gets it right, always makes it better when he revises.

When I asked her what she thought of the O-groans, the final four *O*'s Hamlet is called upon to utter in the Folio after "The rest is silence," she was equally open-minded about the alternatives. She cited Harold Jenkins's conjecture that they were "playhouse interpolations" by a hammy actor, but then added that this didn't necessarily (as Jenkins believed) disqualify them from consideration:

"Perhaps one *can* imagine Shakespeare having gone through a period of rehearsal or having seen the thing [meaning *Hamlet*'s swan song] performed and then tinkered with it afterwards and thinking 'Burbage did rather a *good* dying groan, I'll put that down to remind me.' You *could* imagine that," she says.

"Publishing all three texts allows us to do that, to display the possibilities. If you're going to publish one text you're driven to excluding things. Therefore you have to persuade yourself the readings you've chosen are authentic and superior. What the three texts allow us to do is to say, 'These are the differences, these are the passages that are in one text and not the others. We can say there are arguments for, reasons for the differences but we don't have to attribute all difference to a single factor or theory. What I've been finding is that we can be more inclusive. You know, the eighteenth-century editors I've been studying in the Folger were tolerant of these differences. Recent editors have become obsessed with the idea 'I have to have a theory of the text and everything else follows from my theory.' "

It was at this point I couldn't resist asking her about a phrase that had occurred to me: "American feminists have a phrase—'Male Answer Syndrome'—for the tendency of men to insist they've always got things figured out. I wonder if your willingness to entertain conflicting theories, this inclusiveness the three-text solution offers, comes from a feminist perspective?"

"It's kind of nice to think so," she mused, although characteristically she demurred at anything that might sound like a countervailing certainty about her position.

Still she has not been shy in bringing a female if not explicitly feminist perspective to editing Shakespeare and particularly *Hamlet.*

At first, she told me, she resisted being drawn into the textual-editing labyrinth. "I did my Ph.D. with Richard Proudfoot," she said. "He encouraged me to edit a relatively obscure apocryphal text, which I refused to do, working instead on Shakespeare's use of Chaucer. Several years later, I got into editing when I was invited to do *The Taming of the Shrew* for the New Cambridge Shakespeare. I discovered I enjoyed editing." She had begun editing the Arden *Cymbeline* when Arden invited her to become a general editor, along with Proudfoot and Columbia's David Scott Kastan—a position of considerable influence in the world of Shakespeare studies.

Her rapid ascent, she told me, may in part have been a response to her critique of the male-dominated textual-editing establishment. "I had noticed how few women were involved in editing, and how they always did the same 'easy' Folio-only comedies," she said. "And I'd given a couple of conference papers on the topic, pointing out the absence of female editors of the major 'difficult' tragedies, so I more or less talked myself into editing *Hamlet*—*Othello* and *Lear* having already been assigned to senior male editors."

Thompson's assertiveness has caused some grumbling among some "senior male editors." But the groundbreaking step she's taking in deconflating *Hamlet* should not be interpreted as an outgrowth of the gender wars. She has worked closely with male Shakespeare scholars; she made her *Hamlet*-text decision in collaboration with a colleague, Neil Taylor, whom she brought in as her coeditor on *Hamlet.* (She has also coedited a book, *Shakespeare: Meaning and Metaphor,* with her husband, John O. Thompson, a film scholar.)

For two years after receiving her *Hamlet* assignment in 1993, Thompson immersed herself in the play's textual problems. She came to the conclusion—as she told her fellow editors at Arden in a heated confrontation—that it would be a mistake to do another conflated version of *Hamlet.* "Harold Jenkins had already done that very well," she said. "I would not have wanted to edit *Hamlet* if I had to do that. I would not have felt it was worth doing."

Her colleagues—and executives at Routledge, the publishing house that owned the Arden imprint at the time—had some practical concerns. The three-text version she proposed—the 1603, 1604 and 1623 *Hamlets*—would be at least a thousand pages long, making it hard to sell to the college market as a single volume.

Oxford's Stanley Wells once called for editors of courage to "take the risk" and divide *Hamlet* the way he and Gary Taylor had divided *Lear*—something they had avoided in their *Hamlet.* Such multi-text editions, Wells said, had the potential to "open up the most illuminating discussion of Shakespeare's creative processes since the plays were first reprinted." But Wells expressed concern to me, more recently, that a proliferation of *Hamlets* might be "confusing to the general reader."

Still, Thompson made it clear to the other two general editors of the Arden imprint at the time that she wasn't going to do it in the traditional way even if it came to forcing a showdown with the publisher. Which it did.

She felt strongly that a century of bibliographical scholarship had corroded the foundation, the rationale for trying to confect a single Lost Archetype of *Hamlet* from the found objects of the three imperfect *Hamlet* texts we have. Conflated texts might well be presenting a *Hamlet* that Shakespeare never wrote and the Globe never staged. (Even the Bad Quarto had a stronger claim than the conflated text in that respect: a claim to have actually been staged in Shakespeare's lifetime for better or worse.)

But unlike the other anti-conflationist *Hamlet* editors, Thompson doesn't necessarily endorse the Folio edition as the superior nonconflated text; she doesn't feel the case that it's closer to Shakespeare's "final intentions" has been proven. Nor on the other hand does she feel the partisans of the 1604 Good Quarto have proved their case that Q2 (as this version is called, since the Bad Quarto, Q1, was published a year earlier) is the purer expression of Shakespeare as dramatic poet (rather than poetic dramatist) before its "debasement" in the playhouse by theater managers and actors who—some believe—simplified and dumbed it down to cut it for time.

The wintry afternoon I spoke to Ann Thompson in London she'd just come back from a sojourn at the Folger, and said she was less than a year away from completion of a draft of the edition she and Neil Taylor had been working on for some five years. (In fact it would take five more years.) And she said she was perfectly prepared to produce an edition that didn't claim to explain with any surety the relationship between the three *Hamlet* texts.

In particular, and most controversially, she says the evidence was not sufficient to characterize with certainty the black sheep 1603 Bad Quarto.

"I don't think either those like Eric Sams who attack the 'memorial reconstruction' theory of Q1 and argue it's an early draft, or those like Harold Jenkins who defend 'memorial reconstruction' and disparage the Bad Quarto, have proven their case. It's possible to conjecture it's some form of both—perhaps a bad reconstruction of an early draft—but the evidence is not strong enough to do more than speculate."

But if the evidence is not there, the text *should* be there, in any scrupulous scholarly edition of *Hamlet,* she believes. "It does seem likely this [the Bad Quarto] was a *Hamlet* performed during Shakespeare's lifetime, whatever his actual relation to it, and it plays a role"—as we've seen with Harold Jenkins, a ghostly triangulation role—in conjectures about enigmas in the two longer texts.

It all seemed logical and defensible to me, but to the prospective publisher of the edition it still seemed impractical and uneconomical.

"There was a resistance to publishing not so much more than one text, but more than one volume," Thompson recalled. Oxford has published a two-text *Lear,* but in the context of a three-thousand-page Complete Works edition. (Subsequently they've issued a separate Quarto volume edited by Stanley Wells.) Same with the American Norton edition and its three-text *Lear,* also a relatively small part of a huge volume. But the economics of academic publishing are predicated on "course adoptions"—getting professors of literature, for instance, to assign the Arden over an Oxford, Cambridge, Signet, Penguin or Folger single-volume edition of *Hamlet.* Harold Jenkins's second Arden *Hamlet* was a voluminous six hundred pages for a single conflated text. Everything about a three-text *Hamlet* would be *in*flated at a cost that would restrict it to the graduate rather than the undergraduate student market. The showdown came in the summer of 1995.

"We had a meeting that went on all day with the publisher and the other general editors who were initially against it. And it was tough going. There was a lot of resistance. Arden had decided to do the two other plays where there was a similar dispute—*Lear* and *Othello*—Quarto and Folio in single-volume conflated editions. But I would not have wanted to edit *Hamlet* if one had to do that. I wouldn't have felt it was worth doing. What we're doing is completely different from what other people have done and it affords an opportunity to discover new things and discuss the play in different ways. But yeah, there was resistance."

What carried the day was Ms. Thompson's ingenious proposal for packaging the plays in two volumes. There would be a first volume consisting of an extensively footnoted version of the Good Quarto text preceded by the traditional Arden scholarly apparatus of textual and thematic commentary, and performance history that would cover all three *Hamlet* texts. A volume that could be a stand-alone for undergraduate course adoption. But it would be published simultaneously with a second volume containing the Bad Quarto and Folio versions (with annotations of their unique words and passages), the two volumes designed more for advanced students and scholars.

Ann Thompson overcame internal resistance at Arden. But the two-volume, three-text *Hamlet* will not appear without carping from outsiders. "They say they're not choosing one text over the other," Gary Taylor told me, "but choosing Q2 for the single volume, isn't that an implicit endorsement?" And, Taylor argues, including the 1603 Bad Quarto, whatever the rationale, gives unjustified prominence to what he disparages forthrightly as "a bad text." Including it, he says, amounts to "unediting."

It will be controversial, it may well be attacked for the wrong reasons, as a product of deconstructive theory rather than scrupulous bibliographic research. Still there is no doubt, as Ann Thompson said, that they are "doing something completely different." Something that will dismay those who long for the certainty (or the illusion) of one true *Hamlet.* It will offer a new way of reading and experiencing an old play that has become an ossified compendium of famous quotations to many. A version that requires the reader to engage actively with the texts, to make choices, to try to investigate it, not as some granitic cultural monument, but one that has to be constructed—not deconstructed—by the reader, director, player. Of course actors and directors always have taken the liberty of cutting, of deciding what had to be left in and out for reasons of time and pacing. But now readers must decide what *they* want, what alternative, which branch in the garden of forking paths to take.

Ann Thompson says she sees it work this way teaching *Hamlet* to undergraduates: "I use the two texts and their differences to get them arguing about alternative readings, which causes them to think more deeply about *Hamlet.* It's not more confusing, it's exciting to them."

Her fierce commitment to restoring the distinct identities of the three early texts of *Hamlet,* their lost integrity and individuality, is impressive. I asked her if she felt an affinity with the first woman to attempt to divide *Hamlet,* the Victorian prodigy Teena Rochfort-Smith, whose tragic death I'd become fascinated with.

"Teena Rochfort-Smith, yes!" she said. "You know, I've just published a paper on her in the new issue of *Shakespeare Quarterly.*" Not that surprising, it's a tragedy spawned by a tragedy, not a *Hamlet* tragedy so much as an exemplary *Hamlet* editor's tragedy.

Teena Rochfort-Smith was a young woman adopted professionally and romantically in the early 1880s by F. J. Furnivall, an original sponsor of the *Oxford English Dictionary,* a Victorian gentleman who had a penchant as well for sponsoring "young ladies' rowing clubs" and becoming involved with the young ladies. Furnivall was director of the New Shakspere Society, a group dedicated to restoring Shakespeare's texts to their "original purity." As such, he fostered the ambition of a prodigiously gifted young woman, Teena Rochfort-Smith, then only twenty-one, to produce "the four-text *Hamlet* in Parallel Columns." An insanely complicated task, a kind of Grand Dis-Unification of conflated *Hamlets* that offered a comparative vista of the three original *Hamlet* texts and a fourth, conflated one.

It was, as Ann Thompson put it, "a wonderfully complicated manuscript page that used four different colors of ink and three different forms of underlining as well as numerous signs and symbols, six varieties of type and a formidable battery of asterisks, daggers, and other indicators, to signal the variation in the four parallel texts." She looked through her files and retrieved a photocopy of the sample of the work Teena Rochfort-Smith had published before she perished. Just the "instructions for reading" with which Rochfort-Smith preceded her four-text version "dizzy the arithmetic of memory," as Hamlet put it. One sample from her guide to reading the Folio column's typographical signals:

> BLACK LETTER, where F1 differs from Q2. When this difference (if of word, and not of letter only) agrees with Q1, a dagger is added. Differently spelt words are shown thus: F1 do, Q2 doE. Thus F1 is collated with Q2, but *not* with Q1, except where F1 differs from Q2 and agrees with Q1.

If following the instructions is difficult, imagine the intensity of concentration, the destabilizing multiple four-part focus that each line, each word of *Hamlet* required for the young woman trying to construct it. It's a project that might have consumed much of her life if she had lived. But in fact her life was consumed in a far more brief and terrible fashion: Teena Rochfort-Smith was burned to death when she set fire to her dress, apparently while she was burning some letters with a candle. Like Ophelia, who in effect killed herself for Hamlet, drowned by the weight of her garments, Rochfort-Smith was killed by her clothes, ignited by text.

Ann Thompson maintains her death was most likely an accident, one that had nothing to do with her *Hamlet* editing project. But there's no doubt such an accident could have been the product of strain and distraction.

I had a sense that part of Ann Thompson's special interest in the story of Teena Rochfort-Smith—the fact that she took time out from a crushing deadline schedule for her *Hamlet* edition to research and write a substantial scholarly article on the brief life and doomed project of the unfortunate young *Hamlet* editor—derived from a kind of identification with her predecessor.

But when I pressed Ann Thompson a little further she just demurred and allowed, laconically, "It's a very sad story."

SHAKESPEARE IN REWRITE: SECRETS OF THE ENFOLDED *HAMLET*

At this point the reader might be forgiven if it has not become apparent which *Hamlet* one should read, what *Hamlet* we talk about when we talk about *Hamlet.*

If the new Arden three-text, divided *Hamlet* will do anything, it will make it dramatically clear that to read a *Hamlet* is to make a choice between *Hamlet*s, that there is no longer a default *Hamlet* so to speak. There is a Quarto *Hamlet,* a Folio *Hamlet,* and scores of conflated *Hamlet*s each with claims to be the more poetical, the more theatrical, or the more inclusive. There is a highly regarded "synoptic edition" of the two texts edited by Jesús Tronch-Pérez. And for those who want to triangulate those *Hamlet* texts with a putative predecessor, the Bad Quarto, there are two versions of a three-text *Hamlet:* the Arden, which will print the three texts in succession (over two volumes), and two editions that print them in parallel columns across the page.

But for those who want to catch what the Revisers believe are glimpses of Shakespeare at work, Shakespeare making changes, to my mind Bernice Kliman's *Enfolded Hamlet* best dramatizes the variants.

The origins of Bernice Kliman's *Enfolded Hamlet* can be found in the MLA's *Hamlet Variorum* project, the new version of the ultimate illuminated *Hamlet* text, the volume that surrounds the text of *Hamlet* with a vast inky penumbra of exegesis that sums up four centuries of *Hamlet* commentary and disputation by poets, scholars and madmen on virtually every phrase in the text: the *Hamlet di tutti Hamlet*s.

The term "variorum"—short for the Latin *"cum notis variorum"* (with notes of various persons)—is the scholarly rubric for an edition of a classic work that attempts to record not just all the variations and suggested emendations in the text or texts of the work in question, but to cite and quote what every significant scholar and editor and littérateur has said about every single enigma, every problematic moment, every "site of contestation" as the academics like to say today, that has ever prompted comment.

The most recent *Hamlet Variorum,* the 1877 *New Variorum* edition edited by H. H. Furness (one of those prodigiously erudite and energetic Victorian polymaths), is an amazing volume. A veritable *grimoire* of quaint and curious *Hamlet* lore, it takes some nine hundred pages in two volumes of minuscule type to do the job. Seven-page-long footnotes are not uncommon and often quite wonderful. (Long out of print, the 1877 edition has been reprinted in an affordable Dover Press facsimile.) It's an important document in intellectual history in its chronicle of the evolution of thinking about perhaps the most emblematic work of English-speaking culture, the evolution of the fantasies, longings, visions and delusions projected upon *Hamlet* as well. And it reveals something of the world-historical relevance *Hamlet* has taken on beyond the English-speaking realm.

There's a chilling instance of this in the dedicatory page of the Furness *Hamlet Variorum.* Furness had included voluminous excerpts from the prodigious outpouring of German *Hamlet* scholarship in the century before the *Variorum* was published. Hamlet was, after all, in a very important respect, a German intellectual: he was educated at Wittenberg in the era of Luther's Reformation. A version of *Hamlet* (*Der Bestrafte Brudermord—The Fratricide Punished*) played Germany as early as 1605.

The outpouring of German commentary was, in part, initiated by Goethe's rhapsodies about *Hamlet.* His novel *Wilhelm Meister*—about a young German who succumbs to what became known in Germany as "Hamletism," a veritable frenzy of *Hamlet* fever—inspired one commentator to say that "Germany *is* Hamlet." By "Germany is Hamlet" he meant in its romanticism, its feverish intellectualism, its moody dividedness both spiritual and geopolitical. This was before the triumphalism of the German victory in the 1870–71 Franco-Prussian War, which created the modern united and militarized German empire. Furness's 1877 *Variorum* reflects the seismic shift in German national character in the following dedication:

> TO THE GERMAN SHAKESPEARE SOCIETY OF WEIMAR, REPRESENTATIVE OF A PEOPLE WHOSE RECENT HISTORY PROVED ONCE AND FOR ALL 'GERMANY IS *NOT* HAMLET,' THESE VOLUMES ARE DEDICATED.

Furness must have regarded this as a harmless bit of witty tribute. But looked upon from what we know of subsequent German history, it's possible to observe that if "Hamletism" was the disease, the cure was worse. It's possible to wonder darkly just how much the shift in German character was a conscious redefining itself *against* Hamlet's character. Critics who focus censoriously on Hamlet's indecisiveness as a character flaw might meditate on the consequences of over-decisiveness. Whether the vice of "thinking too precisely" on a subject is worse than the vice of not thinking precisely at all, and whether it was a good thing that Germany became "Not Hamlet."

But once past that chilling dedication, the Furness *Variorum* is a thrilling testament to the enduring power of *Hamlet* and *Hamlet* enigmas to engage the intellect and imagination, to the seductive lure of the textual and thematic labyrinth of the play. To plunge into one of the Furness *Variorum*'s multipage, tiny-type footnote compendiums of commentary is to lose oneself in the pleasures of the penumbral *Hamlet,* the extratextual *Hamlet.* Just to take one example, there is the mystery of the "dozen or sixteen lines."

These are the lines Hamlet privily asks the chief Player to insert into *The Murder of Gonzago,* the better to "catch the conscience of the King." It is the moment when Hamlet himself becomes playwright, and naturally we'd like to know which lines of the hundred or so that we get to hear of *Gonzago* are supposed to have been written by Hamlet himself. Unfortunately the answer's not obvious and has sparked centuries of debate. It's not an insignificant controversy when you consider that Hamlet is a rather prolific writer in *Hamlet.* He writes (and we hear parts of) three letters in the play, one to Ophelia, one to the King, one to Horatio, and then there are those "dozen or sixteen lines," whatever they are. Alas, at the end of eight pages of *Variorum* commentary it's still a controversy that goes unresolved, as it does today. Hamlet has proven quite productive of—but also quite resistant to—definitive, reductive or overly schematized solutions.

The Enfolded Hamlet was Bernice Kliman's invention for the new *New Variorum Hamlet.* More than a century after Furness's *Variorum,* the Modern Language Association, the umbrella organization of literary scholars, began commissioning new variorum versions of Shakespeare's major plays. And in 1990 the assignment to lead a *Hamlet Variorum* team was given to Ms. Kliman.

Ten years later, when I first met her, she and her team of three coeditors (Eric Rasmussen, Hardin Aasand and Nick Clary) were still several years from completing their task of sorting through and knitting together four centuries of *Hamlet* dispute and commentary, but they have made already two breakthroughs that are likely to transform the way *Hamlet* is transmitted to the unfolding future.

There was, first, the breakthrough into the digital realm. If the last *Variorum* took nine hundred pages for three centuries of commentary, the hard-copy version of the new one will certainly exceed a thousand, reaching a point of unwieldiness and inaccessibility that might require a curtailing of the wonderful digressive penumbral quality of a *Hamlet Variorum.* Making a Web-based electronic version correlated with the hardcover, on the other hand, will allow expansion in space and time—more expansive individual entries in the cyberspace version and additive extension in time, theoretically into the infinite future of *Hamlet* commentary.

And at the heart of all that—or so it seemed back then (plans are still in flux)—will be a version of Bernice Kliman's *Enfolded Hamlet,* a hybrid *Hamlet* text she designed herself, one that was first published in a special edition of *The Shakespeare Newsletter* in 1996. It is now also available on the Web in a somewhat different form (www.hamletworks.org) and in 2004 was published in amended hardback form. It's an ingenious design solution initially meant to create a template for the *Variorum,* one that displays and contrasts the two primary *Hamlet* texts simultaneously to the eye, rather than sequentially or in parallel. And in doing so may offer a window, a portal that tantalizes with glimpses of what *appears* to be Shakespeare at work, Shakespeare revising himself, Shakespeare in the act of creation.

Bernice Kliman came to the problem of the *Hamlet Variorum* as something of an outsider. She had founded and edited the *Shakespeare on Film* quarterly; she teaches at Long Island's Nassau Community College; she had written a scholarly paper on the theatricality of Olivier's filmed *Hamlet.* But what she lacked in experience and elite institutional affiliation, she made up in enthusiasm and ingenuity.

Particularly ingenuity. Her *Enfolded Hamlet* solved a problem that had defeated previous editors of multiple-text *Hamlet*s for generations: How do you represent the variant texts and variant words visually in a way that permits comparison?

The solution of traditional conflated editions such as Harold Jenkins's second Arden *Hamlet* was to present a mix-and-match inclusive text and note the additions, omissions and variants in the tiny-type "collation" section beneath the text, a section sandwiched between the lines of the play and the footnotes. (Graduate students have been known to call this "the band of terror.")

Ann Thompson's new Arden edition presents the three texts one after the other in the pages of two volumes. Bernice Kliman herself produced a three-text parallel-column *Hamlet* in the early nineties with a collaborator, Paul Bertram, as a study for the *Variorum.* Teena Rochfort-Smith died in the midst of attempting a four-column parallel edition (the three texts plus a conflation). But none of these methods captures the texture of the *Hamlet* variations (or revisions) in their context the way *The Enfolded Hamlet* does. In sequential *Hamlets*, one has to shift back and forth hundreds of pages, from Quarto to Folio; in conflated *Hamlet*s, one's eyes have to shift up and down the page from text to collations; in parallel *Hamlet*s, one shifts back and forth from column to column, a process that soon induces nystagmus if not nausea.

But *The Enfolded Hamlet* does something the other arrays of *Hamlet*s don't: it juxtaposes the alternatives face-to-face so to speak—and thereby dramatizes the subtle shifts, the single word and phrase alterations between the two major texts. And it does so in a way that makes a more persuasive case than any single academic treatise has for me that we are watching Shakespeare at work, Shakespeare hovering over the text of *Hamlet* like a ghost, and fine-tuning it.

In designing *The Enfolded Hamlet* it was not her intention to give support to either side of the Shakespeare-as-Reviser hypothesis, Bernice Kliman told me when I visited her at her home on Long Island's North Shore.

In her sunlit office which serves as the headquarters for the *Variorum* task force, she makes it clear repeatedly that she has no investment in proving or disproving either side of any of the controversies that swirl around the *Hamlet* texts. Rather than striving to reduce them to a single Right Answer, Male Answer Syndrome style, she *celebrates* the proliferation of *Hamlet* arguments.

And one could with some caution conjecture that there is something conversely feminine about *The Enfolded Hamlet,* beyond the name itself: the "enfolding" is in effect a twining, a braiding, and interleaving of the two primary texts. In this regard it's probably no accident that the example Bernice Kliman uses in the introduction to the first published version of *The Enfolded Hamlet* is a passage involving Ophelia, whose signature gesture is the braiding together of the stems and vines of flowers and herbs.

There is, it might also be noted, something Ophelia-like about Ms. Kliman, who is one of those rare academics who has not lost a kind of innocent celebratory joy in the literature she studies. Ophelia-like in that she is a weaver and binder of leaves even if they be the leaves of old *Hamlet* texts and commentaries. And Ophelia-like in the kind of pure Romantic joy she takes in *Hamlet:* she loves *Hamlet* the way Ophelia loved Hamlet. But it's a generous rather than jealous love: she loves the fierce way *others* have loved *Hamlet,* the way *Hamlet* has been enhanced, elaborated, illuminated, fought over by commentators over the centuries. "I love the infighting and the backbiting and the multiplicity of possibilities you find over the centuries," she tells me. And she sees the *Variorum* she now presides over not just as a reading experience:

"The variations and the variant interpretations are important not just for scholars," she tells me, "but for actors and for directors. They offer a range of ways to play the lines, they expand the possibilities implicit in the ambiguities of the text."

Here's the Ophelia-related passage she uses to illustrate the way *The Enfolded Hamlet* works. A passage that counterposes the play's sententious old courtier Polonius (talk about Male Answer Syndrome) and his daughter Ophelia, a spirited soul striving to break free from her father's strictures.

In the first act, Polonius warns his daughter against any further contact of any kind with Hamlet. In the Quarto this is rendered

. . . From this time
Be something scanter of your maiden presence . . .

While in the Folio it's

. . . For this time daughter
Be somewhat scanter of your maiden presence.

Reading most editions of *Hamlet* in sequence, parallel or up and down the page, the differences might escape notice of the nonspecialist.

Here is how both texts and their differences are rendered simultaneously in *The Enfolded Hamlet:*

. . . {From} <For> this time <daughter>
Be {something} <somewhat> scanter of your maiden presence.

And here is how Ms. Kliman explains how to read the initially confusing-looking braiding of the two texts:

"To unfold Q2 [the Good Quarto] read all the words with no brackets and the words within curly brackets. To unfold F1 [the First Folio version] read all the words with no brackets and the words in pointed brackets."

And here is how Ms. Kliman comments on the shifts visible in the *Enfolded* version: "F1 is milder because the command 'For this time . . .' is more provisional than 'From this time . . .' and because adding 'daughter' has a softening effect. . . ."

Her other introductory example is more famous and even more telling:

There are more things in heaven and earth, Horatio,
Than are dreamt of in {your} <our> philosophy.

The Folio version, "our philosophy" as opposed to "your philosophy," sharpens Hamlet's sense of bewilderment. He's not telling Horatio how clueless *he* (Horatio) is from the point of view of a more knowing philosopher. He's rather saying he, Hamlet, is just as clueless; it baffles the resources of *his* philosophy as well, implicitly baffles human comprehension itself. (And yet, can we be sure the removal of the "y" was the work of Shakespeare's deliberation or the accidental or purposeful work of a scribe, compositor or editor?)

It takes a little getting used to, reading the different brackets, but after a while they take on the minimalist elegance of the solution to a difficult chess problem. Ms. Kliman had designed it to serve as the template for the

Variorum, the text to which the footnotes of commentary would be keyed; it solved the problem of displaying and arraying the two texts and the comments on them in an easy-to-read way.

But it does something more. Once you get used to it, it offers an utterly new way to read *Hamlet.* One that allows the two texts to call each other into question and thereby causes a kind of attentiveness to the choices made (whether by Shakespeare or not we cannot know for sure) to words and passages otherwise often glossed over—but which Shakespeare (or someone) *seemed* to worry over. In a way reading *The Enfolded Hamlet* or the *Variorum,* or any of the multiple-text versions for that matter, is almost like attending a *Hamlet* rehearsal, Shakespeare himself as well as his commentators trying out alternative readings. No one knows in fact whether Shakespeare took any kind of director-like role in the staging of his plays. But it's possible to imagine one is seeing him rehearsing alternative phrasings in the theater of his mind.

Another way of looking at the penumbra of *Hamlet* variations is to use a Heisenbergian metaphor: as a wave-array of possible variations and interpretations of a single word or phrase, a wave-array of possibilities a reader can entertain that doesn't have to be "collapsed" into singularity until an actor makes a choice of one in performance.

MADNESS, LUST AND ANGELS

And *The Enfolded Hamlet* is perhaps the best way, the best textual stage to see certain of these variants acted out, in particular the ones that Shakespeare himself may have played with in moving between the Quarto and the Folio.

It's true you can get a feeling for certain striking thematic differences between the Quarto and Folio in other editorial designs for *Hamlet.* G. R. Hibbard's single-volume Folio-based edition of *Hamlet* in the Oxford series (produced under the guidelines laid down by Gary Taylor and Stanley Wells) does something striking with the long- and medium-length passages that appear in the Quarto but are omitted from Oxford's Folio-based text: it groups them together in an appendix where, cumulatively, one *could* say they tell a story. A story about a level of madness beyond madness, a level of madness that can be found in one *Hamlet* but is lost or has been deliberately cut from the other. A level of madness that "breaks down the pales and forts of reason" (a passage omitted from the Folio), a level of madness that "puts toys of desperation . . . into every brain" (omitted from the Folio). A level of madness that "dizz[ies] the arithmetic of memory" (omitted from the Folio). A level of madness that is unprecedented in life as well as in art: Hamlet declares that his mother's choice of Claudius over her first husband, the murdered King Hamlet, is an utterly fathomless mystery—a choice beyond any madness ever seen before:

"Madness would not err / Nor sense to ecstasy was ne'er so thralled," as he says.

In other words, never in the history of madness was madness like this witnessed. That's madness. Or it was until, for some reason, it was omitted from the Folio, as were the other passages I've cited evoking this extraordinary level of madness. In a play that is in some sense *about* the varieties of madness—true madness, feigned madness, love madness, melancholy madness, revenge madness, the madness of the abyss—the absence or presence of that higher level of madness—bottomless madness one might say, unbearable madness—makes the *Hamlet* with, and the *Hamlet* without, that level of madness subtly different works of art.

It's hard to deny the apparent thematic relatedness of these cuts—or additions. Of course there is one problem which few of the Reviser enthusiasts wish to face. It came up in my conversation with Barbara Mowat of the Folger. I told her that I'd admired the exegesis of the *Hamlet* variations by Oxford's John Jones in *Shakespeare at Work* and Ms. Mowat, a formidable scholar, replied a bit tartly, "Well, he must be very sure that the Quarto preceded the Folio and not the other way around." She points out that as editor of *Shakespeare Quarterly* she published an essay by one scholar who argued the heretical case that the 1623 Folio version, although published last, was *written* first, or at least before the 1604 Quarto. If so, these madness passages would have been *added* to the Quarto to increase the level of madness, rather than removed to tone it down. But whichever it was, it *seems* there was a guiding artistic intelligence behind many of the correlated cuts and additions.

I feel that reading Hibbard's Quarto-only appendix made me think more deeply about what had become a convention—"the madness of Hamlet." Most commentary has focused on when and where the madness is feigned and when real. Hibbard's appendix had me thinking about madness in *Hamlet* in a new way, thinking about *degrees* of madness and what they might mean.

But for the most part, in the same way that "Nature is fine in love," *The Enfolded Hamlet* suggests that Shakespeare is fine (or fine-grained) in rewrite, focused not only on large thematic alterations but on fine-tuning at the single word and phrase level.

Two examples from the very first scene of *Hamlet:* Up on the battlements of Elsinore the shivering sentinels who have seen the Ghost before, and their skeptical friends Horatio and Marcellus, suddenly glimpse the chilling apparition.

"Speak to it, Horatio," says Marcellus in the Quarto.

"Question it, Horatio," he says in the Folio.

"{Speak to} <Question> it, Horatio" is the way it's rendered in *The Enfolded Hamlet.* Someone—if not Shakespeare, then who?—sought to sharpen "speak to it" to "question it," a double-edged sharpening that carries with it the sense of "question its existence" as well.

Later in that scene, after the Ghost has disappeared with the coming of dawn, Marcellus speaks of "that season . . . Wherein our Savior's birth is celebrated" when, in the Quarto, "they say no spirit *dare stir.*" But in the Folio, it's "no spirit *can walk.*" (In the Bad Quarto, there's a confusing amalgam of "dare stir" and "can walk": "dare walk.") Seeing "dare stir" and "can walk" juxtaposed in the *Enfolded* version invites further reflection: it *appears* that someone sought to change the balance between the holy and unholy. In the Quarto the unholy is far more fearfully inhibited by the holy: it does not *dare* stir. In the Folio it is instead merely mildly disabled: no spirit *can* walk. Someone cared enough to make this slight but significant alteration.

Are we seeing Shakespeare's hand fine-tuning his greatest creation in these alterations? It's hard to imagine some theatrical manager—the usual culprit invoked by those who dispute the Shakespeare Reviser hypothesis—taking time to make this kind of change. One can easily imagine such a person cutting whole lines and passages for time and pace but not as easily altering individual words for subtle thematic effects.

Even more persuasive evidence for Shakespearean revision can be found in the apparently correlated changes made in the language Hamlet uses to chastise his mother in the so-called closet scene. One is easy to see in the *Enfolded* version. When his mother chides Hamlet that "You answer with an idle tongue," he replies, "Goe, goe, you question with {a wicked} <an idle> tongue."

A gentler Hamlet in the Folio sees his mother as "idle" rather than "wicked." An even more decisive gentling can be found enfolded a bit later.

Gertrude asks Hamlet, "Have you forgot me?"

"No," says Hamlet, he has not forgotten who she is. "You are the Queene, your husband's brother's wife."

In the Quarto he goes on to say, "And would it were not so, you are my mother."

In other words, he wants to disclaim utterly his maternal connection with her, because of her hasty marriage to Claudius (her "husband's brother").

A slap in the face which is transformed in the Folio into a wistful caress: "But would you were not so. You are my mother."

The change from a comma in the Quarto to a period between "so" and "You" in the Folio shifts things utterly. Now he's not disclaiming her but frankly and directly *claiming* her: "You *are* my mother," rather than "would it were not so, you are my mother." Now it is "would it were not so you are connected to Claudius," but you are still my mother.

It is difficult not to think of these two alterations in conjunction and just as difficult not to see them as the thoughts of a playwright looking for a way to make the relationship between mother and son more tender and complex. Yes, either one or both could be an accident or a compositor's whim, but the fact they are altered in the same way at least *argues* for intention.

The value of noticing these particular changes is more than academic: they can be signals to the actors who play Hamlet and Gertrude to focus on calibrating the tenderness between them, as close to "notes" direct from the playwright as anything we have. The revised version suggests the same kind of tenderness the Folio version gives Laertes in the "precious instance" passage.

The Enfolded Hamlet dramatizes what seems like another precious instance of the playwright wrestling with the nature of love. There is a wonderful moment when one can almost see Shakespeare grappling with the attempt to express a complex thought about the nature of women's love, a moment dramatized in *The Enfolded Hamlet*'s rendition of a speech by the Player Queen. This comes in the midst of *The Murder of Gonzago,* the look-alike royal murder-plot play that Hamlet has specially asked the Players to perform in order "to catch the conscience of the King." The play to which Hamlet has said he will add "a speech of some dozen or sixteen lines." Where in the hundred or so lines of *The Murder of Gonzago* are Hamlet's "dozen or sixteen"? Could it be in this passage in which Shakespeare attempts to evoke the nature of women's love?

The Player Queen is trying to tell her husband the King that she's concerned about his health but he shouldn't get too upset. "Discomfort you . . . it nothing must."

Why shouldn't it bother him? Because of the nature of women's love, she says:

> {*For women feare too much, even as they love*}
> {*And*} <*For*> *women's fear and love* {*hold*} <*holds*> *quantitie,*
> {*Eyther none*} *in neither ought, or in extremity. . . .*

Harold Jenkins and others have argued that these lines represent an instance of Shakespeare changing his mind *in currente calamo,* as the scholars call it—"in the heat of the moment," or more literally as the ink flowed.

The first line, according to this conjecture, "For women feare too much, even as they love," was Shakespeare's first draft of the second line—"For women's fear and love holds quantitie."

After trying the second version of the first line out, the argument goes, he forgot to cross out the first version and both became incorporated into the Quarto text by an unwitting typesetter reading the handwritten manuscript. In the Folio the implication is, Shakespeare left out that first attempt but continued to work on the next two lines.

So, if we are tracking a shift from first to second try and looking at the change in the third line, we can imagine we are watching Shakespeare working out a thought about love that is almost as difficult to express as the "precious instance" passage, the one that opened "Nature is fine in love . . ."

Women, he seems to be trying to say, are not "fine" in love in that sense, but fierce: They are either all or nothing. When they do love, they love more intensely than men and because they love more intensely, they fear for their love more intensely, in equal "quantitie" as the intensity of their love, to the point of extremity.

It is, like the thought behind the "precious instance" passage, an idea that somehow hovers above these three lines like a soul preparing for incarnation in the body of a newborn child, but a bit before the child has been brought to term. The Word not quite made flesh.

Shakespeare *seems* to have decided to move on without resolving the difficulty—but couldn't quite move on. He tries another version—or if you will, portrays Hamlet (if this is part of the "dozen or sixteen lines") trying another version just a few lines later where that thought about women's love (or something close to it) is embodied in these further words of the Player Queen:

"Where love is great, the littlest doubts are fear; / Where little fears grow great, great love grows there."

It's fascinating the way so many of the *Hamlet* passages that suggest Shakespeare worried over most involve meditations on the extremities, the degrees of love and madness. It is in surfacing precious instances such as these that textual studies redeem the mind-numbing mental labor, the sight-destroying close focus, the combat and backbiting among *Hamlet* editors over the centuries.

Bernice Kliman loves the backbiting and the combat, but she also loves rescuing obscure *Hamlet* explainers from obloquy and oblivion as well. When I met with her she'd just come back from the Folger Shakespeare Library in Washington, where she'd made a discovery while burrowing into the Library's unrivaled collection of eighteenth-century literary manuscripts and books.

"I was able to identify the author of some extremely thoughtful Shakespearean commentary that appeared without a byline in the *Gentleman's Magazine* and which turns out to have been written by George Eliot's love and mentor, George Henry Lewes.

"The more voices the better," she says. She's fascinated by *Hamlet*'s ability to strike so many chords however discordant, and she has made it her mission to make the new *New Variorum* even more inclusive than Furness's, extending even to some of the further, wilder shores of *Hamlet* speculation.

Now comes what I'd say was the second most gratifying moment in my odyssey among the textual scholars. Did I hear you say you wanted to know the *first* most gratifying moment? I'm glad you asked. It took place in an exchange I had in the office of Barbara Mowat of the Folger. She had just taken me down into the Folger vaults to show me their unrivaled collections of Quarto *Hamlet*s (five of the seven in the world in addition to numerous First Folios).

Mowat is coediting all of the plays for the Folger edition (with Paul Werstine) and has done textual scholarship at its most sophisticated. I was in awe of her expertise and grateful she'd been willing to spend a considerable time addressing my questions on the questions. Toward the end I was telling her how, even after two years of studying the *Hamlet* text problem and the Reviser question, I felt swayed almost too easily by the powerful polemics on both sides.

"I'll read one then the other and feel batted back and forth to the point where I wasn't sure I knew what I was talking about."

"Oh you know what you're talking about," she said, apparently, to my great delight, *without irony.* I felt like I'd received a blessing for my outsider's odyssey into the innermost citadels of scholarship.

The second most gratifying moment? The upshot of my conversation with Bernice Kliman about the "lust and angels" passage in *Hamlet.* It's the passage in which the ghost of Hamlet's father tries to describe his horror and disgust at his wife Gertrude's consorting with his murderer Claudius.

It is here, in the "lust and angels" passage, that another important feature of *The Enfolded Hamlet* plays a role. It's an "original spelling" version of *Hamlet,* an unmodernized *Hamlet,* a *Hamlet* that is a virtual facsimile of the way that the words were printed, read and played from when Shakespeare was alive (with certain exceptions such as the substitution of a modern *s* for the elongated *s* that looks like an *f*). A text closer to the one Shakespeare himself wrote and perhaps revised.

In the "lust and angels" lines Hamlet's ghostly father calls Claudius an "incestuous beast" who won the Queen to his lust. But the Queen shares a responsibility for this "falling-off," the Ghost tells Hamlet bitterly. Because true virtue can't be seduced,

Though lewdness court it in a shape of heauen
{So} but <lust> though to a radiant angel linct
Will {sort} <sate> itself on a celestial bed
And pray on garbage.

It's an extraordinarily violent, sexual and mystifying passage. To sort it out in an unfolded way, in the Quarto, the Ghost tells Hamlet, "lewdness"

So but though to a radiant Angel linckt,
Will sort itselfe in a celestiall bed
And pray on garbage . . .

This doesn't quite make sense unless it's meant to read, "If lewdness" (from the previous line) "is linked to a radiant angel, it will degrade the angel's bed to a place of garbage," to a "waste of shame" (to quote one of the Sonnets on lust). It's a link made more explicit in the Folio when the Ghost says

But lust though to a radiant Angel linct,
Will sate itselfe in a celestiall bed
And prey on garbage.

Once again, we have an extreme, almost incendiary image, an image of sexuality and degradation, a marriage of heaven and hell that hovers just out of reach of complete articulation. To parse it out at its most basic level, it *seems* to be saying that a virtuous person, though courted by a heavenly looking seducer, will be unmoved, while a lustful person will drag down even a radiant angel to degradation. But even that's perhaps imposing more rationality on a feverish vision of sex with angels that doesn't quite sort (or sate) itself into easy paraphrase.

And what about that final image: "pray on garbage." It was here I made a suggestion about a slight omission in *The Enfolded Hamlet's* enfolding—and a conjecture about what was enfolded within that omission—that Ms. Kliman felt was worth entering into her *Variorum* database. For centuries almost every commentator had read "pray on garbage" as "prey on garbage" because "prey" was the Folio reading and "pray" was often an old-spelling version of "prey." *The Enfolded Hamlet* went with the Quarto "pray" but did *not* unfold this as a {pray} <prey> variation because Ms. Kliman told me it was assumed to be an incidental or accidental alternate spelling rather than an alternative meaning.

But, I asked Ms. Kliman, why *not* an alternate meaning? Why not "pray," why not an image of someone who would kneel down and pray on (a heap of) garbage? To "prey on garbage" in the predatory sense is not necessarily the obvious choice. What does it mean to "prey" on garbage? Generally, a predator preys on some lesser fleeing animal. To prey on inanimate garbage, to slaver, to scavenge like a jackal or a rat, over refuse is a graphic image, certainly, but "prey" in this predator sense is not an obvious choice over "pray"—not to the point of excluding the possibility of a religious connotation.

A case could be made, I suggested to Ms. Kliman, that "pray" is just as coherent and perhaps more consistent than "prey." After all, the previous lines are filled with religious references—"a shape of heaven," a "radiant Angel," "a celestial bed." "Pray" would not be out of place in that celestial chain of images. In fact, it might heighten the sense of degradation by sharpening the degree and intensity of the contrast between the heavenly and the hellish. To *pray* on garbage is more than an image of degradation. It carries a suggestion of deliberate blasphemy, almost Satanic mockery of prayer and reverence. Harold Jenkins in fact has made the suggestion in his *Hamlet* edition that there is a submerged reference to Lucifer in the "radiant angel" image. Jenkins cites the line in Corinthians in which Lucifer (a name which means "light bearer") is referred to as "an angel of light"—a radiant angel. And later, in fact, Hamlet observes that "th'Devill hath power to assume a pleasing shape"—perhaps the pleasing "shape of heaven" evoked in this passage.

One doesn't necessarily need to find Lucifer flickering beneath the surface of these lines to see that "pray" is, in certain respects, a more poetically resonant image than "prey." After all, the previous images in the passage have embodied heaven-hell contrasts: virtue and lewdness, lewdness and heaven, lust and angel. Similarly, with "pray" and "garbage." While *prey* and garbage lacks that contrast; they are reinforcing images of appetite and degradation rather than contrasts like virtue and lewdness.

All of this I expounded to Bernice Kliman who went to her computer, opened up the *Variorum* database and, either in the spirit of inclusiveness or of humoring a guest, asked me to dictate a compressed version of this conjecture for her to input into the provisional electronic version of the *Variorum.* She also told me that she planned to unfold "pray" and "prey" in the revised version of the *Enfolded* template for the *Variorum.* It now appears in the hardcover version of *The Enfolded Hamlet.*

I must admit to experiencing a kind of thrill at having my conjecture entered into the slipstream of the *Variorum Hamlet,* into the ongoing centuries-old discourse over *Hamlet* even by drawing attention to the significance of a variation in a *single letter.* I had always envied a fellow I knew, Timothy Ferris, who was involved with Carl Sagan in choosing exactly what emblems of human civilization would be inscribed on the information-bearing module to be launched into space on the *Voyager* deep space probe and boosted out of the solar system's orbit on an interstellar voyage in search of an alien intelligence that might somehow respond to the symbols and tokens of human civilization. Ferris, now a professor of astrophysics at USC, had been the one to choose which one song would be put in the module to represent rock 'n' roll in the infinite depths of time and space (he chose Chuck Berry's "Johnny B. Goode").

Somehow the possibility of having my conjecture about the "angels and lust" passage inscribed in the *Variorum* gave me a similar feeling of satisfaction. *Hamlet* is, after all, the artifact of our culture most likely to continue to sail on into time, the *Variorum* its ever-expanding comet trail.

THE ARDEN DECLARATION THAT ALL *HAMLET* MUST BE DIVIDED into three parts is likely to set off a new round of *Hamlet* wars. But the upheaval will produce more than scholarly fratricide; it will give all of us a new lens with which to look at the play. The conflicts are not just about the texts but about what *Hamlet* means and who Hamlet is.

It may inspire some readers to go deeper into the play. It is likely to excite echoes and ripples in the expanding cosmos of the *Hamlet Variorum,* that record of the love and madness of *Hamlet* scholars. Indeed, the fact that so many variant *Hamlet* passages involve meditations on the extremities of love and madness may apply to its exegetes: the love and madness of *Hamlet* scholars has deepened our sense of the play's inexhaustible mysteries. Hamlet's last words may be "The rest is silence." But *Hamlet* continues to speak.

O, o, o, o.

Epilogue

In January 2006, as I was sending the manuscript of this book to the copy editor, I checked in with Ann Thompson and heard some remarkable news: the Arden *Hamlet* that she and Neil Taylor had been working on for nearly a decade, initially scheduled to appear in 2002, was at last ready to go to the printers and would receive its debut at the April 2006 Shakespeare Association of America Conference in Philadelphia, and shortly thereafter at a reception at the Globe Theatre in London.

Shortly after that I received from Arden (now a publishing division of London's Thomson Learning) the page proofs of the massive two-volume edition, nearly a thousand pages altogether, with prefaces and appendices. I was surprised at how faithfully the basic formal plan Ann Thompson had been arguing for since as long ago as 1995 had been followed: two separate volumes, the first containing the 1604 Good Quarto (Q2) and a long introductory essay of remarkable clarity and comprehensiveness, along with a second volume containing the earliest Quarto (Q1) printed in 1603 (the so-called Bad Quarto) followed by the Folio text (F) of the play printed in 1623. (The second volume would be a hardcover-only edition for the moment, and there have been some complaints about its price.)

What impressed me even more was the steadfast commitment to what you might call scholarly humility in the treatment of the centuries of contentions over *Hamlet*'s textual identity.

In commenting, in appendix 2, on the complexities of the theories of "transmission" (was F derived from an annotated copy of Q2, with reference to Q1, for instance, or derived from a separate annotated derivation of a transcription, with reference to an annotated copy of a theatrical "promptbook"?) they are unafraid to say: "We do not feel that there is any clinching evidence to render definitive any of the competing theories outlined above. The temptation to deny that we have a theory for any one text, let alone all three, is almost overwhelming. Our disposition is agnostic . . ."

They take the same agnostic position on the crucial question of Shakespeare's "intentions": Does the Folio text represent Shakespeare's "final intention" for *Hamlet,* or his "theatrical intention" but not his "literary" intention as some have argued Q2 was?

They don't condemn conflation out of hand as the work of the devil, but point out that the drive by past editors "to establish a final, definitive text" leads to arbitrary choices based on inadequate evidence and subjective considerations about what "belongs" and doesn't "belong" in *Hamlet.*

They have rejected conflation they say, "preferring to treat each text as an independent entity. This is not because we believe that they were, in fact, entirely independent, but because none of the evidence of possible dependence is sufficiently overwhelming or widespread to oblige us to make any specific act of conflation as a result. And these three texts are remarkably distinct entities."

That last statement may prove to be the most controversial, particularly when it comes to choosing the text for the first, stand-alone volume. In choosing Q2, they frankly concede they are "settl[ing] for the most probable" of the choices, rather than anything "provable." In fact they flatly state, "None is proven (or as we imagine, finally provable) and none can be dismissed out of hand."

And elsewhere they state: "Nearly 400 years [after publication of the last of the three texts], there is still no consensus of what constitutes the true text of *Hamlet.*" If humility ever could be said to be "shocking" one must praise this as a shining instance in scholarly literature of shocking—and praiseworthy—humility. It is a recognition that before we even grapple with *Hamlet*'s haunting opening question—"Who's there?"—we must admit that when it comes to the play itself we can't even know "what's there."

Yes, they offer complex and well-reasoned conjectures, they offer a menu of theories, they offer *three* charts of potential relationships between the three texts. But they do not pretend to offer certainty on any of these questions.

And indeed if, in the play, Hamlet himself, the character, has trouble defining himself, deciding on a course of action—on an identity—the fact that *we* cannot, after all this time, decide what the true identity of the text of *Hamlet* is or how it came to be, may well be, for want of a better phrase, poetic justice.

Chapter Three

A Digressive Comic Interlude Featuring Shakespeare's Ambiguously Revised Testimony in the Wigmakers' Lawsuit

As you know I feel strongly that the biographical approach to Shakespeare is usually futile. I've sought to avoid, for the most part, making inferences from the life to the work, or vice versa. And I distrust attempts to reconstruct Shakespeare "the man" as much as I do attempts to deconstruct Shakespeare's body of work (deconstruction of course is not exegesis, which seeks to find coherences; deconstruction is the attempt to prove that there are no, can never be any, coherences because of the self-subverting nature of language—that works of literature, like all works of speech and writing, are ultimately incoherent).

Still . . . Shakespeare's deposition in the Wigmakers' Lawsuit is not speculation, but genuine, documentary evidence of his testimony. And documentary evidence of how he revised it. And before moving on to the weighty matter of how the revision question affects our view of King Lear's dying words, I'd like to pause for a digression upon that testimony, those revisions.

I'm not saying it's evidence in the contention over whether he revised his work, but it is an instance in his life when he revised his *own words* under oath. And so ought to be worth paying some attention to, if only because the circumstances surrounding Shakespeare's deposition—the comic intrigue—are entertaining. And in part because it may be the closest we can come to hearing Shakespeare speaking in his own voice—Shakespeare playing the part of Shakespeare.

My attention was drawn to the wigmakers' lawsuit by two disparate references to it. First from Professor Richard Wilson of Lancashire University, one of the earliest popularizers, through an influential article in the *TLS,* of the "Shakeshafte" theory of Shakespeare's Lost Years. I hope you will bear with me, because Wilson and the Shakeshafte theory will require a digression within a digression that I would defend as illustrative of the *perils* of biographical bubbles, and will, I hope, establish the Wigmakers' Lawsuit as a defensible limited exception to my strictures against bio-criticism.

And not to address the Shakeshafte theory would be to ignore entirely what Professor Wilson characterized to me as "an earthquake" in Shakespeare biographical studies, "one of only two biographical discoveries in the entire twentieth century"—the other being the Wigmakers' Lawsuit. And the Wigmakers' Lawsuit has received none of the virtually frenzied attention the Shakeshafte theory has from fact-starved biographers (most recently Stephen Greenblatt in *Will in the World*) who have given the Shakeshafte theory a prominence and a significance that may have no foundation in fact. Indeed, as I write, the backlash against its overreaching has already begun and it may be remembered as an insubstantial bubble deserving little more weight than the misattributed "Funeral Elegy" bubble.

The Shakeshafte bubble, which is only now beginning to deflate, makes a grander claim—about the nature of Shakespeare's soul—than any conclusion that can be drawn from the Wigmakers' Lawsuit testimony. But the latter is at least based on solid evidence, not the *possible* identification of a certain William Shakespeare with a certain William Shakeshafte. To illustrate the point requires a *further* digression into the terra incognita of Shakespeare's "Lost Years" and the way Shakespearean biographers have sought to fill them.

"The Lost Years" is a term popularized by the respected textual scholar Ernst Honigmann to refer to the period from 1579 when Shakespeare was fifteen years old and *may* have completed Stratford grammar school (although no record survives of his attending) to 1593 when he becomes a celebrated poet and dramatist with the publication of the notoriously erotic *Venus and Adonis* and the success of his first real masterpiece for the stage, *Richard III*.

The Lost Years are the longest gap in a series of gaps and absences in the fragmentary documentary record of Shakespeare's life, particularly his early life. We don't have many biographical documents from his later playwriting life, either (setting aside the work itself, from which inferences about the life cannot be securely made).

The later documents mainly testify to his involvement in petty Stratford lawsuits and various land transactions involving the theater company ownership in London. But the record of his youth and early years is largely, well, lost.

Lost in the Lost Years is any reliable account of transformation: how the provincial glover's boy from Stratford became the sophisticated cosmopolitan poet and playwright of London.

The Lost Years exemplify what I once characterized as "evidentiary despair." The phrase is a way of summarizing the argument made to me (in *Explaining Hitler*) by Yehuda Bauer, then head of Jerusalem's Yad Vashem Holocaust Museum. He was attempting to counter various "mystifying" explanations of Hitler that relied on the absence of contradictory evidence—of any evidence—for their persistence. Especially the trope that Hitler is "inexplicable" because he represented some numinous form of superhuman evil. No, said Bauer, Hitler is not inexplicable—in theory.

Rather he may be inexplicable in *practice* to biographers, in part because Hitler's own Lost Years, the thirty years before he suddenly became a public figure in 1920, left behind a similar mystery of transformation: How exactly did this nonentity develop into the charismatic world-war-making mass murderer?

Yehuda Bauer argued forcefully that we view this as mysterious not because of some occluded, occult mystical cause, but because there are just too many gaps in the evidence, too many missing or dead eyewitnesses, too few documents, too many contradictory or unreliable anecdotes. Too much lost in the Lost Years. Thus: "evidentiary despair," which applies even more to Shakespeare's irretrievable four-centuries-old Lost Years.

The man who popularized the term in Shakespeare studies, Ernst Honigmann (in his 1985 book *Shakespeare: The Lost Years*), was not the first to argue that the Shakeshafte theory was a "solution" to the Lost Years (a Jesuit scholar, Father Peter Milward, deserves credit for that). But Honigmann was the first influential scholarly insider to start people talking about the Shakeshafte theory.

Of course the documentary record before the Lost Years is not exactly rich with indisputable evidence. Even the day of his birth is a little slippery. People like to say it was April 23, 1564, in part because it was registered then and in part because of the symmetry: April 23 (1616) is the day he died. How neat! Dare we say mystical? Almost too perfect, the twinned birth and death moments. And April 23 also happens to be the birthday of Vladimir

Nabokov. An added bonus for those of us who like to see him as the only contemporary analogue of Shakespearean genius.

But the problem with this all-too-convenient date of birth is that, as biographer Peter Ackroyd summarizes the controversy, "the date may have been April 21 or April 22," but only *assigned* to April 23 because that was the day it was registered and it was an important national feast day.

This slipperiness is symptomatic of the uncertainty that pervades the entire fragmentary biographical record. We know the date of Shakespeare's marriage to Anne Hathaway in November 1582, when he was eighteen and she was twenty-six, although there's a troubling record of a William Shakespeare being betrothed in a nearby village to one "Anne Whately," and entire comic-romantic biographical fantasies about "the other woman" have been spun out of what may be a clerical error in spelling the name of the same person.

And entire cloud castles of unfounded, or certainly unprovable, biographical fantasies have been built upon the slender foundation of the age disparity between Shakespeare and his bride and the fact that she must have been three months' pregnant before they married since she gave birth to their first daughter, Susanna, in May of 1583.

Urgent love, or forced marriage by a scheming older woman? Unfounded inferences about this question have been put to service as lenses through which to look at Shakespeare's attitude toward love and sex in the plays and poems.

We know that his wife gave birth to twins in 1585, and we know that one of those twins, Hamnet, died at age eleven in 1596, and that James Joyce spent more than fifty pages of *Ulysses* spinning out a theory of *Hamlet* on the basis of it (as does Stephen Greenblatt among many others). But the sad truth about such inferences is reflected in Peter Ackroyd's hopeless locution: "We know that Shakespeare either was or was not inconsolable upon his son's death." Precisely: he either was or was not many other things in many other biographies. A schoolteacher in the countryside? A deer poacher? A lawyer's clerk?

But until the Shakeshafte theory, the Shakeshafte "earthquake," came along there was little to found even a cloud castle upon in the Lost Years.

Thus the popularity of the Shakeshafte theory as adumbrated by Milward, Honigmann, Richard Wilson, Park Honan, Anthony Holden, Stephen Greenblatt, Peter Ackroyd, just about every recent biographer except the relentlessly and refreshingly skeptical Katherine Duncan-Jones, the Oxford-based author of *Ungentle Shakespeare.*

All of it founded on the discovery of someone called William Shakeshafte—in a will registered two hundred miles north of William Shakespeare's Stratford, during the Lost Years.

Back in the 1920s and '30s two archivists called attention to the will of one Alexander Hoghton of Lancashire, who had made a special request in his will that his "players' clothes" be given into the care of a local Lancastrian lord named Hesketh, along with a request that Hesketh take care of two of his attendants, one of whom was named "William Shakeshafte."

Voilà! The Shakeshafte theory: William Shakeshafte is identical to young William Shakespeare and he was a player in the household theater troupe of someone who turned out to be a secret Catholic sympathizer. But was this Shakespeare? Was Shakespeare Shakeshafte? Spellings were fluid and variant then, but there were a number of Shakeshafte families in Lancashire, so the similarity of spelling is in no way conclusive.

Undaunted, Shakeshafte theory has forged a link between the alleged identity of Shakeshafte/Shakespeare and the theatrical world since Hoghton and Hesketh had connections with Lord Strange, later a patron of William Shakespeare's theatrical company. But there is no record or testimony of Shakespeare's association with Lord Strange's company until the 1590s, more than a decade later.

Connections have been found or forged between the Lancashire barons and the underground of secret "recusant" Catholics in Elizabeth's Protestant theocracy. And between those secret Catholics and Shakespeare's father, John, who may have been a secret Catholic and may have been in possession of a "spiritual testament" circulated by an underground Jesuit operative, Father Edmund Campion, who may have met William Shakespeare in the household of the northern baron if Shakespeare was the same person as William Shakeshafte, the attendant in the Lancastrian household.

But was Shakeshafte Shakespeare? No way of telling. Utterly unprovable four hundred years later. And was William Shakespeare a secret Catholic who wove into his plays secret Catholic allegories, Da Vinci code style, as some of the more extreme Shakeshafte theorists have argued? No way of knowing, or proving it.

But given the poverty of evidence in the Lost Years, few biographers have been able to resist making the Shakeshafte connection. Even if they hedge it heroically with might-have-beens and could-have-beens, they proceed to run with it. And yet it all depends on assuming an identity between the "shafte" and the "speare." An all-too-shaky foundation upon which to make all too many assumptions about what Shakespeare's personal religious beliefs were and what was reflected in the plays. As the author of a recent study, *Shakespeare's Religious Language,* R. Chris Hassel Jr., put it, "various readers have tried to argue Shakespeare's faith as well as his position on Reformation controversies. Yet . . . most readers, myself included, still reserve judgment on just what and how Shakespeare believed. . . ." The plays can supply evidence for almost every point of view about such beliefs, but, again, nothing indisputable.

How unsatisfying, compared with the all-too-neat Shakeshafte theory, which solves so many questions at once: how he became a dramatist, what his secret faith was, what the plays are *really* about. No wonder Richard Wilson called it "an earthquake" when I spoke to him. But alas it's an earthquake built on a fault, one might say, an absence of proof. (Professor Wilson, to his credit, does not take the line that the Shakeshafte theory *proves* Shakespeare was a secret Catholic in league with Catholic martyrs like Campion or that the plays contain secret Catholic messages. In fact Wilson told me he believes, if anything, the plays offer a "critique of martyrdom," of fanatical true believers.)

Which brings us to the Wigmakers' Lawsuit. To me, by far a more interesting and significant and well-founded, if not well-known, biographical fragment by comparison. It came up indirectly in my conversation with Wilson when he spoke of the Shakeshafte discovery as one of "only two" new biographical discoveries about Shakespeare in the twentieth century.

As it happened he didn't name the other one, but I was familiar with what he was referring to. My attention had recently been drawn to the Wigmakers' Lawsuit by a thread on SHAKSPER, the Shakespeare scholars' electronic discussion list. Someone had posted the question: Where, if anywhere, do we find a credible record of Shakespeare speaking in his own voice? Not necessarily, or provably, in the characters in the plays—those are staged voices. Not necessarily the voice of the Sonnets, whose narrator may be as much literary convention as personal confessional. Wordsworth thought the Sonnets were the key to unlock Shakespeare's heart. Perhaps, although they may more likely be a key to unlock Shakespeare's art. There's no evidence he's speaking in his own voice as opposed to that of a *persona* in them. Nor can his voice be found necessarily even in his will, where some would like to find it, but which might be just so much lawyers' boilerplate.

So is it possible we have *no* reliable record of Shakespeare in his own voice? Well, there is that one unverifiable anecdote, the "William the Conqueror's Story." In which an ardent female fan was said to be so mesmerized by Richard Burbage's portrayal of seductive evil in *Richard III* that she sent a note or proposition backstage, suggesting Burbage come to her abode following the play. A proposition which was, according to the anecdote, intercepted or overheard by Shakespeare, who showed up first at the woman's lodging and talked her into letting him serve in Burbage's place in her bed. At which point, or in the midst of which, Burbage banged on the door braying, "It is I, Richard the Third." To which, we are told by tradition, Shakespeare replied, "William the Conqueror came before Richard the Third!" Talk about a self-serving anecdote. Perhaps it happened and perhaps it's Shakespeare's voice, but a more extensive and less suppositional place to find that voice is in the Wigmakers' Lawsuit.

That was the conjecture of one of the scholars on the electronic discussion list. Perhaps someone could recover Shakespeare's *testimony* in that lawsuit, she suggested. In fact someone had, and as it turns out the Wigmakers' Lawsuit is a useful counterbalance to others' speculation about the secret spirituality, because it gives us something, the texture of the life led by "someone writing at the time transcendent tragedies"—but not above getting involved in some seedy domestic comedy, what sounds like a tawdry sex farce. And it suggests a link between something going on in Shakespeare's voice and something that goes on in Shakespearean language.

The suit was brought, Shakespeare's testimony was taken, in 1612 when he was forty-eight years old, four years away from his death, close to the time when he'd virtually abandoned his solo playwriting career, shortly before retiring (as much as we can tell) to Stratford to indulge in the petty litigation that came with his new gentrified landowner status.

The Wigmakers' Lawsuit, however, referred back to a cryptic episode in the past, eight years earlier in 1604 when he had been a lodger in the home of the wigmaker Christopher Mountjoy and his wife Lucy and their daughter Mary and their servant/apprentice Stephen Belott. This cast of characters produced *some* kind of secret farce beneath the surface of their domestic arrangements that would later result in litigation—and in Shakespeare giving a deposition. The seventeenth-century Litigation Roll record did not surface until 1910 and the transcript of the Elizabethan legal-hand document by C. W. Wallace was published in modern type the following year; I found it in a 1911 issue of *University of Nebraska Studies* in the NYU Library.

In the years he was living with the Mountjoys Shakespeare was producing dramas such as *Hamlet* and *Lear* and some of his trickiest comedies such as *All's Well That Ends Well* and *Measure for Measure.* At the time his own wife and family were living in Stratford, the Mountjoy house was a pied-à-terre in London, although he's portrayed in the depositions as a full-time resident rather than a commuter.

From the evidence available it is tempting to see the Mountjoy establishment as a hotbed of sexual intrigue. The Mountjoys were Huguenots who had fled anti-Protestant persecution in France. Christopher Mountjoy, the head of the family, was not so much a wig- as a "tire-maker," someone who crafted ornate, often-bejeweled frameworks and headpieces for women who wore elaborate wigs. His clientele were wealthy women who cared about attractiveness.

They had a daughter, Mary, but there seemed to be a problem marrying her off. Else why would so many "conferences" between William Shakespeare and Mrs. Lucy Mountjoy be required for them to form a plan wherein William Shakespeare would approach the servant and apprentice wigmaker and make him an offer of a generous settlement on behalf of Christopher Mountjoy if Belott married the daughter Mary? Shakespeare, in other words, did the financial wooing.

We don't know for sure why a servant and apprentice would require such blandishments, but the depositions indicate that Shakespeare was successful in his surrogate wooing on behalf of Mary, or at least his promises were. But what were Shakespeare's promises? That was the issue of the lawsuit, although only long after the alleged promises were made.

A few years after the marriage, there's some split between the wigmaker and the son-in-law, and he and the daughter he married moved out; then they move back in with the Mountjoys, and then there's this lawsuit—eight years later!—where the servant turned son-in-law declares that all that time ago he was promised by Mr. Shakespeare (on behalf of the wigmaker) a payment upon marriage and a substantial settlement—some two hundred pounds—after the wigmaker's death. And that the wigmaker never gave him a penny.

Again one of those affairs whose combinational and permutational possibilities "dizzy the arithmetic of memory." Anthony Holden suggests an affair between the wigmaker's wife and Shakespeare, the two of them scheming to get the prying daughter out of the house—or the prying apprentice. I personally suspect Shakespeare and the daughter herself—which would explain why there was some difficulty, some negotiations necessary, to get her married off to the servant. Of course, neither the estimable Holden nor I have any proof for our suspicions. But the raw material of Shakespearean comedy is there: the cynical go-between (Shakespeare as Pandarus), the scheming servant, the flighty daughter, the amorous mother, the foolish wigmaker.

All this, a farce that could be called "Shakespeare and the Wigmaker's Daughter," lurks beneath the surface of the depositions of the wigmaker family and in particular the deposition of "William Shakespeare of Stratford-upon-Avon in the Countye of Waricke, gentleman of the age of xlviij [48] or thereaboutes."

At first when I got the *University of Nebraska Studies* version of the Shakespeare deposition I was slightly disappointed. The question had been, initially, did we have any indisputable instance of Shakespeare's own voice, and yes this *was* Shakespeare's own voice although slightly filtered through a kind of court reporter.

As in: "To the second interrogatory this deponent [Shakespeare] sayeth he did know the complainant [the son-in-law] when he was servant with the defendant and that during the time of the complainant's service with the said defendant he, the said complainant, to this deponent's [Shakespeare's] knowledge did well and honestly behave himself, but to this deponent's remembrance he hath not heard the defendant confesses that he had got any great profit and commodity by the service of the said complainant, but this deponent saith he verily thinketh that the said complainant was a very good and industrious servant in the said service."

There's a filter but it can't filter out the patterned ambiguity, the alternation of assertions and retractions. Stephen was a good servant, says Shakespeare, but on the other hand he never *heard* the master say he got much from his service. But on the other hand he thinks he *was* a good servant.

This ambivalence or ambiguity reaches a kind of fever pitch in the fourth interrogatory, where you stop wondering about whether Shakespeare was screwing the wigmaker's daughter or wife or both and wonder if you are getting a glimpse of his mind at work doing something that is, in a primal way, *Shakespearean:* creating double meanings, revising himself, rewriting himself. I'm speaking of Shakespeare's "Corrections."

The grail of recent textual scholarship has been to discover whether we can glimpse Shakespeare in the act of rewriting, rethinking his words. For the most part the debate has focused on his dramatic works, his playwriting, but here in the fourth interrogatory, because of the way the document has come down to us in the original—with handwritten cross-outs and substitutions—we get something even more unique and indisputable: Shakespeare rewriting not his plays but his own dialogue.

It is in the fourth interrogatory that Shakespeare is pressed on the key question in the case: What *exactly* did he, Shakespeare, in his role of go-between, tell the servant that the master had promised as a payment in return for the hand of the daughter? It's an interrogatory in which Shakespeare's answer sounds as shaky and fungible as Falstaff describing the seven (or was it eleven) "men in buckram" who robbed his robbery. Here it is, beginning with the third interrogatory to put it in context:

3. To the third Interrogatory this deponent [Shakespeare] sayethe that it did evydentlye appeare that the said defft [defendant, Christopher Mountjoy] did all the tyme of the said compltes [complainant's, the servant, now son-in-law, Belott] service wth him beare and shew great good will and affeccion towardes the said complt, [the servant] and that he hath heard the defft and his wyefe diuerse and sundry tymes saye and reporte that the said complt was a very honest fellowe: And this depont [Shakespeare] sayethe that the said defendant [Mountjoy] did make a mocion vnto the complainant of marriadge wth the said Mary in the bill mencioned, beinge the said defftes sole chyld and daughter, and willinglye offered to performe the same yf the said Complainant shold seeme to be content and well like thereof: And further this deponent [Shakespeare] sayethe that the said defftes wyeffe did sollicitt and entreat this deponent [Shakespeare] to moue and perswade the said Complainant to effect the said Marriadge, and accourdingly this deponent did moue and perswade the complainant therto: And more this in Interrogatorye he cann[ot depose].

Now we come to the corrections: note carefully that which is "stricken out":

4. To the ffourth Interr[ogatory] this deponent [Shakespeare] sayth that the defend[an]t promised to geue [give] the said Complainant a porcion ["of monie and goodes"—those four words are stricken out in the original] in Marriadg w[th] Marye his daughter. but what certayne porcion he Rememberithe not. Nor when to be payed ["yf any summe weare promised"—(stricken out in the original)] nor knoweth that the defend[an]t promissed

> the ["defendt" (stricken out)] plaintiff twoe hundered poundes wth his daughter Marye at the tyme of his decease. But sayth that the plaintiff was dwelling wth the defendant in his house And they had Amongeste themselues manye Conferences about there Marriadge w[hich] [afterwardes] was Consumated and Solempnized. And more he cann[ot depose.]

Consider the first instance in which Shakespeare turns a statement that might have been definitive evidence into utter ambiguity: "the defend[an]t promiced . . . a porcion of monie and goodes" becomes "the defend[an]t promiced . . . a porcion."

A portion of what, Mr. Shakespeare? By striking out "of monie and goodes" he leaves us with an abstraction, a "portion" that could be anything, any portion of anything, an infinite array of possible portions. The possibilities are now endless if not bottomless. It all depends on what portion you think portion should mean. A very Clintonian Bill Shakespeare here.

And then he goes a little *too* far in the second statement. When he says not only doesn't he remember what portion nor when to be paid nor "yf any summe weare promised" (stricken).

Evidently he must have given this bit a rethink: Hmm, that's going a bit too far, denying knowledge of *any* sum. There was *some* summe. And one begins to suspect that the landlord's pledge of that sum—or the size of it—was a fiction Shakespeare fabricated to seal the deal.

You can almost see and hear Shakespeare squirming. And then as a way to get out of it, almost as if he is sending a signal not to look too closely into how this marriage was arranged and what was really promised, he makes an apparently irrelevant addendum about the fact that the plaintiff was dwelling in the house: "And they had Amongeste themselues manye Conferences about there Marriadge w[hich] [afterwardes] was Consumated and Solempnized. And more he cann." "Cann" is rendered as an abbreviation for "cannot" in the University of Nebraska edition, but by itself, it could also read "cann [tell]." Or even if it means "cannot," *cannot* could mean *could but isn't willing to* rather than *can't.*

Almost without meaning to—although who can know for sure?—Shakespeare seems to be creating himself or re-creating himself as a comic caricature with his transparent Falstaffian attempts to avoid being pinned down. He seems caught between two opposing factions (because of his fictions), each of whom he wants to please, because each of them, one imagines, has something *on* him.

He's Pandarus, the comic, lascivious go-between from *Troilus and Cressida,* he's Slippery Will of the anecdote about William the Conqueror coming before Richard the Third, he's the double-talking con man Autolycus, the ballad seller in *The Winter's Tale* who serves as go-between as well.

The biographers, needless to say, are attracted to the Mountjoy depositions because they suggest something juicy going on in Shakespeare's *life* at a crucial point in his creative development, something that may have fed into his "problem" comedies, as they are called, a secret play on the order of Shakespeare and the Wigmaker's Wife—or Daughter. Perhaps there is something irresistible about the juxtaposition of wigmaker and bald Shakespeare (there is even a scholarly book devoted, in a postmodern way, to the deeper meaning of *Shakespeare's Baldness*). One begins to imagine scenes: Shakespeare and the wigmaker's wife—or daughter—trying on hairpieces together. . . .

All harmless fun, this speculation. The Wigmakers' Lawsuit may seem like a digression but it could be taken as a token of a phenomenon in the *work* as well.

In the Wigmakers' Lawsuit we see Shakespeare almost literally, almost simultaneously, speaking out of both sides of his mouth, creating double meanings on the fly. He had apparently, on the one hand, convinced the servant there's a rich dowry in prospect if he'll marry the daughter, and he's promised the master he hasn't *really* promised much at *all* to get the servant to agree. Then in his deposition he compounds the doublespeak with another level of ambiguity and leaves a legible record of what he's first advanced and then retracted. (His initial testimony isn't erased—it's crossed out in a way that makes it still readable.)

So the statement and its negation are both present, almost like matter and antimatter, assertion and denial—much à deux of two contraries that adds up to be nothing. The dowry was both "to be" and "not to be."

Again let me make clear that this is not necessarily evidence that Shakespeare revised his *work.* As we'll see in the next chapter the tide has begun to turn against the sweeping claims of the "Reviser" faction. But Shakespeare's deposition is one of the few biographical fragments that suggest something one *can* find in the work: a predisposition to ambiguity, which is not the same as a predisposition to rewriting. Rewriting, or revision, in most cases changes one meaning to another meaning. Ambiguity endows one word with two meanings, sometimes multiple, multiplying, meanings. So that it's always revising itself. Nonetheless Shakespeare's shaky testimony has to be taken with a grain (a shaker?) of salt. Maybe he'd just flipped his wig.

Chapter Four

"Look There, Look There . . .": The Scandal of Lear's Last Words

IT IS, TO MY MIND, PERHAPS THE MOST IMPORTANT, DIFFICULT, complex, embarrassing, humbling, *scandalous,* unresolved question in Shakespeare studies: the question of Lear's last words. The fact, the veritable scandal, that we have two versions of those last words and can't be sure which is the more "Shakespearean."

Two versions that differ more perplexingly, even profoundly to some, than the two versions of Hamlet's last words. Those, you'll recall, consist only of the addition (in the Folio version) of the four "O-groans." And though the *Hamlet* question is not simple, the two versions don't *necessarily* contradict each other.

But with the two versions of *Lear,* one set of dying words *replaces* the other. There is, as well, a pronounced, undeniable difference in sentiment and significance between the last words in the 1608 Quarto and the last words in the 1623 Folio version. The Folio version of Lear's last words is one of the most memorable passages in all Shakespeare. Lines that virtually define what we think of when we think of what is "Shakespearean."

They are the last lines a dying Lear utters while cradling the dead body of his daughter Cordelia and desperately hoping that she still has the breath of life in her. Hoping or deceiving himself that he sees the breath of life on her lips. Which prompts him to cry out:

Do you see this? Look on her! Look her lips,
Look there, look there.

He then dies thinking (or deluding himself) that she lives. He dies, some say, with a redemptive, even hopeful vision emerging provisionally, perhaps delusively from the suffering of the tragedy. A redemptive potential far different from the unrelieved, unredeemed suffering in the Quarto version.

In the Quarto last words, which have long been occluded by neglect, Lear cries out, apparently without hope of any kind, real or delusional:

"Break, heart, I prithee break." Words which some scholars see not just as a cry of brokenheartedness, but as a wish for self-annihilation.

And judging from the ongoing argument among scholars, the difference in the last words makes a difference thematically as well. Poses a question about the poetic, emotional and thematic implications not just of Lear's last words, but of *Lear* itself.

The pronounced preference of scholars, actors and directors for the more obviously redemptive Folio version, and the favor it has received from readers and playgoers (most unaware of the alternative), has gone a long way to establish it as the *only* version of the last words. But one wonders if that preference has something to do with what seems to be the hope, the hint of redemptiveness those words bring to the unbearability of the end of *Lear*—"the most terrifying five minutes in literature" as Stephen Booth describes it.

In its mixture of tenderness, tragedy, love and madness the Folio version is nigh unto irresistible. And yet are they Shakespeare's words? Just about everyone likes them so much that we don't like to linger on the question, on the doubts.

I'd like to linger on the question, on the doubts, for a moment or two. After all it could be said the entire weight of Shakespeare's greatest tragedy comes to rest on those last words.

Do we have a Lear who, in despair over the death of his daughter, and the morally bankrupt universe it betokens, cries out, "Break, heart, I prithee break," and by some interpretations, in effect, brings on the death he cries out for?

Or does *Lear*'s final impact rest on the Folio version of his last words, which have been interpreted as a moment of either real or imagined communion with his lost daughter, a delusion (or less pejoratively, a vision) based on the belief she is yet breathing:

"Look on her! Look her lips, / Look there, look there."

As if the final mutual gaze, the one denied the dying Romeo and Juliet, is envisioned here—at least in Lear's mind. Or—and not all interpretations of the Folio last words are redemptive—they could suggest something even more crushingly bleak: a grief-maddened tragic folly on the part of the foolish old man, whose earlier delusions about love and Cordelia plunged him and his kingdom into destruction and death.

The possibilities engendered, the thematic, even theological implications, the question of which ending for Lear is more "Shakespearean," encourage closer examination of what each choice could imply.

Not just which is *more* Shakespearean, but whether *either* can be said to be with certainty. Or do they represent different stages in the evolution of Shakespeare as an artist and thus different versions that are both, in their way, "Shakespearean"? If it was he who made the change.

It doesn't mean the goal of such an examination must be to rule one implication in or others out. But it's remarkable how often and how confidently people make allusions to the literary and existential meanings of *Lear* without even an awareness that there's a *problem,* a complication, a bit of uncertainty: two endings can imply two thematically differing narratives since the final words define the final shape of the play's arc, the place to which all before has led. And we have two different places.

The imperative which Philip Edwards (editor of the New Cambridge *Hamlet*) asserted about the differences in the *Hamlet* texts certainly applies to the endings of *Lear:* "Everyone who wants to understand" the play, "as reader, actor or director needs to understand the nature of the play's textual questions and to have his or her own view of the questions in order to approach the ambiguities in the meaning."

All those who read *Lear*—most certainly everyone who stages it, acts it, everyone who alludes to *Lear* in their discussion of literature, in their discussion of the meaning of tragedy, the meaning of life, the meaning of meaninglessness—must think they know what they're talking about, right? Which means they have a reasoned position on the two texts of *Lear* and in particular on the two versions of Lear's last words, no?

All those millions of words written about *Lear* can't be based on a foundation that lacks certainty about Lear's *own* final view of the cosmos, can they?

All those thematic inferences, philosophic extrapolations, excursions about the redemptive or nihilistic nature of the cosmos are based on the choice of one set of those words or another—and that choice must rest on a solid foundation, no? It would be scandalous otherwise, wouldn't it?

That's what I mean by the scandal of Lear's last words. We talk about Lear as if we know for sure who he finally became.

Believe me, I've wrestled with the question for some years and find the problem deepens the more one looks at it, involving questions of not just what we mean by "Shakespearean" but what we mean by an author's intentions, and how much weight we should put on what we conjecture them to be. Are we reading ourselves into Shakespeare at some disputed points?

And I'm not alone; many scholars continue to wrestle with these questions. So I decided to wrestle with their wrestling and see if I could come closer to a conjecture of my own than I had before.

THE GAME IS STILL ON

So how *do* we evaluate the two versions of *Lear* if neither we nor the specialists can be sure which version of the last words is more "Shakespearean"? Or, rather, when claims to what is more "Shakespearean" turn out to be, necessarily, subjective.

Two years after publishing a report on the *Hamlet*-text revision controversy in *The New Yorker* I returned to the world of textual scholars to see if I could at least find more clarity on the questions raised by the two-*Lear* problem. Whether the ongoing war over the *Lear* texts between the Revisers and the believers in a "Lost Archetype" was moving toward a resolution of at least one question: Lear's last words. In the hopes of giving readers the last word on Lear's last words.

I found the landscape had changed dramatically.

Up until the late nineties, the world of Shakespearean scholarship was "swimming with promise," as John Jones, the former Oxford professor of poetry, exclaimed in his 1995 study of "Shakespearean" revisions in *Shakespeare at Work*.

"Swimming with promise"? Because the Shakespeare-as-reviser thesis had triumphed—"the game was up," Jones declared. Gary Taylor's "palace coup" had been an unqualified success. And dividing the texts of *Hamlet* and *Lear* had bequeathed us a powerful new tool for reading Shakespeare's great works in greater depth. In stereo one might say, holding both versions in mind at the same time, the dual focus deepening each alternate choice the way a chord deepens each individual note, or a rhyme chimes.

But it was a method that depended on the assumption that the major variations between the texts were, in fact, made by Shakespeare himself.

A method that made the claim that a close reading of "Shakespeare's own changes" from one version to another would tell us more about the author's understanding of, and intention for, his work. And that despite the strictures of the so-called intentional fallacy—that a work's meaning should not depend on what we intuit or divine about the author's intention—nonetheless, such evidence, if it is trustworthy, should not be summarily dismissed or ignored.

And in 1995, for John Jones, the only question left in the revision controversy was whether one calls the Folio text of *Hamlet* "a revision," and whether one called the two texts of *Lear* not a revision but two different *versions.*

But in fact the game was *not* really up and over as John Jones optimistically reported. The game was still on. I had registered the opposition case to the Revisers in my magazine piece, which was published in 2002, but it had seemed to me at the time that the Revisers had indeed, as Gary Taylor put it, executed a successful "palace coup" at least within academia and in Shakespeare publishing, since more and more publishers began offering two *Lear*s in different arrays, and Arden was de-conflating *Hamlet.* The Lost Archetype school seemed to have lost.

But Jones wrote "the game was up" before the powerful counterattack on the revisionist hypothesis made itself felt.

The game was on because influential figures such as Frank Kermode in the United Kingdom and David Bevington and Richard Knowles (editor of the MLA's *Lear Variorum*) among others in the United States raised difficult questions about the rush to judgment over Shakespearean revision.

None more difficult than this question: How can we be sure that the major changes, the ones with thematic and esthetic implications, were the work of Shakespeare's own hand, and not that of some theater manager, compositor or journeyman company playwright adapting Shakespeare's version for the stage? Was there an infallible, nonsubjective way of knowing what was a Shakespearean revision and what was not?

If we can conjecture an actor (not Shakespeare) adding O-groans to Hamlet's last words (as many do), why can't we conjecture an actor or playwright altering Lear's last words sometime between the 1608 Quarto and the 1623 Folio, published seven years after Shakespeare's death?

And even assuming the changes *were* in Shakespeare's own hand, how can we be sure that the Folio changes were his *preferred* literary refinements, his thematic rethinking, his sculpting and clarifying of plot and character—as the Revisers tend to assume? Or whether instead some changes represented the exigencies of stage production, the need to cut because of time limitations, additions that might be designed to pander to a theater audience's easily distracted attention rather than a reader's close relationship to a text.

The renewed assertions by some scholars, in particular Lukas Erne (in *Shakespeare as a Literary Artist,* 2002), that Shakespeare thought of himself as a "literary artist," that he considered his longer playscripts to be his truest, fullest realization of the work—rather than the shorter Folio versions regarded by many as cut for the stage—undermine the largely faith-based case made by most of the revisionists that because the Folio versions were stage-oriented they must represent Shakespeare's "final intentions" rather than, say, his final *compromises.*

The game was on because a persuasive review article (in *The Shakespeare Newsletter*) on a new anthology about the controversy (*Lear from Study to Stage,* edited by James Ogden and Arthur H. Scouten) by Thomas Pendleton suggested the battle had swung back against the Revisers. That among textual scholars the burden of proof was now on the Revisers to demonstrate why we should believe that any given Q to F variant represented "Shakespeare's considered second thoughts"—as the technical term of art coined by textual mandarin T. Howard-Hill had it—rather than a host of other possible causes.

"Of course there were changes," Richard Knowles, the *Lear Variorum* editor, and leader of the resistance to the Revisers, told me over the phone. "The question is, did Shakespeare make the changes"—and did he make the changes to change the meaning he intended for the play or to make it move more swiftly, take less time on stage because the company demanded he do so? Is there any way of knowing whether the "Shakespearean" changes can be identified with enough certainty to make the case that he willingly re-envisioned both or either *Hamlet* or *Lear*?

The response from those who are determined to draw firm conclusions from the textual variants has been, largely: well, the changes *seem* Shakespearean and they can be wrenched into some conceptual correlation to tell a different story from the putative first version—a different, "more Shakespearean" story we're told—so the new account of the play must have Shakespeare as its source. An argument that can seem circular.

John Jones for instance contends *Hamlet* is improved by having just one, not two, "delay soliloquies," so the Folio does the right thing, the Shakespearean thing, in cutting the thirty-five-line "How all occasions do inform against me" fourth-act soliloquy.

Here are those cut lines:

How all occasions do inform against me,
And spur my dull revenge! What is a man,
If his chief good and market of his time
Be but to sleep and feed? a beast, no more.
Sure He that made us with such large discourse,
Looking before and after, gave us not
That capability and godlike reason
To fust in us unus'd. Now whether it be
Bestial oblivion, or some craven scruple
Of thinking too precisely on th' event—
A thought which quarter'd hath but one part wisdom
And ever three parts coward—I do not know
Why yet I live to say, "This thing's to do,"
Sith I have cause, and will, and strength, and means
To do't. Examples gross as earth exhort me:
Witness this army of such mass and charge,
Led by a delicate and tender prince,
Whose spirit with divine ambition puff'd
Makes mouths at the invisible event,
Exposing what is mortal and unsure
To all that fortune, death, and danger dare,
Even for an egg-shell. Rightly to be great
Is not to stir without great argument,
But greatly to find quarrel in a straw
When honor's at the stake. How stand I then,
That have a father kill'd, a mother stain'd,
Excitements of my reason and my blood,
And let all sleep, while to my shame I see
The imminent death of twenty thousand men,
That for a fantasy and trick of fame
Go to their graves like beds, fight for a plot
Whereon the numbers cannot try the cause,
Which is not tomb enough and continent
To hide the slain? O, from this time forth,
My thoughts to be bloody, or be nothing worth!

I don't believe they should be cut. Look at how much further they take us into Hamlet's thought process (and what else is *Hamlet* about if it is *not* about that?). I believe having two delay soliloquies is what makes *Hamlet Hamlet* (and Hamlet Hamlet) rather than a more streamlined, no-delay *Hamlet* and Hamlet.

In *1599,* James Shapiro follows Jones in arguing for the cut; arguing that the elimination of Hamlet's last soliloquy was Shakespeare's choice, although neither Jones nor Shapiro provides any evidence why we must believe it was *Shakespeare's* own deliberate choice, rather than, say, a theatrical manager's cut that got incorporated into the source of the Folio text version.

Shapiro tells us that the thirty-five-line final soliloquy belongs in *Hamlet* "only if we want to see the play as dark and existential." (*Hamlet* "dark and existential"? Who could *possibly* want that? Let's have a Hamlet who becomes an action-film hero!)

Instead Shapiro reads Shakespeare's mind to divine that "In allowing his writing to take him where it would in his first draft Shakespeare had created his greatest protagonist, but the trajectory of Hamlet's soliloquies had left the resolution of the play incoherent and broken too radically from the conventions of the revenge plot that *had* to sweep both protagonist and play to a satisfying conclusion. Shakespeare now had to choose between the integrity of his character and his plot and he chose plot. Hamlet's climactic soliloquy *had* to be cut." (Italics mine.)

In other words Shakespeare took his "greatest protagonist" and chose deliberately to make him less "great" in order to provide something more conventional. That's our Shakespeare—always taking the easy way out. (If it *was* Shakespeare.)

Note the assumption that ambiguity must mean "incoheren[ce]." Note the assumption by Shapiro that Shakespeare *himself* would have seen things Shapiro's way: that his original draft was "incoherent" and that he had to make a choice between "the integrity of his character and his plot." That Shakespeare preferred conventional revenge-plot simplification to anything too "dark and existential."

Note the way all these pronouncements are based on the shaky assumption that the cut is "Shakespearean" in origin, although a case could be made that removing unresolved ambiguities diminishes not just what makes Hamlet Hamlet, but what makes *Hamlet* Shakespearean as opposed to a more conventional contemporary's work.

This preference for simplifed, some might say dumbed-down versions of Shakespeare can be found in arguments over *Lear* as well. A particularly analogous example is the argument that the elimination of Lear's third-act mad-scene mock trial of his daughters in the Folio version makes for similarly more clear-cut and direct action, less "digression." While some might argue that one reason we value Shakespeare is for his digressive excessiveness, that he would not *be* Shakespeare if we eliminated the alleged digressiveness in *Hamlet* and *Lear.* That, in fact, it is Lear's madness, the degree of Lear's madness exemplified in the scene in which he puts his invisible daughters on an invisible witness stand, that is the very height of Shakespearean inventiveness, the loss of which diminishes the character and the play for the sake of more direct action, the way the loss of Hamlet's last soliloquy does.

The kind of thinking exemplified in Shapiro's analysis is the subject of a scathing critique by the textual and theoretical scholar Edward Pechter in an issue of the journal *Textual Practice.* Pechter laments that in preferring the direct-action, no-digression version of Shakespeare, "Shakespeareans have given way to a diminished version of literary art which emphasizes the value of directness over digressiveness 'without any foundation but their own taste."

So the question of Lear's last words is at the heart of a Gordian knot of snarling academic argument perhaps because in this case the stakes are genuinely high. I spent a year at least focused, if not totally, then persistently on the issue. It became a kind of quest: What should we make of the two versions of Lear's last words? What can the question tell us about two *Lear*s?

AN EMBLEM OF THE APOCALYPSE

The close of *Lear* you may recall has been characterized by Stephen Booth as "the most terrifying five minutes in literature."

The terrifying five minutes begin with one of those moments of raised then dashed expectations that recur throughout the play. Cordelia has come at the head of an army to rescue her dispossessed father; she and Lear have been captured and imprisoned. Then the tide shifts once more and the forces allied with Cordelia take charge again. Their new ally, the Duke of Albany, remembers too late—"Great thing of us forgot!"—to send an officer to free Lear and Cordelia from their death sentence.

Many have been struck by the farcical crudeness of that line: "Great thing of us forgot!" It really is a line from a Monty Python sketch, to use an anachronism, and yet it precipitates one of the most profound moments of tragedy in literature. A deliberate juxtaposition? A way of heightening the Beckett-like absurdity? One can't help wondering what was going on in Shakespeare's mind when he wrote "Great thing of us forgot!"—and if he then looked over the play and let it stand. Perhaps he liked the conspicuous irrelevance of its tone. Or perhaps he never looked back at it at all. But I digress.

In fact the messenger Albany sends arrives too late. They hang Cordelia. Something we learn only when Lear enters carrying her dead or near-dead body, literally howling with grief.

"She's dead as earth," he says in both versions as he sets her body down and calls out for a mirror. One he can hold up to his daughter's lips in a desperate effort to see, "If that her breath will mist or stain the stone, / Why then she lives."

The tragic spectacle evokes from Kent and Edgar this shocked and sorrowful exchange, which alludes to more than merely the sight of Lear bending over the dead body of Cordelia. Makes it an emblem of the apocalypse.

KENT: *Is this the promis'd end?*
EDGAR: *Or image of that horror?*

So Lear has called out for a mirror (or reflective "stone") but there's a puzzling shift in his next speech, when, instead of a mirror, he seems to be holding up a feather to Cordelia's lips to see if there's any breath to stir the feather. Has a mirror not been forthcoming and a feather (perhaps from his or another's costume) been found and substituted? (How to play the mirror-and-feather moment is a question debated by scholars and directors for centuries.)

In any case, after holding the feather up to Cordelia's lips, Lear suddenly exclaims:

This feather stirs, she lives. If it be so,
It is a chance which does redeem all sorrows . . .

The teasing moment of apparent redemption doesn't last more than an instant before Lear seems to have lost hope:

I might have sav'd her, now she's gone for ever!

Then the next moment he seems to imagine he hears her alive and uttering something:

Cordelia, Cordelia, stay a little. Ha!
What is't thou say'st? Her voice was ever soft,
Gentle, and low . . .

Like Lear we, the audience, are jolted back and forth between hope and despair.

But then Lear seems to lose interest, or give up the delusion that she lives. He talks to his long-lost loyal retainer, Kent; a messenger arrives to announce the villainous Edmund's death; Edgar and Albany and Kent converse, tying up loose ends of the plot. Then suddenly Lear breaks into the play again, does something that catches their attention once more as he cries out in his very last utterance in the play:

And my poor fool is hang'd. No, no life!
Why should a dog, a horse, a rat, have life,
And thou no breath at all? O thou wilt come no more,
Never, never, never.
Pray you undo this button. Thank you, sir.
O, o, o, o . . .
[and after a brief interval] *Break, heart, I prithee break.*

Again these are his last utterances in the earliest of the two *Lear* texts, the Quarto first published in 1608. But in the Folio version of 1623, the last two lines above—"O, o, o, o . . . Break, heart, I prithee break"—are omitted. (Actually the "Break, heart . . ." line is assigned to Kent after he sees Lear and Cordelia dead.) The four O-groans just like those added to Folio Hamlet's dying words are cut from Folio Lear's—perhaps someone was conscious of the potential repetition in the two tragedies. And there are now five "nevers": "Never, never, never, never, never." An order of magnitude difference from three "nevers." (Try saying first three, then five.) And the following two lines, two lines that are, to some, the most powerful in Shakespeare, are added:

Do you see this? Look on her! Look her lips,
Look there, look there.
(He dies.)

TWO VISIONS OF "LOOK THERE"

"Look there," indeed. Almost an echo of *Hamlet*'s opening line, "Who's there?", with its evocation of a deeper mystery than the name of a sentry—the mystery of who's *out* there, who's the moving spirit or being out there in the cosmos? "Look there, look there" may be the greatest mystery of *Lear,* one of the greatest in all Shakespeare, and at the very heart of the controversy over who "Shakespeare the Writer" was, as well.

The Folio addition has generated two major schools of thought. The first was articulated most colorfully by the Edwardian-era critic A. C. Bradley, who argued that when Lear says, "Look her lips, / Look there, look there," Lear is witnessing Cordelia showing signs of life. Bradley ascribed to Lear's Folio dying words what has become a famous phrase: "unbearable joy" at the sight.

By which he meant that Lear had been granted "an ecstatic vision that Cordelia is alive, that at last she speaks the words he wants so to hear; a vision of some supernatural aura about her, presumably beatific, even an apparent glimpse of her spirit rising toward heaven; or a horror of the ultimate silence that has stilled her."

Over the years Bradley has become identified with the former rather than the latter vision—the redemptive and beatific rather than the horrific. Recent support for this position has come from some of the Revisers who believe that the Folio *Lear* vision of Cordelia at least momentarily resurrected is an instance that prefigures the Shakespeare of the Late Romances—the Shakespeare of miraculous resurrections and reunions—returning to the grimmest, most terrifyingly bleak moment of his pre-Romance works and adding that beatific touch.

The choice of how to play Lear's death has divided actors, directors and scholars long before the Revisers came along. Alexander Leggatt, in an unpublished paper entitled "How Lear Dies," says "John Gielgud chose joy, Morris Carnovsky, despair." Many attempt some conflation of the two.

After Bradley the second turning point in the modern debate over Lear's last words might be the moment in 1962 when Peter Brook put on his *Lear* at the RSC with Paul Scofield playing the King.

It's hard to overestimate how influential Brook's production was. Some who saw it, such as the critic Frank Rich (who told me he saw it when it came to New York), said it changed their lives. The icy bleakness of the Brook-Scofield *Lear* derived in part from the Polish-born critic Jan Kott's essay "*Lear* as *Endgame*"—*Lear,* in other words, as a Beckett-like broken hymn to hopelessness.

Which made the alteration of Lear's dying words all the more central to the argument about whether the play was ultimately redemptive—was it about the wisdom, even the vision earned through suffering—or about the *denial* of redemption, the futility of suffering, the absence of justice in the moral order of the cosmos? The absence *of* a moral order in the cosmos.

The bleak Brookean view suggests that Lear's final vision, the one he refers to in "Look there, look there," is a sad delusion, a delusion that is not a blissful comfort, but one further flawed and failed attempt to find solace in a hostile cosmos. One where "As flies to wanton boys are we to the gods. They kill us for their sport," as Gloucester puts it. Thus, at the end, Lear realizes his vision is a cruel deception, like all the other things he believed in about this world and the next. False hope unmasked and dashed again.

These are not the only possible positions to take on the Folio addition (and cut: remember the four O-groans are excised as well). In addition to the party of redemption and the party of bleakness, R. A. Foakes, the editor of the Arden *Lear,* offers a third vision of "Look there," one might say, one that gazes upon the last words of Lear in the Folio and finds, "There can be no return to simply optimistic or pessimistic readings of the play, and the difficulty of reconciling them has helped to promote a deep distrust of all attempts at closure in *King Lear,* a negation of the possibility of unity, coherence and resolution." Undecidability.

So it's unbearable joy, unbearable bleakness, or unbearable undecidability, depending on how one interprets Lear's dying words in the Folio text. Unbearable any way you see it. Exit, pursued by an unbear, you might say.

The presence of two endings has produced a continuing torrent of scholarly polemics. Is the new ending one of Shakespeare's "considered second thoughts," as those who believe he revised his work like to call them?

A "considered second thought" about the nature of tragedy, of the cosmos, its cruelty or redemptiveness? What status do the revised dying words of *Lear* have if they are incorporated into just about every production of *Lear* ever staged, and yet we cannot be sure Shakespeare wrote them? Do they *become* Shakespearean by usage, and if so do we mean something different when we say "Shakespearean" than we thought we did? Do we redefine "Shakespearean," as some of the more postmodern textual theorists do, as any version produced by his collaborative theatrical company?

Perhaps, like their respective tragic heroes, *Hamlet* scholars are more at home with doubt and ambiguity, and *Lear* scholars must (in a scholarly way) rage. There is a kind of anger and bitterness now between the two *Lear* camps (and *within* one camp) that doesn't seem to obtain with the *Hamlet* specialists. I know that one *Lear* scholar uses a classical Greek obscenity that translates as "goatsucker" to refer to another scholar. ("Tragedy" of course is derived from the Greek for "goat song," but I don't think that's the referent here.)

And the goatsucker was his ally! Well, they were, intellectually, predisposed to the same position in the *Lear* text conflict. (It had something to do with who got credit for publishing something first.)

It's fascinating to me that controversy over the two *Lear*s and revision hasn't broken out into the public realm among educated nonspecialists.* It's almost like the engine room refusing to report to the captain on deck that the *Titanic* had a hole breached below the water level. The apparent unsolvability of the two-*Lear* problem is a similar kind of damaging—if not physically dangerous—breach in literary culture. Damaging to any attempt to form a coherent picture of perhaps the most formidable and influential work in the language.

This is why I use the term "scandalous" for this situation: we are a culture which at least professes reverence for *Lear* as one of the great works in the language, one of the great works of the human spirit, blah, blah, blah. What are the last words, the final reflections of the tormented human spirit at the heart of it? Must we be condemned to choose one answer from column A, another from column B? It's something worth caring about.

Or maybe it says we don't care. I don't think so. I think more people would care if more were aware of the problem. I think it's important at least to try to bring the news of the problem, and the implications of the various solutions, to the attention of a wider audience.

* Although a recent reference to my story in a volume of textual scholar essays (*Textual Performances,* edited by Lukas Erne and Margaret Jane Kidnie) refers to it as a "hot topic even in *The New Yorker.*" Scholars' views of what constitutes a "hot topic" in the world outside the academy may reflect a certain insularity.

GREENBLATT'S CHALLENGE: OR A GREENBLATTIAN DIGRESSION UPON STEPHEN GREENBLATT AND THE "THIRTY-SECOND-DEGREE ADEPTS"

But there are some who disagree, who think it's too complicated for the nonspecialist and can cause undue worries. In other words: you, the educated general reader, can't handle the truth.

Stanley Wells, who was, in his Oxford edition, the first to divide *Lear* and later called for "editors of courage" to divide *Hamlet,* became trepidatious when an editor of courage, Ann Thompson, did so. On a BBC program prompted by my *New Yorker* piece about Ann Thompson's three-text *Hamlet,* Wells argued the general public would be too confused by the problem.

Then Stephen Greenblatt said something remarkable to me when I raised the question with him. It was a semipublic context in which he made the remark, one that consigned the *Lear* text question to "thirty-second-degree adepts." The occasion for this pronouncement, which I have come to think of as "Greenblatt's Challenge," was a rather posh luncheon for Greenblatt, perhaps the most eminent of Shakespearean scholars in America, if you don't count Harold Bloom (and many serious scholars just don't).

Star of the English department at Harvard, successor to Bloom as the most famous explainer of Shakespeare, founder of the most influential academic school of Shakespeare theory, the one known as the New Historicism, Greenblatt was about to launch a book designed to launch *him* out of the academic world and—like Bloom—onto the bestseller list.

His publisher, well-respected W. W. Norton, for whom Greenblatt had edited an American version of the Oxford *Complete Works* edition of Shakespeare widely used in colleges—the only Complete Works edition to publish not one, not two, but *three* versions of *King Lear*—was putting on this luncheon for some twenty-five editors, writers and reviewers. Not to celebrate publication of the book, but release of the *galleys*—four months before publication of the book *Will in the World,* his exploration of "the ways in which Shakespeare's life experiences inform his writings."

The luncheon was designed to indicate just how important an occasion the forthcoming publication of the book (for which they'd paid Greenblatt a reported million-dollar advance) would be. After cocktails and hors d'oeuvres the guests would be seated for a formal three-course meal, before which Greenblatt would give a little talk; between courses Greenblatt would shift from table to table for a little informal conversation with those attending. My table had him for dessert.

Given the limited amount of time I'd have with Greenblatt, time shared with the others at my table (although it turned out he was seated next to me during his dessert appearance), I spent the first two courses trying to think of the single unanswered question about Shakespeare and Shakespeare scholarship I found most important, the one in any case I most wanted to hear from Greenblatt about. I wanted to ask him about the question of revision in *King Lear,* to learn what his answer would say about *Lear,* what it said about Shakespeare. And, I guess, what his answer would say about Greenblatt. And so as I finished off my extremely good molten-centered chocolate disk, I asked him.

But since Greenblatt is famous for framing his scholarly discourses with unhurried personal anecdotes which turn out to bear upon the Shakespearean and theatrical issues he subsequently addresses, perhaps the reader will permit me a Greenblattian digression about Greenblatt and myself which bears upon the recent trajectory of Shakespearean theory.

I had known Greenblatt, though not well, since we had both been Junior Fellows at Yale, at Jonathan Edwards College there. He was far more serious about academia than I was at the time, but I had a number of rewarding conversations with him about literature and politics, and one of them has remained in my mind.

Remained because it had an important effect on my thinking back then, and because of the way it can historicize, let's say, the fascinating trajectory of Greenblatt's own thinking. His thinking about Shakespeare as an author. That conversation back at Yale was not explicitly about Shakespeare, but rather about the Black Panthers. It was at a time when protests against the murder trial of a Black Panther leader were causing disruption in the Yale community. One aspect of the contention had to do with whether white supporters of the Panthers had the "right" to criticize the tactics of the Panthers (for example, allegedly murdering those alleged to be "informers").

At the time, I was an impressionable reader of Left publications, some of which had advanced the view that "fact"—objectivity about evidence—was merely "a liberal concept." That reality was a matter of the racial perspective—essentially the racial identity—of the person apprehending it. As I recall Greenblatt and I were having an after-dinner drink in Greenblatt's suite in Jonathan Edwards, talking about this question, and I said I thought there was merit in the argument that it was inappropriate for whites on the Left to criticize the strategies and tactics of black "revolutionaries," because we could not possibly enter into their consciousness and understand "reality" the way they did—we lacked their history of oppression, hence we could not shed our "white skin privilege." And since our consciousness was ineluctably shaped by our racial identity, our criticism was not appropriate or relevant to those engaged in "the struggle."

That sort of thing. (I was, in effect, a New Historicist *avant la lettre:* I was expressing a historicist view of the self, that it was not autonomous, that my consciousness could not escape the determinisms of my identity and the culture that shaped it.)

Greenblatt's response back then was basically to say "that's nonsense." That one always has the right to think for oneself, to assess a situation as objectively as one can, to offer an opinion, a criticism if one felt it was warranted. That the opinion needed to be tested, challenged, of course, but that one's thoughts were not the inevitable product of one's perspective. Implicitly one could enter, sympathetically, into a perspectival world shared with others. Which is what he attempts, by the way, in *Will in the World*—as well as anybody has, considering the dubious fragments of Shakespearean biographical evidence that he builds on. But the journey from our conversation to that endeavor would be a roundabout one.

Before leaving behind that long-ago conversation, I want to say Greenblatt's words then were—and remain—important to me. To my own life, at a time when perspectivist historicist arguments were coming to be considered the most intellectually sophisticated. Greenblatt's calm defense, back then, of the validity of personal reflection, of the possibility of an autonomous, intellectual free will seeking truth (rather than the notion that one's thoughts, one's will, one's truth were historically, culturally, racially "determined"—"authored" by the culture), had an impact on me back then as it does now in assessing the claims of much of lit crit theory (claims Greenblatt paradoxically ended up shaping). The conviction Greenblatt brought to the belief in autonomy, the *responsibility* to exercise autonomy, impressed me and I think influenced me at a formative time of my life in a way I'm still grateful for.

But Greenblatt had already begun moving away from autonomy when he'd gone to study in England on a fellowship to Cambridge, where he came under the influence of the then-fashionable "cultural materialist" Raymond Williams, an extremely influential neo-Marxist, or cultural Marxist. Greenblatt absorbed the British strain of historicism, and it seemed to me changed his mind—autonomously?—about autonomy. Going far in the direction of belief in "culturally determined" consciousness that internalized the power relations of a society at every expressive and representational level. Consciousness and literature were both "constructed" by the "material culture," and only the elite who developed "critical consciousness" could deconstruct the fiction of individual creativity—historicize the self—by specifying ("unpacking") the material forces that determined it.

Greenblatt brought to British cultural materialism the anthropological perspective of the American scholar Clifford Geertz. And from these materials he crafted what came to be known in the United States as "the New Historicism," more cultural, poststructural, less Marxist than British cultural materialism, but that was more a matter of degree.

Later, at Berkeley, he absorbed Michel Foucault's determinist critique of the illusion of autonomy, founded an influential New Historicist quarterly called *Representations* and began earning a well-deserved reputation for himself by bringing first-person confessional storytelling into his scholarship—he framed his linkages between literary and nonliterary texts with anecdotes about crazed airline seating companions and the like.

But soon, it is no exaggeration to say, he became the center of a cult worthy of anthropological study. Graduate students in theory-centered comparative literature departments all aped his style so sedulously that, in 1996, when I noticed and pointed out in print that the quarterly *Raritan* had published a parody of Greenblattian New Historicism (written pseudonymously by Ed Mendelson and David Bromwich), it turned out that virtually no one outside *Raritan* had noticed its parodic intent: the style itself had become indistinguishable from its own parody. (The parody had been dutifully and obliviously incorporated into scholarly databases.)

When Greenblatt became the academic equivalent of a guru for the New Historicism, what surprised me most personally was how the New Historicism constituted an almost precise reversal of the sensible argument Greenblatt made to me back at Yale. Historicism suggests there is no such thing as autonomous "agency," that free will was an illusion, in life or art as well.

In the epilogue to the book that made his reputation, *Renaissance Self-Fashioning,* Greenblatt tells us of the transition that took place in his attempt "to understand the role of human autonomy in the construction of identity."

He began with a belief in autonomy, but "as my work progressed, I perceived that fashioning oneself and being fashioned by cultural institutions—family, religion, state—were inseparably intertwined. In all my texts and documents, there were, so far as I could tell, no moments of pure, unfettered subjectivity. . . ."

"Unfettered subjectivity": a way of saying free will, the ability to author one's acts and (if one was an artist) author one's works freely. Instead, "the human subject itself began to seem remarkably unfree, the ideological product of the relations of power in a particular society," he wrote. "If there remained traces of free choice, the choice was among possibilities whose range was strictly delineated by the social and ideological system in force."

The implications of this disbelief in autonomy, free will, authorship of self or work—disbelief in the self itself as having any meaningful role to play in selfhood—were both radical and illogical: How did the "social and ideological system in force" that limited free will or choice come to be if not through the choice, or accumulated choices, of somebody somewhere?

Even among postmodernists, many (especially some feminist critics) have questioned this radical dismissal of free will or "agency," as the jargon had it, because it seemed to argue that change was impossible, because of the invisible shackles of the hegemony on autonomy.

In its more extreme forms it denies the existence of the so-called bourgeois self, otherwise known often as "the Romantically constructed illusion of individual subjectivity." And some of Greenblatt's acolytes took denial of a belief in autonomy all the way to denial of belief in authorship itself. It was now outmoded to believe that a text was the product of an "author," a word usually written with scare quotes. Instead a text was "produced" by an "author function," the real "author" was the historical moment, which inscribed itself on the waxen tablet, the blank slate of the nominal creator's mind.

The more stringently postmodern historicists essentially say that authors as individual consciousness are irrelevant, that authorial free will does not, in effect, exist. Texts are there to be dusted for fingerprints of the power relations of the culture that gives birth to them.

Needless to say one of the authors who didn't really exist was William Shakespeare, whose individual identity, Theory partisans insisted in various ways, was shaped by "the hegemony," the patriarchy, the hierarchy of royalty, every archy but autarchy. Shakespeare, like everyone else, was not possessed of an autonomous self.

But—and here was the Great Admission, the Great Rebuke really to virtually all postmodern lit crit, that Greenblatt had now made. He now clearly believed, or at least *professed* to believe, that such a creature as an author existed, in a significant way. And that the author's life—his self!—could be—in a (gasp!) biography, autonomously!—used by said author to shape his art. (My problem with Shakespearean biography has been lack of facts; for postmodernists it has been lack of subject—lack of "author.")

They say that in America there are no second acts, but really there are no second *glances.* That whole author-doesn't-exist thing no longer existed! Might as well never have.

I'D LAST BEEN IN TOUCH WITH GREENBLATT WHEN WE EXCHANGED faxes about the "Funeral Elegy" Donald Foster had been promoting as Shakespearean. Greenblatt had somehow been persuaded by the American branch of the Norton imprint to include the Elegy in his *Norton Shakespeare* Complete Works edition. Foster was at that time claiming the inclusion as an endorsement, and, when I inquired, Greenblatt faxed me back from Berlin where he'd been on fellowship, to make sure I knew that "It doesn't sound like Shakespeare to me" and that he had included it only for the purposes of studying "questions of attribution and authorship." A hedge, but an important one.

I had the feeling that his offhand concession that there *was* something definably "Shakespearean" that can be distinguished from the non-Shakespearean ("doesn't sound like Shakespeare to me") was important.

It comported with something I'd felt while reading his most recent book (the one before *Will in the World*), his best book to my mind, *Hamlet in Purgatory.* It was an exemplary work of scholarship which placed *Hamlet* in the context of the debate over the fate of souls supposedly in Purgatory—after the English Protestant Reformation had abolished the existence of Purgatory. It was a book in which he'd abandoned postmodern jargon almost entirely for the kind of historical literary scholarship that set him apart from Historicist theory and justified his reputation as a leading Shakespearean. Greenblatt seized upon two warring pamphlets published in the 1530s and 1540s that debated the fate of the souls in Purgatory after Purgatory was abolished. One was ingeniously written in the voice of the supposed souls in Purgatory bemoaning their sudden unexpected abandonment. Before the English Protestant Reformation there was an entire monastic social establishment devoted to the souls in Purgatory—the chantries and their chanters, subsidized by the relatives of the dead to say constant prayers for their lost loved ones, paid prayers which were said to be a way of speeding the dead through the purgatorial fires (in which Hamlet's father's ghost was purportedly confined) to the bliss of God's heavenly Paradise.

Now with the abandonment of the chantries and the chanters, they were, the inhabitants of Purgatory complain in this pamphlet, stuck forever in a Purgatory that no longer had an officially approved theological existence. They felt the loss of all those living humans who had been devoted to praying for their release.

There was a reply pamphlet written on the question—by Sir Thomas More, in fact. But I was fascinated by Greenblatt's discussion of the plea from Purgatory in relation to Greenblatt's own intellectual trajectory. It was almost as if this touching sympathy for these fictional souls abandoned and trapped in Purgatory could be seen as a kind of sympathy for the "authors" abandoned by postmodernists, whose existence they'd denied, consigned to the realm of superstition and myth—the Purgatory of nonbeing—for so long.

Will in the World could then be seen as a further reversal; it represented, in effect, Greenblatt's return to rescue them, or at least one of those authors. If *Hamlet in Purgatory* signaled Greenblatt's almost total rejection of fashionable jargon and theoretical sophistry, *Will in the World* is almost defiantly unfashionable, indeed unashamedly Old-Fashioned.

Still, it was absolutely stunning to see how far along this road Greenblatt has traveled—or traveled back—in the glimpse of his method (and his book) he gave the luncheon in his talk, which essentially summarized his novel argument about Shakespeare and Shylock. ("Novel" is a word I use advisedly. As Rachel Donadio put it in a *New York Times Book Review* essay, "Whether it belongs on the nonfiction list . . . or the fiction one is a matter of some debate.")

Will in the World does have the sustaining virtue of Greenblatt's intelligence. He's acutely self-conscious that he's weaving the few tattered, picked-over rags and bones of Shakespearean biographical anecdotes and old wives' tales that have come down to us from a variety of narrators of unprovable reliability over the centuries into a tapestry of sometimes ingenious, sometimes strained conjecture about the relationship of these alleged episodes in Shakespeare's life (a Catholic Lancashire stay? a deer poaching charge?) to moments in the plays.

Often the point he wants to make is so smart it scarcely needs the shaky foundation of the grab bag of anecdotes and suppositions that make up the usual ragtag Shakespearean biography.

In his talk that day he gave us one of his most precarious leaning towers of suppositions, one that allows him, he says, to connect the life of Shakespeare with the character called Shylock he created. This one involves an absolutely unfounded conjecture that Shakespeare witnessed the execution of a Jew, the queen's physician, Roderigo Lopez, a Jew converted to Protestantism, but still under suspicion that treacherous Jewishness lay beneath the professed conversion. And that all this tells us something about *The Merchant of Venice.*

There is no doubt Lopez was executed, not much doubt that his Jewishness was a known factor and a factor in his conviction. But there is no evidence that Shakespeare witnessed the public execution, which included the cutting out of the intestines, and burning them in front of the still-living condemned man along with further butchery as required by "drawing and quartering." And there's no evidence of Shakespeare witnessing or overhearing any one specific crowd reaction at that execution. Nor is there any evidence that Marlowe's play *The Jew of Malta* was the source of the crowd's reaction. Nor that any of this had a crucial effect on Shakespeare's depiction of the Jew, Shylock, in *The Merchant of Venice.*

Nevertheless Greenblatt gives us a graphic description of the execution of the (converted) Jew Lopez, and then asks, "Was William Shakespeare in this crowd?" that witnessed the execution. And answers only that we "know" he "was interested in executions . . . [and] mobs" and "the comportment" of men and women facing the end. So he must have been there, then! It's not impossible!

Or as Greenblatt puts it in his book, "It is reasonable to suppose [Shakespeare] had witnessed executions for himself," and "the execution of Dr. Lopez was a public event. If Shakespeare did personally witness it, he would have seen . . . a ghastly display. . . ."

And now he's off on a tear. Assuming what is pure supposition, he makes an elaborate argument about Shakespeare's reaction to the crowd's reaction to the Jew's reaction to being executed.

It all rests on the secondhand report of an Elizabethan historian, William Camden, who tells us that before Lopez was hanged and butchered alive, the allegedly treasonous and treacherous Jew-turned-Christian prisoner (convicted on the basis of torture-extracted testimony from his "confederates") cried out that he, Lopez, "loved the Queen as he loved Jesus Christ." A remark which, Camden tells us, "drewe no small Laughter in the Standers-by."

Then Greenblatt tries to see, to hear, actually, that remark and that laughter *through Shakespeare's eyes and ears.* Assuming of course, without evidence, that Shakespeare was there, Greenblatt tells us that Shakespeare *would* have reacted by seeing the laughter at the foot of the scaffold as the product of the crowd's familiarity with *The Jew of Malta,* the work of Shakespeare's playwright rival Christopher Marlowe. Marlowe made his Jew, Barabas, a comic villain, someone who courted and indulged in laughter at the extremity of his melodramatic villainousness. A treacherous former doctor and poisoner in fact, Marlowe's Jew of Malta had the over-the-top mustache-twirling generic evil glee of a cartoon villain.

Thus, according to Greenblatt (and again he's reading Shakespeare's mind) what was in the mind of the spectators, or at least in the mind of Shakespeare reading the mind of the spectators—in the mind of Greenblatt—was this:

"These laughing spectators thought . . . they were watching a real-life version of *The Jew of Malta.* . . ."

Because the crowd at the execution had seen *The Jew of Malta* (Greenblatt insists) they interpreted the condemned man's last words as ironic. "I love the Queen as I love Jesus Christ" really meant he hated them both because his conversion to Christianity was a sham, a Jewish trick. He *didn't* love Jesus, thus not the queen either.

So Greenblatt told the luncheon, and tells us at greater length in his book. He believes that *Shakespeare* believed that the spectators laughed at Lopez's last words—because, *Greenblatt* believes, *Shakespeare* believed these laughing witnesses had seen that particular play.

From questioning the author's "agency," the freedom of his (or anyone's) choices, Greenblatt is making up incredibly elaborate fictions about him and his choices, which he then applies to the author's fictional character Shylock in *The Merchant of Venice.* A character which, according to Greenblatt, grew out of Shakespeare's discomfort with the cruelty of the ironic laughter he thinks Shakespeare thinks Marlowe inspired at the execution of Lopez, the one Shakespeare may or may not have attended. And this discomfort led Shakespeare to choose to create his own Jew, who would have more humanity than the Marlovian butt of laughter and cruelty he chose to feel sympathy for.

Shylock is different, Greenblatt says, because of Shakespeare's reaction to the crowd's reaction at the execution: "Did he admire the [alleged] way Marlowe's dark comedy had helped to shape the crowd's response?"

And then without answering the question he tells us that Shakespeare wanted, it seems, "to excite laughter at the wicked Jew's discomfiture [as Marlowe had] and he wanted at the same time to call the laughter into question, to make the amusement excruciatingly uncomfortable."

Voilà! *The Merchant of Venice.*

Well, it's a nice fantasy.

All this strenuous supposition brings Greenblatt gasping close to the finish line for his thesis, in which he again reads Shakespeare's mind for us:

> . . . it is as if Shakespeare had looked too closely at the faces of the crowd, as if he were repelled as well as fascinated by the mockery of the vanquished alien, as if he understood the mass appeal of the ancient game he was playing, but suddenly felt queasy about the rules.

Well, maybe or maybe not, it makes for good speculative reading, but it's an instance of Greenblatt's new method, no longer denying "the author" or his autonomy here, but *authoring* the author—making a fictional narrative about the author's thought process. And of course, in doing so, tacitly asking us to believe that Shakespeare has given us a more humane Jew, and thus, tacitly exculpating the play from what some might call an even deeper anti-Semitism than Marlowe's. Shakespeare can do no wrong. He can see through false prejudices the way Superman can see through walls, and build us all a new Jew: it's the New Historicist become bardolater.

It was a dazzling performance, but clearly, a performance, a multi-suppositioned notion, with conjecture piled on conjecture. An elephant dancing on a shot glass mounted on top of a beach ball. It seemed to me that one could applaud it. It was his way of engaging with the text, his way of attempting to bring Shakespeare the man closer to Shakespeare the text. Or at least it brought Greenblatt the man closer to Shakespeare the text.

To me the close examination of the way the variant versions of certain plays such as *Hamlet* and *Lear* interrogate each other may be less glamorous than a fantasy of some imagined *Shakespeare in Love* figure watching executions in London and suddenly feeling compassion for the Jews—less glamorous but in some way more genuinely exciting. Exciting because textual scholarship focuses close attention on conjecture about what Shakespeare wrote, and perhaps rewrote, and challenges us to ask why, and how we decide. It takes us inside Shakespeare's actual language and characters rather than into a fantasy of his life. It allows us to imagine Shakespeare's work through Shakespeare's eyes, the eyes that *could* have reread, rethought, revised.

So (and this is the point of my Greenblattian digression) I decided, when Greenblatt seated himself next to me during the dessert course, to ask him where he stood on the *Lear* revision question. After all, his Norton edition printed three versions of *Lear:* a Quarto and a Folio (on facing pages) and a traditional conflated edition with the editor, Barbara K. Lewalski's, choice of the best bits from both Q and F incorporated.

Clearly Greenblatt thought the contention over *Lear* texts was important enough to preserve the separation of Quarto and Folio texts that he adopted from Gary Taylor and Stanley Wells's Oxford edition. But on the other hand he didn't wish to commit himself to a strict anticonflationist dogma, thus the third, traditional conflated text as well. So I asked him over dessert: Did he think Shakespeare was a reviser, did Shakespeare revise *Lear* to the extent that the two versions are different enough to be considered not just separate texts but separate works of art?

He did not give me a definitive answer; he circled around the question of whether the changes resulted from revision or errors of transmission, or the intervention of someone in the company. He communicated a sense that Shakespeare did revise, but rather than going further turned to the rest of the table and said, "Ron asked me a question that thirty-second-degree adepts of textual scholarship argue about."

The effect, if not the intent, of what he was saying was to dismiss the revision question, which in fact has been—most others agree—the single most divisive and important "site of contention" in Shakespeare scholarship for the past quarter century, as if it were merely an arcane (tacit implication: irrelevant) controversy of interest to specialists and pedants and decipherable only by them.

I took it as a challenge. I felt I had succeeded in making the complex controversy over three *Hamlet*s clear to *New Yorker* readers. Did Greenblatt think intelligent readers were incapable of appreciating the complexities of two *Lear*s? I didn't think they were.

IN WHICH TWO ADEPTS ARE QUESTIONED

And since the argument over texts and revision was still ongoing and evolving, I wanted to step back and examine the opposing points of view more closely before proceeding to the local question—if one can call such a profound problem "local"—of Lear's last words.

I wanted to begin by getting to know better the positions of two of the leading advocates for each pole of the revision question especially as it pertained to *Lear*—a revisionist and an antirevisionist. I chose two of the most adept of the thirty-second-degree adepts: Steven Urkowitz and Richard Knowles.

What surprised me was that their positions were not simply oppositional, there was a complexity to both the revisionist and antirevisionist positions that had consequences for how one decides which version of the last words of Lear was more "Shakespearean."

Still, talking to Urkowitz and Knowles in succession about the two versions of *Lear,* and the two versions of how there came to *be* two versions, is akin to stepping back and forth between two visions of Shakespeare.

I met Urkowitz, a founding figure of the *Lear* revisionists, a CCNY professor and professional theater director as well, at a restaurant near his Greenwich Village apartment.

I told him about Stephen Greenblatt's "thirty-second-degree adept" remark about the controversy.

Urkowitz responded by saying that one unfortunate consequence of defining the conflict as too arcane for ordinary readers is denying those outside the small circle of scholars the benefits of reflecting upon the differences, great and small, between the two *Lear*s. "Knowing both versions can mean knowing each of them better." It is the same, rather persuasive, argument Ann Thompson gives for introducing nonadepts (even undergraduates!) to the variations in the *Hamlet* texts.

"That 'thirty-second-degree adept' response," Urkowitz said, "has long been the authoritarian response to textual problems. It's what Fredson Bowers back in the fifties and sixties was pushing, the idea that this is too complicated, leave it to us, dears . . ."

"We'll give you the texts and—"

"It's so condescending, it's condescending because usually the people who say it have only minimal appreciation of how the texts work and differ dramatically. . . ."

He goes on to denounce conflated texts from the perspective of a director who has found that stage directions from one version imported into another text's version of a scene can render the scene incoherent dramatically and thematically.

But before going further into the Urkowitz analysis of the two-text problem, let me introduce Richard Knowles, Urkowitz's arch-foe in the *Lear* debate. (The one thing the two of them do agree on is that the two-*Lear* question is important outside a small circle of adepts.)

You might recall Knowles from the previous chapter. It was his attack on the revisionists in the *International Shakespeare Yearbook* that brought pleasure to Frank Kermode—long a skeptic about the Revisers' case—when I faxed it to him.

Knowles is the editor of the *Lear Variorum,* the new Modern Language Association–sponsored compendium of textual and interpretive commentary designed to succeed the 1908 Furness version. As such Knowles is a powerful institutional figure. (He's been working on the *Variorum* for more than two decades.) The closest thing to a king in the divided realm of *King Lear* studies. And yet his dogged opposition to the revisionists' case has never seemed to me the product of an elitist possessiveness and resistance to "disintegration"—the division of *his* kingdom—on principle. He genuinely believes the arguments of the revisionists are flawed, even destructive in their implications.

In fact for some time Knowles was, it seems to me, quite the loner; if not a complete outsider, certainly a lonely dissident going against the tide of Reviser thought that seemed to have swept the field in Shakespeare studies in the eighties and nineties. If one wants to use Gary Taylor's *Hamlet*-inflected "palace coup" image, Knowles was the deposed occupant of the palace who dared to continue to speak up in opposition to the new regime.

Nonetheless, in a relatively short time Knowles, firing off powerfully argued polemics, has almost single-handedly stemmed, if not reversed, the results of the coup. The rush to divide and distinguish the two versions of *Lear* at least. When I first spoke to him at a Folger Library MLA reception in 2001, he'd seemed to me to represent a resistance that was receding into the past. But by the time I spoke to him for the second time, four years later, the tide seemed to be shifting to his side of the battle, largely through his persistence.

In polemic after polemic, including one anthologized in *Lear from Study to Stage* entitled "Two *Lear*s? By Shakespeare?", Knowles had pointed out the weak points of the Revisers' case. First their inability to say with any certainty that the Folio changes had in fact been made *by* Shakespeare. Which were errors of transmission by scribes and compositors, which were actors' or stage managers' interpolations and which might have been Shakespeare's "considered second thoughts" as the Revisers liked to believe? "The questions," Knowles has written, "have not been answered, or are perhaps no longer answerable."

Knowles went on to raise the related objection that the arguments presented by the Revisers—that we were seeing Shakespeare's own second thoughts—were often circular: the changes must be by Shakespeare because they were so perfectly brilliant; they were perfectly brilliant because they must have been by Shakespeare.

The Revisers' contention that the two *Lear*s represent two separate works of art doesn't always rely on a belief that all the changes were for the better, but it's a habit some find hard to break.

And then in a phone conversation with me Knowles disclosed an argument—an evidence-based argument—I hadn't heard before.

It was an argument he said he first made in a paper he delivered to an Atlanta conference of scholars. In the past he had focused on the weaknesses of the Revisers' case for describing some changes as "Shakespeare's considered second thoughts." Here he was addressing what I'd always thought was the Revisers' strongest argument: the additions that appear in the Folio texts of *Hamlet* and *Lear.* Unlike cuts, which could be done by taking something away that was already there, revisions for the Folio had to be created (unless one accepts one of Harold Jenkins's weaker arguments that they were there, but were mistakenly deleted from the original Quarto draft).

The Revisers had been coasting on the assumption that what was newly written in the Folio was something newly *rewritten* by Shakespeare. But now Knowles was citing to me on the phone his study of the language of the Folio additions. In which he'd found there was a far greater percentage of words in those additions that had never appeared, or only appeared rarely, in Shakespeare's previous work. Which would argue that the Folio additions were not necessarily—or always—Shakespeare's considered second thoughts, but rather the thoughts of a second *hand,* another writer entirely.

It's an argument that goes against instinct, perhaps, or one's subjective sense of what is "Shakespearean," when one considers the "precious instance" passage in *Hamlet* and the "Look her lips, / Look there, look there" lines in *Lear.* Could someone else have written them? Someone in Shakespeare's company? The same person who may have revised *Hamlet*? Could a skilled imitator have fabricated "Shakespearean" additions? Again, study of the variants leads to a fascinating if subjective question: what one thinks Shakespeare capable of that others are not.

Do words, lines, passages seem "Shakespearean" because we had always *assumed* only Shakespeare could write them? Was Shakespeare incapable of imitation? Could none of his cowriters—Fletcher, Middleton, Wilkins—be capable of imitating his voice? Knowles cites a study by *Hamlet Variorum* coeditor Eric Rasmussen, which suggests that the vocabulary of the *Hamlet* additions is subtly different in its rare-word usage from that of the *Lear* additions. The implication is that Shakespeare could have been responsible for one or neither set of additions—but not both.

The mind reels. At what point then do we incorporate a putative "imitation"—or a line we may never know the provenance of—into the thing being imitated? Can we imagine *Lear* without "Look her lips . . ." merely because we cannot be absolutely sure it is an addition by Shakespeare?

Does the loss—or at least the reduction to conjecture—of a Shakespearean origin of Lear's dying words, of "Look her lips, / Look there, look there," diminish our sense of Shakespeare? Of *Lear*? Can we entertain the idea that someone else could do those dying words just as well, indistinguishably from Shakespeare—even better than he could? Or if it's "better," is it less Shakespearean? Should purists cease speaking it on stage?

These are important questions in esthetic theory, but Knowles feels there's more to the story, indeed there's a *moral* to the story of the rise and fall of the Revisers, a fall he assumes, since it hasn't quite happened yet.

For one thing he sees the Revision theory as a kind of marketing phenomenon, the scholarly equivalent of other speculative bubbles in its history—akin to "Tulipmania" and the nineties dot-com bubble—an emblem of all that has gone wrong with Shakespeare scholarship. (Indeed David Bevington, the prominent Shakespearean editor, compared it to "New Coke," to the fury of Gary Taylor, who resented comparison by "reactionaries" to "a sugary beverage." Other recent Shakespeare "bubbles": the "Funeral Elegy"; the "Shakeshafte" theory.)

After mocking the Revisers' pretenses to a "Copernican revolution" in Shakespeare studies, Knowles says "the idea of two *Lears* was very aggressively and successfully marketed . . . to some . . . the notion of multiple and unstable texts of *Lear* seemed to offer a golden opportunity. In the words of Honigmann, 'a gold rush, with more and more speculators jostling or encouraging each other.' Before long the theories of revision and multiple versions of plays were further extended into other theories about textual instability: the 'politics' of editing, a putative 'crisis' in editing, hypertext and genetic editing, collaborative authorship and publication, the immateriality of the text and the immateriality of the author, the indeterminacy of meaning, the relation of literature to power and censorship and other notions and issues dear to recent critics who have in one way or another found the ideas of revision and multiple versions of Shakespeare's plays, and particularly the exemplary disintegration of the standard version of his greatest tragedy, congenial and supportive to their own views."

Knowles's catalog of the sins of postmodernist literary fads fed, in his view, by the Revisers, focused on *Lear,* does not, for me anyway, *necessarily* discount any element of the Revisers' case: we don't judge a theory by the motivations or subsequent generalizations of its believers but by the evidence that supports it. Nonetheless, what he says about the way the Revisers' cause has been taken up by postmodern Theorists rings true.

His caustic vision of those who profit from the Revisers' separation of the texts is almost akin to Stephen Greenblatt's vision of the scoffers at the base of the scaffold, laughing as the head and body of the condemned person were separated. Separated abruptly as the texts of *Lear* were separated by the "palace coup."

All of which is to say it has consequences outside a circle of adepts, consequences for what readers will—from now on—be given to read (and see) as Shakespeare, as *Lear,* as several of the other most consequential works of art in the language.

The most surprising thing Knowles said to me was in his response to this question: Does he rule out Shakespeare's revising hand in the changes entirely?

No, he said, he doesn't. He just suggests that such judgments are essentially critical decisions based on subjective considerations about what is "Shakespearean." In his essay in *Lear from Study to Stage* Knowles tells us that "Given [the] limits of factual knowledge, conclusions about the authenticity of the Q and F versions must rest mainly upon *critical impressions*" (my italics). He goes on to say that "in the first half of the 20th century when Q was widely held to be an imperfectly reconstructed version of some kind of lost origin and F was accordingly regarded as superior, most editors and critics thought that the three hundred lines unique to Q *seemed authentically Shakespearean* . . ." (my italics).

In other words decisions about the differences between Q and F *Lear* were really esthetic judgments about what we decide is more "Shakespearean"—judgments about *us,* about what *we* value—rather than the product of bibliographic "science."

Here Knowles converges again with Urkowitz, in this sense: Urkowitz departs, or did in conversation with me, from some of his fellow Revisers in that he doesn't make the assumption that the Folio changes must always be *superior* to the earlier Quarto version (usually because of the assumption that as the more theatrical version the Folio is more truly "Shakespearean" because Shakespeare felt his work was most fully realized on stage). Nor does he insist that the changes must be *improvements,* because a genius like Shakespeare can only improve.

Like Knowles, Urkowitz believes there can be merits to both versions—that these are subjective judgments about what one considers Shakespearean rather than matters of "scientific" determination. Rather than arguing over which version is superior, or "more Shakespearean," he suggests it's better to spend time in teasing out the implications of each variant. Here he joins Knowles in endorsing a subjective critical and esthetic examination of the versions.

This is more than a subject for leisurely open-ended reflection for some. It's an urgent matter for directors, Urkowitz reminds me, because directors have to make choices between the two versions, whether one can (as almost all do) include variants from both. But in each case it's a choice that requires an esthetic strategy or theory about why one includes and omits what one does. To use a metaphor from physics, readers and scholars can forever entertain the potential for each version; directors must end the indeterminacy, "collapse the wave," choose one variant to be uttered on stage.

My choice of a metaphor from physics is not idle; both Urkowitz and Knowles had something else unexpected in common: they both began studying physics before they turned to Shakespeare.

For Urkowitz more than Knowles, this has had a profound effect. In Urkowitz's case his talent for physics fed a facility for extrapolating spatial/temporal relationships from reading Shakespeare and became, he told me, the basis for his ultimate vocation: directing Shakespeare. He discovered that he had an ability to read a scene in a text and then somehow visualize the potential array of spatial—and emotional—relationships between the bodies in motion on the stage and the expressive and thematic significance each potential constellation of forces could evoke.

The way Urkowitz described it to me, it recalled Nabokov's description of the way chess wizards could view the board, not as peopled by individual pieces, but rather as vectors of force projected by pieces, vectors of force that radiated, and reflected and intersected, other vectors of force.

It was actually the study of the physics of bodies in motion that got him interested in the two-*Lear* problem. Dead bodies in motion.

"I was working up the action in the last scene of *Lear,* figuring out how many people you need to carry off the bodies," he told me.

"You know, can you get away with two? Well, [in addition to Goneril and Regan,] you have to carry Edmund's [dying but not dead] body off stage. And I'm looking at the stage directions in the two versions and the moment when Edmund is carried off is different in each."

It led Urkowitz, who was at the University of Chicago at the time, to begin writing a paper on the importance of the differences in the two *Lear*s. At the same time, Michael Warren at Berkeley and Gary Taylor and Peter Blayney at Cambridge were working on similar efforts to convince the world that we can no longer believe there is just one *Lear,* the ideal Lost Archetype *Lear* that all the differently conflated *Lear*s strive for.

It's fascinating when Urkowitz recites the roll call of his old allies, how many divisions there now are between the rebels who divided the kingdom. Very *Henry IV.* Urkowitz has issues with Gary Taylor on scholarly grounds; Taylor says Blayney hates him; Blayney has mysteriously abandoned his projected second volume on the two texts of *Lear.*

But entering into a labyrinth of *Lear* variations has its rewards if one is not an embattled partisan. It encourages a closer study, entangles one more deeply in the language and in some quieter, lesser known lines that might have otherwise escaped attention in the focus on mighty themes.

I'd asked Steven Urkowitz during our dinner the same question I'd asked Stephen Greenblatt: if he thought the differences between the Quarto and Folio were so great they marked them as different works of art.

"Well, yeah, I think on issues of personal responsibility, some in Lear, mostly in Albany, but also in the audience."

"In the audience?"

"The things that are being changed that matter here affect the comfort/discomfort axis of the audience."

To explain, he invokes an influential (okay, "influential" here perhaps mainly among adepts) book by Stephen Booth, *King Lear, Macbeth, Indefinition, and Tragedy.*

"Booth refers to Olivier's famous preface to his film version of *Hamlet*—

'This is the tragedy of a man who could not make up his mind.' No, Booth says, and this goes for *Lear* as well, it's the tragedy of an *audience* that can't make up its mind. In *Hamlet* we're whipsawed from hating Claudius to being in sympathy with him, from believing the Ghost to agreeing with Hamlet there is no such thing and back—these torment the audience."

And *Lear*? Here he takes a position opposite to Gary Taylor's: Urkowitz believes the Quarto is the more redemptive version.

"What happens in *Lear,* there are certain spots where in the first [Quarto] version we agree with various ameliorative visions of the world—"

"The servants who offer to heal Gloucester's bleeding eyes . . ."

"Yes, and these are stripped out in the Folio version. You are going to get a much harsher experience, not just the servants but things like Edgar's heartfelt reaction before he sees Gloucester, Kent and the Gentleman talking about Cordelia and Lear being reunited. Over and over again though we return to the experience *as an audience* of undecidability."

I should say I'm undecided about the undecidedness alternative, myself. I'm not sure the Folio dying words alone can turn the play on its head from tragic to redemptive. I'm not sure how undecided we feel. I'm undecided about whether a playwright would wield his most powerful dramatic gifts over the course of a three- to four-hour production mainly to leave the audience . . . undecided. Although on the other hand one could say undecidedness—about the moral nature of the cosmos—is an intrinsic element of tragedy. I know I found myself in a constant state of undecidedness while weighing the conflicting claims of the two factions in the two-*Lear* controversy.

Gary Taylor was one of the first contemporary scholars to argue the case that the new ending of *Lear,* the Folio last words, represents the intervention of a later Shakespeare, the Shakespeare of the Late Romances. And thus a different *Lear:* "Some sense of hope, transcendence, spiritual consolation the Folio version surely offers. The interrelated changes in the Folio's dramatization of the ending of *King Lear* produce an effect strikingly similar to the resonant emotional complexity of the most memorable scenes in *The Winter's Tale* and *Cymbeline.*"

In other words—as with the addition of the "precious instance" passage in *Hamlet,* the addition of "the silver livery of age" passage that Richard Proudfoot pointed out in *Henry VI*—the Folio ending of *Lear,* Taylor seemed to be saying, drapes the tragedy in the silver livery of a Late Romance. But let's return to a close focus on the last words. On one of the most heroic efforts to rationalize the variations. Does it offer a way out of the labyrinth of undecidability?

A FEARFUL SYMMETRY? OR SUICIDE BY SIGHS

The quest to define the nature of the shift between the Quarto and Folio versions of Lear's dying words may have found its most strenuous exegete in the scholar Alexander Leggatt and his paper "How Lear Dies," which he delivered at a seminar at a Shakespeare Association of America conference. It's a thesis anyone such as myself seeking *some* resolution of the question must contend with.

Leggatt begins with something I had a particular interest in: the disappearing O-groans in the Folio *Lear.* Recall that Shakespeare (or someone) had added four O-groans to Hamlet's last words in the Quarto: "The rest is silence." And that Shakespeare (or someone) had subtracted four O-groans from Lear's dying words in the Folio.

Leggatt attempts to convince us there is something more to Lear's (and possibly Hamlet's) O-groans than potentially expressive swan songs.

He suggests there is evidence that the O-groans were meant not to suggest the effect of dying but the *cause.* That emitting O-groan-like sighs was recognized as a method of committing suicide in Elizabethan literary convention—bringing one's life to a close, expelling one's spirit. Suicide by sighs.

"In Shakespeare's time," Leggatt tells us, "sighs and groans were thought to shorten life." Leggatt argues that Lear's four O-groans in the Quarto would be designed to be seen (and heard) by audiences as his deliberate attempts to take control of his death, to shorten his life, cause himself to die by successive life-shortening sighs. Something he achieves moments after he utters "O, o, o, o," when he commands himself to die:

"Break, heart, I prithee break!"

Citing the O-groans added to the Folio version of *Hamlet,* Leggatt argues that Hamlet, "like Lear, will[s] his own death," doing literally what Ophelia earlier imagined him doing:

> *He rais'd a sigh so piteous and profound* [Ophelia says]
> *As it did seem to shatter all his bulk*
> *And end his being.*

Life-shattering sighs: Lear's death in the Quarto, Leggatt suggests, is similarly "not something that happens to him but something he does." Suicide by sighs.

Not so in the Folio version of *Lear,* Leggatt maintains. In the Folio, he says, Lear is not focused on himself and ending his being through suicidal sighs; instead "Lear's focus on Cordelia is much stronger and his own will and self-consciousness are more suppressed. He does not control his death and does not even seem aware that it is coming, so little does he care about himself . . ." In other words the Folio's "Look her lips, / Look there . . ." is about *her* heart. The Quarto's "Break, heart," is about his.

It's an interesting contrast, but is it the only contrast, is it the most important contrast between the two endings? I'm not sure, but Leggatt has a schematic notion, into which he wants to fit this contrast between Lear's last words in the Quarto and his last words in the Folio.

To oversimplify somewhat, Leggatt sees a correlation, a thematic coherence in the Folio revisions, the ones leading up to Lear's last words. He sees these Folio alterations, the ones he regards as "considered second thoughts," giving us a Lear in the Folio who is more in control *up till the end:* "The Lear of Q is more a creature of impulse, less reflective and less in control [than the Folio Lear]. This means that in each case the death scene *reverses* the main pattern: in Q an unreflective Lear comes to clarity and asserts control over his own death; in F a commanding, thinking, assertive Lear surrenders himself in his total focus on Cordelia, and his language moves beyond meaning into an inarticulate sound [the dying fall of "Look there, look there . . ." fading into silence]. Each Lear is reversed at the point of death."

Well, there's no doubt he's presented us with a neat pattern, or imagined one, at the very least. It's a noble attempt to give classic Newtonian symmetry to something that may have more in common with the positional uncertainty, the both/and resonating ambiguity of post-Newtonian theory.

One flaw is that—even if you accept his binary assumptions about the two versions of the play *before* the final words—that does not mean that there are only two possible ways the final words can spin what has come before. Or that there are only two ways to characterize the Lear of the last words: controlled or out of control.

This reduces the dazzling array of ambiguities each ending offers, and the array of relationships between the two endings available, some of which are more interesting and less symmetrical than Leggatt's control versus out-of-control and subsequent last words "reversal" schematics. It makes everything too simple, too pat. It replaces the often unbearable pleasures of undecidability with the comforts of certainty.

Having suggested Leggatt may have been too schematic in "How Lear Dies" I don't want to rule out all conjectures about the implications of Lear's last words and the way they change from Quarto to Folio. Especially since I have a conjecture of my own.

"SMILING EXTREMITY OUT OF ACT," OR WHAT DOES *PERICLES* TELL US ABOUT THE ENDING OF *LEAR*?

My conjecture grows out of a feeling that if Shakespeare wanted to "rewrite," in the sense of reconceive, the ending of *Lear* he could have done it less ambiguously. Because there is a sense in which he did "rewrite" the ending of *Lear* in what seems to be a remarkably explicit and unambiguous way at the climax of what is regarded as the earliest of the Late Romances, *Pericles.*

Could a comparison between the father-daughter recognition scene in *Lear,* one of the last of the tragedies, and the one in *Pericles,* probably the first of the Late Romances, suggest something about the way Shakespeare revised or re-wrote? Could it dramatize the way Shakespeare's vision of the world *changed* in the interval between the last tragedies and the first romances? The way in which the Late Romances are, in great and small ways, his way of re-writing the tragedies in a redemptive key?

It was something I first considered when the New York Shakespeare Festival asked me to write the program essay for Brian Kulick's production of *Pericles* at the Joseph Papp Public Theater. In rereading *Pericles* I was transfixed by the reunion scene and its echoes of *Lear.* The whole play has echoes of *Lear* in a new key.

Pericles was written—or cowritten (Brian Vickers, in the latest, most persuasive version of this argument, makes the case that one George Wilkins, author of a prose Pericles saga, wrote most of the first two acts)—not long after *Lear.*

Lear is said to have been performed as early as 1605 or 1606, and *Pericles* is now thought to have been written in 1607 or 1608. And yet there is a world of difference between the plays of the late tragic period, including *Lear, Macbeth, Coriolanus* and *Timon of Athens,* and the world of the Late Romances, the sequence of plays beginning with *Pericles* and continuing with *The Winter's Tale, Cymbeline* and *The Tempest.*

In some ways the wandering prince, Pericles, is Shakespeare's Odysseus, and like *The Odyssey* the play is about the struggle for return and reunion. The plot sends Pericles reeling around the Mediterranean, from one disturbing, but largely disconnected, episode to another. By the fifth act his wife Thaisa has apparently died in a storm at sea; he believes his daughter Marina dead too. In his grief, Pericles has become, in a way akin to Lear, Shakespeare's Job.

When his ship reaches its final harbor Pericles is disintegrating, his berth virtually a floating bier. There is little to distinguish Pericles from the dying Lear. And little to distinguish his daughter, Marina, from Lear's daughter, Cordelia. Unbeknownst to Pericles Marina has survived the tempest at sea and grown into an iconic figure of mercy like Cordelia. Loving and forgiving, Marina is a spiritually redemptive figure (forced to take shelter in a brothel, her radiant innocence somehow transforms its customers into humane protectors).

Circumstances have at last brought Marina to her father's side, just as it seems he is about to die of melancholy or commit suicide by sighs.

The shipboard reunion scene that follows, tentative, skeptical, then tender and overwhelming, is to my mind one of the most powerful and beautiful in all Shakespeare. It is almost as if it were set down amidst the somewhat chaotic plot of *Pericles* from another play. Almost as if its heightened language were lifted intact from *Lear.* Indeed from another sphere, another spiritual dimension than we've seen before in *Pericles.* In fact the scene reaches a climax when Pericles, finally convinced that Marina—the daughter he thought dead—has been restored almost miraculously to him, actually *hears* what he describes as "the music of the spheres."

I think the *Pericles* reunion scene, some 150 lines, has suffered from being set late in a play that is rarely produced or read because of its irregularities, its uneven quality and the belief by many scholars that the first two acts were not even written by Shakespeare. And so a scene that might otherwise achieve the recognition of some of the celebrated scenes in *Lear* or *Romeo and Juliet* is hardly known, rarely referred to, a rare exception being the T. S. Eliot poem "Marina."

But the reunion scene in *Pericles* comes in the last act, one almost universally credited to Shakespeare, and in addition to its lovely emotional intensity, the scene is rife with explicit echoes and redemptive rewrites (one might say) of lines, of scenes, in the last two acts of *Lear.*

There is that moment in act 4 of *Lear* in which the King, exhausted by madness, has fallen into a deep sleep and awakens to find he is in the kind custody of his daughter, who has returned to England at the head of an army to rescue him and reunite his divided kingdom.

"Pray do not mock me," Lear pleads, heartbreakingly, when he sees his daughter, but can't believe his eyes.

I am a very foolish fond old man . . .
I fear I am not in my perfect mind.
Methinks I should know you . . .
Yet I am doubtful . . .
Do not laugh at me,
For (as I am a man) I think this lady
To be my child Cordelia.

It may be the most deeply moving moment in *Lear.* It's hesitant, this recognition, questioning, then tentatively joyful. It is followed by Lear's abject apology to Cordelia:

LEAR: *I know you do not love me, for your sisters*
Have (as I do remember) done me wrong:
You have some cause, they have not.
CORDELIA: *No cause, no cause.*

Those words: "No cause, no cause." I am not the first to say they may represent the most sublime compression of compassion, grace and forgiveness in all Shakespeare. (Is there another instance in literature where four words carry such weight, such release?)

It's a fusion of lovingness and forgiveness that makes the imminent denouement at the close of the final act—Cordelia's death in Lear's arms—all the more shattering.

Lear's hesitancy in believing his good fortune in awakening to his daughter's loving gaze is mirrored and mocked by the cruel fortune of imagining, in his dying words (in the Folio), that his daughter is once again alive to gaze at him.

Now consider the echoes in *Pericles* of those two linked scenes from *Lear.*

"Methinks I should know you," an awakening Lear says to his daughter Cordelia.

". . . thou lookest / Like one I loved indeed," says an awakened Pericles to his daughter Marina.

And then the language of Pericles seems to point to the final act of *Lear:*

"Yet thou dost look," Pericles says to Marina, "Like Patience gazing on kings' graves, and smiling / Extremity out of act."

"Kings' graves": the bitter ends of tragedy.

Smiling extremity out of act: a remarkably resonant locution. "Smiling extremity out of act" even suggests a theatrical connotation: the extremity of a play is its last *act,* the act that determines whether it will feel tragic or redemptive.

"Smiling extremity out of act": that is how Shakespeare's Late Romances in effect "revise" the tragedies that precede them—they smile the terminal extremity *out* of the last act. Smile the extremity into some miraculous act of redemption and promise.

And indeed, the echoes in *Pericles'* father-daughter reunion almost explicitly reflect Lear's last moments holding the dying or dead body of Cordelia—the extremity that can't be smiled out of *Lear*'s last act.

After Marina tells Pericles her name and that she was a daughter of a king, he wonders if she's a living being—". . . are you flesh and blood? / Have you a working pulse . . ."—with the same apprehension with which Lear holds a feather to Cordelia's lips to see if she has breath (in both the Quarto and the Folio). One searches for breath, the other for a pulse, evanescent signs of life.

Lear is asking if Cordelia lives and breathes. His daughter does not, Pericles' daughter does. The fact that they both ask that desperate question, that both fathers seek signs of life in their daughters, makes the parallelism of the scenes hard to ignore.

But Pericles still can't believe such a redemptive denouement can be possible, that the apparition of a living daughter he thought dead isn't a delusion like Lear's "Look her lips . . ."

It must be a dream, Pericles insists, a delusion: "This is the rarest dream that e'er dull'd sleep / Did mock sad fools withal."

The way Lear's last delusion mocked him as a terminally sad fool? But Pericles' "rarest dream"—beautiful locution, no? an echo of Bottom's "most rare vision," is it not?—is no delusion.

Finally Pericles experiences it fully, experiences at last what A. C. Bradley attributes to Lear in the final lines the Folio gives the dying king—an ecstatic vision of bliss:

> . . . *this great sea of joys rushing upon me* [Pericles exclaims]
> *O'erbear the shores of my mortality,*
> *And drown me with their sweetness.*

Instead of Lear dying of sighs with his daughter, we have Pericles near-drowning in sweetness with his. Something he experiences as "o'er-bearing"—in a sense, unbearable.

In a moment, "wild in his beholding" (another lovely locution), Pericles is finally convinced he recognizes his daughter. Finally convinced, he hears the "music of the spheres." As Bradley's Lear sees a vision of Cordelia ascending to heaven.

But—and here's the point of my conjecture—in a way this *Pericles* scene could be taken as a *refutation* of Bradley's blissfully redemptive interpretation of the final Folio words of Lear. The *Pericles* recognition scene suggests that when Shakespeare wants to make a redemptive father-daughter reunion scene he doesn't need it to rest perilously, ambiguously, on what is read into it, making it radically undecidable. He can heighten the drama of the resolution—incorporate the dashed hopes and doomed expectations of the tragedies by enclosing them within a stirringly redemptive framework. He can celebrate redemption unambiguously in the Late Romances. He could have made us believe, share in Lear's last imagined communion with Cordelia; believe it was no delusion. He may not have been ready to, not unambiguously, in the tragedies.

Indeed in *Pericles,* especially in Marina, he seems to want to redeem all his tragic heroines at once. She becomes, I once wrote, "all the lost heroines of Shakespearean tragedy—Ophelia, Desdemona, Cordelia—risen from their untimely graves and given radiant life again." In Marina's first words in *Pericles* she speaks of strewing the green with violets and marigolds, which echoes Ophelia's despairing near-dying words about withered violets: "I would give you some violets, but they wither'd all when my father died." It echoes Desdemona's weeping "willow song" in a redemptive key.

Ophelia's violets bloom again in Marina's hands. Both Ophelia and Marina weave garlands; Ophelia's help drag her down to death, Marina places garlands upon a grave, the grave of her mother, who turns out, miraculously, to be alive, figuratively turning the graves of Cordelia, Ophelia and Desdemona into places of rebirth.

Marina embodies the grace we're given—occasionally, unpredictably, unmeritably for the fates we're forced to suffer; for the way injustice seems to single out those who most deserve to be blessed. As does Cordelia in *Lear,* especially when Lear tells us if she lives it will "redeem all sorrows." In other words, should a miracle occur and Cordelia live, it would represent a spiritual trumph of a higher order—the way Marina's reunion with her father does. But Cordelia does not live. *Lear* remains a tragedy, whatever inscrutable vision ("Look there, look there . . .") passes before Lear's dying eyes. A tragedy awaiting the scene in *Pericles* that will belatedly offer recompense.

When thinking about the recognition scene in *Pericles,* it occurred to me to wonder: Was *this* why it was so drawn out, why Pericles first believed then disbelieved, then thought he was in a dream: "This is the rarest dream that e'er dull'd sleep / Did mock sad fools withal"?

Before he will allow himself to believe his daughter has been miraculously restored to him, the half-mad Pericles requires proof after proof it *is* his daughter, tests hope against doubt, beyond the point when it should be clear to all—even him—this is his daughter. Could it be that the need to prolong—so conspicuously—this doubt and disbelief comes not merely from the exigency of *Pericles* but from the double duty it does in "rewriting," reenvisioning the final scene in *Lear*? To prolong the doubt, to savor it, to wring out every unbearably heartbreaking moment of unbelief, raises the stakes for the Romantic ending. Will this scene, like *Lear*'s last one, dash the hopes so pitifully raised once again by a doubting father? Or fulfill them?

The more prolonged and excruciating the doubt in *Pericles,* the better to redeem and recuperate the unbearable loss at the close of *Lear.*

In other words you might say the reunion scene in *Pericles* presents us with such an explicit revision of the end of *Lear,* it suggests Shakespeare did not intend the close of *Lear* as a moment of ecstatic bliss and unbearable joy, but as a denial of the redemptive ending he would in effect give *Pericles.* A denial with just enough ambiguity to raise impossible hopes, and thus doubly dash them. Just my conjecture, but again an example of how suggestive the contemplation of textual variation can be. How perplexing and suggestive the problem of Lear's dying words can be. I don't claim to have resolved the problem. I want to emphasize how problematic it is. But as the British philosopher Simon Blackburn put it, of particularly recalcitrant problems in the philosophy of mind: "The process of understanding the problem is itself a good thing."

III

The War over What Is—and What Isn't—"Shakespearean"

Chapter Five

The Great Shakespeare "Funeral Elegy" Fiasco

In which the question "What do we mean by 'Shakespearean'?" becomes front-page news.

PERHAPS THE ELEGY FIASCO, SCANDAL, WHATEVER YOU WISH to call it, should be thought of as a Shakespearean comedy. To compare it to *The Comedy of Errors* might be too obvious. In some ways—and perhaps it's the Peter Brook effect—it could be compared to the *Dream.*

The love potion in this case was the overfond intoxication, the starry-eyed vision, that the prospect of a "new" Shakespearean work produced when it was dropped into the eyes of the Shakespeare studies publishing-industrial complex.

And then there was the Mechanical (Don Foster's digital database) raised to virtual godhead and then proven to be an ass.

But it wasn't a pure comedy either. There were moments when it suggested something menacingly Macbeth-like—what happens when someone is driven by ambition to seek a crown, here, the virtual crown of a scholar's lifetime, a "Shakespearean discovery."

I know I'll never forget the moment when I first spoke with Don Foster on his purported Great Shakespeare Discovery. The moment when Don Foster cheerfully told me, "I could destroy you."

I'm sure he didn't mean it literally, it was a pose; it was Don Foster at his most Don Corleone. It was Don Foster at the height of his fame as "Shakespeare super-sleuth" as the London *Sunday Times* would call him, "the world's first literary detective" as the jacket cover for his book *Author Unknown* described him.

It was the Don Foster who had been lifted by the wave of celebrity generated by his "Shakespeare discovery" from obscure Vassar professor of English to (as he describes his new celebrity life in *Author Unknown*) the sort of person who was lifted by helicopter from the Vassar campus to the network TV studios of Manhattan to explain his triumphant unveiling of the true identity of "Anonymous," the author of *Primary Colors* in 1996—considered, back then, a coup to surpass even his Shakespearean "discovery." A coup that appeared to validate the all-but-unquestioning acceptance (at least in the American media) of Foster's Great Shakespeare Discovery.

This was the Don Foster whose self-regard was fueled by adulatory profiles on Barbara Walters's *20/20* and the BBC, which portrayed him as parlaying his Shakespearean discovery and his "literary sleuthing" into a career as a Sherlockian consultant in high-profile tabloid-headline criminal cases such as the JonBenét Ramsey murder, the investigation of the Unabomber, even the anthrax-letters case.

Foster's new career of fame and crime-fighting was founded upon the strength of his Great Shakespeare Discovery (or Rediscovery, or, as the scholars like to say, the *attribution*), the one front-paged by newspapers throughout the world in 1996. All hailing Foster's declaration that a long-ignored, nearly six-hundred-line poem, authored by someone who signed it only "W.S.," was in fact by William Shakespeare. The long, tediously pious, clumsily convoluted poem had been published in 1612 as "A FUNERALL Elegye *In memory of the late Vertuous Maister* William Peeter of Whipton neere Excester. By W.S." (from here on we'll just call it the "Funeral Elegy"). If Foster was right, it was not a negligible discovery, like the dubious claim made a decade before on behalf of a doggerel-like piece of poetry called "Shall I Die? Shall I Fly?", attributed to Shakespeare by Oxford University Press editors Gary Taylor and Stanley Wells. Ironically it was the same Don Foster who led the charge in denouncing that discovery as a non-Shakespearean impostor.

No, if Shakespeare wrote the "Funeral Elegy" as Foster claimed, it would not only mean we had a new long poem by Shakespeare; it would mean Don Foster had given us in effect *a new Shakespeare.* The Elegy would have been his last known nondramatic work, his most personal poem, in a sense, the only poem that could be said to have been written "in his own voice," one supposedly written in memory of a dear dead friend. Shakespeare's most explicitly devotional and religious work. If Wordsworth claimed the Sonnets unlocked Shakespeare's heart, this "new" poem about life, death, mortality, faith and fate written four years before his death might unlock Shakespeare's secret *soul*. Might serve in a way as the closest thing to a Last Testament.

If. By the time I first talked to Don Foster, he had succeeded in silencing most of his other critics, at least on this side of the Atlantic where few outside the academy seemed to care, and hardly anyone inside did.* Few seemed concerned that the Elegy would rewrite Shakespeare's identity—perhaps even the interpretation of his work—almost as radically as the "anti-Stratfordians" who claimed "Shakespeare" wasn't Shakespeare anyway. The Elegy attribution might be used to confirm or misattribute other disputed "Shakespearean" texts. It would forever skew our understanding of his intellectual evolution. Much was at stake it seemed to me.

My strained conversation with Foster followed publication of my second skeptical essay on Foster's "discovery" in *The New York Observer*. By that time I had read and reread the Elegy (a punishing task) several times and it seemed clear to me from a lifetime of reading and rereading Shakespeare that the Elegy was, in the sodden piety of its language and the stilted delivery of its language and of its themes, just *not* Shakespearean. Yes, this was "subjective," speaking strictly, but I thought my informed subjectivity trumped the faux "objectivity" of Foster's computer database. I predicted that the Elegy was destined for "the dust heap of literary history."

When Foster called me up, it was in the context of the reply letter to an anti-Elegy essay I'd written. The letter he was drafting, he magnanimously told me, *could* "destroy" me but wouldn't.

It was of course a magnanimity designed as much as a warning as a gesture of generosity. In his reply letter, which was, in parts, gracious, he nonetheless maintained:

"My Funeral Elegy won't be getting the funeral [Rosenbaum thinks] it deserves any time soon." (He was right about that. It took five more years before Foster was forced to inter "his" "Funeral Elegy" himself.)

Note that Foster was calling it "my Funeral Elegy." In a sense it *was* his, certainly more than Shakespeare's. In any case a couple of years later Foster felt secure enough in relation to me to shift from tough-guy talk to triumphalist condescension. There it is, prominently featured on page 45 of *Author Unknown*, Foster's 2000 book, the one he subtitled "Tales of a Literary Detective." Featured, as an epigraph to the opening section of his

* Notable American exceptions: A. Kent Hieatt and the Shakespeare Authorship Clinic and its directors, Ward Elliott and Robert J. Valenza.

account of his "Shakespearean discovery," was the following quotation from my critical attack on Foster's attribution:

> The alleged "Shakespeare" elegy: Shall it die or shall it fly? . . . relentlessly sententious, mind-numbingly mediocre, destabilizingly dull-witted . . . a poem that I believe will eventually end up in the dust heap of literary history. . . .
>
> —RON ROSENBAUM, *NEW YORK OBSERVER*
> (24 FEBRUARY 1997) [caps in Foster's original]

There could be no doubt of its intent: secure and confident in his Great Discovery, Foster wanted to show "what fools these doubters be"—the ones who made fools of themselves by raising their voices against Foster's purportedly crushing arguments for the Shakespearean attribution, which at the time seemed to have swept the field. It was a famous victory and he was singling me out as symbol of the vanquished. But then suddenly it all came tumbling down for Don Foster. It truly became his funeral, if not "his" "Funeral Elegy."

I could destroy you . . . I couldn't help thinking of that line, five years later, when I read Don Foster's astonishing admission that his Great Shakespeare Discovery had been a Great Big Mistake. When Don Foster, in effect, buried his "Funeral Elegy."

The whole tragicomic episode is an instructive tribute to the intoxicant power Shakespeare has over our imagination.

A BRIEF HISTORY OF PHONY SHAKESPEARE

Of course, passions have always run high when alleged "New Shakespearean Works" are brought forth to the world. Even during Shakespeare's lifetime some unscrupulous printers sought to cash in on his fame by putting his name or initials on plays such as *A Yorkshire Tragedy* that few scholars believe he wrote.

The momentousness and the divisiveness of Shakespearean discoveries—and the question of how to define what was "Shakespearean"—first became evident a century and a half after Shakespeare's death when a frenzy of bardolatry seized England and the first Great Shakespeare Discovery, or as it should more accurately be called, "The First Purely and Simply Fraudulent Shakespearean Discovery," made headlines in 1796. The discovery or, more properly, the William Henry Ireland "discoveries," included letters, poems and even an alleged "new play" by Shakespeare called *Vortigern* that actually had a debut in the Drury Lane Theater, temple of bardolatry.

William Henry Ireland is a great character, almost a Shakespearean character (think Autolycus, the con man who peddles "famous" ballads in *The Winter's Tale*), and there's a wonderful book about the Ireland forgeries by Bernard Grebanier (*The Great Shakespeare Forgery*) which portrays the nineteen-year-old boy William Henry driven by a desperate desire to please his father, Samuel Ireland, one of those early mad bardolaters who gave bardolatry the bad name it has suffered from ever since. Samuel Ireland displayed virtually *no* interest in the subtleties and complexities of the plays (and their language) but was obsessed with accumulating mute relics of the "true cross" one might say, autographs, letters, deeds, laundry lists. While the explosion of fraud ruined the market for material remnants for the most part, the attempt to attach Shakespeare's name to non-Shakespearean works continues, viz: the Elegy.

Samuel Ireland's son William Henry Ireland produced both relics and words enough to fulfill his father's wildest dreams. His con consisted of claiming he'd been befriended by a "wealthy patron" who wished to remain anonymous, but who had in his possession an "oaken strong box bound in gold clasps" (recall the secret book, similarly bound "in clasps of gold" in *Romeo and Juliet*) from which he would tantalizingly produce Shakespearean relics and manuscripts, one bit at a time, to take home to his greedy father. Of course William Henry concocted all these false documents himself.

Many of Ireland's forgeries were targeted at, and provided convenient solutions to, such genuine questions as Shakespeare's spiritual orientation, and such biographical cruxes as whether Shakespeare really did receive a gift of one thousand pounds from his patron the Earl of Southampton.

Consider the amateurish effort at supplying an answer to this which Ireland produced, a supposed Shakespearean thank-you note:

> Copye of mye Letter toe hys grace offe Southampton Mye Lorde.
>
> Doe notte esteeme me a sluggarde nor tardye for thus havynge delayed to answerre or rather toe thank you for youre greate Bountye I doe assure you my graciouse ande good Lorde that thryce I have essayed toe wryte and thryce mye efforts have benne fruitlesse I knowe notte what

> toe saye Prose Verse alle all is naughte gratitude is all I have toe utter and that is tooe greate ande tooe sublyme a feeling for poore mortalls toe expresse O my Lord itte is a Budde which Bllossommes Bllooms butte never dyes itte cherishes sweete Nature ande lulls the calme Breaste toe softe softe repose Butte mye goode Lorde forgive thys mye departure fromme mye Subjecte which was toe retturne thankes and thankes I Doe retturne O excuse mee mye Lorde more at presente I cannotte
>
> Yours devotedlye and with due respecte
> Wm Shakspeare

You have to love "itte is a Budde which Bllossommes Bllooms . . ." Double letters mean he's Extra Poetic, that Shakespeare.

Later there would come Shakespeare's "spiritual confession" and a slew of phony documents which happened to solve many Shakespearean biographic mysteries.

Why did so many fall for these pathetic frauds with their eccentrically antiquated spelling, supposedly found in a "secret chest"? It occurred to me it's not so different from a phenomenon I found in Hitler studies: the belief that the real truth about Hitler's psyche or his sexuality had been secreted away (and usually lost to the world) in some "lost safe deposit box." The difference was that William Henry Ireland's "safe deposit box," his oaken casket, was ready and willing to deliver up on order whatever solutions to whatever mysteries bardolaters like his father demanded.

It has been asserted, however—and I tend to agree—that it was the Ireland forgeries—and their refutation—that gave birth to a *true* Shakespearean scholarship, to a far more rational, systematic if not scientific scholarship, which developed out of the effort to make informed judgments about what was "Shakespearean" and what was not. One of the most definitive refutations of the Ireland forgeries, a daring act at the time, considering that the prince regent himself was an enthusiastic endorser of the documents' legitimacy, was written by Edmond Malone, author of "An Inquiry into the Authenticity of Certain Miscellaneous Papers and Legal Instruments." This modestly titled pamphlet pretty much settled the case (for all but poor William Henry's father, who sadly maintained that his youngest son was too stupid to have written anything "Shakespearean," so the forgeries *must* be real).

Malone had made his reputation exposing a previous eighteenth-century forgery—the works of "Rowley," an allegedly medieval "bard" invented by one Thomas Chatterton. Malone's research for his never-finished *Life of Shakespeare* exposed numerous frauds and turned up a number of authentic Shakespearean documents, and Malone's evaluations of what was claimed to be "Shakespearean" have held up well. Malone's methods have been so successful, in fact, that he is regarded as one of the greatest, if not the first, serious Shakespeare scholar. It is not uncommon to say Malone *created* the Shakespeare we know or half-know.

At this point, and indeed for another two centuries, the lively debate over Shakespearean apocrypha had not even made the "Funeral Elegy" an object of scrutiny and consideration, despite the fact it was signed in two places "W.S." In 1984, at the time of Don Foster's first fatal encounter with the "Funeral Elegy," contestations over Shakespearean "*dubia*" (from the Latin *dubium,* or doubt), as Foster liked to call them (or "*dubiosa,*" as others did), were focused on a few disputed plays and poems.

There was, for instance, the difficult matter of the inauspiciously titled play *The Double Falsehood.* An eighteenth-century Shakespearean editor, Lewis Theobald, the play's "author," said he'd based it on a manuscript in his possession of a seventeenth-century play called *Cardenio,* one which *had* been registered in 1612 as written by John Fletcher and Shakespeare.

The problem here is that Theobald never showed the world his copy of *Cardenio,* never explained why he didn't just produce *it,* rather than his adaptation (*The Double Falsehood*). And then, when pressed, Theobald claimed that the original *Cardenio* manuscript had been "destroyed by a fire" in his quarters. It was the Shakespearean *dubia* version of "The dog ate my homework."

Nonetheless many scholars have accepted Theobald's claim and believe there are elements, at least, of the original Shakespeare in Theobald's *Double Falsehood.* So many that at the time of Don Foster's astonishing retraction of his claim for the "Funeral Elegy," the Arden Shakespeare announced that it would bring out an edition of *Cardenio* in its *Double Falsehood* form.

Two other plays have been hanging around the portals of the canon hoping for admission for some time, *Edward III* and *Edmund Ironside.* The first has already been accepted as partly Shakespearean by major scholarly editions such as the Riverside and Cambridge. The latter, *Ironside,* most vigorously championed by the late Eric Sams, has won less acceptance.

In addition there has been a long-running contention over the three

Henry VI plays, the earliest works Shakespeare wrote according to many. But how much of them did he actually write and in what order? Was *Henry VI, Part 1* the first of a planned trilogy, or a "prequel" added later, after the success of what are now known as parts 2 and 3?

And then there was the fragment known as "Hand D," which has been stirring a lesser-known but far more important controversy than the Elegy since 1871, when Richard Simpson called attention to an unpublished manuscript of a play called *Sir Thomas More* from around Shakespeare's time. Simpson and his followers argued that some three handwritten pages of *Sir Thomas More,* a 147-line-long scene, and possibly a 21-line soliloquy, were the work of Shakespeare, perhaps in Shakespeare's own handwriting. If so it would be the *only* instance of Shakespeare captured in the process of composition, deletion and revision. I'll address this important controversy in the next chapter.

ENTER SHAXICON

Until Don Foster made headlines with his claim that the "Funeral Elegy" was a "new," that is, unrecognized, poem by Shakespeare, no one else had paid the Elegy much attention. Here are the opening 50 lines of the poem, just to give those who haven't experienced its unique paralyzing effect on the mind an idea. Read them—I dare you—and imagine trying to read all 579 lines.

A FUNERALL ELEGYE

Since Time, *and his predestinated end,*
Abridg'd the circuit of his hope-full dayes;
Whiles both his Youth *and* Vertue *did intend,*
The good indeuor's, of deseruing praise:
What memorable monument can last,
Whereon to build his neuer blemisht name?
But his owne worth, wherein his life was grac't?
Sith as [*that*] *euer hee maintain'd the same.*
Obliuion in the darkest day to come,
When sinne shall tread on merit in the dust;
Cannot rase out the lamentable tombe
Of his Short-liu'd desert's: *but still they must*

Euen in the hearts and memories of men,
Claime fit Respect; *that they, in euery lim,*
Remembring what he was, with comfort then
May patterne out, One truly good *by him.*
For hee was truly good; if honest care,
Of harmlesse conuersation, may commend
A life free from such staines, as follyes are;
Ill recompenced onely in his end.
Nor can the toung of him who lou'd him least,
(If there can bee minority of loue,
To one superlatiue aboue the rest,
Of many men in steddy faith) reproue
His constant temper, in the equall weight
Of thankfulnesse, *and* kindnesse: Truth *doth leaue*
Sufficient proofe, he was in euery right,
As kinde to giue, *as thankfull to* receaue.
The curious eye, of a quick-brain'd suruey,
Could scantly find a mote amidst the sun,
Of his too-shortned dayes: or make a prey
Of any faulty errors he had done.
Not that he was aboue the spleenful sence
And spight of mallice; but for that he had
Warrant enough in his owne innocence,
Against the sting of some in nature bad.
Yet who is hee so absolutely blest,
That liues incompast in a mortall frame?
Some-time in reputation not opprest?
By some in nothing famous but defame?
Such in the By-path *and the* Ridg-way *lurke*
That leades to ruine; in a smooth pretence
Of what they doe, to be a speciall worke,
Of singlenesse, not tending to offence.
Whose very vertues are not to detract,
Whiles hope remaines of gaine (base fee of slaues)
Despising chiefly, men in fortunes wrackt,
But death to such giues vnremembered graues.
Now therein liu'd he happy, if to bee
Free from detraction, happinesse it bee.

Little surprise few found this "Shakespearean" until Foster came along. But Foster wheeled out an intimidating new weapon in support of his claim, one that impressed the media and silenced many academics: the computer. More specifically the great and mighty "SHAXICON," as Foster dubbed his digitized database of Renaissance-era literature, a database he never quite got around to sharing with the world, and later mysteriously caused to disappear from his account of his Great Shakespeare Discovery. His digital Wizard of Oz remained the man behind the curtain, but at the time SHAXICON was credited with "proving" that Shakespeare wrote the Elegy, with the precision of "scientific objectivity" beyond mere fuzzily subjective judgment about "literary value."

That's the heart of the matter: Can literary judgments be reduced to, improved upon by, digital and statistical methods? Is all the evocative power of language translatable into and out of numbers? Is there, in effect, an *equation* for Shakespearean language, or an algorithm that fits him and only him?

But it was more than methodology at stake. Unlike "Shall I Die? Shall I Fly?"—which even supporters conceded was likely to be Shakespearean "juvenilia"—the "Funeral Elegy" was written in 1612, four years before Shakespeare's death. If it was Shakespeare's, it was Shakespeare meditating on profound questions of the meaning of life, meditations which could not help but lead future students to look at all his greatest earlier works through the lens of the Elegy. In deciding, for instance, whether Shakespeare was at some point a secret Catholic, whether he was or wasn't being ironic or skeptical about salvation in his dramatic works, how to read *Lear*—the Elegy would inevitably have a bearing upon all these questions. The Elegy would, if accepted, become a master key to the culmination of the evolution and arc of Shakespeare's work.

So the rise and fall of the Elegy and the rise and fall of Don Foster along with the rise and mysterious exit of SHAXICON, the computerized database that was Foster's secret weapon, are phenomena worth further study. Let's begin with a compressed four-century-long time line, based upon Don Foster's account.

February 1612

Following a day-long drinking binge and a slow-motion drunken pub crawl in Essex—one of the greatest strengths of Don Foster's research (however flawed his conclusion) is the reconstruction of this incident—a man named William Peter, an Oxford-educated landowner, is stabbed to death with a sword that pierces his head (through the skull) by a drunken neighbor on horseback.

March 1612

A pamphlet is published by Thomas Thorpe, a printer who published *Shakespeare's Sonnets* in 1609. The pamphlet contains a 579-line poem, a memorial poem for the dead man: "A Funeral Elegy [for] Master William Peter." It is signed only with the initials "W.S."

There is no surviving evidence that contemporaries considered it a work of Shakespeare—or that they considered it at all.

1612–1984

Virtually everyone in the world continued to ignore the Elegy for 370 years and by the time Don Foster came upon it, only two copies were known to remain in existence, both of them in Oxford's Bodleian Library. It is (to digress for a moment) one of the sad facts, indeed a tragedy not incommensurate with the burning of the Great Library of Alexandria, that Oxford's Bodleian Library, the key repository of literary materials from Shakespeare's time, had disdained back then to acquire and preserve *theatrical* manuscripts of that era (with only a few exceptions) because the theater was considered a lower form, base popular entertainment. So who knows how many lost Shakespearean plays, perhaps at the very least the elusive *Love's Labor's Wonne,* a putative sequel to *Love's Labor's Lost* attributed to Shakespeare in three different seventeenth-century book-trade sources, would be there. Along perhaps with scores of plays by lesser-known brilliant but forgotten playwrights of the age. That's all gone, but the "Funeral Elegy," that black hole of pious tedium—because it was "poetic" and not dramatic—was preserved. This sense of loss may explain some of the animus I felt at the suspect "find."

1984

This was the year that Oxford began making copies of its Bodleian collection available to other universities on microfilm. And this was the year that Don Foster, then a graduate student in English at the University of California at Santa Barbara, came face-to-face with the "Funeral Elegy" in the UCLA library microfilm room.

As he describes the moment, he immediately felt he heard "frequent echoing of Shakespeare in the 'Funeral Elegy.' " The only echo he mentions explicitly in *Author Unknown* is a line in the "Funeral Elegy" with the phrase "we will all go weeping to our beds." There is a line in *Richard II,* "and send the hearers weeping to their beds." For some reason the possibility that *another* poet might be consciously, ineptly, echoing (or stealing) a locution *from* Shakespeare—who was by that time quite famous—did not shoulder itself to the fore in Foster's mind.

No: this was *Shakespeare himself,* echoing *himself,* Foster instinctively felt. That Foster should take this position may be less a surprise if we consider the context in which he made his "wild surmise."

At the time Foster was working on a project, one of the most vexed Shakespearean biographical-bibliographical mysteries at that time: the identity of "Mr. W.H." the "onlie begetter" of the Sonnets as the dedication of the 1609 edition of Shakespeare's Sonnets calls him. Entire library shelves have been filled with books speculating on the nature of "Mr. W.H.": Was he Shakespeare's patron (or lover), and was the dedication *by* Shakespeare to *him,* or was "Mr. W.H." the person who procured (perhaps even illicitly, without Shakespeare's express written consent) the poems for publication? Was he patron, poltroon or publisher, and what *did* the initials "W.H." stand for?

It's another manifestation of the biographical obsession spinning its wheels furiously but fruitlessly. There's no indication that certitude on this question will tell us anything valuable about the Sonnets themselves, but Donald Foster had a bee in his bonnet which he was later to let out in a scholarly article. A bee in his bonnet that there *was* no "Mr. W.H." at all. That "Mr. W.H." was just a *misprint* for "Mr. W.Sh." Mr. William Shakespeare! The printer made a mistake and didn't notice he'd got the initials of the author he's celebrating wrong!

Despite the fact that it's hard to take this solution very seriously anymore, it is interesting in retrospect that here, too, Foster found Shakespeare lurking behind a pair of initials even if he had to *change* the initials as they appeared on the page to slip Shakespeare in. Interesting that some, initially—at least some American academics—bought it, even gave Foster a prize for his essay, even though it's an unprovable conjecture.

And this time, with the "Funeral Elegy by W.S." in front of him on the microfilm screen, there was no need to posit a misprint. (As if somehow the printer of "Mr. W.H." didn't notice he got it wrong when it came off the press, and would not have corrected it the way scores of on-press corrections were made to Shakespeare's dramatic texts in the printing shops. As if, in Foster's theory, it would somehow have slipped the printer's notice that he got the *author's* initials wrong when the first sheet came off the press.)

Nonetheless, the "Funeral Elegy" text had *two* sets of "W.S." bylines. Under the title: "by W.S." And at the bottom of the dedicatory epistle to the dead man's brother: just plain "W.S."

It was this dedicatory epistle, even more than the poem's alleged "echoes of Shakespeare," that first convinced Foster that W.S. = William Shakespeare. The dedicatory epistle in the Elegy "echoed," Foster believes, the dedicatory epistles Shakespeare wrote to patrons for his long narrative poems such as *Venus and Adonis* and *The Rape of Lucrece.* Apparently Foster did not consider the possibility that "W.S." might have been influenced by Shakespeare's *style* or the style of the times in penning "dedicatory epistles." Rather Foster jumped to the conclusion that it was Shakespeare himself. That he had found that grail of all grails: a "new" poem by Shakespeare.

1984–1989

Don Foster devoted five years to producing first a Ph.D. thesis then a book, *Elegy by W.S.: A Study in Attribution,* which came very close to declaring definitively that Shakespeare wrote the "Funeral Elegy," but which held back, out of scholarly caution, from going all the way. And thus, when it was published by a respected academic press (University of Delaware, which specialized in Shakespeare studies) after having been rejected by Oxford and Harvard's university presses, Foster's book received very little attention outside the academy and mixed reviews within.

In a way this was a shame because Foster's *Study in Attribution* was a serious work of scholarship and he may have learned the wrong lesson from its reception: abandon all inhibitions ye who wish to make worldwide headlines and become a "Shakespeare super-sleuth."

But before getting further into Foster's Fall, let us give Foster credit for some of his achievements in the course of coming to what turned out to be a Spectacularly Mistaken Conclusion.

After his epiphany reading the "Funeral Elegy" on microfilm, Foster began years of research by going to England to study the original relic of the true cross, the version of the Elegy in Oxford's Bodleian Library.

But Foster did something remarkable in investigating the death mourned in the "Funeral Elegy." There was no evidence in the poem itself, which was mainly composed of abstract pieties on the goodness of the dead man, that he had been killed in a drunken brawl. But Foster dug out the ancient records of the inquest into the death of William Peter in rural Essex and got all the gory drinking-binge details behind the sword-through-the-skull murder. It suggested either that the author who portrayed William Peter as a model of piety didn't know the drunken lout he appeared to be or did know him, and suppressed what he knew.

Stabbed to death though the skull. A horrible way to die. But when Don Foster examined the question of the Elegy for the dead man, it might be said that—behind the scrim of scholarly objectivity—he had blinded himself, or at least half-blinded himself by his initial predisposition to believe "W.S." was William Shakespeare.

There was a far greater (metaphorical) pot of gold at the end of *that* rainbow, a consideration that doesn't seem to have escaped Foster, since he did something unusual in scholarly publishing when he finally submitted the manuscript of his Elegy book to Oxford: he made those who read his manuscript sign "confidentiality" agreements—that they wouldn't speak of the Great Discovery to anyone else in the world, the better to ensure that Foster received all the credit and benefits that would accrue from being the "onlie begetter" of the Great Discovery. This is the sort of thing that has become standard practice for celebrity tell-all bios about the likes of Princess Di and Michael Jackson. And while the confidentiality clause may be understandable, it somewhat contravenes Foster's portrait of himself as some cloistered naïf, a fawn in the forest tiptoeing into the limelight, all astonished at the media attention that picked him up on the placid Poughkeepsie campus and swept him away by copter into the spotlight of the massive publicity industrial complex.

THE CLUE OF THE TOPLESS MAIDENS

In the light of the tragicomic denouement it's hard to resist noting the way Foster's invective against Gary Taylor's earlier Great Shakespeare Discovery applies to his own. As for instance, in Foster's article " 'Shall I Die' Post Mortem," the way Foster sneers that the Oxford editors' "decision to include the poem raises the spectre of a lyric that will not die after all, but that will return to haunt all future editions of Shakespeare." Exactly what threatened to happen with Foster's own Great Discovery.

Gary Taylor first made his claim for "Shall I Die?" in 1985. Foster's most sustained attack appeared in *Shakespeare Quarterly.* Going back and reading Foster's assault on the other Shakespeare "discovery" is instructive now, since it reveals him using *exactly* the kind of qualitative, subjective language of literary judgment and value that he sniffed at disdainfully in the critiques of his own discovery.

Foster's discussion here of the key division in "attributional studies"—the one between "external" and "internal" evidence—is useful and illuminating: he admits the existence and validity of literary quality and literary judgment. "External evidence" means facts in the world outside the poem—such as the fact that the Elegy was signed "W.S.," which are William Shakespeare's initials. ("External evidence" to the *contrary* would also include the fact that printers eager to cash in on Shakespeare's name had used the device of putting the initials "W.S." on *non*-Shakespearean works before.)

"Internal evidence," Foster tells us, "includes such variables as diction, prosody, imagery, word frequencies, and authorial voice."

Wait: "authorial voice"? Doesn't that sound a bit like a distinction to be made by much-despised "subjective literary judgment"? Then he asks, "If we could find in 'Shall I Die?' a single distinctive *Shakespearean* phrase . . ." (italics mine).

Remarkable: an assertion that there *is* something "Shakespearean," something distinctive about his *particular* authorial voice that can be securely discerned by human readers as opposed to silicon chips. And how do we decide what is "Shakespearean"? Here are words Foster wrote which one wishes (indeed one imagines Foster wishes) he had kept in mind:

> We must present our data responsibly, truthfully and with humility, that is, with a recognition under whose jurisdiction the verdict properly belongs: it belongs to all informed readers, to all those who have come to know William Shakespeare through the words he left behind. No one can add to the canon a single word, even by way of emendation, by personal fiat; for there is no individual, whether stationer, scribe, editor or scholar who can speak for that larger community of readers who will exercise their communal authority. The wise editor is therefore sensitive, not just to the integrity of the text, but to the integrity of shared opinion concerning what constitutes "Shakespeare."

"What constitutes 'Shakespeare.' " Here he verges on suggesting something interesting: that the definition of what is Shakespearean should be a kind of vote of the cognoscenti. But he does admit the value of expertise, literary judgment and discernment by educated humans, something he seemed to abandon once he was seduced and betrayed by the computer.

There is one other odd feature of Foster's attack on Gary Taylor's "Shall I Die?" attribution that deserves mention because it calls into question one facet that is at the heart of literary judgment—at the heart of the entire Elegy controversy: close reading. A talent for which is not one of Foster's strengths, as demonstrated by his odd digression on bare-breasted fashions in his refutation of the Gary Taylor "discovery."

Foster introduces the topless issue as part of his argument against Gary Taylor's dating of "Shall I Die?": Taylor contended it was probably written before 1595 or earlier. The earlier the date, the easier its clumsy infelicities can be explained by Shakespeare's youth, his experimentation with an unfamiliar form he never returned to.

No, says Foster: "That 'Shall I Die?' was written later than 1595 and probably after 1610" is confirmed "by another clue that the Oxford editors overlooked or simply misunderstood."

Ah yes, a missing clue that only the future "super-sleuth" detects! But let's see who misunderstood what. Foster claims that "the woman described in 'Shall I Die?' wears her breasts bare"—a fashion that only took hold after 1595 and especially "From about 1610 [when] naked breasts are a frequent concern of English ministers and moralists," Foster says. He spends considerable time adducing denunciations (and descriptions) of bare-breasted fashions from that era.

But wait, all that may be true, but what in the language of "Shall I Die?" indicates the "fair beloved" to whom it is addressed goes around bare-breasted in public?

Foster's evidence for this is stanza 8 of "Shall I Die?" (of the nine total), one that follows stanzas praising the beloved's hair, her forehead, her eyebrows, her eyes, her cheeks, her lips, her chin, her neck. Clearly the catalog is heading downward to the breasts and the eighth stanza runs, in its hobbledehoy way:

A pretty bare, past compare
parts those plots (which besots)

still asunder
It is meet, nought but sweet
Should come nere, that soe rarre
tis a wonder
No mishap, noe scape
Inferior to nature's perfection
noe blot, noe spot
She's beawties queene in election.

"The besotting plots mentioned here," Foster declares, "are the woman's nipples, exposed by a low-cut bodice."

To which one wants to say, *huh?* His only evidence for this is that "plots" according to the *OED* could, at the time, denote "birthmarks, age-spots, or any relatively darker patch of skin," but Foster has no doubt the verse means "the woman described in 'Shall I Die?' wears her breasts bare." But even if one accepts Foster's dubious assertion that "plots" equal "nipples," why is it necessary to believe she publicly bares her "nipples, exposed by a low-cut bodice"? Why not just as easily read the verse as a lover describing his lady's private nakedness in bed, or in his mind? Why? Because Foster conjures up, in his imagination, a nipple-baring *dress* that will put the fashion-date of the poem fifteen years later than Gary Taylor wants it.

This tendentious exegesis suggests a failure of close reading that would eventually cause Foster's downfall, because the scholarly refutation that led Foster to retract his thesis was founded on one demonstration after another of Foster's failure to read closely the context of what he claimed were "Shakespearean parallels" in the "Funeral Elegy." His reliance on counting word usage, rather than careful contextualizing.

The counting—which Foster first did by hand—may explain Foster's turn to the computer; he was substituting a silicon chip for a tin ear. He turned to the computer after his historical research into the "external evidence" had reached a dead end. It's evident from his 1989 book, although *never mentioned again,* that Foster had a working theory about why Shakespeare would have come out of virtual retirement to write six hundred tedious lines of abstract and windy piety about someone he hardly seemed to know (on the evidence of the poem anyway, which basically says nothing more than that the deceased was good and his death was bad).

Foster's initial working theory, which survives in traces in his 1989 book, was that the dead man was actually a part-time actor in Shakespeare's theatrical troupe.

To this end the industrious Foster, whom one must credit for investigative energy, however misguided, dug up the 370-year-old Oxford "buttery" (dining hall) records for the dead man, William Peter, when he was an Oxford student, and used them to try to correlate Peter's absences from the buttery with the dates when Shakespeare's company was playing or traveling nearby.

Nothing much came of this, nothing definitive anyway, and the state of the "external evidence" that linked the "W.S." on the Elegy pamphlet and William Shakespeare (and the dead man William Peter) was limited to the initials' similarity—and undermined by the meretricious use of the initials "W.S." in previous cases, and the existence of several religiously inclined writers of memorial verse with the real initials "W.S."

Foster did, however, demonstrate that the dead man's path had, on numerous occasions, crossed that of a John Ford at Oxford who seems to have been the same John Ford who later became a playwright in Shakespeare's company. Ford had also gone through an intense devotional period (of which there is little evidence in Shakespeare's life) around the time of the "Funeral Elegy," in which Ford himself wrote funeral elegies and religious poems with titles like "Christe's Bloodie Sweat." (I even discovered a line in one of Ford's lesser-known plays, *Love's Melancholy,* that reads: "a funeral elegy of tears.")

Foster examined the possibility of Ford's authorship of the Elegy in his 1989 book, *A Study in Attribution,* and admitted that this John Ford and his brother were more likely, based on the record, to have known the dead man in the "Funeral Elegy" than Shakespeare was. And while there were stylistic similarities and echoed phrases in both the "Funeral Elegy" and Ford's work, Foster concluded, largely on the basis of statistical evidence, that it was more likely that Ford borrowed from "Shakespeare's" "Funeral Elegy" for his own work than that he wrote it himself.

DON FOSTER'S FATAL CLEOPATRA

Too bad that, his quest for external evidence frustrated, Foster was led astray by the siren song of statistics and the newly fashionable "science" of "stylometrics." Because he might have gotten it right the first time with Ford, although there was little glory to be gathered from identifying a relentlessly mediocre poem by Ford, who is mainly admired for such lively Jacobean plays as *'Tis Pity She's a Whore.* The "Funeral Elegy"—" 'Tis Pity He's Dead" you might call it—is sub-sub-standard Ford.

But Foster's fate was sealed when he turned to statistics. They were, as Samuel Johnson said of Shakespeare's puns, "his fatal Cleopatra." The "science" of the statistical analysis of literary style and identity, sometimes called "stylometrics" (although Foster unconvincingly claims that his methods are really not stylometrics), was then in its largely pre-digitized infancy and relied a lot on hand-counting prepositions and conjunctions ("function words") to arrive at comparative percentages of "ifs" and "buts" in a known author—which were then matched with an as-yet-unattributed work.

Statistics and stylometrics implicitly argued that style could be atomized into numbers, that one could at the very least define an author's identity, his "fingerprints" by counting his characteristic percentages of word use, especially "function words" such as "and" or "but."

So poor Don Foster spends *years* hand-counting "ands" and "buts" in Shakespeare's work as well as in the work of scores of forgotten funeral elegy writers, working without computerized help—which perhaps explains his overreliance on SHAXICON, his computerized database, once he got it up and running. He confesses, toward the end of *A Study in Attribution:*

> I am nonetheless left with the impression that my methods have been terribly rudimentary in some respects due to the lack of available tools. The word-counts present in Table 1.9 are the partial product of many tedious weeks counting "nots" and "buts" and "so's" and "that's" . . . in the process I discovered a maddening tendency to arrive at *a different count for my several variables no matter how many times I tallied a particular poem, and am not certain even now, that my tables are perfectly accurate.* (Italics mine.)

A maddening tendency indeed. One has to feel, once one has glanced at Foster's astonishingly complex tables, that it was *this,* this maddening slipperiness more than anything that led to his fatal infatuation with SHAXICON: anger, perhaps rage at the slipperiness of Shakespeare's language, the words that somehow just wouldn't stay counted precisely, almost a metaphor for the way Shakespeare's words resisted, in a larger sense, reduction to a single meaning. No matter how many times Foster set them down "in the tables of his memory" as Hamlet put it, they would "dizzy the arithmetic of memory" as Hamlet also put it.

So Foster's Fall, like Hamlet's, could be construed as a revenge plot gone wrong: he'd show *them,* these slippery uncountable words—he'd turn them into numbers and crunch them, crunch the hell out of them in his computer, and *make* them say what he wanted to hear. He devised a "mousetrap" that would "catch the conscience of the king," catch the presence of the Bard.

Staring at Foster's tables, I thought of another set of maddening tables, one that I had come across in researching my Hitler book. They were the tables compiled by Hitler scholar Rudolph Binion, a Brandeis professor, to defend his theory of the origin of Hitler's evil, the grail of the Hitler explainers.

Binion's theory focused on young Adolf's reaction to his mother's fatal breast cancer. Binion believed, from his study of the medical records of Hitler's mother's Jewish doctor, one Eduard Bloch, that Bloch had over-applied the standard ineffective remedy of the time—the caustic and searing chemical iodoform—to Hitler's mother's cancerous breast tumor, causing her more agony than necessary. Suffering which, Binion believed, Hitler blamed on the Jewish doctor but repressed, because unbearable, and later projected upon the Jewish people as a whole.

Then another writer, a psychoanalyst named John Kafka (a distant relative of Franz, and *also* a descendant of Hitler's Jewish doctor) disputed Binion's calculation of Bloch's use of iodoform. Binion went back to his archival researches—into the price in Austrian kroners and the standard number of grams and meters of Austrian iodoform gauze prescribed in 1908—and constructed a table similar in complexity to Foster's.

It looks incomprehensible and a bit silly, in the sense that it reduces the vast question of the genesis of Hitler's evil to kroners-per-meter-of-gauze. But it is another instance of the persistent longing to believe that something as numinous and awesome and bottomless and inexplicable as Hitler's evil or Shakespeare's genius could somehow be captured by reducing it to numbers. Captured and somehow tamed, made less unbearable because less incomprehensible.

One can see why this has more of a maddening than illuminating effect on those who seek elusive truths through numerical calculations. At first, in Foster's case, it seemed to have a salutary inhibiting effect as well. Foster's awareness of the imprecision of his counting, the incompleteness of his database, the impossibility of getting a perfect hand-count of all the "ifs," "ands" and "buts" in all the funeral elegies composed in the decades before and after 1612, may have inhibited Foster from claiming a certainty for his Shakespearean attribution in his 1989 book.

1995

Enter SHAXICON. Now it was no more Mr. Nice Guy. No more shrinking violet. Foster's initial claim was that SHAXICON was a digitized database of "rare words" in Shakespeare's plays and other texts from that era. Rare words, in this definition, are words that appear in Shakespeare's entire canon less than twelve times. In Foster's theory this would allow him to compare the frequency of rare words in Shakespeare with the frequency of those rare words in a disputed text such as the "Funeral Elegy." A test which Foster claims the "Funeral Elegy" passed with flying colors. Then Foster went on to try to use SHAXICON to tell us which speaking parts Shakespeare played as an actor in his own plays, by "showing" that the frequency of rare words that had appeared in earlier plays would sometimes spike in later plays. Foster's theory was that, while Shakespeare was *writing* the later play, he was *acting* in the earlier play and this accounted for the spike in early-play rare words in the late plays he was writing. And the early-play rare words could point us to what role in the early plays Shakespeare might be working on. He called this particular category of rare words "Egeon words," after Egeon the father of the twins in *The Comedy of Errors,* one of the "old man" parts Shakespeare was said (in one uncorroborated apocryphal report) to have specialized in playing himself.

Few serious scholars have Foster's confidence in his ascriptions of Shakespeare's speaking parts. But for the media it was not so much what Foster did with his digitized database as the fact that he used one at all. It made such a seductive story: wonkish scholar finds "new" Shakespeare poem overlooked by old-fashioned professors with new-fashioned techno-geek computer program. A program with the sleek James Bondish name of SHAXICON. It played to the techno-optimism of the age. A new age has dawned when the numinous secrets of literature will be served up on a silicon platter by our powerful computers.

Armed with SHAXICON, Foster now had the confidence, or chutzpah, to abandon his previous hedgings and to declare that he had *proved* the Elegy was by Shakespeare. The subsequent worldwide headlines obscured the fact that Foster never made public for examination what was *in* his SHAXICON database. He kept claiming, for some seven years, that he was about to make it publicly available, but recurrently gave the excuse that he was too busy with his very important, very high-profile criminal work, claiming to have invented the science of "forensic linguistics." A claim that apparently impressed some folks at the FBI who, despite—or because of—repeated embarrassing failures of their self-promoting "profilers," believed Foster's techniques would add to their arsenal of "scientific" crime-detecting techniques.

Alas for his future crime-fighting prospects, Foster told Caleb Crain of *Lingua Franca* in 1997, "All I need is to get *one* attribution wrong *ever,* and it will discredit me, not just as an expert witness in criminal cases, but in the academy as well" (italics mine).

Still, for a time, SHAXICON served its purpose. In December 1995 at the Modern Language Association convention in Chicago, Foster and Professor Richard Abrams made an unequivocal declaration that Shakespeare wrote the "Funeral Elegy," a claim Foster backed with the elusive SHAXICON and Abrams supported with his "close reading" which "proved" that the dullness of the poem was deliberate. That the poem was "an intimate document from the poet's final years," Abrams argued, in which the death of William Peter in that drunken brawl caused Shakespeare to "reconsider theatricality" itself because it might be a source of murderous passion (the drunken brawl).

Stephen Booth would later characterize Abrams's reading as an example of what others have called "The Fallacy of Imitative Form":

"William Peter, a dull plodding man who lived a dull plodding life, was a good man. The dull plodding Funerall Elegye is imitative of its dull plodding subject, and is, if looked at in that light, a good poem."

But Booth did, alas, title his talk on the Elegy "A Long Dull Poem *by William Shakespeare*" (italics mine).

THE MARKETING OF THE SHAKESPEAREAN CLAIM

Looking back on it, it was remarkable to see the apparent coordination of allies, publishers, scholarly publications and conferences that Don Foster marshaled to bolster his Shakespearean claim for the Elegy.

Another indication that, like Gary Taylor, some contemporary Shakespearean scholars are scarcely shrinking violets, but are forced, perhaps because of the economics of the profession, to become warriors (or entrepreneurs) for their cause.

In *Counterfeiting Shakespeare,* his book on the Elegy question, Brian Vickers, one of the first to call Foster's "discovery" into question, calls it an instance of "the politics of attribution." Vickers documents elements of the campaign Foster waged for the Elegy, in particular his triumphalist efforts to delegitimize dissent.

Politics is one way to characterize it. Marketing is another. In both cases the selling of the Elegy depended on Foster's getting the most validation and canonization for the Elegy with the least possible skeptical scrutiny.

The first target was the academic press. According to Vickers's account Foster and Abrams made their decision to make a definitive claim for the "Funeral Elegy" after Foster was persuaded by Abrams to become more bold and forthcoming in April of 1994, at a meeting of the Shakespeare Association of America, and they both began to prepare papers for the *Publications of the Modern Language Association* (*PMLA*) from their statistical and "close reading" perspectives respectively.

Vickers believed that it was the prospective entry of the British *Norton Shakespeare* into the American market at this moment that was crucial. The Norton decision to include the "Funeral Elegy" in the American edition, even though the edition distanced itself by describing it as "a poem . . . that raises important questions about the attribution of works to Shakespeare," was the key to setting off a kind of marketing feeding frenzy over the Elegy among the *other* two American Complete Works that were also about to go to press with new editions: the Riverside and the Addison-Wesley.

Once Foster got the Elegy under the tent, so to speak, in the guise of a poem "raising questions" about attribution in the Norton, the other Complete Works followed suit and included it.

The Norton edition had a competitive edge because it engaged Foster himself to edit and introduce "his" Elegy for them. The editors of the rival editions were clearly not happy with their publisher's decision to include the "long dull poem" in their editions as a "work of Shakespeare," but, it seems, publishing and marketing people craved "The New Shakespeare Poem." What resulted in both cases was a kind of inclusion hedged so strongly by its editors, it verged on an attempt to quarantine the Elegy, if not reject it entirely. As David Bevington, the respected University of Chicago scholar and editor of the Addison-Wesley edition concluded, after summarizing Foster's case for the Elegy:

> To skeptics, on the other hand, *A Funeral Elegy* remains too piously conventional in its treatment of the great themes of slander, death, and immortality through poetry, to be attributable to Shakespeare even as an occasion piece. Not all tests of vocabulary uniformly endorse his authorship. The attribution remains uncertain.

But the poem entered the edition anyway. Similarly with the Houghton-Mifflin Riverside edition in which the poem's editor, J. J. M. Tobin, also made clear that he thought there was something missing from the poem, something one could define as Shakespearean. He defined what was missing as "the philosophical tolerance and psychological profundity that we expect in Shakespeare's work." Take *that,* marketing department!

But the damage had been done. The triple inclusion allowed Foster to make the inflated claim that his Elegy had been "accepted by the three major scholarly publishers of Complete Works editions." For Foster, evidently, "accepted" was a flexible enough term to cover these emphatically unenthusiastic and distanced inclusions.

And then came the headlines, first in the *Chicago Sun-Times,* then *The New York Times,* then the world. Despite widespread acceptance in the media, especially in America, Foster likes to portray the reception of his Elegy as deeply embattled. Indeed the first sentence of his retraction in 2002 reads, "In 1996, having ventured an attribution of W.S.'s A Funeral Elegy I was blasted in the pages of the *TLS.*" And in fact in the *TLS,* Stanley Wells (who had been himself the subject of attack by Foster for his endorsement of the inclusion of "Shall I Die?" in the Oxford edition) did have his (well-reasoned) revenge by heaping contempt on the attribution of the Elegy. As did several other U.K. scholars (such as Brian Vickers and Katherine Duncan-Jones) with no evident axe to grind other than their common horror at the idea that a soulless computer program identified this particularly soulless poem (on ostensibly soulful subjects) as "Shakespearean."

WHY IT MATTERS

Still, despite Foster's own warning about the danger of a false attribution coming to "haunt" Shakespeare studies "forever," this long tedious non-Shakespearean poem was worming its way into the canon.

That's why the controversy matters. The "Funeral Elegy" is a kind of "false bottom" to the bottomlessness of Shakespeare. If one has the slightest belief that Shakespeare's body of work is an interesting phenomenon, one that repays attention and deeper study, one in which every part resonates with the whole, the acceptance or rejection of the "Funeral Elegy" makes a big difference. If the Elegy, and not *The Tempest* for instance, is construed as Shakespeare's final vision, one gets a different picture of the entire Shakespearean phenomenon, the arc of his intellect. (The way Chaucer's deathbed "retraction" of his best work can't help but become a distorting lens through which to re-envision all that previous beauty and comedy.)

In any case making generalizations about Shakespeare that derive from the Elegy is akin to making generalizations about the complexity of women based on the study of a plastic blow-up doll.

And it matters, Foster's claim, if one believes in the idea of an author, of the individual dignity of an artist, as opposed to thinking of an author as merely an "author function," one that has no free will or creative autonomy, but whose identity and work are purely the deterministic product of the power relations of his moment in history (as the more stringent New Historicists have it). It matters if one believes that the body of work is as important to define as the body of the author. Even those who don't believe Shakespeare ("the Stratford man" as the anti-Stratfordians dismissively call him) wrote Shakespeare's works do believe there *is* something *distinctive* about the works, whether they were written by Bacon, Marlowe or the Earl of Oxford. Even they believe that any significant part of the canon defines, or at least irrevocably colors, the interpretation of the rest.

But Don Foster and his "author function" computer database were riding high in the years following the front pages and the worldwide headlines. His Great Shakespeare Discovery was followed by his even greater media splash in the *Primary Colors* affair, and suddenly he was catapulted, not just to media fame but to the forefront of the criminal justice system, as law enforcement agencies sought to use the alleged science of "forensic linguistics" Foster had confected to crack crimes that involved disputed documents.

Foster's involvement in the JonBenét Ramsey case should have caused law enforcement people (and Shakespeareans) to have second thoughts about his methods and conclusions. I'd known something about it: the reports that Foster had first leapt in to declare in a letter to the mother of the murdered child, Mrs. Ramsey, that his scientific methods would clear her of any implication she had written the suspect "ransom note" herself. And then he reversed course and aligned himself on the opposite side. And in his book *Author Unknown,* he admits he "made a mistake." But not until I'd read Brian Vickers's book on Foster and the Elegy did I realize how intoxicated Foster had become with his reputation as "Shakespeare super-sleuth."

According to Vickers, Foster omits from his brief reference to his JonBenét case "mistake" the fact that "Donald Foster intervened in it *twice,* entirely on his own initiative, and that his authorship methodology twice produced an erroneous identification." (The second Foster suspect turned out to be a housewife from North Carolina with no connection to the crime aside from having written about it on the Web, thus subjecting her text to Fosterian analysis.)

It's comic, yes, but perhaps tragic as well, considering that—despite all this, because of his supposed Shakespearean discovery—law enforcement authorities continued to consult the "Shakespeare super-sleuth" long after the JonBenét embarrassment, up to and including the anthrax letter scare in the aftermath of September 11, 2001. In fact the BBC did a documentary celebration of the "Shakespeare super-sleuth's" involvement in the anthrax case that aired in 2002, just a few weeks before Foster was forced to make his big retraction—and in effect pull the rug out from under the crime-fighting career he'd built upon the Great Shakespeare Discovery. Recall, after all, that Foster himself proclaimed that "one mistake" would destroy his super-sleuth role forever. (Foster's "anthrax suspect" has never been charged and, in fact, is suing the government for pursuing him.)

What struck me most personally, though, was Vickers's account of Foster's treatment of those who disagreed with him. Foster told one opponent that he (the opponent) would "destroy" himself; specifically, according to one of Foster's computer methodology critics, Foster told him that "any attempt to publish your findings or present them at conferences on 'Funeral Elegy' would destroy your reputation. . . ."

BUT I THINK WHAT SET MY TEETH ON EDGE FROM THE BEGINNING was not these tactics so much as the triumphalism about the computer and the reductivism about literature that accompanied Foster's claim. Even though Foster later made SHAXICON disappear from his narrative like the Ghost in *Hamlet* at the crowing of the cock, the message that had been transmitted was clear: it was SHAXICON that had made him a literary superman, or at the very least "super-sleuth." SHAXICON was his Frankenstein creation. Now all that wooly literary judgment stuff could be junked—number-crunching had arrived at a state of Fosterian sophistication. Literary value was to be defined by digitized statistics. And the only reason his opponents, mostly in the United Kingdom, couldn't abide his claim was that they were—like fearful and ignorant primitives (bardolaters, idolaters)—primitives now forced to bow before the superior judgmental power of the number-crunching computer.

Literary judgment, literary value was already under assault from the pseudo-science of Theory whose partisans believed their job was to demonstrate that literary judgment was *always* inherently incoherent, inconsistent, irredeemably subjective, the product of unacknowledged personal prejudice. Or that "literary value" was just a construct, a slavish reflection of the internalized values of the power relations of an oppressive hegemony. Now in Foster's methodology literary judgment was shown to be reducible to nothing more than the zeroes and ones of a digital database far more qualified than any individual human sensibility to "hear" such things as "authorial voice."

The over-optimism of technology and the over-pessimism of Theory were squeezing literary judgment out of existence, or sending it to stand in the corner with a dunce cap for lacking the resources or the self-awareness to realize that an "author" was nothing more than an "author function."

Rereading the first column I did on the Elegy question in 1996 I can see I was initially torn on the question. But in reading over my initial column on the Elegy I also came upon something I'd forgotten: I'd had a phone conversation with Foster's colleague Richard Abrams in which he made an intelligent-sounding case for the attribution (I had not yet read the poem).

But Abrams said something else remarkable, another aspect of the Great Shakespeare Discovery when it first burst upon the world that had later been discarded by Don Foster, but had done a lot to sell it. Abrams told me that he and Foster "believe that Shakespeare wrote the Elegy to the memory of the same man to whom he wrote the early flattering homoerotic sonnets."

A little frisson that didn't last much longer than its initial market-testing, but which showed up in the original *New York Times* front-page story ("A Literary Sleuth Finds His Man"). A little frisson that didn't hurt the marketing campaign (sex never does). Back then Foster had called attention to a line in the Elegy referring to the "brand of some former shame." And, Abrams told me, they both believed that this *could* be a reference to a Shakespearean scandal, perhaps over a homosexual liaison with the male subject of the Sonnets, the reality of whom, the nature of the relationship with whom, the historical identity (if real at all) of whom, has been the subject of inconclusive debate for four centuries.

By suggesting the dead man might have been Shakespeare's same-sex lover they were implying that the Elegy was not only a new discovery in the Shakespeare poetic canon, but one that may well have solved one of the great biographical riddles of Shakespearean scholarship. It was beginning to seem too neat, the Elegy like Casaubon's *Key to All Mythologies* in *Middlemarch.*

I must admit I began to see it in folktale terms as a kind of "John Henry versus the Steam Drill" battle, with myself playing the John Henry doomed-humanist role, against the silicon steam drill that SHAXICON represented. But I thought it would be a useful test: I wasn't claiming to be the most well-versed and erudite Shakespeare scholar in the realm, but I thought my nearly three decades of reading and playgoing were more than a match for Foster's number-crunching in making a judgment about the Elegy.

"FABRIC" OR FABRICATION

What kept irritating me about Foster was his dismissal of literary value, literary judgment as worthless in deciding whether an "authorial voice"—Shakespeare's voice—can be or not be identified through reading rather than computing. The point he didn't seem to get, or polemically misconstrued, about his critics was not merely that the poem was bad, but that it was bad in a non-Shakespearean way.

I think what brought matters to a head between me and Foster was not my reporting on his exaggerated claims of "acceptance." Rather, I believe, what prompted his cheerful "I could destroy you" imprecation was the "indistinguishable fabric" question I'd raised.

It was a phrase I discovered at the very close of Foster's *PMLA* article. The *PMLA* piece was filled with intimidating tables, all of which Foster employed to make the case that his statistical "tests" proved positively by number-crunch word counts that the Elegy could only have been written by Shakespeare.

Or *is* that what he proved? What Foster actually said in his conclusion was this:

The "Funeral Elegy" "belongs hereafter with Shakespeare's poems and plays," he declared, "not because there is incontrovertible proof that the man Shakespeare wrote it (there is not)"—this is not the message the "Shakespeare super-sleuth" and "world's first literary detective" had conveyed to the press, when he proclaimed his Great Shakespeare Discovery. But wait, there's more. "Not even because it is an esthetically satisfying poem (it is not), but rather because it is *formed from textual and linguistic fabric indistinguishable from that of canonical Shakespeare*" (italics mine).

This is a remarkable *failure* to make the claim the media thought he had made. And that he made his reputation on. Here he wouldn't even say the terrible poem was *by Shakespeare.* Now it's "formed"—whatever that means—"from textual and linguistic fabric indistinguishable from Shakespeare." Which is very different from saying it's *by* Shakespeare. Two twins, to use a Shakespearean example, are "formed" from "fabric indistinguishable" from each other, one might say, but that doesn't make them the same person.

I was puzzled at first by Foster's use of this "fabric indistinguishable" phrasing. First because I thought it was still wrong. And second because it suggested to me that beneath the bravado Foster might have some doubt.

This is what I wrote at the time, five and a half years before Foster admitted his error:

"I think the shabby 'fabric' (of the Elegy) is quite easily 'distinguishable': by a human if not a computer. It sounds almost as if Professor Foster would dearly love to retreat to his agnosticism [the hedging in his 1989 book], but realizes he's got three publishers out there already flogging their new editions on the basis of the Elegy's inclusion. He has to give them *some* cover. So he retreats to the extremely strained 'linguistic fabric indistinguishable from canonical Shakespeare' argument."

"Linguistic fabric": you have to love the evasiveness of that. I called it "an argument that tells us exactly why we should *reject* the attribution." I used the analogy of a freshly killed corpse: "one could just as easily say that a newly dead body is 'formed from a fabric' of flesh 'indistinguishable' from that of a living body: after all a computerized scan of all the chemical elements in a newly dead body would prove it 'indistinguishable' from a living one. The only difference—the difference that makes *all* the difference, the difference between a work by Shakespeare and the Elegy (a distinction that the tone-deaf, tin-eared SHAXICON can't make) is that one is a living being. And the other is a corpse. Perhaps it's time to give 'A Funeral Elegy' the funeral it deserves."

Well, those *were* strong words, I admit. And I reprint them not (merely) to gloat over being right. Because I was, I think, wrong about at least one thing: when I speculated that Foster really wanted to retreat with that "fabric indistinguishable" locution. It's true he may have wanted to hedge his bets for the academy in the *PMLA* story, a hesitant caution that he displayed when he identified *Primary Colors'* Anonymous. (In fact, as has been widely reported, in his original draft of his story for *New York* magazine he hedged his certainty that it was Joe Klein at the close of his story, and then-editor Kurt Andersen stepped in and rewrote Foster's conclusion to say *unequivocally*—and correctly—it was Joe Klein. Foster might have preferred "fabric indistinguishable from Joe Klein.")

But with the Elegy, although he may have been initially hesitant and equivocal in the *PMLA* article, the attacks on it, not mine necessarily, but particularly from the mandarins of the British Shakespeare establishment such as Stanley Wells, may have galled Foster into convincing himself there was no doubt. At least that's the way he began to act, dismissing his opponents as "fools" and "dopes"—words he used in referring to specific scholars in conversations with me. He took to using violent metaphors like "I blew her out of the water."

Still, by 2000, when Foster published *Author Unknown,* his self-congratulatory memoir, things had quieted down on the Elegy front. Foster's pointed attempt, in citing my dissent (in *Author Unknown*), to make me seem one of the antiquated crowd that foolishly still believed in human literary judgment, and persisted in resisting the triumph of his computerized "scientific methods," was written from the perspective of someone serenely certain he had decisively won the battle.

THE FALL

And there the matter stood between us: Foster bestriding the "forensic" and academic world like a colossus, and poor uncredentialed me continuing at every opportunity to denounce the Elegy attribution. Until the beginning of the end. The beginning of the Fall for Don Foster was signaled (to those of us who noticed it) by a brief paragraph at the close of a review in the *TLS:* Brian Vickers's April 2001 review of Foster's *Author Unknown,* when it came out in the United Kingdom.

It was interesting that, in that review, Vickers also noted the Don Corleone vibe that I had picked up in the triumphant Don Foster's polemic style: "He comes across as a combative person, very tough about his professional reputation and slow to forgive offense."

Vickers cites the way that in going after Joe Klein in the *Primary Colors* affair, "Foster confess[es] to a little bit of harmless mischief"—this being the suggestion that "Anonymous" could be gay, thus "poking fun at the author's evident sore spot, his masculine anxiety."

Vickers is briskly dismissive of Foster's altered narrative of his Elegy discovery (which omits SHAXICON's importance, even existence): "Foster's summary of the arguments for Shakespeare's authorship of the Funeral Elegy can be shown to be *wrong in every detail*" (italics mine).

Then in the final paragraph came the bombshell:

"Happily three independent studies [of the Elegy] to be published shortly will identify it as the work of John Ford. As Don Foster puts it 'in the end truth usually prevails.' "

Rarely has a single paragraph given me such pleasure, and in a matter of hours I was on the phone to Vickers in Zurich, where he was teaching at the Institute of Renaissance Studies. It was exciting to think not only that three more scholars had joined the struggle against the Elegy attribution, but that they had named John Ford as the author, which I had done four years earlier—prompted by a 1997 letter to the *TLS* from Vickers himself suggesting Ford as a candidate. (The *very* first person to have suggested Ford appears to be the independent scholar Richard Kennedy, who posted it on the SHAKSPER electronic discussion list in 1996.)

When I reached Vickers in Zurich and asked him what the three studies were, he mentioned a forthcoming study in the *Review of English Studies,* a widely respected academic journal, by someone named Monsarrat; a new study of Foster's computer methodology mistakes by members of the Shakespeare Authorship Clinic; and Vickers's own Cambridge University Press book *Counterfeiting Shakespeare,* due out the following year.

But it was more than a year until Foster felt forced to make his retraction. It's hard to think of a bigger reversal, and everything about it—the timing, the manner, the venue and the explanation he gave for it—is intriguing.

Foster says that he decided to make his retraction after he and Richard Abrams both read G. D. Monsarrat's article in the *Review of English Studies* May 2002 issue. It's a devastating analysis of Foster's methods and conclusions which names John Ford as the true author of the awful Elegy.

Some speculated that, since Foster knew Vickers's five-hundred-page book on the Elegy was soon to appear (an announcement had been made in Cambridge University Press's catalog), Foster rushed to concede defeat to a relatively obscure scholar, Monsarrat, rather than to Vickers with whom he'd been dueling publicly, sometimes bitterly in print, for six years.

When Foster made the announcement of his retraction, he made it to a small-circulation (approximately 1,200 scholars) electronic discussion list on the Web called SHAKSPER, on June 12, after most scholars had departed from their campuses, many leaving behind summer protocol instructions to hold off on delivery of their daily dozen or so e-mail posts from SHAKSPER. In other words he wasn't advertising it on the front page of *The New York Times,* as he had his original claim.

And he also phrased the retraction to make sure it was spun as a retraction caused by reading Monsarrat, not Vickers's book (although he did mention Vickers's forthcoming book as an additional factor).

Still, I never expected the day to come. It was one of those moments when you remember exactly where you were. I was sitting in my living room, surfing the Net with my morning coffee, coming upon a couple of new communiqués on the SHAKSPER discussion list (which are automatically delivered to members' in-boxes) when I saw the subject line: "ABRAMS AND FOSTER ON THE FUNERAL EL——" (there was no more room on the subject line).

At first I thought: What more can they say at this point? Or could it be an attempt to refute, preemptively, the three coming attacks on the attribution that Vickers had heralded?

But when I opened that post I couldn't believe what I was seeing. First Abrams, then Foster, in an obviously coordinated move, both admitted they were wrong. They took it all back. It wasn't Shakespeare after all. It was

John Ford. All this after nearly *seven years* of strenuous insistence that it *was* Shakespeare—and that everyone who disagreed was a fool. All their computer tests, their "close reading" had collapsed like a house of cards—all because of a single scholarly article, the one by G. D. Monsarrat in *Review of English Studies.*

Frankly I couldn't believe what I was reading at first. The notion that SHAKSPER had been hoaxed crossed my mind, as it did more than one other initial reader. But it was real.

As another list member expressed it, using the earthquake imagery which is, it seems, endemic among excited scholars: *"This is seismic!"*

Here is a sample and summary of what Foster wrote. Ostensibly an admission of error, it's actually a marvelous comic tour de force of spin that comes close to suggesting that in many ways his big mistake was somehow a *vindication.*

First Foster attacks a number of scholars who had, early on, rejected his headline-making attribution to Shakespeare and had initially suggested some minor poets (less well known than Ford) as alternatives to Shakespeare. In other words, people who were right about the large claim. These suggestions "failed for a good reason," Foster scolds, "They were mistakes."

Foster then concedes Monsarrat was right about Ford because "I know good evidence when I see it." Is this the right time for him to boast of his expertise on good evidence?

Then he quotes a passage from the Elegy—about "answers which the wise embrace [rather] than busy questions such as talkers make." A passage that seems to imply that all his opponents until now—who just happened to be *right* when he was strenuously, loudly, aggressively wrong—were just "busy talkers" while he was somehow "wise." (Wise but wrong.)

At which point Foster temporarily switches gears and offers a lovely, gracious sentence: "No one who cannot rejoice at the discovery of his own mistake deserves to be called a scholar."

But he returns from that note of graceful, high-minded humility to an unconvincing self-defense: he's moved far beyond the question of the Elegy; he barely remembers it. Years ago he too considered Ford, but the numbers just weren't right: "Ford's 'rate of enjambment' was too low." In other words, he had a good statistical excuse for his mistake, but he should have paid more attention to "internal"—nonstatistical—evidence, something he claims to have "insisted on in arguing the case for Shakespeare."

(This will come as a surprise to those who tried to argue "internal evidence"—the words as opposed to the numbers—in disputes with Foster.)

But in any case, he was using all the right methods, there was just some unexplained glitch in the answer that the methodology produced. No matter, he assures us. After having almost succeeded in distorting the Shakespeare canon for all time, he's moved on to true crime stories: "Since 1997 I have had a second career in criminology and forensic linguistics." (In other words, he's left ivory-tower pedants behind for more relevant and important work—built of course upon the fame achieved as a "Shakespeare supersleuth"—on the same tools and methods that led him to believe in a bogus identification for so long.) "Nor have I yet determined where I went wrong with statistical evidence." (Implicit but unstated assumption: statistical evidence is *still* the right way to make literary attributions, he may have just made a mistake in what statistics he used, or how he manipulated them.)

"Still, my experience in recent years with police detectives, FBI agents, lawyers and juries has, I hope, made me a better scholar." (If you don't count the fact that he tried to jump into the JonBenét case with risible results. Instead he implies his "experience" with the justice system has been an unending series of triumphs for him and his methods.)

Then he takes another slap at people who were right when he was wrong. He now looks down his nose at them anyway, because he's identifying himself with the supposedly infallible criminal justice system with its "higher standards."

And once again he mischaracterizes his opponents as merely fusty bardolaters who believed Shakespeare "was simply not a man to write that sort of thing." This is the key sentence, what all the griping and grudging in the nominally "gracious" concession has been leading to: the old charge of bardolatry. Foster is still alleging that his opponents' argument was nothing more than the snobbish belief that Shakespeare was "simply not a man to write that sort of thing." Here Foster's disingenuous condemnation of his opponents as snooty bardolaters surfaces again despite the discovery that they were right and he was wrong. They were right for the *wrong reasons,* he's saying in effect. They were right by *accident,* while concomitantly, he suggests, he was wrong for the *right* reasons. Those who doubted him were not doing so because such a thing as literary judgment, stylistic attentiveness or any of the imprecise methods have value; Foster's "scientific" conclusion was completely off, but still, he implies, *theoretically superior.*

Having admitted he was defeated by "good evidence," he still accuses his opponents of mere subjectivity: "Personal opinions cannot stand for evidence nor can personal rhetoric." In other words, the scholars who opposed him were basing their opinions not on a lifetime of literary scholarship but merely on "personal opinions," while *his* bullying predictions that opponents would be "destroyed" were not "personal rhetoric," but pure scholarly discourse.

Summing up, Foster tells us Monsarrat used Fosterian methods to prove Foster wrong. Thus, even though he was dead wrong, his *methods* have been vindicated, because they were slavishly adopted by the guy who got it right—which as we shall see is far from the case.

CLOSE READING TRUMPS MARKETING (AT LEAST THIS TIME)

Looking back on what I wrote about the Foster retraction (and Ford attribution) at the time, I feel I tried to be gracious in singling out the one gracious sentence in Foster's retraction for special attention and glossing over the grudging and bitter tone of most of it.

In any case, that one sentence I singled out is the one that read: "No one who cannot rejoice at the discovery of his own mistake deserves to be called a scholar." It is a beautifully written sentence and I made a special point of highlighting it and giving Foster credit for it—although in order to do so I had to gloss over Foster's own history of scorn for the possibility that he had made a mistake, and disdain for those who dared suggest it.

I'd gone out of my way to be kind to Foster in that first published story in more than one way: I omitted the fact that the Monsarrat article that ostensibly forced Foster to concede also pointed out several instances in which Monsarrat disputed Foster's use of evidence to make his case.

Instead I focused on what I thought—and still think—is the most important phenomenon disclosed by Monsarrat's analysis, the true source of the whole scandal: a failure of close reading in deciding what is Shakespearean. Foster's choice instead was number-crunching *counting*—counting words as bits, bytes, atoms, isolated from their context, often mistaking their context or ignoring the different context in which Shakespeare and Ford might use the same word. Vickers calls it "atomizing" language into word-units for the purpose of a one-zero digital analysis that fails to capture context.

But first, I found out a little more about this fellow G. D. Monsarrat and how he got on the Foster case. As soon as I saw Foster's post, I obtained a copy of Monsarrat's article, which identified him only as a professor of English studies at the Université de Bourgogne.

Within a day of reading Foster's retraction and the Monsarrat attack that prompted it, I once again called Brian Vickers in Zurich. He filled me in on the origin of Monsarrat's paper. Vickers seemed pleased and, to my mind, very generous in an old-fashioned scholar's way in being unperturbed that Monsarrat might have gotten credit for disproving the Foster attribution and nominating John Ford as the man behind the initials "W.S." (and getting Foster to retract)—all before Vickers's already completed book came out.

Vickers told me a fascinating story about Monsarrat, this apparent academic giant-killer. About the way the relentless marketing of the Elegy finally backfired. Monsarrat was a specialist in English religious poetry and prose of the seventeenth century; he had been called upon by a French publisher, which was preparing a bilingual edition of Shakespeare, to do a French translation of the "Funeral Elegy." Just as in America, there was marketing pressure to include the "new Shakespeare poem" in the edition. Another instance of the insidious creep of the mistaken Foster attribution beyond the realm of English to corrupt the way the rest of the world saw Shakespeare's body of work as well.

But fortunately Monsarrat was well versed in the religious and devotional poetry of John Ford, and as soon as he began studying the Elegy for translation purposes he began to feel that it was the "authorial voice" of Ford, not Shakespeare.

Vickers told me that as Monsarrat "worked on translating the Elegy into French, he began to find that in virtually every line of the Elegy there were parallels to Ford coming to mind. Not just verbal—since he's written on English stoicism, he found echoes of Ford's version of stoic philosophy."

Time after time Monsarrat found reason to challenge Foster's attempt to discount the Elegy's parallels to Ford. Foster claimed that they were there because Ford had "plagiarized" from the Elegy, thus, in his view, plagiarized from Shakespeare. Instead, Monsarrat suggested, there is evidence that Ford's post-Elegy works weren't borrowing from "Shakespeare's" Elegy—they were borrowing from *himself.*

How did he know? Monsarrat reexamined the places in the Elegy that Foster said were Shakespearean echoes rather than Ford echoes, despite their parallels to Ford. And in case after case, after reading the words and phrases *in context* Monsarrat found that (read carefully, read closely) the Elegy's use of the phrase was more consonant with Ford's customary usage than with Shakespeare's usage of the same word or phrase.

Consider two examples: First the phrase "pure simplicitie." The word "simplicitie" appears in both Shakespeare and Ford, but, Monsarrat argues, "Ford used the word with *synonymous* adjectives, 'artless simplicities' . . . 'spotless simplicities' . . . Shakespeare never uses the expression ['pure simplicitie'] and only uses 'simplicitie' with *pejorative* adjectives: 'Twice-sod simplicitie' . . . 'low simplicitie' " (my italics).

(Fascinating: Aside from its implications for the Ford-Shakespeare Elegy identification question, the fact that Shakespeare, when he spoke of it, was an enemy of "simplicity" is worth noting for those of us obsessed with his bottomless complexity.)

It was really more than anything else the *dumb* simplicity of the Elegy that made me averse, nearly allergic to it from the beginning. In clumsy ways that define the difference between complicated and complex, the Elegy would appear to be expressing a complex thought but in fact be spinning out complicated verbiage to disguise simplemindedness, the inability to think. When Shakespeare is purely simple, if he can ever be said to be purely simple, it works the other way: simplicity concealing complexity, not complicatedness concealing dumb simplicity.

On to a second example: the use of "bread" in Shakespeare, the "Funeral Elegy," and Ford. Monsarrat points out, "Foster considers that 'the bread of rest' [in the Elegy] is an echo of 'the bitter bread of banishment' [in Shakespeare] but it is in fact closer to Ford's 'Sweet is the bread of content' and 'sleep of securitie is a bread of sweetnesse.' In Shakespeare the bread is 'bitter,' in Ford it is pleasant.' "

As I was discovering these examples of Foster isolating, counting, atomizing the words without close or closer-reading context, Brian Vickers faxed me from Zurich a similar example from the galleys of his book *Counterfeiting Shakespeare.* In Ford, Vickers says, "a word like 'steddiness' is not a linguistic *counter* [my italics] . . . that can be found with an electronic search function, but a term having specific connotation within a philosophical system"—connotations (of Ford's stoic philosophy in the Elegy) that Vickers, like Monsarrat, argues were ignored or simply misunderstood by Foster in his tunnel-vision reliance on mere counting and crunching.

Essentially what Monsarrat and Vickers were demonstrating was that

Don Foster had been, in Hamlet's words, the "engineer hoist with his own petard." Foster's "petard" being his computerized counting methods, which allowed him to count a lot more words and turn them into bits, but left him analyzing only bits and pieces, not contexts, connections, resonances, ambiguities, relationships with other words. Without, in other words, everything that makes poetry untranslatable into bits and pieces, everything that distinguishes a living body from a corpse.

Postscript

Have I been harsh on Don Foster? Certainly less harsh than he has been on his critics when he was riding high. One scholar who thought I'd been, well, stringent, added that "If you were to say of Foster, 'Well, he asked for it,' I would be hard-pressed to argue the contrary." In fairness, though, I should say that Foster turned out to be more right than I was—and I've credited him in print for it—about one literary controversy in which I was agnostic: whether some letters written under the name "Wanda Tinasky" were actually the work of Thomas Pynchon. Using traditional, nondigital methods of literary analysis, Foster cleverly identified the real, non-Pynchon author; I'd written "I can't make up my mind" about it. If only Foster had remained agnostic about the Elegy.

But in fact I see this chapter as a tribute to Foster, or at least to his vulnerability to the Shakespearean spell and the intoxicating effects it can have. In fact I don't think one can place the blame for his mistaken fervor entirely on Foster. It's in great measure Shakespeare's fault, it's bardolatry's fault, it's celebrity culture's fault, it's the "frenzy of renown" that Shakespeare has generated.

It could be argued that to become intoxicated by seeing Peter Brook's *Dream* might have a different effect from becoming intoxicated by faux-Shakespeare like the "Funeral Elegy." I hadn't "discovered" anything new at the Brook *Dream,* not a new work. I had discovered something that was always there, waiting to be released. But who knows how I might have acted if I'd been in Don Foster's position and thought I'd discovered something more apparently "Shakespearean" than the pathetic Elegy?

Chapter Six

The Indian, the Judean and Hand D

A true scholar—or is he a "scholarly nihilist"?—and a real dilemma.

IT HASN'T MADE FRONT-PAGE HEADLINES THE WAY THE ELEGY DID, but the Hand D controversy has an excitement of its own. An importance all its own.

And a Hand of its own. If Hand D becomes accepted, canonical Shakespeare, it will suddenly mean that we believe we have something only dreamt of by scholars for centuries. A manuscript in Shakespeare's hand. Not a complete manuscript, just a single scene. But a scene of genuine thematic significance if "Shakespearean." At the moment we barely have more than a single word, aside from the six sacred signatures.

At the moment most scholars recognize only six instances of Shakespeare's actual handwriting. Six "authentic signatures." One from his deposition in the so-called Wigmakers' Lawsuit, the rest from mortgage and property transactions and his will.

And oh yes, two words: "By me." The words that preface one of the signatures on the last page of the will.

"By me"—isn't it ironic that of all the words written by the hand behind the "veil of print," the only two words we can be certain of: "By me."

Unless you believe in Hand D. In which case we have an entire dramatic scene, 147 lines in Shakespeare's own handwriting. A veritable exhibition of his writing process, his hesitations, his habitual spelling and metrical tics, not to mention thematic preoccupations. A secret book of golden clasps that contains golden keys to many unresolved issues, centuries-old debates such as that over the Indian and the Judean in Othello's final words.

But is the hand behind Hand D truly William Shakespeare's? The contention over Hand D has been conducted over more than a century by serious-minded scholars open to arguing with skeptics. And no one has been more skeptical than Paul Werstine, whose challenge to Hand D is even more urgent in the light of the Elegy fiasco.

But first some background on Hand D . . .

"Hand D" is the literally disembodied phrase for the author of a handwritten section of a never-printed play manuscript called *Sir Thomas More,* a kind of panoramic biopic, you might say, about the martyred "Man for All Seasons." More, the son of a tradesman who rose to become Henry VIII's secretary of state, who temporized about Henry's breach with Rome but took a stand against a royal divorce that cost him his head.

The Hand D section of the play manuscript (it was never, so far as we know, printed) is one of the least known, most intriguing potential additions to the Shakespeare canon. Few had paid much attention to the *Sir Thomas More* manuscript until 1871, when a scholar, Richard Simpson, made an argument that the manuscript consisted of several distinctive handwriting styles, which he denoted Hands A, B, C, D, etc. And that Hand D was the actual handwriting of William Shakespeare.

It seemed to be a collaborative work by people associated with a theatrical company contemporary with Shakespeare's. A play that may never have been staged because it ran into trouble with the censors, involving as it did touchy questions of Catholic and Protestant conflict and civil unrest by the poor. Indeed the manuscript (now in the British Library) bears the literal "hand" of the official censors.

One passage that apparently caused difficulty with the censors was from More's earlier career when he was high sheriff of London and quelled an anti-immigrant mob riot that had defied the lord mayor. Censors were always touchy about scenes of riot and rebellion. And this scene, written in what is known as Hand D, seems, according to Simpson, to have been a late, rewritten response to the censors' objections. And Simpson believed 147 lines of it bore the marks of Shakespeare in handwriting, spelling and theme. Later, others would suggest a 21-line soliloquy by Thomas More in Hand C might also be a Shakespearean contribution, transcribed by a theatrical scribe ("C").

Fifty years later, in 1923, a then-famous Shakespeare textual scholar, A. W. Pollard, published a collection of essays by himself and other eminent scholars that solidified Simpson's Shakespearean claim. And some seventy years after that, in 1989, another collection of scholarly essays appeared, *Shakespeare and "Sir Thomas More": Essays on the Play and Its Shakespearian*

Interest, edited by T. H. Howard-Hill, most of which took it as settled that the Hand D scene was Shakespeare's work—and most that it was his own handwriting.

The latter is a particularly exciting conjecture, because the Hand D portion of the manuscript is replete with lines crossed out, and substitutions superscripted, words deleted and altered. It's almost as if we were catching Shakespeare in the act. Catching him at work, rewriting and rethinking, changing his mind: Shakespeare in *currente calamo* as the scholarly term has it, in the heat of the moment, in the very act of creation.

But suddenly in 2002, just as the *Oxford Companion to Shakespeare* was declaring Hand D "no longer apocryphal," in other words indubitably "Shakespearean," suddenly—in *currente calamo,* one might say—two formidable challenges to the attribution of Hand D emerged. First and most thoroughgoing came from Paul Werstine, a Canadian-based scholar who had earned a reputation as one of the most stringently skeptical analysts of the assumptions of textual scholarship. Werstine's attack appeared in an issue of *Florilegium,* the Canadian journal of medieval studies. Although first published in 1999 it only came to my attention when I came across a thread in the free-for-all Shakespeare electronic bulletin board, alt.humanities.lit.shakespeare, which—compared to, say, the more carefully moderated SHAKSPER scholars' list—is more like the World Wrestling Federation. There out of the blue was a subject line, "Werstine on Pollard (75 posts)," which brought the Werstine attack to my attention.

I'd already seen another attack on Hand D by Katherine Duncan-Jones, a rising star in Shakespeare studies who had edited the new Arden edition of the Sonnets, and in her unusual biographical study *Ungentle Shakespeare* opened a fascinating window into the internecine interchanges between Shakespeare and his contemporary rivals and collaborators in the "War of the Theaters." In the introduction to *Ungentle Shakespeare* she had expressed strong doubt about the case for Hand D.

To me these attacks on Hand D were far more "seismic" than Foster's Elegy retraction, because I never bought Foster's claim in the first place. But from the very first I felt that in Hand D, especially in one extended speech by Thomas More, one could hear the "authorial voice" of Shakespeare. And that in the Hand C soliloquy, one could find images that were far more telling thematic "fingerprints" of Shakespeare than any of the "stylometric" statistical "fingerprints" that led Don Foster astray. Could I have been intuitively right about the Elegy, but intuitively wrong about Hand D?

Wrong about my sense of what is "Shakespearean"? Hand D might be a more stringent test of the validity of literary judgment in deciding what was "Shakespearean."

Let's begin with Werstine's attack on A. W. Pollard, long the most influential advocate for Hand D and one of the founding giants of the so-called New Bibliography that dominated twentieth-century Shakespearean textual scholarship. A movement whose arguments Werstine has devoted his life to dismantling—not deconstructing, but more literally taking apart. Deconstructionists argue that all speech is ultimately incoherent. Werstine argued that Pollard and his colleagues were coherent but *wrong,* in an old-fashioned way.

In any case Werstine finds a curious, hidden agenda behind Pollard's Hand D arguments that I had been unaware of. That an argument has an agenda doesn't disqualify it out of hand, but Werstine thought it (mis)guided Pollard's own hand in the Hand D question.

Werstine points out that there was, in the early twentieth century, a very vigorous and "very successful resistance movement against the 'anti-Stratfordians' [those who refused to believe Shakespeare, the "Stratford man," wrote Shakespeare] that was led by A. W. Pollard." Werstine notes that in Pollard's tone-setting Preface to his 1923 book that virtually canonized Hand D, one of the values Pollard ascribed to the demonstration that Hand D was "Shakespearean" was the ability to argue that "if Shakespeare wrote these three pages, the discrepant theories which unite in regarding the 'Stratford man'[i.e., Shakespeare] as a mere mask concealing the activity of some noble lord (a 17th Earl of Oxford, a 6th Earl of Derby or a Viscount St. Albans [Francis Bacon]) come crashing to the ground."

Crashing to the ground, in part at least, because one of the arguments the anti-Stratfordians use is the absence of virtually any sample of Shakespeare's handwriting. The only undisputed samples of Shakespeare's handwriting that survive are those signatures, none of his dramatic or poetic writing. Until Hand D. Hand D would flesh out his existence as a playwright.

Werstine is emphatically *not* an anti-Stratfordian. He is coeditor of the Folger Library edition of Shakespeare and he believes that the works he edited were written by "the Stratford man." However, one of the arguments he makes in the *Florilegium* paper ("Shakespeare, More or Less: A. W. Pollard and Twentieth Century Shakespeare Editing") is that Pollard was swayed by his campaign against the anti-Stratfordians to favor arguments that the hand-(writing) of Hand D matched the handwriting in the six signatures, as well as matching certain idiosyncratic spellings in the printed texts of Shakespeare's plays.

This is more than a tempest in a teapot, Werstine demonstrates: it's a tempest in *The Tempest.* Because, as he articulates the stakes in his paper, the enshrinement of Hand D in the Shakespeare canon means that it is being used as a *referent* in decisions about doubtful passages in other Shakespeare plays. In a small but important way Hand D is *rewriting* Shakespeare. Or as Werstine puts it: "What [we decide] Shakespeare wrote is being determined by how Hand D may have shaped the letters comprising what Shakespeare wrote."

THERE WAS SOMETHING REFRESHINGLY DOWN-TO-EARTH ABOUT Paul Werstine that stood out among the nobs of Shakespeare studies gathered amidst the riches, both physical and intellectual, of the Folger Library, where I first ran into him in a group of textual scholars at an MLA reception—among them Barbara Mowat, editor of *Shakespeare Quarterly* (and Werstine's coeditor on the Folger Library edition of Shakespeare), and Richard Knowles, editor of the MLA's *King Lear Variorum* edition.

Werstine stood out because he reminded me more of investigative reporters I knew than most textual scholars. In fact he reminded me, physically, of a somewhat younger version of Seymour Hersh. Same black glasses hiding intense eyes, slightly disheveled look, skeptical angle of the head—really he was almost a dead ringer for Sy Hersh. And in a similar way he was renowned and feared in his field for a Sy Hershian take-no-prisoners investigative skepticism: his belief that elaborate edifices of textual theory were essentially cover-ups for ignorance. He is much admired (and I suspect, like Hersh, feared) but he also has his critics such as the equally admired textual specialist Ed Pechter. Pechter has called Werstine a "textual nihilist."

I wonder if some of the aura of the ink-stained wretch (and I mean this as a compliment) came from the fact that Werstine's original specialty was the study of the ink-stained compositors in the type shops that produced Shakespeare's printed texts.

It was when Werstine turned from the type shops to the project of the New Bibliography, the textual studies tendency that dominated the twentieth century, that his investigative skepticism came into play. The New Bibliography hoped to work back from the printed texts in the type shops to find, beneath "the veil of print," the true hand of Shakespeare himself, the hand found in the lost manuscripts, the hand that would reveal which variations in two or more printed versions of the same play were printer's errors and which were Shakespeare's own reconsiderations, rethinking, rewriting, *currente calamo.*

Werstine's skepticism was a fierce weapon, Ockham's razor with a very sharp edge. Our conversation at the Folger reception, for instance, featured a fascinating (to me anyway) exchange about the so-called Bad Quarto ("Q1," 1603) of *Hamlet,* the truncated, garbled (but first published) printed text of *Hamlet* that preceded by a year the far fuller and more "Shakespearean" Good Quarto version, and the Folio version which wasn't published until seven years after Shakespeare's death in 1623.

Up until Werstine came along there were two main theories to explain the relationship of the Bad Quarto to the other two *Hamlets*. After Werstine (in a famous journal article) finished with them, there were *no* theories left standing.

Werstine had undermined the evidence the New Bibliographers used to prove the Bad Quarto was a "memorial reconstruction"—that is, cobbled together from memory by some actors who'd played parts in *Hamlet,* but who lacked a playhouse script perhaps because they were traveling in the provinces during the plague. An entire novelistic narrative of these imaginary wandering players, the putative memorial reconstructors, had been constructed with virtually no convincing evidence or historical corroboration, as Werstine (among others, including Eric Sams) had shown.

Then Werstine took on the new substitute explanation for the Bad Quarto by some of the so-called revisionists of the 1980s who argued that the Bad Quarto was not bad so much as *early*—Shakespeare's first draft, perhaps even a version of the lost ur-*Hamlet,* subsequently revised successively to produce the Good Quarto and then the Folio. Werstine made a powerful argument that this too was an evidence-challenged fantasy.

But, I asked Werstine, once you've demolished both explanations for the origin of the Bad Quarto, you've removed *any* explanation of how it got to be. And yet it *does exist;* it got there *somehow.* To which he said, essentially, "that's not my problem." It's not his problem, nonetheless it was a problem. But in a way he was not utterly disqualifying either solution, he was just demolishing the existing evidence for them. A fine distinction but an important one. I don't think Hand D came up in this discussion at the Folger but of course I was fascinated when I saw that he wanted to cast it too into the all-devouring black hole of his bottomless textual skepticism, his "textual nihilism" as Edward Pechter calls it.

And the Hand D controversy is at least as important in its own way as the Bad Quarto or the Elegy controversy in raising the question: Can we define and detect the "Shakespearean" and how? Here might be a good place to quote the key passages from Hand D (and the Hand C soliloquy) which had been widely accepted as "Shakespearean" before Werstine's attack. Still are, in fact.

The 147-line scene in question is particularly provocative politically because, if it's Shakespeare, it raises the question of Shakespeare's attitude toward authority, toward order and hierarchy, and in doing so invokes one of Shakespeare's signature images: violent self-devouring bestiality as—absent external restraint—the true nature of human nature.

Here's the situation: In 1517 during Thomas More's tenure as high sheriff of London a riot broke out among native (and nativist) London tradesmen and apprentices, a riot against foreigners, an anti-immigrant riot. To some degree, in that many of the immigrants were Italian or "swarthy," a race riot. The immigrants were accused of offering goods and services so cheaply they were ruining native merchants (it might be seen as one of the earliest anti-globalization riots).

There was a comic but sinister element to the riot, at least as depicted in Hand D: the "parsnip" allegation. The mob, often depicted in Shakespeare as filled with ignorant fools, blames the foreigners for spreading the plague, because the foreigners allegedly introduced the practice of eating root vegetables such as parsnips, which, one member of the mob says, "grow in dung [and thus] have infected us, and it is our infection will make the city shake [from a plague of palsy], which partly comes through the eating of parsnips."

It's clownish, but it echoes the allegations of "poisoning the wells" and causing plague which were a frequent excuse for murderous pogroms against Jews throughout medieval Europe. The suggestion that mob stupidity has its cruel and sinister side, one that turns on the weak and innocent, can be found just about anywhere a crowd is found in canonical Shakespeare.

And yet in the opening scenes of the play, as G. Blakemore Evans's edition of Hand D points out, in the non–Hand D scenes, the sympathy is with the immigrant-bashing nativist poor. One of the things that stands out about

Hand D is the apparent reversal and the sympathy shown for the immigrants.

In any case in the Hand D scene several high figures in the realm, including the lord mayor, fail to quiet the riot, until at last the crowd allows that it will hear from Thomas More, primarily because he came from humble origins like them. More then begins by asking the anti-immigrant crowd, What if we gave you what you asked for: the expulsion of foreigners? Here's how he conjures up the consequences for the mob:

Grant them removed and grant that this your noise
Hath chid down all the majesty of England,
Imagine that you see the wretched strangers,
Their babies at their backs, with their poor luggage
Plodding to th' ports and coasts for transportation,
And that you sit as kings in your desires,
Authority quite silenc'd by your brawl,
And you in ruff of your opinions cloth'd,
What had you got? I'll tell you: you had taught
How insolence and strong hand should prevail,
How [order] *should be quell'd . . .*

Okay then, More is saying, having painted a sorrowful picture of the victims of the mob's wrath, "babies at their backs, with their poor luggage / Plodding to th' ports . . .", if that's what you want, here are the consequences:

. . . and by this pattern
Not one of you should live an aged man,
For other ruffians, as their fancies wrought,
With self-same hand, self reasons, and self right,
Would shark on you, and men like ravenous fishes
Would feed on one another.

It was this passage, those last two lines in particular, that struck me immediately, intuitively as right—as having the unmistakable ring of Shakespeare's "authorial voice." This is true despite the fact that I'd first read the Hand D passage when I was in the midst of my polemical crusade against the Elegy's bogus attribution to Shakespeare, which made me even more predisposed to be doubtful of "Shakespearean" claims. But Hand D was suggestive in several ways.

First the "wretched strangers" passage with its echoes of those lines in *Lear* about the fugitive Edgar being watched for at "ports and coasts."

Then that image of the mob sitting as "kings in your desires": a critique of the mob, of unchecked narcissistic desire—and implicitly, almost subversively, of kingship—in a way that echoes the "hollow crown" soliloquy in *Richard II*.

Then that little flourish, that nice riff on "ruff" and "ruffians"—"in ruff of your opinions cloth'd" followed by "other ruffians," luxurious ruffs and roughnecks conflated—suggests the tossed-off metaphoric facility we find in what we know is "Shakespearean" dramatic verse.

SELF-DEVOURING

And finally, most suggestively, there is the thematic attitude toward authority, order and hierarchy in Hand D. Not one that derives from Divine Right, but a different attitude toward authority found in canonical Shakespeare. One that doesn't favor order for order's sake, for tradition's sake, for the sake of preserving the privileges of the privileged class. That's all ruff. It's rather an attitude that favors authority because it is often the only thing that protects the weak from the strong, restrains the unleashed tyranny of appetite, of self-devouring human nature—restrains the rough beast *within* human nature.

But more than anything it was the specific image the Hand D author used to embody that theme: an image of a future in which—if the mob had its way—a future mob would turn on this mob and "With self-same hand, self reasons, and self right, / Would shark on you, and men like ravenous fishes / Would feed on one another."

This image of self as self-devourer was at the heart of the thematic case made for Hand D, a case first made back in 1931 by a scholar named R. W. Chambers, when he compared it to a similar image, the locus classicus of self-devouring in canonical Shakespeare, the image that appears in the famous speech on "degree" Ulysses makes in *Troilus and Cressida*. This passage in Ulysses' speech in particular:

Take but degree away, untune that string,
And hark what discord follows. Each thing meets
In mere oppugnancy: the bounded waters
Should lift their bosoms higher than the shores,
And make a sop of all this solid globe;
Strength should be lord of imbecility,
And the rude son should strike his father dead . . .
And appetite, an universal wolf
(So doubly seconded with will and power),
Must make perforce an universal prey,
And last eat up himself. . . .

Ravenous fishes eating themselves up in *Sir Thomas More* and appetite a universal wolf that devours itself in *Troilus and Cressida.*

That just begins to catalog the places that self-devouring image appears in Shakespeare. The horrible line in *Lear* in which he consigns Cordelia to the company of savage cannibals who don't just eat each other but make their "generation messes." That is, make meals of their own progeny, eat their children.

And then there's the remarkable passage in *Macbeth,* one that describes the dark portents that follow the murder of King Duncan. It's a conversation between the all-purpose factotum and stolid reporter of war news, Ross, and a mysterious "Old Man."

ROSS: *And Duncan's horses (a thing most strange and certain),*
Beauteous and swift, the minions of their race,
Turn'd wild in nature, broke their stalls, flung out,
Contending 'gainst obedience, as they would make
War with mankind.

OLD MAN: *'Tis said, they eat each other.*

ROSS: *They did so—to th' amazement of mine eyes*
That look'd upon't.

What an amazing recurrent image. The passage first conjures up the wild and beautiful stallions and then makes a point of insisting that it was not a metaphor, not some folk tale with mythic resonance. No, when the Old Man raises the stakes and says " 'Tis *said,* they eat each other," the play's chief witness, Ross, affirms it—"They did so"—and reiterates that he was an eyewitness, and not just to the stallions going wild, "contending 'gainst obedience," but to the astonishing "fact" that the horses did "eat each other."

Again it's explicitly related to the breakdown of authority, but as in Hand D, where the self-devouring fishes "feed on one another," in *Lear* where fear is expressed that "Humanity must peforce / Feed on itself like monsters of the deep," and in *Troilus,* "appetite, an universal wolf," eats itself up—when you think about it, this is a physical impossibility. When you think about it further it's a metaphysical impossibility as well. Matter turning on itself and consuming itself. If, as it's said, you can't get something from nothing, neither can you get nothing from something. (In the most mundane terms if the horses in *Macbeth* did "eat each other" they both would grow fat with each other and yet disappear into each other—if you take the image literally. This reciprocal devouring seems to imply their mutual disappearance, just like the wolf which consumes itself into nonbeing. In a way just like Paul Werstine's polemics devouring both sides of an argument at once.)

It is almost as if this image, like the image of the exchange of bodies, souls, eyes, is one of those rich and strange, recurrent images that Shakespeare was drawn back repeatedly to worry over, revise, re-envision. That in these images of self-devouring we are somehow brought closer to Shakespeare, to his mind, to his imaginative preoccupations—his imaginative fingerprints if you will. The fact those fingerprints can be found in Hand D goes a long way to making it seem "Shakespearean" to me, indeed to help define what "Shakespearean" is—even though this is exactly what Paul Werstine warns against.

Perhaps even more interesting in this regard is another of what might be called "fingerprint passages" in *Sir Thomas More,* this one in what's known as the "Hand C addition," which many have also attributed to Shakespeare, although unlike Hand D it is not argued to be in his handwriting, but more likely that of a theatrical scribe who may have copied a Shakespearean handwritten addition to the play.

It's a twenty-one-line soliloquy that goes like this:

MORE: *It is in heaven that I am thus and thus,*
And that which we profanely term our fortunes

Is the provision of the power above,
Fitted and shap'd just to that strength of nature
Which we are born [withal]. Good God, good God,
That I from such an humble bench of birth
Should step up as 'twere to my country's head
And give the law out there. I in my father's life
To take prerogative and tithe of knees
From elder kinsmen, and him bind by my place
To give the smooth and dexter way to me
That owe it him by nature. Sure these things
Not physick'd by respect might turn our blood
To much corruption. But, More, the more thou hast
Either of honor, office, wealth, and calling
Which might accite thee to embrace and hug them,
The more do thou in serpents' natures think them,
Fear their gay skins with thought of their sharp
state,
And let this be thy maxime: to be great
Is, when the thread of hazard is once spun,
A bottom great wound up, greatly undone.

Setting aside its putative biographical interest—if it's Shakespeare, one could read into it more than a meditation on the rise of More from humble provincial beginnings; one could read into it Shakespeare meditating on his own rise ("in my father's life") to prominence in London from humble provincial beginnings.

And setting aside the stylistic tics that have the ring of Shakespeare—the two hendiadys ("smooth and dexter way" and "prerogative and tithe of knees")—there is that final couplet which invokes the image of a "bottom."

. . . to be great
Is, when the thread of hazard is once spun,
A bottom great wound up, greatly undone.

To be great, to be *at the top,* is to be "a bottom," literally a big old weaver's spool with the thread wound up on it. But to be great is simultaneously to come unwound, to come undone, to become—one almost might say—bottomless.

There is much unresolved controversy over the dating of *Sir Thomas More,* which makes it impossible to say whether the passage about the bottom was written before *A Midsummer's Night Dream* with *its* Bottom, and Bottom's bottomless dream.

But before or after, whichever way the influence might run, I felt an unmistakable kinship between the two "bottoms." The use of "bottom" in Hand C in the sense of spinning a thread (creating a story) is somehow connected with the undoing, the uncreating of a once-fat and solid bottom to the bottomlessness of a dream, of the *Dream*. And there is, I'd argue as well, a link between that image and the image of self-devouring in Hand D.

All in all, despite my Elegy-bred skepticism it was that bottom image that made me feel there was something to the *Thomas More* attributions.

Not so fast, says Paul Werstine. Not so fast, says Katherine Duncan-Jones. Duncan-Jones's disavowal comes mainly in passing in the Preface to her book *Ungentle Shakespeare,* so I asked her, in an e-mail, if she wanted to expand on her dismissal of Hand D. And before getting more deeply engaged with Paul Werstine's more comprehensive attack let me report what she replied:

> My doubts arise a) from the fact that half a dozen [alleged Shakespeare] signatures, all very late, and all giving the appearance of a hand in decay/haste do not constitute a sufficient sample for secure identification of the appearance of that hand overall; and from b) from the problematic nature of Shakespeare acting as scribe and/or poet for a rival playing company at a period of his career when he was particularly busy and successful. I know that at least one senior manuscripts expert at the British Library shares my skepticism,—but of course the BL has a lot "invested" in believing they hold a literary manuscript in Shakespeare's hand.

"INDIAN" OR "JUDEAN"?

So academic politics may play a hand in the Hand D controversy, but Paul Werstine felt the issue was more than academic, indeed, went to the heart of how we define Shakespeare, how Shakespeare is being redefined even now.

The example he cites of the consequences to what he believes is the over-hasty adoption of Hand D into the canon is its effect on one of the oldest, longest-lasting controversies in all Shakespearean textual scholarship. It has to do with Othello's final words. The almost unbearable farewell speech he makes in the wake of his discovery he'd been tricked by Iago into murdering the wife he loved to distraction, Desdemona. (Fascinating the way the last words of the great tragic figures—Hamlet, Lear, Othello—are all in dispute.)

In Othello's case, he pleads with the stunned witnesses to his deed to

Speak of me as I am . . .
Of one that lov'd not wisely but too well;
Of one not easily jealous, but being wrought,
Perplexed in the extreme; of one whose hand
(Like the base Indian) threw a pearl away
Richer than all his tribe . . .

Or is it not "Like the base Indian" but rather "Like the base Judean"? It's "Indian" in the 1608 Quarto of *Othello;* it's "Judean" in the 1623 Folio version—and the difference is not trivial. While "Indian" is found elsewhere in Shakespeare—the "spicy Indian night" in the *Dream,* for instance—if it's "Judean," it carries multiple deeper resonances. Othello as a Judas figure (*the base* Judean); the pearl, as in the biblical parable of pearls before swine, a Jesus parable reference. Combined with Othello's utterance immediately following this, his dying boast that "in Aleppo once" he "smote" a "turban'd Turk" as a loyal servant of a Christian state, it gives the tragedy a multiply ramified Christian framework focused on that single word, "Judean." If it is "Judean," and not "Indian."

Werstine points out how a recent editor, the much laureled textual scholar Ernst Honigmann, has used Hand D to come to a conclusion about whether it should be "Indian" or "Judean."

Honigmann is the author of the groundbreaking 1965 book *The Stability of Shakespeare's Text,* which actually argues for the *instability* of Shakespeare's text—because of the difficulty of deciding which variants are printers' or scribes' errors and which might be Shakespeare's changes, and how to decide between alternatives.

Werstine depicts Honigmann as having decided the Indian/Judean issue by examining the way the letters of the problematic word were formed, when those letters were used in the handwriting of Hand D, which is supposedly Shakespeare's. On the basis of Hand D's letter-shaping formation (the *I* a *J*? the *e* an *i*?), Honigmann believes the compositor of the Quarto

Othello misread Shakespeare's handwritten "Judean" as "Indian" and someone, maybe Shakespeare, thought the error serious enough to change it to "Judean" in the Folio version.

This is Werstine's problem: not that Honigmann is necessarily wrong about "Indian" or "Judean," but that he has made a crucial decision—a decision with implications for how we construe the theological vision of one of Shakespeare's greatest tragedies—on the basis of the hand of Hand D. This is what Werstine warned against when he said that the hand of Hand D was in a subtle way playing a part in "writing" or creating Shakespeare. All on the basis of what Werstine believes is inadequate evidence.

When I questioned him on the phone Werstine told me he never took the "Funeral Elegy" seriously, but said, yes, "this sort of thing" (deciding "Indian/Judean"-type questions) would be likely to happen if the "Funeral Elegy" attribution had not been discredited: decisions on crucial Shakespearean textual questions might well come to be decided on the basis of what we now see is an unquestionably discredited attribution.

Werstine's *Florilegium* attack on the Hand D attribution is strongest on the handwriting and spelling evidence. He points out that the argument that occasional idiosyncratic spellings in Hand D match some idiosyncratic spellings in the early printed texts of Shakespeare's plays falls apart without conclusive evidence that the early printed versions we have were set up *from* Shakespeare's handwriting and not (for instance) from earlier, no longer available printed versions or scribal transcriptions that reflect the scribe's, not Shakespeare's, spelling tics. "If some were and some were not" printed from Shakespeare's handwriting, as a critic Werstine quotes puts it, "the argument cuts its own throat." Self-devouring again.

That's harsh, but again Werstine isn't saying Hand D can't possibly be Shakespeare, he's saying that arguments on the basis of handwriting (the sacred "Six Signatures" matched to Hand D's controversial "Three Pages") and spelling are not strong enough to support any certainty.

But I found Werstine's arguments uncharacteristically less persuasive when it came to the *thematic* affinities between Hand D and canonical Shakespeare: the wolfish appetite devouring itself in *Troilus* and the devouring fishes feeding on themselves in Hand D, the parallel first suggested by R. W. Chambers. "In the Hand D segments," Werstine writes, the wolf from *Troilus,* which is paradoxically its own prey, and Hand D's fish that feed on each other both suggest "cannibal monsters" to Chambers. "To arrive at this parallel," Werstine says, "Chambers had to equate a creature's eating itself, which is hardly cannibalism in any sense of the word, to its eating another member of its own species."

A man devouring himself not cannibalism? Perhaps it's an arcane point, but here I felt like rising to Chambers's defense: if he hasn't expressed with exactitude the nature of the resonance between the wolf devouring itself and the fish feeding on themselves (by describing it as cannibalism, as opposed to "self-devouring," say), that doesn't deny that a resonance exists. To me it's still a significant point that Werstine doesn't really succeed in knocking down by knocking over the straw horse of "cannibalism." In attempting to dismiss the case for imagistic parallelism, one might say, Werstine mentions—without engaging—other such self-devouring image analogues found by other scholars in *Coriolanus, Richard II, King John, 2 Henry IV, Henry V, Julius Caesar, Othello, Timon of Athens* and *Macbeth.*

I was surprised to see the way he attempted to discredit these parallels: "in presuming that such patterns were self-evident in all these texts, none of these investigators offered a rationale for how their predecessors, who had also searched for the same patterns, had failed to find them."

This seems to be an argument that because everyone didn't see everything all at once, nothing is really there. It is skepticism as a ravenous wolf devouring itself, one might say. One might also point out that a reprint of the manuscript of *More* was not widely available until relatively recently, and the fact that earlier commentators had not thoroughly scoured all Shakespeare and thus missed some parallels, however derelict this might make them, shouldn't necessarily imply the parallels are false. The argument of one critic of the attribution cited by Werstine, MacDonald Jackson, that by 1985 there had been a "total absence of restraint" in finding further parallels to Hand D, may be just, but it does not necessarily entail that all parallels previously found are invalidated.

I must admit I was curious about this section of Werstine's paper since I'd always admired his skeptical restraint, always found the logical discipline of his argumentation so impressive. Here, however, with his attack on the Hand D thematic arguments, he seemed to skip a step or two in his eagerness to dismiss them.

For instance Werstine proceeds from MacDonald Jackson's objection to a bald assertion that "Shakespeareans do not seem to have noticed how they have knocked out *all* the support for Hand D's identification of Shakespeare" (italics mine). But he has not demonstrated this is true. He has shown that the support on the grounds of handwriting and spelling is weak and inadequate. But he has not demonstrated to my satisfaction that support on thematic and stylistic grounds has been "knocked out" by his quibble over "cannibalism," or the assertion that too *many* thematic parallels have been made.

He repeats this overstatement a few pages later, after scolding Honigmann over the Judean/Indian issue. Honigmann makes judgments based on Hand D "even after Shakespeareans have lost confidence in each kind of evidence . . . for the identification of Hand D as Shakespeare." But saying "Shakespeareans" he implies, without evidence, that *all* Shakespeareans have lost confidence in *each* kind of evidence, which is not the case. And he concludes by saying "all" the evidence "has been dismissed as inconclusive by Shakespeareans themselves."

Saying this three times does not make it true. I wondered what the source of this curious illogical animus on the part of the brilliant skeptical analyst of illogical agendas might be.

I began to get a hint of the frustration behind Werstine's uncharacteristic hyperassertiveness on Hand D when I spent an hour or so on the phone with him after reading his Hand D paper. He is, in person and on the phone, such a low-key, self-effacing, just-the-facts-ma'am sort of fellow that sometimes it's hard to connect this persona with the polemicist who becomes a sort of demon barber with Ockham's razor in his hand in his textual-skeptical prose.

But I sensed, as well, that his has been, in some ways, a thankless task. I mean *I'm* thankful for his work, but it's thankless in the sense that telling people we don't have the Answer, without offering a substitute Answer, by emphasizing all we do not know—rather than the little we can say with confidence we do know—about the heart of Shakespeare's mystery, is not felt as a comforting thing by many who would prefer not to live with uncertainty. Werstine was paying the price for the integrity of his negative capability: there was just so much supposition passing for truth out there in Shakespeare studies, he told me. So much supposition, so little time, so hard to scotch the snake(s).

One way of defining Werstine's role in Shakespearean controversy—and the controversy over what we call "Shakespearean"—can be found in a story he told me about meeting Harold Jenkins, the legendary editor of the 1982 second Arden *Hamlet,* one of the last avatars of the achievements and flaws of the twentieth-century school of Shakespearean textual scholarship known as the New Bibliography.

"You know," Werstine told me, "I read your piece on Harold in *The New Yorker* and it reminded me of the time I met him—only once in my life and that was in 1990 at the Malone Society's celebration of the two hundred years since Malone published his 1790 edition [of Shakespeare]. It was at Stratford-on-Avon, and I did something there [his characteristically self-effacing way of saying he gave a paper at that erudite gathering] and Harold approached me earlier, and you know in 1990 things were in ferment in textual studies—"

"The Oxford edition with two *Lear*s based on the principle of revision had just been published . . ."

"Yes, and it had raised a huge amount of controversy and things were really unsettled and so Harold approached me to caution me that what was most important in textual studies was 'good order.' "

"Good order meaning cleansing the text of ambiguities, resolving textual cruxes one way or another, making firm choices between 'sullied,' 'sallied' and 'solid,' for instance?" I asked.

"Yes, 'good order,' " Werstine repeated. "He definitely wanted to communicate this to me above all else."

"And your project really has been to unsettle good order, right?"

"Oh, I grant you that," he said, "I do. I do grant you that."

"Your project has been to make things messy."

"You're right. I have to confess," he said, laughing.

"I mean, you're not *against* 'good order,' you just feel there's not enough evidence to sustain some of these positions."

"Precisely. I have nothing against 'good order.' I just don't think the order we've had stands up. I don't think we have enough evidence."

I sought to trace the source of his skepticism about twentieth-century textual scholarship and discovered that he began his career pursuing the same dream as the so-called New Bibliographers: the dream of finding the true face of Shakespeare beneath "the veil of print." Werstine wanted to study with the man who coined that phrase, Fredson Bowers, whose lifelong project was to seek to reconstruct Shakespeare's lost handwritten manuscripts—to reconstruct his "original intentions" by working backward, so to speak, from the conflicts and idiosyncrasies in the early printed texts to the lost handwriting behind it.

Werstine, who had grown up in western Ontario, ended up studying at the University of South Carolina with T. H. Howard-Hill, an associate of Bowers, because he'd been deeply impressed by Howard-Hill's reconstruction of a shadowy little known figure in Shakespeare's life: Ralph Crane. Crane was a theatrical scribe employed by Shakespeare's company, and is known to have transcribed some of Shakespeare's now-lost manuscripts to make them readable and accessible for the playhouse and the printing house. Crane seems to have felt the liberty to add his own touches, including his own punctuation—often a crucial interpretive function. Crane's way of reading Shakespeare became his way of writing and, sometimes, some suggest, rewriting Shakespeare.

"The way I got into Shakespeare was through the back door," Werstine told me. "I got interested in the way that printing affects the texts we have and the best developed work, the leading edge of the field at the time in the early seventies was being done by T. Howard Hill and Leeds Barroll at South Carolina. My first textual essay was on the printing of the 1598 Quarto of *Love's Labor's Lost.* I looked at all the surviving copies in the British Isles, even one in Switzerland, and compared them letter by letter, punctuation mark by punctuation mark, and found some variants that hadn't been previously recorded. I used the Hinman Collator for identifying individually distinguishable damaged type and I did that with a magnifying glass and tried to plot the way it had been printed—very blindingly meticulous research."

The Hinman Collator: I'd read about this notorious Shakespearean textual editing machine, a contraption of lights and mirrors and magnifying lenses that Charlton Hinman, the legendary modern editor of Shakespeare's First Folio, used to locate the variants in the various printings of the First Folio (many changes were made during the print run resulting in many variations within copies of the First Folio) and the differences between Folio and Quarto versions of the same plays. I told Werstine about my conversation with Richard Proudfoot, specialist in Shakespearean apocrypha, in which he spoke of the experience of using the Hinman Collator, which Proudfoot described as like riding a stationary bicycle with flashing lights and mirrors.

"Oh yeah," Werstine said, "it is that. It's wonderful, a very spectacular thing to look at, but it's hard. Poor Hinman was almost blind by the end. And you get—you're pressing your head against the headset and you get this telltale angry red band across your forehead and this incredibly glazed look from being in strobe lights for hours. You're really quite a picture when you're done."

I liked the notion of the Scarlet Letter–like red brand of textual scholars.

And if it sounds a little silly, Werstine insists you could accomplish serious work with it.

"In this work it was possible, in some cases, to come up with some very substantial dependable evidence for certain arguments about the order in which the text was printed, which of the workmen was responsible for setting type for which page. In other words there was a level of probability you could achieve in studying the printing, something that I found very satisfying."

One could argue over the significance of the results. When I asked him, Werstine couldn't pinpoint any of the variants he'd discovered in his labor of love on *Love's Labor's Lost* that offered different *interpretive* readings of the passages involved. But on the other hand he was able to make a conjecture that might have tremendous importance: he came to believe there was a "Lost Archetype" of *LLL*—a lost manuscript or earlier printed version from which both the 1598 Quarto and the 1623 Folio were printed.

In fact, a couple of months before we spoke, evidence turned up, from an auction of a seventeenth-century bookseller's list, of a previously unknown *1597* Quarto of *LLL*. Not the thing itself, but a record of its existence. The significance of which helps confirm Werstine's suspicion of a Lost Archetype, but also corroborates speculations by others (not Werstine, who has not entered this controversy) that *Love's Labor's Lost* may have originally been printed with a sequel, *Love's Labor's Wonne,* a putative now-lost Shakespearean play that is mentioned in three different contemporaneous documents, but which (if it ever existed—many argue it's an alternative title for a play we already know by another name) has not survived.

So Werstine found his print shop work "very satisfying," but when he began to read more closely some of the "textual criticism or theories about the kinds of manuscripts that were supposed to lie *behind* the printed text," he told me, "it didn't seem one could achieve demonstrations of the same level of probability there at all. So you may say that my skepticism arose from that stuff."

"That stuff" being what he regards as generalizations unsupported by evidence. For instance the argument the New Bibliographers made that texts in which speech headings are more regularized (in which, say, "Queen" becomes more consistently "Gertrude") were more likely texts prepared for the theater, thus more likely a later draft and thus more likely to represent Shakespeare's alleged "final intentions" for his play as opposed to his "original intentions." It's a key component of the argument that the Folio versions of plays like *Hamlet, Lear,* and *Othello*—often filled with significant variations—are to be preferred to the earlier Quarto versions.

"That stuff"—claims based on unreliable suppositions—is clearly what Werstine believes the Hand D attribution is. And one senses he believes it will matter, because of the way Hand D is being used to rewrite Shakespeare in further Indian/Judean-type editorial decisions.

Gingerly, because I was reluctant to cross swords with a scholar who (unlike Don Foster) I actually thought *could* "destroy" me—in the sense that the depth of his grasp on these matters was bottomless compared to mine—I told Werstine that while I found his counterarguments against the handwriting and spelling evidence for the Hand D attribution formidable, I was less impressed with his argument against the thematic evidence. His attempt to discredit R. W. Chambers's focus on images of self-devouring—the ravenous wolf in *Troilus,* the ravening fishes in Hand D—with a quibble over Chambers's use of "cannibalism" to describe the images, for instance.

"Chambers did a splendid rhetorical job of bringing those passages into relationship," Werstine said. "But to the point of identity? I thought his way of doing it was more like *constructing* the relationship between the images."

I persisted, again gingerly, asking him about the image of the horses devouring each other.

Werstine knew it instantly and got the Folger edition of *Macbeth,* which he coedited with Barbara Mowat, and read it to me. "Duncan's horses . . . Beauteous and swift . . . 'Tis said, they eat each other."

"Isn't that meaningful?" I asked him, in relation to Hand D's evidence of mutual devouring.

"The thing that strikes me about the devouring images," he replied, "is that we read Shakespeare over and over again and we see correspondences like that, but we don't read the 350 other plays written before the closing of the theaters [by the Puritan regime] in 1642. I do, now, read a lot of those plays, they're not as accessible, popularly."

"And thus passages we think are echoes of Shakespeare may be echoes of other playwrights?" I asked.

"Yes, that's it," he said. It's also possible of course that the Hand D author was someone who read and mimicked Shakespeare.

But Werstine wanted to clarify, he told me, that he doesn't feel one could *rule out* Hand D as Shakespeare. He just feels the arguments for it are not decisive enough to use it as a foundation for making decisive arguments on other questions about plays we feel confident Shakespeare did write, such as *Othello*.

In fact, Werstine told me that when a book of essays—edited by one of his mentors, Howard-Hill—on Hand D came out in 1989, he reviewed it rather favorably without taking issue with the attribution.

"But then in a seminar on scholarly editing at the MLA in 1995 I heard skepticism expressed about Hand D being Shakespeare and I collected everything written about Hand D, and I saw how many people were abandoning different aspects of the evidence, but clinging to the belief in it because of what they'd call 'cumulative evidence' even though each aspect of the cumulative evidence had been abandoned."

The argument had become self-devouring! Or so he thought. I just couldn't go that final step with him to agree that the "self-devouring" image argument had been self-devoured, so to speak.

So was Hand D "Shakespearean"? To my mind far more probably than the "Funeral Elegy" ever was. But Werstine was a more formidable scholar than Don Foster. He was the real deal "Shakespeare super-sleuth." I don't feel as confident in staking my intuition as to what is and isn't Shakespearean against his skepticism. Not as confident as I was in staking my intuition against Don Foster's credulousness. Not confident enough in the handwriting evidence to believe *it* should decide the Indian/Judean matter (although I'd agree with Honigmann's "Judean" on other grounds).

Not confident certainly because of the self-devouring image alone. More persuaded rather because of the soliloquy (in Hand C), the one in which Sir Thomas More compares himself to a "bottom" whose thread is wound up and wound out.

To me, to my intuition, that bottom is the hint that the *Sir Thomas More* fragments partake of the bottomlessness that is uniquely "Shakespearean." But I wouldn't claim this is more than a subjective judgment. Not that the truth is relative here: Shakespeare either wrote or didn't write it. Some passages are "Shakespearean," some are not. But the fragmentary historical record does not afford the certainty that lies, in the philosophers' shorthand, "in the mind of God." Ultimately no matter how many numbers we crunch or stylistic tics we tick off, what we call Shakespearean will at times depend on the idea of "the Shakespearean" we project upon it.

IV

The Promise and Perils of Shakespearean "Originalism"

Chapter Seven

The Search for the Shakespearean in a Delicate Pause

I DON'T THINK I'LL EVER FORGET THE MOMENT. SIR PETER HALL, founder of the renowned Royal Shakespeare Company—who will certainly figure as one of the great Shakespearean directors, one of the great Shakespeareans, even in a history already four centuries long—is pounding the table in the small Greenwich Village restaurant in which we've been drinking and dining. He's accompanying his pounding fist, which is rattling the silverware in precise iambic pentameter time, with a booming vocal counterpoint: "daDUM, daDUM, daDUM, daDUM, daDUM . . . PAUSE."

It is that last word, that last command—"PAUSE"—that is at the heart, that is, one might say, the heartbeat, of Peter Hall's re-creation of Shakespeare's language, certainly his dramatic poetry. That PAUSE, it could be said, is the foundation stone upon which he built the grand edifice, both physical and cultural, that is the Royal Shakespeare Company. The troupe he founded to play at Stratford-on-Avon in 1959 has since become an international cultural institution that has embodied Shakespeare—some of the best, most dazzling Shakespeare of the twentieth century—including of course Peter Brook's *Dream,* Hall and John Barton's *Wars of the Roses,* and Trevor Nunn, Adrian Noble, Terry Hands and Nicholas Hytner's remarkable series of eye-opening productions.

Of course to say that the PAUSE, that moment for breath, that delicate moment of hesitant stasis, that brief instant of intentional silence at the end of an iambic pentameter line, is alone responsible for these achievements is to use a bit of hyperbole as well as synecdoche (the part, the pause, standing for the whole). The whole being what Hall calls "the Poel principles," after William Poel, who led a movement beginning in the late nineteenth century to return Shakespearean performance to its origins, to its original staging and verse-speaking styles—as much as they could be recovered or conjectured. A movement designed, at the very least, to strip away grandiose, scenery-centered stage conventions and florid, grandiloquent verse-speaking that had come, Poel believed, to obscure Shakespeare beneath a veil of kitsch. For Sir Peter the Poel principles were a way to unlock and release the power of Shakespeare's language, the "infinite energies" Peter Brook spoke of. The source of the spell.

For Sir Peter—who was in America to direct a New York production of *Troilus and Cressida* with American actors when we met—the Poel principles, which he learned at Cambridge along with his frequent collaborator (and sometimes dissenter) John Barton and Trevor Nunn, the third of the founding RSC trilogy, had their triumphant realization when, in the last half of the twentieth century, the RSC revolutionized the way Shakespeare was played and spoken. But the revolution's victories now seem imperiled to Hall, the gains about to be lost again, and he is genuinely upset.

"Only about fifty actors are left in the theater who really understand them," he'd told me bitterly as he worked himself up to a table-pounding fury over lack of respect for the Poel principles—and particularly the pause.

That pause at the end of the five-foot, ten-syllable iambic pentameter line in which almost all Shakespeare's dramatic verse is written, the pause he insists must be observed even in cases of "enjambment" (when the clause begun in one line doesn't end at the end of the line, but winds itself snake-like around to the middle of the next line, or the line after that). That pause *must* be marked by a brief intake of breath, Hall told me.

"John Gielgud once told me that he could go three lines without a breath, but if you study his work closely you will see that he often took a *small* breath"—the all-important PAUSE—"at the end of each line regardless," Sir Peter told me that evening.

"Now you've got my adrenaline going," he says as he returns to banging out the rhythm and the pause on the dinner linen. What got the adrenaline going was the sense of urgency he felt when I'd asked him about verse-speaking, about the "iambic fundamentalism" for which he's famous. An urgency, almost a desperation, that the key to speaking Shakespeare, to experiencing that which is truly Shakespearean, to getting *closer*—deeper inside—the language, is maintaining what Hall calls "line structure"—line structure that is *given* structure by that pause.

But before getting deeper into Sir Peter's anguished rhapsodic tribute to "line structure," to "iambic fundamentalism," to the neoclassical purity of the "Poel principles," I'd like to put his passions in the perspective of a broader, more multifarious, equally impassioned, sometimes table-pounding passion: the persistent search for Shakespearean origins. The persistent (if sometimes futile and inconclusive) search for the original way Shakespeare was spoken, written, played, heard. The search for the way Shakespeare himself heard the words in his head, when he wrote them, the way he heard the words as they were spoken in his Globe.

The search for origins is a search for Shakespeare's Shakespeare—and for whatever it was in his work that endowed it with the power to mesmerize his original audiences. What "Shakespearean" meant to Shakespeare and his audiences.

It's a quest that has led some to find the spellbinding power in the spelling itself: the "unmodernized spelling movement" argues that it can bring us closer not merely to the way Shakespeare spelled his words but to the way he *thought.* (See the following chapter.)

If the "unmodernized spelling movement" sounds a bit antiquarian, it is, in fact, when looked at closely, with the help of unmodernized spelling advocate John Andrews, an unexpectedly exciting approach to the quest for the Shakespearean.

And one could say that actor Steven Berkoff's quest for the symbolic "sword of Kean" (which was presented by Lord Byron to the eighteenth-century actor Edmund Kean after Kean made Byron faint from the power of his Othello) is a quest for what Berkoff believes was the original sword-to-the-heart *emotion* that Shakespearean acting evoked in audiences—spellbinding, faint- and fit-inducing emotion that reaches a horrid epitome with Berkoff's hellish re-creation of "the Original Shylock."

And it includes as well certain techniques of Shakespearean film—however anachronistic it might seem to view film as an Originalist mode. Peter Hall, for instance, spoke of the way Shakespeare's original, virtually bare-stage theater spaces at the Globe and Blackfriars allowed—in their very bareness, blankness and lack of cumbersome scenery and sets that had to be shunted off and on—the lightning-like "cinematic" jump cuts that Shakespeare built into his dramas, ones that would take you in an instant from Caesar's Tiber to Cleopatra's Nile.

But this sequence on origins really ought to begin with that night with Peter Hall, with that original table-pounding, grape-and-adrenaline-fueled tirade.

"THE NAKED SHAKESPEARE"

Though the subject of verse-speaking has "got his adrenaline going," he says, Hall hardly seemed the sort to need any artificial boost in adrenaline levels. Then past seventy, he was still a whirling dervish of theatrical fecundity and Falstaffian appetite. He'd just flown in from Denver, where he'd directed his massive ten-play, ten-and-a-half-hour Greek-myth marathon known as *Tantalus,* written by his longtime RSC collaborator John Barton. The two of them had made the RSC famous in the early sixties with another kind of marathon—their epic staging of Shakespeare's history plays under the rubric *The Wars of the Roses.*

And after a casting session for *Troilus and Cressida* here, he would fly to L.A. to direct *Romeo and Juliet* at the Ahmanson Theatre, after which he returns to New York to rehearse *Troilus* for an April opening at the Theater for a New Audience.

Jeffrey Horowitz, artistic director of TNA, had asked me if I'd like to appear on a panel about *Troilus* with Sir Peter and others, and so I ended up joining the two of them to discuss the play over dinner at a cozy Hudson Street place called the Greenhouse.

Troilus, of course, is perhaps the most bitter play Shakespeare wrote. For centuries, it had been a minority taste because it's so vicious and dark, but really, who in our time could *not* love a play that ends with a dying pimp wishing his venereal diseases upon the audience?

It's a play so relentlessly caustic and corrosive, so bleak and melancholy, it's almost as if it were written not in ink but in black bile. But it's fun, too, to see all the piety that Western culture has lavished upon mythic, Homeric warrior-heroes such as Achilles and Agamemnon lampooned as wickedly and savagely as Shakespeare does in *Troilus.* One way to think of *Troilus* is not merely as a satiric revision of Chaucer's lovely *Troilus and Criseyde,* but as Shakespeare's disillusioned and hostile rewrite of the romanticism of *Romeo and Juliet,* played by a cast of fools and degenerates from Homer.

As Sir Peter summed up its unappetizing cast of characters that evening: "Troilus is in many respects a fool, Cressida a manipulative tart, Ulysses a very scheming, amoral politician; Pandarus is a pimp; Agamemnon's a fool; Ajax is a dope; Achilles is a narcissistic, irresponsible queen. I mean, one could go on. You know, if you asked a Broadway producer whether we should do this, he'd say no. He'd say—"

"Where's the love?"

He laughs. "Pandarus—I mean, please, that last speech . . ."

Pandarus' final speech: it takes place after Troilus has been betrayed by Cressida, after the one unblemished hero in the play, Hector, is killed and mutilated on the field before Troy, and Troilus takes out his rage at Cressida's betrayal by striking Pandarus. End of play. At which point Pandarus steps forward—much as Puck does at the end of the *Dream.* But not with a humble plea, rather with a curse. Pandarus steps forward from the world of Troy, the world of the play, and turns upon the audience and addresses them directly, addresses them as if they were fellow pimps:

"O traders and bawds, how earnestly are you set a-work, and how ill requited! Why should our endeavor be so lov'd and the performance so loath'd?"

After some further abuse, again addressing the audience as fellow pimps, he foretells his own death:

Brethren and sisters of the hold-door trade,
Some two months hence my will shall here be made.
It should be now, but that my fear is this,
Some galled goose of Winchester would hiss.

Winchester was a precinct that permitted prostitution; "a galled goose" is a whore covered with venereal sores—sweet, no? Then the final vicious couplet:

Till then I'll sweat and seek about for eases,
And at that time bequeath you my diseases.

I asked Sir Peter for a reaction to a question Shakespearean biographers have been debating about *Troilus:* "Do you think *Troilus* reflects some sort of Shakespearean nervous breakdown into a kind of utter, bitter bleakness, or is it the play when the mask drops and the bleakness that was *always* there in Shakespeare makes itself apparent?"

"I think *that's* the reality, yes," he says, meaning the latter. "I think it's the reality. I think he wrote two plays with an absolute, arrogant indifference to the public or whether the public liked them or understood them. And one is *Troilus* and the other is *Hamlet.* I mean, *Hamlet* lasts four hours fifteen minutes. And he didn't care a fuck. 'Really,' he said, 'this is what I want to write.' And with *Troilus*—"

"He gave Pandarus that last speech, wishing venereal disease on the audience."

"Oh, amazing," he says. "I mean, that is a man who hates his audience. Really."

"So this is the naked Shakespeare, do you think?"

"I think it is the naked Shakespeare, yes. Because there's something of the same note in *Timon of Athens.* But there's nothing bleaker, I think, in the whole canon than *Troilus.* The eighteenth and nineteenth centuries couldn't abide the play. I mean, the Enlightenment—[*Troilus*] reduces the whole of human life to lechery and war, and the Victorians were shocked out of their minds by it."

The naked Shakespeare: Perhaps we'll never know if this Shakespeare, the Shakespeare of *Troilus,* is a more true and authentic Shakespeare—the "original" Shakespeare—than the one of *Romeo and Juliet* or *As You Like It,* or just another mask.

But there is a way, Sir Peter believes, to get closer to the language in which that nakedness is clothed. If dreams are "the royal road to the unconscious," as Freud maintained, then verse-speaking, line structure—those "Poel principles" Sir Peter devoutly believes in and crusades for, the ones that he believes return us to origins, Shakespeare's original intention for speaking and staging his work, the ones that "get his adrenaline going"—are the royal road to Shakespeare's soul. In any case, it was the Royal Shakespeare Company's royal road from its founding in 1959, for the fifteen years Sir Peter presided over it, a period that revolutionized Shakespearean staging until he left to take over the Royal National Theatre from Laurence Olivier.

And it all comes down to those Poel principles, he says.

THE STATIONMASTER'S SON

The Poel principles: "Only fifty actors who know the Poel principles?" I asked.

"And about a half-dozen directors, and that's it," he said. "The actors are all avid for it; directors aren't. Directors tend to pretend to know about verse when they don't."

William Poel (1852–1934) sought to replace the leaden pace of plays originally played on bare stages with rapid, fluid scene changes. Poel and his disciples, such as Harley Granville-Barker, and supporters such as George

Bernard Shaw sought to restore what they believed made Shakespearean staging so unique—those fluid lightning-like scene changes that anticipated cinema. (Many of the first printed texts of Shakespeare's plays are almost completely without act and scene divisions, just entrances and exits—implying that the action should be continuous—or at least not formally, laboriously, divided up.)

Even more important, Poel sought to restore what he believed to be the way Shakespeare was originally spoken, "trippingly on the tongue," as Hamlet tells the Players, rapidly but in a way that preserved the pentameter rhythm and the "line structure."

Enter Peter Hall. He was born in 1930, the son of a railway stationmaster, something I find fascinating for someone who is famous for wanting to make the verse run on time, so to speak; to make it follow a rhythm he might have become attuned to from the iambic beat of the steam-engine pistons, or the click-clack of the tracks. (The celebrated Shakespearean voice coach Patsy Rodenburg compares the iambic beat to the heartbeat—the lub/DUP, lub/DUP.) It turns out that his father's occupation was crucial to his finding his calling in Shakespeare, he tells me: a free rail pass permitted him to travel to London at an early age to see a lot of theater, but his life changed when he was twelve years old and saw John Gielgud's legendary *Hamlet.*

The transformative moment occurred in Cambridge. "I saw Gielgud play Hamlet in 1942 when I was twelve, and that was what fixed me. I saw Olivier play Richard III and Ralph [Richardson] play Falstaff; Peggy Ashcroft." He still prefers Gielgud's Hamlet over Olivier's more famous film performance, he says: "The problem with Olivier's Hamlet on film is that [the way he played the prince] he would have killed Claudius very quickly. He's too direct. There's this forty-year-old man who would obviously kill *anybody.*"

And Gielgud?

"Oh, tortured, tortured. But I never—I mean, I was friends with them both and I worked with them both later, but I never took the view they were opposite poles. They're much more like each other than they gave out." An emotional iambic—complementary elements, with different stresses, but the same heartbeat.

And Ralph Richardson's Falstaff?

"Oh, probably the best performance I've ever seen. He was great, great—greatest actor I've ever seen."

Charged up by these electrifying performances, Hall went to Cambridge as an undergraduate in order to learn how to direct Shakespeare. There he encountered two major literary figures who influenced the way he'd do it: F. R. Leavis, who inculcated an attentiveness to the text, to close reading; and George Rylands, a disciple of William Poel whom Hall met as a member of the influential Cambridge Marlowe Society.

"It [the Marlowe Society] was started in 1907, the idea being to speak Shakespeare as Poel taught it and bring Shakespeare back to the clarity Poel preached. George Rylands, by the time I got there, which was forty years later, was the don in charge and he taught all of us—John Barton, Trevor Nunn, Jonathan Miller, Richard Eyre—the principles of Poel's verse-speaking." It is a stunning list, those Poel disciples, some of the greatest Shakespearean directors of the past century.

There are two chief elements to the Poel principles of verse-speaking, and Peter Hall is known far and wide for the first one, for what some have called "iambic fundamentalism," his stress on respecting the five-beat da-DUM, da-DUM meter in speaking Shakespearean verse. And he hasn't retreated from that one bit, even if it's responsible for a reported esthetic rift with his collaborator John Barton, who has dared to depart from Hall's strict fundamentalism with his emphasis not on the pause but on the *antithesis*—the way Shakespeare builds "speech structure," you might say, upon the foundation of oppositional pairs such as—at its most basic—"To be or not to be."

But during dinner Hall's emphasis was less on the internal iambic stresses of the line and more on the second element in Poel's verse-speaking dictates: the line-ending pause that defines and preserves what he calls "line structure": the integrity of the single line of Shakespearean verse as an esthetic unity. It's all about the pause at the end, regardless of whether the line is "enjambed"—that is, when the sense or "natural progression" of a sentence or clause runs around the end of a line.

The principles of line structure "are very simple," Hall told me that evening: "You breathe on the end of a line; you never breathe in the middle. You think of it as a whole line, not as a series of words. You find where the meter makes your accent, which is usually alliterative." He's speaking of "accent" as opposed to "stress"—not the five stressed syllables in the ten-syllable iambic line. By accent he means those words in a line which receive a *special* stress.

To illustrate, he intones Antonio's famous opening line from *The Merchant of Venice:* "In sooth, I know not why I am so sad."

" 'Sooth' and 'sad' are the accented words," he says. As I understand Hall, such dictates are not designed to regiment reading in a metrical straitjacket, but to allow the internal dynamics counterpoised within the line to emerge, to allow the relationships between sound, stress and sense implicit in the ordering to blossom, to allow notes to merge as chords rather than jangle in discord. Indeed, Hall prefers to refer to the Shakespearean text as "the score" or the "scoring" (he's directed numerous operas as well), and it's only proper verse-speaking that, he believes, can unlock the musical potential in each line of the score.

"You can't appreciate Mozart if you play the wrong notes or the wrong tempo; you've got to start by getting that bit right."

And a delicate pause at the end of each line is essential to line structure. In his recent book *Shakespeare's Advice to the Players,* Hall refines the reference so it's no longer a "pause" but "a tiny sense break (not a stop)." A more delicate, elegant interval than a naked "pause" suggests.

Hall recited the opening lines of *Troilus and Cressida* as an example:

In Troy, there lies the scene. From isles of Greece [*pause*]
The princes orgulous, their high blood chaf'd, [*pause*]
Have to the port of Athens sent their ships . . . [*pause*]

"Now if you run on around the line ends, you don't understand it."

EXPOSED BY THE MASK

The trouble in reconstructing the original form of Shakespearean acting, the original form of Shakespearean *anything,* is the tragic historical pause, really a gap: the closing of the theaters in 1642 by order of the Puritan Parliament (which thought the playhouse Satan's playground), a gap that lasts some two decades until the Restoration relaxed the ban.

Up till the 1640s most of those who played Shakespeare could do so with the living memory of how it was played and spoken in Shakespeare's own lifetime, often by Shakespeare's own company of players.

By the 1660s anyone who saw *Hamlet* when it was first performed in 1601 or so would likely be in his eighties at least; there were very few actors whose careers spanned the gap and almost none from Shakespeare's time. (I suppose you could imagine one of the boy actors who played women in Shakespeare's company tutoring an actor in the 1660s.)

I've mentioned the conjecture about an "Unbroken Chain of Hamlets"—the theory that at least one actor who saw the first Hamlet, Richard Burbage, then played Hamlet and was then seen playing Hamlet by another actor, who was then seen playing Hamlet by a person who would have seen the person who saw Burbage etc., etc., down through the centuries to John Gielgud and then finally to Laurence Olivier who made a movie which could be seen forever by anyone. The implication—that knowledge or witness of playing Hamlet, traces of Shakespeare's original Hamlet, have somehow been preserved to this day—is hard to sustain. Indeed some might say earlier is not necessarily better, that there might even be improvements, if one isn't a purist or doesn't believe that Richard Burbage must have done it definitively for all time.

Thus "Originalism" in the strictest sense is a pretty shaky theory on which to found any conclusions on how Hamlet was or should be played, alas, and very little description of "original" acting styles and direction has survived from Shakespeare's time anyway.

More is known about the Shakespearean stage, in particular its absence of scenery, its relative bareness (based on a single surviving contemporary sketch of the Globe stage, most believe there were just two pillars on either side of the stage, two doors in the rear, and a smaller "second story" for balcony scenes and the like). A stage like this served as a blank screen on which the audience was invited to project its own imaginative (filmic one might say) background for the action and characters.

As for how to speak Shakespeare, we do have Hamlet's famous advice to the Players, but even if we make the risky assumption that this is the "naked Shakespeare" speaking through his character, rather than an expression of that *character's* character, so to speak, it doesn't tell us everything. Or it gives license for a number of variant styles that can claim they're following Hamlet's dicta. "Suit the action to the words," for instance, is a coat of many colors that could cover any number of emotional colorations and gestures.

But since it is the locus classicus for all Originalist attempts to reconstruct the naked Shakespeare, it is worth reprinting in full Hamlet's advice to the Players:

> Speak the speech, I pray you, as I pronounc'd it to you, trippingly on the tongue, but if you mouth it, as many of our players do, I had as lief the town-crier spoke my lines. Nor do not saw the air too much with your hand, thus, but use all gently, for in the very torrent, tempest, and, as I may say, whirlwind of your passion, you must acquire and beget a temperance that may give it smoothness. O, it offends me to the soul to hear a robustious periwig-pated fellow tear a passion to tatters, to very rags, to split the ears of the groundlings, who for the most part are capable of nothing but inexplicable dumb shows and noise. I would have such a fellow whipt for o'erdoing Termagant [a stock character in crude Punch and Judy type shows], it out-Herods Herod [a stock villain in medieval mystery plays], pray you avoid it.

The tenor of Hamlet's speech argues for naturalism, as we'd call it, against melodramatizing. And yet it must be recalled that earlier in the play when Hamlet asks the Players for a "taste of your quality" when they first arrive at Elsinore, the speech he specifies he most wants to hear is one of the most purple-passaged tear-jerkers anyone can imagine—the one about the murder of Troy's King Priam and the maddened grief of Hecuba his wife. And yet Hamlet seems to admire this "dream of passion," indeed he has it memorized and begins it himself, and later admits to envy the Player's ability to drive himself to tears with his own hyperbolic passion. "What's Hecuba to him?" Hamlet marvels. Is the fact that Hamlet is unmoved a critique of Hamlet (his comparative numbness) or the lines (their melodramatizing)?

Hamlet's advice to the Players seems almost overdone in its animus toward over-emoting, "tearing a passion to tatters." There is a disdain for the multitude ("the groundlings . . . are capable of nothing"), for common humanity, that could be taken as condescension. It makes one wonder whether one can confidently say that Hamlet's words faithfully reproduce Shakespeare's own attitude or whether they might instead mock the sort who sneer that a truly good play is "caviar to the general"—too rich for common taste. On the other hand one could believe him to be reacting judiciously to the over-purpling of the passage.

What *was* Shakespeare's own attitude? Ever since that maddening gap, when the theaters were closed, theories about "original" Shakespearean speech are largely conjectures based less on evidence than on the temperament and projection of the theorist.

Acting styles have tended to alter in an iambic rhythm. The Restoration productions of Shakespeare were often ridiculously altered (the most famous example being Nahum Tate's *Lear,* which has a happy ending—Cordelia rescued to marry Edgar at the end) and were said to have featured a high-flown poesy-like style of recitation, a style eclipsed by the riveting naturalism of David Garrick, the first post-Restoration Shakespearean "star." Whose style was succeeded by the hyperemotionalism of Edmund Kean, famous for causing Lord Byron to swoon into a dead faint at his production of *Othello.* Variations on Kean's stagy but mesmeric expressionist style that "tore a passion to tatters" were the ideal until the advent of the Poel disciples, who sought restoration of Hamlet's more naturalistic advice to the Players. And recently, in certain respects, Shakespeare-on-film also paradoxically permitted a return to a more modest, reinvigorated naturalism.

Actually "formalism" or "neoclassicism" is a better word for what Hall and Barton reinvigorated at the RSC. (Hall called his *Troilus* "neo-classical.") At the time Hall was called upon to form the company in Stratford in 1959, Shakespearean acting was wavering between the poles of Olivier's staccato expressionism and Gielgud's refined and melodic intellectualism.

But Poel's vision offered something to Hall deeper than these mood swings. The focus on Poel principles, on the "integrity of the line structure," had its own intrinsic esthetic reward to Hall. It made Shakespeare *work,* he felt, in a way that Hall could hear—and learn from, get deeper into.

"I remember, about 1961 or '62," he told me, "in the old rehearsal room at Stratford, suddenly knowing that I *knew,* and that I would *always* know, what the line structure was when I heard a Shakespearean speech. Just from listening. And that's because I had done so many years of it that it was ingrained in me, and I remember it clicked and I thought, *'Christ!'* And the consequence is I can hardly watch most Shakespeare, because it irritates me when it's not used. It does have an effect on you. It's like learning music."

The integrity of line structure: it must be maintained even when a single line of five beats is split between two characters. Particularly then.

Hall cites an example from *Twelfth Night,* a key line shared between Olivia and Viola. Disguised as the male page Cesario, Viola has come to Olivia on behalf of her patron Orlando, to woo Olivia on Orlando's behalf. Olivia has refused to respond to Orlando, but does respond to the male impersonator intermediary Viola, who tells Olivia how he/she would woo Olivia if it were him/her and not his/her lord, Orlando, doing the wooing. How she would be relentless:

VIOLA/CESARIO: . . . *O, you should not rest*
Between the elements of air and earth
But you should pity me!
OLIVIA: *You might do much.*

"Read it as one line—'But you should pity me!' 'You might do much'—and it's beautiful. She's in love! But if you do it with a pause between the two half lines, you lose fifteen to twenty seconds. You lose everything! I've done this for forty years, and if you do it right it always, *always* works! So many productions take much too long because actors are inserting unnecessary heavy pauses and sighs when it should move along lightly, like Mozart."

Agree or disagree—and I'm not sure a lovelorn pause there doesn't work as well—you must give the man credit. He really, urgently cares about this. With all his achievements, all his laurels, his knighthood, you sense that Sir Peter feels deeply embattled, fighting what might be a losing battle on a question whose stakes are immensely high: recovering, rescuing from obfuscation the naked Shakespeare—or at least the most fully embodied Shakespeare. Releasing, unleashing, uncoupling from the line structure the full power, depth and musicality of an artist who is inexorably slipping further and further and further from our grasp across the abyss of centuries.

Hall spoke of attending a conference on verse-speaking sponsored by the Royal National Theatre the previous year, 1999, in which it was generally agreed that we are perhaps the last generation for whom Shakespearean speech will be immediately intelligible at *all*—as opposed to intelligible only through the kind of half-translation often used to render Chaucer's Middle English. That precarious intelligibility is what makes the disappearing art of verse-speaking even more vital to preserve, since he believes the One True Way is known now to but fifty actors and a half-dozen directors.

It may sound fanatical, and it should be said that many scholars and directors dissent from the Poel principles or the strictness with which Hall applies them. But I know I've profited immensely from Peter Hall's method. I know I found exposure to the Royal Shakespeare Company verse-speaking style transformative when I first experienced it at Stratford, when I saw, back-to-back, two amazing RSC productions: Trevor Nunn's *Hamlet* and Peter Brook's *Midsummer Night's Dream.*

Nothing prepared me for the astonishing offhand *clarity* of the verse-speaking. It wasn't conspicuously emoted; it was expressed as if the actors were thinking it up for the first time. It was like experiencing Shakespeare for the first time. After Hall and Nunn left, the sparkling clarity of the verse-speaking has been maintained at a high level by their longtime associate Cicely Berry.

I loved talking about *Troilus* with Sir Peter. It's a play that I've found more and more depths to each time I reread it. It's a play he's been wanting to do again for nearly four decades, he told me, ever since he did it at Stratford in 1962, in a run that derived an added antiwar frisson when it coincided with the Cuban missile crisis.

But it's more than an antiwar play, he suggests: "It's a play about lust in *all* its forms"—warlike lust for blood, the lust for power, as well as plain old lechery and the war between the sexes.

One of the things that occurred to me while rereading *Troilus* this time was that there was a deeper connection between Peter Hall's verse-speaking obsession and a preoccupation close to the heart of this particular play.

Consider that most famous and controversial speech in the play, Ulysses' praise of "degree," the one whose image of self-devouring is so crucial to the Hand D debate. Consider the way the speech at one point describes degree and order with a musical metaphor:

Take but degree away, untune that string,
And hark what discord follows.

Reading the degree speech this time, it struck me (I'm sure it's occurred to others) how it was as much a meditation on order and structure in *art* as it was on politics and statecraft.

The invocation in the degree speech, to "Insisture . . . proportion . . . [the] line of order," could be Peter Hall insisting upon the importance of metrical regularity and ordered line structure. ("Insisture" carries connotations of persistence and regularity.)

That these are esthetic as much as political preoccupations is signaled by the central metaphor in the degree speech, which comes from music: "Take but degree away, untune that string, / And hark what discord follows."

The pentameter-ending pause and the line structure it preserves, Hall insists, are not repressive and confining, but can be expressive and liberating. The way (to use an anachronism) the sense of formal containment of one of Pope's rhyming couplets allows it to resonate—ring with precision, ring in tune—within its expansive two-line architecture. The way the grace of the ballet depends on the base of rhythmic structure from which the balletic leaps, the graceful spins and pirouettes take off. The way much improvisation in jazz arises not from nothing, not from noise, but from a melodic or rhythmic base. "Untune that string," the degree speech concludes, on an apocalyptic note, and "the bounded waters" of the earth will overflow "and make a sop of all this solid globe"—return it to the formless mud that preceded creation. The iambic line is like a "bounded water" whose boundedness—that pause—gives resonance and definition to its waves and tides, its riptides and undertows, whose complex interactions are so characteristic of what we call "Shakespearean."

There's an ambiguous reference to masks in the "degree" speech* that reminded me of a conversation I had about Peter Hall with a somewhat embittered Shakespearean actor (Steven Berkoff) who complained—without having seen it—about Peter Hall's use of masks in his ten-part *Tantalus* epic. Of course, almost all classical Greek drama was played with masks, but Berkoff argued, in a very actor-centric way, that Sir Peter's use of masks would deprive the actors of their identities, their gratifying audience recognition, their chance to make individual impressions, their chance to be *stars.* Instead it made the director (Sir Peter) the star.

But in fact, by all accounts, Hall used a different kind of mask in *Tantalus*—not traditional rigid masks that obscured the facial expressions of the actors, but flexible masks that clung to the contours of the features and gave an expressive structure to the face, one they could play up or play against, heightening and complexifying the drama of their utterances.

The masks were analogous, in a way, to Hall's notion of line structure and "iambic fundamentalism": line structure is a kind of esthetic mask, a structure, a fundamental (in the musical sense) that heightens expressiveness by playing up the tension between form and feeling within each line, tensions that would slacken, lose their riptides and overtones if lines were run around willy-nilly without the defining pause, or moment of *poise,* at the end.

An expressiveness that is "Exposed by the Mask"—to use the ironic title Hall gave to the recently published version of the Clark Lectures he delivered at Cambridge, the place he first encountered the Poel principles.

But this is a rather academic defense of line structure. I came across a rather more playful and seductive one later on in *Troilus.* A Shakespearean defense of line structure. It's at the heart of one of the most controversial

* ". . . Degree being vizarded, / Th' unworthiest shows as fairly in the mask."

moments in the play. Troilus and Cressida's *Romeo and Juliet*–like rendezvous has been interrupted: she is told she must be taken from Troy and from Troilus to join her father in the Greek camp. Unlike Romeo, Troilus doesn't put up much of a fight, and unlike Juliet, Cressida doesn't try to remain faithful 'til death.

Instead, when she gets to the Greek camp, she exchanges repartee and kisses with the Greek generals who greet her; soon she'll become the concubine of one of them.

Here's how Ulysses characterizes Cressida's initial flirtatious behavior:

There's language in her eye, her cheek, her lip,
Nay, her foot speaks; her wanton spirits look out
At every joint and motive of her body.

So ostensibly it's about seductive behavior by a woman—but couldn't it also be seen as evoking the seductive power of language? There's "language in her eye," "her foot speaks." And perhaps that last phrase, "her foot speaks," suggests that it's about a particular kind of language, poetic language—whose unit is the line made up of iambic "feet," the technical term for a da-DUM unit of iambic pentameter. It could suggest an analogy between the way a woman deploys the "line structure" of her body ("every joint and motive") and the way the body of a poem deploys the line structure of verse: each releases "wanton spirits," seductive energy. It could suggest one of those moments in which Shakespeare's language can be felt expressing pleasure in its own art. The seductiveness of language and the language of seductiveness in those lines about Cressida subvert Ulysses' official disapproval of her behavior. It suggests that both he and Shakespeare are really on her side, seduced by Cressida's poetry in motion—her *lines*—almost against their will.

How then explain what Sir Peter called Shakespeare's hostile attitude toward sex in some of those bleak, middle-period, "nervous breakdown" plays?

"I believe he was betrayed very badly," he said over dinner. "And I believe he tried to hate sex. And I believe he couldn't."

It's the very dynamic that seems to be going on in Ulysses' description of Cressida's "wanton spirits." He tries to condemn her, but he can't. The seductiveness of "line structure"—in every sense of the phrase—is just impossible to resist.

THE EDELSTEIN VARIATION ON THE HALL PAUSE

While I took much away from my exposure to Peter Hall's impassioned pleas for iambic fundamentalism, it wasn't until a couple of months later that it *clicked* for me in the same way it "clicked" for Peter Hall in a rehearsal room in Stratford. It clicked for me in a rehearsal room on Thirteenth Street in New York City, in a Shakespeare-speaking workshop conducted by Barry Edelstein, artistic director of the Classic Stage Company.

Edelstein had founded the CSC after studying Shakespeare at Oxford as a Rhodes scholar, teaching seven years at the Juilliard School and directing a number of productions for Joe Papp's New York Shakespeare Festival. He's considered, along with Brian Kulick and Karen Coonrod, to be one of the rising stars among American Shakespearean directors, and this workshop was attended mainly by actors who wanted to get deeper into Shakespearean verse-speaking. I felt fortunate to be invited but could not have expected the way Edelstein's interpretation of Hall's line structure suddenly made it leap into focus for me—and changed the way I read and spoke Shakespeare. Edelstein had studied with Hall and with the RSC's Cicely Berry, but he'd developed his own rationale for that all-important pause that defined Hall's line structure.

I asked Edelstein how he came up with his interpretation of Hall's stricture on structure. "Barton and Hall had codified the traditions, but when I was studying in England," he told me, "I had an old friend, Robert Clare, who was an actor in the theater who had assisted Peter Hall on the late plays [*The Winter's Tale, Cymbeline, The Tempest*], and he had become a Shakespeare teacher and he took me through what Hall was doing. And then when I got back to New York I started directing and started teaching, and I basically reshuffled and straightened out in my mind what was going on and it's just evolved over years working with students and directors to what you saw in that workshop. And it was my own reading and experimenting and having to explain it to young drama students."

"What puzzles me," I said, "is that your notion makes so much sense of what Hall was doing. Why wouldn't Hall himself, in the course of his long tirade on the pause, have mentioned this interpretation of it, which makes so much more than technical esthetic sense out of line structure? It is from him, isn't it?"

"Well, no, that's *my* interpretation of the source of its power," Edelstein said.

Perhaps it's past time to disclose what Edelstein has done to explain and energize Hall's neoclassical notion of line structure, how Edelstein explains that all-important pause.

Up until then I had what I think was an imperfect, only partial understanding of Hall's line structure. I've made the anachronistic analogy to Alexander Pope's eighteenth-century rhymed couplets, each of which created a self-contained crystalline world of echoes, resonances, reverberations contained in the mirrored, jewel box–like interior of the two-line couplet. An interior that was dazzling and fiery and yet (and only *because*) self-contained. As I'd understood Peter Hall before Edelstein's workshop, the ten-syllable pentameter line was its own self-contained jewel box whose containment, whose internal dynamic, depends on the esthetic closure given it by that final pause for breath.

There's another more explicitly Shakespearean analogy one can make: the restrictive form of the Sonnets—a delimited architecture of fourteen lines, a formal rhyme scheme concluding with a couplet, an architecture whose formality defines and contains the pulsating language within. As a devotee of close reading, Hall's line-structure-punctuated-by-a-pause had a particular appeal to me because in effect it made each line a single poem to be read closely. Not that this was the only way to read Shakespeare's lines but that it revealed just how much was going on in each one that might otherwise be overlooked.

But Edelstein had a (literally) breathtaking interpretation of that pause. A more dynamic than static sense of the line's structure. He saw the pause as the moment the actor, as the character, takes *to think up the next line.* Needless to say, actors don't really think up the next line on the spot, but Edelstein asks them to act as if the pause was the moment they did. A deceptively simple concept, a kind of imitation of spontaneity if such a thing is possible, or Hall might say a recognition of the apparent *inevitability* of what comes next. But one that gives a kind of dramatic momentum and freshness, an illusion of both spontaneity and inevitability, to what follows. As if it were being thought up for the first time, but—as it's revealed in that dramatic pause, a pause for thought, a pause for invention—as if it's the only possible thing that could be said.

"It was Barton and Hall who inspired me to look at the verse one line at a time, and then as I worked with actors," Edelstein continued, he found "the whole thing is to make them *find the thought,* live in the moment in front of the audience, and Barton has a saying, 'Why am I using these words *now*?'

And it eventually then occurred to me that there's a moment there at the end of each line, that pause, a moment to reach into yourself and find the next set of words. It's in that pause that, given the idea that you're trying to express, you choose words to express them." In Edelstein's interpretation the pause is a moment of *poise*—not unlike what Frank Kermode has called "the beautifully poised" moment in Shakespeare in which one finds oneself on the very "threshold of comprehension."

It sounds simple but it's transformative; it makes the end of each line not a dead pause but a live pause, a kind of kinetic (linguistically and intellectually) poised springboard to launch with new energy and momentum into the line following. A moment of dramatic suspense or suspension at the end of every line.

In some ways this was one of the most exciting moments in my peregrinations among Shakespeareans, the realization that every line is a self-contained drama, or more precisely a self-contained first act, one that made that pause a pivotal moment of dramatic reflection. A delicate moment of silent stasis and realization that conceives, gives birth to the second act, the next thought, the next line, the next threshold of comprehension.

Edelstein told me he used three Shakespearean passages to get this point across: "I use Portia's third-act speech in *Merchant of Venice,* 'You see me, Lord Bassanio, where I stand,' and I also used Leontes' 'Inch-thick, knee-deep, head-and-ears a forked one,' from *Winter's Tale,* and sometimes I will go through the opening chorus of *Henry V* as well. . . ."

For reasons that will soon become apparent, I'd like to look more closely at that "Muse of fire" prologue from *Henry V.* In part because it suggests Shakespeare talking about his art, in part because the next chapter examines the way Shakespeare's "Muse of fire" relates to the New Testament "tongues of flame." And in a subsequent chapter, the relation between the "Muse of fire" and the flickering muse of film becomes an issue. It's a remarkable passage, the "Muse of fire" speech, not least because it embodies what it disclaims it possesses.

I'd suggest as an experiment: read these opening lines of *Henry V,* the passage delivered by a character called "Chorus." Read it with Barry Edelstein's injunction in mind: the pause at the end of each line is a moment of invention. In fact invention is the subject of the first two lines:

O for a Muse of fire, that would ascend
The brightest heaven of invention!

A kingdom for a stage, princes to act,
And monarchs to behold the swelling scene!
Then should the warlike Harry, like himself,
Assume the port of Mars, and at his heels
(Leash'd in, like hounds) should famine, sword, and fire
Crouch for employment. But pardon, gentles all,
The flat unraised spirits that hath dar'd
On this unworthy scaffold to bring forth
So great an object. Can this cockpit hold
The vasty fields of France? Or may we cram
Within this wooden O the very casques
That did affright the air at Agincourt?
O, pardon! since a crooked figure may
Attest in little place a million,
And let us, ciphers to this great accompt,
On your imaginary forces work.
Suppose within the girdle of these walls
Are now confin'd two mighty monarchies,
Whose high, upreared, and abutting fronts
The perilous narrow ocean parts asunder.
Piece out our imperfections with your thoughts;
Into a thousand parts divide one man,
And make imaginary puissance;
Think, when we talk of horses, that you see them
Printing their proud hoofs i' th' receiving earth;
For 'tis your thoughts that now must deck our kings,
Carry them here and there, jumping o'er times,
Turning th' accomplishment of many years
Into an hour-glass: for the which supply,
Admit me Chorus to this history;
Who, Prologue-like, your humble patience pray,
Gently to hear, kindly to judge, our play.

Just consider the first four lines:

O for a Muse of fire, that would ascend
The brightest heaven of invention!

A kingdom for a stage, princes to act,
And monarchs to behold the swelling scene!

"Invention," the Riverside edition notes remind us, was more than its modern meaning suggests. It was back then, "in rhetorical theory, the 'finding' of suitable topics." The *finding.* This is what Barry Edelstein is suggesting one does or what a skilled actor suggests in that end-of-line pause: a finding, a reaching into oneself to find what comes next.

So if one reads aloud the first line with the idea that when one comes to the word "ascend" at the end of the line, one pauses to invent, one pauses to find, to ascend to the stunning notion of the "brightest heaven of invention." One invents invention in this ascension, one is almost being instructed by the verse in how to speak it, how to leap it.

Something similar seems to happen in the second set of two lines:

A kingdom for a stage, princes to act . . .

It's a line that seems to call for sweeping gestures by the Chorus, gestures of a magician of invention. One can see the Chorus flourishing his hand at the stage to accompany "a kingdom for a stage." One can imagine him summoning into being with a flourish the entrance of the players on "princes to act"—and then a moment of invention. One can imagine the inventive Chorus thinking up—in that all-important pause after "princes to act"—a gesture to accompany, to transform, the next line:

And monarchs to behold the swelling scene!

One can imagine him finding, inventing the idea of a flourishing gesture of comic grandiose flattery *at* the audience on "monarchs to behold": *they* are the real kings. It's a lovely way to curry favor and to conjure up the true rulers of the Globe, the inhabitants of this bright heaven of invention, the audience.

It's a compliment that works best dramatically if it invents its own authenticity, if it seems to come from a spontaneous end-line pause in which the notion is invented to turn from the players to the beholders, to turn on a dime and turn it into a charming act of generosity as well as flattery. A fusion or bonding of the audience's "imaginary forces" with the players.

"Swelling" with a hint of metaphoric pregnancy in the intercourse between *their* good will of invention and the players' Good Will (Shakespeare).

Did Shakespeare think this way or expect his actors to deliver their lines with the Hall-Edelstein end-stopped springboard pause? It's impossible to know. But it's possible to experience the heuristic value of the Hall-Edelstein concept. It seems to energize the language in such a way that it doesn't become mere recitation. And certainly, at one point, when Shakespeare was writing, there *was* a moment of invention at the end of each line when he thought up what came next and how to contain it within the pentameter line structure. So in speaking the lines this way, theoretically, one is returning, or getting closer, in some way, to *that* moment of Shakespeare's creation.

EPILOGUE: JUDI DENCH DEFENDS THE PAUSE

There are dissenters to Hall's fundamentalism. His longtime collaborator and acting teacher John Barton for instance. Barton does not deny the importance of the pause, but argues that it must at times give way to the flow of emotion and passion that spills over into the following line. There are reports that the pause has at times caused a division (a "slight sense break"?) between the two, although they still work together closely and the difference is more one of emphasis than of theory.

And, it must be said, there are pauses and there are pauses. One could envision an entire Ph.D. thesis devoted to "The Pause in Shakespeare." About the way brief moments of silence can speak, or be made to speak, so eloquently. (Actually whole books have been written about Shakespeare's silences.)

Peter Brook virtually made his reputation as a director with an eloquent pause: the pause he drew out into an extended silent rebellion at the end of his 1954 *Measure for Measure,* when Isabella draws out her silence in response to the duke's marriage proposal. A controversial pause that made her silence a repudiation of the conventional assumption that the play would end in a reconciliatory marriage.

There are, as well, the two pivotal pauses in *Hamlet:* the moment in the Player King's recitation of the melodramatic description of the death of Priam when his executioner, the bloody Pyrrhus, raises his sword—and then pauses—before slaughtering the king of Troy. And the corresponding moment when Hamlet himself draws his sword prepared to slaughter

Claudius, King of Denmark—and then pauses and, unlike Pyrrhus, forgoes the fatal stroke.

In his book *Shakespeare's Advice to the Players,* Hall has strong words about that pause. The passage goes thus:

> HAMLET: *And now I'll do't—and so 'a goes to heaven,*
> *And so am I reveng'd. That would be scanned . . .*

For Hall it's all about *when* Hamlet draws his sword in the course of the line, and thus when that act creates a pause.

Hamlet must draw his sword at the *end* of the line, not in the middle after "And now I'll do't," Hall insists.

"There is no justification for the stage practice of breaking the line to draw the sword," he maintains quite sharply.

In fact Hall's insistence on this is problematical. He wants Hamlet to stop and reflect only after the end of the line, at the beginning of the next: so that "and so 'a goes to heaven" is merely a conventional way of saying "and so he dies," not, as some see it, an ironic reflection on the fact that a murderer will end up in heaven among the blessed. Which would make the following line, especially "reveng'd," already consciously ironic, rather than an utterance that discovers the irony of "reveng'd" in the course of thinking it up and speaking it.

> *And so am I reveng'd. That would be scanned . . .*

"Scanned," indeed: a pause in the middle rather than the end of the preceding line, a pause after "And now I'll do't" rather than after "and so 'a goes to heaven" suggests that Hamlet's second thoughts *begin* with "and so 'a goes to heaven," rather than undergoing a metaphysical double-take after "heaven," as Hall insists.

It's a subtle, important distinction; one can agree with Hall's interpretation, though, without thinking it's the only alternative. He can tend to be absolutist about what his pause dictates, and in this instance, I tend to disagree.

But if Hall has a reputation of being all about pauses, in his book *Shakespeare's Advice to the Players* he insists he is really all about "smoothness." That Shakespeare was about smoothness. "Speak the speech . . . trippingly on the tongue," yes, but even within a whirlwind of passion find "a temperance that may give it smoothness," Hamlet says. In other words, Hall now seeks to emphasize that his pause, which he now calls "slight sensory break," is not the problem, does not ruffle the smoothness he seeks. What's wrong with contemporary Shakespeare, he tells us, are unnecessary, self-indulgently actorish pauses that chop up and slow down the lines, which should go smoothly and swiftly with just a hint of a hesitation.

Hall blames American Method acting with its heavy emotive underlining of each word.

Shakespeare's "form is destroyed by acting single words rather than lines . . . chopping up lines into little naturalistic gobbets may sound 'modern,' but it plays hell with the meaning . . . the sanctity of the line is betrayed and Shakespeare's primary means of giving out information rapidly and holding our attention is destroyed."

"The sanctity of the line": the man is possessed, he is a priest of the pause.

But Hall has supporters among academics as well as directors such as Edelstein and the "fifty actors" Hall cited as truly understanding the importance of the deceptively evanescent pause. Perhaps the most impressive testament to the pause from a mainstream scholar was the one I elicited a few years later from Russ McDonald, who I suspect will be remembered as one of the most illuminating Shakespearean scholars of the twenty-first century.

McDonald's study—in the Oxford University Press book *Shakespeare and the Arts of Language*—was, to me, the epitome of contemporary scholarship at its best, both post-postmodern and premodern you might say. His careful reading of Renaissance books on Greek and Latin rhetorical tropes (*antanaclasis, hyperbaton,* and the like) and the way they are echoed and transmuted in Shakespeare's figures of speech and linguistic patternings was exhilarating in its lucidity and sophistication.

I raised the question of Hall's pause with McDonald in the course of asking him about the research he was then doing at the British Library in London. He told me in an e-mail that he was studying the culture of visual symmetry in Elizabethan England, the belief among sixteenth-century theorists of art and architecture that repetition, and patterning, order and rhythm—*correspondence* in its largest sense—were somehow fundamental to esthetic pleasure. He said he believed that Elizabethan poets and Shakespeare in particular were deeply concerned with the "aural equivalents of such visual patternings" and that the discourse of visual symmetries was an important context for the way sounds and words were arranged, patterned and correlated in Shakespeare's poetry.

Something in what he was saying led me to mention to McDonald my evening with Peter Hall, and his ferocious insistence on "line structure" and the importance of the pause to maintaining it. I wondered if that might relate to McDonald's work on the discourse of formal gardens and visually pleasing symmetries. Invoking a term I'd recalled from a long-ago college seminar on Edmund Spenser, I suggested to McDonald that Hall's pause transformed each individual line of Shakespeare into a *hortus conclusus,* Latin for "enclosed garden," whose very closure was necessary to structure its visual symmetries.

"I never quite believed Hall's rabid argument either," at least at first, McDonald replied, "but then something convinced me. I have a book coming out this month called *Look to the Lady: Sarah Siddons, Ellen Terry and Judi Dench on the Shakespearean Stage.* In order to do the thing I managed to arrange an interview with Judi Dench and so I asked her about verse-speaking, who taught her. She immediately mentioned Trevor Nunn, and John Barton and Peter Hall, all of whom, as she said, learned from Dadie [George] Rylands [Poel's disciple at Cambridge]. . . .

"And she gave the Hall line about pausing and then she launched into 'I dreamt there was an Emperor Antony . . .' and gave the whole speech and I nearly [lost control]."

Hearing Judi Dench, one of the great Shakespearean actresses of the past century, insist the pause was essential to the delivery of one of Shakespeare's most impassioned dramatic arias was a kind of conversion experience for McDonald, as hearing Edelstein's explication of Hall had been for me.

Dame Judi, he continued, "went on to explain the pause, and the way she talked about it made me see it in a new way. The very slight, almost inaudible pause seems to segment the speech into equivalent units, serves very delicately to underline the ten-syllable unit without insisting on it or making it sound clunky. This pretty much convinced me, partly because I'd been thinking in just those terms of balance or equivalence. I am looking at visual symmetries in this project [at the British Library] but mainly as a means of establishing a cultural context for further understanding the pleasing units of the aural text."

Here are the lines Judi Dench recited, from *Antony and Cleopatra,* to illustrate the Hall pause, the lines that put Russ McDonald into an altered state. It's the fifth-act speech, shortly after Antony's death, the one in which Cleopatra tells Caesar's messenger:

I dreamt there was an Emperor Antony.
O, such another sleep, that I might see
But such another man! . . .
His face was as the heav'ns, and therein stuck
A sun and moon, which kept their course, and lighted
The little O, th' earth. . . .
His legs bestrid the ocean, his rear'd arm
Crested the world, his voice was propertied
As all the tuned spheres, and that to friends;
But when he meant to quail and shake the orb,
He was as rattling thunder. For his bounty,
There was no winter in't; an [autumn] *it was*
That grew the more by reaping. His delights
Were dolphin-like, they show'd his back above
The element they liv'd in. In his livery
Walk'd crowns and crownets; realms and islands were
As plates dropp'd from his pocket. . . .
Think you there was or might be such a man
As this I dreamt of?

At this point Caesar's messenger says "Gentle madam, no." Which provokes this final outburst:

You lie up to the hearing of the gods!
But if there be, nor ever were one such,
It's past the size of dreaming. Nature wants stuff
To vie strange forms with fancy; yet t' imagine
An Antony were nature's piece 'gainst fancy,
Condemning shadows quite.

One could imagine that hearing these lines read by Judi Dench would make one amenable to any theory they were said to confirm. But before returning to the question of the pause I cannot resist pointing out the echoes of *A Midsummer Night's Dream* and Bottom's Dream in particular, in this dream-besotted invocation.

Cleopatra's dream is "past the size of dreaming." Bottom's Dream is "past the wit of man to say what dream it was."

Both dreams suggest the possibility of the power, of something beyond nature to confuse sight and sound, hearing and seeing, as the dream does for Bottom. These are, one might say, "exceptionalist" dreams, off the continuum of all other dreams ever dreamed or dreamable. The very notion of an undreamable dream is itself an almost impossible paradox whose contemplation destabilizes our notion of the finite limits of the dreaming imagination.

Fascinating that Shakespeare should return under tragic circumstances to a phenomenon he conjured up in comic guise: the dream beyond dreaming.

As for the pause, since I wasn't there, I can't attest how delicately or pronouncedly Dame Judi employed it. I imagine a spectrum of potentialities. But the one line that exemplifies it for me in that passage is the one in which ". . . his rear'd arm / Crested the world."

The "rear'd arm"—suggesting he's holding a spear just about to be released—is placed at the end of the line where the pause should come: it perfectly epitomizes that moment of tension and equipoise before release. A moment of poise. In fact perhaps that's what Hall and Edelstein (in his interpretation of Hall) are getting at: a moment of poise (or rather, a poised moment) as much as a moment of pause.

But there are further moments in that Cleopatra speech that are worth attending to in the light of the controversy over "unmodernized spelling" that is the subject of the next chapter.

I had been reading, as will become evident, the scholar John Andrews's unmodernized, or as some call it "original spelling," text of *Antony and Cleopatra.* The lines of Cleopatra spoken by Judi Dench quoted above are rendered in the more conventionally modernized-spelling *Riverside Shakespeare,* a widely respected Complete Works edition used in many universities (and except where indicated the default source herein).

The *Riverside* makes two departures from the unmodernized text worth noting.

First, in the unmodernized version (essentially the Folio as printed in 1623) the line reads "the Sun and the Moon lighted . . . the Little o' the earth," implying that the glowing orbs lit the little people who populated the great globe.

Perhaps with the Globe Theatre in mind as a punning allusion (the "wooden O," as the stage is called in *Henry V*), most contemporary editors change this to "The little O, the earth," meaning the sun and moon lit the globe or the Globe, in any case, not "the Little o' the earth," the little people when seen from above, as the unmodernized spelling version has it.

It's just the addition of a comma and capitalization of *o,* but it's too clever by half I'd say, about this emendation. I'd agree with John Andrews in his note to this line in his *Everyman Shakespeare* edition: "not only is this change unnecessary; it obscures Cleopatra's praise for Antony's generosity of spirit."

But Andrews has an even more insistent and important dissent from another modernizing emendation in this passage. In the line as rendered by the *Riverside* edition, in speaking of Antony's bounty Cleopatra says, "There was no winter in't; an [autumn] it was / That grew the more by reaping."

Note the brackets the *Riverside* places around "autumn." The original Folio version where the bracket now says "autumn" reads "an *Antony* it was, / That grew the more by reaping."

Why replace "Antony" with "autumn"?

This is one of those small but resonant moments in which the debate over what is "Shakespearean" comes down to an argument over a single word in the text—and the impulse to change or "improve" it.

"Most editions emend to *autumn,*" Andrews observes in his footnote. But Cleopatra's point is that Antony's "bounty" *exceeded* autumn, exceeded even that of the season proverbial for "reaping"—for its plenteous harvest. Being unique, Antony can be likened only to his own: "semblable" (III.iv.3) or "spacious mirror" (V.i.34) . . . "Antony / Will be himself" (I.i.42–43) in a realm that lies beyond this world's "dreaming" . . . "past the size of dreaming" in the passage Judi Dench recited.

The change from "Antony" to "autumn," then, erases this further reference to a realm beyond imagining, that realm of the infinite and bottomless, that appears recurrently in Shakespeare's verse.

This was one of the things that convinced me to take seriously what I'd initially thought of as neoclassical pedantry: the "unmodernized spelling movement," which I'll explore in the next chapter.

Chapter Eight

The Spell of the Shakespearean in "Original Spelling"

It may seem an abrupt shift from the Muse of fire to what might be called the "Muse of spelling." But there is—I am determined to convince you—excitement to be found in pursuing what is usually called the "unmodernized spelling" argument. Or, as I prefer to call it, the "unanchored spelling" debate.

It is, in its own way, a no less fiery disputation than that over verse-speaking. And it turned out that, not ten minutes into my conversation with John Andrews, the most persuasive modern advocate of "unmodernized spelling," he made an allusion, if not to a Muse of fire, then to "tongues of flame." As fusty and pedantic a preoccupation as "unmodernized spelling" might sound, it attempts something similar to Peter Hall's pause: a return to origins to discover what has been lost by some all-too-user-friendly contemporary practices. An attempt that may be neoclassical in form, yet is Romantic in its belief that it can take us deeper inside Shakespearean language, the way it was written, the way it was heard by others, the way it was heard perhaps in Shakespeare's own mind.

I had initially sought to avoid the unmodernized spelling argument like a plague. From my initial, superficial knowledge of it, I didn't see how it could be of interest to any but the most antiquarian-minded of scholars. I thought of it as analogous to the mindset of Civil War "reenactors" who are so concerned that the thread stitching the buttons on their uniforms be "authentic" or "original."

My first inkling that the spelling question ought to be taken more seriously was a sudden impassioned outburst from my ordinarily mild-mannered friend Jesse Sheidlower, who is the American editor of the *Oxford*

English Dictionary. We had been discussing the unexpected pleasures we both found in textual editing questions.

"What I don't understand," Jesse said, "is why people don't care more about reading Shakespeare in original spelling editions."

It seemed at the time such a Jesse-like obsession. I mean that as a compliment: no one cares more intelligently about words, their history, evolution and the precise linguistic coloration they have at any moment in history than Jesse. That's his life work, and one could understand why he would care about the shades of coloration the words Shakespeare used had on Shakespeare's palette, or palate for that matter. Still, how much difference could mere spelling make?

In addition it seemed to me, when Jesse first brought up the spelling issue, that it was too late to care: that we were living in an age when most people already felt Shakespeare was written in a foreign language—the mandarins of British Shakespeare were warning that Shakespeare would soon seem as foreign as Chaucer's Middle English to even the most erudite, and most people read Chaucer, if they do at all, in "translation."

So to insist—as Jesse did and John Andrews, editor of the Everyman editions of Shakespeare, did—that one wasn't *really* ever reading Shakespeare *in the original* unless one read it in the original late sixteenth–early seventeenth century spelling, seemed a bit . . . well, *unrealistic,* however well intentioned.

And besides there were arguments to be made that the original spellings we have available did not necessarily issue from Shakespeare's hand; they were rather the original spellings of the scribes who copied over his manuscripts, or the type-shop compositors who took the manuscripts, or the scribes' copies, and set them into type for the printed versions that are all that we have left. (Aside perhaps from Hand D, *if* one believes it is Shakespeare's own handwriting.) But on the other hand, even if this is the case, it represented the spellings of those who *heard* the same language, heard the same sounds shaped into speech as Shakespeare.

My interest in original spelling was initially awakened a couple of weeks after my piece on *Hamlet* texts appeared, when I was contacted by John Andrews, who, while polite and respectful, clearly felt that I should have addressed the unmodernized spelling question. I tried to explain how many complex issues I had to *omit* from the original thirty-thousand-word draft of the piece to fit it into the magazine's ten-thousand-word limit. But I knew

Andrews was a substantial figure in Shakespeare scholarship. A longtime editor of *Shakespeare Quarterly,* a director of academic programs at the Folger Library, he subsequently founded his own Washington-based Shakespeare Guild, which gave a highly regarded annual Gielgud Award to Shakespearean actors. The latter fact suggested Andrews brought to unmodernized spelling not the perspective of an antiquarian pedant, but of someone who also appreciated the embodiment of Shakespeare's language in its spoken, dramatized (modern) form. And so I asked him to send me a couple of the scholarly papers he'd written on the original spelling question along with his (mostly) unmodernized Everyman edition of *Hamlet,* not expecting to find the subject as exciting as in fact I did.

Exciting because what Andrews was getting at went far beyond the original way the words were printed on the page. It offered a new way of hearing them on the stage, a new way of thinking about how they were first formed on the stage of Shakespeare's mind.

It's not that I'd never seen an unmodernized spelling edition before. I'd made Bernice Kliman's original spelling *Enfolded Hamlet* my well-worn bible for more than a year as I sought to tease out the significant single-word and phrase differences it spotlighted in the two main *Hamlet* texts.

But I found reading straight through the largely unmodernized Everyman *Hamlet* (a mostly Quarto version)—especially through the lens of John Andrews's formidable arguments in his paper "Sight Reading Shakespeare's Scores"—a new way of experiencing *Hamlet.*

Consider the Everyman *Hamlet* version of the first-act ghost scene, which in almost every modern edition begins with Hamlet observing the cold by saying, "The air bites shrewdly," the 1623 Folio version.

But in the Everyman edition, based on the 1604 Second Quarto spelling, Hamlet says, "The air bites Shroudly."

Shroudly! Even if we take it that "Shroudly" is an alternate spelling of that quality we know now as "shrewdly" (which is itself only a conjecture, not a given, even though "shrewdly" is the version in the Folio), nonetheless, spelling *shrewdly* "Shroudly," or just spelling *shroudly* "Shroudly," gives the word a dimension more than temperature. Gives a more frightening resonance to Horatio's response—"It is a nipping and an eager air"—which is often read as having erotic overtones, but which could just as well—with "Shroudly"—express the apprehension that death is nipping eagerly at our heels.

Which is not even to mention the more explicit ghostly connotations: a shroud being the usual costume of stage ghosts. Andrews's point is that you get *all* this—and "shrewdly," in all *its* implications as well—when you read it, when you print it, when you pronounce it, as it once was ("Shroudly") and you miss all that if you modernize it to "shrewdly."

REAMBIGUATING THE DISAMBIGUATED

As I was reading the original spelling *Hamlet* I was also getting a sense from John Andrews's scholarly papers of the larger stakes in the spelling question.

At its deepest level Andrews's argument is that this is not a question of Shakespearean spelling habits, but the nature of Shakespearean *thought,* his original way of using language to create meaning. Andrews calls the spelling of the time "unanchored." It was a century and a half before English spelling was first regularized, "anchored" (in Dr. Johnson's famous dictionary). By "unanchored" Andrews means more slippery, free-floating, not just in word-letter formations but in meaning. It is not, to use the famous example from *Hamlet,* that we must make a choice between "too too sullied flesh," "too too sallied flesh" and "too too solid flesh." But that *each* spelling gives one *all three* overlapping colorations of the word. As did each *spoken* utterance of the word. And that the multiple forms of words, such as "shrewdly" and "Shroudly," the unanchored, nonreductive variant spellings, either created or reflected a more fluid, unanchored, polysemous way of reading, hearing and thinking that found its epitome in Shakespeare's language and thought. (*Polysemous,* by the way, pronounced "po*liss*imus," one of my favorite new locutions, means offering many potential meanings.)

Andrews points out some telling examples in building this case. In *Macbeth* for instance the unmodernized spelling renders the line about the arrival of the soon-to-be-murdered sovereign "Duncan comes here To night." As opposed to the commonly modernized version: "Duncan comes here tonight." If "to" and "night" are not compressed, it's more than a scheduling announcement. "Duncan comes here To night" has a deeply ominous resonance, less temporal: Night is a destination, not a time. Duncan comes here to Eternal Night.

Even more convincing on the question of spelling and temporality and eternity is the original spelling version of perhaps the most famous speech in *Macbeth:*

Instead of "Tomorrow and tomorrow and tomorrow" it goes:

To morrow and to morrow and to morrow
Creeps in this petty pace from day to day
To the last Syllable of recorded time:
And all our yesterdays have lighted Fooles
The way to dusty death.

The full force of that slow creep toward Eternal Night is felt far more strongly as "To morrow and to morrow" than as "Tomorrow and tomorrow." With "to morrow" one has to cross the gap *to* a morrow, morrow is *both* a time and a destination. With "tomorrow" one is already there.

Andrews calls "to morrow" and "tomorrow" "not discrete words but a potential multivalent word pairing." A pairing that, particularly when *heard,* would be simultaneously apprehended as "to morrow" with the emphasis on the travel (or "travail"—another multivalent word pairing in Shakespeare: travel/travail)—and "tomorrow" with its emphasis on the time of arrival.

Other examples of multivalent pairings Andrews points out include "mettle" and "metal" and the way the witches in *Macbeth* were not originally spelled "Weird Sisters" as modernized editions have it, but "Weyward sisters." I was particularly intrigued with "loose" and "lose" because to illustrate Andrews's point he refers to what I have always believed is one of the signature passages in early Shakespeare, from *The Comedy of Errors.*

One of the lost twins bemoans his fate:

I to the world am like a drop of water,
That in the ocean seeks another drop,
Who, falling there to find his fellow forth
(Unseen, inquisitive), confounds himself.
So I, to find a mother and a brother,
In quest of them (unhappy), ah, lose myself.

Or as the unmodernized spelling edition has it, "ah, *loose* myself."

Lose myself, loose myself. Subtly different: "loose myself" is slightly more deliberate, more a willed loss than "lose myself." On the other hand "lose myself" has connotations that "loose myself" doesn't: lose my *self* and lose my *way.* Or perhaps, as Andrews conjectures, they were both present, both connotations, in Shakespeare's mind when he wrote it, just as they are both present when we hear them spoken, rather than read them reduced to one or the other version on the page.

Andrews emphasizes the way what we *hear* is essential to the unanchored senses that original spelling evokes on the page. He's particularly good on what has been lost in the regularizing of names. The original spelling of Montague in *Romeo and Juliet,* or one of the spellings, was "Mountague." Since "ague" is an ache (often in Shakespeare an ache resulting from mounting—a sexually transmitted disease) "Mountague" embeds an embittered vision of tainted love in Romeo's last name. What's in a name indeed.

And more recently in an essay on the unmodernized spelling text of *Merchant of Venice* Andrews points out that the original spelling of the name of the strange clown modern editions call "Launcelot Gobbo" is Launcelot *Iobbe.* And that in Venice at that time there was a prominent church of St. Iobbe, a church dedicated to the biblical sufferer Job. I've always thought that there was far more to Gobbo's presence in the play, particularly in his initial monologue, which (for a clown) is curiously, heavily, freighted with Old and New Testament images. But that Gobbo might conceal Job in a play about a suffering Jew . . . !

Andrews's essays, introductions and annotations are filled with exciting and suggestive examples such as that. He traces the original sin of spelling modernizers and conventionalizers to "Pope and all the editors who've sanctioned this disambiguating modification of Shakespeare's script."

"Disambiguating"—a great word for a reductive "either/or" approach to ambiguity. And in service of this point, what Andrews does with his examples and his arguments is—one might say—to *re-ambiguate* what Pope and the others disambiguated. To give us back the original "rapt" in *Macbeth* so that it can mean enraptured as well as the modernized "wrapped" we get in most editions. And to give us back "wrack" for "wreck" in *The Tempest.*

And in one of his tour de force readings, to give us back the pluripotential, polysemous sense of passages in which we restore "Ay" to "I" (and to "eye").

There is the crucial passage in *Richard II,* in part of what is known as "the deposition scene." It is the moment when rebellious Henry Bolingbroke (later Henry IV) asks King Richard if he is ready to resign his crown to him. As Andrews points out, most modern editions render Richard's reply as:

Ay, no, no ay; for I must nothing be . . .

Here Andrews tells us that the 1608 Quarto of *Richard II,* the one purportedly closer to Shakespeare's manuscript than the 1623 Folio, reads like this:

I, no; no I, for I must nothing be . . .

Suddenly, read this way we realize we have come upon one of the most complex meditations on the first person, the subject I, the subjective eye, in all Shakespeare.

This version, Andrews says, "permits each 'I' to indicate either 'ay' (as in, 'ay, yes') or 'I' ('I' being a normal spelling for 'ay' in Shakespeare's day). Understanding 'I' as 'I' [and not 'ay'] permits corollary word play on 'no,' which can be heard, at least in its first occurrence as 'know' [as in 'know I' rather than 'no, ay']. At the same time the second and third soundings of 'I,' if not the first, can also be heard as 'eye.' In the situation in which this speech occurs, that construction echoes a thematically pertinent exhortation from Matthew 18:9—'if thine eye offend thee, pluck it out.'

"But these are not all the meanings 'I' can have here," Andrews continues. " 'I' can also represent the Roman numeral for '1' which will soon be diminished, as Richard explains, to 'nothing,' (0), zero along with the speaker's title, his worldly possession . . . his life . . . to become 'no thing' or at best 'an O-thing.' In addition to its other dimensions, then, Richard's response is a statement that can be formulated mathematically, and in symbols that adumbrate the binary system behind today's computer technology: '1, 0, 0, 1 for 1 must 0 be.' "

I'm still not sure I completely follow that last step into ones and zeroes, but I do follow Andrews's larger point: that the ambiguity of spelling releases us to focus on *sound.* Thus restores, reambiguates Shakespeare's language. The multiply spelled, ambiguous word when spoken aloud gives us the richness of the unanchored, multiple meanings of its sound.

This eye-ear distinction is an important one to Andrews, a key reason he believes the unmodernized spelling question matters so much, and he expresses its importance in a passage that returns us once again to Bottom and his dream:

"As the word 'audience' may help us to remember, people who frequented the Globe usually spoke of 'hearing' rather than 'seeing' a play. If we're serious about analyzing and reanimating the works we know to have been composed for that magic circle [the original Globe audience] we will learn to do likewise." When we read unmodernized spelling editions, "We'll reacquire the capacity to listen with our eyes." Once again that eye/ear reversal!

Recent Shakespearean biographer Peter Ackroyd also argues the case for unmodernized spelling and uses it in all his citations, even to the point of printing the original "u" for "v" as in "loue." Ackroyd argues "the fussing of successive printers and editors has curbed and flattened [Shakespeare's] native sonority. Any standardization or modernization of Shakespeare's language robs it of half its strength." So Andrews is not alone in making this argument. Or in seeing that it is not pedantic, fussy or arcane but rather seeks to *undo* fussiness.

To "listen with our eyes." Andrews was referring to the ability when "sight-reading a Shakespearean score" in the original spelling, to *hear* both "I" and "ay" (and "eye") for instance, when we read it silently. Rather than only seeing and reading "ay," as the more modern editions have it.

But I was fascinated by the recollection, the not-so-buried allusion in "listening with the eyes" to the delirious dreamlike synesthesia in Bottom's recollection of his dream: "The eye of man hath not heard, the ear of man hath not seen."

Original spelling, Andrews seemed to be arguing, brings us closer to the original delirious synesthesia that so successfully put a spell on Shakespeare's original audiences, the spell that unanchored spelling liberates.

Andrews builds upon this point in the textual introduction to his Everyman editions (which he describes as "hybrids" that return as much as possible to the unmodernized versions of the plays) when he says, "Shakespeare revelled in the freedom a largely unanchored language provided."

Shakespeare reveled . . . I thought Andrews seemed to be coming close to saying something beyond original spelling, beyond polysemy (multiple potential meanings), something about the way Shakespeare *thought.*

When I first spoke to Andrews over the phone I read him that line about Shakespeare reveling in the unanchored language. Did he mean Shakespeare thought differently from the way we think in our now-anchored language—is that why the original spelling question has the fascination it does? Because language affects, shapes thought as much as the reverse?

"Yes," he said. "You know it seems to me that what we're gradually beginning to recover is something of the sensibility of the period, and it's happening in a lot of different ways. In the archaeology that has gone into restoring the Globe and the Blackfriars [theaters] and a lot of the work that other scholars have done to try to recover the manners and the intellectual life of the period. But one of the things that surprises me is that there has been so little focus on the degree to which the language that we use differs, in I think rather fundamental ways, from the language of Shakespeare and his contemporaries. And I think it's partly because we're used to thinking of Shakespeare as a modern writer, because virtually every contemporary edition *translates* Shakespeare—and I don't think 'translates' is too strong a word—into modern orthography, modern punctuation, often modern grammar.

"It's amazing to me," he continued, "how much we've adapted Shakespeare to our time and our sense of what the language ought to be." Adapted it, that is, without most people realizing that what they're reading and hearing *is* an adaptation.

It's interesting to put Andrews's complaint alongside those of the so-called purists who reject "adaptation" of Shakespeare for film, and yet read and often see and hear onstage a Shakespeare whose language is adapted, in effect, rendered in (to use Don Foster's term) a different "linguistic fabric" entirely, more like contemporary polyester than Shakespeare's more rough-hewn, irregularly colored linsey-woolsey.

"And yet we don't do that with Chaucer or Milton," Andrews said.

"And what's lost, you're saying, is what the language was like at its very origins," I asked, "the way Shakespeare thought of the words he wrote, the way his actors thought of them as they spoke them, the way the audience heard them?"

TONGUES OF FLAME

And then Andrews said something that both captured the stakes in the question and raised them immeasurably:

"There was an essay that C. S. Lewis wrote called 'Transposition,' " he said. "I think it was a sermon actually delivered on a Pentecost Sunday, a celebration based on the incident in the Book of the Acts of the Apostles, when all of a sudden there were tongues of fire that descended and the apostles all began speaking in different languages—the 'speaking in tongues' passage.

"And Lewis was trying to account for that and what he ended up with was what I thought was a very striking analogy that has to do with translating something that is in effect three-dimensional into something that is a two-dimensional reality. What we do [in reverse] when we use perspective in painting."

"So Lewis was saying . . ."

"What I think he was trying to do was account for the difficulty of translating a spiritual experience into ordinary language."

"So the analogy is that translating Shakespeare from the polysemous unanchored original spelling is in a way a 'transposition' from a richer to a lesser dimensionality?" I asked. "A sphere to a flat plane?"

"I think that's right," he said. "For example just to take spellings, when you think of a word like 'rack,' there are at least two ways in which it can be spelled in Shakespeare's time, 'r-a-c-k' and 'w-r-a-c-k.' And if you're a member of an audience and you hear that word spoken and you don't see it printed one way or another in a book, you don't know how it's spelled, so it can have more than one possibility" hanging in the insubstantial unanchored air that is the medium of sound that unites actor and audience.

To push Andrews's "tongues of fire" analogy a little further than Lewis and even Andrews might have wanted (and in a slightly different direction), the "tongues of fire" that represent the dimensionality of Shakespeare that modernized editions lose could suggest as well the mystery that surrounds the "tongue of fire"—Shakespeare's own tongue, the special dimension of linguistic genius Shakespeare possessed. Or it could suggest the "Muse of fire" he called upon in the prologue of *Henry V,* who began that play with the line "O for a Muse of fire . . . and monarchs to behold the swelling scene!" A muse to swell its stage-born flatness with a dimensionality, to effect a transposition of the narrow confines of the Globe Theatre into the spherical expansiveness of the globe, in the sense of the entire human cosmos.

Restoring the original spelling is for Andrews a way back to more than orthographic origins, but a way—through the polyphony and polysemy unleashed by the unanchored orthography—of restoring the missing dimensionality, the source of the tongue of fire within Shakespeare's thought itself, the bottomless dimensionality of his flickering linguistic resonances.

Andrews cites another example of dimensionality that has been lost. "There's a passage at the end of *King Lear* as Lear is dying and either Edgar or Albany (depending on the text used) says, 'let him passe, he hates him / That would upon the rack of this tough world / Stretch him out longer.' In every modern edition except for mine," Andrews said, " 'rack' is spelled 'r-a-c-k' and that's what the image encourages us to think, because 'stretched' suggests the idea of the rack as instrument of torture."

In the unmodernized spelling however it's "wracke," which can also mean "wreck" or "wreckage."

"Which suggests a more 'Waste Land'–like image?" I asked. "Lear stretched out over the wreck of this tough world is less a physical stretching out than a stretching out over time in this realm of ruin?" (I couldn't help thinking about "prey" and "pray" on garbage.)

"Yes, or rather 'wracke' gives you both."

What struck me about Andrews was his willingness to admit the contingency of some of his arguments. There is undoubtedly a certain extent to which the strongest version of his case is contingent on a strong connection between the spelling that appears in the early printed texts and Shakespeare's own (lost) handwritten spelling. A connection impossible to make absent any surviving handwritten manuscript (aside from the conjectural Hand D). We just have no certain evidence whose spelling "wracke" is.

But Andrews's argument does not depend solely on a direct link. In its broadest sense, it depends more on the fact that the language shared by Shakespeare, the scribes and compositors was far more "unanchored": pluripotentiality and polysemousness were built into it regardless of how any one word was spelled, or by whom it was spelled. Any version of "wracke" would have given you every version of wracke. Each word was a "drop in the ocean" of a different sort of sea from the one we swim in, a more fluid ocean of words.

I raised an objection to Andrews that I had heard posed to the different but not unrelated "original punctuation" movement. The latter has had a particular appeal to American actors having trouble "sight-reading" Shakespeare's language. It argues that, when seeking for moments of dramatic pause, forget Peter Hall's end-stopped line structure, but rather follow religiously the punctuation to be found in the First Folio edition of the plays because the First Folio versions of the plays were the ones "prepared" for the theater or reflected the way they were performed at the theater. In any case they argue that First Folio punctuation was closer to Shakespeare's own "final intentions" for how his lines should be read.

But subsequent skeptical investigation of the Folio and its compositors has undermined confidence that the Folio punctuation can be reliably said to reflect Shakespeare's wishes as opposed to the type shop compositors' whims.

The original spelling argument depends less on an imagined Shakespearean origin of the spelling, more on the fabric of the language he used, the potentially shifting coloration of the words with their multiple spellings and concomitant multiple meanings. Unmodernized spelling theory as adumbrated by Andrews depicts Shakespeare writing what he *heard* in his head rather than hearing the meaning a particular spelling dictated.

Still Andrews displayed a commendable and rare scholarly modesty when he admitted that the evidence linking the spelling, say, of "Shroudly" in the Quarto to Shakespeare's own hand in the original manuscript version was conjectural and that "Shroudly" could be a compositor's choice or error.

But Andrews did point out several examples of places where there is some suggestive indication that Shakespeare did supervise *some* punctuation—traces of Shakespeare's supervisory presence.

Andrews referred me to a hilarious passage in *Midsummer Night's Dream* involving Peter Quince, the author of the comically primitive version of *Pyramus and Thisby* which Bottom and his fellow Mechanicals present at the wedding of the Athenian nobles in the final act of the *Dream.*

Quince, as author, comes on first as a character called "Prologue," to address the Athenian wedding feast audience with, yes, a prologue. One that becomes a comic tour de force entirely by means of punctuation. Or rather mispunctuation. Mispunctuation which expresses Peter Quince's nervous, halting, hesitant delivery in front of such an august audience.

Here's how Quince's Prologue reads in the modernized Folio version (take note of the role punctuation plays):

If we offend, it is with our good will.
That you should think, we come not to offend,
But with good will. To show our simple skill
That is the true beginning of our end.
Consider then, we come but in despite.
We do not come, as minding to content you,
Our true intent is. All for your delight,
We are not here. That you should here repent you,
The actors are at hand; and, by their show,
You shall know all, that you are like to know.

My favorite part is, "All for your delight, / We are not here." Theseus, who gets the joke, makes a comment on "pointing," as punctuation was (and among scholars, still is) known:

"This fellow doth not stand upon points."

And Lysander adds, almost as if channeling the voice of Peter Hall: "He had rid his prologue like a rough colt; he knows not the stop."

There is so much to love, so much surefire comic business in this halting prologue that Peter Quince has become a favorite minor part of major actors. If done right—and it's hard to do wrong—it always gets serial bursts of sympathetic laughter, because it plays on, brings to the fore, the great fear we all feel of appearing, being observed on stage, the fear we admire actors for overcoming.

But there's something haunting and forlorn that struck me about the passage after my attention was drawn to it again by John Andrews:

> *. . . All for your delight,*
> *We are not here.*

We are not here. It anticipates Theseus's beautiful line about the unreality of all actors good or bad: "The best in this kind are but shadows."

We are not here: this self-canceling line beautifully captures the unreal world that actors on stage occupy: here but not here. To have being and not to have being. "Here" enough to express the fact they're not here.

And then there's the self-referential allusion to "Good Will" as in Good Will Shakespeare: "we come not to offend, / But with Good Will."

One does not have to go Good Will hunting to figure out which Will the Prologue (who, it is often suggested, was played by Good Will, typecast as a playwright) is speaking of with such self-referential self-deprecation.

And it all depends on punctuation, on "pointing," on Good Will pointing to himself in fact. Andrews argues that this is one place of all places where we might expect that Shakespeare would have been present at some point to supervise the punctuation of those lines, in the printed text, since everything—selling all that great comic business—depends on getting the punctuation wrong in the right way.

This is another one of those passages that, once I had my attention drawn to it for one reason, I found myself looking at it more closely than before, and suddenly felt the presence of Shakespeare, the imprint of "the Shakespearean."

After all, Peter Quince was a playwright as well as an actor, and as an actor he's playing a playwright, actually he's playing a part called "Prologue," and there's a relationship here I'd suggest between his Prologue and the figure called "Prologue" in *Henry V.* Both are stand-ins for the playwright, for Shakespeare, and both in their own comic and serious ways expound upon the insubstantiality of the pageant they play in. And, in some touching and moving way, the insubstantiality of the pageant we are all actors in, on the other side of the division between stage and pit. The "vast insubstantial pageant," the "little life rounded with a dream" which that final playwright figure in Shakespeare, Prospero, finally abjures.

Indeed Peter Quince's comic "repent you, / The actors are at hand" (I think we're meant to think *he'd* meant to say "attend you") carries with it the echo of "Repent ye, for the kingdom of heaven is at hand"—the New Testament invocation of the end of this insubstantial world.

SLIPPERY, LIKE FISHES

Andrews had a couple of other fascinating examples of what seems like Good Will's presence, supervising his manuscripts' printing, but let me first put Andrews himself in perspective. In a sense he represents the opposite pole of Paul Werstine's epistemological skepticism about Shakespearean texts. Andrews is a defender of *some* of the optimism of the New Bibliographers: that one could conjecture a glimpse of the true face of Shakespeare beneath the veil of print. It's a particularly interesting opposition since, like Werstine, Andrews emerged from a similar scholarly focus early in his career: the inky realm of the type shops and the murky, shadowy personae of the alphabetically denoted type-shop compositors, the elusive actors in the incomplete dramatic narrative of the printing of Shakespeare: "Compositor A," "Compositor B," "C," etc. Andrews for instance is credited with identifying the particularly elusive "Compositor G," who may have a double identity.

It turns out that Andrews and Werstine had a mentor in common, Leeds Barroll, himself a colleague of Fredson Bowers, the man who coined the phrase "the veil of print."

Andrews had been inspired to take up the study of Shakespeare as a Princeton undergraduate, but it wasn't until doing graduate study at Vanderbilt, "when I ended up being assigned as an assistant editor for a new journal called *Shakespeare Studies* edited by Leeds Barroll, that I really got into the subject matter, particularly textual matters. As it turned out I did a dissertation on the typesetters and compositors who had worked on the

First Folio. There had been a dissertation that had been published in the sixties by an associate of Fredson Bowers, William S. Kable, and Leeds had published that dissertation in a monograph and what Kable was doing was analyzing the spelling patterns in the Pavier Quartos."

Ah, the Pavier Quartos.* Bear with me, ye faint of heart who might not yet have come to see the elusive, arcane allure of textual studies, in which such delicious mysteries as the Pavier Quartos thrive. One of those veils within the veil of print, the Pavier Quartos were a set of ten single-play quarto-size versions of Shakespeare's plays that appeared in 1619, three years after his death and four years before the 1623 First Folio with its thirty-six plays.

Some of them seem to have been backdated versions of earlier Quartos. Some scholars believe they can be mined for clues to the "original Shakespeare" beneath the veil of type.

So after much microscopic study of spelling problems and—yes—a disorienting spell on the Hinman Collator ("I couldn't take it, it made me seasick"), Andrews told me, "I ended up refuting the thesis I was going to base my thesis on [the Kable thesis, that *Lear*'s Compositor B was involved in the Pavier Quartos] and discovered that the Pavier Quartos were set as much by another figure who I named 'Compositor G.' "

Another shadowy figure in the subterranean drama of the print shops, another nameless figure beneath the veil of print—one whom no scholar had thought to envision before.

"And it turned out at the same time that Peter Blayney who was working at Cambridge came up with the same theory."

Blayney is a living legend among textual scholars—long considered the ne plus ultra of that elite breed, particularly when it came to *Lear.* His vast book about the printing of the 1608 Quarto of *Lear* is regarded as the last word on the idiosyncrasies of that document, and for two decades now scholars have been waiting for him to finish its counterpart, his study of the printing of the 1623 Folio version of *Lear.* Many hoped Blayney's second book would clarify at last the question of whether the differences between

* Named after Thomas Pavier, whose unauthorized edition was halted by an injunction from Shakespeare's company, but who may by his transgression have inspired compilation of the 1623 Folio, which preserved from oblivion half of Shakespeare's plays, the ones that exist only in Folio versions.

the two *Lears* were the result of print-shop compositors' idiosyncrasies or of Shakespeare's own revisions—one of the great controversies in all Shakespeare studies (see chapter 4).

But I'd kept hearing word that Blayney had abandoned the project, that in some sense the magnitude of it had devoured him.

"People are in awe or despair about Blayney, aren't they, about the fate of the second volume?" I asked Andrews.

"Yes," said Andrews a bit reticently, as if he knew more than he could say.

"What have you heard?"

"Well, he's very *meticulous.* It takes him a long time. But it may not be definitive. I don't think anything is ever definitive. . . ."

Nothing is ever definitive . . . Is this the tragic epitaph for the encounter between some of the most brilliant minds in the scholarly world and the recalcitrant mysteries that lie behind the veil of print in Shakespeare studies?

I took this opportunity to ask Andrews about Hand D and found he tended to agree with me that the *thematic* argument that it was Shakespeare's work was persuasive. But he also adduced a remarkable *theatrical* moment in support of Hand D's Shakespearean authenticity:

"Back in 1996 I had formed an organization called the Shakespeare Guild and we had organized an award in honor of John Gielgud and we presented the award for the first time to Ian McKellen, and he accepted it—in a ceremony in May of '96—at the Folger. And he talked about Sir John [Gielgud] and he said that if there might have been any point at which Sir John had envied Ian McKellen, it was that perhaps he [McKellen] was the first to do on stage the lines that Shakespeare had written for *Sir Thomas More* [from Hand D]. And what he did that night was the speech of More reproving the mob."

"The poor expelled immigrants heading for the ports?"

"Yes, and of course he related it to his own cause [gay rights] you know, strangers . . . And it was powerful, and as he read it you could very readily think that only Shakespeare could have written it."

Andrews does, however, agree with one of Paul Werstine's critiques of the Hand D attribution: that too many conclusions can be drawn from Hand D's lack of punctuation.

"If we concede, as I think we should, that Shakespeare must have overseen the deliberate mispunctuation of the Peter Quince Prologue in *Midsummer Night's Dream,* why shouldn't we assume that the rest of the punctuation—especially in a Quarto as good as the 1598 *Dream,* or the *Mer-*

chant of Venice, which was published in the following year—why shouldn't we take seriously the notion that he actually prepared a script, whether or not for publication, that was carefully pointed. I must say that the [new skeptical orthodoxy] that we can't draw *any* conclusions, that we can't draw any conclusions about Shakespeare's punctuation and spelling from especially the good Quartos, goes too far. Now I may draw too *many* inferences. But I find there is a consistency, evidence of care in overseeing the manuscript, whether or not he saw it through press."

It seemed to me that what Andrews was advancing was a neo–New Bibliography theory of a more sophisticated and limited sort than that advanced by those who thought we could remove the veil of print entirely. What Andrews is suggesting is that we can at times part the veil, get some glimpses of Shakespeare paying careful attention to the preparation of his theatrical manuscripts—unlike the now-popular image from *Shakespeare in Love* of someone who dashed off scripts and sent them to the playhouse and went on to the next without looking back.

I asked Andrews whether there was much of a movement to return to unmodernized spelling editions.

"To a limited extent," he said, "the variorum editions used basically a transcription of the facsimile of the original texts. But even the [1986] Oxford original spelling edition which was, in the scholarly realm, at least a major victory for the *concept* of original spelling, often wasn't—often didn't present the original text but included editors' emendations."

So how did he end up producing a major edition of Shakespeare that few knew they needed, fewer had ever seen, but which changes the way one reads Shakespeare, changes the way one hears Shakespeare in one's mind? I found reading Andrews's original spelling *Hamlet* for instance a striking experience because of the way it defamiliarized the all-too-familiar text, and gave me a strange sense of coming upon the play for the first time.

It began, Andrews told me, when he was invited by the Doubleday Literary Guild imprint to do a deluxe edition of Shakespeare. "I had originally intended to do what most editors do, which is start with someone's modernized version and add my own notes and introduction, but I decided to look back at some of the original facsimiles and again it was *Midsummer Night's Dream* which caught my attention. One line in particular in the original edition. In the very first speech of Hippolyta, in which she refers to 'the moon, like to a silver Bow / *Now* bent in heaven . . . ' Which every subsequent editor has changed to 'the moon, like to a silver bow / *New* bent in heaven . . .' "

Here was an instance he thought where the original "now" is just as good, or even better, in emphasizing imminence than the emendation to "new."

The more he looked the more he felt that, after the Literary Guild edition (which contained some, but not many, reversions to original spelling), he wanted to produce a more thoroughly unmodernized spelling edition. In his Everyman edition he only made two minor compromises, he says: he reduced the long *S*'s (the ones that are easily confused with *f*'s) to contemporary-looking *s*'s and he distinguished between the *u* and *v* letters in a way such that "love" was printed "love," not "loue." Andrews also retained much of the promiscuous, often irregular and arbitrary capitalization and got Everyman, the British publisher, to go along with it.

"So how did you convince Everyman to do it?" I asked Andrews.

"I'm not sure," he said. "And I'm not sure if they'd do it over again if they had the choice," he said laughing.

I told Andrews I wanted to get back to that line in his Everyman textual introduction in which he speaks of the way "Shakespeare revelled in the freedom a largely unanchored language provided."

"That phrase, 'unanchored language': Are you implying that Shakespeare was thinking and writing in a different way than we imagine ourselves thinking and using words?"

"I think so, yes," he said. "You know [T. S.] Eliot—I don't think he was talking about this specifically, but Eliot talked about the 'dissociation of sensibility' and his sense that somehow there was a change in our relationship to language that was related to the very way we think and feel. Something that happened sometime after the time of Shakespeare and Donne. And I think that he's speaking about the language before it became rigidified, before it became codified and ruled out multiplicity. You know I once heard Robert Fagles [the acclaimed translator of Homer] speak at Princeton, and he quoted D. H. Lawrence who said something like, 'Before Plato told the great lie about Ideas, men went slippery like fishes and didn't care.' I'm not sure what exactly Lawrence was getting at but I do think Shakespeare was using language in that way, 'slippery like fishes,' malleable. You didn't have any grammars, no one had codified grammar or spelling. I think for Shakespeare spelling was a *trope*—you could play around with the form of words just the way you could do other figurative things with words."

This seemed important to me: spelling as a trope, Shakespeare deliberately using the unanchored multiplicity of the spelling of the time to create a cloud of potential meanings hanging in the air when the words were uttered, radiating polysemy on the page. Which makes a return to something closer to, if not assuredly identical with, the original important, a way of deepening an experience of "the Shakespearean."

I thought of Jonathan Bate's analogy to the Cambridge physicists and the Copenhagen model of the atom, a nucleus surrounded by a cloud of possible electron paths, none of which could be pinned down without uncertainty about their position—a cloud of unanchored meanings all potentially valid, none pinned down, though some ruled out by quantum limitations.

I tried this out on Andrews, who didn't recoil at the metaphor from physics.

"Yes, if one approaches language with an awareness that the language as spoken and heard at that time was a richer medium than when committed to manuscript or print. You have a sound, and when you hear the 'Ay/I' sound, sitting in the Globe in *Richard II,* you don't know how those lines should read on paper. There are multiple possibilities in the spoken language that you can't preserve when you put it in a single written form. And so the written form is a *transposition* from a richer medium to a medium that is more limited."

Transposition. It's that tongues-of-flame trope again. The paradoxical notion that the original spelling has less to do with letters on the page than the sound in the air, freeing letters on the page to enjoy their full efflorescence, one might say, in the multiplicities of tone and coloration that the ear, the mind, afford sounds.

AT SIXES AND SEVENS

"And I think Shakespeare must have known it," Andrews told me. "I find this over and over in the works: if there's any possibility for it to have multiple implications, it will. For example at the end of *The Tempest* there's a passage where Ariel is telling Prospero about the state of Prospero's captive enemies and Ariel says, 'they cannot budge till your release.' And the way we would naturally interpret that is 'they cannot budge till you release them.' But it's not very long after that that Ariel tells Prospero what *he* would do if he were human and then Prospero decides that he'll forgive his captives. And I think that what happens there is that Prospero experiences 'your release' no longer as 'you releasing them,' but 'your release,' as in *his* release, a personal release, from the tyranny of his own self that allows him to forgive and release his enemies."

Andrews's choice of "release" as an example is a fortuitous one in the larger sense. In a peculiar way that I was becoming convinced was important, related to Peter Brook's belief that splitting open a line of Shakespeare will release infinite energies, unmodernized spelling can release from mere lettering the polysemous radiant cloud of unanchored—but nonrandom—meaning.

What Andrews is suggesting is a deepening of the notion of close reading to close *listening*. That close reading isn't close enough unless it takes into account the "trope of spelling" as Andrews puts it—the way unanchored spelling, multiple ambiguous letter combinations are only truly "released" when they are released from the page to be experienced as spoken and heard on the stage.

I asked him if he thought there was a kind of hierarchy of the most complete, the deepest way of experiencing Shakespeare.

"Are you saying that reading aloud or hearing players speak aloud from an original spelling text is going to be closer than anything else?"

"I would think so," he said, "I think what we need is to recover the ability to hear the words as we read them, even if we're reading them silently, and to be alert to the possibility that when we read it, a word that has one form on the page may have other possible forms when it's embodied in sound."

It would in addition be not without interest to get closer if possible to the way Shakespeare heard and pronounced his own words, an attempt that may not yield certainty but might often yield surprises like "Shroudly" casting a subterranean chill on "shrewdly."

I asked Andrews why he thought more companies didn't do Shakespeare from original spelling texts. He said he'd spoken with the conductors who design the music for the restored Globe. "They're part of the early music movement, playing Bach on the clavichord and all that. The Globe is doing some of it musically, but I don't think they've addressed the language. I remember seeing a Globe production of *Henry V* in which they had the traditional all-male cast, in costumes that were Elizabethan, in a staging that was Elizabethan, or as near an approximation as they could find—and then you had various characters referring to 'the Dauphin' as the heir to the French throne, while in the early printings of course they say 'Dolphin.' And if you Frenchify it you lose something."

"You lose the subcurrent of ridicule in calling him 'Dolphin'?"

"Yes, and there's one place where there's a reference to Louvre—'the Louvre's balls.' And in the Folio 'Louvre' is spelled 'Lover,' so you lose the pun 'Lover's Balls.' "

Andrews's passion for the original printing extends beyond original spelling and original punctuation to original lineation. Or perhaps it's more fair to his point of view to say that he's anti-*tampering:* that he believes one ought to adopt the Hippocratic philosophy when approaching the original printings: first do no harm, don't tamper with irregularities and idiosyncrasies, because in doing so one risks missing what might be hidden within the apparently irrelevant irregularity. In support of original lineation he cites the way many contemporary editors rearrange two crucial lines in *Richard II.*

"York comes in after hearing three or four pieces of bad news at a time. And he has a long speech that is very messy metrically, and every editor tries to realign it into some pattern that would make it more regular. And then I noticed the final line, which is too long, the line that ends with 'everything is at six and seven.' " In the unmodernized Folio version of *Richard II* this is rendered:

I should to Plashy too, but time will not permit,
All is uneven and every thing is left at six and seven.

The problem with these lines is that they depart radically from the standard ten-syllable iambic pentameter line. The last line containing "six and seven" consists of a full fourteen syllables. In the *Riverside* edition of Shakespeare's complete works the editor treats the fourteen-syllable line as a mistake and rearranges the last lines like this:

I should to Plashy too,
But time will not permit. All is uneven,
And every thing is left at six and seven.

It leaves two lines regularized at ten syllables each (and almost rhyming), but Andrews noticed something when preparing the Literary Guild edition of *Richard II.* "In that final line with 'every thing is left at six and seven' if you keep the original fourteen-syllable version you find in the sixth metrical unit is the word 'six' and in the seventh is the word 'seven.' "

Not only is it an instance of the jeweled clockwork of Shakespearean verse, not only is it another instance, he suggests, in which one imagines that Shakespeare may have overseen the printing in order to ensure that the expressive irregularity of the meter was preserved in the lineation, just as with the expressive mispunctuation of Peter Quince's Prologue. But also, as Andrews points out, "It accounts for everything that precedes that speech." He argues the irregularity is a deliberate expression of a disordered mind. At Yale the New Critics used to call this the fallacy of imitative form—disordered verse expressing a disordered mind. But here disorder is both expressed and captured by a higher order.

Impressed as I was by Andrews's arguments, even more by such instances of his attentiveness to Shakespeare's language, I was, I admit, reluctant to concede that in effect I'd been "doing it wrong" all my life, by reading Shakespeare in modern spelling editions. And yet I found myself not alone in seeing some merit in Andrews's arguments. Peter Ackroyd's a true believer. The *OED*'s Jesse Sheidlower, no inconsiderable student of language, felt impassioned on the question. It's not for nothing that Stephen Booth and Helen Vendler both include facsimile unmodernized versions of the Sonnets in their editions. And shortly after interviewing Andrews I was visiting one of the most erudite nonacademic writers I knew, Daniel Kunitz, who writes art criticism for venues that range from *Harper's* to the *New Criterion.* The grandson of a poet, he had studied pre-seventeenth-century poetry as a graduate student at Columbia with a legendary Shakespearean teacher, Ted Tayler; he knew his Shakespeare and he knew his metrics. He was skeptical about Peter Hall's end-stopped line structure argument. And at first when I reviewed for him John Andrews's arguments for unmodernized spelling editions, he was incredulous.

"What do you mean?" he said. "I haven't been reading Shakespeare in the original?" I took out my copy of Andrews's Everyman edition of *Hamlet* and handed it to him. He looked it over for some time and then got up and dug out his copy of Harold Jenkins's Arden edition of *Hamlet,* and started comparing passages.

"I can't believe this," he finally said. "I feel cheated"—cheated out of an authentic Shakespearean experience by modernization and conventionalizing of spelling and capitalization.

So where does that leave us? Frankly it convinced me that in my next round of rereading Shakespeare I'd do it in the original spelling editions.* In the original tongue of flame, so to speak, before the "transposition."

That is of course in addition to reading it *aloud* in the Hall-Edelstein line-structure method. Originalist arguments can make great demands. And offer great rewards.

* And why not in this book? It was not an easy decision, but since it's not an *edition* of the plays, but a book that cites passages, I thought the interest in making the quotations more accessible to more readers outweighed the alternative. That it was better to familiarize readers before presuming to de-familiarize them with the passages in question. But I would encourage readers to seek out unmodernized editions for their next rereading of the plays.

Chapter Nine

Dueling Shylocks

Olivier, Goodman, Berkoff, Pacino, Mostel: Whose is more "authentic"?

IF THE DEBATES OVER HOW TO SPEAK IT, HOW TO SPELL IT, ARE highly fraught, sometimes bitter, the debates over how to act it, how to *feel* it, what emotion to depict in the character, what emotions to induce in the audience, are even deeper and more long-standing.

I was struck by a remarkable quote on this issue from Samuel Johnson, who asked a radical question about acting. To the modern ear Johnson can sometimes come across as a stuffy fussbudget, or perhaps he is most often quoted by stuffy fussbudgets, but his responses to Shakespeare are often uniquely valuable both because of his extraordinary intelligence and because of the moment he was situated in time in respect to Shakespeare: some one hundred fifty years after Shakespeare died.

The distance made it possible for the first time to begin to see the magnitude of the achievement for the bottomless phenomenon it was. As if until that time, Shakespeare's closeness had obscured, overwhelmed any chance of seeing it with any perspective. The way an astronaut floating in space close to the surface of the moon sees less of the surface than an astronomer with a telescope 200,000 miles away.

In any case one of the radical things Samuel Johnson said about Shakespearean acting was cited in a *TLS* essay by the scholar Paula Byrne, reviewing several books about eighteenth-century Shakespearean acting. It was in the eighteenth century that arguments about Shakespearean acting had begun to appear in other literature, from Fielding's *Tom Jones* to Jane Austen's *Mansfield Park*.

In each of the latter works the arguments centered around the revolution in Shakespearean acting effected by David Garrick, and what was seen as his radical naturalism back then.

Byrne cites Garrick's first biographer, who said, "Mr. Garrick shone forth like a theatrical Newton . . . he banished ranting, bombast and grimace, and restored nature, ease, simplicity and genuine humor."

Byrne portrays Garrick almost as an anticipation of Strasbergian Method acting: "Garrick worked on the principle of emotional identification with the part, though not all of his friends supported his approach . . ."

Here she cites that jolting, radical Samuel Johnson remark about acting and "authentic" emotion:

"Johnson challenged the actor John Kemble, 'Are you sir, one of those enthusiasts who believe yourself transformed into the very character you represent?' When Kemble answered in the negative Johnson concurred: 'The thing is impossible. And if Garrick really believed himself to be that monster, Richard III, *he deserved to be hanged every time he performed it*' " (italics mine).

An amazing statement about a certain kind of acting. Johnson disparages it, but raises the possibility that to play Richard III's evil one must become as evil as the character (and deserve punishment for having effected such a transformation—or transposition, one might say). Does an actor who plays Shakespearean evil risk his soul whatever method he uses? Is such success a Faustian bargain as Johnson implies?*

But if the actor does *not* attempt to risk becoming the evil being Shakespeare originally conceived, or gives us a denatured, distanced simulacrum, is he denying us that original, unbearable intensity?

These were some questions raised by my encounter with the actor Steven Berkoff, by witnessing his embodiments of Shakespearean evil. Particularly his reversion to what might be called an Originalist Shylock.

I'd heard a couple of misleading things about Steven Berkoff before he came to New York City's Public Theater with his one-man show *Shake-*

* Johnson's question may sound naïve, or old-fashioned, but I was struck recently by the way it was raised in January 2006, by one of the foremost philosophers of our time, Saul Kripke. In a report on a Kripke lecture by Charles McGrath in *The New York Times,* we learn that Kripke—in the course of a talk called "The First Person"—expressed concern that "it's one thing when writing about a historical character to try to become that character, and something else again when that character is Hitler." Essentially the same concern Johnson expressed about acting Richard III.

speare's Villains. I knew vaguely he was a British actor-director, considered an outsider and some kind of avant-garde critic of establishment Shakespeare.

Misleading.

And then there was a remark Gary Taylor made to me about Berkoff's *Hamlet.* Recall, I'd asked Taylor, co-editor of *The Oxford Shakespeare,* a notoriously cantankerous and hard-to-please fellow, what was the most impressive performance of *Hamlet* he'd ever seen. "Steven Berkoff's," he said, without hesitation. "It sounds kind of wild and crazy when you describe it though," he added, "because for instance, in the closet scene, his Hamlet fucks Gertrude."

Also misleading. Well, as we'll see, *partly* misleading.

But I think what's most misleading about Berkoff, sixty-four when I met him, is the avant-garde label. True, he likes to say that most contemporary directors and players of Shakespeare are still "working with a telescope" while what he does is "comparable to the electron microscope."

But I think the best way to look at Berkoff is not as an *avant-gardiste* but as a kind of flamboyant throwback: a throwback to an earlier, more grandiose age of Shakespearean players, the age of Garrick and Kean, and Edwin and John Wilkes Booth. An era in which Shakespearean actors—when they weren't assassinating presidents—were slaying audiences. An era when grand, operatic, gestural histrionics caused weeping, wailing, fainting and frenzy. When Shakespearean actors did to audiences what rock stars—and demagogues like Hitler—did.

I bring up Hitler again because Berkoff, a Jew, actually played Hitler—in the 1990s miniseries *War and Remembrance.* He has supported his Shakespearean barnstorming with lucrative film villain roles in Bond movies, *Rambo* and *Attila* (he was the Hun). I mention Hitler because in his one-man show on Shakespeare's villains Berkoff attempts to find in those fictional figures a hierarchy of evil, and an etiology of evil that, he believes, casts light on historical figures such as Hitler.

Berkoff's one-man show consists of Berkoff tearing into some of the juiciest, most operatically villainous moments in Shakespeare, giving us Iago, Macbeth and Richard III (along with some less obvious but villainous aspects of Hamlet and Oberon), combined with a running commentary that is part essay on evil, part actor's memoir and part stand-up patter. It's a thought-provoking entertainment, but what's most revelatory about it, I believe, is the way it's a kind of throwback.

The very form of it, for instance: There's a venerable tradition of British Shakespearean actors touring the colonies, so to speak, giving one-man shows, wowing the yokels with some best bits from the Bard. Mark Twain satirized it in *Huck Finn.* John Gielgud earned some well-deserved plaudits and paydays touring with his *Ages of Man* one-man show of Shakespearean high points. You could think of Berkoff's one-man show as *The Rages of Man.*

But rage is a usefully polysemous word in this context. Because Berkoff's show harks back to the days of a different kind of actor, a different kind of acting, when Shakespeare was, literally, all the rage. Not merely respected and revered as he is now, but wildly, deliriously mesmerizing. You read accounts of the grand old histrionic figures of the Shakespearean stage and repeatedly, inevitably, they speak of women fainting and men weeping, of the histrionics on stage provoking a histrionic, virtually hysterical response in the audiences.

It's a style of acting most modern Shakespeareans have abandoned, virtually fled from, in order to seek the subtleties and the subtexts in a more "naturalistic" manner. But Shakespeare wasn't always a naturalist. After all, he wrote in iambic pentameter, not prose, for the most part, and even his prose is heightened, not prosaic. And watching Berkoff one wonders if there's something that's been lost, something missing in even the very best of contemporary players: the pure relish for the grand gestural moment, the operatic passion that made Shakespeare the rage, rather than just a sage.

Berkoff's impassioned embodiments of Shakespearean evil are often electrifying in that old-fashioned throwback way. He endows his personations with a disturbing power, far more profound than Berkoff's intellectual *explanation* of evil, which relies a bit too much to my mind, on social worker victimology: people like Richard III turn bad because they "don't get enough love" or, in Shylock's case, they're "cut off from community." If only it were that simple. If only Berkoff's own malevolent Shylock were so easily explained away.

But I've sometimes found, in talking to talented actors, that they need an intellectual rationale to hang on to in order to liberate—give them permission to unleash—performances that strike chords far deeper than the abstract rationales. And when I say Berkoff's histrionic style is a throwback, I mean that as a compliment. Not throwback in the sense of antiquated, but throwback in the sense that you feel hurled back in time to a kind of experience whose raw power made original Shakespeare the rage. Closer to what it was like to be present when larger-than-life acting sensations like Burbage, Garrick and Kean stalked the stage.

In fact when we met at his hotel in Gramercy Park to talk about Shakespeare and acting, Berkoff told me a remarkably emblematic story about the histrionic tradition: the story of the sword.

It was in the context of a lengthy denunciation of what Berkoff contends is the dull, pedestrian quality of almost all Shakespeare since Olivier. Olivier was his idol. Watching Olivier's Shakespearean films changed his life, Berkoff told me. It was Olivier who introduced him to a transformative level of Shakespearean experience, "supernatural" as opposed to naturalistic acting.

"Because he," meaning Olivier, "is the great one. He *carries the sword.* Do you know the story of the sword?"

At the time I didn't know the story of the sword.

It's a story that begins with Byron and Edmund Kean, one of the great Shakespearean actors of the early nineteenth century. Coleridge famously remarked that watching Kean act was "like reading Shakespeare by flashes of lightning."

"Kean!" Berkoff exclaims. "He was our greatest, our patron saint of the theater. He is the true *tiger* of the theater. So great—even by reputation, people would faint. Even Byron apparently, in the box one night when Kean was playing, I think it might have been *Othello,* and Byron is a quite tough guy you know. He's a poet but he's tough and he's seen it all, and he got so excited he actually *passed out* watching. He passed out like people did when they saw Olivier." He sighs. "And he was—he got so excited as he"—Berkoff sighs even more violently, almost suggesting he too will pass out in a violent fit at just the thought of it: "God! Kean! His voice and his projection, it was—*frightening!* Byron thought he was so unbelievable that he had a sword made. He had a sword inscribed to Kean. And Kean was very flattered because he was a little bit feeling inferior to these educated poets, you know, Oxford-trained and cultivated. Kean tried to learn, to teach himself Latin. It was very moving. . . ."

There is perhaps a bit of self-identification here with Kean. Berkoff too was self-educated, the product of the mean streets of East London's Jewish slum. He does not share in the Oxbridge background of the main line of Royal Shakespeare Company types in the United Kingdom. He dropped out of school at fifteen and sometimes betrays a touching insecurity about his lack of Latin—like Kean, indeed like Shakespeare, who was mocked for having "small Latin and lesse Greeke." But he's touchingly intoxicated with the history of Shakespearean acting.

To return to the story of the sword: "Then Kean died. The sword was auctioned off and then got into the hands of a dealer. And one day Gielgud in 1935, I think, was playing Hamlet. Someone managed, a dealer, to come backstage and brought the sword and said, 'This is the most amazing performance I have ever seen on any stage anywhere in my life,' and presented him with Kean's sword. He said, 'You must keep this sword, John.' So John was thrilled and he kept the sword for about fifteen years. Then one day Gielgud went to see Olivier playing Richard III and he says"—Berkoff does a beautiful Gielgud imitation, urgent, faint and musical: 'I can't—I can't carry the sword! This is impossible. This man is *mad,* wonderful, exotic. Really I would feel *guilty* to have the sword in my cupboard. I'll give it to Larry. I don't give a damn, I'm done with it.'

"So Gielgud goes to Larry and says, 'Please take this as my respect for your wonderful performance.' And Larry said, 'Well John, are you sure you want to give it to me because it's . . . ' 'Well, we should pass it *on,* Larry. If *you* see somebody, somebody fantastic, something moves you, let's pass this wonderful thing on, because it comes from Byron to Kean to me. I don't think I really deserved it, but it came to me. But you, Larry—wonderful, *wonderful* performance. Take it, take it, Larry.'

" 'Thank you very much, John, John, it's beautiful and thank you, darling.' "

Berkoff has shifted from playing Gielgud to playing Olivier.

"Olivier took the sword and then he keeps the sword and he's thinking, 'Oh shit, who should I give it to?' See? And he goes to the theaters and he thinks, 'This one? Burton? Hmmmm, no, no, no. Scofield? Yes, he's pretty good, pretty good. Alec McCowan? Excellent, excellent, um, no one *really.*' And then he's dying and Joan [Olivier's wife Joan Plowright] is saying 'Larry, what about the sword, the sword?' 'Well, uh, I haven't *seen* anybody really that I felt like giving it to'—This is what I'm imagining now." Berkoff says, "But in the end he didn't give it to anybody. They were not good enough. He knew his standard and he wanted someone that would thrill him and he never gave the sword. . . ."

I was fascinated by Berkoff's rhapsodic account of Olivier because he's an actor who's become so much a cliché for acting "greatness" that one forgets, if one has not seen him, the force of that greatness. Berkoff can't forget Olivier was a force, a power that changed his life. One he first experienced when he was an acting student with little interest in Shakespeare until he saw Olivier on film.

"I was never into Shakespeare at all as a youth," he told me. "I didn't know anything about Shakespeare. Only when I started drama school—I had a limited education and when I went to an evening class for working men and women, they said, 'You have to audition you know, Shakespeare.' So I suddenly started looking and reading and studying Shakespeare. But I didn't have any kind of, you know, revelatory experience really, except when I started watching Olivier's films.

"I watched his Richard, his Hamlet, and his Othello and I thought they were unbelievable. I thought they were almost like something transcendental. I found his performances beyond human. I thought they were something of such an extraordinary power it made me feel that acting could be one of the world's great arts, greater than anything.

"It was that experience, seeing him and wanting to *be* him in a way, like Muhammad Ali wanted to be like Joe Louis. Olivier was my mentor, my master, I became obsessed with Olivier, totally obsessed, and I felt that his daring—what he did was to take the craft into a kind of an almost supernatural realm, a ferocity, an energy that I thought was just kind of quite incredible."

Did you know him? I asked Berkoff.

"No, no, I met him once or twice but didn't know him. I *wanted* to know him. I worshiped him, I dreamed of him. I was obsessed by him and I started to model myself on him. Then one day I was acting and I suddenly heard his voice coming out of my mouth and I thought, this is terrible! I've got to get rid of him! He possessed me like a dybbuk and I became very, very, very close, in a sense, in my spirit. And then one or two reviews mentioned me in the same breath, as if to say, 'Like Olivier, he tried to do this,' and I was terribly thrilled to get such a review."

"What was that for?"

"I think it was when I did *Macbeth* on the radio. But that daring, Olivier's physical daring, I got closer to him . . . Then for many years I'd been trying to get back to the [Royal] National Theatre [the prestigious South Bank venue founded by Olivier and Sir Peter Hall] and I thought if Olivier was there *I* should be there because he would appreciate me."

He proceeds to tell a kind of showbizzy story about a supposedly fateful "intervention" by Olivier that was a turning point in Berkoff's theatrical career. How Olivier's death, in effect, handed "the sword" to him.

"Olivier died in '89 I think it was, and his wife Joan Plowright was about to do a play. And she canceled. They rang around everywhere, you know, 'We've got a space to fill for two months.' So I received a call because I had a production which I had been touring of *Salome* [the Oscar Wilde play] and would I go in that spot? And I went there and that was the most successful production I've ever done. It was at the National Theatre and it was virtually the first time *Salome* had ever been seen on stage. And that came from Olivier, damn it! Through his death. So I thought that was a kind of sign. I took it as a sign in my kind of like fantasy. That he gave me more than any other human being in terms of my profession. And he even gave me—even when he died, he gave me more than any of these other people gave me by living. Even as he died he passed the baton to me somehow . . . I was only there doing it because of Olivier. Kind of a weird story. And then *Salome* was successful, I always thought it had to be, and we were sold out. It was the most successful production they've had there in years."

Despite that acclaim, he's still at odds with the theatrical establishment. I'd asked him if he had a critique of current Shakespearean productions in England, establishment Shakespeare. At first he tried to sound dispassionate.

"I don't really give a—I don't really think too much about them, because I do my own thing. So I mean, I don't regard them in any particular way."

And then slowly, well, not *that* slowly, he segues into a rage.

"I think they are traditional and they are still working with the same telescope—the same microscope that Pasteur used. They have not yet invented the electron microscope, so they are still looking at things in a very simplistic way.

"They're looking at things through a milk bottle lens. They're not allowing the insight of the unconscious or its physical manifestations. No shortcuts of using modern techniques that we use in film of fast forward or flashback. It's pedestrian, simplistic and eventually damaging. *Deeply* damaging to Shakespeare because the human mind is now so sophisticated through the kind of swift-moving inventive shortcuts you find in literature, television, movies, even video.

"But to go back to pedestrianism, they're asking us to accept it in the name of fundamentalism, the name of THEE-AY-TER, in the name of culture. And it is *appalling* what they're doing. They are taking, dragging Shakespeare to his knees. They're not taking advantage of making it valid for twentieth-century man. All they're doing is fulfilling a guilt trip for the older people who go and say, 'Oh very, very nice.' They rely on one or two stars and surround it with a tepid, insipid, ridiculous, dull, placid, old-fashioned, decayed, pedestrian production."

"But do you have a *critique*?" I asked (jokingly). Not pausing, he continued to rage on.

"It's awful, I mean it's *so* awful, not only is it awful, it's awful because they consciously resist anyone like myself or any innovator saying, 'Let us have a go.' But they persist in doing the same old crap. Bring on the dry ice machines. If I see another ice machine and steam, I think I'm going to kill somebody."

THE NIGHT EVERYONE CHANGED

I asked him whether his critique extended to Shakespeare at Trevor Nunn's then-new Royal National Theater Company.

"I've never seen *any* Shakespeare done well in the last thirty years, not one. The only thing I've ever seen that was thrilling was a German production of *Macbeth* which knocked me sideways. It was in Düsseldorf, I was directing there—it's a translation by the German writer Heiner Müller. It was done very quietly and I thought, here is something exciting.

"But," he says, if one goes a bit further back than thirty years there was *the* defining Shakespearean performance of his lifetime: "There was Olivier as Othello. I saw him at Chichester, which is a three-sided theater, but he'd played it at the Old Vic, for a season, maybe thirty performances, forty performances. Big theater, the Vic, those days. Unlike today, they didn't use mikes. So your voice got quite big. His voice was stretched. So when he was in Chichester, he had the voice which had been expanded for the Old Vic.

"I was very excited, of course, seeing my idol. And he came on and the whole audience *froze.* I mean really frightened, frozen awestruck. Because he's kind of like—this is an acting *machine,* this is, you know, the Rocky of the classical theater. And he came on with the robe and he had this white costume and his black makeup that took three hours to put on, and he'd polished his face, even the eyelids and under the eyelids and inside the eye, the white and everything, and pink palms, everything *worked,* so it was beautiful. And you have this voice, really deep, wonderful voice: [quoting Olivier as Othello] *'Keep up your bright swords . . .'*

"And I was thrilled of course. We're watching him like he's taking us to another world, the world of the super-actor. Something thrilling about that, quite thrilling, like seeing Kean. As he got into it, as Iago put the poison in and he [Olivier] starts getting into second gear, you know, he starts to do things vocally and physically which are strange and bizarre. And with his hands and fingers and teeth. And he gets excited and starts going into the *furore,* the fit: *'Be sure of proof, the occular proof . . .'* And he grabs himself and suddenly he becomes—his hips are moving and there's excitement and he *comes*! Fantastic!

"It's the end of the first act, you know, and the curtain comes down, the audience can't clap, because it seemed silly. You couldn't clap. Clapping was not *enough.* It seemed like you've seen a human *sacrifice,* and you could not *clap* that. You couldn't even *live* anymore."

He laughs. "You felt having seen this, how can you go to the *bar*? How can you say, 'Do you have a gin and tonic?' It seemed absurd. You felt, just get on the *floor.* Howl, scream, do something. But you can't go, 'Shall we have a drink, dear?' And so nobody spoke to each other.

"That was a fantastic night. Everybody *changed* that night. Nobody remained ever the same. And then gradually people shifted in their seats and got up. Nobody spoke. People could barely speak to their partners. Their voices sounded thin, empty. You couldn't speak, you were like awestruck. You couldn't say—you know, 'What did you *think*?' to your lady friend. It was fantastic. So that was something I never *ever* witnessed. An audience that was stunned into fright. Stunned. And then that night, everybody changed. People who had never made love to their wives in thirty years fucked like pokers."

"Like pokers?"

"You know, when you stoke the fire? Suddenly everybody was—*he attacked* something in you. I mean it was hideous to watch, it was frightening, unbelievable." Berkoff, it occurred to me, was conjuring up once again a variety of the unbearable, not exactly unbearable pleasure (this was a tragedy after all), but pleasure of some kind in the unbearable suffering or the unbearable *accuracy.* The fidelity with which Olivier depicts murderously unbearable suffering.

"Was it his charisma or was it, did he have some vision of Othello that was different from—?"

"It was charisma, power, it was a daring movement, strange absurd mannerisms, howls, screams, crying. I mean, heaving, you know, weeping. And crazy gestures. Like when he had the fit: cross-eyed, smelling his hands and all kind of things he'd worked out or had read about, epilepsy when the smell comes and the—you know, it was the beauty of the *gesture* . . ."

THE GARRICK GESTURE

The beauty of the gesture, yes. While Berkoff likes to style himself an innovator, a rebel, a modernizer, an electron microscope guy, what seems to me to be the source of his power and distinction as an actor is the way it is a *return* to the grand histrionic gestural language of eighteenth- and nineteenth-century Shakespeareans like Garrick and Kean. It's what he admires most in contemporary actors such as Christopher Plummer.

"I thought *he* was very much in the Olivier mode. I worked with him when they did a *Hamlet* at Elsinore for the BBC. And I thought this actor can wipe the floor with any English actor. He had a purity and he had this voice. He influenced me. Watching him, I had to keep switching between Olivier and Plummer, who was best? Especially in the *Hamlet.* What Plummer was doing in the *Hamlet* was a tremendous, vivacious, electrifying vocal delivery. Plus almost balletic and perfect use of gesture. And utter madness and brilliance and daring to push the envelope of madness—of Hamlet's madness. A completely satanic, revelatory performance. And his voice was like nothing else. It was beautiful. When he hit a note it was—the whole room at the rehearsal all shriveled. Fantastic! So I was watching, I thought this guy was genius. *Genius!* And I watched his gestures and I learned. Then after that I did a play in London, *Zoo Story,* which is actually quite different. But having absorbed Plummer, I was released in gestural expression and I got the most fantastic reviews I ever had."

It's this gestural power I believe that makes Berkoff's Shakespeare so distinctive, links it to the era of Garrick and Kean. Makes it a theory not just about playing Shakespeare, but a theory about what the "Shakespearean" is. An implicit assumption that Shakespeare wouldn't have written plays and passages that had the *potential* to drive people to fainting and frenzy if he hadn't *wanted* that kind of frenzy unleashed by actors in the theater.

It's what makes Berkoff's brief embodiment of Richard III in the "Villains" piece such a tour de force. Again Berkoff's intellectual analysis of Richard's evil didn't seem to do justice to the depths of Richard's wickedness the way his acting emphatically does. He appears to buy into Richard's self-exculpation: the way the hunchback schemer blames his wicked nature on his deformity, on his hump. Virtually asks for our pity. Do we really think Richard III wants our pity, cares what we think except to deceive us as he dissembles with all?

As someone wrote recently, it may be a mistake to take literally Richard's "victim defense" of himself, rather than looking at it as "a transparently cynical parody of the victim defense by someone whose predilection for evil is far deeper and more complex than some all too easily understandable compensation for his conspicuous hump." Okay, that was me, in *Explaining Hitler,* comparing the "victim" explanations of Hitler—the attempt to blame his malevolence on some deformity—with Richard III's disingenuous rationale for his "motiveless malignancy" (Coleridge on Iago). A level of evil for the sake of evil, evil for the art of evil, that defies easy explanation.

But when Berkoff *becomes* Richard rather than explains him, when he embodies Richard not just verbally, but gesturally, emotionally, primally, the effect is sensational.

You can see it in one particular speech—Richard's first soliloquy—in the predecessor history play that introduces his character, *Henry VI, Part 3.* It's not merely Richard's first soliloquy, it's sometimes regarded as Shakespeare's first soliloquy, the first extended instance of villainous introspection by the character who first made Shakespeare the rage. A character who has continued to fascinate and terrify for centuries afterward.

It's one of the longest soliloquies in Shakespeare in addition to being one of the first. It's one of those moments in which you can virtually watch Shakespeare's genius unfold before your eyes, watch Shakespeare becoming *Shakespearean,* as he shows us a man becoming a monster before our eyes.

It's the one that begins with Richard contemplating all the obstacles—all the intervening successors to the throne he must murder before he can become king.

"Well, say there is no kingdom then for Richard . . ." he jests bitterly, "I'll make my heaven in a lady's lap."

A thought that devolves into an ecstasy of self-loathing (if you believe he's "sincere"):

Why, love forswore me in my mother's womb;
And for I should not deal in her soft laws,
She did corrupt frail nature with some bribe,
To shrink mine arm up like a wither'd shrub,
To make an envious mountain on my back,

Where sits deformity to mock my body;
To shape my legs of an unequal size,
To disproportion me in every part,
Like to a chaos, or an unlick'd bear-whelp . . .

Watching Berkoff play this on a bare stage, watching him as he twists his body into a writhing serpentine corkscrew of malice, watching him as he becomes possessed by the beat and power of the pentameter is, well . . . Once in Haiti I was driven far into the backwoods beyond Port-au-Prince to attend a voodoo ceremony. Watching Berkoff was like watching the *hougan,* the voodoo priest, being seized by the *loa,* the serpentine spirit of darkness. With Richard it's an evil spirit within that causes the metaphysical deformity, not the physical deformity that gives rise to the evil.

And then, in the concluding lines he becomes all gesture, clawing the air as he describes himself fighting to find his way to the throne:

. . . like one lost in a thorny wood,
That rents the thorns, and is rent with the thorns,
Seeking a way, and straying from the way,
Not knowing how to find the open air,
But toiling desperately to find it out—
Torment myself to catch the English crown;
And from that torment I will free myself,
Or hew my way out with a bloody axe.
Why, I can smile, and murther whiles I smile . . .
Change shapes with Proteus for advantages,
And set the murtherous Machevil to school.
Can I do this, and can not get a crown?
Tut, were it farther off, I'll pluck it down.

It becomes like the birth pangs of a demon child struggling to escape the womb, to be born into the full flowering of his wickedness. It's excessive, but it's beautifully, theatrically excessive. Not designed for subtlety. Climaxing with the murderously ecstatic boast that he "can smile, and murther whiles I smile . . . / Can I do this, and can not get a crown? / Tut, were it farther off, I'll pluck it down."

Suddenly, shockingly flourishing thorn-rent hands to the audience, Berkoff opens his fists to display the sticky stigmata of evil: hands dripping with blood. Stage blood, yes, an actor's trick, it too is *way* over the top, but it didn't feel that way at the time. It felt like the appropriately bloody climax to a black mass.

Behind the melodrama is an attempt—in that line about someone who can "smile, and murther," an image Hamlet reprises (Claudius "can smile and smile and be a villain")—to capture some higher consciousness of evil, to capture the delight—the deep pleasure—in evil for the sake of evil. Not ordinary evil, not crippled-inner-child, low-self-esteem psychological evil, but a radical, smiling evil that is chillingly modern.

Most scholars date *Richard III* at or before 1593, before Shakespeare turned thirty. Some six or seven years later, as we've seen, his Hamlet would advise the Players who arrive at Elsinore, "do not saw the air too much with your hand, thus . . . for in the very torrent, tempest, and, as I may say, whirlwind of your passion, you must acquire and beget a temperance that may give it smoothness."

But what we also see is that while Shakespeare was capable of a temperance, he never lost, even in *Hamlet,* an affection for the "torrent, tempest, and . . . whirlwind" of passion. Whatever lip service he gives to temperance, Hamlet seems to admire acting that amazes, goes beyond the natural to the supernatural.

Berkoff does a number of thought-provoking riffs from *Hamlet* in his "Villains" piece. He has an interesting notion that in certain respects, Hamlet should be seen not as a blameless or tragic hero, but as a callous villain. He singles out the moment after Hamlet kills Polonius, for instance, thinking it's the king hiding "behind the arras" in Gertrude's chamber.

Berkoff seizes on what he characterizes as Hamlet's boastful indifference to the killing. The way Hamlet virtually sneers at Polonius's corpse. The way he tells the dead body: "I took thee for thy better. . . . / Thou find'st to be too busy is some danger."

Berkoff repeats the line like an incantation: "Thou find'st to be too busy is some danger," sneering at Hamlet's sneering. Contemptuous of this casual indifference, all the more reprehensible for its offhandedness. It's a good point. (Berkoff once told me in all seriousness that he believed Polonius's precepts—"To thine own self be true," etc.—can, indeed should, be taken non-ironically despite the comic sententiousness with which they are most often delivered. And it turns out there's a long tradition of scholarly dispute on just this question, in which one faction maintains it is Shakespeare's challenge to us—a test—to see if we can get beyond the comic messenger to the substantive message.) But the most fascinating moment in Berkoff's riff on Hamlet was, to me, the Garrick gesture.

I might not have noticed it for what it was if I hadn't recently read about it, but there it was, when Berkoff was doing a bit from the scene when Hamlet first sees the ghost of his father.

The Ghost catches Hamlet by surprise. It's midnight on the battlements of Elsinore, where Hamlet's come with Horatio to seek to glimpse the specter he's heard about. As he waits, he delivers (in the Folio version) a long meditation on the origin of evil—the "vicious mole of nature" speech—when suddenly Horatio interrupts:

"Look, my lord, it comes!"

It's the moment when the supernatural suddenly breaks into Hamlet's previously naturalistic world (in which he sees evil as merely psychological, its source some "vicious mole of nature").

It's at this moment—at first glimpsing the Ghost—Berkoff, as Hamlet, slowly turns on stage and then gives a sudden, exaggerated gesture: one hand flies up to his face as if to hide from the dread sight, the other shoots out and up as if to seek to forfend—or to touch—the specter. I'd just seen a drawing of that very gesture, one of the most famous in theatrical history. The gesture made by the legendary eighteenth-century Shakespearean David Garrick, when he played Hamlet in Drury Lane. Hamlet suddenly thrust onto the threshold of apprehension.

"Were you consciously replicating Garrick's gesture?" I asked Berkoff.

"Oh yes," he said. "One critic, I forget who it was, said that when Garrick saw the Ghost, he did more than make the whole audience think there *was* a ghost there. *The temperature of the theater went down.* The critic actually felt it getting *cold.* He *did* something. It started very, very slow, and then he sees it, and then he goes—from the slowness and people getting used to slowness . . ."

We were in the bright-lit dining room of the Gramercy Park Hotel as Berkoff began to act out the Garrick-seeing-the-Ghost gesture. It's late morning, the place is empty except for a waiter rattling a tray of coffee cups. Nothing could be further from the chill, midnight parapets of Elsinore. And yet . . . Berkoff begins the gesture just as slowly as he says. He turns in his seat toward me, glances up to his left, and suddenly without warning, like some swift Bruce Lee *kata,* one hand shoots up, fending off the supernatural, the other shielding his eyes from the terror.

I must admit it snuck up and chilled me, that gesture: a representation of terror that was itself terrifying. All the more impressive because Berkoff did not avail himself of any of Garrick's ingenious artifices to achieve his effect: Garrick, for instance, was said to have engaged a skilled wigmaker who designed hair that would *stand on end* when Garrick saw the Ghost.

There was, however, one gesture (shall we say) from Berkoff's own production of *Hamlet* that he didn't reproduce in his one-man "Villains" show: the gesture that led *Oxford Shakespeare* coeditor Gary Taylor (who thought Berkoff's Hamlet the best he'd ever seen) to recall that Berkoff's Hamlet "fucks Gertrude." Of course, ever since Olivier's film version it is not novel to play up the Oedipal tension between Hamlet and his mother, particularly in the so-called closet scene in Gertrude's chamber, when Hamlet confronts her with her sexual guilt for betraying his father (lust linked to a radiant angel prays on garbage). But to "fuck Gertrude"—was it an effort to top Olivier, so to speak?

Berkoff had been talking about that scene when I raised the subject, because it's the scene in which Hamlet kills Polonius—evidence, Berkoff believes, of the prince's villainy.

"Hamlet," Berkoff was saying, "is corrupted by the very things we have to do, as many people are. The man starts out as a revolutionary or radical. In the end, he becomes a kind of dictator because he becomes contaminated by the very weapons, the very methods, of his enemy. So I mean, Hamlet causes—has caused—more deaths than practically anyone else in the whole of Shakespeare. But because he's charming from time to time, people forget that. And he drives Ophelia into suicide. And everybody thinks it's a charming scene of, you know, young man's passionate rage against a woman who has kind of collaborated with her father out of a weakness. Well, I mean, he drives her to *suicide,* and after the killing of Polonius, he doesn't react very much. He makes jokes about it. And when Rosencrantz and Guildenstern go to their deaths, he says, 'Why, man, they did make love to this employment.' "

With this cue ("make love") I mentioned what Gary Taylor had told me and asked him, "Did you 'fuck Gertrude'?"

"No, not at all," he says.

It turns out to be a "depends on what you mean by 'fuck' " answer.

"It *looked* as if I was," he says, "because it's a very dramatic scene and I do have Gertrude on the floor. We had no bed in our production. And as I'm telling her, you know, 'Refrain, et cetera, et cetera,' refrain from having sex with Claudius, your husband's murderer and usurper, I'm on top of her by that time, not kind of crotch to crotch, but just on my knees holding her down. And I say, 'It shall go *hard,* / But I will delve one yard below their mines, / And blow them at the moon,' and it was almost orgasmic when I say this to her . . . I tried to make the words fit and I pressed myself right into her crotch. I didn't fuck her, of course, but I pressed myself right into her crotch and had an orgasm. It's quite disgusting." He laughs. "Because I got up and loosened my trouser where the sperm flowed down the leg."

Where the sperm flowed . . . ? I *think* (I hope) he means "*as if* it flowed."

"So you did [fuck Gertrude], right? Well, you came."

"Yes, well, a little *frottage,*" he says. "I was using her body as a kind of metaphor, to point [punctuate] the lines." It was violent, he says. "It was sex and murder."

Berkoff has an interesting theory that sex or talk of sex in Shakespeare is almost inevitably followed by violence, even murder. He believes that "in Shakespeare's warped mind" there is some unhealthy connection between the two. (It's not too dissimilar to Peter Hall's belief that at one point at least "Shakespeare hated sex.")

"Shakespeare's warped mind": I think it's valuable and important that Berkoff is capable of an unsparing critique of Shakespeare, a refreshing departure from the kind of bardolatry that insists on seeing Shakespeare exempt from all mortal and moral flaw.

Which brings us to Berkoff's Shylock.

WHICH SHYLOCK?

It's the most truthful and the most terrible moment in his "Villains" piece. It's the most truthful and the most terrible Shylock I've seen. Truthful, in part, because it's a throwback to the original, a throwback to the deeply repellent character Shakespeare created. A throwback that has no truck with contemporary cant of the sort that attempts to exculpate Shakespeare and Shylock, evade or explain away the anti-Semitism. It doesn't fall victim to the intellectual fallacy, the comforting but deluded evasion that has pervaded many recent productions of *The Merchant of Venice:* the belief that if you make Shylock a *nicer guy,* play him with more dignity, play up the cruelty of the Christians as well, you can somehow transcend the ineradicable anti-Semitism of the caricature.

The problem with the warm and fuzzy Shylock, the feel-good Shylock, you might say, is that it doesn't diminish, it actually exacerbates, deepens the anti-Semitism of the play as a whole. The more "nice" you make the moneylender, the more you end up making the play not about the villainy of one Jew, but the villainy of *all* Jews, a deep-seated villainy that subsists beneath the surface even in those who appear "nice" on the surface. The more warm and fuzzy you make Shylock, the more you make it a play about the fact that even such a Jew will not hesitate, when it comes down to it, to take a knife and cut the heart out of a Christian.

And so I have seen Shylock played as a kind of lovable schlemiel by Dustin Hoffman (in a production directed by Peter Hall), and I have seen Shylock performed by the great English actor Henry Goodman (in a production directed by Trevor Nunn) as a tweedy academic type. And I've watched Olivier play him on film as a distinguished-looking Edwardian banker type, and in each case no matter how dignified and complex a Jew he's costumed as, ultimately he's forced by the text to remove the mask and reveal the bloodthirsty Jew of anti-Semitic imagery beneath the dignified garb. Beneath even the most civilized, gentlemanly, gentrified Jew is—if the production has any fidelity to the text—a vengeful, heartless creature prepared to cut out the heart (or more precisely a pound of flesh "nearest" the heart) of a Christian with a knife.

The intention of all these recent feel-good Shylocks is to remove the sting of anti-Semitism, but to my mind they succeed inadvertently in driving the sting deeper. The Trevor Nunn production can't resist, in the scene where Shylock unsheathes his knife, having Antonio assume the pose of a bare-chested and bound Jesus about to be pierced by the cruel nails of his crucifiers, thus making apparent and visible the Christ-killing imagery in the language of *The Merchant,* and making inescapable the implication: within every Jew, however smooth the surface, lurks a Christ-killer.

For some reason some of the most extreme attempts to exculpate Shakespeare and Shylock have come from Jews. One of the most brilliant of the younger generation of Shakespearean scholars, Kenneth Gross, shocked me when he told me he was working up a theory that Shakespeare *was* Shylock, both literally—that Shakespeare was a Jew or had Jewish blood—and figuratively: that Shylock was Shakespeare's self-portrait. In his otherwise valuable study *Shakespeare and the Jews,* James Shapiro "explains" Shylock by revealing that the "pound of flesh" Shylock wants to cut out of Antonio is really a "displaced" castration fantasy, the "flesh" in question lying below the belt. So it is some Freudian complex that is implicitly at fault, not the embedded anti-Semitism. That sounds like a displacement to me. And we've seen how Stephen Greenblatt would have us believe a conjecture based on an unfounded supposition that Shakespeare witnessed the execution of a Jew—and that when he heard the crowd laugh at the hanging, he blamed Marlowe's *Jew of Malta* for their heartlessness and made up his mind to give us a more "humanized" Jew.

And then there is the mad obsession of Arnold Wesker, the British Jewish playwright. I saw him read aloud from a play that was an attempt to rewrite Shakespeare: Wesker's *The Merchant.* I've read the play and I've read Wesker's diary in book form of his quarter-century-long effort to get it properly produced: *The Birth of "Shylock" and the Death of Zero Mostel,* one of the great quixotic sagas of Shakespearean—and Jewish—folly, I believe. Worth recounting as a prime instance of what one might call contemporary "Shylock denial"—the fear of facing Shakespeare's original Jew.

For those unfamiliar with Wesker, he leapt to fame as one of the Angry Young Men generation of British playwrights, along with John Osborne and Joe Orton. While not as famous as *Look Back in Anger,* Wesker's plays, which include *The Kitchen* and *Chips with Everything,* gave him a substantial reputation in Europe and in his diary/book he's always jetting off to Denmark or Sweden for some new state-theater production of some work rarely produced in English anymore.

But back in 1975 when he could still command the elite talent of the theater, he developed an ambition to rewrite Shakespeare, specifically to rewrite Shylock, to make him not a nicer moneylender, but not a moneylender at all. He made his Shylock a bibliophile, a rare-book collector, not someone the patrician Antonio spat upon, but someone Antonio shared fine wines and true friendship with.

Wesker at least has no illusions about Shakespeare's Shylock. As an epigraph to his *Birth of "Shylock" and the Death of Zero Mostel* he quotes from the British critic John Gross (who writes for *The New York Review of Books* as well). Gross is the author of *Shylock: A Legend and Its Legacy,* perhaps the definitive treatment of the question. Wesker's epigraph from Gross reads thus:

"Shylock is meant to be a villain. There can be arguments about his motives and his personality, but there can be no serious argument about his behavior. Given the opportunity—an opportunity which he himself has created—he attempts to commit legalized murder.

"He is also a Jewish villain. He did not have to be: Christians were moneylenders too, and the story would have worked perfectly well with a Christian villain. [. . .] He belongs inescapably to the history of anti-Semitism. [. . .] at no point does anyone (any other character) suggest that there might be a distinction to be drawn between his being a Jew and his being an obnoxious individual. The result is ugly . . . the ground for the Holocaust was well prepared. . . ."*

But what about Shylock's famous speech in his defense: "Hath not a Jew eyes? . . . If you prick us, do we not bleed?" one is inevitably asked. Some might argue that this indicated that Shakespeare had a more advanced consciousness than the medieval anti-Semitism that persisted into his time. Perhaps. But if the speech is read to the bitter end "do we not bleed" bleeds any poignancy dry as it turns out to be a rationale for vengefulness: If we are alike in these respects, "If you wrong us shall we [just as you] not revenge?" as well.

And even if it were true that the speech indicates Shakespeare's consciousness was "ahead of its time" it does not seem to have diminished the *effect* of the play, the way it drew deep from and gravely exacerbated anti-Semitic stereotypes: even with "good Jews," prick them and they bleed, but scratch the surface and they're vengeful butchers.

Shylock's speech of self-defense may tell us something about Shakespeare's consciousness but it doesn't, it hasn't, defused the historical effects of the play. Hitler and Goebbels were not somehow *deluded* when the Nazis sponsored no less than fifty productions of the play during the Third Reich. They knew the effect if not the intent of the play. In a persuasive essay on the origins of English anti-Semitism the British author and barrister Anthony Julius argued that, unlike most European nations where theological and racial anti-Semitism had the most malign influence, in Britain it was *literary* anti-Semitism that was more influential. Two literary characters in particular: Shakespeare's Shylock and his reembodiment in Dickens's Fagin.

Wesker's solution, his way of remedying the harm that Shylock has done, is to rewrite Shylock entirely, to make him into a perfect and perfectly lovable English gentleman, to make him (although Wesker wouldn't say it this way) into a "respectable gentile." To make him not a moneylender but

* Gross's actual conclusion is more modulated: "I personally think it is absurd to suppose that there is a direct line of descent from Antonio to Hitler or Portia to the SS, but that is because I do not believe that the Holocaust was in any way inevitable. . . ."

a bibliophile, a bon vivant, a connoisseur-like companion to Antonio. Not someone whom Antonio would "void his *rheum*" on—spit upon in public. Rather someone Antonio would invite into his *room.*

Wesker tells us he had this insight back in 1975 after seeing Laurence Olivier play Shylock as what Wesker characterized as an "oi-yoi-yoi" Jew. Here Wesker gives away the game: it sounds as if he's ashamed of Shylock for his lack of gentility. He's unconsciously internalized the values of English gentility and thinks somehow it helps matters to give us a gentile-friendly Jew. An aristo-Jew. In any case an essentially gentrified Shylock was born in Wesker's mind during that Olivier performance.

"Then came the moment," Wesker tells us, "when Portia announced Shylock couldn't have his pound of flesh because it would involve spilling blood, which wasn't in the contract, and I was struck with what I felt to be an insight: the real Shylock would not have torn his hair and raged for being denied his gruesome prize, but would have said, 'Thank God! Thank God to be relieved of the burden of taking a life.' "

"The real Shylock"! As if there were some historical Jew Shakespeare misrepresented. Twenty years of suffering and madness followed Wesker's "insight," this insight that depended on a ridiculous category error (as the logicians would call it): "the real Shylock" wouldn't have behaved badly, because "real" Jews are nice! Well, sure they are, many of them, but there *was* no "real Shylock," there is only Shakespeare's Shylock. A different Shylock wouldn't be Shylock, and it doesn't help erase the legacy or the reality of Shakespeare's original Shylock to confect a saccharine Shylock.

But Wesker felt that by rewriting *The Merchant of Venice* so that the civilized bibliophile and student of history and culture, his Shylock, would be Antonio's friend, he would somehow remedy the anti-Semitism of Shakespeare's play.

But in an epic act of self-deception he didn't realize that this left him without a coherent play, or with a play that was even *more* anti-Semitic in effect if not intent. Wesker was for some reason intent on changing the character of Shylock but preserving the ugly heart of the plot: the moment when Shylock would seek to cut the heart out of Antonio, conceived now not as a Christian who spat on him, but as his best friend. Which makes things, makes Shylock, far worse!

Wesker's play, originally called *The Merchant,* later retitled *Shylock,* then was the ultimate reductio ad absurdum of all modern attempts to gentrify Shylock: the nicer you make Shylock, the more you endow him with "gentility" in every sense of the word, the uglier you make the Jew within when the moment comes to draw the knife. I wish intelligent directors, actors and academics would stop trying to defend Shylock—and Shakespeare—in this incredibly naïve way. This is true bardolatry of the worst kind: Shakespeare can do no wrong, cannot be guilty of an attitude his entire culture shared, must be absolved and shown to be a Higher Being in all respects—by making Shylock nice. Please.

And yet Wesker's reputation back in '75 was enough to enable him to enlist in this project none other than Zero Mostel to play this new improved Shylock on Broadway. Zero Mostel of *The Producers;* Zero Mostel of *Fiddler on the Roof.* One might have wanted to see Zero Mostel wrestle with the real Shylock, Shakespeare's Shylock. But alas the contradictions of Wesker's play may have been too much for Mostel. There was a lot of strife in rehearsal and Mostel died after the very first performance of the Wesker *Shylock's* out-of-town tryouts in Philadelphia, and the play died shortly thereafter on Broadway. One doesn't blame Wesker for Mostel's death, but the strain of attempting to make coherent the absurd, incoherent role couldn't have helped. But Wesker still doesn't get it. He thinks flaws in the production (not the script) *and* the loss of Mostel were responsible for the play's failure.

What followed was a twenty-year ordeal in which Wesker attempted to get the play produced in English. I felt for Wesker's desperation; Shylock had driven him mad in a way, but everything he did to the Shylock story seemed to confirm John Gross's judgment of the ineradicable, irredeemable anti-Semitism of the play. It was as if Wesker had been both possessed and cursed by Shylock. And at one point in the midst of an argument with his close friend, and the director of the play, John Dexter, Wesker tells us in his disarmingly honest if confused book that, to his horror, he'd become Shylockized, one might say. He finds himself telling Dexter that if *he* (Wesker) were Shylock and Dexter were Antonio, yes he *would* draw a knife and use it on Dexter to enforce a Shylockian bond. It becomes a horror story almost, Wesker possessed by the malign spirit of the "real Shylock," the "original Shylock," while trying to make a "nice" Shylock.

Sorry, it's just not a character you can make nice about, or rationalize as some do, by emphasizing the play's critique of the cruel mockery of the money-hungry Christians as well. Christians weren't slaughtered for their religious stereotypes in Europe; Jews were. None of the Christian characters played the ugly and vicious role Shylock did in Nazi propaganda.

When one encounters this allegedly sophisticated Shakespeare-made-the-Christians-worse evasion, one has to ask why the Nazis put on fifty productions of *Merchant.* Because of its critique of the Christians?

I felt so strongly about this that, when I heard the actor Henry Goodman give a talk about his Shakespearean roles, particularly his Shylock (in the Trevor Nunn National Theatre production I'd seen), I forsook my reluctance to speak up at public talks—and asked him a pointed question.

My reluctance to challenge Henry Goodman came from the same kind of respect I had for someone like Peter Brook. Goodman was an actor of undeniable brilliance, a Jew who was, in playing Shylock, conscientiously trying to do the right thing. Who certainly wouldn't have done it if he felt he were in any way advancing a more sophisticated—any kind of—anti-Semitism. Someone who clearly had taken the question seriously and sincerely believed in his rationale.

And had been rewarded by almost universal praise in the British press for his achievement. In John O'Connor's survey of "Shylock in Performance" (in Mahon and Mahon's *The Merchant of Venice: New Critical Essays*) he cites ecstatic reviews of Goodman in Nunn's production (for which he won the Olivier Award for Best Actor in 1999). Reviewers call Goodman "overwhelming," "superb," "magnificent," "magnificently perceptive," "brilliantly conceived, superlatively detailed," "penetrating, complex and . . . moving."

When I saw it I was less overwhelmed. I think there is a tendency among reviewers of *Merchant* who wish to avoid the difficult issue of the play's anti-Semitism to overpraise the actor playing Shylock (particularly when he's a Jew). But Goodman's skill was undeniable and he was so smart and engaging in talking about other aspects of Shakespeare that evening (he said something about Richard III—which he was preparing to play for the RSC—which suddenly made Shakespeare's method in that play "click" for me, as Peter Hall might say).

Still I had my problems with Goodman's Shylock, which his skill could not transcend. Problems with the ultra-restrained, genteel, even gentile, tweedy Shylock he played, virtually like an Oxbridge intellectual in Nunn's 1930s setting.

I had problems as well with Nunn's decision, as O'Connor points out, to soften both the anti-Semitism of the Christians (Antonio never spits at Shylock in this production) and the anti-Christian animus of Shylock. Nunn radically shifted the position of a key Shylock speech early in the "original" play. It's a speech in which Shylock viciously invokes not a personal grudge against Antonio, but the purported "ancient grudge" of his "tribe," of all Jews in other words, against all Christians.

By shifting that speech from early in the play, when it is portrayed as part of the essence of his, of a Jew's, essential character, till much later when it can be seen as Shylock's more justifiable personal emotional reaction to the theft of his daughter by the Christians, Nunn gives us a more humane Shylock than Shakespeare's original.

And in Goodman's talk he used the *Jew of Malta* evasion which has become quite popular in recent years: Marlowe's Jew, in this view, was far more wicked than the oh-so-human Shylock Shakespeare gave us.

But Marlowe's Jew, Barabas, is such an obvious, over-the-top caricature of a stock-comic villain, it makes *The Jew of Malta* far less *insidiously* anti-Semitic than Shakespeare's play in my view. So I felt I had to challenge Goodman's goody-goody Shylock during the question period, although I tried to do it in the most respectful manner:

"I was privileged to see your Shylock," I told Goodman, "and you played him with great dignity, but isn't there a danger when you play him with such dignity that you exacerbate the anti-Semitism by showing that beneath the most dignified, civilized Jew there is someone who is willing to take out a knife and cut the heart out of a Christian for a debt? As opposed to Marlowe's obvious stock villain in *The Jew of Malta,* isn't a Shylock who's given a more dignified façade a more dangerously anti-Semitic Shylock?"

Goodman took the question seriously enough to give a long, heartfelt and occasionally surprising reply:

"I think that underneath *any* person, whether it be Jew, Christian or any other type person, there is that possibility. It's not a danger, it's what Shakespeare offered us to *explore.* But you have to admit there is that prospect, you've got to admit it's there."

Then he shifted abruptly and conceded, "It's almost impossible to put on this play after the Holocaust, there's something distasteful about it. My job in that context—and Trevor and I talked about this—is if you're going to do it in this context, show a man in all his dimensions."

There is a questionable assumption here, to me at least, that one should start with the belief that it's a "job" worth doing, just because somebody, even Trevor Nunn, asks you to do it. Especially if the job calls for the rationalizing, gentling, gentrifying of this distasteful play "after the Holocaust." It seems to come from an apparently desperate need to believe that Shakespeare cannot be flawed, can never be at fault, that everything he did had to have transcended the prejudices of his time—my least favorite form of bardolatry. That Shylock was a universal, not a Jewish, villain ("a man in all his dimensions"), and not even much of a villain at that.

Nonetheless Goodman was just getting started; he proceeded to justify taking this "job" by veering into a curiously hostile-sounding description of the Jews he'd grown up among:

"I grew up with Orthodox Jews all around me and I saw these people do the most appalling things. I saw it every day of my life. So I've seen people do what you're frightened of—beat their wives, viciously curse their children, become arrogant, vicious religious bigots. I've seen it day after day after day for years. I've also seen there are Christians who are warm, wonderful, uplifting—magnificent people who helped me and my community, which was very poor. So I don't have this exclusion theory that Jews are better than others."

It was interesting, something I didn't notice at the time, only later when listening to the tape, a little bit of hostile projection on me: that I was "frightened" of seeing an unsympathetic Jew. That I had an "exclusion theory" that "Jews are better." One doesn't have to believe "Jews are better" to register dismay at the evasion of the anti-Jewish animus in the play. It's true that I called the warm and dignified Shylock potentially more "dangerously anti-Semitic," so I suppose in a pejorative way you could say I was "frightened" of the consequences of perpetuating, however unintentionally, an essentialist anti-Semitic stereotype that Jews had been murdered for. But Goodman seemed to think I was frightened of *any* potentially negative reflection on Jews (not true of someone who loves *Portnoy's Complaint*).

I don't think that's what I meant. I think that I was trying to say that, in fact, one should not attempt to hide from, evade or disguise the reality of *The Merchant of Venice*. That it is not some inoffensive universalist critique of the potential for darkness in the human nature shared by *all* human beings of all religions, but specifically a critique of something essential, something theologically specific to Jews. That one cannot ignore the play's embrace of the notion that Christian mercy is superior when juxtaposed to a pejorative vision of a specifically Jewish lust for vengeance.

That Goodman believed the former, universalist interpretation was evident as he continued his remarkably extended response to my question:

"I think we are all in the same boat. I'm not saying the world is not unjust, I'm saying what psychologists learn day after day: that inside all civilized people there are terrible, awful things that affect every single one of us. I've never yet met a decent human being that doesn't have indecency in him but they learn to deal with it decently." So in this view Shylock was just a decent ordinary fellow who happened to be Jewish, letting his dark side out.

He's such a decent fellow, Henry Goodman, that I wanted to agree with his universalist interpretation; it would make my admiration of Shakespeare in general less problematic if I could embrace this play fully too. But the problem, as John Gross pointed out, is that the terrible things that are done by Shylock are identified specifically as *Jewish* things, ineluctable aspects of a specifically Jewish stereotype.

Shylock's obsession with vengeful fulfillment of his bond no matter how cruel the consequences (cutting out the pound of flesh "nearest the heart") is specifically cast as an imprint of Old Testament, Old Law, Jewish theology, the Old Law "superseded" by the New Testament's new dispensation of mercy, invoked theologically in Portia's famous "quality of mercy" speech.

A DIFFERENT PERSPECTIVE: THE SOCINIAN HERESY

Still I believe there is an aspect of the play's theological debate that has been overlooked. I think it *is* possible to think of *The Merchant of Venice* as anti-Christian as *well* as anti-Semitic. Critical of Christian orthodoxy in a subtle, profound and little noticed way. Not anti-Christian in the sense of the currently fashionable defense of *Merchant* you hear from actors and directors longing for a fig leaf for putting on an undeniably seductive theatrical work with many tour de force parts: the superficial notion that the Christians in the play are "just as bad" as the Jew, just as money-hungry, just as cruel in their way. It's an interpretation that is strained in that it is forced to ignore the profound theological anti-Semitism in the play: the Christians may betray their ideals, but their ideals are noble, while the Jews are ignoble at heart.

But I think there is a different, more searching theological critique of Christian doctrine available, barely submerged, in some ways right in your face in *Merchant.* It's a critique I came to be attentive to while rereading the play in conjunction with reading William Empson's scathing work *Milton's God.*

It is one of the last works by the godfather of the New Criticism (my edition was published in 1961). And it expressed a seething rage against an aspect of Christian orthodoxy Empson had expressed repeatedly in other contexts. Empson was obsessed with what he felt was a kind of barbaric and bloodthirsty doctrine at the heart of Christian orthodoxy, one he believed Milton wrestled unsuccessfully with: the Doctrine of Satisfaction. The way most orthodox Christianity explains the meaning and necessity of the Crucifixion: that God would not extend his mercy to man, his absolution for Original Sin, that God would not spare man from everlasting damnation without "satisfaction": without man having to pay a *debt.* The Doctrine of Satisfaction holds in effect that the Christian God demanded a blood sacrifice, the sacrifice of his only begotten son-become-man as "satisfaction" for man's debt of sin.

That God, in other words, shared something with Shylock: they both, in effect, demanded a bloody pound of flesh to settle a debt. That Jesus was the Christian God's pound of flesh.

Those who quarrel with the Doctrine of Satisfaction were said by most orthodox Christian theologians to be guilty of the "Socinian heresy," after the sixteenth-century theologian Faustus (!) Socinus, who contested the Doctrine of Satisfaction. And argued that Christ's suffering on the cross was meant to be an exemplum of his identification with human suffering—that forgiveness for original sin was not something "bought" by Christ's bloody death, but freely granted by God. Would that make Shakespeare a secret Socinian? Impossible to know, but at least as probable or provable as the belief his work should be read as a secret Catholic allegory.

I don't offer this as a way of absolving the play's anti-Semitism or of restoring Shakespeare to uncritical bardolatry-worthiness, but to show there may be a theme genuinely subversive of Christian orthodoxy that has been ignored by those who attempt to absolve Shakespeare and Shylock on more superficial and unconvincing grounds.

It was a thought I had again when Henry Goodman concluded his response to my question by counterposing his universalist Everyman Shylock to what he called "the old-fashioned stereotypes in which Shylock was always played in a red wig."

The red wig reference is not insignificant. The red wig had become a convention of theatrical Shylocks up until the nineteenth century. A sinister convention because the red wig was long the mark of Judas, the ultimate Jewish villain, betrayer of Jesus, in the medieval Mystery Plays that survived till Shakespeare's time. Playing Shylock in a red wig, linking him to Judas, was not, in my view, an antiquated *exacerbation* of the anti-Semitism of the play that (as Goodman seemed to believe) one could cast off as one could a hairpiece. The red wig was rather the outward manifestation of the deep theological anti-Semitism inextricably embedded in the play.

And one of the things that struck me when Steven Berkoff talked about playing Shylock is that he *preferred* to play him in the traditional red wig. He didn't use a wig when he did passages from Shylock's speeches in his *Shakespeare's Villains* traveling show at the Public Theater. He didn't use any costumes at all, just casual black garb on a bare stage. But the difference over the wig was, I think, a symbol of why I preferred Berkoff's more honest, more true-to-the-original, true to the play, Shylock, to Henry Goodman's user-friendly Jew, so to speak.

That's why I found Berkoff's Shylock courageous, utterly uncompromising. Such a convincing contrast to the gentrified Shylocks one sees in almost every misguided contemporary production. It's profoundly disturbing because the unvarnished loathsomeness of his characterization brings to the surface on stage something the feel-good Shylocks avert their eyes from. Berkoff's Shylock is the Jew in the medieval woodcut—the woodcut of the sort that depicts the ritual-murder blood-libel: the caftan-clad, hook-nosed, bearded Jewish rabbi, making an incision in the body of a Christian child to extract the blood for ritual use. Berkoff's Shylock is not a figure out of Victorian drawing rooms or Oxford common rooms that the likes of Olivier and Henry Goodman have given us. His Shylock comes from deep in the fevered unconscious of medieval Jew-hatred.

And it's *there*. Berkoff is not fabricating it, he finds it in the language. In a certain way the spittle is the key. Shylock is both spit upon (except in Trevor Nunn's production) and spitter. Shakespeare wrote Shylock's lines in such a way, with so many explosive and hissing *S*'s, that they virtually burst with an emotionally poisonous spittle. Consider Shylock's first address to Antonio, the man whose heart he will later seek to cut out. This first speech is Shylock's response to Antonio's request for a loan on behalf of his friend Bassanio:

Signior Antonio, many a time and oft
In the Rialto you have rated me
About my moneys and my usances.
Still have I borne it with a patient shrug

(For suff'rance is the badge of all our tribe).
You call me misbeliever, cut-throat dog,
And spet upon my Jewish gaberdine,
And all for use of that which is mine own.
Well then, it now appears you need my help.
Go to then, you come to me, and you say,
"Shylock, we would have moneys," you say so—
You, that did void your rheum upon my beard,
And foot me as you spurn a stranger cur
Over your threshold; moneys is your suit.
What should I say to you: Should I not say,
"Hath a dog money? Is it possible
A cur can lend three thousand ducats?" Or
Shall I bend low and in a bondman's key,
With bated breath and whisp'ring humbleness,
Say this:
"Fair sir, you spet on me on Wednesday last,
You spurn'd me such a day, another time
You call'd me dog, and for these courtesies
I'll lend you thus much moneys"?

When Berkoff did this passage as part of his *Shakespeare's Villains* one-man show at the Public Theater, I felt I was coming face-to-face for the first time with the original Shylock, with the full force, the living embodiment, the deeply repellent image of the anti-Semite's Jew: Shakespeare's Shylock.

Even if one reads that passage silently one can't help but notice how packed with hissing *S*'s it is, serpentine, satanic hissing *S*'s. Not only is it packed with repeated references to spitting—"You . . . spet upon my Jewish gaberdine"; you "did void your rheum upon my beard"; "you spet on me on Wednesday last"—but there's spittle built into every line.

Antonio spat, but Shylock *is* spittle, formed from "linguistic fabric indistinguishable" (as Don Foster might say) from venomous spittle.

In Berkoff's hissing, sniveling rendition of this passage he hits every *S* with a small explosion. Berkoff's spittle could be seen exploding into the spotlit air of the stage. His Shylock was wronged, yes, but repulsive in his feigned obsequiousness to his tormentors.

Berkoff did this at New York's Public Theater without costume, caftan, red wig, stage beard or stage blood. He did it by finding it in the language, the way the language Shakespeare has given Shylock twists him into a writhing creature of spittle, obsequiousness and malice—as much Uriah Heep as Fagin.

This is Berkoff's talent, this is what he did with his Richard III: nothing "avant-garde" but quite the opposite. He reaches back and draws upon the original primal emotional power of Shakespeare's villains there in the language. A power that depends on a belief in evil as a profound factor, a real source of human behavior, not just an unfortunate effect of low self-esteem, say. He reaches back before psychologizing explanations for villainy made the villains into victims (of some syndrome or other) and robbed them of their original malevolent power to put us in touch with something more adamantine and frightening, an evil one senses Shakespeare believed in and endowed certain of his characters with. Fathomless—or not easily fathomed—malignity.

Berkoff didn't create or confect this primal creature of spittle. He found it there, once he scraped away the incrustations of embarrassed, evasive attempts to dignify an undignifiable character.

Again, Berkoff's achievement as an actor is far more impressive than his intellectual rationale, which seems to me to let Shakespeare off the hook by arguing that since Shakespeare didn't really know any Jews (most of them had been expelled from England in the thirteenth century—although recently James Shapiro's research has found more Jews than previously thought living in London), his Shylock is just taking a stock villain stereotype "down from the shelf." No special animus. Berkoff compares Shakespeare's Jewish villain to his use of Italian villains, the way they reflect *their* stereotype, of the scheming "machiavel."

But Shakespeare's Italian villains, however sinister, are more commedia dell'arte stock-villain types, they don't partake of the deep theological hatred Christian anti-Semitism endowed Jews with, the sick Christ-killing imagery Shakespeare endows his Jew with. And for every Italian Iago, there's a Romeo.

Nor was I persuaded that Shakespeare's Shylock became antisocial because he was excluded from "community" and thus lacked the experience of love and sociability, as Berkoff explains him offstage. I think, in his defense, it can certainly be said Shakespeare wasn't *consumed* by anti-Semitism; nothing like this shows up elsewhere in his other plays—but that does not vitiate the ineradicable ugliness of its appearance in *The Merchant of Venice.*

But Berkoff's embodiment of Shylock (as opposed to his exculpatory intellectual rationale) is a powerful piece of truth-telling and an important reproof to the feel-good Shylocks of late.

Which made the applause even more puzzling. In the version of the *Villains* piece I saw at the Public Theater, Berkoff's Shylock was the last bit before the intermission. And after a slight pause to register that it *was* the intermission, the crowd burst into prolonged applause. Applause, it *seemed,* for Shylock. Of course, it could be interpreted as applause for Berkoff's performance in general, and not for his Shylock. But it didn't leave me feeling like applauding, precisely because it was so truthful. Perhaps the audience had bought into Berkoff's intellectual rationale—Shylock's just another colorful Shakespearean villain—but the flesh and blood embodiment was something more profound and disturbing than that. It deserved praise for being truthful, yes, but applause seemed all wrong. As Berkoff said of Olivier's Othello, "It seemed like you've seen a human *sacrifice,* and you could not *clap* that."

PACINO: THE USURER ON THE ROOF

But wait. There are those who believe you *can* "clap that." There are those, at least, who are capable of clapping themselves on the back for giving us a *Merchant of Venice* that is an exemplary lesson in tolerance, featuring an utterly unproblematic Shylock.

I'm speaking of the people who made what is familiarly known as "the Al Pacino *Merchant,*" the Michael Radford film of *Merchant* that was released to the accompaniment of torrents of self-congratulation in December 2004.

If one had to devise a production of Shakespeare's *Merchant* that incorporated just about every technique of evasion, every effort to sanitize the anti-Semitism, it would look something like this film.

It's an effort worth looking at in detail because already more people have seen, in movie theaters, on VHS and DVD, this version of *The Merchant of Venice* than (in all likelihood) the total number of people who have seen staged performances in the past century. It is this *Merchant* that will be likely to be *the Merchant* for the foreseeable future.

It asks the question: How much can you sanitize, denature, gentrify *Merchant,* how much can you subdue Shylock, make Shakespeare's villain a hardworkin', loving Jewish father with a bit of a temper, cut the nasty bits, and cleanse (or at least launder) the anti-Semitism that weighs it down like a metaphorical pound of flesh?

At what point in this process does the play become no longer Shakespeare's but something other, someone else's—some bowdlerized, unrecognizable, unthreatening, harmless schoolchild's tale?

Not merely a different interpretation but a different play. If you remove the note of the sinister, of the Jewish-identified malevolence unmistakably embedded in Shakespeare's language, what do you have left? What do you have left anyway that might be called Shakespearean? Again the question of the *Merchant* comes down to a question of: What do we mean when we say something is Shakespearean or not?

But I want to preface my thoughts on Michael Radford's film (it's more his responsibility than Pacino's—Radford even gives himself a "screenplay by Michael Radford" credit for his cut-and-paste sanitizing of Shakespeare) by bringing to your attention an exegesis of the words and image of Shylock from an unexpected quarter. It's an exegesis I've not seen referred to in the academic literature and yet one that makes its point with a forceful polemical intelligence, and probably shaped my antithetical response to the Radford *Merchant*.

I'm speaking of the remarkably eloquent excursus on the subject of Shylock written by Philip Roth and delivered by one of the characters in Roth's 1993 novel *Operation Shylock*.

I might not have reread Roth's remarkable passage had I not been asked to give a talk about *Merchant* at a Fairleigh Dickinson University conference, "Shakespeare and Politics." The conference took place about ten days before the first screening of the Pacino *Merchant* as it happened, and in the course of preparation for the talk, I reread the Roth passage and was stunned by its rhetorical power. It was, as well, a remarkable piece of close reading. An impassioned close reading of just three words in *Merchant*—the first three words Shylock speaks.

The passage on Shylock takes up only two pages in Roth's four-hundred-page novel and is delivered by a character named Supposnik, an antiquarian book dealer in Jerusalem and perhaps an Israeli intelligence agent.

Supposnik's extraordinary outburst comes out of nowhere—although I suspect Roth's reading of John Gross's contemporaneous *Shylock* might have had something to do with his remarkably erudite railing. And, indeed, it could be seen as the heart of the novel's meditation on anti-Semitism, on the Jew and Western civilization and the question Shakespeare's *Merchant*—its reception and influence—poses to both.

The speech begins with Supposnik's reading—his impassioned, hostile close reading of Shylock's first three words:

"I studied those three words," Supposnik begins, the three words "by which the savage, repellant and villainous Jew, deformed by hatred and revenge, entered as our doppelganger into the consciousness of the enlightened West. Three words encompassing all that is hateful in the Jew, three words that have stigmatized the Jew through two Christian millennia and that determine the Jewish fate until this very day, and that only the greatest English writer of them all could have had the prescience to isolate and dramatize as he did. You remember Shylock's opening line? You remember the three words? What Jew can forget them? *'Three thousand ducats.'* "

He has only begun to get revved up, having named the three words:

"Five blunt, unbeautiful English syllables and the stage Jew is elevated to its apogee by a genius, catapulted into eternal notoriety by 'Three thousand ducats.' "

"Elevated to its apogee by a genius." Here almost in passing is a point that is often neglected in discussion of the play: *Merchant* is so malevolent precisely because Shakespeare is so good. So good at what he does. When he wanted, for opportunistic theatrical reasons, to raise the stakes in conventional representation of the Jew, to take the latent theological and characterological hostile suspicion of Jews to its most sinister, threatening, crowd-thrilling limits, no one else could have or has bettered him. And he did it not by making him a comic demon as did Marlowe, but rather by knowing the paradoxical effect of giving him a touch of humanity, just enough to make his departure from humanity more repellent.

You might say that in Supposnik Roth elevates the *critique* of Shylock and Shakespeare to its apogee by an act of lesser but impressive genius.

After his exegesis of the "three words," the relentless Supposnik gives us a bit of the stage history of Shylock and the three thousand ducats: "The English actor who performed as Shylock for fifty years during the eighteenth century, the Shylock of his day was a Mr. Charles Macklin. We are told that Mr. Macklin would mouth the two *'th's'* in 'three thousand ducats' with such oiliness that he instantaneously aroused, with just those three words, all of the audiences' hatred of Shylock's race. 'Th-th-th-three thous-s-s-sand ducats-s-s.' "

It's Berkoff's creature of spittle!

"When Mr. Macklin whetted his knife to carve from Antonio's chest his pound of flesh, people in the pit fell unconscious—and this at the zenith of the Age of Reason. Admirable Macklin! The Victorian conception of Shylock, however—Shylock as a wronged Jew rightfully vengeful—the portrayal that descends through the Keans to Irving and into our century is a vulgar sentimental offense, not only against the genuine abhorrence of the Jew that animated Shakespeare and his era, but to the long illustrious chronicle of European Jew-baiting, the hateful hateable Jew whose artistic roots extended back into the Crucification pageants at York, the Jew whose endurance as the villain of history no less than of drama is unparalleled, the hook-nosed money lender, the miserly money-maddened, egotistical degenerate, the Jew who goes to *synagogue* to plan the murder of the virtuous Christian—*this* is Europe's Jew, the Jew expelled in 1290 by the English, the Jew banished in 1492 by the Spanish, the Jew terrorized by Poles, butchered by Russians, incinerated by Germans, spurned by the British and Americans while the furnaces roared at Treblinka. The vile Victorian varnish that sought to humanize the Jew, to dignify the Jew has never deceived the enlightened European mind about the three thousand ducats, never has and never will."

An astonishing rhetorical performance whether you agree entirely with it or not. (I would disagree when he insists on Shakespeare's "genuine abhorrence of the Jew": one does not have to have deep-rooted abhorrence to create an abhorrent character if one is a great dramatist whose true passion is not anti-Semitism but theatrical power and the intensification of an audience's emotional response.)

But focusing on those three sibilant words intuitively draws our attention to the unmistakable hiss of the serpent in them. Sharpening the point of the spear within *Merchant.* Whetting the knife.

It's an intelligence sadly lacking in the doggedly oblivious Michael Radford production. One that summons up another three words, of Supposnik's: "vulgar sentimental offense." Add three other words as well—"vile Victorian varnish"—and you have defined the Michael Radford–Al Pacino *Merchant of Venice.*

Actually this production doesn't merely varnish the serpentine hostility, it *burnishes* it. In trying so strenuously to distort the play into a civics lesson it exposes what it tries to hide. Nothing anti-Semitic here, it insistently claims. It's not anti-Semitic, it's "*about* anti-Semitism."

Here are some of the statements contained in the hysterically defensive promotional material reviewers were handed at the prerelease screenings of Radford's *Merchant of Venice.*

First the producer: "This is a play about Anti-Semitism . . . and about discrimination and about prejudice but it is not Anti-Semitic. Shylock is a very sympathetic character. We understand his pain, we understand the toll of discrimination he's faced throughout his life and we understand why he acts in a way that is perceived to be extremely vengeful."

Yes, all those Nazi productions of *Merchant* were designed to promote "understanding" between Jews and Germans, to help the latter "feel the pain" of the former, not to encourage them to inflict pain. Makes sense. Or maybe the Nazis just had a failure of the kind of discerning close reading Michael Radford announced he has attained.

Radford—who we are told "added moments that he felt the play was lacking"—informs us in the screening notes:

"It's so clear that Shakespeare is writing about racism but he's not racist and the play is not racist. It's a true statement about culture at a particular time."

This is a fascinating point of view. By this reasoning D. W. Griffith's *Birth of a Nation,* which rationalized Ku Klux Klan lynchings of black people in the post–Civil War era by giving the audience ugly racist caricatures of blacks, is "a true statement about culture at a particular time." And perhaps with a little fixing up—a pre-credit sequence showing the downside of slave culture, perhaps—the racist film could be presented as being "about racism."

Note Radford's evasive universalizing use of "racism" rather than "anti-Semitism," the elision of the theological bias—the play's triumphalist celebration of New Testament mercy over Old Testament Jewish vengefulness. This has nothing to do with "racism" because a Jew could be of any "race" and still suffer from the theological prejudice that was the driving force of Judeaophobia throughout the centuries before "racial anti-Semitism" was invented.

But Radford went even further in an online interview in which he proclaimed that "his" *Merchant* wasn't even about Christians and Jews.

Instead, he told one interviewer, "*The Merchant of Venice* I saw as a piece that basically spoke not just of Jews and Venetians. But using the epoch of the 1500s it spoke of a very modern situation—that is two cultures that don't understand each other in terms of culture and beliefs. I think it's a film that's talking about something other than the controversy between the Jews and Christians. It does speak of that, but it's a text set back then. We hope that people understand what we are saying."

Note first how eager he is to make the film not about the whole distasteful Jewish thing, the "controversy between the Jews and Christians" as he calls it. It's fascinating in itself that he chooses to call the centuries of murderous slaughter, pogroms, persecution, the cruel and degrading ghettoization of Jews by Christian Europe, leading to the Holocaust, as "the controversy between the Jews and Christians" as if it were some sort of long-running debating-society matter. I'm sure Radford is an admirably tolerant gentleman, but look at the knots he must tie himself into to neuter the play.

But setting that aside, what of the cryptic "We hope that people understand what we are saying"? What's the secret meant "for those who have ears to hear"?

Apparently (I'm not the only one to advance this interpretation of the cryptic remark; Jonathan Freedland of *The Guardian* had the same impression) what Radford's saying is that the whole Jewish thing is old hat, that the way to make Shakespeare's play matter today is to see it as an allegory of "two cultures that don't understand each other." Which two cultures would that be? For a Briton with a Eurocentric vision, this would seem to be a reference to the lack of "understanding" between the "two cultures" of Muslim immigrants and the Western Europe to which they've immigrated, and live, often in impoverished circumstances.

So no worries about Jews here. This *Merchant* is really about persecuted Muslims!

People will do anything, it seems, to find an excuse to avoid the sinister heart of Shakespeare's play. It's hard to say which is sillier, this making *Merchant Judenrein,* so to speak, a universal fable of persecution, or the resultant incoherent production. Incoherent because Radford has to hack away pounds of flesh from the play, so to speak, to make his film the bloodless, weightless falsification it is.

"He made the right cuts," the producer averred. In addition to the obvious ones—"I hate him because he is a Christian"—he edits and invents at will. At Will's expense, one might say.

Consider how Radford "fixed" just one speech. It's not one of the most renowned speeches in the play but in certain ways it's one of the most definitive. It speaks to the argument that Shakespeare did not portray Shylock in an anti-Semitic light, in terms of age-old specifically Jewish stereotypes, but rather as someone "wronged and justly vengeful" because Antonio's friends had stolen his daughter from him.

Most will recall Solanio, one of the Christian cronies, depicting Shylock running through the streets of Venice, lamenting the loss of his daughter,

Jessica, and the money she'd absconded with when she eloped with a Christian, Lorenzo.

As Solanio reports on Shylock:

I never heard a passion so confus'd,
So strange, outrageous, and so variable
As the dog Jew did utter in the streets.
"My daughter! O my ducats! O my daughter!

That's all we hear in the film: Radford has cut the last seven lines of Shylock's words as quoted by Bassanio. The lines that go:

Fled with a Christian! O my Christian ducats!
Justice! the law! my ducats, and my daughter!
A sealed bag, two sealed bags of ducats,
Of double ducats, stol'n from me by my daughter!
And jewels, two stones, two rich and precious stones,
Stol'n by my daughter! Justice! find the girl,
She hath the stones upon her, and the ducats."

The cut eliminates precisely the greedy excessiveness of Shylock, his inability to separate or even consider the loss of his daughter as much as he feels the loss of his money. In the initial lines Radford uses they are given roughly equal weight. No prize for paternal love here; nonetheless the lines that are cut give us the full measure of the inhumanity Shylock is endowed with by Shakespeare's language.

In the cut lines we see the transition from Shylock's initially divided sense of loss—daughter and ducats—his normal human feeling as father, subverted by his lust for lucre and become something far worse as it mutates into a kind of inhuman, even demonic obsession with his ducats alone. In the latter seven lines he doesn't want his daughter back, he wants his daughter locked up.

Not just locked up but dead: Radford cuts lines from Shylock's subsequent speech in which he wishes his daughter were dead and "the ducats in her coffin."

Cutting this makes for a nicer, or less repellent, Shylock, but Shakespeare clearly wasn't attempting to give us a more gentle portrait of Shylock with those lines that were cut. He was whetting the knife, so to speak, making the hatefulness of Shylock cut deeper, and Radford's edit dulls that knife, whatever we may think of it.

THE MYSTERY OF THE RING

And here is the least discussed, most ingenious (or dissembling) little trick Radford plays. I have not seen anyone comment on its inept meretriciousness. But it shouldn't go unchallenged since this will be the version of *Merchant* most people will see for a long time.

It's an instance of how film directors have found a way to use the beginnings and endings of Shakespeare films to "contextualize," or more mundanely, put their spin on, the play that comes before or after.

At its best this can be an intellectually provocative ploy, as in Michael Hoffman's way with the ending of his film of *A Midsummer Night's Dream.* He gives us an ending that does not stop with Puck's blessing of the marriage beds, gives us an addendum in which we follow Kevin Kline's dapper, guileless, charming Bottom home to the domestic confines of his real life and his real wife. Without adding a word of dialogue Hoffman is subtly asserting his vision of *A Midsummer Night's Dream:* that it is, at bottom, Bottom's play, that Bottom is the one who has traversed all realms of human and godlike fantasy—and that he, like us, must somehow learn to live with the memory once he returns home.

But in his *Merchant* Radford does something more tricky. He adds two scenes after Shakespeare ends the play. First he shows Shylock, who has been forced to convert to Christianity, seeking to enter—and being barred from—the synagogue of his friends and fellow Jews. Shylock looking, silently, more crushed than ever. (Radford, apparently thinking this will make us feel bad for Shylock, is apparently unaware that this makes the Jews look more cruel than the Christians.)

After this non-Shakespearean play for sympathy for Shylock, we then get another such ploy: what is meant to be a poignant shot of Shylock's daughter, Jessica, the one who has run off with a thieving Christian, the daughter who has stolen his ducats and his jewels. Shakespeare's *Merchant,* you'll recall, ends with some bawdy jollity from Gratiano about his new wife Nerissa's "ring," which has been the subject of erotic raillery at the close of the play (Portia and Nerissa disguised as lawyer and law clerk have cozened Bassanio and Gratiano, their newly betrothed, out of their rings in return for having saved Antonio's life from Shylock).

After the merry disguise and ring ruse has been resolved, Gratiano takes his bride to bed with the words:

Well, while I live I'll fear no other thing
So sore, as keeping safe Nerissa's ring.

So Shakespeare's *Merchant* ends on a note of bawdy reconciliation. But for contemporary directors eager to evade the failure of Shakespeare to be contrite about the anti-Semitism, the end of *Merchant* has become their "Jewish moment," so to speak.

So it was for Trevor Nunn in his Royal National Theatre production, which ends not with unapologetic comic bawdiness but rather with the return of a mournful, remorseful Jessica, alone on stage accompanied by keening Jewish vocal music, gazing off (we're apparently meant to believe) toward her abandoned father.

In searching for justification for, in effect, silently rewriting the concluding tone and content of Shakespeare's *Merchant,* directors have looked to a single line in the last act. When Jessica and Lorenzo are stargazing at lovely Belmont, they hear music and she says, cryptically, "I am never merry when I hear sweet music."

This can be a beautiful, subtle touch—perhaps it's not the sweet music that's making her melancholy; it's her separation from her father, her faith, her former life.

But this subtle moment, by no means the note on which Shakespeare ended *Merchant,* has licensed well-meaning philosemitic directors to attempt to redeem the play from its anti-Semitism at its very last moment, by giving Jessica a star-turn in order to conclude the play with a sorrowful Jew feeling the weight of an anti-Semitic world.

We are supposed to intuit in her deep feelings of regret and affection for her abandoned Jewish identity. And of course recognize the deep reverence for Jewishness on the part of the people behind the production.

Radford's approach might be seen as even more heavy-handed were it not so curiously inept in its O. Henry-ish ambitions.

Once again Jessica stars in a concluding "Jewish moment" (actually the second Jewish moment after the spectacle of Shylock's exclusion from the synagogue). Radford makes his Jewish moment about Jessica's turquoise ring.

You'll recall that momentary flash of human feeling Shylock displays when his moneylender friend Tubal tells him of the reports he's heard about the behavior of Shylock's absconded daughter.

Tubal claims he was shown a ring by one of Antonio's creditors. One "that he had of your daughter for a monkey."

This cuts Shylock to the quick:

"Out upon her! Thou torturest me, Tubal. It was my turkis [turquoise], I had it of [his dead wife] Leah when I was a bachelor. I would not have given it for a wilderness of monkeys."

A wilderness of monkeys! A phrase with an eerie, chilling, heartbreaking, expressive power. One of those strange memorable phrases that is Shakespeare at his most "Shakespearean." Radford accompanies it with a quick flashback cut to a scene of a flushed, wanton-looking Jessica apparently in some tavern laughing as she trades her ring for a monkey, an animal traditionally associated with brazen lust (as is "ring" given salacious connotation in the very last exchange of the play).

But Radford apparently doesn't want to give us a Jew, Jessica, with any flaws. Having needlessly conjured up the picture of the wanton vixen Jessica, he seems to want to undo it. No anti-Semitism here, remember. No bad behavior by Jews. Not in *The Merchant of Venice.*

And so in the final shot of the movie we see Jessica, separated from the Christians at Belmont in what has now become the traditional non-Shakespearean "Jewish moment." But unlike Nunn's silently weeping Jessica hearing Hebrew melodies, here she's doing something strange: she's gazing at the turquoise ring on her finger, and—clearly—thinking longingly of her father and mother.

But how did she get the turquoise ring back? Or did she ever give it away? Did the monkey have a money-back guarantee? Was the vivid flashback to the flushed and wanton Jessica just Shylock's tormented imagination, inflamed by a false story told to torment him by his false Jewish friend Tubal?

To saddle one of Shakespeare's most difficult, important, problematic plays with some labored attempt at an O. Henry "surprise" ending seems, if not beneath contempt, beyond comment. The only thing one can say for it is that most people I spoke to who'd seen it couldn't figure out what it was supposed to be doing there. What it was attempting to add to Shakespeare's conception of Jessica, the play, Jews, monkeys, you name it. All it conjured up was a poorly focused desperation to prove that Shakespeare had somehow written a philosemitic play, a desperation that spoke more clearly than anything of the anti-Semitism it sought to cover up.

Any attentive spectator's thoughts leaving the movie theater are less likely to be about "racism" or "anti-Semitism" or the relationship between justice and mercy but rather: What *was* that ring thing about? What happened to the monkey?

The most "logical" (if that is the word) possibility that suggests itself is that Tubal's account to Shylock of Jessica's ring-for-monkey trade was false. A malicious falsehood designed to hurt him—whether by one of Antonio's creditors or by Tubal himself. Though why would Tubal, his supposed friend, seek to torture Shylock as he does? (Because he's a Jew, and that's a typically Jewish thing to do? No, no anti-Semitism here, can't be.)

Radford's motivations for this unnecessary and over-ingenious, poorly thought out device (which will nonetheless become *the* ending of *Merchant* for the millions now and in the future) are as incoherent as the device.* I wish I didn't feel an obligation to point out this deceit posing as a Shakespearean finale, but alas, none of the critics I read paid it any attention, nobody seemed to care. It's not as if the way Shakespeare's plays end matters much, does it? Or that we should pay any attention to *his* last word on such a question when there are so many more things to say in the director's head.

POOR AL

Of course Radford's chief "device," one might say, is Al Pacino and the way he had him play the Jew.

It's deeply sad watching Pacino's denatured Shylock. Especially when you revisit *Looking for Richard*—which contains a few scenes of Pacino playing Richard III with a brilliant malevolence: to see all that talent for malice subdued here, despite the language that licenses it.

Resolutely stifling his talent, Pacino plays Shylock as nothing more than a hard-pressed workingman, and a dull one at that. A blue-collar "Joe Sixpack Shylock" I called him in an essay at the time of the release. A Shylock

* I've omitted any attempt to explain the baffling scene of men shooting arrows (at fish?) in the lagoon that is the very final image in the film. Needless to say another Radford "improvement" on Shakespeare.

who's just a harassed Jewish father worried about his daughter, almost like Tevye in *Fiddler on the Roof.* I suggested they retitle Radford's film *The Usurer on the Roof.*

This was a bit unkind, but I felt Pacino's studied, sedulous sullenness was a mistake, robbed his Shylock of his inherent theatricality as a character for the sake of some dumbed-down idea that Shakespeare didn't think of him as malevolent but merely dumb and wronged.

I saw the Radford/Pacino *Merchant* twice within a two-week interval just to make sure I was seeing what I thought I saw, and I must say the second time it seemed even worse. The second time I found myself fascinated by a moment in the trial scene when Shylock is seen whetting his knife, sharpening the blade the better to carry out his "forfeiture" by using that knife to cut a pound of flesh from Antonio, "nearest the heart."

"Why dost thou whet thy knife so earnestly?" Bassanio asks, in the text, making it clear Shylock is doing his chilling knife-sharpening in full view of all, seeking to torment and terrify, before exacting his revenge.

Here is the most vile anti-Semitic scene in the play, one which would inevitably call up in the minds of Shakespeare's audiences ingrained cultural memories of ritual murder accusations against Jews (the "blood libel"). Shakespeare certainly knew what he was doing when he had Shylock demonstratively, eagerly and greedily whet his knife for Christian blood.

And it is, in a way, a metaphor for the relationship between Shakespeare and anti-Semitism in this play. Shakespeare takes the seldom used (because there were so few Jews in England) old rusty knife of anti-Semitism from the musty drawer, and hones and sharpens it to a vicious cutting edge.

This aspect of the Jew is what Michael Radford chooses to be faithful to. Because it's all about Muslims anyway, right? In any case I was amazed that such a travesty was welcomed with open arms by so many film reviewers. It was Shakespeare! The Great Bard! One of his most famous plays! A stellar cast, lavish luxuriant sets, a big budget, Al Pacino. Who would dare question it?

There were so many oblivious, nearly idiotic quotes from reviewers. "If you've never seen Shakespeare on the screen before, this may be the one to see!" said one. And indeed that is the tragedy, it's likely this is the only Shakespeare on film many *will* see, and it's a meretricious impostor from beginning to end. (Well, except for Jeremy Irons as Antonio.)

As far as I can tell there were only two major reviewers who put their finger on what was really wrong with what has now become the Revised

Standard Version of *Merchant* and Shylock—it's not anti-Semitic, but *about* anti-Semitism.

One was James Bowman, a former editor of the *TLS* reviewing in *The New York Sun,* who said this production convinced him that *Merchant* was just no longer playable. If it had to be transformed into something else from Shakespeare's *Merchant* in order to render it inoffensive, why do it at all?

And Jonathan Freedland, reviewing it in *The Guardian,* went further in at least one respect than I did in saying that this bowdlerized production was even more anti-Semitic than those productions that didn't try as hard to deny the reality of what was in the text.

"It's clear," Freedland wrote, "that director Michael Radford does not want to make an anti-semitic film. But he has two big problems. The first is the play. The second is the medium."

As for the play, Freedland tells us, "We may want it to be a handy, sixth-form-friendly text exposing the horrors of racism, but Shakespeare refuses to play along. . . . Harold Bloom has declared, 'One would have to be blind, deaf and dumb not to recognise that Shakespeare's grand, equivocal comedy *The Merchant of Venice* is nevertheless a profoundly anti-semitic work.'

"There is no getting away from it," Freedland continued: "Shylock is the villain, bent on disproportionate vengeance. Crucially, his villainy is not shown as a quirk of his own, individual personality [the Henry Goodman rationale], but is rooted overtly in his Jewishness."

This is similar to my thinking, and I repeat his views at least in part to suggest that I am not alone in my view. Freedland, Bloom, John Gross find that, with all the equivocations you want to find, there is a unified attempt in Shakespeare's play to evoke anti-Semitic sentiments and bring them to bear not just on Shylock, but on Jews in general.

What I suggested in my talk at the Fairleigh Dickinson colloquium is that Keats's "negative capability" is useful here. Shakespeare was undeniably the greatest playwright in the language. *Merchant* (the one he wrote, not the travesty Radford filmed) is undeniably anti-Semitic. Negative capability requires us to hold these two opposed concepts in our mind without reducing them to a single conclusion. It doesn't necessarily make Shakespeare a committed anti-Semite. There is little in the other plays to suggest it was a preoccupation. It does make him an opportunistic dramatist. But we don't have to distort his drama in order to remove all imperfection from his being.

But Freedland makes another point worth paying attention to. He says there is something about "the medium," about film, that exacerbates the worst aspects of the play.

He argues that Radford "has deepened his trouble by making a film. For the very nature of the medium aggravates the traditional dilemmas of staging *The Merchant of Venice.* We may want to dismiss Portia and friends as ghastly airheads, in contrast with weighty Shylock, but that's tricky when they are played by beautiful A-list film stars, in gorgeous locations accompanied by delightful music. How can we do anything but sympathise with Antonio, when he's played by Jeremy Irons—exposing his chest to Shylock's knife in an almost Christlike pose?

"Film is an emotive medium, uniquely able to manipulate through lighting and music as well as words. . . . More importantly, Shakespeare is simply experienced differently on stage. . . . To hear the words 'dog Jew' shouted on Dolby Surround speakers; to see a Jew fall to his knees and forced to convert to Christianity on a wide screen, cannot fail to have a different, and greater power."

He adds, "That doesn't mean that such scenes should never be shown on film." And I would agree with him—I don't believe that *Merchant* should be banned or never shown. I'm just not sure of the rationale for showing it rather than *reading* it. One could study it as a historical artifact. One could study its language and patterns of imagery in relation to their use in other plays. But one can't airbrush it.

In any case, Freedland concluded, "there should be films that take on anti-semitism. But Michael Radford is not in that game. Amazingly, he told last week's *Jewish Chronicle,* 'I was never worried about the anti-semitism of the play.' "

And it shows. It shows. But I would like to take up Jonathan Freedland's point about film and Shakespeare and the different effects of film and staged Shakespeare. A subject that requires another chapter, entirely: the next one.

Chapter Ten

Shakespeare on Film: A Contrarian Argument

I WILL BE CANDID AND CONCEDE AT THE OUTSET THAT I HAVE A case I want to make in this chapter. A case that might seem at first paradoxical, perverse, anachronistic, even (horrors) philistine (to certain theater snobs whose pretense to purism outweighs the sophistication of their scholarship).

A case that, right now, at this very moment, one can see more great Shakespeare, one can find more transformative Shakespearean experiences, from what is already on film *even in the form of tape or DVD on a television screen* than the average person, even the average critic, will see on stage in a lifetime. A case as well that if you see just *four* Shakespearean films I'm going to speak of you will have seen more truly Shakespearean performances than all the stage productions you are likely to see in a lifetime. And I will make a further even more controversial claim that in certain ways certain films can be more "Shakespearean" than Shakespeare on stage.

This is a function both of the greatness one can find on film, and the prevailing mediocrity of Shakespeare on stage, a mediocrity that makes it unlikely one will encounter anything of truly Shakespearean electricity in most Shakespearean productions you will see in your lifetime. You only have to see *one* to see what you're missing, and then you'll face a lifetime of missing it. Better almost you had not known it.

And even if one sees some superior productions in one's lifetime, superior to the run of the mill, one could still never have the good fortune to see a single Shakespearean performance that comes close to some of the astonishing work one can watch over and over and over again on film. Not just watch once in its entirety, as in even the best stage performances, but rewind repeatedly, study closely on tape or DVD. Anatomize like a patient etherized on a table? Don't disparage it until you've freeze-framed Welles's Falstaff.

Watch every gesture of Olivier until you begin to grasp how thoughtful even his wildest responses can be. Listen to every quaver in Gielgud's voice (in *Prospero's Books,* Peter Greenway's eccentric version of *The Tempest,* in which Gielgud speaks all the roles) for their complex emotional resonances. Burton, Scofield, McKellen, Dench, Bloom—watch them all and then watch them frame by frame. Rewind scene by scene, gesture by gesture. See them, study their gestures, examine their departures from the text, their departures from the past, their departures from your expectations. Discover readings expressed with voice and body you hadn't imagined before, ones that make you think more deeply about the passages—split them open and release infinite energies—ones you might not have noticed without rewinding and rewatching a third time. Do I need to add that even with a great stage performance you can't do that (unless it's filmed for posterity)?

You will know Shakespeare far more deeply watching and rewatching a few select films that have the touch of greatness in them, than catching every touring company that comes through town, no matter what town.

Believe me, I live in a Shakespeare-saturated city and about half the time I walk out at intermission. I used to think one could learn something even from poor Shakespeare productions and sometimes that's been true, but the unbearable pain of mediocre Shakespeare has become too much. With few exceptions contemporary stagings of Shakespeare productions fail to measure up to the unbearable pleasures and intensities to be found on the page—and in just a few films.

I say that as someone whose life was changed by a stage performance, not a film—Brook's *Dream.* But also as someone who has come to realize—after a lifetime of hoping to find something that approached that electrifying intensity on stage—very little ever approaches it. Trevor Nunn's *Troilus and Cressida* with Roger Allam as Ulysses? Maybe yes in a darker key, in the ecstasy of its irony and anger.

Moments in other productions, certainly, individual characters in plays, yes, but it is rare to find even those. I don't think people realize it's rarely *their* fault if they don't "get" Shakespeare. Shakespeare done right is supposed to get *you.* That is an almost ineluctable element of the Shakespearean experience. It's likely if you didn't get it, it's not your fault; it wasn't there in the production in the first place. It didn't happen.

There's something tragic about this, about the vast mediocrity of most Shakespeare on stage and the pro forma "elevating" obeisance critics and audiences pay to the experience. There's something irritating about the snobbish disdain accorded Shakespeare on film by the middle-brow mentality that assumes that stage must always be a higher art than its successor, film. Stage must always be preferable to film, however electrifying the film, because of some vague existential argument stage partisans make that there is something "special" about being "in the same moment" with the actors. A stage performance offers "existential contingency." This defense of stage superiority may seem to have merit in the abstract but just doesn't survive a comparison of the experience of seeing Olivier's theatrically malevolent *Richard III* on a small-screen tape with, frankly, every *Richard III* I've seen "in the moment" on stage. Who wants to be "in the moment" with mediocrity?

Or to make another comparison, a tape of an opera sung by one of the great voices of our time seems preferable to being "in the moment" at a performance by lesser voices. Shakespeare is like opera in that way. There are a very few, one, two, sometimes three actors or actresses in a generation who rise to empyrean heights on waves of pentameter and applause. We only remember a few: Burbage, Kean, Macklin, the Booths, Barrymore from past centuries, and we only have written accounts of them. But we can *see* Burton, *see* Olivier, Welles, Gielgud, on film. We should not take this good fortune for granted.

In practice the "existential contingency" of most stage performances means you rarely know from moment to moment how disappointed you'll be. It becomes less about Shakespeare than it is about how tense and upset you are when it's done ineptly.

And in fact most people will see very little good Shakespeare on stage in the course of their lives and only rare moments of greatness. This is a tragedy because they will be right to wonder "what the fuss is all about," as Stephen Booth puts it. But you can find out on film. Think of the hundreds of millions of Anglophone people who have no access to the very best staged Shakespeare: no opportunity to see the Royal Shakespeare Company, Royal National Theatre Shakespeare, the occasional Lincoln Center and New York Shakespeare Festival triumphs, the Folger Library Theater, the Old Globe, even the widely traveled Shenandoah Shakespeare company, to name a few. Not to say these are the only places that passable Shakespeare can be seen on the stage, but it's such a hit-or-miss thing even there. And when something is really good anywhere it sells out so rapidly only a tiny percentage who might want to see it get to see it.

And the difference between great Shakespeare and indifferent or dutiful Shakespeare is not one of degree but of kind. Indifferent or dutiful Shakespeare has questionable qualifications to be called Shakespearean at all, sharing more with the slack tedium of pretenders like the "Funeral Elegy."

And yet so many people are not aware of how much important, memorable, compelling Shakespeare is as close as their video store. I can't tell you the number of times people have said to me something on the order of "I haven't read much Shakespeare since high school [or college]. I mean I want to get started again, I feel I've missed something, but . . ." But they don't want to start out reading and the productions they've seen have likely been the mediocrities I'm speaking of, so they lose any sense of urgency about Shakespeare—that sense of urgency you feel watching great Shakespeare. They shut Shakespeare out of their lives, because it seems inaccessible or tolerable only for its cultural capital, when they are so close to greatness, when a few select films are enough to ignite a passion to read that makes the dutiful productions irrelevant.

What I say to them is something like: Don't bother to *try* to start reading it, if it seems in the slightest like a chore. This is the most exciting phenomenon devised by the human imagination. Drop everything, race to your video store and pick up a VHS or a DVD of Olivier's *Richard III*. It's not the only *Richard III* possible but it's a breathtaking, charismatic embodiment of the play that explains why it became Shakespeare's first sensational triumph on stage in 1593 and why Richard remains one of his most powerful creations. It's amazing to me that so many have not given themselves the gift of this experience.

If you're talking about "getting started," this is how the world got started on Shakespeare—on the malevolent intensity of Richard, who touched some deep chords, evoked some primal fears of the depths to which human nature can plunge. Once you see Olivier's version you will be compelled to read it, you won't have "trouble getting started." And you'll want more.

And then for those who have mainly seen mediocre Shakespeare on stage or "can't get started" reading I'll ask: Have you seen Richard Burton's *Hamlet*? It's just a videotape of a stage production but perhaps the most exciting *Hamlet* I've ever seen. I'd almost say you haven't seen *Hamlet* if you haven't seen what Burton does with the "rogue and peasant slave" soliloquy, even on a grainy kinescope of a 1964 Broadway stage performance. And please don't tell me it's "not like being there." You weren't there, you never will be, but it's unlikely you'll ever "be there" for anything that can equal seeing *this* on your humble screen.

And then if my interlocutor hasn't slipped away from a certain over-intensity I bring to this conversation, I'd ask, ominously, please don't tell me you haven't seen Orson Welles's *Chimes at Midnight* (his *Henry IV* conflation), please don't tell me you haven't seen Peter Brook's film of *Lear.* Because I feel we don't inhabit the same reality if you haven't.

Here are some of the great Shakespearean actors and directors of the century giving you versions of some of the plays that one is likely never to see equaled in a lifetime of theatergoing. Tell me all you want about being in the existential moment in a live production, I won't quarrel with you. But only tell me that after you've seen four stage productions that come within a light-year of the thrilling intensity of just those four tapes, the Olivier *Richard III,* the Burton *Hamlet,* the Brook *Lear* and the Welles *Henry IV*. One could watch them over and over and get deeper into Shakespeare than one could from seeing all of the stage productions one is likely to see.

Again I put it down to a snobbery about film, a snobbery the academic profession to its credit has gotten over, with some excellent recent studies of Shakespeare on film from Herbert Coursen, Samuel Crowl, Anthony Davies and Kenneth Rothwell, among others. But still, stage is seen as prima facie a mark of superiority among those who are unfamiliar with just how electrifying, exhilarating, challenging some of these films can be.

But there's another even more radical level to the argument about film I'd like to make. That in some cases film techniques allow us access to a vision of Shakespeare that is closer to the original than most stage productions allow us to get, despite—precisely because of—the differences in the medium. This is, of course, not true of all films or even many. But the few . . .

It's a case I'd begun to feel strongly enough about to make it the focus of a public forum on film and staged Shakespeare I moderated.

IT'S NOT THE HORSES

In the summer of 2001 New York's Shakespeare Society, which had put on some distinguished programs at the Hunter College Theater featuring actors, directors and scholars including Claire Bloom, Derek Jacobi, Harold Bloom and the like, asked me to put together a program and panel on the question "Shakespeare: Stage vs. Film." While I had some reservations about the premise (why either/or instead of both/and?) and didn't consider myself a credentialed expert on Shakespeare on film or stage, or "performance studies" as it's called, obviously I did have some strong feelings about the subject. And a paradoxical Originalist thesis about filmed Shakespeare I wanted to test out.

Preparing the program was the test. One could fill a small library with the growing number of academic works on filmed Shakespeare, but what I wanted to test out is one narrowly focused aspect of the subject, one way into the question, one of the most controversial, counterintuitive, anachronistic ways into the question: the notion that in some ways film, a medium invented three centuries after Shakespeare wrote, could bring us closer to something, or some things, "Shakespearean" that the stage can't do or rarely does. That there are ways in which film can take us deeper into the language, the thought, sometimes the spirit if not the letter of original Shakespeare. And that, on the other hand, there are ways in which filmed Shakespeare can go dreadfully wrong in attempting to be too "original."

What started me thinking about film as an Originalist medium was the remark Peter Hall made about one of the advantages offered by the original conditions of Shakespeare's playing: bare stage, virtually without scenery, certainly no cumbersome movable sets to lower down or roll off. It was this, Hall believed, that allowed Shakespeare to write drama with lightning-like cuts that moved at the speed of thought from Rome to Egypt, England to France. It was Sir Peter who used the phrase "cinematic cutting" to describe the way Shakespeare is best played with no pronounced scenic breaks.

So there's cinematic cutting and then there's the great innovation of performance on film: the close-up. It's hard to overstate what the filmed close-up has brought to Shakespeare, although Peter Brook came *close* to overstating it with his calm, measured, but utterly radical and astonishing remarks in *Looking for Richard* (the Al Pacino film about not making a film of *Richard III* that featured some important directors and scholars). Brook spoke about the effect of the filmed Shakespeare close-up on the closeness we can get to Shakespeare's language:

"This language," Shakespeare's language, Brook said, "is the language of *thought*. In a theater to do this right you have to speak loud [to reach the back rows] and still be truthful. That's the actor's problem: every actor knows the quieter he can be, the closer he can be to himself.

"And when you play Shakespeare in close-up, in film, and have a mike and can really speak the verse as quietly as this [as quietly and meditatively as *he* was speaking then], you're not going against the nature of verse, but going in the right direction. Because you're really allowing the verse to be a man speaking his inner world."

This is—like most Peter Brook statements—a quietly astonishing, slow-burning fuse. It is a critique in some respects of his own theatrical past, a critique in some respects of all stage acting, not excluding, one must suppose, even the stage acting by Shakespeare's *own* company, performed in Shakespeare's presence, often acted *by* Shakespeare. You could say that Brook is making an argument that the filmed close-up allows us to become more truly original than *the* original, than Shakespeare himself, if that is conceivable.

It's an argument that raises many questions and potential objections: Is the actor's goal to be "closer to himself" or closer to Shakespeare? Do the two goals always coincide? It is possible to argue that Shakespeare wrote language meant to be "projected."

He does suggest that a few great stage actors have solved "the actor's problem" of expressing thought without seeming to rant to the rafter seats, but even then it is *felt* as a problem.

This is the language of thought, Brook said. Certainly one could describe the soliloquies that way, and one of the great breakthroughs in filmed Shakespeare, one of the moments that most strikingly posed the question of whether film in some way was an Originalist medium, was Laurence Olivier's treatment of the soliloquies in his 1948 film of *Hamlet* when he did "To be or not to be" as pure *unuttered* thought.* Unuttered in the sense that Olivier filled the screen with a close-up of his silent countenance—just his head—as we heard, as a voiceover on the soundtrack, Olivier doing the soliloquy. As if we were not just "close-up" but rather inside his head overhearing his unspoken thoughts. Soliloquy as internal monologue. Meanwhile allowing us to watch the play of emotions across his troubled brow as the conflicted thoughts roiled and eddied up from inside, like the surging tide far below.

About a week before my Shakespeare Society presentation and panel discussion (we had enlisted critic John Simon, noted Shakespearean stage director Michael Kahn, the actor Liev Schreiber, who had played a creditable Hamlet on stage, and director Michael Almereyda, who made the

* Olivier experimented with the technique in one soliloquy in his earlier film of *Henry V.*

controversial film that's come to be known as "the Ethan Hawke *Hamlet,*" although that doesn't do justice to Almereyda's wit and daring), I happened to hear a remarkable quotation which adds to the Peter Brook argument. The highly regarded historian of filmed Shakespeare Kenneth Rothwell (author of the Cambridge University Press *History of Shakespeare on Film*) tossed it off at a talk he gave at a conference on the subject at Fairleigh Dickinson University. It was a line from the Russian director Grigori Kozintsev, who'd made a Russian-language *Hamlet* widely admired by film and Shakespeare scholars.

What Kozintsev said was that the advantage of doing Shakespeare on film is "not that you can use horses, but that you can look deeper into a man's eyes."

BRANDO'S BROW

It's deceptively simple—"you can look deeper into a man's eyes"—until you think about how much one is missing from great stage acting because, even from the best seats, one can't gaze as closely into the eyes of a Paul Scofield, an Olivier, a Welles, a Richard Burton, a Claire Bloom, an Irene Worth, as one can when one is watching them on film, in close-up, even at home on a TV, a VCR or DVD.

And when Kozintsev spoke of looking more deeply into a man's eyes it was assuredly a synecdoche for looking more deeply into a man's soul, glimpsing what Patsy Rodenburg, the famous Shakespearean voice teacher, calls "the pentameter of the soul" through which the pentameter of the language is filtered.

And then there is that line from Marlon Brando (anyway one attributed to Brando) that goes: the difference between stage and film acting is that "in stage acting you have to show what you feel. In film acting you just have to feel it." All because of the close-up!

I opened my Shakespeare Society presentation by showing clips from three extraordinary sets of eyes: Paul Scofield's in the opening of Peter Brook's electrifying and chilling 1972 film of *King Lear;* Orson Welles's as Falstaff, in the remarkable Welles-directed version of the *Henry IV* plays, *Chimes at Midnight* (1966); and Brando himself from the underrated Joseph L. Mankiewicz–directed *Julius Caesar* in which Brando plays Mark Antony.

A film which I proposed to the Shakespeare Society audience as a kind of test case for film versus stage Shakespeare.

I'd said that the Joseph L. Mankiewicz *Julius Caesar* was underrated perhaps *because* it featured Brando playing Mark Antony. It was released in 1953, a year before *On the Waterfront,* when Brando was still known mainly for *Streetcar* and *The Wild One* and contemporaries did not give him credit for Shakespearean gravitas. But the cast featured John Gielgud as Cassius, a role that Stephen Booth, another hard-to-please critic, thought was Gielgud's great Shakespearean achievement on film, and one of the rare preserved Shakespearean appearances by Gielgud (if you don't count the Ghost in Burton's *Hamlet,* a silent Priam in Branagh's *Hamlet* and of course his naked-in-the-bath narrator and player of *The Tempest* in Peter Greenway's production *Prospero's Books*).

Mankiewicz cast James Mason as Brutus, as good a Brutus as any I've seen on stage, in a part that Stephen Booth calls a "Kamikaze role" for actors, in that so many self-destruct in attempting to resolve its contradictions. One of the achievements of the film is to give the Cassius-Brutus relationship the weight it deserves in a play that is as much or more about them than about the title character.

And then there's Brando. Well, two Brandos. There's the Brando who delivers the famous funeral oration over Caesar's body ("I come to bury Caesar, not to praise him"), the one who turns the fickle Roman crowd from sympathy with Brutus and the assassins of Caesar into a frenzy of remorse and rage against them.

Brando delivers the oration itself in a fairly formal style, almost as if to say, "I'm quite capable of doing this in a traditional way if that's what you want." It is reported that he took careful advice from John Gielgud about doing that speech and he did it without tripping on his tongue. But it had no magic, little charisma, there was no Muse of fire at work in his words, not to my mind.

But then Brando surveys the vast assemblage, filled with extras in togas making mindless riot; in response he turns and faces the camera and Mankiewicz gives us a close-up moment in which Brando's face fills two thirds of the screen. A moment that delivers what Peter Brook said Shakespearean acting should aspire to, what film alone, the film close-up alone, can supply at times: a representation of the language of thought, of thought itself.

For one silent moment we see thought, or rather conflicting thoughts, conflicting aspects of the thinker play upon the stage of Brando's brow, almost like watching riptides crisscross each other in the aftermath of a retreating wave. It is certainly true that a soliloquy on stage isolates our attention on the (usually) distant actor. But in a film close-up we are as close to an actor as if he or she were looking in a mirror.

And when I say we "see thought," I mean we see mirrored in Brando's enigmatic smile and expressive brow the different ways of construing Mark Antony—loyal impassioned friend of Caesar, or cynical political opportunist, or both contending—and the different ways Mark Antony construes himself and what he's wrought. I can (and do) run and rerun this moment and still find it hard to fathom the drama the conflicting Antonys are playing out on Brando's brow. He gives us the irresolution of the conflict as well as the conflict in a half-bemused, half-cynical half-smile. Amazing the power film close-up can endow even a silence with.

But then there is something else film can do that—used wisely (not always the case)—stage cannot: the long shot. Consider the *long* long shot that Orson Welles chose as a prologue of sorts to *Chimes at Midnight.*

What we see as the film opens is a vast snowy landscape, and deep, deep in the deep-focus shot, two virtual specks resolve themselves into human figures, one fat, one thin, picking their way through the snow, obscured in the distance by the twisted limbs of an ancient tree in the foreground.

It's Falstaff and Justice Shallow in that lovely, melancholy scene from the second part of *Henry IV* where Falstaff has come to extract a loan of a thousand pounds from his old schoolmate, Shallow, on the strength of his prospects should his partner in crime, Prince Hal, take the throne. The doddering Justice Shallow insists on reminiscing to Falstaff about their allegedly wild and lecherous youth together, looking like and reminding Falstaff of a bony death's head—Shallow is the skull beneath Falstaff's skin.

Welles may have chosen this scene as a prologue because it contains the line that became the title for his compression of the two *Henry IV* plays—*Chimes at Midnight.* Whatever the reason, it represents the melancholy, emotional heart of the film. That snowy field they emerge from is, in some way, the wilderness of chilly age they both find themselves lost in. As they pick their way toward us through the snow out of the long, long shot we hear their dialogue in voice-over. It's a moment I'll never forget ever since I first saw it as a youth; it's a moment that grows more powerful the more I watch it, the longer I live.

Welles has edited and compressed and slightly altered it: he inserts Shallow's first name here. And one has to hear Justice Shallow's (Alan Webb) high-pitched, enfeebled but excited voice contrasted with Welles's rumbling basso to appreciate it, but here it is:

SHALLOW: *Do you remember since we lay all night in the Windmill* [an inn/brothel] *in Saint George's Field?*

FALSTAFF: *No more of that, Master Shallow.*

SHALLOW: *Ha, ha, ha, 'twas a merry night.*

FALSTAFF: [Silence as they approach and enter a barnlike structure and warm themselves in front of a rusty metal brazier pockmarked with holes flickering with light and smoke from the glowing coals within.]

SHALLOW: *Is Jane Nightwork* [some wench from their student debauchery days] *alive?*

FALSTAFF: *She lives, Master Shallow.*

By now the two of them are seated on a bench before the brazier, Welles's Falstaff wearing an antic death's-head smile that seems to combine mimed hilarity and frozen horror at age and death, a horror that Shallow seems obliviously intent on exacerbating.

SHALLOW: *Does she* [Jane Nightwork] *hold her own well?*

FALSTAFF: *Old, Master Shallow, old.*

SHALLOW: *Certain she's old. Nay, she must be old. She cannot choose but be old.*

FALSTAFF: [Close-up: Welles's painfully frozen grinning silence]

SHALLOW: *Jesu, the days that we have seen. Ay, Sir John, said I well?*

FALSTAFF: *We have heard the chimes of midnight, Master Robert Shallow.*

SHALLOW: *That we have. That we have, Sir John. In faith we have.*

FALSTAFF: [Close-up: silence]

SHALLOW: *Jesu, the days that we have seen.*

And then for a beautiful moment before the opening credits roll there is a lingering close-up of Falstaff and Shallow side by side, the firelight flickering on Welles's face illuminating the strangest grin poised on the knife edge of horror and laughter, flickering back and forth between him and Shallow's blissfully oblivious grin, both reflecting the dying fire.

There is something unspeakably, unbearably lovely and sad about that moment. It's there in the words and it's there written on Welles's face in close-up. This is part of the power of Shakespeare on film: the ability to emerge from a long, long shot and then focus at such close range upon the faces of great Shakespeareans.

I'll never forget seeing *Chimes at Midnight* for the first time, during its brief first run in Manhattan. (The *Times'* reviewer Bosley Crowther disliked it, although Pauline Kael gave it one of her signature rhapsodic raves in *The New Yorker,* which propelled me down from New Haven to see it.) I was still in college but somehow watching it, watching that scene in particular, I felt I'd learned something about age that would stay with me forever.

Watching it again, watching it over and over preparing for the Shakespeare Society program where I would show it, staring at the flickering shadows from the fire and thinking about the "Muse of fire" that Shakespeare's Prologue had called for in *Henry V,* I suddenly thought: Fire, flickering light: film.

O for a Muse of fire, that would ascend
The brightest heaven of invention!

Was film in some sense the "invention" that Shakespeare had been calling for? The one he was asking his audiences to *create* with the silent power of thought? Did film play that role: a medium able to join with the "imaginary forces" of his audience to *project* the "swelling scene," to raise "flat unraised spirits" to larger-than-life dimensions, in the grand illusion of cinema?

One can get carried away. The close-up for instance: one gains a lot from looking more deeply into a man's eyes as Kozintsev said, but on the other hand one loses something, as well. One loses the presence of the other characters excluded from view during the close-up moment (unless it's a soliloquy), the other characters always present or at least visible on stage, ones that can give context and reaction to whatever it is going on deep within the eyes one is focusing on. Who can say for sure this is something Shakespeare would have wanted, this isolation?

But on the *other,* other hand, with film one can cut back and forth from close-up to wide shot, one has more alternatives, more perspectives at one's command. Individual and individual-in-context can be shown in counterpoint. "Command" may be a key word: film reverses the power relationship between the play and the audience. In a stage production the audience can choose on whom to focus, where to look, no matter who's speaking. Film chooses for you, most of the time exercises command over what you see.

On the *other,* other, other hand, a VCR or DVD turns the tables again and puts the film, to a limited extent anyway, its pace, its direction and momentum, in the viewer's command. I will get more deeply into the arguments against film or the ways in which film can go wrong. But even in some overenthusiastic construals of the relationship between Shakespeare and film there are some intriguing connections to be made between the playwright and the medium that developed three centuries after his death.

In the midst of writing this chapter for instance I came across a provocative remark by Norman Mailer in a rambling essay about modes of dramatic writing in *The New Yorker.* Mailer is recalling an anecdote about Chekhov and Tolstoy in which the younger Chekhov visits the elder Tolstoy at his estate, and according to Mailer's version of the anecdote, Tolstoy concluded the evening by saying, "Chekhov, you are a very good writer [of short stories] . . . but Chekhov, I must tell you, you are a terrible playwright. You are awful! You are even worse than Shakespeare."

According to Mailer, Chekhov goes off into the night ecstatic that he's even been *compared* to Shakespeare, even by a notorious Shakespeare-hater (well, skeptic) such as Tolstoy.

But Mailer has his own theory of Tolstoy's dissent. He asks, "Why did Tolstoy dislike Shakespeare so?" He speculates, "The answer is that Tolstoy was always searching for subtle but precise moral judgment. That required a detailed sense of the sequence of events that could produce a dramatic or tragic event. You had to know how to assess blame. For that you needed to know exactly when and why things happen.

"But there, very much in the way, was Shakespeare, the greatest movie writer there ever existed—centuries before cinema had a silver screen."

What does Mailer mean by "Shakespeare, the greatest movie writer there ever existed"? Shakespeare, Mailer says, "was not interested in making careful connections with his characters. Shakespeare was looking to get the most dynamic actors together under any circumstances available, no matter how contrived. He was looking for superb exchanges of dialogue and fantastic moments, vertiginous possibilities for the English language, whereas Tolstoy lived for the sobriety of moral judgment. So he considered Shakespeare a monster who paid attention to causality only when it was useful to him. Will's people do incredible things, fall in love and/or murder usually with a minimum of preparation—Hamlet—and then deliver exceptional speeches that sear an audience's consciousness. To Tolstoy this was monstrous."

I would disagree with some of Mailer's characterizations of Shakespeare ("not interested in making careful connections with his characters" should read "not always interested in making explicit and obvious the links between characters," if you ask me). But there is a germ of truth in the way Mailer links Shakespeare's lack of preoccupation with the "sobriety" of moral judgment (this should read "disdain for a single perspective for judging his characters," if you ask me) and his being "the greatest movie writer there ever existed." There is something cinematic in his ability to cast light upon his characters from all possible POV's, as they say in scriptese. To do psychologically what a film camera can do physically: see a character from 360 different angles and degrees of perspective. As opposed to stage Shakespeare where in most cases the spectator stares straight ahead from one fixed, usually frontal point of view. In film, connections are elided, causality established often by cutting rather than explanation, understood in shifting close-ups, in exchanged glances. In cinema we can see one character *through another's eyes,* and then the other through the *other's* eyes. And then see them both from outside.

WHEN SHAKESPEARE ON FILM GOES WRONG

To some this can be esthetic tyranny, the tyranny over the gaze, but in invoking the Tolstoyan fullness of causality as opposed to film's sly cutting elision, Mailer suggests the sort of thing that filmed Shakespeare probably should *not* do, or goes wrong when it does: transform Shakespearean drama, written for the stage, into novelistic film. Make it try to imitate Tolstoy in novelistic fullness and sobriety, rather than give us flashes of illumination in the darkness that Shakespeare's scenes suggest.

An unfortunate example of where film can go wrong in this fashion is Trevor Nunn's film of *Twelfth Night,* which I saw shortly before seeing the Shenandoah Shakespeare company's staged version of *Twelfth Night* at the Folger Library Theater, and after Nicholas Hytner's Chekhovian staging at Lincoln Center.

I expected so much from Trevor Nunn's film since as a Shakespearean director he's given me almost as many peak experiences on stage as Peter Brook himself. It was, you may recall, Trevor Nunn's *Hamlet* that played back-to-back with Peter Brook's *Dream* that weekend in Stratford that changed my life. It was a *Hamlet* still not surpassed by any I've seen live on stage (although nothing is likely to surpass the electrifying Richard Burton "Electrono-vision" taped-from-stage-performance *Hamlet*). And Trevor Nunn's 1999 *Troilus and Cressida* was perhaps the most powerful stage Shakespeare I'd seen in the past decade.

If I had to find a single word to sum up what went wrong with Nunn's *Twelfth Night* it would be *landscape.* Nunn made the decision to "open up" the play, to give it the look and feel of a film of a Thomas Hardy novel, all grassy moors and wild seacoasts. He fills in all the intervening space between the courts of Orsino and Olivia with landscape, he gives us long heroic vistas of the page Cesario (Viola in disguise) spurring his/her horse across the landscape. He "opens it up" as they say to represent "real" space and extension as opposed to theatrical space—different locations in the same staged space. He gives us not a stage but a world, not a Globe but a globe, and in doing so somehow the comedy is lost in the vistas.

All the world's a stage, but the stage is not meant to *be* the world. Comedy, we suddenly realize, is more dependent than we imagined on the confinement of the characters on a stage, on the "esthetic microcosm" as the scholar Anthony Davies put it, the closed-off cloud chamber of the stage where vectors of emotion like charged particles bounce off the boundaries and collide. Where the comic mathematics of doubling and cross-dressing and subterfuge and deceit work upon each other, where they can, in effect, bounce off the fourth wall. The confines of the stage are like the confines of Peter Hall's pause-enclosed "line structure."

By removing *all* the walls, in effect, Nunn's film version removes, slackens, empties out all the tension of confinement, the confinement that is the subtext of *Twelfth Night* itself, the confinement of sexual roles, of sexually signifying clothes, the confinement of Malvolio's "cross-gartering," the final cruel confinement of the maddened Malvolio in the "dark house." A madhouse needs walls, not open landscape. One understands Peter Hall's insistence on enclosure when one sees what results from its removal.

Perhaps that's why, of the two staged *Twelfth Nights* I saw nearly simultaneously—the bare-stage, bare-bones, natural light–lit *Twelfth Night* by the Shenandoah Shakespeare company at the Folger (codirected by Stephen Booth and Ralph Alan Cohen), and the lush Lincoln Center *Twelfth Night* by RSC alumnus Nicholas Hytner—I felt the cubicle of the Folger Library Theater far more effective in representing the vectored mathematics of the comedy than the spacious set at Lincoln Center (which featured its own little real-water "seashore" on stage).

Seeing them made the case that Shakespeare contained the cosmos in the "esthetic microcosm"—and that opening the microcosm to the cosmos loses the kind of esthetic closure that, for instance, Peter Hall seeks in line structure. One feels lack of closure too often in Kenneth Branagh's *Much Ado*—the young stud soldiers galloping home from the wars, then washing the sweat off their naked bodies. One doesn't feel that in Julie Taymor's film version of *Titus Andronicus,* which was made with an intensity so breathtaking one forgets the rest of the world.

Stage structure, like line structure, is not inconsiderable both in its power—with a few cinematic exceptions—and in its loss. The exceptions being, in fact, not when film opens *up* the stage, but sometimes when it closes in and confines it even more, in the full-frame close-up.

So I am not unaware of the limitations of Shakespeare on film. I've even had some second thoughts on *thought.* Recall Peter Brook in *Looking for Richard:* Shakespeare's language "is the language of *thought.* In a theater to do this right you have to speak loud and still be truthful. . . . Every actor knows the quieter he can be, the closer he can be to himself."

I was moved to rethink this question while attending a Shakespeare Guild dialogue featuring Guild founder John Andrews, the unmodernized-spelling advocate, and Jeffrey Horowitz, the artistic director of the Theater for a New Audience who was present at my table-thumping dinner with Sir Peter Hall.

Jeff Horowitz had recently been invited to bring his company's production of *Cymbeline* to the United Kingdom under the auspices of the Royal Shakespeare Company, where it received an enthusiastic reception. During the run he participated in a panel on the state of Shakespearean theater to which Peter Brook had been invited. Brook couldn't make it, Horowitz said, but "he sent a letter in which he said, 'The next revolution in verse-speaking will be a return to the original grammar that released the energy of the language. The next revolution may learn from film; we've all been influenced by film and seeing thought, the natural rhythms of thought.' "

Brook's reiteration of this point brought out something contrarian in me. Was it always true, as Brook had said, that "the quieter [an actor] can be, the closer he can be to himself"? How often did Shakespeare write seeking his words to be spoken quietly?

Wasn't it true, I asked Horowitz in the question period, that Shakespeare had written much of what he wrote to be *declaimed,* to be uttered at a higher pitch of intensity, and yes decibels, than the "natural" quiet language of thought that would be drowned out in most of the theaters he was writing for?

It may be true that the filmed close-ups are "closer to the actor, closer to himself," but are they closer to Shakespeare? Might we lose something if all Shakespeare was turned into quiet, thoughtful soliloquized close-ups?

John Andrews responded by bringing up Hamlet's advice to the actors in which he advises them not to "split the heavens" with declamation nor "saw the air" in overly declamatory fashion. I countered by pointing to the purple passage Hamlet specially requested from the Players when they first arrived at Elsinore, the soaring declamatory depiction of the death of Priam and the maddened grief of Hecuba, the Pyrrhus speech.

To which Jeffrey Horowitz replied that he had once heard that very speech done on stage quietly and thoughtfully and with devastating effectiveness.

LET US ACCEPT, FOR THE SAKE OF ARGUMENT, THAT ALL FILMS ARE adaptations, even translations, into another medium. Shakespeare didn't write camera directions such as CLOSE-UP or LONG-SHOT, to accompany his playscripts. He wrote for a relatively bare stage. Nonetheless, films can go awry in ways similar to staged Shakespeare when the director's hand weights too heavily on the delicately counterpoised scale of forces in the text.

As an instance take Peter Brook's *Lear,* which I've argued is one of the four essential Shakespeare films that offer experiences that equal or exceed any Shakespearean performance you are likely to see in a lifetime.

When I first saw it in a big-screen theater I left stunned and shaken. It still gives me a chill watching a videotape on a TV screen, almost as if I had inhabited the icy landscape Brook chose for the film, a vast arctic stage for the bitter exposition of the tragedy.

Brook shot it in stark black and white with a Cro-Magnon-like costume design that suggested a Stonehenge-era setting, almost as if at the very dawn of human nature.

Brook brought his own intensity to the filmmaking. He cuts from icy face to icy landscape, and from face to face, with a kind of savage brutality, as with a butcher's knife. You might see an equal, but to my mind you'll never see a better Lear than Paul Scofield's in this film.

The problem, if it could be said to be a problem and not a "directorial point of view," is in what Brook chooses to cut from the text and what to play up. As Thomas Pendleton, multifaceted Shakespeare scholar and co-editor of *The Shakespeare Newsletter,* pointed out in a critique of the Brook film at a Fairleigh Dickinson symposium, Brook's cuts constitute a kind of polemic: they all tend to omit the often small telling acts of human kindness—the servant who tends to the blinded Gloucester for instance,

Edmund's deathbed attempt to save Cordelia. Moments that, when omitted, Pendleton argues, serve Brook's intent to recast Shakespeare's *Lear* as Beckett's bleak *Endgame.*

Is this "playing fair," so to speak, or robbing the play of a Shakespearean balance that makes Beckett seem more one-dimensional? But these things Brook did on film are things he just as likely could have done on stage.

Then there are things films can do—such as flashbacks for instance—that they shouldn't necessarily do just because they can. Consider Kenneth Branagh's decision in his often admirable full-length four-hour *Hamlet* to give us a flashback scene of Hamlet and Ophelia rolling around naked in bed making love. Setting aside the fact that it offers an all-too-confident answer to a question that Shakespeare seems deliberately to have left unresolved in the play—were Hamlet and Ophelia sexually involved?—and setting aside Branagh's understandable decision to err on the side of rolling around naked with Kate Winslet, who plays Ophelia, it's not exactly an Originalist device. On the other hand neither is Branagh's decision to allow us to visualize on film the tragic moment depicted in that Pyrrhus speech that Hamlet called for when the Players arrive.

But I was grateful that he did it and in doing so gave us John Gielgud's last Shakespearean moment, playing a mute Priam wielding a futile sword about to be cut down by Pyrrhus in the burning ruins of Troy. A sad, beautiful, silent farewell for Gielgud.

And yet such choices, good and bad, are not remarkably different in kind from the kinds of choices good and bad that stage directors make. An exception—not really a *Hamlet* film per se—is the film version of Tom Stoppard's *Rosencrantz and Guildenstern Are Dead.* Which offers in sidelong glances, and overheard moments, some of the best pieces of *Hamlet* to be found on film.

THE GREAT DIVIDE

The deeper argument about film is about the appropriateness, the legitimacy of such an anachronistic medium itself to Shakespeare—and, to my mind, whether in fact it offers a way to illuminate aspects of Shakespeare that give us greater access to the mysterious original power of his work.

And if there is a single film that divides Shakespeare scholars, amateurs, film historians and film fanatics on this question it is Baz Luhrmann's idiosyncratically titled *William Shakespeare's Romeo + Juliet.* (Yes, those of us who defend the film have to live with Luhrmann's + in the title; it is, so to speak, our cross to bear. We also have to live with gibes about the necessity or justice of calling it *William Shakespeare's.*)

It's a film which, along with Michael Almereyda's *Hamlet* and to a lesser extent Richard Loncraine's more traditional *Richard III* (with Ian McKellen magnificent in the title role), represents a new and controversial wave of Shakespearean adaptations that emerged in the nineties alongside Kenneth Branagh's more traditional film versions. Of the three, *R+J* is the focal point. Because it's such a radical adaptation, and because it's so smart about it.

It's remarkable how few people are neutral on the question of the Luhrmann adaptation. To my, admittedly partisan, mind it's a kind of test: those who hate and denounce it do so out of a misplaced reverential gentility: to be truly "Shakespearean" an adaptation must be presented in stately fashion in Received Pronunciation. Those of us—and this includes a number of well-credentialed academics—who admire the film do so not because it is a triumph of RSC-style verse-speaking (it's not), but because in totality it captures the spirit if not the letter of *R&J*'s passion, better than many stage versions that give us the letter (if that) but not the spirit. To have both would be ideal; we're not saying Luhrmann's *R+J* is the ne plus ultra adaptation that makes others unnecessary. Let a hundred flowers bloom, but don't deny this blossom its place.

Perhaps to understand the dimension of the controversy, it's useful to place it in the context of the evolution of Shakespeare on film. It's a genre that ranges from early silent versions, to faithful one-camera recordings of stage performances, to surprising oddities such as Max Reinhardt's 1935 *Midsummer Night's Dream* (the one with Mickey Rooney as Puck). A genre that really comes into its own with Laurence Olivier's 1944 *Henry V,* and his subsequent *Hamlet* (1948) and *Richard III* (1955), films that Olivier both directed and starred in.

There's some truth to the tendency to disparage the rah-rah spirit of Olivier's rousing wartime *Henry V,* which eliminates or underplays the countervailing antiwar ironies that Kenneth Branagh played up in his 1990 film version. Although even Branagh has been criticized for lacking the nerve to include the scene in which Henry orders the slaughter of the French prisoners, a war crime (by most standards) that Shakespeare made a point of including.

But whatever one thinks of its politics, Olivier's *Henry V* points the way to a new era of filmed Shakespeare by foregrounding the mechanics of the transition itself.

He opened his *Henry V* with a conspicuously anachronistic, simulated aerial shot of a simulated "original" Globe Theatre in 1600. Then he takes us "inside" this theater by cutting to interiors of the mock Globe's backstage, where the actors are preparing a production of *Henry V.* Takes us into the pit where the rowdy groundlings are awaiting it, and finally with a trumpet blast the play begins. Clearly Olivier is having irreverent fun with the anachronistic contradictions of filming a staged stage play, with filming, supposedly, the "original" production of *Henry V.* The snake swallowing its tail or vice versa.

Then Olivier makes another metaphysical transition. We start out at the Globe with the Prologue asking for a "Muse of fire." Then the actual play begins with a comic take on the clerics' reading of the Salic law, all on stage, along with the court scene featuring the French ambassador's tennis ball mockery and Henry's defiance.

But then at the opening of the Olivier film's second act, when the chorus reappears to proclaim a change of scene ("the scene / Is now transported, gentles, to Southampton . . ."), suddenly we are out of the Globe into the "world," into a realm without a stage and an audience—the seemingly unbounded realm of film (or film sets) in full. Occasionally to reinforce the defamiliarizing effect of film, Olivier will return to the Globe, to the stage and the backstage hubbub, and then take us back to the open landscape of France. In a way these shifts may have reflected Olivier's own internal division over whether Shakespeare *should* be represented in an anachronistic medium such as film—and the division within himself between the stage and the film actor.

By the time of his 1948 *Hamlet,* however, Olivier had abandoned all inhibitions about film, the camera's mobility and the illusion of reality it offered. Indeed in that *Hamlet* he made the camera a character, no, a *stalker* who virtually chased Hamlet up the winding stone stairs to the parapets of Elsinore castle, then peered down with him at the boiling sea far below, reflecting in its wild surge the wild surging emotions in Hamlet's head. And then the camera seems as if it has entered his head and looks out from within Hamlet's eyes, while overhearing his very thoughts.

By 1955, in his *Richard III,* Olivier has turned the tables and is spending half his time as Richard looking into the camera, stalking the camera, unctuously, familiarly, leeringly, almost too familiarly invading our own space with his insinuating invasive probing of our reaction to his outrages.

It was Henry Goodman who pointed out something important about Olivier's *Richard III* that the film medium exploits. Goodman argues that *Richard* is the only play of Shakespeare's that opens with the main character addressing the audience directly (with "Now is the winter of our discontent / Made glorious . . .").

In doing so Richard establishes, seduces us into a "bond of complicity" in what becomes a series of ever more repellent acts of betrayal and murder. The subtextual drama then becomes our relationship to Richard—at what point will we realize our guilt and complicity in Richard's crimes and refuse his charming but insidious importunings? Speaking to us directly through the close-up camera lens initiates, intensifies this tension, in which we find ourselves seduced, tempted, even though we know he's evil, or (as the line from Milton has it) "surpriz'd by sin."

All of which is to say that, while Olivier's films represent the first widely distributed mainstream film adaptations, and they may seem, in some ways, antiquated to us, he was in fact from the very beginning doing very sophisticated things with the medium.

But in the Originalist sense, another thing Olivier did was bring us closer to what might be called the Great Actor aspect of Shakespeare, the way so many of his plays were written to throw the spotlight on stars and star-turns. Indeed, in his *Henry V,* in the scenes supposedly set in a sixteenth-century production of the play at the Globe, Olivier is playing Richard Burbage playing Henry V. He's inhabiting the role not just of Henry but of Shakespeare's original star.

Critics such as Anthony Davies have done much to elucidate the sophistication of this film, arguing for instance that while Godard's 1968 *Weekend* is often credited with the first use of "double diagesis," Olivier used it first in his 1944 *Henry.* (Diagesis is the manipulation of conflicting time frames in the same film.)

But to me the wittiest diagesis, if that's what we're calling it, occurs when we get that glimpse of "Shakespeare" playing prompter in the 1600 stage play (in Elizabethan dress, but wearing a pair of twentieth-century-looking eyeglasses). It is Olivier's sly way of proposing that he's giving us the text as Shakespeare himself would have seen it through twentieth-century *lenses,* which of course are the lenses of the motion picture camera.

ROMEO AND JULIET VS. *ROMEO + JULIET*

Following the Olivier age, the sixties and seventies saw three landmarks in Shakespearean film that pointed in three different directions. There was Peter Brook's *Lear* with Paul Scofield as the old king. There was Orson Welles's less widely distributed *Chimes at Midnight,* and there was Franco Zeffirelli's *Romeo and Juliet,* a huge popular success.

The first two offer the cinematic pleasures of great actors and actresses in close-up, and the remarkable use of expressive landscape and interiors (Brook's bleak snowy realm in *Lear* is soul chilling; and in *Chimes* the warm-blooded interior of Falstaff's inn throws into sharp relief the frosty, cold-blooded exterior realm of power politics captured in the visible cloud of condensed breath John Gielgud exhales in Henry IV's chill throne room).

Which brings us to the Zeffirelli *R&J.* What's been surprising over the years is the growing scholarly and academic appreciation for Zeffirelli's film, a work originally not taken very seriously because of its lush Technicolor costume-drama ambiance, and its literal teen romance which dared to cast a Juliet virtually as young as she was in the play (not yet fourteen when she dies).

I know that for many years I myself didn't give it the respect it deserved because I'd felt it too personally at the time: it affected me in what I recalled as perhaps a too emotional or sentimental way the first time I saw it. Maybe, I now realize, that was the point: Zeffirelli had designed his film to go for the gut, evoke a kind of visceral romantic-tragic impact that according to contemporaneous commentators made the play such a sensation from the beginning, gave it such an enduring power.

A useful contrast is with the BBC-TV version of *R&J* circa 1985. The eighties were the era of BBC-TV Shakespeare, an era when all the best Shakespearean talent—actors and directors—were drawn into the vast, worthy, uneven but invaluable BBC enterprise of producing serious versions of the entire Shakespeare canon for television. An enterprise that virtually shut down Shakespeare on film. And for the most part offered televised versions of staged plays.

But while I've found many of the BBC-TV Shakespeare productions powerful and evocative—the *Tempest,* the *Lear,* the *Troilus* (and the *Love's Labor's Lost,* a revelation, the best I've seen)—the *R&J* was just too refined and cold. It was a pious homage whose sober, somber seriousness conjures up its comic antithesis: the travestied version of *R&J* put on by the Crummles Theatrical Troupe in Trevor Nunn's RSC production of *Nicholas Nickleby.*

Which is why one has to admire the boldness with which Baz Luhrmann walks the line between tragedy and travesty in his *R+J.* Doesn't walk it, races madly across a tightrope, seemingly heedless of risk, capturing in his film's mad rush the mad rush of first love at first sight.

Luhrmann captures the spirit rather than the letter, but there's more than that. He finds a way of translating Shakespeare's verbal wit into visual terms, captures the dizzying, breathtaking madness of it all.

The prologue, for instance. It's surprising how often Shakespeare's prologues reveal the unexpected, in themselves and in the way directors and actors play them. Luhrmann's film opens with a TV set suspended in space, a set that first bursts briefly into buzzing static electricity then dissolves to a TV anchor in a CNN-type setting. Then in perfect anchorwoman mode she recites the prologue as one thing it is: *news,* or the simulacrum of news, the entire play compressed into fourteen lines—a broadcast sonnet:

Two households, both alike in dignity,
In fair Verona, where we lay our scene,
From ancient grudge break to new mutiny,
Where civil blood makes civil hands unclean.
From forth the fatal loins of these two foes
A pair of star-cross'd lovers take their life;
Whose misadventur'd piteous overthrows
Doth with their death bury their parents' strife.
The fearful passage of their death-mark'd love,
And the continuance of their parents' rage,
Which, but their children's end, nought could remove,
Is now the two hours' traffic of our stage;
The which if you with patient ears attend,
What here shall miss, our toil shall strive to mend.

When you think about it, it's a breathtaking compression of the story which practically mates in two-word phrases the beginning—the "fatal loins" of the parents—with the end (the "death-mark'd love" that leads to their children's end). It's a hectic compression that, once unlocked, Luhrmann virtually *explodes* by doing the prologue not once but twice. First the CNN anchoress, then suddenly we are in "fair Verona" for a visual recapitulation (with the prologue voice-over) done like late Scorsese to a soundtrack of operatic ecstatic chants and subtitled cameo shots which introduce the main characters and then give way to angry hip-hop and the opening quarrel scene. Which takes place at a gas station where the warring Capulet and Montague gangs of "Verona Beach" brandish their "Sword 9mm" guns and set the fuel on fire.

Don't dismiss it for its sheer (or mere) ingenuity. I've seen this opening quarrel scene done on film, I've seen it done on stage. It's usually done in a strained, clownish manner, as if the players are embarrassed by the puns. Rarely with the menacing, fiery explosiveness of Luhrmann's amazing opening (post-prologue) scene. What is often treated as a perfunctory preliminary to the advent of the lovers becomes the murderous, mad violence of clashing male vanity which puts its brand on the entire drama to follow. Suddenly the pretty teenage romance which *R&J* has devolved into in the popular imagination becomes an expression of something malign and deep-rooted and dangerous. Not just two star-crossed lovers but star-blighted, destructively inflamed human nature.

In the Cambridge performance-history edition of *Romeo and Juliet,* I came across something Peter Brook said about his controversial 1947 stage version, produced when Brook was just twenty-one at Stratford-on-Avon's Memorial Theatre:

"What I have attempted is to break away from the popular conception of *Romeo and Juliet* as a pretty-pretty sentimental love story and to get back to the violence, the passion and the excitement of the stinking crowds, the feud, the intrigues. To recapture the poetry and the beauty that arise from the Veronese sewer, and to which the story of the two lovers is merely incidental."

The two lovers are not incidental to Luhrmann, but, as in many productions, his Mercutio, here Harold Perrineau, steals the show, and watching him while writing this chapter suggested for the first time a connection I'd never made before. I'd always been fascinated not just by Mercutio but by the Mercutio *type* in Shakespeare, the fast-talking, mercurial, mad, bad and dangerous-to-know character. Someone, I think it was Dryden, wondered if Shakespeare *had* to kill Mercutio off in the midst of *R&J* or Mercutio might have (metaphorically) killed him, killed Shakespeare, somehow eclipsed him at least. Doom haunts the other Mercutio types in Shakespeare like Hotspur, Cassius, Hamlet, Edmund, Iago. But something more emerges from Luhrmann's Mercutio: Mercutio as Marlowe.

Part of it of course is the way Luhrmann casts and costumes Mercutio for the "Queen Mab" speech: in a two-piece sequined drag-queen disco-ball skirt and top.

But first let me say the surprising thing about Luhrmann's film is that he doesn't rewrite Shakespeare. If you read along with the text while seeing the film (not the ideal *first* way to experience it) you see that Luhrmann has cut, often drastically, but that his actors are all speaking Shakespeare's words. Not, as in some current adaptations such as the lamentable *O* (the high-school basketball team *Othello*), speaking high-school-equivalent words.

Not all the verse-speaking is the best I've ever heard, I'll concede. Leonardo DiCaprio and Claire Danes don't have the flawless verbal command of the couple in the BBC *R&J,* even that of Leonard Whiting and Olivia Hussey in the Zeffirelli version. But they do have something (especially the effortlessly radiant Claire Danes) the BBC couple lack (and Olivia Hussey has): an almost deliquescent romantic charisma. And by the time one meets them one is so charged up by Luhrmann's opening, their blushing restraint is a welcome contrast.

Another stunning thing Luhrmann does is with that great speech about spells in *Romeo and Juliet,* Mercutio's "Queen Mab" speech, the dizzying, delirious ode to the mischievous-verging-on-malicious muse of dreams. Since dreams are such a central preoccupation of Shakespeare, since Mercutio's Mab speech is such a signature Shakespearean tour de force, a defining actor's moment—especially since Mercutio and the Mercutio type seem such a recurrent fascination for Shakespeare—one wonders where this comes from, this fast-talking wit whose verbal facility whips itself into a dangerous, near self-destructive madness. One finally fatal to him. Anything that does something to illuminate Mercutio and Mab is as rare and exhilarating as Mercutio himself and I have to give credit to Luhrmann's film for the suggestion that one can find mad self-destructive, word-drunk, sword-struck Christopher Marlowe in Mercutio.

Shakespeare's relationship to his predecessor, the murdered genius Marlowe, is a much and bitterly debated one. When it was asked whether Shakespeare had to kill Mercutio or he would have been killed by him, the same might be said of Marlowe. Not that Shakespeare had him killed but that had he not died the Shakespearean might not have escaped the shadow of the Marlovian.

Somehow Marlowe's spirit seems to haunt this version. Luhrmann cannot be accused of lack of boldness: in addition to cross-dressing his Mercutio, a black (cross-racial you might say) actor, in a disco-queen outfit, he gives him a silvery acrylic Afro, heavy lipstick beneath his mustache, and has Mercutio accompany his famous declaration to Romeo, "You have been with Queen Mab," by extracting, from a silver snuff box, a pill with an arrow-struck heart on it: a love drug.

The other thing, among many other things actually, that Luhrmann's *R+J* does, perhaps the most controversial, is to restage the ending. One perceptive thing the actor Henry Goodman said in the talk I attended is that the point of seeing and reading Shakespeare is not to find out what to think, but what to think *about.* And restaging the end of *R+J* in a way possible only on film gives one a lot to think about.

A FINAL GLANCE?

Staging the conclusion of *Romeo and Juliet* is one of *the* famous conundrums for Shakespearean directors, Trevor Nunn had told me. Nunn brilliantly expressed the comic impossibilities implicit in the tragic denouement in the demented road show *Romeo* put on by the Crummles Theatrical Troupe in the RSC's amazing nine-hour-long *Nicholas Nickleby.* It's a production that reminds us in many ways how preoccupied Dickens was with Shakespeare (not just in *Nickleby* either). There is in *Nickleby,* for instance, a parodic version of a Shakespearean textual scholar who has an idiosyncratic scheme for restoring the lost truths of Shakespeare by repunctuating it so that, for example, the "To be or not to be" soliloquy would be pronounced:

> *To be or not to be* that?
> *Is the question, whether 'tis*
> *Nobler in mind . . .* [etc.]

But the tour de force of Dickens's serio-comic commentary on Shakespeare in *Nickleby* is the Crummles' madly hammy *Romeo.* It's Dickens's *Pyramus and Thisby*–type parody of *Romeo and Juliet.* The moment of pure genius, in particular, is the "revision" of the tragic ending.

The always thought-provoking scholar Peter Holland begins his introduction to the Pelican edition of *R&J* by taking note of the tradition, dating back to Garrick, of rewriting the final scene to give Romeo and Juliet a moment together of conscious communion as they lie side by side in the Capulet tomb before their misbegotten mutual deaths.

As you'll recall, the plan was for Juliet to take a potion that would mimic death to avoid being married to her father's choice, Count Paris (since she's already been secretly married to Romeo). While the seemingly dead Juliet is installed on a bier in the Capulet "monument," Friar Lawrence (who secretly married her to Romeo and provided the potion for Juliet) is to send word of Juliet's fake death to Romeo, who's been banished to Mantua (for killing Tybalt). Of course the Friar's messenger doesn't reach Romeo with word of the false-death-inducing potion. Instead a servant from Verona who's not in on the scheme (Romeo rescuing the "dead" Juliet when she comes to life) reaches Romeo first and tells Romeo that Juliet is dead, as in *really* dead. A stricken Romeo then buys poison from a seedy apothecary, races off to Verona and breaks into the Capulet monument with the intention of killing himself by his dead lover's side. He sees what he thinks is a dead Juliet (still under the spell of the potion), voices a farewell to her (apparently) lifeless, actually comatose, body, then takes the poison, killing himself. (If they weren't endowed with tragic weight by the way the two lovers have stirred us in the first four acts these complications might be comic—a funereal French farce.)

Meanwhile the well-intentioned but bumbling Friar Lawrence arrives just as Juliet awakes from the potion's spell; they see Romeo's dead body, Friar Lawrence flees the oncoming Watch, Juliet stabs herself in order to join Romeo in death. It has always vexed actors that Romeo and Juliet never speak to each other in this scene, never have a final love-duet so to speak, in the tomb, and recurrently some of them have sought to remedy Shakespeare's supposed neglect by rewriting the scene to provide one.

"At the climax of David Garrick's adaptation of *Romeo and Juliet* first performed at the Theatre Royal, Drury Lane, on November 29, 1748," Peter Holland writes, "Juliet wakes up in the tomb before Friar Lawrence arrives, but also, much more significantly, before Romeo has died. Romeo, forgetting for the moment that he has already taken the poison and is dying, is in raptures: 'She speaks, she lives! And we shall still be blessed!' For a brief moment the lovers' passion seems able to conquer the threat of impending death. But the poison has taken hold and Romeo, explaining to Juliet what has happened, cannot resist its power and dies."

Holland argues that, however misguided one might think it, it's a significant recurrent impulse because it highlights Shakespeare's conscious decision *not* to give the lovers a final mutually aware moment of farewell.

Garrick even claimed it was "injudicious" of Shakespeare to have omitted "this addition to the catastrophe." And Baz Luhrmann revives the Garrick tradition in a subtle way, Holland notes: Luhrmann's "Juliet wakes just a few seconds too late and sees Romeo take the poison though she cannot prevent it. Appalled, the lovers have to share the recognition that nothing can be done, that Romeo will die and that Juliet must watch him die." In other words they don't speak, but they share a final unspoken communion.

Does this deepen the tragedy? Does it prefigure the ambiguous suggestion of a final communion between Lear and Cordelia in the Folio version of *Lear*? Luhrmann, it should be noted, in his thrillingly illuminated tomb scene, doesn't invent dialogue the way Garrick did. He invents a silent communion that the text doesn't rule out. Just one shared conscious glance between the star-crossed lovers before they, each in their own way, succumb to their chosen form of suicide. (Luhrmann's Juliet, seeing Romeo die, then shoots herself.) But it's a solution to the "problem" that has bothered actors and directors for centuries, one that only really could have worked on film. A stage representation of the silent shared glances is unlikely to communicate much beyond the footlights, but with filmed close-ups Luhrmann can give us what so many stagers of *R&J* have longed for.

Not everyone approves of this choice of course. Holland argues that in withholding such a moment, "the scene as Shakespeare wrote it is one of a desolate series of gaps and mistakes. As such it [the lack of a final moment of living communion between the lovers] brings to an apt conclusion the gaps and errors that have impelled it into being, one more part of the play's exploration of the tragedy of incompletion." I'd suggest that while Garrick's version violates that "tragedy of incompletion," Luhrmann's mute mutual exchanged gaze of loss and horror could be said to have illuminated rather than contradicted Holland's vision of Shakespeare's "tragedy of incompletion."

In this context you must forgive me for digressing, but I can't resist quoting from Trevor Nunn's staging of the Crummles Theatrical Troupe's *R&J* in *Nicholas Nickleby*. It's a hilarious—and brilliantly savvy—reductio ad absurdum of the alterations that Holland criticizes: just about everybody wakes up from death. Romeo (Nicholas as played by the brilliant Roger Rees, who in this loving comic mockery of the play is somehow better than most deadly serious Romeos I've seen) is the first to awake.

Juliet cries out when she sees his prostrate body, the cup of poison dangling from his grasp.

"Romeo dead!"

Rees as Romeo suddenly bolts up and cries, *"Hold! Hold! I live!"* in his most stentorian mock-theatrical, mock-nineteenth-century, melodramatic, grandiose Shakespearean style. As he proclaims in Crummles-invented dialogue:

The potent poison coursed through my veins—
A dizziness that I mistook for the numb torpor
That doth presage death. But in an instant
It hath passed!

Suddenly it crosses his mind that the Juliet who cried out to him and woke him up was the Juliet he thought was dead, a death that had caused him to take the poison in the first place:

"What? Juliet?!" he exclaims.

"Romeo, thou starts!" she cries out. *"I am not dead for I too drank a draft / That had the same benign effect."*

Suddenly Count Paris (but recently stabbed to death by Romeo in a duel, at least in Shakespeare's "original" version) awakes! What appeared to be a sword through the heart, he tells us, was but a glancing blow that "did for a moment give appearance of death."

Then to compound the comic resurrections and reversals of *R&J,* who but Mercutio should appear all hale and hardy, revealing that he too, though apparently fatally stabbed in his duel with Tybalt, had been taken away by Benvolio and cured by "surgeons of great renown." For good measure, to compound the echt-Shakespearean reversals, Benvolio then reveals that "he" has all along been a woman disguised in men's garb. All the risen dead and un-cross-dressed then join together in song.

Yes, I laughed—probably as hard as I'd ever laughed in my life—but I've come to think of it, like Luhrmann's version, as a kind of commentary, an exegesis of that final moment.

But the brilliance of it, and the brilliance of Luhrmann's far more sophisticated, subtle, troubling and perhaps even more deeply tragic glance of mutual communion between the dying lovers, is that it presses on the nerve, the node of an original highly consequential Shakespearean decision: the decision to withhold completion, withhold a *Liebestod* duet. Violating or elaborating on Shakespeare's decision highlights it in a way we might not notice otherwise. And nobody has violated it so stylishly, no one has highlighted that original decision more shrewdly and beautifully, than Luhrmann's film.

It's not the play, it's a filmed adaptation. One could say the best in this kind are but shadows, or the best in this kind are but flickers. But like the best in this kind, it doesn't tell us what to think, but what to think *about.*

WELLES AND OLIVIER: RIVAL OTHELLOS

One last thing: I want you to watch Laurence Olivier and Orson Welles act and direct dueling *Othello*s. Of all the many pleasures the great Shakespeare films afford, one of the rarest is that of comparing at close range the visions of great actor/directors as they make the same play into different films, different works of art.

Such an opportunity to compare is rare, but it's there. It's there in the Welles and Olivier films of *Othello,* which are easily available from video stores, amazon.com, or Shakespeare-on-film mail order specialist "Poor Yorick" (www.bardcentral.com).

IT'S AN OPPORTUNITY WHICH ONLY BECAME AVAILABLE IN 1997, when Welles's 1952 *Othello* was unearthed from a warehouse with a damaged soundtrack and remastered to the point where, while rough in places, it could take its place in the canon—of both Shakespeare and Welles.

An exciting aspect of the reemergence of Welles's film is that it makes comparison with Olivier's 1965 version possible. This is Olivier in the film version—and with the cast—of the famous stage production Steven Berkoff raved about as breathtaking, life-changing.

Comparing the two—both Welles and Olivier at the height of their powers (though Welles's version was, like *Chimes at Midnight,* not made at the height of his fortunes)—offers some of the excitement, the meta-drama one can find in comparing the Quarto and Folio versions of *Hamlet* and *Lear* side by side.

The resonance of the contrasting choices in each version deepens one's sense of what the other one is doing or not doing, makes one reflect on the question of which choice is more "Shakespearean"—that recurrent question for scholars, directors and actors.

Welles's restored 1952 version is an expressionist nightmare. Olivier's controversial radical blackface version is more traditional in form, more of a film of a stage play than a film per se.

Nonetheless: Olivier! Welles! Othello! Absolutely thrilling. I loved watching both versions in succession, act by act, moment by moment. They critique and illuminate each other as performances, as genres. As visions of tragedy.

Welles's film is in black and white, but it is a creation of shadows. There is so much focus on barred shadows, constricting passages, twisting stairways, dank basements and precarious parapets that one almost comes to think Othello is a victim not so much of Iago, of jealousy, of his inner demons, but of architecture.

And in fact I think that is Welles's metaphoric vision: Othello as victim of the *moral* architecture of a universe of shadows that deceives, traps, imprisons and tortures noble souls. The shadowy enclosures, confusingly constructed interiors of archways, latticework, barred apertures, grim sweating stone walls, low ceilings and the characteristic cages of light and shadows, embody Welles's vision of a prison universe. Or one might say, a penitential universe of shadows. Alternately one could argue all that architecture was an externalization of Welles's vision of the baroque interior architecture of human nature.

Olivier's *Othello* is filmed in color but obsessive about black and white, as in the blindingly bright-white garments he wears, obviously designed to heighten the contrast with the blackness of his heavily caked blacked-up skin.

This is perhaps the deepest variation. In Welles's version, shadow and darkness are the fabric of the world; for Olivier we lose that sense but are forced almost at knifepoint to face our feelings about blackness. In curious, unexpected ways both press upon the racial question in a way that Laurence Fishburne's excellent 1995 filmed *Othello* (with Kenneth Branagh as Iago) doesn't—or does so in a different way—because Fishburne is black.

The white actors' Othellos, the differing masks of blackness they offer the world, emphasize that Shakespeare's Othello, Welles's and Olivier's

Othellos, were about white conceptions—and misconceptions—about blackness, more problematic than anything that could be impersonated with makeup. Racism after all is a problem of whites, one that makeup, however thorough, reveals rather than conceals.

Watching Olivier and then Welles; Welles, then Olivier, you suddenly find yourself wondering whether Shakespeare saw Othello in terms of shadows or starkly contrasting black and white—and the different implications of the two visions.

I found both versions unbearable because I find *Othello* unbearable. Who can enjoy the sight of a great spirit being cruelly tortured in front of one's eyes? Tortured, driven mad, driven to horrible murder and self-annihilation.

The Welles version was more Welles than Shakespeare, a spirit-rather-than-letter affair, but in a mad disordered way, not dissimilar from the mad disorder of the Moor. The deranged architecture of light and shadow, stone and bars, that is a feature of the film becomes an objective correlative, cause and reflection, of Othello's derangement.

The puzzle to me was that the Olivier version, as intense and disturbing as it was, did not seem to me to possess the visceral power that Steven Berkoff raved about. It led me to wonder if he was magnifying it in retrospect.

But then somebody told me about the cast recording of the Olivier *Othello.* And after searching for months, a chance conversation led me to the discovery that a rare copy of this 33 ⅓ rpm vinyl disc was in the possession of a friend of mine, the writer Alfred Gingold.

Apparently in order to make an LP of the production the cast had gone into a recording studio, almost directly from the stage, and had produced an album.

It took me one hearing of the last side, actually one moment, to make me understand, make me give more credit to Berkoff's account. Give more credit to Olivier, who offers on this vinyl version one of the most heartbreaking moments in all Shakespeare.

The moment came late in the final act, when Othello is finally convinced he's been duped by Iago, and that he has murdered his beloved wife Desdemona out of a delusion.

After lashing himself rhetorically—"roast me in sulphur! / Wash me in steep-down gulfs of liquid fire!"—he finds such words inadequate, and gives way to wailing:

O Desdemon! dead, Desdemon! dead!
O, O!

O-groans again! But here the fulcrum, the focal point of all the tragic grief comes not from the *O*'s but from the *o,* the moan within "Desdemon."

In saying "Desdemon! dead!" Olivier's voice cracks on the syllable "mon" in Desdemon, in a way that splits your heart open. The crack in the voice—who knows how it was achieved, by acting process or naturalistically, it was almost like a jeweler's tap in its subtlety and profundity. I will never forget "Desdemon! dead, Desdemon! dead!" as long as I live.

When I heard that I suddenly felt I could credit Steven Berkoff's memory of the devastating effect of Olivier's Othello. Finding exactly the—unmarked—crack in the voice. Finding the final focal point of *Othello*'s unbearability is what great actors do.

Of course I am making a case here *against* film, aren't I? Not necessarily: I'd say I was making a case for voice, whether it be on a film soundtrack, stage, a vinyl platter, a tape or digital file.

And I suppose I am returning to my argument, my personal discovery that voice recordings can sometimes be the best way of experiencing Shakespeare.

And so I want to plead with you that you pick up John Gielgud's audio version of *Lear.* Gielgud's voice here—toward the end of his and Lear's life—becomes a kind of riveting extended vocal aria.

And Paul Scofield's audio version of *Hamlet.* Yes, you miss the visual dimension of watching the actors on stage, but often as not that can distract from the language. You get so much, much more than watching the full theatrical panoply of mediocre productions of Shakespeare. Audiotape Shakespeare, especially with headphones, turns the mind into a virtual stage.

I could go on but perhaps I should not leave the subject of film without a word about *Shakespeare in Love,* a film that's probably been seen by more people than all the film versions of Shakespeare's actual plays combined, and has, for better or worse, created the reigning popular culture image of Shakespeare.

Look, I liked *Shakespeare in Love* in a spirit-rather-than-letter way. But what is less widely noted and perhaps more troublesome is that it has created an image of Shakespeare as an artist—an image that takes sides in one of the most crucial controversies in all Shakespeare studies: the question of revision.

The Shakespeare of *Shakespeare in Love* dashes off playscripts in the midst of drinking and wenching, sends them off to the theater and never has another care about what he writes.

Taken the wrong way it can seem to be a disparaging vision of the artistic process, or Shakespeare's. He didn't take his plays very seriously, why should we? Perhaps we're making too much of a "fuss" about it.

On the other hand it can be a tribute to his offhand genius, but in either case it clearly suggests that he never has second thoughts, not even a second look, much less undertakes a careful revision of his first draft, as a large and influential faction of scholars have argued for the past three decades. (Unless you count his revision of "Bertha and the Pirates" into *Twelfth Night.*)

I'm enormously fond of Tom Stoppard's work (especially *Rosencrantz and Guildenstern Are Dead,* one of the very best non-Shakespearean Shakespearean films ever made, with many great moments of *Hamlet* as well). And there are some truly dazzling sequences in *Shakespeare in Love* (the *Romeo and Juliet* interchangeable parts duet, for instance). Again it's not a polemic, it's a spirited conjecture. Again we're not told what to think—but what to think about.

V

Three Giants

Chapter Eleven

Peter Brook: The Search for the Secret Play

In which an attempt to plumb the depths of bottomlessness in Shakespeare leads to an embarrassing public incident involving Peter Brook, whose disclosure of the notion of a "Secret Play" beneath each of Shakespeare's plays leads to an intimation of a "Secret Play" beneath all the plays.

There are three kinds of audiences [for Shakespeare]: a normal audience, an audience with Peter Brook in it, and you lot.

—Patrick Stewart (former Royal Shakespeare Company member) speaking to the 18th International Conference of Shakespeare Scholars at Stratford-on-Avon

I FEEL I HAVE TO BEGIN THIS INQUIRY WITH MY APOLOGY TO Peter Brook. It was Brook's *Dream* that changed my life by initiating me into a realm I might otherwise never have known. It's possible to go through life, through literature, even as a compulsive reader (as I was) and not to have had that kind of experience. Until Brook's *Dream,* with the exception of that strange moment with the sonnet at the blackboard at Yale, I had found literary intensities not in Shakespeare but rather from the seventeenth-century Metaphysical poets, from Milton and Keats and to a certain extent Hart Crane among the moderns.

But Peter Brook's *Dream* introduced me to something I had not imagined, nor been prepared for by other literary experiences. Looking back it reminds me of the curious opening to *The Taming of the Shrew*—the so-called Induction—in which a Stratford-area lowlife, Christopher Sly, awakened from a drunken stupor, is duped into believing he is a highborn nobleman and that his lowlife past is but a dream from which he's been awakened, just in time to witness a performance of a play ("The Taming of the Shrew"). It evokes what may have been Shakespeare's own sense of "induction," his elevation from Stratford yokel to royal poet and playwright. It evokes, that induction, my own sense of induction that night in Stratford: from waking life to Shakespearean dream state. I can't help identifying with Christopher Sly, drunken tinker; it was Peter Brook who tricked me into thinking I'd awakened *into* a dream.

What that experience was, what gave the *Dream* the power to cast that kind of spell—one I feel that I'm still under at this very moment three decades later—is a mystery that deserved further investigation, particularly as I began to learn I was not alone in having had this sort of experience with that *Dream.*

It was Brook as well who said something that crystallized my desire to write this book and helped define what it is I was seeking to discover in the process of doing it. This was back in September 1998 when I first met him face-to-face and he gave me a remarkable response to what might be called "the exceptionalist question" on Shakespeare.

And then after I'd begun writing this book there were two further encounters with Peter Brook in which I sought desperately to get deeper into the question of bottomlessness: another one-on-one interview that was followed, shortly thereafter, by what can only be called an Embarrassing Public Incident. The kind that calls for an apology.

Although, in my defense, I felt driven to it by the urgency I felt about understanding Peter Brook's vision. He was, it could be argued, one of the greatest if not *the* greatest and most influential Shakespeareans of the past century. He'd brought Shakespeare to life in a life-changing way not just for me but for countless other Shakespeareans. He had a vision of Shakespeare which was powerful and suggestive but also elusive. He was seventy years old and inevitably there was a feeling that if I did not press him further upon it then, when I had a chance, I might never get such an opportunity again.

And then, on the evening of the Embarrassing Public Incident, Brook made what to me was a novel and sensational disclosure: the notion of a "secret play" to be found beneath each of Shakespeare's plays.

It was this, more than anything, that precipitated the Embarrassing Incident.

Perhaps without much further ado I should reproduce the letter of apology I sent to Peter Brook the morning after the incident. It's still a bit painful to me, but the reader might find it amusing evidence of the urgency I felt.

Dear Peter Brook,

I feel I owe you an apology for something that happened at your "BAM* Dialogue" last Thursday. Please understand that I am such a self-conscious person that I rarely venture even to ask a question at a public forum such as that. But I must confess: I was the person who—to my own astonishment—could not stop myself from calling out to interrupt a long-winded questioner that night. The questioner who seemed intent on telling us everything he knew about your work, thus devouring the time left to hear *you* tell us about your work.

In what I thought was a well-meaning attempt to move things along and cut short his Polonian rambling, I made a caustic remark out loud ("Thank you for the *lecture*") that I probably should have muttered under my breath.

I don't think I was being intolerant so much as impatient; impatient in the way that everyone in *Hamlet* is impatient with Polonius. But impatience is not necessarily a virtue, and even though others assured me afterward they felt the same way, I probably should have suffered in silence. To say that I spoke out because I was dying to hear more from you rather than from the questioner does not exonerate me from the charge of unkindness to him—and of taxing you by raising the drama level in the hall in a way that may not have been of your choosing.

Happily you were able to be more gracious than I was to the questioner. You made amends, you made concord of my discord, and went on to say many more exciting things in the time left. I'm not sure what to make of my unaccustomed outspokenness (unaccustomed anyway in myself, although not uncommon in New York forums where I've witnessed numerous "Question, please!" outcries in similar circumstances). I think it was the excitement of your ideas. I think I was responding to the thrilling notion you introduced in your pre-question-period remarks, the notion of finding "the secret play" beneath the surface of the

* Brooklyn Academy of Music.

text in the experience of performance. So much of what you say matters to me, so much of what you've done has mattered to me in a life-changing way, it felt unendurable to put up with the questioner's pontification in preference to hearing from you. Although, in fairness to him, I guess we were both, in our own ways expressing an urgency about your work.

Still I feel terrible if I offended or disturbed you. I apologize for that and hope you may find it possible to "assault mercy" and grant me pardon.

Yours truly,
[signed]
Ron Rosenbaum

The letter speaks for itself, alas, and I want to say that my deferential tone to Brook, my apologetic fervor, was utterly sincere if (as Brook gently pointed out in the generous letter he wrote in reply) a bit long-windedly Polonian itself. The one thing my letter *does* play down, I'll admit, is my still-seething irritation at the long-winded questioner.

I'm sure you know the type, the ones who love to seize the opportunity to preen (at the expense of the speaker and his audience), with a self-congratulatory expansiveness, their profound understanding of the artist in question. To let everyone know how *conversant* they are with the theoretical ramifications of everything.

In this case it was particularly irritating because the questioner focused his discourse almost entirely and obtusely on the least interesting, most misleading aspect of Peter Brook's career: his flirtation with the alleged breakthroughs of sixties experimental theater and meta-theater, including Antonin Artaud's Theater of Cruelty and Jerzy Grotowski's Theater Workshop. These may have been experiments Brook learned from, and the sterile, stunted, minimalist meta-theatrical dogmas still appeal to antiquated academic *avant-gardistes* who can't get over the stunning revelation that a play isn't *real* ("It's, like, *artificial,* man!"). Those who believe that the entire function of theater is to *expose* theater, with an immature Holden Caulfield–like equation of artifice with "phoniness."

But while it is part of Brook's past and he may have incorporated an aspect of it into his Shakespeare, it doesn't speak at all to Brook's uniqueness. Everybody was doing that kind of stuff in the sixties and seventies. But from the forties through the seventies, *nobody* in the world was doing what Peter

Brook was doing. Nobody in the world, no scholar, no individual actor, was reinventing Shakespeare, bringing electrifying new life to one play after another. And he was talking about *that,* that night at BAM, he was revealing an aspect of that process, the method to making it new: the search for "the secret play." To me it was unbearably exciting to hear Brook speak about it and unbearable to have to listen to someone else drone on about "metatheatricality," eating up Brook's time.

So I don't repudiate the emotion behind my outburst, I just regret the outburst. Believe me I tried to suppress and stifle it, but after it seemed that the talk given by the questioner would never, ever get round to terminating in a question, I lost it. And so I called out:

Thank you for the lecture!

Well, it did stop him; it stopped everything. There were muted gasps, the well-behaved audience craned its neck in my direction, seeking the transgressor. And then looked back to Peter Brook to take a cue from his reaction.

It was then that Brook ever-so-smoothly turned this small bit of drama into a Theater of Cruelty Moment. Turned it on me.

He could have treated my interruption good-naturedly ("Well, yes, this *is* New York, isn't it?"—something like that) and really it was pretty mild for a New York forum on anything. But instead Brook focused a serenely steely gaze up in my direction. I couldn't tell if he recognized me in the darkened recesses of the hall as the person who'd interviewed him about the "metaphysical dimension" of Shakespeare's bottomlessness a few days before. (I'll get to that.) But it was *some gaze:* a gaze one felt had stared down some of the most powerful and irritable theatrical egos of the century—Welles, Gielgud, Olivier, Scofield—and made them do his bidding. A gaze that had surveyed the world from the heights of ancient Persepolis and the bottomless depths of disciplined meditation. I was no match for it, nor for what he was about to say.

It was one of those moments when you could sense the sentiment in the audience wavering. One of those recurrent moments beloved by Shakespeare when the outcome of a battle, a combat, a test of wills is poised at a moment of irresolution, wavering "like a vagabond flag on a stream" (in *Antony and Cleopatra*).

I felt I might have had some support, that I wasn't alone in feeling impatient. I thought Brook himself might have secretly welcomed an interruption of the time-devouring questioner. But that was not the way he made it sound. In the most mellifluous voice imaginable he turned first to the questioner and said, "I'd like to apologize for the fact that *some* here tonight"—and here he flicked a dismissive glance in my direction—"cannot be more patient."

And in that one instant I could feel the sentiment in the room shift abruptly against me. The force of the sudden shift—prompted as if by the flick of Prospero's wand—was like a palpable blow. And in that instant I learned a lesson: that's what great directors do. They *direct:* turn language into palpable, focused physical vectors of powerful emotion.

I suppose I should have been grateful as well to have a momentary glimpse of what Peter Brook's directorial style might be—the iron hand in the velvet glove—even as its object.

David Selbourne, who had attended the rehearsals of the *Dream* at Brook's invitation and had published a fascinating rehearsal diary called *The Making of A Midsummer Night's Dream,* told me about several cast members who found Brook's rehearsal process for the *Dream* almost too unbearably intense and—as a consequence—suffered breakdowns.

By all accounts putting together the *Dream* was no dreamy affair. Trevor Nunn told me of the initial dismay with which he had watched the evolution of Brook's production from the very beginning at Stratford back in 1970.

Nunn had been the one who had called on Peter Brook to do the *Dream* at a point when Brook had already left Stratford and the Royal Shakespeare Company to launch an experimental "International Center for Theater Research" in Paris. Nunn told me he'd begged Brook to come back and do the *Dream,* and Brook had balked "and then said he'd only do it if we could recruit *a hundred schoolchildren* from the neighborhood to play the fairies. He was worried about the fairy problem—how do you depict them without looking silly. And I said, 'Yes of course, of course, Peter, one hundred children, whatever you want.' " Nunn ended up doing most of the casting for the *Dream* from the Royal Shakespeare Company's fairly extraordinary stock company and then Brook came over to re-audition everyone and finally begin the rehearsal process (by that time he'd dropped the *kinder*-fairy-battalion idea). I remember Nunn's still mystified look as he told me how everything he saw Brook doing with his actors during the rehearsal process—the staring exercises, the touchy-feely interaction, the nonsense sounds he had actors chant to the pentameter beat, all this Brookian psychodrama—was impressive in its way. But, Nunn says, using a phrase I'd never heard before, but one which I instantly came to love: "I didn't see anything you might call *theater-filling.*"

There was nothing in the evolution of the rehearsal process that prepared him for what happened opening night. Until, he said, the technical rehearsal two days before the opening. Up till then Brook had *withheld* direction, in a New Age collaborative way, refraining from giving the cast line readings, refraining from taking control of the production, from *directing.* But suddenly, Nunn said, "Peter began to bark out orders and then everything fell into place like magic, like he'd snapped a whip." And the night of the first performance "something happened I'll never forget," Nunn told me. And, recall, Nunn is a man who had gone on to direct some of the most celebrated Shakespearean productions of the late twentieth century—including one I'd just seen, at the National Theater, his devastating *Troilus and Cressida.*

The opening night of Brook's *Dream,* though, "was a revelation from the first moment. And at the first interval [Anglicism for "intermission"] we *knew.* You have to understand about that interval," Nunn was telling me. "*Nobody* gets a standing ovation at a first interval. It just had never happened before. But that moment before the interval with Titania and Bottom borne aloft to the Mendelssohn 'Wedding March' with the fist coming up triumphantly between his legs . . ."

That last bit needs a little explication for those who weren't there. It's the moment when Bottom, transformed to a hairy-eared ass, is lifted up on the shoulders of the fairies and workmen who bear him to his tryst with Titania the Fairy Queen. She of course has fallen madly in love with Bottom-as-ass under the influence of Puck's love potion. Now there is much scholarly debate over whether Bottom and Titania physically consummate their love potion–induced union, the mating of an ass and a goddess. Brook's production jubilantly takes the position that it's more than a nesting and cuddling moment. A gesture had developed in rehearsal that captured the spirit of it all. Just as the "Wedding March" breaks out, confetti explodes from the heavens; one of the workman bearing Bottom to his bed swings a forearm and clenched fist up between Bottom's legs.

It was more than a metaphor. "Peter used to tell us that the ass has the largest penis in the animal world," Sara Kestelman (who played the Fairy Queen and the mortal Amazon Queen Hippolyta in the production) told me, and there is even a scholarly debate about whether Bottom is endowed with more than an ass's *ears* during his transformation. But in any case, the moment, the gesture, was the climax of an electrifying scene. It only would have worked if the gesture genuinely embodied the physical excitement, the almost aphrodisiac energy the play itself imparted. It only would have worked if everything else worked. But everything did work brilliantly. That triumphant fist brought the audience to a standing position as well, for an explosive standing ovation.

"I've never seen anything like it in the theater before," Trevor Nunn told me. The *Dream* was suddenly in every sense of the word "theater-filling."

All of which is to say (as I learned to my cost), Peter Brook is no experimental theater flower child. He can crack a whip (I felt its lash). For all his rhetoric of collaboration, there is a single mind, a single vision behind what happens on the stage when Brook does Shakespeare. He's a terrifying perfectionist who feels the stakes in Shakespeare are high enough to warrant whatever mind-games and psychodrama manipulations are necessary to produce a single embodiment of Brook's vision. To make the company, make the language into a single-minded organism with "a single beating heart" (as he would call it on the night of the Embarrassing Incident).

On the night of the Embarrassing Incident, however, I felt hurt by Brook's disapproval. Hurt most of all because I appeared to have offended someone to whom I owed a lifelong debt of gratitude. For having given me a unique gift, with that *Dream.*

Some sort of powerful initiating experience turns out to be common to lifelong Shakespeareans. It came up in a number of my conversations with Shakespeareans. For Harold Bloom the revelatory encounter was a role—seeing Ralph Richardson play Falstaff, when Bloom was just fourteen. For Ann Thompson, the editor of the Arden three-text *Hamlet,* it was a moment during an outdoor production of *King Lear.* For Frank Rich it was Peter Brook's stage version of *King Lear* with Paul Scofield.

But more often than not, among an impressive array of directors, scholars, actors, critics and private citizens it was Peter Brook's *Dream.* From the moment it opened to ecstatic reviews in 1970 to the end of the long world tour some four years later, Brook's *Dream* drew people to it and changed them. Made them *see* differently, the way Puck's love potion dropped into the eyes transforms all to love at first sight in the *Dream.*

Think of it this way: there are biographers and collectors and antiquarians who might give their lives to find some lost artifact of "the real Shakespeare," the tiniest unintelligible scrap of his handwriting, not so much for its monetary value (although that might be inestimable) but out of the belief that such an icon might somehow bring us closer to Shakespeare.

It's the illusion, even the delusion, behind the impulse to believe certain verbal icons—like the "Funeral Elegy"—might bring us closer to Shakespeare. It's the illusion that portraits of Shakespeare—every decade or so someone claims to have uncovered another one, mostly of dubious provenance—might bring us closer to Shakespeare.

It's the illusion that may be what's really behind the "authorship" controversy: the illusion that since we can't know Shakespeare, since there's not enough material evidence to paint a complete portrait, let's select someone else that we *can* know *as* our Shakespeare. A different more knowable Shakespeare. One we can get closer to.

It was a similar illusion in another realm that sparked the frenzy behind the phony Hitler "diaries": the longing to believe that somehow these dubious scribblings would bring us closer to the mystery Hitler represented.

But even if we could find some Hitler-diary-equivalent for Shakespeare, I'm not sure it would bring us closer to what matters most about Shakespeare—the work, the spell—than Peter Brook has. He is the icon who gave us what no antiquarian relic possibly could: an experience of Shakespeare's *presence,* the spell Shakespeare cast—the most unbearably real thing about him.

THE SHOCK OF THE *DREAM*

Brook had this effect on people from the beginning. He was in many ways an Orson Welles–like prodigy whom Shakespeareans took note of, argued about, loved and hated from the moment when Brook was an Oxford undergraduate and John Gielgud lent him some old movie sets which Brook used to make his first film, an adaptation of Laurence Sterne's *Sentimental Journey.* (According to Gielgud's biographer, Sheridan Morley, "Already Gielgud knew that Brook was going to be one of those rare directors from whom an old dog could learn new tricks." Brook was nineteen at the time.)

He soon made a name, Morley reports, "with Paul Scofield in some early seasons at the Birmingham Rep," and followed this with a revelatory *Measure for Measure* at Stratford featuring John Gielgud as the repressed lecher Angelo. Kenneth Tynan said the role gave Gielgud's acting "a second lease of life." After that Brook became a fixture at Stratford with an eye-opening *Romeo and Juliet* and a *Titus Andronicus* that almost single-handedly transformed that neglected early tragedy from a disparaged relic whose violence many were embarrassed about to an utterly modern, eloquent realization of the heart of Shakespearean darkness. People still talk about the red ribbons of "blood" that streamed from the mouth of the mutilated Lavinia (played by Vivien Leigh to Olivier's Titus).

And then in the early sixties Brook's *Lear* with Paul Scofield playing the King (first on stage and then on screen) found some fusion of bleakness and dread that left audiences devastated and cathartically exhilarated and marked the moment when *Lear* displaced *Hamlet* in the minds of many as the more profound Shakespearean experience.

Until Brook's *Dream.* Which, like *Titus,* was in a kind of reputational decline at the time, burdened with the encrustations of Victorian fairy imagery, elaborate woodsy sets, some of which featured real rabbits hopping about. It was considered Shakespeare-for-children by some.

What Brook succeeded in doing was to reawaken people to the centrality of the *Dream* to Shakespeare's cosmos; he led many to see that the *Dream* is, in effect, the *King Lear* of Shakespeare's comedies, a work just as dizzying and profound.

He also achieved an astonishing popular success. The reviews were so sensational that suddenly "helicopters were landing in Stratford," as Sara Kestelman recalled it. "People were jetting in from all over the world." One of them was Clive Barnes, then chief drama critic of *The New York Times.* He called it "a magnificent production, the most important work yet of the world's most imaginative and inventive director . . . the greatest Shakespearean production I have seen in my life." In the London *Sunday Times* Harold Hobson called it "magnificent, the sort of thing one sees only once in a lifetime and then only from a man of genius." An enormously intense spotlight was focused upon the production and the players. And an enduring mystery was created as well: What *had* Brook wrought? Why was this *Dream* different from all other *Dreams*? What made it exceptional?

Since seeing it I've seen a lot of misguided explanations which all too often focus on surface aspects of the production. For some reason Brook's detractors, many of whom never saw the production, only still pictures or the ten-second film clip that is all that survives, focus on the eerie circus-like costumes and props, the bare bright-lit white cube of a set.

In my first interview with him Brook told me that what he'd seen when he first saw the Peking Opera Circus perform in Paris was a way to capture the *spirit* of the fairies, the lighter-than-air, globe-girdling swiftness and grace—without being imprisoned by the antiquated fairy convention of centuries of stage cliché that had deadened the exhilaration implicit in Shakespeare's language. "I wanted to capture their *lightness,*" he told me.

By clearing away all the scenic underbrush, so to speak, what Brook had done was allow the language itself to flourish, for the language to be the star. He allowed the language of the play to achieve what Brook had once spoken of as his goal: to bring the actors so deeply into their interrelated roles in the rigorous rehearsal process that the words didn't seem to be recited but *uttered for the first time.* Minted at the moment of speaking as if they were utterly inevitable and spontaneous: as if they had never been uttered by anyone before. Permit me to utter *this* again: what Brook was doing was not making the *Dream* something radically new, but rather something radically *old.* Making it seem as if we were watching it, experiencing it as if in a dream, performed for the first time, on its first night.

This was a physical as well as metaphysical effect. A physicality that was captured beautifully by veteran Shakespearean actress Zoe Caldwell, who saw the *Dream* in her youth and saw vast quantities of Shakespeare at its best since then. And yet still remembers her first exposure to the *Dream* as unique.

"The effect was truly dreamlike," Ms. Caldwell wrote in her memoir, "but the main difference was the incredible clarity of the play. I had never heard and understood every syllable of the text before and it was *shocking* to sit in an audience and never for a moment have your attention wander. I remember feeling a breeze around my neck and I realized that it was because my head had sat high on my spine as a child's does at a circus for the entire evening." There's that word: "shocking." It's overused these days, but for me it was a shock that has left me still shaken.

What impressed me most, once I began seeking out Shakespeareans in a more systematic fashion, was the way the most discerning and attentive scholars of Shakespearean language turned out to have feelings like mine about Brook's *Dream.* Stephen Booth and Russ McDonald, for instance. Both of them told me they'd seen the Brook *Dream* and had felt much like I had about its language. I recall the three of us speaking about it at a lunch during a scholars' and directors' conference in Staunton, Virginia. As soon as we started talking about it, for all three of us the excitement of that *Dream* was as fresh as the moment it transfixed us first.

It was the remarkable enthusiasm of these two that fortified me against the objections of the two foremost anti-Brookians, John Simon and Harold Bloom, because frankly, whatever the virtues of the latter two, their attunement to Shakespeare's language pales before that of Booth and McDonald in my estimation. And my sense is that even Bloom and Simon insist on seeing Brook through the wrong lens, as some kind of experimentalist, rather than as someone more deeply classical than the classicists.

THE EXCEPTION TO EVERY RULE

In any case it was something Peter Brook said about Shakespeare in my first personal encounter with him, nearly three decades after the *Dream,* that helped crystallize the idea for this book. If seeing the *Dream* had been the distant cause of this book, an initiating cause had been that first encounter, two years before the Embarrassing Incident, when Brook had come to New York on the book tour for his memoir, *Threads of Time,* and I spent an hour with him talking about Shakespeare in a hotel lobby bar. Here are some of the things I recall about Peter Brook's persona from that first meeting:

First how pale he was. Not in an unhealthy way, something more ethereal. An aura of serenity bordering on (doubling as?) a cool hauteur that radiated from pale blue eyes. The simplicity of his garb: black blazer, gray slacks, dark turtleneck. And the style of his greeting: no handshake but a polite Zen-master-like nod-bow with hands pressed together beneath his chin as if in blessing, briefly dipped toward one in acknowledgment.

As he tells us in his memoir, Brook's father was originally called Bryck; his parents were Russian-Jewish immigrants to England in the early twentieth century. Those eyes are Baltic blue. Brook himself is not conventionally religious although he does follow a spiritual discipline which he began practicing in the forties known as the "Gurdjieff work," an esoteric Eastern- and Western-based spiritual path with some roots in Sufi mysticism brought to the West by the Russian writer P. D. Ouspensky. Brook would eventually make Gurdjieff's account of travels in Central Asia in search of enlightenment, *Meetings with Remarkable Men,* into a film. (In addition to *Meetings* and *Lear,* Brook's films include *Marat/Sade,* based on his sensational stage production, and *Lord of the Flies,* an adaptation of the William Golding novel.)

I frankly have never been able to glimpse profound depths in what I've read of Gurdjieff but he seems to have attracted an array of highly educated followers. The best brief definition of what they were seeking may be the one in the *Skeptics Dictionary* which calls Gurdjieff a spiritual "con man" but describes his appeal thus: "he offered to show his followers the way to true wakefulness, a state of awareness that transcends ordinary consciousness." Sometimes con men have the power to con the receptive into a new consciousness.

What makes "the Gurdjieff work" unique and arduous (and thus, somewhat self-importantly, called "work") as I understand it is the emphasis on confrontational self-examination designed to uncover layers of self-deception. And although Brook has frequently disclaimed any Gurdjieffian influence on his Shakespeare, according to many I spoke to it may well have influenced his all-important rehearsal techniques.

When we met that first time in 1998 Brook had not done Shakespeare in any traditional sense for nearly a quarter century, since his *Antony and Cleopatra* with the Royal Shakespeare Company (starring Alan Howard and Glenda Jackson). In fact one could almost say he'd *fled* Shakespeare. Which was why what he had to say about Shakespeare and the "exceptionalist question" had such an impact on me.

You'll recall the exceptionalist question with Shakespeare: Is he on the continuum of other great writers, perhaps the greatest, but still understandable in the same terms as other great writers, or does he occupy—has he *created*—some realm of his own, beyond others?

The reason Brook's experience seemed so pertinent to this question is that he cannot be easily accused of culture-bound "bardolatry" as some of those who take the exceptionalist position on Shakespeare have been.

At the peak of his success and celebrity as a Shakespearean director in the U.K. with "people jetting in from all over the world" to see his productions, he had already uprooted himself and moved to an abandoned music hall in an industrial suburb north of Paris where his Centre for Theater Research was located. And neither the spectacular success of the *Dream* nor the world tour could lure him back.

Instead he abandoned traditional English-language theater entirely, abandoned *language itself* entirely for a time, when he and the poet Ted Hughes took a huge company to the shah's Iran where they staged a play on the ancient cliffside ruins of Persepolis, a play in which the actors spoke an entirely invented—and to everyone else *unintelligible*—language that Ted Hughes devised ("Orghast"). One which he and Brook in their sublime if dizzy madness insisted would convey more authentic meaning than mere words in any specific language. (Of course the dream of all mystics, conjurers, alchemists and fraudulent spiritualists in Shakespeare's time was to discover just such an ineffable universal language, the language God taught Adam in the Garden, the language lost in the mists before Babel.)

In other words Brook not only fled Shakespeare, he fled Shakespeare so violently he fled language itself. He fled it, I suspect, as one flees a violent consuming love affair because it became so unbearably intense he had to question the experience—see it from the outside in, from as great a distance—culturally, theatrically, geographically—as possible.

And so from the invented language in Persepolis he took his troupe to Africa, out to villages where no one had seen theater in any Western sense before, unrolling a carpet amidst mud huts and seeing what could hold the attention of these virgin spectators. It was a kind of madness, but he had a Pied Piper appeal: many people left their lives to follow Brook and never returned to them in any conventional sense even after Brook's hejira ended.

Then there was a flight into another kind of theatrical realm which seemed to offer a bottomless infinitude similar to Shakespeare's: the years Brook spent transforming the many thousand pages of the Hindu epic the *Mahabharata* into a nine-hour theater experience.

When I met with him in 1998 he'd been staging operas, most recently *Carmen* and *Don Giovanni,* but at the time he had no immediate plans to do any Shakespeare (although he conceded there were three plays that might tempt him—*Othello, Troilus and Cressida* and *Hamlet,* which he'd last done in 1961 with the Royal Shakespeare Company, with Paul Scofield playing the prince).

So at the time I first met him Brook seemed a long way from Shakespeare. Someone who had gone deep inside Shakespeare, come out the other side perhaps. He was in other words the perfect person to ask the exceptionalist question about Shakespeare. And here is the hesitant, awkward way I raised the question.

"You're a man who has explored the great theaters of the world. Setting aside naïve bardolatry, is there something unique or exceptional about Shakespeare, something that makes Shakespeare a realm of its own beyond that which you've experienced in the theaters of other cultures, something that *isn't* culture bound—"

He interrupted me with a reply that was stunning in its unambiguous conviction:

"I think he is a unique case and I think the uniqueness inheres in his generosity. I think there's no one else who manages to insert himself totally in such a wide range of human beings. If you count how many human beings [he created] . . . That he could have, in the act of writing, instead of using them partly to express what he himself wants to say, lets *them* say what *they* want to say . . . to be such a highly developed, highly acute servant of other people's truths is unique."

A "highly developed, highly acute servant of other people's truths"—it occurred to me that Brook was, perhaps unconsciously, perhaps not, describing his own relationship to Shakespeare's "truths."

"One level of author, Shaw," Brook continued, "uses his characters as his mouthpiece. The next level of author uses human beings but only aspects of them, their humanity is not complete; another level can give brief life but to a small cast, small parts. But Shakespeare's sense of each character having *endless facets* so you can see year after year, after year, new interpretations can be given to any character and they're *always* based on truths which are *there*—that is what is unique and I think this is inseparable from Shakespeare being so anonymous. One thing everyone can agree about him is that he is the least known of any great writer."

The so-called authorship obsessives, Brook says, the "anti-Stratfordians," are misled by this anonymity into a search for someone else who "really" wrote Shakespeare, "quite simply because he *does* disappear, dissolve, parcel himself out to his characters"—an echo perhaps of Juliet's line about cutting up Romeo and parceling his incandescence out to the night sky as stars.

"And yet none of his plays could have been written by themselves," Brook continued, "they have to have one person using the vision and craft of playwriting. For mysterious reasons this [Shakespeare] was the exception to every rule."

The exception to every rule. It's a lovely way to express an exceptionalist position. A powerful and complex one as well. It defines Shakespeare's exceptionalism in the negative, a negation of all rules. It goes along with what seems to be a similarly negative way of defining Shakespeare's exceptional genius as a playwright: he's someone who *empties himself out.* But it is not mere emptiness; the absence of evidence about him becomes something more than mere anonymity: it becomes a highly charged void.

Brook invokes the imagery of infinitude when he speaks of the "endless facets" of Shakespeare's characters, endlessness being the horizontal equivalent of bottomlessness's depths, you might say.

I was only beginning to become aware of what I now see as Brook's preoccupation with the infinitude in Shakespeare. It was in fact at the close of this first interview that Brook called my attention to a lecture he'd recently given in Berlin, the one published in the slim book *Evoking Shakespeare.* The one in which Brook spoke of the way "each line of Shakespeare is an atom. The energy that can be released is infinite—if we can split it open."

I'd come to suspect that Brook's sense of Shakespeare's exceptionalism and his preoccupation with Shakespeare's apparently bottomless infinitude are linked: that the latter is at the heart of the former. And so when I learned, some two and a half years after my first interview with Brook, that he was coming back to New York again, this time with a Shakespearean production, a controversial *Hamlet,* I made a determined effort to secure another interview. For me, by that time, after some two years of working on this book, Brook had grown even more in importance. I felt gratified that I might have another chance to get to the bottom of the question of bottomlessness with Brook.

Indeed there was a kind of Brookian convergence in the spring of 2001. In addition to Brook himself bringing his *Hamlet* to New York for a one-week run at the Brooklyn Academy of Music, there was another *Hamlet* on a near-collision course with Brook's: the Royal National Theatre (artistic director: Trevor Nunn) version of *Hamlet,* directed by John Caird and starring Simon Russell Beale. But featuring—and here my heart stood still when I found out—Sara Kestelman, the brilliant redheaded actress who had been Brook's leading lady in the *Dream,* playing both Hippolyta, Queen of the Amazons, and Titania, Queen of the Fairies, now playing another queen, the tormented Gertrude in *Hamlet.*

Sara Kestelman not only played a goddess role in the *Dream,* she played a heroic role in my life—in the meta-drama that erupted the second time I saw Brook's *Dream.* When the production came to Broadway and a fire broke out on stage in the fifth-act wedding banquet scene, and the audience began a dangerously panicked exit from the theater until—as I recall it—Ms. Kestelman stepped forward to prevent the comedy from turning into a tragedy by insisting the crowd not panic. At least I thought it was her—my interviews with Brook, Ms. Kestelman and later John Kane, who played Puck, raised new questions about the source of the Mysterious Voice who intervened to prevent the *Dream* from turning into a nightmare.

ENTER "THE SECRET PLAY"

Meanwhile as Brook and his Queen from the *Dream* were heading to New York, I was heading for the hospital for a fairly serious operation, one I actually postponed to make sure I would be able to see the two *Hamlets* and secure interviews with Brook and Kestelman. I have a feeling that the imminence of the surgery, the pain I experienced during the postponement, was less important than a different kind of pain: my conviction—my delusion—that I had somehow failed utterly during my interview with Brook three days before the Embarrassing Incident. Failed to get to the bottom of his bottomlessness. It meant so much to me by that time to get at least a glimpse of what it was like to see Shakespeare through Peter Brook's eyes, and somehow I was certain that I'd failed. So convinced was I of my failure that it took a full *eight months* before I could force myself to listen to the tape of my interview with Brook and realize how much was there. Realize that in my pain I had blocked out some remarkable things Brook said on the question of infinitude, bottomlessness and Shakespeare's "metaphysical dimension."

I'll get to those things, but on the evening of the Embarrassing Incident as I raced up the steps of the Brooklyn Academy of Music it seemed to me 1) this was the last chance I'd get to hear Brook and get to the bottom of his vision, and 2) even that chance was slipping away from me because a traffic tie-up on the Brooklyn Bridge had made me very late. When I arrived breathless at the top balcony of the BAM Rose Theater, scene of Brook's "BAM dialogue," Brook had already been speaking for at least twenty minutes, and it seemed I'd missed the beginning of some strange but fascinating Brookian riff that involved *percentages.* One that led to the even more provocative notion of the "secret play." I was bitter at myself, convinced it would be too late for me to ever reconstruct it and apprehend it in its entirety.

Things started to go wrong as soon as I whipped out my tape recorder to catch what Brook was saying. And was almost immediately busted by one of the BAM monitors who instructed me that no taping was allowed. Shamed, I stumbled down the steeply raked steps of the small auditorium and found a place to hide on the side, although I found it hard to focus my attention again until I heard Brook utter the phrase "secret play."

Fortunately, even though I wasn't allowed to tape, there was an official

BAM tape being made of the occasion, and a couple of months later, after I got out of the hospital, I persuaded the people at BAM to play for me, over the phone, the recording of what I'd missed, of what led up to that mystifying "secret play" disclosure.

Brook led up to the notion of a secret play by suggesting a sort of secret play going on *within* Shakespeare.

He began with a deceptively simple inquiry: Just how *alive* was William Shakespeare?

"With Shakespeare I like to stick to things that are beyond dispute," he began. "And one of the few things we can say about Shakespeare that is beyond dispute is that he was alive. But to say someone is alive is not enough. You can be one percent alive, you can be twenty percent alive. With Shakespeare one has something very extraordinary: a man who was not only one hundred percent alive, but perhaps a thousand, even ten thousand—a *million* percent alive. Now what is the difference between being one percent, ten percent, a thousand percent alive?

"This person walking through the streets of London [Shakespeare] must have lived each single moment with an incredible richness of awareness. So many levels, infinite levels of meaning."

Infinite levels of meaning! It becomes clear that what Brook has been leading up to with his deceptively simple discourse about percentages of aliveness is the phenomenon of infinitude.

"A million percent alive," I'd suggest, is actually a way of expressing that specific recurrent preoccupation of Peter Brook: the challenging, dizzying, even destabilizing apprehension of bottomlessness, endlessness, limitlessness in Shakespeare's work. Brook seems to be suggesting that it is a reflection of some state of being, some state of dizzying elevation within Shakespeare's mind. A state Shakespeare sought—at times at least—to evoke, to conjure up in his work.

Consider that moment when Edgar is conjuring up the dizzying view from the top of Dover Cliffs for his blind father, Gloucester. Edgar warns "How fearful / And dizzy 'tis to cast one's eyes so low! . . . I'll look no more, / Lest my brain turn, and the deficient sight / Topple down headlong."

This last moment is particularly apropos because Edgar is trying to explain, conjure up the vista, the visual experience of dizzying bottomlessness to a blind man, with words. And, in a way, Brook is trying to be *our* Edgar, to make apparent to us in *our* blindness, the infinitude that can be glimpsed in Shakespeare, indeed within a single line.

I was fascinated by Brook's use of *numbers* to invoke this vision; it seemed oversimplified to quantify it. But looked at more closely, listened to reflectively rather than in the hectic circumstances at the BAM dialogue and the Embarrassing Public Incident, the choice of numbers is suggestive.

If one hundred percent alive is almost by definition as alive as one could *be,* that is already, one might say, infinitely alive. Then a thousand, ten thousand, one million percent alive, are what you might call *transfinite* levels of aliveness. "Transfinite" in the sense that Georg Cantor, the inventor of the mathematics of infinity, meant the word when he was the first to categorize the "transfinite numbers"—degrees of infinity beyond the infinite. For instance, the way the infinity of integers—1, 2, 3, 4—while undeniably infinite, endless, bottomless, must necessarily be a lesser level of infinity than the infinity of the number of points on a line. Because the latter would include all the fractional points *between* the points on a line represented by the integers.

It is not without interest or significance, I believe, that, as I recently learned, Cantor was widely supposed to have been driven mad by the contemplation of the ultimate unbearable enigma of bottomlessness—"the continuum problem"—and had to spend much of the latter half of his life in a residence for the mentally disturbed. During which time Cantor became obsessed with Shakespeare. He became a Baconian enthusiast who believed Shakespeare encoded cabalistically in his language hidden revelations about its true author—a Gnostic version of the search for the true occluded deity which is a different kind of "authorship" question. (The Gnostics—some of them—believed it was not God but a lesser demon who is the author of our world.)

So in speaking in thousand and million percentages Brook is trying in a way to open our mind to what it's like to gaze into Shakespeare's mind. For Brook the lip of the stage is like the cliff's edge in *Lear:* the boundary of a bottomless abyss.

"When I say 'infinite levels of meaning,' " Brook continued, "the only reason his plays are redone, rediscovered for centuries, is the phenomenon that a line of ten syllables has within it level after level of meaning.

"But where did these meanings [the infinite levels within the line] come from?" Brook asks. "From his surroundings, yes. This extraordinary person hearing the sounds around him, hearing through his eyes."

Did I hear that right? "Hearing through his eyes"? It seems as if Brook is making an explicit reference to the language of synesthesia Bottom used to describe his dream: "The eye of man hath not heard, the ear of man hath not seen" the stuff of Bottom's Dream, the dream that "hath no bottom."

In doing so Brook comes close to suggesting that Shakespeare *had* some version of Bottom's Dream, or experienced, walking through the streets of London, some analogy to Bottom's synesthesia. Brook goes on to conjure up what he imagines it's like to, well, hear through Shakespeare's eyes, you might say:

"He can overhear and notice two kinds of things: all the life and noise pouring out with great excitement. Yet at the same time, even though he's a very practical man, he can evoke in words faraway worlds, strange tales, astonishing ideas, and develop and link them to an intimation of meaning in society, in regard to the gods, a sense of cosmic reality—these were *all* pulsing through his mind, all these levels *at the same time.*"

Pulsation and simultaneity. I'll be dwelling further on Peter Brook's pairing of these phenomena in chapter 13, in which I explore the way Stephen Booth's exegesis of the Sonnets transforms them into exquisite devices that *produce* a sense of pulsation and simultaneity in the reader—the sort that shocked me when I first experienced just that, banging chalk on a blackboard in a Yale classroom.

But at this point Brook shifted from a discussion of Shakespeare's mind to that of his audience, a discussion which leads up to his disclosure of the notion of a "secret play."

"He didn't have a lot of quiet, attentive people in a dark room such as this," Brook said. "It was, rather, the most mixed audience that ever existed in the theater: thieves, pickpockets, whores, drunks, half-drunks, brawling in fights. As well of course as the bourgeoisie, there for entertainment, sophisticates looking for things that are sharp, witty, erudite. It is difficult to understand how deeply *difficult* the task was: Shakespeare at every moment had to bring *all* those along. Because if you learn anything from the theater it's that if you lose part of an audience, you're *dead.* The work is to bring them all together into one organism beating with one heart. . . ."

By now he had the audience at the BAM dialogue "beating with one heart."

All of which, this discourse on the audience, was preparation for his conjecture—no, his lived *certainty*—about Shakespeare's work:

"In all his plays there is the outer life of the play and the inner life of the play. Sometimes within one single line—which on the surface is so clear it registers in the most crude, vulgar level, yet within that line there may be an adjective, some *vibrant word* that both keeps that clarity on the surface, but at the same time suggests something *way* beyond it."

Something way beyond it! Is he speaking here of the infinite energies released by splitting open a line of Shakespeare, or does that "vibrant word" unlock something else?

"Plays exist for one purpose only: to be brought to life. To be this million percent alive. A performance should bring the plays, with the audience, to the highest level of life within them."

So that's where the million percent enters the picture. But it is here he gets into strange territory:

"In every play there is the *inner* play. When we were doing *Midsummer Night's Dream* with the actors we called it the *secret* play. It can't be analyzed, it can't be described, it can only be *experienced.* But the secret cannot be unveiled unless there is also the outer play, aware of the needs of the theater and audience. Shakespeare used all the conventions of his time. That is why today one has to balance these two aspects. What is the inner aspect, what is the secret play? It's why we bother to do Shakespeare instead of any given modern story: The secret play of Shakespeare is deeper, finer, more important to us than any other writer."

What was fascinating and frustrating to me about this notion of the "secret play"—and what lent urgency to my impatience with the long-winded questioner who was bent on demonstrating how familiar he was with aspects of Brook utterly irrelevant to that question or to Brook's talk in general—was Brook's insistence that this experience of the secret play is not one that can be obtained from reading and interpreting, even from seeing and apprehending the plays. But rather that it may be the esoteric possession of players and directors alone—because it can *only* be experienced in rehearsing and staging the play.

But Brook was onto something even deeper I suspected. Of course for centuries there have been poets, lovers and madmen who have claimed to have discovered secret codes, secret messages, secret anagrams, secret authors, secret esoteric doctrines embedded in the language of Shakespeare.

But this was Peter Brook, someone who had brought Shakespeare to life in a way that few others in a century have. When Peter Brook speaks of coming upon a "secret play," it carries with it some authority. He's been inside the plays, deep inside, he's gotten a glimpse of the bottomlessness, he returns to report that *one* thing one discovers in the process of staging them—knowledge apparently privy only to those on the other side of the footlights from us—is something, some experience he calls a "secret play."

I was suddenly immensely envious of that experience, that knowledge. But beyond that it struck a chord because it recalled to me a momentary disclosure of some secret level of apprehension, the one I experienced while attempting to unfold the secrets of the Sonnets to my class of freshmen. It made sense in a way: it makes sense that the secrets of a musical composition for instance are more likely to disclose themselves to the musicians who play it than to mere listeners.

In the month after recovering from my operation—which followed a week after the Embarrassing Incident—I made it a point to look into the literature on Brook, and to make contact with two cast members from the *Dream,* to investigate just what Brook was talking about when he talked about "the secret play."

Most indications are that the concept emerged in the course of producing the *Dream,* although one study of Brook's work reports that in the "late sixties Brook would talk of the existence of a secret play beneath the text and encourage the actors to burrow for it."

But Brook began work on the *Dream* in late 1969, so this could well be what David Selbourne reported on in his valuable but hard-to-locate rehearsal diary of Brook's *Dream,* which I found in the Royal Shakespeare Company archives at Stratford.

"On the first day of rehearsal," Selbourne reports, Brook met with the Mechanicals alone and after rehearsing their various professional duties—Bottom the weaver, Flute the bellows-mender, etc.—Brook had the actors playing the Mechanicals read through the entire text of the *Dream,* taking all the parts.

Then on the second day of rehearsal, "Brook talked to the actors about 'seeking out the mystery' in a play in which there is a 'reality beyond description,' after which he asked actors to explore sounds 'unrelated to verbal equivalents.' He then took the actors into a reading, asking them to 'remember the sounds which came upon the deepest impulse.' At the end of the reading Brook told the actors that *the very last stanzas* of the *Dream* are 'the most inner portion of the whole drama: tantalizingly close to something secret and mysterious. We approach here whatever is behind the whole play' " (italics mine).

Why the "very last stanzas," ones that are often dismissed, or ignored anyway, as comic doggerel, part of the fairy fantasy that made the play seem sadly antiquated to many over the centuries?

Those "very last stanzas": The wedding banquet has concluded; the "entertainment"—*The most lamentable comedy and most cruel death of Pyramus and Thisby*—the inadvertently farcical tragedy put on by the Mechanicals led by Bottom the weaver, comes to an end with Theseus gently cautioning the aristocratic critics of the poor mechanical players with the lovely line, "The best in this kind are but shadows."

The revels are now over, "the iron tongue of midnight hath told twelve," the Duke intones, "Lovers, to bed, 'tis almost fairy time."

The three newlywed royal couples go off to consummate their nuptials in the chambers of the palace. And then Puck emerges with a broom and the final stanzas Brook refers to as the locus of something "secret and mysterious" commence:

Here is how Puck begins:

Now the hungry lion roars,
And the wolf behowls the moon;
Whilst the heavy ploughman snores,
All with weary task foredone.
Now the wasted brands do glow,
Whilst the screech-owl, screeching loud,
Puts the wretch that lies in woe
In remembrance of a shroud.
Now it is the time of night
That the graves, all gaping wide,
Every one lets forth his sprite
In the church-way paths to glide.
And we fairies, that do run
By the triple Hecat's team
From the presence of the sun,
Following darkness like a dream,
Now are frolic. Not a mouse
Shall disturb this hallowed house.
I am sent with broom before
To sweep the dust behind the door.
[emphasis mine]

Look at the world Puck conjures up, in order to apprehend its darkness. One has to overcome centuries of sentimentalizing of "fairies" as cutesy fairytale creatures to see fairy nature "red in tooth and claw." Forget the lion's roar, the wolf's howl, the screech-owl putting "the wretch that lies in woe / In remembrance of a shroud." What is about to take place in the darkness outside the newlyweds' rooms is a horrific dance of death: "the graves, all gaping wide, / Every one lets forth his sprite."

The fairies are identified as minions of Hecate, the witch-queen of hell, "Following darkness like a dream." What is being disclosed more explicitly here, what Brook may have been referring to, is the darkness *of* the *Dream.* This is a Faustian incantation.

After Puck's invocation to the spirits emerging from hell, the King and Queen of the Fairies, the newly reconciled Oberon and Titania, emerge and give orders to their accompanying fairies to fend off the hell spawn. At last Oberon pronounces the protective blessing which mainly involves protecting the newlyweds' newly conceived issue from birth defects. The dance and blessing are designed to prevent "the blots of Nature's hand."

Then Oberon and Titania depart and Puck takes the stage alone, and directly addresses us, the audience. With an "assault on mercy" one might say:

If we shadows have offended,
Think but this, and all is mended,
That you have but slumb'red here,
While these visions did appear.
And this weak and idle theme,
No more yielding but a dream,
Gentles, do not reprehend.
If you pardon, we will mend.
And, as I am an honest Puck,
If we have unearned luck
Now to scape the serpent's tongue,
We will make amends ere long;
Else the Puck a liar call.
So, good night unto you all.
Give me your hands, if we be friends,
And Robin shall restore amends.

So where is the secret play in these last stanzas, which are essentially *spells* cast upon players by the superhuman crew? Spells to ward off evil, spells to ward off misconception, the nightmare of history outside the circumscribed glow of the stage. I've given it a lot of thought and I can't say for sure this was what Brook was referring to, but I think it had something to do with the play itself as spell. With the *Dream* as spell. A work of theater that works like a love potion dropped into the eyes of the audience.

A play as love potion that is designed to alter the way we see things ever after. In the play the love potion works to induce love-at-first-sight, mad love with the first being one sees when one opens one's spellbound eyes. Was the secret play about learning how to turn a text into a spell, a theatrical incantation?

It certainly worked on me long beyond that one night's magic. It worked in a profound, ever-deepening way on me, cast a spell over my life. It worked even more powerfully on others for whom Peter Brook became a kind of Pied Piper leading them across continents, consuming their lives under *his* spell.

Another interesting stray indication that others think of the play as spells has to do with its use as a *counter*spell to the dark spell of "the Scottish play."

It was fascinating to discover, cumulatively, how just about every actor and just about every director I've spoken to in the course of writing this book will refer to *Macbeth* only as "the Scottish play." I thought it was a joke, the superstition that saying *"Macbeth"* out loud brings bad luck. And it is a joke, on one level, I'm sure. But it is also among the most pervasive and persistent theatrical superstitions.* The spell of which will not be diminished by the fact that the curse of "the Scottish play"—the historicity, the origin and meaning of the belief that saying the name "Macbeth" casts an evil spell upon anyone who utters it—was *the* subject that dominated SHAKSPER, the leading Shakespeare scholars' electronic discussion list in America, on September 10, 2001.

It was in the course of this online discussion that I first learned that the only remedy for the supposed "Scottish play" spell, the only possible counterspell to quell the evil before it was too late, was to instantly recite

* On the British version of *The Weakest Link* quiz show, a British actor was disqualified because he insisted on answering a question with "the Scottish play" instead of *"Macbeth."*

some verses from *A Midsummer Night's Dream.* Good magic could drive out bad magic.

Please understand: I'm not endorsing these superstitions, what I'm saying is that it is testament to the belief that the *Dream* has some numinous incantatory power which Brook may be referring to as its "secret play."

More explicit, less suspect and superstitious authority for the notion of a "secret play" in general in Shakespeare can be found in an unusual passage in another play that seems inserted specifically to suggest just such a notion.

As I was writing this chapter I was also watching a tape of the BBC-TV production of *Romeo and Juliet* and found myself arrested by a passage I'd long overlooked, one that almost seems as if Shakespeare were directing our attention to the notion of a secret play. It's a passage in which Juliet's mother is rhapsodizing over the qualities of Paris, the man Juliet's father proposes she marry. In a fourteen-line passage which works as a dramatic sonnet in itself—almost as if composed separately—she compares Paris to a book and asks Juliet:

> *Read o'er the volume of young Paris' face,*
> *And find delight writ there with beauty's pen;*
> *Examine every married lineament,*
> *And see how one another lends content;*
> *And what obscur'd in this fair volume lies*
> *Find written in the margent of his eyes.*
> *This precious book of love, this unbound lover,*
> *To beautify him, only lacks a cover.*
> *The fish lives in the sea, and 'tis much pride*
> *For fair without the fair within to hide.*
> *That book in many's eyes doth share the glory,*
> *That* in gold clasps locks in the golden story;
> *So shall you share all that he doth possess,*
> *By having him, making yourself no less.*
> [emphasis mine]

The gold clasps that lock in the golden story. Yes, on the surface it's just Juliet's mother describing the beauty of her prospective bridegroom, or the secrets that will be unlocked by marriage. But on another level it's about a book, a text that has a secret story locked within it. The secret story to be found "within to hide," obscured from the direct glance perhaps, only to be found "written in the margent."

Only by finding that secret story can one then "share all that he [the author of the secret story, that is Shakespeare] doth possess."

Does the secret story (the secret play?) in *Romeo and Juliet* also partake in the mystery of infinitude? Well, Juliet does invoke it, doesn't she, when in the balcony scene she tells Romeo she gave him her love before he requested it, and wishes she could withdraw it, to give it again, because:

My bounty is as boundless as the sea,
My love as deep; the more I give to thee,
The more I have, for both are infinite.

I'll return to the whole notion that there is a secret play beneath each play—and to the debate over whether there is a secret play that underlies *all* the plays—but I want to get back to Peter Brook at BAM that night in 2001 and the way he related the notion of the secret play to *Hamlet,* both play and person, and then to "the person who was Shakespeare."

He moved from the idea of the inner and the outer play—and the way Shakespeare played to audiences with multiple levels of awareness—to the play going on *within* Shakespeare.

"That," he said, "is the whole complex art of Shakespeare. A complex art that only comes into being if the person who was Shakespeare kept all those whirling levels within him."

All those whirling levels. He's speaking of the mind of Shakespeare as if it were a cosmos, at the very least a microcosm of the cosmos, with infinite levels ever deepening-unto-bottomlessness like a whirlpool in the waves, or, indeed, the whirling internal structure of the atom—the source of its "infinite energies." A mind that is a model of creation, or vice versa. A mind that Brook suddenly, unexpectedly (to me anyway) but unforgettably, suggests is a model of the mind of Hamlet.

Hamlet, Brook says, "is perhaps the only model one can have for Shakespeare's mind." And what does the mind of Hamlet indicate about the mind of Shakespeare? Brook seems to be saying it has something to do with the tragic burden of bottomlessness.

"Who was Hamlet?" Brook asks. "Not just a prince, a courtier, a son with Oedipal problems," not, in other words, all the other reductive theories of who Hamlet was. What was it that made Hamlet exceptional? "Who was Hamlet but a man, a brilliant but normal person who nonetheless exhibited a *million* percent vitality."

So that's another thing this million percent figure is about. It's an almost deliberately, flamboyantly vulgar way of specifying richness beyond vulgar quantification, someone who has within him the vision of bottomless infinitude.

"Now," he said, "we are very close to what is the mystery of *Hamlet.*"

Again, when Peter Brook says we are very close to the mystery of *Hamlet,* a mystery that has confounded four centuries of investigation, conjecture and debate by poets, madmen and lovers, attention must be paid. It seems that what he's saying is that the mystery, the secret of *Hamlet* is the mystery, the tragedy, of bottomless consciousness. Of what it is to walk around with that kind of awareness. The same burden of awareness Brook suggested Shakespeare walked around with. And so what Brook is suggesting is that, in this aspect at least, Hamlet is the closest thing to a portrait of Shakespeare's mind. When you think about it, the other characters in Shakespeare who suggest self-portrait, a portrait of Shakespeare the writer—Mercutio, Falstaff, and Bottom—each to a different degree, in a different mode, are burdened by *knowing too much.* Bottom having just had his dream of bottomlessness. Mercutio, someone for whom language itself is a dizzying spiral into which he almost disappears. Falstaff plumbing the bottomless depths of his own lies.

What does it mean to say the "tragedy" of bottomless consciousness? For one thing awareness of the notion of infinitude, which was only just coming into focus in Shakespeare's time, can be a destabilizing burden. We've seen how contemplation of the maddening paradoxes of transfinite mathematics may have driven their inventor, Georg Cantor, to the madhouse, where he became a Shakespeare obsessive. Not only was the notion of infinitude, or the contemplation of it, relatively new in Shakespeare's time, it was also still controversial. If it drove Cantor mad it drove Giordano Bruno to the stake, where the church burned this Shakespeare contemporary for thinking about such things.

As a scholar noted in *The Shakespeare Newsletter:* "Shakespeare's use of the term 'infinite space' in *Hamlet* . . . invoked the new concept of the infinity of the universe: 'O God I could be bounded in a nutshell and count myself a king of infinite space.' Ideas of the infinity of space or the universe had been discussed by Nicholas of Cusa in the fifteenth century in his famous theological dictum that God is a sphere of which the center is everywhere and the circumference nowhere [stop and think about that for a moment; it's dizzying]. . . . Giordano Bruno lecturing and publishing in England from 1583 to 1588 played an important role in the spread of the concept of the infinity of the universe in . . . writing 'There is a single general space, a single vast immensity which we may freely call "Void" . . . this space we declare to be infinite.' Bruno . . . related his hypothesis of an infinite world in an infinite space to the Copernican solar theory." And died for it: the church burned him as a heretic when he returned to Rome in 1600.

This scholar concludes of Shakespeare's recurrent reference to the infinite:

"There is no reason to believe that anyone in Renaissance England would know or write about infinite space unless he had been exposed to Nicholas of Cusa, Thomas Digges or Giordano Bruno. Copernicus had hedged on the concept of the infinity of the universe. Kepler later rejected the concept. But Shakespeare acknowledges its possibility."

But as Eliot put it, "After such knowledge, what forgiveness?" Such knowledge is a burden, as Brook puts it, to "an otherwise ordinary man walking around" both elevated and burdened by being a million percent alive to the infinitude of creation. Burdened by living with the dizzying apprehension of limitlessness, and the contrary exacerbated awareness of personal limitation—the rock bottom realities of flesh and blood, the unforgiving deadline of mortality. The mind that is indeed "king of infinite space" but also "bounded in a nutshell."

So that was Peter Brook at BAM invoking the unbearable burden of infinitude in Shakespeare. It left many questions. And what surprised me when I finally forced myself to listen to the tape of my interview with Brook, which had taken place a few days earlier, was that he answered some of those questions, and deepened others, as he returned to his near-obsession with the infinitude one encounters in engaging with Shakespeare.

I'm still not sure why I had blocked out some of the exciting things Brook said to me in the Brooklyn Marriott Hotel lounge on that occasion. Perhaps because they were *unbearably* exciting and I was not in the most stable state imaginable when our talk took place, having gotten virtually no sleep the night before, because of preoperative pain and preinterview anxiety.

In any case Brook, at the Brooklyn Marriott: looking a bit closer to his actual age—seventy-seven—than he had two years earlier, a little more frazzled and unsteady, watched over carefully by a French woman who installed us at a table in the lounge and announced that she would return in exactly forty-five minutes to wind things up.

I introduced the subject of bottomlessness with Brook by asking him if he was familiar with the conjecture about the origin of Bottom's name, the one I'd come upon in Peter Holland's footnote (see chapter 1). The conjecture which depends upon the fact that the passage in Corinthians Shakespeare parodies in Bottom's speech about his dream—"The eye of man hath not heard, the ear of man hath not seen" what Bottom's bottomless dream has shown him—is followed immediately by that haunting line in Corinthians about the way "the Spirit searcheth everything, yea *even the bottom of God's secrets.*"

What happened next I've come to think of as a high point of my experience writing this book. It's there on the tape: after I speak of the "bottom of God's secrets," Peter Brook utters what sounds to me like a surprised *"Ah!"*

Both the "Ah" and the surprise are what I treasure. I suppose he could have faked it, Zen master that he was. But at the moment it seemed real, as with Frank Kermode: the simultaneous surprise and appreciation of the significance of this allusion.

In any case the transcript shows that after Brook's "Ah!" I went on to ask him, "Do you feel that in Bottom's Dream Shakespeare was touching on what you call 'the invisible dimension' or 'the metaphysical dimension'?"

"I think what made Shakespeare so extraordinary is that he's a simple, straight, real man with an extraordinary metaphysical awareness. As Gordon Craig [the early twentieth-century influential stage designer and director] said, 'If you take away the supernatural and you don't believe in the supernatural, you might as well burn the entirety of Shakespeare's works.' It's as simple as that. It goes through all his plays."

Burn Shakespeare's works! Brook in his mild way becomes quite fierce on the point: "It's not one person's point of view, that you can *argue* with someone else. Shakespeare is metaphysical because in every line it shows that.

"But what's marvelous is that one of the most, most difficult things, I think, for any human being to do is to link all the levels of existence. And Shakespeare managed to link the highest levels of metaphysical thought with political thought, with a social sense of life, with a sense of human comedy, with a sense of human tragedy. A joy in human vulgarity, a likeness for human likeness and a joy in human grossness. And all of these put in their place, combined, make up the whole of his works."

Brook was on a roll, rhapsodizing over Shakespeare's multifaceted whole, Shakespeare *as* a sphere, the one Nicholas of Cusa described in his "definition of infinitude," the sphere with an infinite number of centers. He's on a roll that takes him from the vulgar to the metaphysical:

"There was nothing in life that was excluded [from Shakespeare]. If you want to be vulgar you could be vulgar, if you want a really crude sort of college-boy humor, you could find it in Shakespeare. If you want purely erotic, you can find it in Shakespeare. If you want *lightness*—that's why the same metaphysical ideas that are there with a different weight in their expression in *King Lear* and in *Hamlet* are there in *A Midsummer Night's Dream.*"

And then he takes it even further, or deeper: "I think you'll find in all great spiritual, mystical writing that sense of that, awareness of the void, of emptiness."

Then he draws upon an unexpected source—neurology—to make a point about void and infinitude.

"I spoke with a neurologist friend of mine yesterday, Nick Goldberg, we were speaking about Oliver Sacks [Brook made a stage play out of *The Man Who Mistook His Wife for a Hat*]. About the way, in all different branches of science, there is this recognition that the void is charged with potential."

He went on to talk about the way in some branches of cosmology there was emerging a belief that the universe was brought into being *from* a charged Void, one that was not pure nothingness but a void filled with (rather ill-defined) vibrant "quantum fluctuations." The theory holds that these notional, random quantum fluctuations, more mathematical than substantial—a virtual mathematical language before there was anyone to speak or read or think it—gave rise to the Big Bang.

"It turns out that Nothing is more vibrant than this mere . . . absence of any form," Brook says.

Reading over the transcript I thought his use of the word "vibrant" was particularly notable; it's the word he used in *Evoking Shakespeare* when he spoke of the potential of "a single vibrant word" to create a world, a universe, to release "infinite energies."

"Shakespeare," Brook continued, "I think felt vitally—through thought and intuition and feeling—he felt and *discovered* this sense." This sense of the vibrancy within the infinite space of void.

Interesting: in his *De l'infinito, universo et mondi* Giordano Bruno wrote, "There is a single general space, a single, vast immensity which we may freely call Void . . . this space we declare to be infinite." A similar paradoxic identification of infinitude with Void, by a contemporary of Shakespeare. If this is beginning to seem a bit too mystical, Brook brings it all back down to bottom, or to Bottom.

After talking about the way he felt Shakespeare had *felt* this intuition of the charged vibrancy of the Void, Brook says, "And it is through the bottom you reach the height and through the height you discover the bottom."

"This vertiginous sense of bottomlessness, Shakespeare seems to like to create?" I asked Brook. "The bottom falling out, dropping out. Horatio warning Hamlet not to go too near the—"

"Precipice," Brook supplied.

"And also that scene in *Lear* where Edgar conjures up the depths from the top of the cliff for Gloucester. What is the relationship of this metaphysical, spiritual-slash-visionary sense you find in Shakespeare to orthodox theology?" I asked. "It's not quite the same is it?"

"You touch on something fundamental, which is whether when you talk about theology you're talking about what the church has turned into doctrine. Or whether one comes to the fact that deep, deep down, at the real bottomless level, Buddhism, Islam, Judaism and Christianity are talking about the same thing. And on that level, on the bottomless level it's the same experience being expressed through different cultures and different languages."

The same experience . . . "Do you have a feeling that Shakespeare had some initiating, mystical or visionary experience?" I asked Brook.

"I would have thought it's so," he said. "I mean there were esoteric groups of course and Shakespeare could have been part of one of those groups. I think it's more probable than improbable. He could have had many, many experiences. I don't think anything suggests a St. Paul–like sudden mystical flare. But a long series of experiences. After all," he concludes, "nothing comes from nothing."

"Nothing will come of nothing" is of course a line from the opening of *King Lear.* And it is of course—1,500 years earlier—the famous line from Lucretius, the Latin author of the epic creation poem *De rerum natura,* the great ode to the creative power of Venus—to the force of love expressed in the personified goddess Venus, which binds the universe together, Lucretius believes, from the lowliest atom to the most elevated souls in love.

"Nothing Will Come of Nothing" is also the title of a lecture Peter Brook gave to a group of Freudian analysts. Clearly, he's fond of the paradox, in *Lear* and Lucretius: if nothing comes from nothing, or if everything comes from Venus, who creates the creator? It is the mystery of creation "in a nutshell." It is a mystery that brings us back to the heart of the *Dream,* to that strange and wonderful verse about poetic creation:

The poet's eye, in a fine frenzy rolling,
Doth glance from heaven to earth, from earth to heaven;
And as imagination bodies forth
The forms of things unknown, the poet's pen
Turns them to shapes, and gives to aery nothing
A local habitation and a name.

Here Shakespeare is writing about creation, about the way imagination in effect "bodies forth" something from nothing. He is also giving us a glimpse of his *experience* of creation: the way the poet's pen "gives to aery nothing" a somethingness, a "local habitation and a name."

At the heart of the *Dream* then is this dual vision of creation, cosmological and poetical, both bringing forth being from nonbeing. We are close here, as Brook would say, to the "bottom of God's secrets." It's a secret Peter Brook seems to suggest that Shakespeare may have in some visionary moment glimpsed himself.

Is this the secret play beneath all the plays? The belief in, the search for some such secret play has obsessed Shakespeareans for centuries. The persistent feeling that there is something exceptional, that he is not just another playwright. That through him we get a glimpse of God's secrets. It's one *possible* secret play. Two subsequent developments—seeing Brook's film of his *Hamlet,* and talking to Cic Berry, verse-speaking guru of Brook's *Dream*—suggested further ways to envision what Brook's "secret play" implied.

WHO'S THERE?

It took me a long time to be able to write about the *Hamlet* Peter Brook brought to Brooklyn. The one that was the occasion for my last two provocative encounters with him in Brooklyn.

Because I found the version staged in Brooklyn so disappointing. Or because I was disappointed in myself for missing something. But at the time I thought there was a lot missing. It was played on a bare stage—well, a stage covered by a bright red carpet and almost nothing else. But that was not the problem, it was the bare minimum of text that was the problem for me. At full length *Hamlet* runs to about four hours. Most directors cut it to three or three and a half hours. (One of the most interesting and remarkably significant controversies in contemporary Shakespeare scholarship is how long most of his plays took on stage. Whether anything like the "full texts that have come down to us from the early printings were actually seen by his contemporary audiences," as Andrew Gurr, the foremost contemporary historian of the Shakespearean stage, puts it. Or were Shakespeare's audiences given cut versions, the "two hours' traffic of our stage," as the Prologue of *Romeo and Juliet* puts it?)

It was not so much that Brook cut the play in half, it was rather that I couldn't divine a unified conception, except for the fact that it both began and ended with someone calling out "Who's there?"

"Who's there?" are in fact the words that open the two "good" texts of *Hamlet,* the Second Quarto and the First Folio. But not the words that close it. In the beginning they are the lines of the nervous sentinel reporting for duty, worrying that the sounds of the watchman on the battlements might be the ghost whose nightly visitation has terrified him.

Who's there? It's a good question. It's a question that one asks of the infinite void: Who—if anyone, or any One—is out there? It's a good beginning. What does it mean if it's the ending as well? That nothing has been learned? That the play has "merely" been a reminder that we don't know the answer? That the play has given us the answer: we'll never know. Or *someone's* there (us) but we don't know who *we* are or how we got here. I don't know the answer, but I admit I liked Brook asking the question at the end, however untraditional it was.

The standard texts of *Hamlet* end with Hamlet's dying—"The rest is silence" (sometimes followed by the O-groans)—then with Horatio intoning, "Good night, sweet prince, / And flights of angels sing thee to thy rest!", followed by Fortinbras commanding, "Go bid the soldiers shoot"—as a final military salute to the dead prince.

But Brook had Horatio step to the lip of the stage and peer out into the darkness, at the audience, at the cosmos, and say "Who's there?"

Still, between the beginning and ending question I didn't find any answers to what Brook was up to. Adrian Lester, who played Hamlet, was energetic and delivered spirited readings of the soliloquies, but I left underwhelmed.

It was not till nearly three years later that I encountered Brook's *Hamlet* again. Or a version of Brook's *Hamlet,* the version he filmed himself at his home theater, the Bouffes des Nordes, the theater in Paris that his company was based in.

In the film it was the same bloodred rug as in Brook's *Hamlet* at BAM but it was a different *Hamlet.* This time no bookended "Who's there?" And deeper cuts. The entire two first scenes—Horatio seeing the ghost, Hamlet in the court of Claudius—had been cut. Instead it began with the first soliloquy:

O that this too too sallied flesh would melt,
*Thaw, and resolve itself into a dew!**

This time, though it took a while to get used to the voids he'd introduced where text had once been, I saw Brook's *Hamlet* in an entirely new way.

The film was a response in part to Brook's own critique of stage versus film productions. His belief that film has something theater can never offer: the close-up. The close-up which can fill a frame and allow an actor to speak as quietly as he wishes short of inaudibility. Not just quiet for its own sake, but because, as Brook has said, "the quieter [an actor] can be the closer he can be to himself," or the character's self.

And this film he made was *very* close up. *Hamlet* in extreme close-up. So intimate one felt one had crossed the fourth wall and was in the same room as the characters. When they sit, we sit, we remain at eye level almost continuously.

Especially Hamlet, the same actor: Adrian Lester, but a different Hamlet from the one he gave us in Brooklyn, where he had to fill the empty space with voice and movement. Now he was more often still, almost quiet. He was a whispering Hamlet, a Hamlet of whispered confidences to himself, as well as others.

When Olivier played Hamlet on film he tried to solve the problem of bombast by giving us the soliloquies in voice-overs as if they were not being

* The *Riverside* text, which I have chiefly relied upon, uses the Quarto's "sallied flesh" as opposed to the Folio's "solid flesh" and the conjectural "sullied flesh."

spoken at all but were just the unuttered thoughts in his head. Adrian Lester gave us spoken thoughts that sounded unuttered even as they were uttered.

Of course there were some weird choices. Doing the Player King's set-piece tale of Pyrrhus and the fall of Troy in ancient Greek was a curious decision. And the silenced—cut—characters and scenes of the play contributed to that sense of silence, stillness, contemplativeness. Made it clear that something unspoken was going on. I felt it might have something to do with the prominence Brook gave to the scene between Hamlet and Rosencrantz and Guildenstern and the recorder.

A recorder is the flutelike instrument Hamlet says R&G want to use him as—to "play upon his stops," the holes that the musician's fingers open and stop up to generate tones. (Each hole a void charged with potential.)

Then there is the way Brook radically shifts the "To be or not to be" soliloquy to make it the last one in the play.

Also remarkable and deliberately so is the way Brook's film ends. Instead of "Who's there?" as in the production I saw, the last words in this film are Hamlet's last words in the play (his last words in the Quarto version; no O-groans). An ecstasy comes over Hamlet's face, a light breaks upon him as he says, "The rest is silence."

Strange the way Brook has changed the close of what will (alas) probably be his last *Hamlet.* He went back from "Who's there?", his own revision, and gave us at least something close to Shakespeare's close: "The rest is silence." Why? It seems an important reversal, the abandonment of "Who's there?" and the return to rest on "silence."

Fortunately, the person who sent me a videotape of the BBC production included on the tape an interview with Brook about this production. I was somewhat disappointed with most of the interview because it largely consisted of the interviewer presenting his theories of *Hamlet*—and Brook politely declining to subscribe to them, until near the end when Brook began to discuss the line "The rest is silence."

He was talking about the question of the afterlife so present in *Hamlet.* The fear in "To be or not to be" of an infinity of bad dreams after death. Ophelia describing Hamlet looking like someone "loosed from hell to speak of horrors"; Hamlet's father's ghost loosed from his afterlife in Purgatory.

"And so when Hamlet says 'The rest is silence,' " Brook tells his interviewer, "one has a choice how to take it. Because entering into eternal silence is not into eternal bleakness, but something of a different order.

"You can say 'The rest is silence' as in 'That's all life is about' in a very Sartrean existential 'Hell-is-other-people' way.

"Or the complete opposite. All this torment, 'To be or not to be,' he talks about—all *that* goes on until all falls into place and the rest is silence. A vibrant silence."

Peter Brook's final word on what kind of spell Shakespeare's most mysterious play casts upon us: "a vibrant silence."

There's that word "vibrant" again. There's that image: a void filled with vibrancy. Words are nothing but vibrations generated by chords, by vocal cords, by the strings of the vocal cords. A vibrant silence uttered by the silent strings of creation. It's Peter Brook's string theory of Shakespeare you might say.

EPILOGUE: STRING THEORY IN PRACTICE, OR THE SECRET PLAY AT LAST?

Of course this can begin to seem at times too abstractly metaphysical. What was refreshing in talking to Cic Berry, who was Peter Brook's verse-speaking lieutenant in the making of the *Dream,* was the way she made physical such metaphysical notions, linked the metaphorical "string theory" to the strings—well, the vocal *cords*—of the actors actually uttering the words.

I met Ms. Berry, eighty now and still with the RSC, when she'd come to New York to work with the American director Karen Coonrod on a *Julius Caesar* for the Theater for a New Audience. I was fortunate to get her to agree to have lunch with me during a break in rehearsals.

I was surprised to learn when we met that Ms. Berry had only just joined the RSC when Peter Brook began to rehearse his production. And I came to believe that what she and Brook did with voice and verse-speaking adds something to our understanding of the secret play that made that production spectacular.

She'd been invited there in 1969, she told me, when Trevor Nunn, then just twenty-nine, took over as artistic director and felt the need, for the first time, to bring in a full-time verse-speaking specialist. In part she said it was because Nunn felt that many talented actors were being drawn to Shakespeare from film and television; they had enormous gifts but lacked classical or Shakespearean voice and verse training and thus had trouble filling the vast space of the Memorial Theatre at Stratford, which was the company's home, and often a graveyard to those whose voices could not carry into its depths. And because Nunn had been impressed with the vision Ms. Berry (now C. Berry, O.B.E.) brought to the concept of voice. Then she met Peter Brook and their collaboration brought out something in that *Dream* that changed both their work, changed contemporary Shakespeare—in addition to changing lives like mine with its electrifying clarity.

Our conversation began with the question of musicality in Shakespeare verse-speaking. As it happened, the morning before meeting Cic Berry I had been watching a videotape of the 1936 George Cukor film of *Romeo and Juliet,* which featured Norma Shearer as Juliet, and more to the point here, and most memorably, John Barrymore as Mercutio. It is said to be the only sustained filmed record of Barrymore doing Shakespeare. It was exactly the sort of Shakespeare Peter Hall, Peter Brook and Cic Berry sought to displace.

Barrymore came from one of the great American Shakespearean dynasties, successors and rivals to the Booths, and he was said to have an Edmund Kean–like swooning-and-faint-inducing power over audiences with his tragic roles. The conscious musicality of his voice can seem hammy to the modern ear, but its vibrancy is impressive.

At fifty-four in Cukor's *Romeo* he's a bit too old for Mercutio, but everybody in the cast, the lovers and their friends anyway, looks too old. They remind you of illustrations of the "robustious periwig-pated fellows" that "tore a passion to tatters" as overaged Romeos in engravings from David Garrick's age.

Not only is Barrymore too old, but he's way old-fashioned-sounding, at least at first. He takes us back, not to original Shakespearean acting, whatever that was, but back a century or so at least, to the florid, musical, operatic style of nineteenth-century Shakespeareans which one can hear still in some rare preserved Edison-era recordings that go back to 1890. And yet the sheer Mozartian beauty of the music in Barrymore's voice is astonishing. It was this vibratory musicality that I found somehow resonated with Cicely Berry's work, and what she achieved with Peter Brook's cast in the *Dream.*

I learned something about musical, harmonic vibrancy in verse-speaking practice from watching Cic Berry work with the *Julius Caesar* cast during the previous week's rehearsal period and had begun to get an intimation of the method to the magic she evokes. The day before, for instance, she called the cast up onto the stage, had them all lie down and begin producing a vibratory series of hums, ahhs and oms that sounded at first like some Eastern monastic practice, but were designed, she said, to get the cast vibrating both individually and in harmony and to expand the space *within* them where the voice lived. Expand it downward, expand the internal volume of space—the theater within—an internal stage on which the voice played.

If it sounds a bit touchy-feely perhaps there's an element of that. But I recalled one Shakespeare scholar compare Peter Brook's concept of "the Empty Space" (the title of his vastly influential book on his methods) with Cicely Berry's voice work: what Berry was doing, this scholar argued, was taking Brook's "empty space"—his phrase for the void theater must fill with life—and *internalizing* it. For Cic Berry the empty space, the empty stage, was a space *inside the body* and must be brought to life within, in the form of sound and voice, before the empty space in the theater outside can be brought to life.

I'm always thrilled to watch any aspect of Shakespeare in rehearsal, the way a production is built from parts (literally) into a whole. But in watching Cic Berry I felt I was witness to a search for a deeper level upon which to found the voice—the vibratory physics of the sound as it shaped itself into language. Getting to watch Cic Berry, I thought I was watching some elemental force in the history of Shakespearean performance, the force that infused the Royal Shakespeare Company's best work.

For the work the day before I met her for lunch, Cic Berry began (after the vibratory hum exercises) with a speech not from *Julius Caesar* but from *Hamlet.* The notorious "Pyrrhus speech." The one that Hamlet called for the Player King to recite when he first arrived at Elsinore. The one that had Hamlet envying the Player King for driving himself to tears in describing the plight of the widowed queen, Hecuba, standing before the body of her slain husband King Priam, while his killer, Pyrrhus, son of Achilles, exults in gory triumph ("What's Hecuba to him, or he to Hecuba?")

Cic Berry handed out sheets with the Pyrrhus speech to the company. And asked them first to recite it together.

Hamlet himself begins it like this:

The rugged Pyrrhus, he whose sable arms,
Black as his purpose, did the night resemble
When he lay couched in th' ominous horse,
Hath now this dread and black complexion smear'd
With heraldy more dismal: head to foot
Now is he total gules, horridly trick'd
With blood of fathers, mothers, daughters, sons,

Bak'd and impasted with the parching streets,
That lend a tyrannous and a damned light
To their lord's murther. Roasted in wrath and fire,
And thus o'er-sized with coagulate gore,
With eyes like carbuncles, the hellish Pyrrhus
Old grandsire Priam seeks.

This is only Hamlet's part of the recitation; he then hands it off to the lead Player, who goes on for more than fifty lines to further describe the slaughter in gory detail.

I think Cic Berry chose the Pyrrhus passage both for its sound and its savagery—a primal early-Shakespearean savage energy not inappropriate for *Julius Caesar,* where ostensibly civilized politics is undergirded with bloody havoc. With Caesar's own "coagulate gore," the blood into which conspirators ritualistically dip their hands.

So what Cic Berry had the cast do was, first, chant the lines together. Then she told them each to take a line and had the cast recite the passage one line per person. Then she had some chant their own line quietly to themselves while the rest of the cast continued to chant them in succession. Then she had them start running around the theater chanting their individual lines. Then she had them continue to run around the theater, only this time when she called "Stop!" each would vocalize his line from whatever location he was in, then run around some more until she called "stop" and they vocalized it from another, different, location.

Over and over—it is her belief that in doing so she imbues the actors with a kind of physical manifestation of the movement of *thought* from line to line. The movement of thought that she believes should go on within the actor, within his voice, as he speaks the lines from a different place, a different space in the mind. And each time he speaks it—sometimes she has them whisper it, hiss it—it must be communicated to someone opposite them in the theater. The day before, I'd seen this exercise work in practice: actually bring some crackling energy to a previously rather lackluster exchange between the actors playing Brutus and Cassius.

At this point, with the bloody thrum of the Pyrrhus speech vibrating in the cast, echoing in the mind, in the diaphragm, and pervading, somehow, the entire theater, she turns to *Caesar.* I'm abbreviating the process but it culminates with Ms. Berry drawing the cast together in a knot in the middle of the stage and asking each cast member to *sing* their favorite line from *Caesar.* They began with someone breaking into a simple *"Hail Caesar"* which was then taken up chorally by the whole cast, which then retreated to a choral hum as the soloist continued with "Hail Caesar." Until someone else broke into *"He doth bestride the narrow world like a colossus."* With beautiful call and response, choral and solo recitatives that seemed to become imbued with the emotion of the line, which somehow shaped the line into a melody with vibratory harmonic undertones. Then a beautiful woman's voice (the voice of the woman playing Brutus's wife, Portia) sang out the embittered line *"Brutus's harlot, not his wife."* Then after the choral responses and reiterations, the other woman in the cast, who played Calpurnia, Caesar's wife, took up *"There is a tide in the affairs of men, which taken at the flood"*—giving the line a lovely spooky lunar embodiment. Finding its musicality.

The origin of this complex choral exercise shouldn't have been surprising. When I asked Ms. Berry about her family background, she told me that she'd grown up poor in the London suburb of Berkhamstead, didn't have an early transformative Shakespearean experience, although she says "I was besotted by poetry from about age three. . . . But my father was interested in music, he used to train the church choir."

It suddenly clicked for me: the choral roots of the exercise I'd seen the day before.

At that time, in the forties, voice-teaching was mainly a kind of polite art known as "diction" taught by devoted spinsters, and although verse-speaking training was a recognized part of an actor's preparation, it was rare that verse-speaking specialists were attached to a company, even a Shakespearean company, until the Royal Shakespeare Company brought in Cic Berry as a resident specialist and brought her unusual methods of verse-speaking to the fore with the kind of excitement the language of their productions was generating. She had come to the attention of Trevor Nunn through her work in the Central Schools of Drama in London and the work she did with several well-known actors whose names she's reluctant to disclose.

By that time she'd been influenced by some, if not all, of the lessons of Method acting (her late husband was a Method actor), not all the overhyped "sense-memory" methods. You might say she believes Shakespeare's language itself serves the function of a kind of built-in "sense memory" for the actors. The Method's emphasis on internalizing is important, but for her it's not necessarily the actor's internalized emotional biography but the internal dynamics of a *character,* dynamics to be found deeply embedded in the words themselves. And then she met Peter Brook and they made theatrical history together.

And what I came away from my conversation with her feeling was that the secret play, so to speak, within the language of Brook's *Dream* had to do with the vibratory dynamics of those vocal exercises. Let me explain by returning for a moment to the musicality of John Barrymore's Mercutio. Cic Berry doesn't favor film Shakespeare, she says, because "one loses the drama of the present moment," but she is not incapable of appreciating some of the present moments, now past, that film preserves.

I mentioned the Barrymore Mercutio I'd just heard to her, and its vibratory, virtually trilled, musicality. "There's a part of us that enjoys that sound even now," she says. "You know I work in prisons"—she's well known for doing Shakespeare and other theater with locked-down prison populations—"and it appeals even to some *very* rough people." (On second thought this might not be the tribute to my taste she sweetly made it seem at the time.)

Anyway we'd been served our lunch—we had met in a tiny Village place called Tartine near the theater and it's a tribute to Cic Berry's own voice that amidst the loud and claustrophobic conversation and clatter surrounding us, her voice came through with ringing clarity on my tape recorder—and I brought up the question of vibratory phenomena in Shakespearean language, both in Barrymore and in the work I'd seen her doing with the Pyrrhus speech the day before.

"I find that area very interesting now," she said. "Finding that kind of [Barrymore] vibration in the voice and yet keeping it sounding *new,* that's very tricky now."

She spoke of the different approaches to language of the three main directors at the RSC when she arrived. Trevor Nunn, who liked a more intimate, informal Method-like approach, "so lovely, so truthful." Terry Hands, "very much the opposite, very much for beating out the rhythm, going fast and loud," a rhythmic style that was "particularly suited to the history plays. When he put them together, as in his *Henry VI* plays, it became one long poem, they were quite stunning."

And then "John Barton of course who is famous for finding the antithesis"—for focusing on a fundamental rhetorical method by which Shakespeare built his speeches: through oppositional phrases, most famously in "To be or not to be" but shot through the rhetoric of his most complex and beautiful verse.

"It was an amazing grounding for me, finding these different approaches to the language and the text. But when I worked with Peter Brook he gave me the confidence to *really* work on text."

I mentioned to her that I'd read somewhere that someone had made the comparison between Brook's use of the term "the Empty Space" as a starting point for thinking about theater, and what she did with voice, that what her work did was internalize Brook's Empty Space, locate it, the space of drama, within the body, make the interior the stage for the voice as it embodied speech and thought within.

"You really read that somewhere?" she said. "Oh! Oh!" expressing surprise, humility and pleasure eloquently with those two lovely vowel sounds. It was the first and perhaps only reaction of that sort I managed to evoke. She's a very pleasant and good-natured woman, and yet very canny in not revealing much about the specifics of her dealings with famous actors and directors (except perhaps Peter Brook) because there are so many sensitive egos to consider when speaking of British Shakespeareans.

And voice- and verse-speaking certainly has not escaped contentiousness. I'd asked her, for instance, if she favored using the Folio punctuation for stops and starts (punctuation RSC founder Peter Hall believes has no foundation in evidence for attributing to Shakespeare as opposed to typeshop compositors). She said, "I don't mind about what system of punctuation, but I do a lot of exercises at the beginning of rehearsal when I get actors to move and change position *on* punctuation. And then they begin to see how thoughts are sometimes very even, other times thoughts are just jumping around."

"Getting people to run around and say these thoughts from different places in the theater," I asked, "for the actors is it like getting thoughts to rocket around to and from different places in themselves?"

"I do a lot of work on that, very specifically on character. For instance what you saw with Brutus and Cassius the other day"—when she had the two actors run around the theater and exchange words across the space from different vantage points—"and Paulina in *The Winter's Tale*"—the deeply moving speech where the outraged handmaiden of the unjustly slandered wife of Leontes denounces the jealous king—"if I get her to do that speech moving around the space, changing direction on every punctuation mark, she suddenly gets the sense of the beating in the blood in her speech."

The beating in the blood . . . It comes back to a drumming of sorts, a tympanic systole/diastole heartbeat rhythm.

It occurred to me to ask her, since sound-and-heard rhythm is so important to her verse-speaking work, if she had an image of how Shakespeare might have written these rhythmic lines. "Would he have spoken them out loud and then have written them down?"

"I think he would have heard them in his head," she said. A fascinating distinction. In the beating of the blood, in his brain, perhaps.

At this point a heretical anti-Originalist thought occurred to me. I'd asked her how important she thought it was to get back to or approximate the way Shakespeare and company might have spoken the lines when they were first performed.

It's interesting, but not necessarily possible to know what the original was, she said. And here's where the heretical thought occurred to me: Perhaps in some rare instances such as the *Dream* she and Brook worked on, we are hearing Shakespeare spoken and performed *better* than the original. Earliest isn't always best or most "Shakespearean" necessarily. Recall that Shakespeare's actors may well have had little sense of the entire play, or of the other actors' parts. According to a fascinating work by the Oxford scholar Tiffany Stern (*Rehearsal from Shakespeare to Sheridan*), all they were given were "cue scripts," which contained the last line or few words of the actor speaking before them, followed by their own speech. Which suggests that Shakespearean actors didn't have the organic awareness of the whole with which to inform their parts—not until something approximating it might have developed in performance eventually.

By contrast the goal of the work Cic Berry and Peter Brook evolved together, beginning with the *Dream,* was to somehow make the whole play resonate in every part. Make every character's part, every character's word, every character's *being,* resonate in every other character's part, by making every actor's voice resonate somehow in every other actor's voice.

She talked about some of the exercises she and Brook would do at the RSC. "There's one where we give each actor a line and they would have to go round in the theater and experiment with the space, seeing what will carry, giving them a sense of lifting the voice, not going higher in pitch. It's very subtle but we do a lot of 'carrying language around.' "

Carrying language around? "We'd get in a circle, take any speech from Shakespeare, say it round [hand the line from one actor to another] so it's like one person speaking at the end. So you become very aware and sensitive to other people's rhythms and other people's pitches and vibrations. It doesn't mean you sound like them, but that *you carry that energy on.*"

I think it finally made sense to me: "So you're saying each actor is responding to the others' sounds and reverberations, and incorporating their reverberations into their own reverberations, which then become slightly altered, and *that* alteration is then incorporated into everyone else's reverberations and echoes, which themselves become altered until each part contains the whole?" I asked. "Is this what you mean when in your books you speak of developing a 'collective voice' in rehearsal?"

"Yes," she said (thank god). Actually, *connective* voice might be just as appropriate as "collective voice." By the end of such exercises the acting company and its language becomes as much an organic whole as the play itself, however divided into parts it is. So that when each individual actor is separate on stage from the others they're still *connected,* they're still somehow on the wavelength of the collective voice. They're one organism, the organism of the language, speaking through separate organs of speech.

I was getting pretty excited thinking that I'd caught on to something important. I was still trying to be analytical, but felt that here was some essential element of what made Brook's *Dream* so stirring to me so long ago—the endlessly echoing reverberation of voice within voice within voice deepening ad infinitum. Deepening into bottomlessness. Here was the vibratory subatomic physics of the *Dream* that changed my life.

"The result," I ventured, "is that the echoes of all the previous iterations of the sound are still echoing, vibrating within each of their voices as they speak?"

"That's right," Cic Berry said.

I'm still not sure I completely understand Peter Brook's "secret play." It's a mystery I feel I've circled around but have not quite grasped. But one can't argue with the achievement, and even if it's something numinous he chooses to *attribute* his experience to, it has that importance.

Still, "The best in this kind"—the best attempts at explication of Peter Brook's secret play—"are but shadows." I think Cic Berry may be offering us a glimpse into at least *one* secret play, or one play of vibratory phenomena, that underlies the words but is made manifest in subtle and even subliminal ways in Brook's best work.

Chapter Twelve

"You Can't Have Him, Harold!": The Battle over Bloom and Bloom's Falstaff

PART 1: LET FALSTAFF BE FALSTAFF!

The director was working himself up to a frenzy over Harold Bloom and Bloom's Falstaff; "You can't *have* him. You can't have him, Harold. You can't contain him. You can't nail him. You can't put him in amber. You can't define him. You can't reduce him."

The director was the well-regarded Jack O'Brien and he was speaking specifically of Bloom's Santa Claus–like interpretation of Falstaff which he intended to challenge with his Lincoln Center production.

But he could have been saying that of Bloom and Shakespeare as well. And if he wasn't, I will: "You can't have him, Harold!"

BLOOM! BLOOM! BLOOM! LIKE THE BEATING OF A BIG BASS DRUM one can't help hearing it, having it drummed into you. Certainly not if you're writing a book involving Shakespeare.

"So what do you think of Bloom?", one will hear approximately one thousand times.

What do I think of Bloom? How much time do you have? Short answer: I'm deeply conflicted, something I realized when I was witness to a remarkable struggle over Bloom's Falstaff—over Falstaff, over Bloom—that played itself out on stage, and dramatized my ambivalence. A struggle, well, a love triangle, pitting Bloom against O'Brien in a tug of war over Kevin Kline, who was playing Falstaff.

Kline's mentor was Bloom, his director was O'Brien, his Falstaff would be . . . I'll get into that, but first a little background, personal and philosophical.

There's little doubt that for most Americans, Bloom's Shakespeare *is* Shakespeare. (His book *Shakespeare: The Invention of the Human* was widely derided in the United Kingdom for both good and bad reasons.) But is Bloom's Shakespeare *Shakespeare's* Shakespeare? Is Bloom's Shakespeare Shakespearean? Is his Falstaff a true or a false-staff?

Bloom! Such a larger-than-life character in brain, body and intellectual hubris. Deserving the Saul Bellow novel the other Bloom (Allan) got in *Ravelstein.* My conflicts are not about him, personally; it's impossible not to feel affection for the larger-than-life Falstaffian *character* he plays. Impossible not to wonder what relation that character has to the man behind the curtain. Impossible not to wonder if it's all—for better or worse—an act, a performance, a conceptual con game worthy of the con artist of braggadocio he most admires, Sir John Falstaff.

Part of me admires Bloom for what—for a long time—was his fairly lonely struggle to assert the existence, the value of "literary value," even literary *greatness* during a period in which academic orthodoxy disdained the concept as a baseless illusion, a Trojan horse of the hegemony designed to sneak its authoritarian values into the unsuspecting minds of readers like you and me.

On the other hand Bloom's bombastic rhetoric about Shakespeare just rings false to my experience of Shakespeare. Bloom's Shakespeare is less about the language than about Big Ideas, Big Themes, Big Characters, Big Bigness. His characteristic rhetoric of overstatement, overinflation, the way he seems to want to beat us over the head with his bardolatry, to make us love Shakespeare not because of what Shakespeare writes but because of what Bloom bellows about him. It's condescending to the reader and—I'd argue—a distortion of Shakespeare.

Bloom suggests one limit of bottomlessness, that it is possible to love Shakespeare too much, to the point where one's love crushes the love object to death in its embrace, or blows it up beyond all recognition.

If Bloom has not reached the bottom of bottomlessness he has in a certain way become Bottom in his dream of union with a divine spirit, inventor of the human, past the wit of man, a veritable God. It's more than bardolatry, it's theology.

Bloom's incessant repetition of variations on the claim that Shakespeare "invented the human," however unfounded in any real way, turned out to be a terrific marketing device. His wasn't just a book about some *writer,* it was about God. By His One True Prophet. It was bardolatry as self-love, what the scholar Linda Charnes—in her brilliant paper on the Bloom phenomenon—was, I believe, the first to call "Bloomolatry."

I can't resist another quote from Charnes's essay—which as I'll explain deserves celebration as a turning point in twenty-first-century Shakespeare studies. This is her way of characterizing Bloom's overblown, overinflated versions of a character like Falstaff. Bloom removes Falstaff from the fabric of the play, and gives us a cartoonish parade float character, "inflated like the Stay-Puft Marshmallow Man in *Ghostbusters*—stomp[ing] through our towns and cities."

Bloom's Falstaff is Stay-Puft Shakespeare.

While Bloom has somehow convinced the towns and cities he stomps through that he is Mr. Shakespeare, I wonder how many people who bought the massive Bloom tome got as far as his Falstaff essay. And how many of those who did take it seriously just because Bloom said it.

How many would defend some of the things that Bloom says about Falstaff:

"Falstaff *is* Shakespeare's wit at its very limits" (his italics). Even as "Hamlet *is* the farthest reach of Shakespeare's cognitive acuity" (his italics).

Note how he says the *character,* whether Falstaff or Hamlet, represents the limits of Shakespeare's wit and intuition, rather than the plays in which they appear. The characters have swallowed the plays for Bloom. It seems obvious and unnecessary to say, but the intellect who created Falstaff and Hamlet and everyone else in their plays is both wittier and more intelligent, Bigger, than Falstaff and Hamlet.

But one doesn't need to make Falstaff and Hamlet Bigger than they are through this puffery. If Bloom is being deliberately paradoxical the device is just a tiresome synecdoche—part invents whole—just as Shakespeare, presumably a human, becomes "the inventor of the human." And "not to appreciate [Falstaff] would be to miss the greatest of Shakespearean originalities: the invention of the human."

And Shakespeare's not merely "inventor of the human." In addition, "Shakespeare essentially invented human personality as we continue to know and value it and Falstaff has priority in this invention."

With Shakespeare inventing the "human," inventing "our feelings," and Falstaff inventing "human personality," there's little left for us to do then, is there? It's all prefab for us. It's as determinist and dismissive of individuality as some of the more extreme versions of Theory he deplores. It's too bad most Americans didn't have access to the brilliant, witty assessment of Bloom's book by John Carey, the lead reviewer for the London *Sunday Times,* formerly a professor of poetry at Oxford, who responded to Bloom's supernatural puffery (Shakespeare as "inventor of the human," i.e., God) by writing:

> It is like chatting with an acquaintance and gradually realizing he believes death rays are issuing from his television screen. An obvious response to Bloom's case is to ask for a single instance of a human faculty that is untraceable before Shakespeare. Mostly, Bloom floats above such tiresome details. But when, towards the end of the book, he briefly descends to specifics, the result is embarrassingly feeble. Our ability to laugh at ourselves, he instances, "owes much to Falstaff." Not a scrap of historical evidence is produced to substantiate even this and, if Bloom himself is anything to go by, an ability to laugh at oneself is far from being an inevitable result of studying Shakespeare.

Carey nails the point, punctures the pretension of "the invention of the human" by simply asking for "a single instance of a human faculty that is untraceable before Shakespeare." Humor? Sadness? Love? Jealousy? Please.

These may have been untraceable in *Bloom* before he read Shakespeare (although even that's hard to believe), but it seems a bit overreaching to generalize from the fact that *he* had to learn to be human this way to the claim that all of humanity did as well.

Bloom's praise for Shakespeare is both shallow and erroneous. His entire "invention of the human" marketing campaign is based on a fallacy: that what makes Shakespeare distinctive, exceptional, Shakespearean is that he was *first.* That he was the Edison of the emotions, rather than that he may well have given us the most profound expressions of them. Not that he was first but that, judging by his durability so far, he may well be, if not the last, the most lasting.

It's a symptom of the insular academic world Bloom inhabits to believe that that which *he* reads, which may have invented *him* in some sense, invented us *all.* In some ways it can be seen as Bloom's unwitting endorsement of the New Historicist ideology he purports to detest: our culture has been so Shakespeareanized, so infused with Shakespearean concepts and characters that it *produces* Shakespeareanized humans whether we know it or like it or not. At the extreme Bloom, like the historicists, denies human autonomy, or limits it to a choice of Shakespearean characters and models whose mold we are poured into.

And Falstaff is a special case, *über*-human. Falstaff, co-inventor of the human, with Hamlet, apparent sole inventor of "human personality," must not be considered an ordinary human in the sense of having any flaws. Bloom tells us: "To reject Falstaff [find any fault] is to reject Shakespeare." He means of course, "to reject my inflated Falstaff is to reject Shakespeare. Worse, to reject me."

And in perhaps the most unself-aware remark about those who dare to criticize Falstaff, he tells us: "After a lifetime surrounded by other professors, I question their experiential qualifications to apprehend, let alone judge, the Immortal Falstaff."

Spending "a lifetime surrounded by other professors" is *precisely* what disqualifies *Bloom* from apprehending, let alone judging, "the Immortal Falstaff." Spending a lifetime surrounded by other professors means that one's view of roguery is limited to the antics of the faculty lounge cut-up. It means one simply lacks the "experiential qualifications" to put Falstaff in perspective.

I don't want to say I'm more qualified than Bloom to appreciate Falstaff, but having left Bloom's faculty lounge sherry parties behind, I have to say I think I've seen more varieties of roguery—from the charming to the venal and vicious and all combinations thereof—than Bloom could imagine. "Experiential qualifications" that find echoes in Falstaff that the well-insulated Bloom might not be able to detect. That alone may not be an argument for a more complex Falstaff than Bloom's "Socrates of Eastcheap." And yet there's no doubt Bloom's faculty lounge point of view gives us a one-dimensional (merely) lovable rogue. Shakespeare gave us one with many more dimensions.

But Bloom insists that to reject his overblown, sacralized, sentimentalized Falstaff (in any way) or to see him as less than a saint or holy man in disguise is to reject Shakespeare. To reject Bloom is to reject Shakespeare. One must accept both. I maintain one has a choice.

Another instance why: Bloom tells us that "Falstaff . . . would be fully present to consciousness if only we could summon up a consciousness in ourselves to *receive* his. It is the comprehensiveness of Falstaff's consciousness that puts him beyond us . . . in Falstaff's way of immanence."

Now we're getting the theology of Bloomolatry. You know immanence, right? In general, the presence of God within, or, in a specifically Christian sense, the Holy Ghost within the world, or within Jesus, or within a single soul who shares communion with Jesus. We must "summon up" a purity of heart to "receive" this spirit the way one receives the body and blood at the Mass.

Before we get to Bloom's Trinitarian view of Falstaff (seriously), we need to address an obvious error in logic: How can we know Falstaff outstrips our consciousness if we can't, by definition, know anything beyond our consciousness? How would we recognize, "receive" it if we can't know it (unless, possibly, one was Bloom, inventor of "the inventor of the human," who like a priest receives it on our behalf)?

This is just careless, lazy sacralizing. Trying to hoist Falstaff and Shakespeare to godhood by the bootstraps of religious rhetoric is unworthy of Bloom, of Shakespeare.

Occasionally Bloom will say something perceptive if not new (as it has been said of Freud: "What's true isn't new, and what's new isn't true"). As when Bloom says, "Falstaff represents . . . the signature of Shakespeare's originality, of his breakthrough into an art more nearly his own" than the earlier Marlowe-influenced works, or plays that worked Marlowe's territory. Nothing in Marlowe approaches Falstaff. True! (But not new.)

But then he will say something that is erudite-sounding nonsense: "Mind in the largest sense, more even than wit, is Falstaff's greatest power; who can settle which is the more intelligent consciousness, Hamlet's or Falstaff's? For all its comprehensiveness, Shakespearean drama is ultimately a theater of mind, and what matters most about Falstaff is his vitalization of the intellect, in direct contrast to Hamlet's conversion of the mind to the vision of annihilation."

A remarkable reductiveness, about Falstaff and Hamlet. And about Shakespeare: "ultimately a theater of mind." Speak for yourself, Mr. Bloom. A theater of mind, yes, but a theater of body and blood, mind and spirit, sex and death all fused into a pageant that is far more than mind alone.

So please, don't tell us Falstaff is only about "vitalization of the intellect," whatever that means. Or that Hamlet converts "the mind to the vision of annihilation." *That's* annihilation: it annihilates the plentitude of Hamlet, leaving us only simple-minded nihilism.

This is not worthy praise, exegesis, critical inquiry—this is making repeated grand rhetorical gestures that one doesn't expect to be examined too closely.

And there are moments of pure lit-crit negligence as when Bloom, obsessively defending Saint Falstaff from any possible alleged fault, tells us: "Falstaff betrays and harms no one."

This is a CliffsNotes-level failure. One of the most famous Falstaff speeches of course is his cruel dismissal of the doomed cripples—the draftees he has corruptly conscripted to die under his "command" in the war—as of no concern to him. They are worth nothing—"food for powder"—essentially condemned to death for their poverty and unfitness by Falstaff. So he can make a celebrated speech on "honor," scorning the pretenses of warriors' "honor." But to say it's merely an "antiwar" speech is to rip it from the context in which it's delivered, from atop a pile of corpses he's sent to an early grave. It flattens and reduces the *Henry IV* plays to a single perspective, rather than the multiple perspectives on the complexities of honor that Hotspur and Hal offer.

Again it ignores both/and ambiguity, Falstaff as a brilliant satirist and skeptic who undermines his own satire with his cold-blooded venality. To do so is to ignore the whole picture Shakespeare gives in favor of Bloom's flawless, faultless Santa Claus Falstaff.

No one wants to turn Falstaff into a villain, just recognize a more complex character than Bloom gives us with his insipid "Falstaff betrays and harms no one."

No one? What about long-suffering Mistress Quickly, cozened with a marriage proposal? And then there are the Canterbury pilgrims robbed (with no intent to—as Hal did—give the gold back). And of course there is Justice Shallow's stolen thousand pounds.

Not that these are mortal sins but they are defining Falstaffian characteristics. At least part of him is an undeniably venal con man, however "immanent."

But it's more than Bloom's Falstaff being without flaw, being without sin; there's the Jesus comparison. We've already had Falstaff as God, inventor of the human; we've had Falstaff as implicitly the Holy Ghost, the immanent Spirit of Shakespeare which the Elect may "receive" into themselves. And here comes the third member of the Holy Falstaff trinity:

"Falstaff . . . is still alive because Shakespeare knew something like the

Gnostic secret of the resurrection, which is that Jesus first arose and *then* he died. Shakespeare shows Falstaff rising from the dead, and only later has Mrs. Quickly narrate the death of Sir John."

This Jesus comparison is a farrago of nonsense beginning with Bloom's view of what "the Gnostic secret of the resurrection is"—a secret *from* most Gnostics. But no matter; Bloom is determined to make a Jesus comparison regardless of whether it falls apart upon closer examination.

But Jesus is not even enough. He's got to be Socrates too, "the Socrates of Eastcheap" Bloom calls him. Oh yes, and "like Socrates," Falstaff is a "great educator," a "sage," and "he is the veritable monarch of language unmatched whether elsewhere in Shakespeare or in all of Western literatures."

Jesus, Socrates, "sage," "great educator." All of this diminishes rather than deepens Falstaff: he is not enough in himself without making him something or someone Other. A Bigger Other. Please, let Falstaff be Falstaff.

What Is Bloom Really Up To?

But could it be that John Carey is being unfair with his TV screen death ray analogy for Bloom's "invention of the human" invention? Could there be a method to Bloom's madness? A con game behind his elevation of con man to God? A hidden agenda behind this play Bloom's not given credit for? I came to suspect, in rereading Bloom's egregious Falstaff chapter, that Bloom *must* be putting us on. He must be doing what Falstaff did in his great post-robbery scene in the first part of *Henry IV.* Remember how Prince Hal and Falstaff plotted to rob a train of rich Canterbury pilgrims, but then the Prince and Poins decide to let Falstaff and friends do the robbery and then (in disguise) rob *them* of their stolen gold.

Back at the tavern, after everything's over, Falstaff tells a tall tale to the Prince about bravely carrying off the robbery but then being attacked by "two men in buckram suits," and as he continues to tell successive episodes in the fictional fight (he actually ran away) it becomes, next, "four men" in buckram, then seven, then—piling fiction upon fiction, invention on invention—nine, then eleven.

Until any pretense at attempting to tell the lies with conviction topples over into ridicule.

"O monstrous!" says the Prince, "Eleven men in buckram grown out of two." (One of the interesting unresolved questions about the scene is at what point—or whether from the very beginning—Falstaff knew the *Prince* knew he was lying and just continued for the sake of making himself "the cause of wit in others.")

It's what we love Falstaff for: his shameless inflated exaggerations and "inventions." "Invention" being, of course, a synonym in this case for "lie."

Suddenly one begins to glimpse, to wonder, if Bloom is *deliberately imitating his hero* in ratcheting up his praise for Falstaff. Bloom's inflating *his* "inventions" to ever more ridiculous levels of invention, until he gets to the "eleven buckram men" of his analysis: "the invention of the human."

The motive? To browbeat the reluctant to care about Shakespeare by deliberately overinflating his most Bloomian character?

There are consequences to this though: inflating Shakespearean characters to the point of overblown parade float caricatures results in their being abstracted from the plays they're embedded in, turned into windy abstractions, hollow personifications, stand-ins for Big Ideas. Big Themes, in effect insisting that *that's* what "all the fuss is about," the Big Big Ideas embedded in the Big Big Characters. What a loss for those who read Bloom and then approach Shakespeare in such a way. One that paradoxically diminishes Shakespeare by making him (merely) Socrates with Big Characters to act out his Big Ideas.

Blame Shelley

Nevertheless I don't think it's Socrates' fault; it's Shelley's. I want to tell you about the Bloom/Kline/O'Brien struggle over Kline's Falstaff. But to place this struggle for possession of Falstaff, the struggle to recapture him from Bloom, this emblematic skirmish in the three-century-long war over Falstaff on stage, I'd like to advance my Shelleyan theory of Bloom's Falstaff, of Bloom's Shakespeare. As in Percy Bysshe Shelley, supreme poet of windy abstractions and empty personifications.

I'll admit this theory may seem parochially derived since it harks back to my having to sit through Bloom's lectures on the Romantic poets as an undergraduate at Yale.

But I think this glimpse of his preoccupation then—and, if one could bear it, the obscurantist critical vocabulary he invented (anyone remember "clinamen"?) but seems to have discarded, one which could vie in jargonic pathos with the worst of the Theory people he supposedly deplores—might shed some light, indeed the pure "white radiance" of Shelleyan Eternity, on the matter of Bloom and Shakespeare.

Once long ago Bloom could actually read poetry closely, rather than merely beat the drum for it. I recall, back then in college, admiring Bloom's provocative exegesis of Keats's ode "To Autumn," a poem that was and is a touchstone for me—one that led me to that last-day-of-summer stubble-fields-of-Winchester vision that probably impelled me to press on to Stratford and get a glimpse of the *Dream* that changed my life. I guess I owe Bloom for this. And this is how I pay him back? Well, I'd say I repay him with honesty I hope he'll be large-spirited enough to respect. He's got enough uncritical adulation. (As I said I'm *conflicted.*)

What made Bloom's "Autumn" exegesis a signature, if perhaps over-ingenious, Bloomian reading was his interpretation of the bleating lambs. Bloom heard in what others had usually read as a harmless pastoral reference in the ode—"lambs loud bleat from hilly bourn"—a virtual sign of the apocalypse. The lambs are "loud bleating," Bloom argued in his edition of the Romantics, because they are either anticipating their slaughter, or are actually being slaughtered, leaving only the echo of their dying bleats behind.

Bloom's reading a premonitory echo of slaughtered lambs in those bleats turns a pastoral ode into quite something else: the Blood of the Lamb, an echo of Exodus, an echo of the Crucifixion's sacred slaughter of the Lamb of God, perhaps a hint of the apocalypse when all us sinners will be led like lambs to slaughter.

No lamb can make a murmur without Harold Bloom hearing the hoof beats of the Four Horsemen! But I liked it at the time, even defended it in a heated session of Carnegie Fellows as I recall, because I love reading and thinking about Keats—I still find in "The Eve of St. Agnes" almost the same unbearable pleasures as I do in Shakespeare's *Venus and Adonis.* And I think that as a Shakespearean commentator, Keats said perhaps the most important two words uttered about Shakespeare: "negative capability." Which he defined as Shakespeare's ability to offer us uncertainty, challenge us to coexist with uncertainty and ambiguity—without rushing to reduce "both/and" to a single "either/or" answer, with what Keats called "an irritable reaching" for certainty. (Bloom's nothing if not an irritable reacher for certainty.)

On the other hand there was the Bloom who sacralized the other Romantic poets, particularly Shelley, whose overblown abstract rhetoric, I'm sorry, with few exceptions I just could not take seriously. Typical is this, from the opening of Shelley's "Hymn to Intellectual Beauty": "The awful shadow of some unseen Power / Floats though unseen among us . . ."

Yes, I think we get the point, it's *unseen.* We just can't see it! Overblown speechifying in verse, emptily raising everything to a Big Idea, inevitably, portentously announced with a boom! boom! boom! amplified in his lectures by Bloom! Bloom! Bloom!

Everything sublime! (and thus, alas, nothing really sublime). Yes, I love that one passage in "Adonais": "Life, like a dome of many-colored glass, / Stains the white radiance of Eternity." And this is precisely the problem. Bloom is always looking for the pure "white radiance of Eternity" in Shakespeare, when in fact Shakespeare is preeminently a poet of many-colored (stained) glass. Shakespeare doesn't regard life as a stain as Shelley does.

Shelleyan sublimity, insisted upon at endless length over tens of thousand of lines, becomes less sublime than tedious in both Shelley and Bloom. Not vatic, or prophetic, barely poetic, but merely . . . windy, repetitive and unpersuasive. Just saying something is sublime doesn't necessarily raise it to sublimity for others beyond the—what shall we call him?—sublimer, so to speak.

I don't think I'm alone in this preference for poetry of a different sensibility (cf. T. S. Eliot and F. R. Leavis). After reading Chaucer, Spenser, Shakespeare, Jonson, Donne, Herbert, Webster and the Metaphysicals, not to mention Pope (and among the Romantics, Byron), poets who can make abstractions somehow a pure pleasure to read (Pope's "Windsor Forest": ravishingly beautiful!), I find it hard to take seriously the iconic Romantic, Shelley, that Bloom was asking us to venerate.

To prefer Shelley to Byron and Keats! It says, alas, everything you really need to know about Bloom's Shakespearean criticism. It takes a tin ear for language and an identification of poetry with the Greatness of its Ideas, for musings however tedious about the soul and of course the Emersonian "Over-Soul."

And while Bloom had obviously been reading Shakespeare all his life, when he turned from writing about the Romantics to writing about Shakespeare (not systematically until 1988) he seems to have seen him through the lens of Shelley. Although he had to turn up the volume.

Having raised the likes of Shelley to the stature of virtual godhood—or prophet of the Emersonian Over-Soul—with his rhetoric, Bloom had nowhere to go but actual godhood with Shakespeare, thus the invention of "the invention of the human." What advertisers and marketers used to call "the unique selling proposition": I bring you not merely Shakespeare, the way other so-called literary critics do. I am not merely the ambassador of a poet, I am the prophet of a God.

Still, even his critics concede that Bloom's deifying belief in literary value has some virtue.

"At least in Bloom's 'zesty' world," his critic and (paradoxically most persuasive) partial admirer Linda Charnes writes, "there's some humor, pleasure and (gasp) an openly avowed Love of Art."

This from one of the most sophisticated Theorists whom Bloom has provoked into at least entertaining the idea of the "Love of Art."

And, as I said, I'm conflicted. I recall flying up to Boston just to hear Bloom do a staged reading as Falstaff sponsored by Robert Brustein's American Repertory Theater. It was a freezing winter night but the place was full and Bloom sat on stage with a lineup of professional actors who fed him his Falstaff cues.

And he was terrible! I was shocked because Bloom is such a scathing critic of stage productions, and of the way most actors and directors falsify the "higher" reality of printed Shakespeare, Shakespeare read silently in the soundproof booth of the mind.

But here he was flattening all Falstaff's energetic, intellect-vitalizing felicities into a dismissive monotone. What was the point? None of his vocalizations had poetic or dramatic inflection, none offered any insight into the lines. He barely mumbled them. He couldn't have believed he was making the case for this semidivinity he'd turned Falstaff into, this character even more deeply implicated in the "invention of the human" than Hamlet, and obviously in Bloom's own self-image.

Was it another Falstaffian joke? Could he be doing this as a kind of reductio ad absurdum of spoken Shakespeare? Saying, in other words, You think this is bad, it's *all* this bad, any attempt by mere humans to utter the immortal Falstaff's godlike words? (But just one viewing of Orson Welles's *Chimes at Midnight* disproves that.)

Still, afterward at the reception I had a brief conversation with Bloom about the Shakespearean experience that changed his life: seeing Ralph Richardson play Falstaff. So he wasn't immune to great acting, but what was the reason for this depressing reading that barely seemed to concern itself with making the words audible? Ill health? He did look like Falstaff as Lear: short of breath, he was a couple of years away from a triple bypass operation.

But it wasn't so much what Bloom said that night as his palpable mournfulness, the knight of the woeful countenance, suffering the unbearable sublimity of Shakespeare for our sake. It's impossible not to feel affection for him the way it's impossible not to feel affection for that aging con man he deifies, Falstaff.

The Bloom Effect: Despite Everything, Maybe It Works

I guess I find Bloom irresistible mainly as a Shakespearean *character,* his criticism a kind of Falstaffian braggadocio. Were it not that so many seem to take it seriously: "My god, Falstaff—eleven men in buckram, what a bold and fearless warrior you are!" Rather than Hal's aware but indulgent "O monstrous!"

I'm not saying he doesn't believe it, I'm suggesting he may be exaggerating for effect. For good and bad effect. Perhaps he saw the hopelessness of getting Americans to read Shakespeare unless he made Shakespeare not just a god, but *the* god, our god, our inventor, which turned the plays into a secular bible.

If Bloom's apocalyptic hectoring jars some part of the populace to read and see Shakespeare, all the better, I guess. But if they read and see it seeking only sublime abstractions Bloom's Shakespeare offers . . .

Here's a carefully chosen excerpt from Bloom on Falstaff in *Shakespeare: The Invention of the Human.* I'll explain why I chose it in a moment. First, listen to Bloom at the close of his chapter on the *Henry IV* plays:

> It is very difficult for me, even painful, to have done with Falstaff, for no other literary character—not even Don Quixote or Sancho Panza, not even Hamlet—seems to me so infinite in provoking thought and in arousing emotion. Falstaff is a miracle in the creation of personality, and his enigmas rival those of Hamlet. . . . Falstaff's prose and Hamlet's verse give us a cognitive music that overwhelms us even as it expands our minds to the ends of thought. They are beyond our last thought and they have an immediacy that by the pragmatic test constitutes a real presence, one that all current theorists and ideologues insist literature cannot even intimate let alone sustain. But Falstaff persists after four centuries, and he will prevail centuries after our fashionable knowers and resenters have become alms for oblivion.

Falstaff's enigmas rival Hamlet's? Please. Falstaff a miracle? Enough already. Yes, there is the matter of the infinite. Bloom finds the "infinite" in the body of Falstaff, I find it in the body of Shakespeare's work, but let's not quibble.

As I said I chose that selection with cause. It was from an essay by the aforementioned Linda Charnes, a leading Theory scholar at Indiana University, who presented an absolutely remarkable, still too-little-noticed paper at a Shakespeare scholars' conference.

It was a paper that I believe will ultimately be seen as a turning point in Shakespeare studies, and it demonstrated that Bloom's *strategy,* outrageous inflation to command attention in order to bully Shakespeare—his Shakespeare—into people's consciousness, was succeeding in earning the respect if not the acquiescence of even a disdainful academy, or one of its brightest stars, as Charnes was.

Charnes's paper was read aloud at a small seminar I was lucky to find myself auditing during the Montreal convention of the Shakespeare Association of America. The seminar was billed as "Harold Bloom and Shakespeare" and I had expected from the names of the participants I was familiar with, such as Jay Halio (pro) and Terrence Hawkes (anti), that there wouldn't be much of a meeting of minds. But I never expected to hear the kind of insightful, self-critical clarity, wit and reflectiveness that I did from Linda Charnes, whose work until then seemed to represent the antithesis of Bloom.

It was absolutely exhilarating, her paper, both a critique of Bloom and a critique of academics like herself. A great cultural essay. After I wrote about the seminar in *The New York Times Book Review,* a collection of the seminar's papers was collected in a book (*Harold Bloom's Shakespeare,* edited by Christy Desmet and Robert Sawyer) and it's worth getting for Charnes's sparkling piece of cultural criticism alone.

What was fascinating was how the clarity of Charnes's paper differed from her customary "practice." I quoted in my *Book Review* account of that turning-point seminar some passages of Charnes's Lacanian analysis of *Hamlet* (Jacques Lacan being the postmodern Freudian the popularity of whose sophistry among influential academics remains a puzzle to me):

> Mass culture is being increasingly "quilted," to use Lacan's term, by the *points de capiton* of what I would call the "apparitional historical." It is

> therefore no accident that "Hamlet" is the play to which contemporary culture most frequently returns. Hamlet-the-prince has come to stand for the dilemma of historicity itself. . . . But the subject of affective time is incommensurable with the order, and the nature, of events. This was one of Lacan's greatest insights, and one of his advances over Freud: his assertion that the true subject of the "impossible real" isn't constituted by her narrative reconstruction of her "story" but rather by the failure of that story to "include" its affective event-horizon—its epistemological starting-and-end-point. As Joan Copjec has recently written about the Lacanian gaze . . .

It's as impenetrable as Bloom's rhetoric is puncturable. But it was almost as if hearing another person entirely in her Montreal talk, so smart, so witty and self-aware, puncturing Bloomian pretensions—and those of her peers. She starts out by contemplating the book jacket of Bloom's *The Invention of the Human*—not Shakespeare or anything Shakespearean, but "a detail of the Delphic sibyl," the famous prophetic figure of the ancient world (guess who the implicit modern equivalent is?) from Michelangelo's Sistine Chapel "as backdrop for a large black boldface type that, if glanced at too hastily," she says, "can easily be misread as 'Shakespeare the Invention of Harold Bloom.' "

She notes that in the sad sack Lear/Falstaff jacket photo of Bloom, "we are asked to contemplate Bloom's wound, as his reciprocal gaze promises access to . . . the deepest mysteries of what it means to be human, as invented, Bloom will claim, by the Deity Shakespeare."

But after her critique of Bloom she turns to her academic peers, and addresses some pointed questions about the implications of Bloom's grand bestseller success with the American public and suggests in a charmingly self-deprecating manner that in some way it "threaten[s] us."

"I'll hazard a guess why," she says. "It's because he comes from here—he comes from our ranks, has contemptuously risen above them, and has written a bestselling and profitable book, that may be what irks us most—the sheer huge FACT of the BOOK itself and (the gorge rises at it) its success! Where does he get off writing a book about ALL of Shakespeare's plays? How dare he profess himself the 'expert' in Shakespeare while 'dissing' the rest of us? Even worse how could he leave us vulnerable to well-meaning family members who say, 'Who is this Bloom guy? Couldn't you write a book about Shakespeare that would be a bestseller?' "

She has many other wise and funny things to say about her and her peers' "practice": "I have to admit most of our criticism wouldn't convince anyone, academic or not, to see the plays."

And then citing another critic, Sharon O'Dair, she makes a remarkable statement. O'Dair argues that it's time to get beyond the " 'institutionalized debunking of the bourgeois autonomous or essentialist humanist self.' I agree," Charnes says. "The time to make a career beating that horse has passed. For more than twenty years, this has been an important and worthy task in rethinking literary culture and the actual politics behind the Western canon. But is this all that we have to offer as critics? A way of endlessly rehearsing our demystifications of the experiences of the bourgeois individuals?"

Wonderful! She has captured all that makes the work of Theory clones so tedious.

But she doesn't let up, she doesn't let the entire Theory generation off the hook:

"Our institutionalist debunking of the bourgeois subject has calcified us into an elite corps of yuppie guerrilla academics. We all avow that we're speaking for the oppressed voices—of class, of race, of gender, of sexuality, of nation. . . . We'd better look very carefully not at what [Bloom's] doing but what we're doing in the academy. . . . If Bloom caricatures us and, in my opinion, Shakespeare, *we have made it too easy for him.* If our admiration of artistic talent, poetic beauty and great intelligence in art is . . . nothing more than the duping of the interpellated subject tricked out in the Trojan horse of the 'esthetic' then Bloom is indeed offering a theory that the public can embrace, and I think wants to embrace now more than ever as cybertechnology virtualizes every social experience and recognizable representations of human character grow scarce" (italics mine).

Love the phrase "an elite corps of yuppie guerrilla academics"! Camille Paglia couldn't have said it better. And a fascinating conjecture about the source of the public's longing for someone like Bloom to *affirm* the human, even if by inventing "the invention of the human." As Shakespeare (remember him?) wrote of poetry: "the truest poetry is the most feigning." Bloom's grand feigning evokes a truth for Linda Charnes: there is a greater enemy than the illusory bourgeois self: digital virtualization of the self. I felt I was witness to something real emerge from Bloom's invention.

I don't know how else to put this but: this was big news! Big news for those who care about literary culture and the academy, anyway. For someone at the very heart of postmodern literary academia to say such things is an astonishing breakthrough. And Bloom's parade float celebrity, his bombastic overstatement, prompted it, because as Ms. Charnes pointed out to her fellow academics, "we lack a compelling alternative model of character and selfhood. Critique it as we may, decenter it to the last instant of recorded time, the post-Enlightenment 'individual' is here to stay."

She's not completely happy about the persistence of this delusion (note the scare quotes around "individual"). But Bloom's success is proof of the persistence of the illusion despite all efforts to deconstruct it.

We owe Bloom a debt for prompting in his bombastic way Ms. Charnes's courageous act of reevaluation. And we owe Ms. Charnes a debt for the acuity and daring it took to make this realization public.

As it turned out when I reported on this paper in the *Book Review* essay, Ms. Charnes was dismayed that even though I called her essay "brave, witty, rueful and irreverent," she felt I had characterized it as a recantation of all Theory. She was unwilling to say that she had recanted the deconstruction of the bourgeois self. It was more "been there/done that, nobody cares anymore. We have more important things to think about." Okay, I'll grant her that and still be thankful for what she's done. Shift to "more important things."

One of those is "the esthetic": the question of beauty and value and how we define it. She admits as well that her fellow Theorists have "cleared the ground for him by ceding the discussion of the Esthetic to Bloom and his fellow reactionaries."

Not only does she speak of reconsidering "the esthetic," but she gives respect to the "love of art" Bloom speaks to.

It was shocking and it probably wouldn't have happened without Bloom's wildly inflated, wildly popular overstatements which spoke to a longing Ms. Charnes knows her "practice" doesn't. "The world doesn't give a fig for our critiques of humanist ideology."

Every postmodern academic should read this essay before burdening us with yet another of those critiques.

But if Bloom has done a service to scholarship by prompting this brilliant essay, what about his Falstaff? Has it done a service to Shakespeare?

That was the issue in Bloom's struggle with Jack O'Brien over Kevin Kline's Falstaff.

PART 2: "YOU CAN'T HAVE HIM, HAROLD!"

Jack O'Brien wasn't seeking to puncture Harold Bloom's balloon so much as recapture, reintegrate Falstaff into the two *Henry IV* plays, level the playing field you might say between Bloom's utterly nonironic Pleasure Principle and, well, other principles. The idea of having principles itself. It was not theoretical for O'Brien; with Falstaff, Bloom is the elephant in the room.

O'Brien was an experienced and much admired Shakespearean director, then the artistic director of San Diego's Old Globe Company, and was putting on a high-profile conflation of the two *Henry IV* plays for Lincoln Center. With a top-notch cast led by Kevin Kline. (And featuring a mixture of RSC regulars such as Richard Easton as Henry IV and earnest but not untalented American aspirants such as Ethan Hawke as Hotspur.)

O'Brien is one of those Shakespearean directors whom I've come to think of as scholars on the fly. Like Trevor Nunn, John Barton and the RSC crew; like Brian Kulick, Barry Edelstein, Karen Coonrod and Jeff Horowitz among American directors. Ones who can drop offhand remarks about characters, language and themes that emerge from the practical questions of staging the plays, remarks that can be as illuminating as those of the best and brightest of academics. I found my talks with traditional scholars exhilarating because so exacting. With directors it was often exhilarating and exacting in a different way.

The behind-the-scenes Lincoln Center drama as I reconstruct it consisted of three acts: The Challenge, The Struggle, The (Two) Ending(s).

The Challenge

It emerged during my dinner with O'Brien when we were discussing the relationship between those two icons of pleasure in Shakespeare, Cleopatra and Falstaff—and Bloom entered the picture.

I'd asked O'Brien if he saw similarities between the two embodiments of the pleasure principle.

He saw differences: "Falstaff is as different in his way as Cleopatra is hers. I don't think her infinite variety is his infinite variety. I think his is almost beyond life."

I asked him to explain what he meant by "beyond life"; it sounded Bloomian. Not quite.

"I mean there's no category over which he doesn't spill. I think it's why Bloom sort of stumbles and falls and gets all gooey and giggly finally about it all. Because you know he's so over the moon, over the top about Falstaff, you get tired of listening to him."

O'Brien is just getting going: "Falstaff is reduced to a kind of Silly Putty, and it's too bad because Bloom is such a wonderful writer and a great mind, and you want to say after a while, 'Oh, shut up, Harold. Enough already—we get it. You can't *have* him! You can't have him, Harold. You can't contain him. You can't nail him. You can't put him in amber. You can't define him. You can't reduce him.' "

And one more time, conclusively: "You can't *have* him."

It was a remarkable tirade, one that reminded me a bit of Sir Peter Hall's table-pounding fury over the delicate pause at the end of the pentameter line. O'Brien never actually pounded the table, but he pounded the point home repeatedly, thumpingly: "You can't have him, Harold."

The phrase not only demonstrates how controversial a figure Falstaff can be. The phrase also made explicit that this was a struggle for *possession*—"You can't *have* him." This is love triangle language. A struggle for possession of Falstaff, a struggle to define Falstaff, for definition of what the most Shakespearean realization of Falstaff might be. And a struggle that replicated the struggle over the love of Prince Hal waged in different ways by Falstaff and King Henry.

In practice it was a struggle for possession, if not for Kevin Kline's soul, certainly for his role.

As someone with a rare combination of film and stage credibility, a combination of fame and talent, Kline was taking on a role that would define his body of Shakespearean work as much as his Hamlet.

It was not a natural for him; Kevin Kline has been more a lean and hungry-looking type most of his Shakespearean career. Can a relatively compact guy convincingly represent the most renowned fat reprobate in literature? Is it something you can put on with a hundred pounds of theatrical padding around the belly—that whole history of gluttonous self-indulgence? Kline was a decade short of Falstaff's seventy and maybe 150 pounds lighter than he would look when he encumbered himself with massive body padding to simulate the lard that is the physical congealment of Falstaff's pleasures of the flesh.

Kline had often consulted Bloom upon Shakespearean roles; they were mutual admirers. So when O'Brien's "You can't have him, Harold" challenge became public through something I was to write, Kline faced a real dilemma that would require him to choose publicly the most "Shakespearean" Falstaff from a position between two opposed mentors.

You can't have him, Harold—there is a rationale for the resistance to all-encompassing Bloominess about Falstaff, especially for those staging the play in the real world, not the "theater of the mind."

The resistance comes in part from the notion that Shakespeare's plays aren't just about "great characters" who like Falstaff have become Dickensian icons of Olde England. That one element of the "Shakespearean" in drama is that of counterpoised characters and the ever-shifting mutual gravitational force they exert on each other.

Characters we see through each other's eyes as in that great scene in which Hal plays his father and Falstaff plays Hal and then they switch.

The *Henry IV* plays, written at the peak of Shakespeare's powers, are Shakespeare at his most symmetrical and complex. A drama of an array of forces acting on—and critiquing—each other, each force embodied by unique characters: Falstaff's appetite for pleasure, and his love of spirits; Hotspur's spirited lust for Honor; Owen Glendower's invocation of a realm of spirits ("I can call spirits from the vasty deep . . . ," an etherealized version of the alcoholic spirits that repose in the vasty deep of Falstaff's belly); Henry IV's dispirited hypocritical Machiavellianism (the principle of being unprincipled); and Prince Hal's attempt to find his way to principle through unprinciple. And yet each containing, reflecting elements of the other.

All those beautifully composed and counterpoised forces, at least on the page. And it offers some of Shakespeare's most powerful, highly charged language, often spoken by others than Falstaff. Consider these opening lines from Part 1 spoken by Henry IV:

> *So shaken as we are, so wan with care,*
> *Find we a time for frighted peace to pant*
> *And breathe short-winded accents of new broils*
> *To be commenc'd in stronds afar remote.*
> *No more the thirsty entrance of this soil*
> *Shall daub her lips with her own children's blood,*
> *Nor more shall trenching war channel her fields,*
> *Nor bruise her flow'rets with the armed hoofs*
> *Of hostile paces. Those opposed eyes,*
> *Which, like the meteors of a troubled heaven,*

All of one nature, of one substance bred,
Did lately meet in the intestine shock
And furious close of civil butchery,
Shall now, in mutual well-beseeming ranks,
March all one way and be no more oppos'd
Against acquaintance, kindred, and allies.
The edge of war, like an ill-sheathed knife,
No more shall cut his master. . . .

It's staggering in its power, just as Hotspur's rhetoric is exalting and exhilarating and Glendower's mystical and romantic.

But on the stage, Falstaff, for all his literary complexity, is an overwhelming crowd-pleasing rogue charmer with an appetite that goes beyond mutton and sack, and extends to chewing scenery and stealing scenes, indeed stealing entire productions. An appetite that audiences have indulged and actors have loved ever since he stepped on stage in 1596 or 1597, even if you don't believe the legend that Falstaff so captivated Queen Elizabeth that she commanded Shakespeare to write a story of "Falstaff in Love." (Which we're told is how *The Merry Wives of Windsor* came to be.)

This was the beginning of Bloom's Falstaff the Beloved, a tradition that has its true apotheosis not in Bloom's inflated cartoon of a joyful liberator (and creator) of the human spirit, but perhaps in Orson Welles's melancholy Lear-like Falstaff who pushed sentiment to the very verge of sentimentality, too far for some, unbearably beautiful to me. Welles wasn't attempting to give us a flawless Falstaff, a superhuman one, but a very human one, whose fall, whose rejection, is all the more affecting.

But for more than a century after Falstaff took the stage, it seems, few had the courage or the caustic intelligence to register dissent from jolly old Saint Falstaff. To say, in effect, "You can't have him, Harold."

It was Samuel Johnson in his 1715 Shakespeare edition who established the Other Pole of the Falstaff argument.

It may, in this age of the Bloom-inflated Stay-Puft Falstaff, be hard to believe that there could be a critique of the mischievous but lovable Santa Claus. But consider two things Samuel Johnson said about Falstaff: "The fat knight has never uttered one sentiment of generosity, and for all his power of exciting mirth, has nothing in him that can be esteemed."

And on Falstaff's famous charm, Johnson admonished us, "No man is more dangerous than he that with a will to corrupt, hath the power to please."

Note the striking connection between pleasure and danger. This is not the puritanical critique of someone who dislikes pleasure, but rather of one who knows pleasure and its seductive power all too well.

It is more a critique of the way pleasure can be treacherous and deceptive: yes, Falstaff can "excite mirth," but there is no generosity in him and "nothing in him that can be esteemed."

Both/and ambiguity: Johnson registers a complexity beyond Bloom's one-dimensional simplicity. But that's an interesting charge: no generosity in him. Falstaff famously is not only witty in himself but "the cause of wit in others." That could be seen as generous, although "cause" here—that so-often-central Shakespearean word—is, typically, ambiguous. It could mean he is the inadvertent cause of jests made at his expense, or it could mean that he creates a world congenial to wit and its mutual evocation that causes everyone in it to be endowed with his radiant wit.

But *no* generosity? Johnson is suggesting selfishness, not selfless congeniality, is hidden beneath Falstaff's charm. Is Johnson being too harsh, or is he asserting something about Falstaff often lost in the warm and fuzzy "appreciations" of him and Shakespeare? Bloom sees Falstaff as all generosity, generous in making the harsh world more tolerable with laughter even at his own expense. The generosity of a creator. Johnson sees it as an act.

Johnson is often caricatured as a puritanical scold for taking this position, but his remarks are not often read closely enough. He seems divided, in a subtle and interesting way, over Falstaff. He can address him as "Falstaff unimitated, inimitable Falstaff," almost sounding like Bloom until he asks, "How shall I describe thee—thou compound of sense and vice; of sense which may be admired but not esteemed, of vice which may be despised but hardly detested."

Now tell me that isn't an interesting distinction: "vice which may be despised but hardly detested." He doesn't detest vice, he may despise himself for liking it too much and find in Falstaff not quite the self-condemnation he feels he should share.

Those who have rushed to defend Falstaff (before Bloom rushed in and emptied the room) range from the painfully earnest to the complex as well.

In a particularly simpleminded attempt to defend his hero and reply to Johnson, one Maurice Morgann published a 1777 pamphlet in which he tried to exempt Falstaff from the charge of cowardice even though his actions typically bore "the external marks of cowardice" (cravenly hiding from the enemy for instance). Even Falstaff wouldn't defend himself against a charge of cowardice: instead he'd *defend* cowardice—on principle. (Bloom praises "Maurice Morgann's defense of Falstaff's pragmatic courage [which] resembles that of Socrates, who knew how to *retreat intrepidly*" (italics mine). I love "pragmatic courage" as a euphemism for cowardice. The man is shameless! Everything Falstaff does reflects Socratic wisdom.)

But again the best, most complex defense of Falstaff I've found is Orson Welles's *Chimes at Midnight.* Welles's unspoken strategy is to play Falstaff as a kind of melancholy comic Lear, the fond, foolish old man revealed finally as a failed fantasist in the rejection scene at the close of *Henry IV, Part 2.* One of the most cruel, heartbreaking moments in all Shakespeare and perhaps Orson Welles's finest moment on film.

It comes at the close of the play as Falstaff charges into the coronation procession that will crown his old tavern buddy Prince Hal, King Henry V.

It's the moment Falstaff has been banking on, literally. He's borrowed a thousand pounds from Justice Shallow on his supposedly rich prospects once his pal the Prince becomes King.

But characteristically, he can't *contain himself.* As soon as he spots the King he cries out, interrupting the solemn coronation procession: "God save thy Grace, King Hal! My royal Hal! . . . God save thee, my sweet boy! . . . My King, my Jove! I speak to thee, my heart!"

To which the newly serious King replies with cold and controlled wrath:

I know thee not, old man, fall to thy prayers,
How ill white hairs becomes a fool and jester!
I have long dreamt of such a kind of man,
So surfeit-swell'd, so old, and so profane;
But being awak'd, I do despise my dream.
Make less thy body (hence) and more thy grace,
Leave gormandizing, know the grave doth gape
For thee thrice wider than for other men.
Reply not to me with a fool-born jest,
Presume not that I am the thing I was,
For God doth know, so shall the world perceive,
That I have turn'd away my former self;
So will I those that kept me company.

When thou dost hear I am as I have been,
Approach me, and thou shalt be as thou wast,
The tutor and the feeder of my riots.
Till then I banish thee, on pain of death,
As I have done the rest of my misleaders,
Not to come near our person by ten mile. . . .

I know thee not, old man. Even in its cruelty there is an echo of something more, something almost Bottom-like: *"I have long dreamt of such a kind of man."* He *says,* "I do despise my dream." And it is the antithesis of Bottom still enchanted by his dream. But in its very overstatement one almost hears a hint of regret and loss that must be surmounted.

Bloom tells us we must choose sides as in a game show, we must "hate" Hal (as he does) for rejecting Falstaff. Or for using Falstaff and then rejecting him. But Falstaff would be less significant if he were not counterpoised against Hal's calculation and Henry IV's Machiavellian authority. If those powers were not real, if it were not a play about clashing perspectives rather than about the deification of Socrates, it would not be much of a play. It would be a one-man show.

Jack O'Brien on the other hand doesn't feel it necessary to take sides for or against Hal or Falstaff as Bloom does. Without saying so, I think he thinks it's a little childish. O'Brien sees and values the complexity of both because their relationship is at the heart of the drama within the comedy within the history.

And O'Brien sees not just the complexity, but the difficulty of Hal's role when compared to the easier crowd-pleasing Falstaff's. He told me he tells actors who play Hal that "your satisfaction is not going to be from getting the love of the audience at the curtain call, but afterward, backstage, when you're removing the makeup and you realize what a difficult task you've pulled off."

What O'Brien said he was seeking when he cried out, "You can't have him, Harold!" was to restore these complexities beyond simplistic love and hate to his Hal and his Falstaff.

Perhaps this is another instance of what Jonathan Bate calls "both/and" ambiguity as opposed to "either/or" ambiguity. Or an instance of what Norman Rabkin, one of the most perceptive critics of the late twentieth century, called "the rabbit/duck" paradox. He was referring to the famous Gestalt psychology line drawing which looked at one way appeared to be a rabbit, while the same figure looked at another way appeared to be a duck. One pattern, two birds. Falstaff, a fat rabbit/duck.

But for some, one must choose sides, and the debate continues: the entry in the 2002 *Cambridge Companion to Shakespeare's History Plays* frostily declares that Falstaff comes to represent a world of "degeneracy" and that his "presumptuous" behavior and "unconcern," even delight, at the death of others "cannot be condoned."

Strong moralizing words from a usually dispassionate academic source. Perhaps a "You can't have him, Harold" reaction to Bloom's suffocating sanctimonious embrace of his antinomian god.

A judiciously compressed summary of the debate over Falstaff can be found in Columbia scholar David Scott Kastan's introduction to his Arden edition of *Henry IV, Part 1*. He asks, is Falstaff "the vitalist truth teller who exposes the life-denying lies of power"—the Bloom view—"Or is he the disruptive force of misrule who threatens the hope for order and coherence?"

Jack O'Brien has a slightly different slant on the "disruptive force of misrule" vision of Falstaff.

He doesn't have a moralist's disdain for Falstaff, he doesn't share in Johnson's denial of his generosity; my impression was that he wanted to rescue Falstaff's roguishness from the kind of Higher Rectitude Bloom ascribes to him. And that "disruptive force of misrule" sounds almost a bit too principled and energetic. O'Brien sees him rather as more of a lounge lizard.

He told me that when he was talking to Kevin Kline about Falstaff and Prince Hal, and how their relationship began, he evoked a kind of fifties Rat Pack Las Vegas analogue. JFK, the Young Prince hanging out with entertainers and "actresses" and rogues in some after-hours joint equivalent to Falstaff's tavern, listening to some fat comic like Don Rickles crack Sinatra up, and thinking, "I want to hang out with this guy."

And "that guy" enjoying the fact that he had the heir on the hook, but not without some genuine friendship developing between the two.

O'Brien sees Falstaff as someone who metaphorically knows how to sing for his supper—keeps the party going afterward, a knowing sycophant. What I liked about the notion was that it restored to Falstaff some of the venality of the character that gets lost in effusive delight in his subversive wit and celebration of hedonic existence.

And O'Brien versus Bloom was a particularly interesting clash because most of the contentions I've dealt with herein have been between scholar and scholar or between director and director. But here it was scholar contending with director over the padded embodiment of an actor, over the way to construe the bloated and overlarded body of Falstaff. Or as the headline writer put it in the piece I did for the *Times:* "Corrupt Buffoon, or Joyous Liberator? Kevin Kline Waddles into the Falstaff Wars."

The Struggle

I mention this because the piece was written and published while the struggle was still going on in rehearsals, before the first previews in fact, and so made public and probably more self-conscious the tug of war over the role.

In the conclusion of *The Times* piece I'd asked Jack O'Brien if he was trying to wrest Falstaff away from Bloom's imprisoning embrace.

"Oh I assure you," O'Brien said, "Falstaff doesn't need my help at all."

But as it turned out, it wasn't that easy. Not judging by some moments of the rehearsal process recounted to me by O'Brien and his dramaturge collaborator Dakin Matthews, who had done the three-and-three-quarters-hour-long conflation of the two parts of *Henry IV.*

"One feature of Falstaff's seductiveness," O'Brien said at one point, one that he keeps discovering in rehearsal, "is this expansive quality: you know when you read something and then you get it up on stage it somehow changes, and even though . . . I've done this version before, when you get it into three dimensions, Falstaff keeps unfolding."

Unfolding and, if not resisted, *enveloping.*

Part of the challenge of containing Falstaff comes from the decision to compress the two *Henry IV* plays into a single evening with two intermissions. Compression itself is not uncommon but not uncontroversial.

"My friend Nick Hytner," O'Brien told me, referring to the new director of the Royal National Theatre in London, "was appalled when he heard we were cutting at all. Why not do it in two evenings? What I couldn't say to him was that for them [in the U.K.] these characters are as familiar as Jefferson, Hamilton and Aaron Burr are to us. So it's different."

In the United States, if a *Henry IV* play is done at all, it's most often the more crowd-pleasing Part 1, which ends with Falstaff fraudulently triumphant and leaves out the more melancholy, dying fall of Part 2, with its climactic rejection scene in which Hal banishes his heartbroken fat friend when the Prince is crowned Henry V.

It's harder to get American theaters—and audiences—to commit to two evenings, two parts, Richard Easton (who played Henry IV in this production) told me. He thought it was these logistical hurdles that prevent the *Henry IV* plays from getting the level of appreciation they deserve—even though they represent Shakespeare at a peak of creativity that rivals the better-known *Hamlet* and *Lear.*

Compression is one solution to putting the entire trajectory of the two plays before a single audience in a single night. It's a tradition with a long history in fact: a manuscript of the two plays compressed into one long one, dating to 1622, just six years after Shakespeare's death, has come to light (the "Dering manuscript"). Whole books have been devoted (without resolving the question) to the mystery of whether Shakespeare composed the two parts of *Henry IV* as separate plays or (as the late textual scholar Harold Jenkins argued) began writing a single play and then realized, halfway through what is now the first part, that he would need two parts to contain its richness.

The problem with compressing the two parts, the problem that O'Brien and Dakin Matthews confront, is that most compressions, like Orson Welles's *Chimes at Midnight,* tend to make the two plays into a single Falstaff play (indeed, *Chimes* was released in America under the title *Falstaff*).

Matthews's compression, first produced some thirty years ago (when Kline saw it as a student at Juilliard), has been a work in progress. O'Brien directed a version at the Old Globe in 1995, with John Goodman as Falstaff. The advantage of the Matthews version is that it preserves the balance between Falstaff and the other major characters. However, in the rehearsal process, the challenge is to control Falstaff's expansiveness. That was the problem with the scene they had been working on the day I had dinner with O'Brien and he declared, "You can't have him, Harold."

That scene is the long, comic confrontation (in Part 2) between Falstaff and the Lord Chief Justice, representative of order and good governance in the play. In which Falstaff, fresh from fraudulent heroics on the battlefield, repeatedly baits the Lord Chief Justice about his age and health. They had tried to cut it at a table reading, but "when we put it up on its feet" in rehearsal, O'Brien said, they couldn't resist giving Falstaff more laugh lines back. Falstaff's part fattened up, although eventually, according to Matthews, "we had to cut it back," put Falstaff on a diet.

That day it was O'Brien who couldn't resist the enchantment of Falstaff's stage turns; often it was Kline who wanted to allow Falstaff full Bloom, so to speak. "I practically have to flail Kevin with a cane because he keeps wanting to restore bits," O'Brien told me.

Matthews talked about several other strategies they have used to contain Falstaff's seductiveness. One is to emphasize often-overlooked colder, darker notes in his character, those that emerge more saliently in the second part of *Henry IV.* There, as Matthews puts it, "he's no longer expansive—he's sponging off the powerful, he's squeezing the powerless."

There's the matter of Falstaff's cold indifference to the fate of the draftees who serve under him in the civil war. He's extracted bribes from those who can afford to buy their way out of the war, and then conscripts the poor and weak, dismissing them, at one point, as "food for powder," mere cannon fodder. More likely to die because he's taken the poor and unfit over the strong who pay to get out. He shows no remorse that their deaths fattened his purse. Nor at mutilating the dead body of Hotspur to bloody his sword, the better to fake his claim for the kill.

"Jack [O'Brien] has been trying to contain the sentimentalism and emotionalism," Matthews told me. "You know, most scholars disagree with Bloom's view" that Falstaff's life-affirming, personality-creating greatness is the heart of the matter in *Henry IV,* and that the *Henry IV* plays are a celebration of hedonic subversion, of wit and play as the supreme human qualities.

In the attempt to achieve balance, Matthews says, Falstaff's cruelly dismissive "food for powder" line "is still in there."

He adds, "It's interesting, Kevin was kind of waffling on how badly he wanted Falstaff to be portrayed in the martial stuff, and he put a fair amount of the negative stuff back in, and then took some of it out."

Indeed the play would turn out to be defined by Mr. Kline's mediation of all the complex contentions over the fat knight.

The Outcome

And so it was, but in a more complicated way than I could have imagined.

I was fortunate to see both the third preview of the Lincoln Center production and the very last performance. Two Falstaffs separated by two and a half months. And I saw two different Falstaffs. Each played by Kevin Kline, each more or less paying respect to his two respective mentors.

I have to admit I felt a genuine state of suspense when I settled into my seat awaiting the opening of that third preview at Lincoln Center. Just how would Kline's Falstaff reflect or reject O'Brien, Matthews, Bloom and a whole host of other Falstaffs' influence?

I found myself absolutely riveted on the very first extended moment of Kline's appearance.

It felt like Kline's own invention and a beautiful one. A gesture really, a prolonged, painfully expressive, silent stage moment that spoke eloquently in silent pentameter of all the contradictions over Falstaff and all the complexities of Shakespearean pleasure.

It was one of those moments that revealed how a gifted actor can find something Shakespearean between the lines on the page. Something that, once seen, is practically emblazoned in memory. It was the first moment we see Falstaff on stage, he's sitting down on a bench. Kline's heavy padding and the stiff leather jerkin over it had made him *huge,* a veritable rhinoceros. His wide white beard and graying pate had made him old.

But it was his attempt, his infinitely labored, shuddering, gasping, grasping (on to others) attempt to lift his vast bulk—it was his attempt *to stand up* that made his Falstaff.

You could hear the stiff leather creaking, you could almost hear the joints creaking, as he first once, then twice, tried to defy gravity and stand up. Defying gravity—in every sense of the word—has been what defined Falstaff. Defying gravitas. Suddenly gravity was having its cruel revenge: defying Falstaff. The entire arc of Falstaff's life was compressed in that losing struggle to bear the unbearable weight of what the pleasures of the past had burdened him with. A revenge play starring gravity as the avenger.

It was ridiculous at first, each oh-so-painful, oh-so-close failed attempt to levitate drawing more and more roars of laughter. It was at once sad and then pathetic. Then, somehow, courageous.

It was the hangover from a sixty-year bender, ruefully acknowledged in his features, both the bender and the unbearable weight it has left behind in its wake. He was a wake for himself, gravity was digging his grave.

He was an embodiment of the heavy burden of pleasure, the image of literally unbearable pleasure in Shakespeare.

It's all there in a kind of mini silent-Shakespearean comedy Kline had crafted. Almost like a Buster Keaton short: *Falstaff Tries to Stand Up.*

Or was it a comedy? There is nothing in the playscript that calls for it. All we are told that is that scene 2 begins "Enter Prince of Wales and Sir John Falstaff." Which seems to imply an already ambulatory Falstaff. Purists might object. But this moment could be said to precede that, it was done as a "reveal"—a previously darkened area of the stage suddenly lit to reveal the seated Falstaff beginning his struggle.

A struggle that doesn't work at first, it doesn't work for several groaning attempts, it doesn't work when assisted by a stout cane, it doesn't work until he is helped unsteadily to his feet by members of his tavern retinue. (A subdued gesture toward the communal bonding of the libertine outlaws of Falstaff's tavern world that have borne him up so that he was a kind of summation, or debauched emblem of their shared pleasures.)

I don't know, I was impressed by the balance, literal and metaphorical, brought to this moment, this Falstaff. Kline made that moment an essay about pleasure and the payment for pleasure, the complexities, the self-destructiveness of devotion to pleasure, the dark side of "unbearable pleasure."

And he played the rest of the role that night with that simultaneous evocation of both aspects of pleasure inflecting his words and being. I thought it was quite good, not a pure celebratory, neo-Bloomian Falstaff, not the attractive alternative melancholy Falstaff of Welles. Neither was it an anti-Falstaff one occasionally sees, *merely* corrupt and venal. But rather a rueful Falstaff, soldiering on in this jester role beyond the point of pleasure, into the realm of pain and regret for the sake of those depending on him for a laugh.

I don't want to oversimplify; I think Kline himself is responsible for what I liked best about his performance, but I thought I felt Jack O'Brien's sensitivity to the duality of Falstaff and our response to him, the way he evoked, as Frank Kermode recently put it, "pleasure and *dismay* at Pleasure."

But this was a preview and I know performances evolve and so I made a point of seeing the very last performance of the extended run. This was nearly two months after the *Times* had published my piece about the contending visions of Bloom and O'Brien over Falstaff. In which I'd included some responses by Harold Bloom to Jack O'Brien's "You can't have him, Harold" outburst.

When I reached Bloom by phone back then he asked me not to refer to his own previously Falstaffian proportions since he'd recently undergone bypass surgery and had lost ninety pounds. He'd lost weight but not his anguished indignation. I read him O'Brien's quote about Bloom being "a great mind, a wonderful writer," but that his ecstatic embrace of Falstaff was "so over the top."

To which Bloom shot back, "You can do a hell of a lot worse than go over the top over Falstaff. I *am* very over the top over Falstaff."

Perhaps this is where I differ from Bloom, in that I'd say, "You *could* do a lot worse than go over the top over *Shakespeare,*" but that does not necessarily entail going over the top over Falstaff. Because it's not clear the Shakespearean Falstaff (if I might subjectively characterize him) is identical with the Bloomian Falstaff. Falstaff is not the coequal of his creator but an element in his complex creation.

And then when I read Bloom O'Brien's quote about him getting "sort of gooey and giggly about it" Bloom replied, "I totally dissent from Mr. O'Brien, although I wish he and Mr. Kline, whom I admire, well with the play."

Publishing this exchange in the Sunday *Times* I'm sure may have put Kline in a more difficult position as first previews approached—spotlighted the fact that he would be choosing whose Falstaff he would embody.

I had thought that Harold Bloom, in part because of O'Brien's "You can't have him, Harold" remarks in *The Times,* wasn't going to see the production. That's what he told me anyway, "I doubt I'll see it."

But I think he'd been prevailed upon and at the final performance I noticed Nancy Becker, cofounder (with Adriana Mnuchin) of New York's Shakespeare Society and friend of Bloom, sitting next to an empty seat before the performance began. "Harold was going to be here," she said, but there was a sudden bout of illness.

I don't know how aware Mr. Kline was of Bloom's presence or absence at that final performance. I suspect, since it was a last minute health-related decision, Kline might well have thought Bloom was going to be in the audience.

And so I don't know if it was a one-off performance for Bloom's benefit, or whether it had evolved this way from the temptations to do a more crowd-pleasing Falstaff, the easy laughs that are readily available, the love that comes to a more lovable Falstaff.

But this was definitely a more lovable, more Bloomian, less infirm, more twinkly, more mischievous and sprightly Falstaff than the one I'd seen in the third preview. Either that's the way things felt most right for Kline in the evolution of the role—maybe it's inevitable playing Falstaff on stage, knowing the audience wants to love him. Not wanting to deny them. Or it was a kind of loving gesture to his (unfortunately absent) mentor.

Still, I couldn't believe my eyes in the opening moment, the way Kline got to his feet without much difficulty. Not nimbly, no. But less *tragically.* So different from the preview I saw. Everything followed from that—the differences were subtle but I felt they were there. Perhaps I'm imagining it, but it felt almost as if, for Kline, the eyes of Bloom were upon him.

Bloom may have won the battle that day, but I think O'Brien displayed exemplary courage in waging the war.

Chapter Thirteen

Stephen Booth: 777 Types of Ambiguity

THE THRESHOLD OF COMPREHENSION

Perhaps the best way of explaining who Stephen Booth is to me, and what place he occupies (or should occupy) in the pantheon of contemporary Shakespeareans, is to put it this way: Booth represents in the realm of close reading what Peter Brook represents to me in the realm of directing. Another way is to think of him as the un-Bloom, a critic undeservedly overshadowed by Bloom's renown, whose fine-grained attention to language contrasts so dramatically with Bloom's overblown abstractions.

The experience of reading Booth on the Sonnets was for me, in its own way, *almost* as electrifying and transformative as seeing Brook's *Dream.* Just as Brook is the director as scholar-exegete, Booth is the scholar-exegete as director, directing our attention to the hidden play of language in the ostensibly "nondramatic" works such as the Sonnets, the way Brook searched for the "secret play" in the dramatic works.

And in the larger perspective, Booth is one of those great critics who have not been distracted by the dubious conjectures of biography, or seduced by the distancing and denigration of Theory, but who return us to a focus on the play within all the plays and poems: the play of words. The dizzying pleasures that are one defining element of Shakespearean language.

An extremely *close* focus. And as we shall see it has cost him, at least in the short run, but as I write (or, actually, rewrite) this chapter I do so with the glad knowledge that the realm of Shakespeare studies is shaking off the spell of Theory and returning to the kind of close reading Booth represents, and to Booth's achievement itself.

Booth's version of "close reading," Extremely Close Reading, one might say, brings one almost *unbearably* close to Shakespeare's language, to the abyss of destabilizing identity. Which I'd suggest may be responsible for the relative eclipse of his work, which blazed a brief path across the academic firmament in the early seventies and then fell victim to a change in critical fashion, in which Extremely Distant Reading (as Theory might be called) supplanted Extremely Close Reading.

It's my belief Booth should occupy the place (and does for many) that Greenblatt and Bloom do today—he does something far different from the celebrity savants of Shakespeare. Perhaps it's because he is neither mystical nor political. He is dangerously, unfashionably, poetical.

It's my belief that Booth's work on the Sonnets will last and stir argument long after the sophistry of Theory is forgotten, and my attempt to approach Booth, to *read* Booth—on the page and in person—is meant as an homage. And ultimately another way of defining what we mean by "Shakespearean."

What ensues is the story of my attempt to come to grips with Booth in his work, a story sometimes as tortured by my own awkwardness as my encounters with Peter Brook, a sign I believe of my deep appreciation for the gift they've both given me.

Booth is best known for his Yale University Press edition of the Sonnets (which first appeared in 1977 and is still widely read and taught), an edition of the 154 poems accompanied by *four hundred pages* of footnotes and commentary.

It was an edition I was familiar with, one I'd get lost in for hours at a time over the years. But it was something else Booth wrote half a decade before that edition, a hugely influential although (because of a sudden change in critical fashion) lamentably out-of-print book: Booth's *Essay on Shakespeare's Sonnets.* A book that had a profound transformative effect on the way the Sonnets were seen, the way Shakespearean poetry itself was read. If this seems like a large claim, consider Frank Kermode's words in *The New York Review of Books* in 1970 about Booth's *Essay:*

> There may be, there is, a moment when one intuits in the complex mesh of conflicting patterns an order; and Booth says that such moments are the happiest the human mind can know, moments when it is beautifully poised on the threshold of comprehension, like, perhaps, the mind of the poet. These large claims suggest that criticism is regaining

> its confidence as it acquires new techniques, which it movingly represents as able to increase our happiness or mitigate our pain. Criticism may thus be both difficult and humane.
>
> Booth's analysis of the sonnets on these new principles seems to me of a high order of criticism and humanity. . . . Any way I can look at it his achievement seems to me extraordinarily impressive.

"Such moments are the happiest the human mind can know . . ." That's a strong statement, even as a description of Booth's position, but Kermode's elaboration upon it is even more thought-provoking. By such "happiest" moments he tells us he means "moments when [the mind] is beautifully poised on the threshold of comprehension, like, perhaps, the mind of the poet."

He's suggesting that Stephen Booth has shown us something about the way the mind of Shakespeare works in the way Shakespearean language works—and that through Booth's exegesis we get a glimpse of what it might be like to experience Shakespeare himself reading Shakespeare, perhaps even to experience Shakespeare *writing* Shakespeare—to look at Shakespeare through Shakespeare's eyes.

And that central to that experience is the sensation of being "beautifully poised on the threshold of comprehension." As Hamlet says, "that would be scanned." What is "the threshold of comprehension"? A moment of dawning awareness of coherence emerging from incoherence? The excitement of a certain kind of *discovery.* Not fully comprehending its magnitude but glimpsing it beginning to unfold, take shape, cohere.

I feel myself only on the threshold of comprehension of what Kermode means by "threshold of comprehension" here, but I like the daring with which he conjectures that this threshold puts us in touch with the mind of the poet. The notion that Booth's exegesis is not about "pinning down" or summarizing meaning, but discovering, experiencing it in the process of creation. Not the already-accomplished feeling of being *across* the threshold of comprehension, but being on the brink of it, the brink of amazement, experiencing the thrill of discovery.

I can't help thinking that was what Keats was conjuring up, in "On First Looking into Chapman's Homer," when he described the moment of "wild surmise" experienced by the explorer Cortez's men, who after trudging through the jungles of Central America in search of the Pacific Ocean, finally, "upon a peak in Darien," first apprehended the ocean's fathomless immensity.

Keats (who notoriously mixed up Cortez and Balboa) is explicitly conjuring up that moment of being on "the threshold of comprehension" in that phrase "wild surmise." The "wild surmise" he's referring to is not the explorer's amazed reaction when *he* first sees the Pacific. Rather it is Keats imagining the wild surmise of the sailors in his party, reading his (Cortez's, Balboa's) excitement. A wild surmise while reading eyes: a particularly Shakespearean threshold of comprehension.

Reading Shakespeare through Booth is like making a wild surmise about the bottomless ocean in his eyes, in his vision. I think of him as our Cortez.

The threshold of comprehension, the brink of amazement, is that cliff overlooking the sea in *Lear,* that parapet overlooking the ocean in *Hamlet,* about both of which we're warned against staring too long from, lest it lead to madness.

Stephen Booth would probably reject the notion that what he's seeking to illuminate in Shakespeare is analogous to the kind of "secret play" Peter Brook was seeking. But Boothian close reading initiates one into a realm of undercurrents, cross currents, tidal flows and undertows beneath the surface of the lines even at their most placid and apparently transparent. Booth's readings split open the ambiguities in the Sonnets and release infinite energies.

It was in the process of attempting a close reading of Booth's close reading, and a close reading of Booth himself, that I began to understand something of that strange experience I had at the blackboard at Yale while explicating a sonnet. A "threshold of comprehension" moment, exhilarating and a bit destabilizing if not frightening. A momentary but memorable—unforgettable—sense of dislocation or double location. When one is on a threshold, one is on both sides and neither.

I referred to this episode briefly in the introduction; to me it goes to the heart of what makes the Sonnets so appealing and disturbing: the utterly excessive, unnecessary, maddening complexity that seems designed to do more, much more, than merely find complex ways of expressing conventional sentiments about love. The way each sonnet seems designed, not as a verbal icon but as a verbal *engine,* a virtual perpetual motion machine with the power to destabilize the reader with its dizzying shifts in perspective, its shimmering, pulsating wordplay—to induce the state of being on that brink-of-amazement threshold. A state not unlike the state of being in love, not merely reading *about* being in love.

I thought at this point I should give the reader a sense of the kind of thing Booth does, and in doing so something surprising happened when I was copying out a few lines of his exegesis of two words—"present-absent"—in the sonnet I believe was responsible for my strange present-absent experience in New Haven.

The words occur in the first four lines of Sonnet 45. In the previous sonnet the poet has described how the two heavier elements (earth and water) of the four (along with air and fire) that compose the self, the two *bodily* elements, can't be with his lover when they are apart. But the other two elements,

> *. . . slight air and purging fire,*
> *Are both with thee, where ever I abide;*
> *The first my thought, the other my desire,*
> *These present-absent with swift motion slide.*

Here is Booth's footnote to "present-absent" in his Yale edition of the Sonnets:

> *present-absent:* 1) Simultaneously both present and absent. 2) now present–now absent, alternately here and away. The hyphen is a standard editorial addition [to the original hyphen-less "present absent" in the original]. These words ["present-absent"]—themselves an oxymoron, a capsule of contraries—act to harmonize a variety of logically incompatible conceits and thus, to facilitate the reader's "swift slide" from one to another. Lines 1–3 have turned a commonplace hyperbole ("my thoughts and desires are always with you"; "half of myself is always with you") into a paradox by equating *thought* and *desire* with *air* and *fire;* the equation invites consideration of the hyperbole as if *with* (line 2) were intended literally; but 50 percent of a human body cannot be anywhere but with the other 50 percent. In sense (1) "present-absent" capsules the paradox, "physically present, spiritually absent." Sense (2) capsules the conceit introduced by *"with swift motion slide";* this new conceit, which takes up the rest of the poem, is logically incompatible with sense (1) and with the assertion in lines 1–3 that *thought/air* and *desire/fire* are always with the beloved, always absent from the speaker.

Note first—if we were to do an exegesis of Booth's exegesis—the distinction he makes about the two ways of reading—experiencing—the state of being "present-absent." It can be simultaneous or alternate. Or perhaps both? The mind begins to "swiftly slide" into an altered state in trying to "capsule" this.

I feel this is important, but I'm barely on the threshold of comprehending why. Help me through it. "Present-absent" could imply self-division, however logically inconsistent that might be. Or it could imply alternate presence and absence as is suggested in "sliding" back and forth. By "alternately" present and absent does Booth mean *alternating* presence and absence? I think so, although I'm now on the brink of that cliff, that abyss, that threshold of comprehension of madness that the phrase conjures up. Almost the same state I was in at the blackboard at Yale. Alternate-alternating? The same, or alternately, different?

The difference between "sliding" back and forth and instantaneously being alternately one place then the other is . . . the difference between being particle and wave?

At this point I suddenly found myself in that very state I was trying to explain. Destabilized, disoriented, sliding swiftly from comprehension to incomprehension. Present-absent to my sense of self, to my sense of "making sense."

Booth's exegesis was doing what the poem had once done. Perhaps an attempt at exegesis of both might help explain.

THE THEORY OF THEORY AND THE DREAM OF THE CHOCOLATE PIE

One of the surprising things I learned (when I eventually had an extended face-to-face interview with Booth) about the origin of his work is—for a man most well known for his exegesis of nondramatic texts—how much Booth is drawn to Shakespeare on stage. Indeed when I asked him about his early transformative experiences of Shakespeare they all took place in a theater.

Beginning with a curious dramatic illusion—and an explosion of cornstarch.

Before the cornstarch there were two early encounters, he told me. Booth grew up in a small Connecticut town, population four thousand, and recalls at age twelve taking his mother, who loved Laurence Olivier, to see the film version of Olivier's *Henry V* for her birthday.

"What I remember was 'the four captains' talking," he told me during our first formal interview. He's speaking of the four soldiers in Henry V's army at Agincourt, each of whom spoke in a dialect: Welsh, Irish, Scottish, Midlands English.

"I knew they were saying *something* in my language," Booth recalls with a hint of his long-ago adolescent plaintiveness, "but I couldn't tell *what,* and I became interested in finding out."

The somewhat alienating duality of language that intrigued him (he loved the dialectic of the dialects: it's English but it's not English he could understand) can be found in much of Shakespeare: it's English but it's not English we really understand at first, not at its deepest levels. It's one of the things that make Shakespeare exceptional. Nobody "gets it" all at once, few come close to the "threshold of comprehension" in a lifetime.

Booth's early fascination with language was supplemented by an early exposure to the double awareness of language when embodied by actors on stage, something *peculiar* about the language when it was embodied on the stage.

"Later I got to see John Carradine playing Hamlet in Litchfield, Connecticut, and it wasn't a very elaborate stage. There was a trapdoor on stage. The trapdoor that serves for the Ghost and for Ophelia's grave. Ophelia was played in the first act by a lovely young woman who—well, at her funeral she was played by a nine-by-twelve rug. She couldn't fit through the trapdoor so they doubled over the rug and shoved it in the trapdoor.

"It showed me clearly an awareness of the physicality of theatricality that is so much part of my experience of the theater."

In a sense, as well, Stephen Booth's way of looking at Shakespeare's dramatic works came to focus on finding the holes, the trapdoors, in the text, the holes that make for a greater whole.

But the other formative stage experience for Booth, he told me, was a remarkable *King Lear.* It was not too surprising to hear that *Lear* should affect him so deeply so early. In preparing for our talk I'd come upon an essay in which Booth described the climactic moments of *Lear*—when Lear learns that Cordelia's reprieve from execution arrives too late, and Lear comes on stage bearing his daughter's body and literally howling with grief—as "the most terrifying five minutes in literature." Terrifying in particular for the way it recurrently raises hopes and then crushes them.

"I saw my first *Lear* at the age of twenty-two. And there was this fellow named Paul Devlin who was in his late twenties or early thirties who was apparently sensationally good at Lear [who is, in the play, an octogenarian] but not good at anything else. He played Lear at the Brattle Theatre," near Harvard, where Booth was writing his soon-to-be-legendary Ph.D. thesis on the Sonnets.

"I went to it and that was the point where I *really* got hooked. Lear was on the heath and his hair was full of cornstarch" (to whiten and age his appearance). "But Devlin's hair still wasn't fully white and he was standing there and Jerry Kilty who was playing the Fool was crouched at Lear's feet, but still taller than his head, and the cornstarch floated up into Kilty's nostrils and Kilty sneezed" into Lear's hair, causing an explosion of cornstarch.

It sounds like a comic moment, the sneeze and the cloud of cornstarch. But Booth saw something more, something strange through the cloud:

"So what I was seeing was a tiny little man [the Fool] crouched at the feet of a tall man [Lear], and what was obviously *there* was a man [Kilty] taller than the 'tall man' [Devlin] who was crouched at his feet but his head was above the head. . . . It was dazzling."

In other words, in real life, Devlin was shorter than Kilty, but his theatrical stature was something else again. (I think.)

"The theatrical illusion [of Lear being taller than the taller Fool] was so complete it was almost like a hallucination then?" I asked Booth.

"Yes, it was like that. And the thing I keep talking about all the time is the essential fact, the essential pleasure we get from drama is generally that one is always looking at two things: what one is being *shown* and what one is *seeing*. This is the quintessential example of that."

What one is being shown, versus what one is seeing? Disjuncture is a recurrent theme, virtually a founding principle of Booth's later criticism. The pleasure to be derived from the disjuncture between the two, an awareness of doubleness, of similitude and difference. Or as Wordsworth puts it in his Preface to the *Lyrical Ballads,* in a quote which, it turns out, is a keynote to Booth's *Essay on Shakespeare's Sonnets:* the pleasure received in literature has much to do with "the pleasure which the mind derives from the perception of similitude and dissimilitude. This principle is the great spring of the activity of our minds and their chief feeder. From this principle the direction of the sexual appetite and all the passions connected with it, take their origin."

It seemed of interest, in the light of his focus on literary pleasure, that Booth recalled for me a dream he had at about the time he was writing his *Essay on Shakespeare's Sonnets* some thirty-five years ago. The dream involved—

on the surface at least—his dilemma about whether to remain at Harvard after completing his dissertation on the Sonnets or to accept offers elsewhere, including Berkeley (where he eventually ended up). But I think there was more to it than that.

There was a powerful professor at Harvard whom Booth didn't feel in synch with when it came to what to focus on in Shakespeare studies. The professor (whom Booth did not want me to name) was known for his detailed studies of Shakespeare's playhouses, his audiences, the material conditions in which Elizabethan drama in general was performed.

"I had a dream," Booth told me, that "X [the professor he'd rather not name] came into my room with a freshly baked potato and told me he knew how long it took to bake a potato and that *from that* he'd know how long it took to bake a chocolate pie. And I realized," Booth told me, "this was information I didn't want to acquire."

In other words, if I can play dream interpreter, or at least dream close reader, here, Booth was in the process of realizing that the academic emphasis at that particular time at Harvard on the analysis of the mechanics of Elizabethan theater in general (i.e., the baked potato offered by the starchy professor) was nothing to be sneered at, solid and nourishing, yes. But in the dream Booth was experiencing resistance to the idea that this kind of analysis was the way to get closer to the uniquely rich pleasures of Shakespeare, i.e., the chocolate pie.

In support of this conjecture about chocolate and pleasure and Shakespeare—and the source of the shift in critical fashion Booth's *Essay* may have precipitated, I'd cite the conclusion of a paper Booth wrote in the late seventies on the second of Shakespeare's *Henry IV* plays. When I reached him on the phone in Berkeley some months after I'd first met him he told me he'd like to send along a few other papers of his that represented his recent direction in criticism more fully. And this *Henry IV, Part 2* paper was one of them.

The *Henry IV* paper was fascinating in several respects but particularly for illustrating the tendency of Booth's criticism, when approaching Shakespeare's dramatic works, to look for holes, for trapdoors in the surface of the language, trapdoors such as the one in the Litchfield Theater *Hamlet* that made him aware, in a double sense, of his theatrical experience.

The trapdoors, the disjunctions in *Henry IV, Part 2,* Booth argues, have to do with expectations raised and then frustrated. Part 2, you'll recall, the somewhat darker sequel to the first Falstaff play, builds up in Falstaff hopes of acquiring power and influence when his tavern crony Prince Hal becomes King Henry V, only to see them dashed in a crushing way in what is known as "the rejection scene." ("I know thee not, old man.") Booth argues that audiences are likely to experience recurrent premonitory versions of this disappointment embedded in the language of the play.

It's about pleasure, the expectation of it, the loss of it. In the remarkable final sentences of his *Henry IV* paper he suggests that "Shakespeare elsewhere experiments successfully with frustrating audiences' dramatic expectations and withholding their moral and esthetic prerequisites, but in *2 Henry IV,* although he may succeed in the perverse rhetorical purposes I propose, he does not succeed in making his audience *like* it. I like thinking about it but I do not *like* it—do not like it as I like *1 Henry IV, Hamlet, Twelfth Night* and chocolate bars. Do you? (in answering that question, do not let yourself be led astray by reason)."

Remarkable for one of America's leading Shakespearean exegetes to close a densely argued textual essay with a question about chocolate bars. But it's a characteristically sly, dry, Boothian question about pleasure—and reason.

Chocolate bars, chocolate pie? This is a critic who is serious about pleasure, but serious in a literary way. The appearance of chocolate pie in the dream, chocolate bars in the paper about *2 Henry IV* and the emphasis on sensual, even sexual pleasure (in the Wordsworth quote about similitude and dissimilitude in poetry), reflect a fascination with pleasure in literature, in Shakespeare specifically. But it is not so much hedonistic, orgiastic pleasure for Booth as it is the graceful pleasure evoked in the mind as it finds itself impelled to graceful balletic leaps, thrilling gymnastic twists and turns in the experience of reading Shakespeare's poetry. The way Shakespearean language can choreograph the mind. This experience, the reader's experience of being transported, a special kind of graceful "transport," is one that later in a phone conversation Booth would analogize to "pole-vaulting on the moon."

But just as a thrill ride or even a rapid elevator lift will cause in some a feeling of both thrill and queasiness in the stomach, just as "pole-vaulting on the moon" may engender a fear of pole-vaulting *off* the moon perhaps, into cold deep space, the focus on the pleasure to be found enfolded in the language, the rush of pleasure opened up by Boothian close reading may have provoked a counterreaction.

This was something—my Theory of Theory and the terror of pleasure that lies beneath it—that began to dawn on me as I prepared to drive south to Staunton, Virginia, to the scholars' conference where I first hoped to meet Stephen Booth. As I searched frantically but fruitlessly to find a copy of Booth's *Essay on Shakespeare's Sonnets,* as I reimmersed myself in the four hundred pages of footnotes and commentary in his still very-much-in-print Yale University Press edition of the Sonnets, I returned again to that strange destabilizing experience I had at Yale when teaching the Sonnets, and to the paradoxes in that sequence that had destabilized me so memorably. That cluster of sonnets beginning with 39 and continuing to 45 is a sequence riddled (in every sense of the word "riddled") with flickering multilayered polysemous wordplay.

It's a sequence (39–45) at the heart of a peculiarly Shakespearean preoccupation: to be or not to be one, or twinned, or, alternately, *both* simultaneously. In this sequence the speaker begins to worry over, to worry to death—or worry into life—the paradox of two lovers being both one and two selves. United by love, although separated by geography. The paradox that results from their being Together in the most profound metaphysical ways, yet separated in the most petty physical ones, so that in some ways they are united *and* divided, twinned *and* twain, double *and* singular selves *at the same time,* or in rapidly flickering pulsation.

Sonnet 40 may be the most dramatic, dazzling and destabilizing of all 154 fourteen-line engines of pleasure and derangement.

Take all my loves, my love, yea, take them all,
What hast thou then more than thou hadst before?
No love, my love, that thou mayst true love call,
All mine was thine, before thou hadst this more.
Then if for my love thou my love receivest,
I cannot blame thee for my love thou usest,
But yet be blam'd, if thou this self deceivest
By willful taste of what thyself refusest.
I do forgive thy robb'ry, gentle thief,
Although thou steal thee all my poverty;
And yet love knows it is a greater grief
To bear love's wrong than hate's known injury.
Lascivious grace, in whom all ill well shows,
Kill me with spites, yet we must not be foes.

The drama stems from the inciting incident: The narrator is in love with someone who has just stolen away the narrator's (somewhat lesser) beloved or mistress. Just how much lesser is evident from the dismissive opening line:

Take all my loves, my love, yea, take them all . . .

He then goes on to make an elaborate argument that, for several complicated reasons, stealing his lover means stealing nothing, or at least gaining nothing:

What hast thou then more than thou hadst before?
No love, my love, that thou mayst true love call,
All mine was thine, before thou hadst this more.

So far *barely* understandable, or at least paraphrasable: Everything that was his—the speaker's—was *already* his lover's. So his lover taking his (the speaker's) other lover from him wasn't getting him (the primary beloved) anything he didn't already have.

But then in the next quatrain, things get really complicated. The apparently maddened speaker can't let go of the conceit and ties himself into mental knots elaborating upon it:

Then if for my love thou my love receivest,
I cannot blame thee for my love thou usest,
But yet be blam'd, if thou this self deceivest
By willful taste of what thyself refusest.

Indulge me: read that over (at least) twice and notice how it drives you not merely to the brink of comprehension but over the cliff of incomprehension, virtually into the abyss of destabilization.

Consider Stephen Booth's annotation, just of the *first* line, of that increasingly complicated quatrain:

5. "Then if for my love thou my love receivest . . ." *For, love,* and *receivest* each has several appropriate and syntactically available meanings here; some of their many combinations are these: (1) if, out of affection for me

> (for love of me), you take my mistress; (2) if, because of my affection for you, you courteously welcome my mistress; (3) if, for yours (as your possession—you being *my love,* my beloved), you take my mistress; (4) if, in place of my affection, you take my mistress; (5) if you understand my mistress to be my true-love; (6) if you understand what I feel for my mistress to be love; (7) if, because of my affection for you (or yours for me), you accept (or suffer) my affection.

Try reading aloud Booth's seven-part explication of the ambiguities; it's criticism that rises to the level of poetry itself. Booth's footnote to line 5 in which he unfolds the dazzling multiplicity of possible meanings of "for," "love" and "receivest," and how each shift in meaning in one unfolds multiple shifts in the others, is an example of the polysemous pleasures of his reading of the Sonnets. Pleasures that almost threaten to dissolve not just the singularity of meaning—but the singularity of self.

Booth doesn't encourage one to choose one particular combination of "for," "love" or "receivest" but rather to contemplate—to revel in—the way the multiple possibilities are choreographed. Change one's way of looking at one word's connotation and the other two dance to a new tune. Look at another word through a different lens and the others shift into a new focus. It's a dizzying but pleasurable destabilization. One won't crack one's head open going off this cliff, but it might open the mind in a way it hasn't been opened before. Something Boothian commentary tries to celebrate. To celebrate the way the words and meanings in effect enact a beautiful and pleasurable dance of significations in which one possible meaning of "for" might combine with four other possibilities for "receivest" and then four more for "love" in an exponentially more complex and yet deeply pleasurable way. The way entertaining all possible, that is *plausible,* meanings at once is preferable to attempting reductively to single out one.

It is more than William Empson's famous "Seven Types of Ambiguity." It is Seven Types of Ambiguity set in motion—taken to the seventh power (at least) and then raised another *n*th degree to the point where the shifting possibilities literally dizzy the arithmetic of consciousness. It has something of the quality of "indistinctness," the term the critic John Carey gave to what David Lodge described as "Carey's idiosyncratic name for what other critics and theorists have called variously ambiguity, polysemy. In other words the capacity of poetic language to generate an inexhaustible but nonrandom supply of meaning in the consciousness of readers." By "indistinctness" Carey doesn't mean *blurriness;* rather it suggests a multiplicity of distinct states.

Inexhaustible, but non-random: an important almost-but-not-quite oxymoronic phrase. It does not mean "anything goes." But, rather, more than you might imagine.

Is this a good thing? Is this what the Sonnets were about, more than about love but about creating a delirium, here the delirium of meaning's shifting, interacting multiplicity? But isn't that *precisely* the maddening and seductive quality—the special delirium and paranoia—of mind-dizzying soul-dissolving love?

Booth's vision of the Sonnets, the vision expressed, unfolded in this endlessly divided and recombinant efflorescence of exegesis, this haze of particles, this cloud of cornstarch, around the words, was in fact an illustration of the secret play he finds beneath the Sonnet language.

A play about the pleasures of polysemy—one that has provoked stimulating debate over the limits of polysemy between Booth and Helen Vendler. In her edition of the Sonnets, Vendler, the distinguished Harvard professor of poetry, made a pointed objection to what she felt could be an out-of-control polysemy. Booth's point as I interpret it is that the Sonnets are designed to induce a state that can feel perilously, destabilizingly "out of control"—one which happens to suggest the state of being in love.

But one thing that can be said about Booth's secret play is that, up until Booth came along, so much of the debate about the Sonnets was devoted either to lesser biographical questions such as who the apparent dedicatee, "Mr. W.H.," was. Or to deducing from the Sonnets the nature of Shakespeare's sexuality, "proving" him one thing or the other.

Recall Booth's way of disposing of the latter controversy was to say, with typical asperity, "William Shakespeare was almost certainly homosexual, bisexual, or heterosexual. The Sonnets provide no evidence on that matter."

Wordsworth famously said that the Sonnets are "the key to Shakespeare's heart." They may or may not be. But to Stephen Booth they are the key to his *art.* One can see that in Booth's beautiful footnote to that single line and those three words: "for," "love" and "receivest." The way they are, one might say, "by love possessed." Booth's exegetical love. In unfolding the manifold possibilities, the shifting, pulsating, flickering patterns of meaning, the interactions of possibilities conjured up, Booth doesn't suggest that one must embrace any one of the seven (or the seven to the seventh power) possible ways he adumbrates. He is suggesting that the pleasure of the Sonnets is that, at some level, not quite conscious, we experience the play of *all* of them, we're not meant to reduce them to a singular meaning but to be subtly stimulated by their dazzling multiplicity.

BOOTH AT THE BLACKFRIARS

I thought about this while driving down to the Shenandoah Shakespeare Scholars' Conference in October a month after the September 11 attacks in New York. My first attempt to talk to Booth. It was a month in the Shenandoah Valley, in the foothills of the Blue Ridge Mountains, when the foliage coloration was at its peak, particularly on the last leg of the journey, the Blue Ridge Parkway. Something about the riotous multiplicity of foliage colors suggested a kind of analogy to Booth's sonnet exegesis. Each word, like a leaf, able to appear in an array of colorations and configurations, depending on angle of light and shift of shadow, affecting and being affected by the array of leaves around it and the way their colors shifted in the shifting sunlight. A spectacle that couldn't be focused or experienced leaf by leaf, but only in its glorious panoply of shifting totalities. (It suggests as well Cic Berry's vision of multiple vocal resonances coloring each other, doesn't it?)

It was almost too much pleasure, unbearable pleasure; the unrelenting beauty of the natural spectacle became oppressive, in almost the same way that reading the Sonnets with Booth's commentary approached the border between ravishment and distaste or at least dismay.

I was almost relieved when I finally arrived at the old antebellum-era town of Staunton. It was the home of the dilapidated Stonewall Jackson Hotel. And, in the middle of the grits joints downtown, the brand-spanking-new Blackfriars Playhouse, Ralph Alan Cohen's field of dreams, its interior glowing with the beautiful sheen of new-hewn wooden planks.

I should explain a bit more about the Shenandoah Scholars' Conference, which was one of the most pleasurable of all the many scholarly conferences I'd been attending. Some of the smartest, wittiest and most engaging scholars in a setting of natural and manmade beauty. It was a fortunate coincidence or confluence of interests that brought me there.

It was something I discovered at the last minute while attending a reception at the Folger Library during one of the Modern Language Association's mass scholar convocations set in Washington, D.C. I was talking about textual matters with the Folger's Barbara Mowat and Paul Werstine and Ms.

Mowat suggested I should meet this bow-tied fellow in tweeds, Ralph Alan Cohen, who had founded the Shenandoah Shakespeare acting troupe. Cohen was soon to open what sounded to me like a bizarre quixotic project, a reconstruction of Shakespeare's "other" theater (other than the Globe), the Blackfriars Theatre. The original Blackfriars was a more intimate indoor torch-and-candle-lit venue, and plunking a replica down in the foothills of the Blue Ridge Mountains two and a half hours southwest of Washington sounded admirably impractical to me, at least at first.

I'd heard of the Shenandoah Shakespeare company, whose bare-bones, back-to-basics, natural-light productions had won favor with scholars at Shakespeare Association of America gatherings for capturing the spirit and the interactive informality and some of the original conditions of Shakespeare's productions at the Globe—which of course were all staged in daylight in an uncovered open-air theater with actors and audience in close proximity.*

When I heard about this mad Blackfriars project (without really believing in it a bit) at the Folger Shakespeare Library reception, what struck me was the enthusiasm with which textual specialists such as Mowat and Werstine—who seem rarely impressed by performances, hyperaware as they are of how the stage can corrupt the page—spoke of Ralph Cohen and his Shenandoah Shakespeare company. They urged me to see the production then running in the Folger Library Theater—a production of *Twelfth Night* which Ralph Alan Cohen had codirected with none other than Stephen Booth.

Booth himself was no longer around. He'd flown back to Berkeley, where he taught, after the opening of the production, but he'd done a typically thought-provoking essay on "doubling and *Twelfth Night*" for the Folger program, and planned to return for the forthcoming conference celebrating the Blackfriars opening.

I suppose, when I was introduced to Ralph Alan Cohen, I was more interested at the time in finding out about the legendary Professor Booth than this fantasy Blackfriars project Cohen kept wanting to talk about. So I focused on something memorable Ralph Alan Cohen said about Stephen Booth: that Booth believes *Twelfth Night* is Shakespeare's supreme creation.

* In a 1992 *Shakespeare Quarterly* review, Booth had written: "I first saw the Shenandoah Shakespeare [company] perform in Washington, D.C., in July 1991. I haven't thought the same since about Shakespeare or the theater."

Surpassing even the Sonnets. A former student of Booth's, Eric Griffin, told me Booth liked to say *Twelfth Night* was not merely Shakespeare's greatest creation, but "the greatest creation of the human mind."

I must admit that at the time this piece of information about Booth's preference for *Twelfth Night* obscured my interest in Cohen's quixotic Blackfriars project. Quixotic because, after all, why would Cohen, who seemed so intelligent, who had accomplished so much with his Shakespeare company, one of whose virtues was its transportability (they hardly needed a stage, they could transform any bare space to a Globe), become involved in the whole dubious "restoration" business in the first place? It would at the very least anchor him to a single piece of land, secondly it sounded like a theme-park-type idea, a Shakespearean version of Dollywood (down at the other end of the Blue Ridge range). And finally I was dubious about the whole restoration craze—including London's Globe—since it seemed to place too much attention on the material conditions of the theater (the baked potato), and not enough on the language (the chocolate pie). It's a fine line between enlightened "Originalism" and pointless antiquarianism, a false Originalism. A lot depends on whether a return to "original conditions" genuinely takes us deeper into the Shakespearean or merely mimics the shell of what has been lost.

I had just spent some time talking to Sir Peter Hall, whose heartfelt and (he felt) historically based insistences about the way Shakespeare's iambic pentameter line should be spoken made such matters seem far more important to me than what kind of wood the theater was made from.

The reconstructed Globe in London was already causing a heated scholarly debate about how much imagined "historicity" was replacing verse-speaking and stage movement as a focus of the best energies for playing Shakespeare.

The Blackfriars replica seemed all the more strange a dream, since it was to be set down in the rural Blue Ridge foothills and the original Blackfriars was, if anything, a much more urban, literary, theatrical venue than the Globe.

Almost everybody knows about the Globe but fewer know, and less is known about, the original Blackfriars Theatre, except that it was a covered indoor venue in which performances could be held at night. A place smaller than the Globe, reputedly more intimate, it was constructed out of the refectory of an abandoned friary and Shakespeare's company the King's Men began using it around 1608—in addition to continuing to play at the Globe.

Still, setting aside the reconstruction/authenticity issue about the Blackfriars, there are those scholars, Frank Kermode among them, who believe that the acquisition of the original Blackfriars Theatre property in 1608 by Shakespeare's company marks a moment of significant change in Shakespeare's dramatic language—and the direction of his art.

There is a school of thought that the candle- or torch-lit, acoustically more intimate setting allowed Shakespeare a freedom to explore a kind of language in his later dramas that became increasingly knotty and complex, in part because it could be better *heard* in a Blackfriars setting, in part because the Blackfriars audience tended to be more sophisticated and literate. There was no open yard for the hubbub of the groundlings to drown the subtleties of language. Some go even further and argue that the magical transformative quality of Shakespeare's Late Romances from *Pericles* to *The Winter's Tale* and *The Tempest* played better there in the more magical candle-lit darkness than in the cruel broad daylight of the Globe.

Whether or not one believes in a "Blackfriars Shakespeare" as opposed to a "Globe Shakespeare," Ralph Alan Cohen felt strongly enough about the project to enlist some of the best theater historians—including Andrew Gurr, who was instrumental in the design of the reconstructed London Globe—to sift through the fragmentary historical evidence about what the Blackfriars Theatre looked like. Meanwhile Cohen, a debonair, charming fellow with remarkable fund-raising charisma among the wealthier sort of literary and theater patrons, combined with the ability to sweet-talk the aldermen of a small Virginia town, managed to raise the money, get the permits and, on the best scholarly advice, build a remarkable Zen-teahouse-like theater in the Blue Ridge foothills. The glowing bamboo-colored hardwood plank walls gave the interior an almost Oriental serenity. Little did I know when I was first captivated by that interior, that a mighty behind-the-scenes debate had been brewing over whether to paint the beautiful bare boards in the gaudy colors more likely to have been slapped on the Elizabethan original. It was a kind of test of Originalism: Should one adhere to the original gaudiness which may easily, for all we know, have looked radiantly beautiful to the seventeenth-century Londoners? Or should one keep to the spirit rather than the letter of "radiance" in the light of changing ideals of beauty: for us, today, radiance is more naturally associated with glowing polished bare wood than with bright painted colors. Which was the more "Shakespearean" paint job?

The scholars' conference I was driving down to that October was timed to celebrate the opening of the reconstructed Blackfriars Theatre, and show off the Shenandoah Shakespeare company in its new venue. And to showcase some brilliant scholars speaking on topics related to Shakespeare and the theater.

One of the extremely astute innovations Ralph Alan Cohen introduced into this particular scholarly conclave was to institute a rule that limited each scholar's talk to ten minutes. *Ten minutes!* It allowed him to schedule more scholars for the five-day conference, but it was an almost unheard of haiku-like length for the kind of talk this caliber of scholar was used to delivering, papers usually running to forty minutes minimum.

With a born dramatist's sense, Cohen demonstrated at the outset of the conference how he would enforce the ten-minute limit. Standing on the luminous stage of the Blackfriars replica, he called forth a "thunder sheet," a twelve-foot-high, four-foot-wide sheet of thick rusty metallic alloy that when shaken produces effects ranging from deep menacing premonitory thunder to mentally deranging Lear-on-the-heath torrents of thunderous sound.

He had his assistant shake it, producing an increasingly loud, threatening, deafening rolling-thunder sound: that was the eight-minute *warning* for the ten-minute time limit. Then from behind the curtain a long earsplitting blast from what sounded like a ram's horn from hell announcing the apocalypse. That would signal the ten-minute termination time.

I have a feeling that one reason Stephen Booth said so *much* in his dazzling disquisition on "The Witty Partition" that weekend was that he was forced to compress his natural expansiveness into that ten-minute time period. And that he was able to articulate something about Shakespearean verse that he had, to my knowledge, not articulated in such a compressed and expressive way before. He actually told us "what all the fuss is about."

That phrase was at the heart of Booth's recurrent response whenever I asked him why he seems to care so little about "theme" in Shakespeare as opposed to a searching exploration of the way the language works. Other great writers can be read for profound themes—as can Shakespeare—he suggests. But that's not what "the fuss is all about" when it comes to Shakespeare, he avers. The fuss is about our feeling that what Shakespeare does with language, what Shakespearean language does to the minds of those who read and hear it.

I first encountered Stephen Booth in person at the opening night cocktail party of the conference. Not at the Blackfriars Playhouse—we were not to see that until we saw the first play on its boards—but in the extraordinary natural theater of the Blue Ridge foothills, which formed a kind of backdrop to the home Ralph Alan Cohen had built for himself and his family.

The sunset was particularly spectacular, some of the sparkling wine being served loosened my tongue and I found I'd fallen in with a particularly congenial group of textual scholars whose work I knew and admired from researching *Hamlet* textual questions. Among them were Thomas Berger, A. R. Braunmuller and George Walton Williams. And one scholar I thought of as one of the most admirably "Boothian," you might say, of current literary scholars: Russ McDonald. His slim Oxford book with the deceptively simple and general title *Shakespeare and the Arts of Language* had proven one of those works where I found myself underlining so much of it that underlining had lost the point of underlining.

I'd met Booth first that evening on the bus that was taking us over rugged mountain roads from the Blackfriars in "downtown" Staunton to Ralph Alan Cohen's mountain aerie. I'd told him of my admiration for his Sonnets edition, and apparently by the time the party had reached its height, I must have been gushing about my enthusiasm for Booth's work to others who knew him, since I heard back from one of their girlfriends, "Booth was gesturing over toward you saying, 'I like that fellow: he thinks I'm smart.' "

It was the perfect Boothian remark, implicating and subverting both his own vanity and my own gushiness simultaneously. Did he really "like that fellow," or was it self-deprecating humility: "I like that fellow" only because "he thinks I'm smart." And is "he thinks I'm smart" really a compliment coming from someone either 1) too gushy or 2) too deceived about Booth's smartness to be trusted? In a funny way, a paradigm for the way he looked at the way the contraries in the Sonnets worked.

In any case one of the things that developed that evening confirmed my sense of Booth's *Essay on Shakespeare's Sonnets* as a kind of transformative icon, almost like forbidden esoteric text. A kind of *Kama Sutra* of Shakespeare, or one of those banned books like *Ulysses* that travelers would smuggle through customs in the barebacked Shakespeare and Company of Paris edition.

It was an impression I got from the textual scholars that evening and over the next four days. I would mention that I had tried every online, used-book, rare-book search engine and hadn't been able to acquire a copy of

Booth's out-of-print *Essay.* All in the hope—hint, hint—that one of them might let me borrow his. I had no takers. They all had the book but none of them was going to let it out of their sight.

Not until several months later did Russ McDonald have mercy on my desperate plea and ask one of his assistants to make a photocopy of his copy, which gave me the added benefit of having the two textual exegetes I'd most admired in a kind of dialogue. In the sense that, not only was I interested in what Booth wrote, I was interested in what McDonald had *underlined* of what Booth wrote—and the occasional, all-too-occasional, marginal comment. One of my favorites of which is, "Not only do we learn about mutability [from the Sonnets], we *participate* in mutability" (my italics). In other words we read about changeableness and find ourselves changeable, changed, changing, exchanging ourselves. Yes—that moment at Yale, that's what was happening: I was "participating in mutability"! It sounds much more dignified than it felt.

In any case, that unique doubling commentary was something I would only get to experience later. But forms of doubling seemed to be the subtext to the Blackfriars conference. The Blackfriars Playhouse was a kind of Shakespearean duplicate. *Twelfth Night,* a play about doubling, was the first play of the conference.

My admiration for Booth only grew the following day after witnessing his extraordinary ten-minute disquisition on "the Wall" in *A Midsummer Night's Dream.* In some ways it offered the lit-crit equivalent of the excitement I felt first seeing Peter Brook's *Dream.*

The Wall is a character in the *Pyramus and Thisby* play put on by the "rude mechanicals." The Wall has a hole in it, a hole that in Booth's vision becomes a trapdoor, somehow a source of greater wholeness.

It's typical of Booth to choose such an apparently low comic device, such as the Wall, and find a way to turn it into a vehicle for some astonishing offhand observations about what makes Shakespeare Shakespearean.

The very existence of the Wall as a *speaking part* is one of the most lovely, comic, yet complex meta-theatrical devices in the *Dream.* The play of *Pyramus and Thisby* is not hard to see as a parody of *Romeo and Juliet* in many ways: the two doomed young lovers of the title are separated by feuding families and here can only speak to each other through a hole or chink in the wall that separates their estates.

The amateur actors in the *Dream,* the Mechanicals who are called upon to put on a play at the wedding feast of Theseus and Hippolyta at the climax of the play, decide that—for "realism"—since they lack an actual portable wall-prop they must have one of the actors play the Wall (they also have another fellow play "Moonshine"—not the moon, but *moonshine*—so that the audience will know the indoor play is set outdoors in the moonlight). Peter Brook considers this one of the great moments of theatrical self-awareness in Shakespeare, so perhaps it's no accident that Stephen Booth happens to focus on it as well.

In any case the Wall, played by Snout the tinker (no accident a tinker—fixer-upper—plays a wall), comes onstage in the midst of the royal wedding pomp and announces

In this same enterlude it doth befall
That I, one Snout by name, present a wall;
And such a wall, as I would have you think,
That had in it a crannied hole or chink . . .

At this point most productions have Snout/Wall hold up two fingers spread apart to form a "chink." Or for actors more inclined to play the obscene low comedy implicit in the "crannied hole," the fingers form a circle with thumb and forefinger. Done with the right oblivious flourish—oblivious on the part of Snout who plays the Wall—the gesture almost never fails to bring down the house. Anyway, Wall presents himself and his hole

Through which the lovers, Pyramus and Thisby,
Did whisper often, very secretly.

Hearing this, one of the Athenian nobles in the audience, Demetrius, says, "It is the wittiest partition that ever I heard discourse, my lord."

"IMPASSIONED DOG TALK"

Stephen Booth began *his* discourse, his ten-minute talk at Blackfriars which he entitled "The Wittiest Partition," with a description of what he called, with typical self-deprecation, the "two largely unsuccessful projects" with which he's occupied his career:

"The first is the campaign for a criticism that looks hard at the esthetic nuts and bolts of great works, recognizes them as significant . . . without feeling obliged to say that such minutiae are significant in the literal sense of something carrying meaning. I stated, as I have long said, to deaf ears everywhere, we should be thinking about what the New Critics made vague, mysterious and dignified with the unusually inaccurate label 'imagery' as *nonsignifying unifiers.*"

In the remaining nine minutes or so—which seemed like an exciting, pleasurable and demanding hour—Booth proceeded to talk about three of these "nonsignifying unifiers" in *A Midsummer Night's Dream:* moonshine, dogs and "parts" or "partitions," including the "witty partition" who called himself Wall.

Before getting to the witty partition itself I will dwell upon just one remarkable aside Booth made on the subject of dogs because it brings up a phrase, "strenuous impertinence," that I think is at the heart of his way of looking at Shakespeare, and in fact, Booth argues, defines the Shakespearean. And, in my reading of Booth's reading, does even more.

In regard to dogs he tells us at one point about how he got to "worrying about the lengthy and unexpected arias on Theseus's hounds and the hounds of Sparta that we hear when Theseus and Hippolyta reenter the play at the beginning of act 4. The idea of 'musical discord' (Theseus says he has never heard 'so musical a discord' . . . as that of his baying hounds)—is a *splendidly accurate definition of literary art in general and of verse in particular.* But the twenty lines of impassioned dog talk feel strenuously impertinent when we hear them in their play."

Musical discord as a "definition of literary art"? Booth's whole critical focus, as we'll see, is to "make concord out of discord" (a line from the *Dream*) in his readings. To seek out apparent holes and make them part of the whole.

But to return to "strenuously impertinent": the phrase reminded me of a very similar two-word verbal formula I'd first heard as an undergraduate at Yale, although for the life of me I'm not sure which of my professors first used it, the two leading suspects being Henry Schroeder the Chaucer scholar and Michael John Kenneth O'Loughlin the late specialist in Milton and the Metaphysical poets. Although it's not even clear to me whether whoever it was might have been quoting someone else. (Harry Berger?)

The phrase, which stayed with me, and which has proven to be an extraordinarily useful device in close reading, the phrase summoned up by "strenuous impertinence," was "conspicuous irrelevance."

It's slightly less judgmental than "strenuous impertinence," but in both cases it's really not meant as a *condemnation:* it's a way of calling attention to lines, phrases, words, passages—like the "twenty lines of impassioned dog talk"—that don't at first seem to belong, which seem somehow off the point, over-the-top, excessive and distracting, but which often, by indirection, reveal more about "the point" than their apparent pointlessness suggests at first. A kind of hole in the text that is key to a larger whole.

Again we can glimpse, in Booth's aside about the "twenty lines of impassioned dog talk," his self-deprecating but deeply serious way of suggesting a "splendidly accurate definition of literary art."

The discussion of the musical voices of the hounds in the *Dream* manifests its "strenuously impertinent," "conspicuous irrelevance" in the aftermath of the night of magic and confusion in the forest outside Athens where the two sets of lovers are first comically disjoined by Puck's misapplied love potion, then finally brought into four-part harmony. They are thrown into discord, then brought into concord through a comedy of Puck's errors.

At dawn, to the sound of hunting horns and barking dogs, Theseus and Hippolyta enter and Theseus begins to boast:

. . . since we have the vaward of the day,
My love shall hear the music of my hounds.
Uncouple in the western valley, let them go. . . .
We will, fair queen, up to the mountain's top,
And mark the musical confusion
Of hounds and echo in conjunction.

Then Hippolyta, the Amazon warrior queen won, but not subdued, by Theseus, comes back at him by recalling (or one-upping) her soon-to-be husband with a memory of even more famous hounds, more mythic hunters:

I was with Hercules and Cadmus once,
When in a wood of Crete they bay'd the bear
With hounds of Sparta. Never did I hear
Such gallant chiding; for besides the groves,
The skies, the fountains, every region near
Seem all one mutual cry. I never heard
So musical a discord, such sweet thunder.

And then, refusing to be topped by this gallant chiding about "gallant chiding," Theseus returns to the subject of *his* hounds. At about this point the audience might be wondering, are we suddenly in a play about competitive hunting dogs? But Theseus's language, like that of Hippolyta, is so musical and evocative itself: that line in which all of nature is united in "one mutual cry," a kind of orgiastic communion of sound, is astonishing. Theseus's counterdescription of his dogs brings us back to earth and then sweeps us into the sky again:

My hounds are bred out of the Spartan kind;
So flew'd, so sanded; and their heads are hung
With ears that sweep away the morning dew;
Crook-knee'd and dewlapp'd like Thessalian bulls;
Slow in pursuit; but match'd in mouth like bells,
Each under each. A cry more tuneable
Was never hollow'd to, nor cheer'd with horn,
In Crete, in Sparta, nor in Thessaly.
Judge when you hear. . . .

It was fascinating to me that Booth should focus on what he calls these "lengthy and unexpected arias on Theseus's hounds and the hounds of Sparta." Fascinating because three years earlier I recall sitting in the Oxford-Cambridge club listening to the erudite international man of mystery David Selbourne,* the author of the rehearsal diary of Peter Brook's *Dream, The Making of A Midsummer Night's Dream,* speak about just those lines with just that kind of conspicuous reverence.

It's one of those passages in Shakespeare that inexplicably take flight, one of those passages where one gets the sense Shakespeare is cruising along, working up a rote passage, and then something lifts him to a level where he's attempting to describe his own experience of creation: "a cry more tuneable." It's one of the passages in the *Dream,* Selbourne said, when he always felt words suddenly transcended themselves to become something beyond words, beyond music even. Not leaving verbal meaning behind: in-

* Selbourne, playwright, polemicist author of influential Blairite manifestos, was at the time I met him involved in a controversy over a manuscript he'd claimed to have discovered that described a Jewish merchant's pre–Marco Polo voyage to China—one whose authenticity had been challenged.

deed one could say that in that passage about hounds, about *animals' voices* becoming *music,* it might be a suggestion that this is what poetry itself is: music made by animals, by ourselves, when our voices rise above ourselves to some higher harmony. It raises us above other animals and yet unites us with them as well, all in "one mutual cry."

This is why I think Booth is on to something when he offhandedly calls the "impassioned dog talk" a "splendidly accurate definition of literary art in general and of verse in particular." It's a splendid example of the way "strenuous impertinence" or "conspicuous irrelevance" in its only *seeming* anomalousness reveals something more profound than the pentameter line expresses on the surface.

A "splendidly accurate definition of literary art," though? How so? After reading over Booth's comments and thinking about them for several years, not constantly, needless to say, but rather frequently, I could suggest an explanation of Booth's explication. I'd suggest the "dog talk" is a kind of allegory of the experience, the exhilaration, the pure pleasure of writing.

Writing as riding—riding to the hounds with a pack of words, trying to keep them all "tun'd" in the mad rush of the hunt. Writers are those who hunt for words, for the meaning to be derived from assembling a pack of words. Where the goal is not the capture of prey—Theseus's hounds are explicitly described as "slow in pursuit"—but rather in the way they are "tun'd" into harmony, their voices conjoined with their echoes, all these vocalizations choreographed into art.

And just as the exhilaration of the hunt is not about seeking the prey, the exhilaration of writing is not in the pursuit of a single prey—a single meaning—which of course would bring the hunt to an end, but in the pursuit of a higher state of being, the "mutual cry" of the hunt in full flight. It suggests Shakespeare giving a sense of what it's like being in hot pursuit of this state, the words surging like the hounds in an echoing crowd—a cloud of sound—around him.

But then Booth went beyond Shakespeare's "splendidly accurate definition of literary art" or this "dog talk" to give a more complex definition of what makes Shakespeare's literary art so unique. To define what it is, technically, that makes the magic possible. What "all the fuss is about."

Here is what Booth called "the second of the two projects I have been so unsuccessfully promoting for so long." The first is to get critics to pay attention to "the esthetic nuts and bolts of great works," in particular "nonsignifying unifiers," by which he means things like dog, moon and partition imagery but more specifically "the *experience* of virtually muffled wordplay and of patterning that does not obtrude upon one's consciousness." Such subliminal consciousness of connection is "more valuable and [should be] more highly valued than the experience of witty connections that invite notice—notice of their wit and therefore of their arbitrary origin." Instead, he argues, "incidental organizations *undemanding of notice* vouch for a sort of organic truth in the work as a whole that makes it feel as if it is as things in nature are."

"Organic truth": them's fightin' words to most postmodern academic Theorists, and it's certainly a concept, dating back to Coleridge's Romantic notion of organic unity, that can be over-applied, over-imposed or imagined. But that doesn't mean some semblance of it doesn't exist or that all analogies from art to nature are invalid, in the sense of a higher coherence that gives "life" to a work of art. I felt that way about the shifting colorations of foliage that lined the Blue Ridge Parkway, an organic analogy, an organic metaphor for the effects the Sonnets' shifting colorations of verbal foliage have in Booth's exegesis. So sue me.

I think that, by "organic truth," when Booth says "as if it is as things in nature are" (note the perfect iambic pentameter in that last clause), he is referring to the subtle holographic unity of Shakespeare, the way every little thing seems in some way related to, reflective of, every other little thing. All the expressions of a single, infinitely almost self-aware unity. The unity *undemanding of notice* that makes Shakespeare seem even more exceptional: the closer one looks at what one does not, at first, consciously notice, the more one senses that there's an unobtrusive necessity, connectedness to all of it.

But that's just part *one* of "the two projects" he says he's been "so unsuccessfully promoting" for so long. When he came to "part two" I think I felt a shock of recognition when I heard him say it, heard him toss it off so casually on the stage of the Blackfriars Theatre replica, with the thunder sheet trembling threateningly behind him.

THE DOUBLE-CHERRY SONATA

Part two is to get critics "to pay attention as critics to things they would not reasonably pay attention to as consumers [i.e., as readers or playgoers] and could not reasonably recommend that consumers pay attention to in the future—that critics pay attention to the *ideational static* generated in Shakespeare's plays, by substantively insignificant, substantively inadmissible, substantively accidental linguistic configurations—configurations in which lurk topics foreign to the sentences in which we hear them [the way "dog talk" turns into a definition, an exemplification of literary art], and 2) to see that such static is probably exciting to the minds it *plays across* and probably brings those listening minds a sense of possessing and casually, effortlessly exercising an athleticism beyond that imaginable in human beings—a sense of being mentally and spiritually sufficient to comprehend 'More than cool reason *ever* comprehends.' Or ever could."

As an example he cites "the incessant hum of 'part' references in *A Midsummer Night's Dream,*" which "hum" is "not only elaborate in its range"—"part" as fraction, "part" as part of "depart," "part" as in "partition," "part" as in role in a play, "part" as in to separate, etc.—"not only elaborate in its range, but in the intricacy with which words and ideas relative to one kind of part or parting interweave with—entwine themselves with—words and ideas relative to other kinds of part or parting."

But before getting deeper into the thicket of entwined "part" references let me return to that remarkable formulation about "ideational static," how the almost subliminal apprehension of connections, configurations brings to us, to our "listening minds a sense of possessing and casually, effortlessly exercising an athleticism beyond that imaginable in human beings. . . ."

He's putting into words in this "ideational static" formulation something I think I've felt occasionally, felt more often the more I read and see and listen to Shakespeare, more frequently in each new cycle of close reading—a kind of ecstatic state of being (ecstatic static?) one can experience in Shakespeare, a state that may define what makes Shakespearean language exceptional. A state that may define that which we call "Shakespearean." Booth's choice of that line "More than cool reason ever comprehends" and that addition "Or ever could" is no accident. It's a reference to Shakespeare's own attempt to define that state. It's a reference to a line a little bit later in *A Midsummer Night's Dream,* the famous passage in which Theseus compares the ecstasy of the poet, the lover and the madman.

After hearing the story of that night in the forest, the confusions, the love-potion-induced changes of heart, the concord finally brought out of discord, Hippolyta says,

" 'Tis strange, my Theseus, that these lovers speak of."

And Theseus replies:

More strange than true. I never may believe
These antic fables, nor these fairy toys.
Lovers and madmen have such seething brains,
Such shaping fantasies, that apprehend
More than cool reason ever comprehends.
The lunatic, the lover, and the poet
Are of imagination all compact . . .
The poet's eye, in a fine frenzy rolling,
Doth glance from heaven to earth, from earth to heaven;
And as imagination bodies forth
The forms of things unknown, the poet's pen
Turns them to shapes, and gives to aery nothing
A local habitation and a name. . . .

It is Shakespeare's most powerful and beautiful description of the poetic imagination; it's difficult not to see it as a portrait of the fine frenzy of his own imagination. Just as, in a way, riding (writing) with the hounds does. And what Booth is doing is describing the experience of reading Shakespeare as affording a similar "fine frenzy," an ability to "apprehend / More than cool reason ever comprehends." Booth is suggesting that in Booth's notion of this "fine frenzy" he situates the reader reading (riding) with Shakespeare in the company of the lunatic, the lover and the poet—that pack of poetic hounds all of whom experience a fine frenzy cool reason can't comprehend.

It is this emphasis on the reader's experience—that what makes Shakespeare different, exceptional, is the way he offers the mind that experience of "casually, effortlessly exercising an athleticism beyond that imaginable in human beings"—that sets Booth's vision of the Shakespearean experience apart, even from other "reader reception" critics as they're sometimes called, in this emphasis on the almost physical virtuosity. The joyful athleticism the mind feels in making concord out of discord.

The secret of Stephen Booth's secret play then is that to read Shakespeare, one must become a *player* of Shakespeare, a player in the sense that a violinist is a player of Mozart. Just as there are levels of the apprehension of Mozart: one can read the score as silent notes on a page; one can hear them played in a concert hall over and over in ever-deepening states of awareness of the connectedness of every note. But the ultimate way of experiencing it is to play it.

This is a question I raised with Booth in one of my talks with him: When he speaks of the experience of "athleticism," of the beautiful "gymnastics" the mind becomes aware it's capable of performing—is inspired to perform, taught to perform by Shakespeare—is this experience, this "fine frenzy" available to everyone? Or can it not be said that just as Isaac Stern probably experiences Mozart in a way you and I are not capable of imagining, perhaps Booth experiences Shakespeare in a way that may be inspiring to us, but represents an exegetical athleticism not available to everyone.

He professed surprise at the question, a surprise that seemed to suggest "of course it's accessible to everyone." But reading Booth on the experience of reading Shakespeare may be like listening to Isaac Stern play Mozart, rather than playing it yourself, even after a lifetime of lessons: one is aware of one's own experience of it, but one wonders what *his* experience of it is like.

Consider what I'd call, in Mozartian terms, Booth's "double-cherry sonata": the final tossed-off tour de force reading he gave down in Staunton of another otherwise "strenuously impertinent," "conspicuously irrelevant" passage in the *Dream.* The moment in that confused night in the forest when Helena upbraids her childhood friend Hermia, whom she mistakenly believes is conspiring against her. She reproves her by summoning up—at strenuous length—her "school-days friendship," when

We, Hermia, like two artificial gods,
Have with our needles created both one flower,
Both on one sampler, sitting on one cushion,
Both warbling of one song, both in one key,
As if our hands, our sides, voices, and minds
Had been incorporate. So we grew together,
Like to a double cherry, seeming parted,
But yet an union in partition,
Two lovely berries moulded on one stem;
So with two seeming bodies, but one heart . . .

Amazing: there's that "witty partition" again: the one between the sentient "double cherries." But the double-cherry division—another "wall"—when looked at as closely as Booth asks us to, turns out to be another kind of partition. A partition that partakes of union, of *communion* in partition, of the pleasures Wordsworth refers to, the almost sexual pleasure one takes in similitude and dissimilitude, one-ness and two-ness. Two be and not two be.

To help us as he launched into his reading of the double-cherry passage Booth had handed out a two-sided, dark-cherry-colored, nearly purple sheet of paper with the passage and his notations on it.

When Booth sent me a copy of the paper, he included his reading of the double-cherry passage typographically entwined with his ecstatic annotation, one might say, and I realized that what I was looking at was a kind of musical score. Booth had turned the passage into a Mozartian score entwining his own voice with Shakespeare. Critic and poet like a double cherry on one stem.

I loved reading Booth's annotated version of the passage with its white-on-black bracketed highlighting. And one of the first things that leapt out at me, the strenuous impertinence to beat all strenuous impertinence, the conspicuous irrelevance to beat all conspicuous irrelevance, was that line, line 203, where Helena begins to unfold her schoolgirl memories:

We, Hermia, like two artificial gods,
Have with our needles created both one flower . . .

Artificial gods? Surely, Shakespeare is not merely speaking of schoolgirls doing needlework patterns when he puts this lofty notion in Helena's words.

Artificial gods? Again, this is one of the passages in which Shakespeare the writer seems to be cruising along working up some schoolgirl memories and suddenly drifts into a meditation on art itself as a kind of godlike, if artificial, creation, an abiding preoccupation in more explicit passages.

But this is not the limit of the artificial godhood invoked. Looking at Booth's annotation one's attention is focused on the strange, strenuous leap from the mundane to the mythological and the theological. It's a young girl describing her prepubescent friendship but in terms that are almost shocking in the ferocity of their coming together:

As if our hands, our sides, voices, and minds
Had been incorporate. So we grew together,
Like to a double cherry, seeming parted,
But yet an union in partition . . .

That double-cherry image: it's a half-formed embryonic twin, it carries suggestion of sweet communion, but also Siamese-twin monstrousness, of a beautiful unified identity and yet a confusion of parts. Concord in discord? Discord in concord? Both/and?

It invokes all the Ovidian metamorphic stories in which, for instance, Daphne is turned into a tree to escape rape by Apollo. But here the metamorphic union is not one forced by fear but formed by some sublime form of love that only "artificial gods" can create and achieve.

Booth has found a passage that one could easily pass by and made us look at something rich and strange: something that seems to link birth, sexuality and creativity with the dramatist as artificial god who embroiders the fates of his characters in the needlepoint of his pen and ink. (A very similar figure linking needlepoint and writing appears in *Pericles:* Marina "would with sharp needle wound / The cambric, which she made more sound by hurting it." She makes holes into a whole.) And links creativity to sexuality—or at least the Wordsworthian sexual pleasure the mind takes in similitude and dissimilitude.

In other words an absolutely bottomless meditation on human creativity, natural creation, sex and drama subverts or disrupts the ostensible insipid purpose of the passage. Strenuous impertinence! Conspicuous irrelevance! They are a double cherry themselves.

Would I have noticed this in a lifetime of reading and seeing the *Dream* if Stephen Booth had not annotated it in his Mozartian score of the double-cherry passage? Perhaps, but I doubt I would have glimpsed its depths without Booth's prompting. It's what he does better and with greater grace and restraint than other close readers. It's one more instance of why I find myself grateful for his Isaac Stern–like reading and playing skill. Why he's the un-Bloom.

A double cherry of course is also another Shakespearean meditation on twinship, imperfectly divided, identical and yet with separate identities. Booth seems to sense, and one senses it in Booth's attention to it, that in the double-cherry passage, in the double-cherry image, we are very close to some primal root of Shakespeare's vision, one that *might*—if one were to give in to the temptation of biographical speculation—be traceable to his own primal experience of twinship, the birth of his male and female twins, Hamnet and Judith, when he was just twenty-one. If so, it transcends biographical fact to become what Wallace Stevens called "supreme fiction."

And then Booth concludes his amazing ten-minute talk on "the witty partition" with a paragraph that is purely Boothian, one in which he finds, in an apparently casual obscenity, the relationship between "hole" and "whole"—the nothingness and the infinitude Peter Brook had spoken of:

"The electricity built up in *A Midsummer Night's Dream* by interplay of ideas relative to the word 'part' is so strong that I am tempted to suggest—although ultimately I am just prudent enough not to suggest—that Wall as partition and the syllable 'whole' (as opposed to a part) flickers behind Thisby's cheerfully obscene 'I kiss the wall's hole, not your lips at all.' "

"Hole"/"whole": they are like a double cherry themselves.

EMPSON: QUANTUM AND CORNSTARCH

But now let us pause, here in the Blue Ridge foothills, where it will be recalled Booth was disclosing all this in an astonishingly compressed ten minutes on the Blackfriars stage. Pause for a moment of intellectual history that might help place Booth in the twentieth-century tradition of close reading and its evolution to "reader reception."

It's an evolution that might better be put in perspective by Booth's response to another gaffe I made in conversation with him. A well-meaning gaffe, to be sure, but one that elicited an unexpectedly revealing reply.

Since I was such an admirer of William Empson's collected *Essays on Shakespeare,* and of the critical method Empson embodied in *Seven Types of Ambiguity* and *Some Versions of Pastoral* and *The Structure of Complex Words,* I made the mistake of asking Booth during a break in the conference how much Empson had been an influence on his own approach. Why this turned out to be a gaffe will become apparent in a moment. But first, for those unfamiliar with Empson, perhaps the best, most novel recent way of explaining the virtual revolution Empson created in literary studies in the twentieth century is the comparison the British Shakespearean Jonathan Bate (author of *The Genius of Shakespeare*) made between Empson's vision of literary ambiguity and the contemporaneous vision of Cambridge quantum physicists of uncertainty in particle and wave theory.

It is ironic, and perhaps not accidental, Bate suggested in *The Genius of Shakespeare,* that William Empson developed his approach to Shakespeare, to literature in general, in the 1920s and '30s, at the same time the Cambridge physicists were working out the paradoxical, ambiguous implications of quantum theory. Both intellectual movements partook, Bate suggested, of a new version of ambiguity: not the usual "either/or ambiguity" but "both/and ambiguity."

I thought it was one of the most illuminating conjectures on intellectual history I'd come across. In physics, the Cambridge adepts who then included Wolfgang Pauli, Paul Dirac and other disciples of the Copenhagen school of Niels Bohr, were wrestling with the troubling paradoxical discovery that the phenomenon of the quantum they all believed in, the infinitesimal discrete unit of energy, could appear at times as *both* a particle and a wave depending on when it was measured (to oversimplify a *lot*). Should the quantum be called a particle, or a wave? No, the Cambridge physicists said, not either/or. Rather, both/and: both particle *and* wave. Bate touches more lightly on the uncertainty principle (aware of the temptation to make overreaching metaphors from mathematics) which in some versions postulated that in certain circumstances a quantum—an electron circling an atom for instance—has no definable, absolutely determinable position but rather just exists as a cloud of probabilities, a haze of uncertainty about where it might actually be. Like the shifting meanings of a word in shifting contexts. Like Lear's actual dimensions obscured in a cloud of cornstarch.

Looking back over the history of Shakespeare criticism, Shakespeare scholarship, it's possible to see just how important a figure Empson was. Until Empson, so much of Shakespeare criticism was glorification of Shakespeare, about his "greatness" and the greatness of his characters. It was about how he told us everything we needed to know about human nature and human character. About the fine sentiments, the exemplary lessons, embodied in his plays which so faithfully reflected human emotions and universal truths and morality. Up until Empson, Shakespeare was celebrated in "the external beauty of holiness," as the Anglican church formulation has it, a line used in defending the spirituality of beautiful cathedrals.

Up until Empson, Shakespearean criticism was in effect much like Newtonian mechanics. It revealed grand truths about the proper order of a stable universe, and the emotional constellations within us. Before quantum theory opened up the strange world of subatomic particles not dreamed of before, where familiar concepts like causality and determinism no longer prevailed.

Similarly Empson might be said to have taken us beneath the Newtonian level of Shakespeare's themes and characters and sentiments and messages to some destabilizing subatomic level within the language, where strange charms prevailed, the kind of rich and strange charms that are, more than any lofty sententiousness, what defines what is most uniquely Shakespearean. The advent of Theory put Empsonian close reading in eclipse, but it's a heartening, hopeful development that, in some quarters at least, Empson's reputation, his contribution, is receiving renewed recognition. There were always those who continued to value his readings. When I visited the brilliant critic Christopher Ricks in his Cambridge, Massachusetts, home there was a picture of Empson on the wall of his sitting room where we talked. Ricks along with Booth is one of the most illuminating contemporary practitioners of Empsonian close reading.

For a long time, though, Empson was spoken of mainly in terms of his eccentricities: the unusual Mandarin-style neck-beard he grew while teaching literature in China during World War II. I've spoken of his obsessive, scorching hostility to Christian doctrine, most particularly the "Doctrine of Satisfaction" (which gives the lie to one of the chief critiques of Empson-derived "New Criticism"—that it was somehow a Christianizing movement with all that searching for Christ-symbols and the like).

But most of all you heard the naughty anecdotes. One Cambridge graduate of the sixties told me he heard that the reason Empson was expelled from Cambridge was that his "bedder" (the now obsolete term for a servant who made up student rooms) found a copious quantity of condoms in Empson's bedroom. Another anecdote had Empson, upon his return to the United Kingdom after the war, setting up unorthodox housekeeping in which he slept in a tent in his living room. Is this, as they say, "too much information"? Perhaps, but Empson is a great character and these anecdotes, curiously, conjure up an actual engagement with the forms and varieties of pleasure, which are at the heart of Empsonian and Boothian close reading.

I recall being surprised and pleased to discover at a Shakespeare Association of America scholarly convocation in April 2000 a "paper session" devoted to Empson along with two other exceptional literary figures who'd written on Shakespeare: T. S. Eliot and Oscar Wilde. The session was entitled ironically (I think) "Before Theory"—as if Theory were somehow the great divide between the nonprofessional, unscientific if nonetheless occasionally artful criticism that came before it, and the purportedly great theoretical achievements of Derrida, DeMan and Foucault that followed after.

Nonetheless I celebrated this appreciation of Empson in a *New York Times Book Review* essay, as a hopeful harbinger of a return from Theory to close reading in the academy. I may have been too optimistic about the larger trend but I think there's no doubt that Bate, for instance, has been successful in reviving interest in Empson. And it is my fond hope to help in a small way to do for Stephen Booth what Bate did for Empson.

There are differences, of course.

Booth is not Empson, or—as he says in his cryptically ambiguous, loving-and-chiding way—"Empson was the only human being who didn't have the advantage of reading Empson." Not quite true, unless he's portraying Empson the way Ben Jonson portrayed Shakespeare: as someone who raced through first drafts and never glanced back to reread or revise. (Empson sometimes *could* seem to write with irascible haste.)

Rather Booth's critique of Empson has to do with Empson not being Empsonian enough: rather than unfolding multiple simultaneous explanations—a haze of possible meanings like the haze of possible positions of a particle—around a word or phrase, Empson often (too often in Booth's view) unfolded the possibilities only to collapse them to a singularity (as Shakespeare calls it in *Twelfth Night:* "the trick of singularity"). Because Empson—"not having the advantage of having read Empson"—thinks he knows the one, singularly correct, interpretation.

But even if Empson *were* Empson to Booth's specifications, Booth goes beyond Empson or takes Empson to a different level, one might say.

While Empson unfolds the ambiguities, sometimes not merely seven types but seven versions of each type, they are nonetheless an almost pictorial array, beautiful but static. Booth's "ideational static" is dynamic, one might say. Not stasis, but rather composed of interacting patterns of interference (or inference). What Booth seems to sense is the pulsating, flickering, mutually subverting relationships between the ambiguities. A dynamic, dyadic alternating current of connections between them, shades of meaning, fluctuations of coloration like the foliage leaves flipping their varying colors back and forth. Empson gone electric.

"Flickering," "pulsating," "vacillating"—these words come up often in Booth's criticism.

Boothian ambiguity is then exponentially more complex, a quantum leap more complex than Empson's both/and. Not a contradiction but an enhancement of Empson at his best, less crankily reductive. Booth, it could be said, puts Empson's ambiguities in motion, sees the Sonnets for instance as perpetual motion machines.

In Booth's *Essay on Shakespeare's Sonnets* and his Yale edition with its four hundred pages of footnotes and commentary one sees how the pulsating ambiguity and the pleasures it offers are what attracts Booth to the Sonnets. Boothian ambiguity flirts with the possibility of endless, bottomless polysemy; it gestures at the Sonnets as endless echo chambers of combinations and permutations of possibilities; dizzying, even threatening, holes in the world.

It is one of the critiques of Booth's approach that he sometimes does seem to go *too* far toward suggesting an infinitude of abundance in the fourteen-line humming machines of pleasure that are the Sonnets. Booth's multiplicity may seem "inexhaustible," but it is not as if *anything* goes, but *many* things go, many more than we can imagine, perhaps many more than we can exhaust in a lifetime.

And then, with all that in play Booth compounds the complexity by introducing a second player, in addition to the sonneteer—the reader—and focusing on the experience of reading or seeing Shakespeare. Here he joins two of his contemporaries, brilliant close readers Harry Berger Jr. and Stanley Fish (before Fish became a postmodernist contrarian), in shifting from close reading of the poem to close reading of the *reader,* of reading itself. I remember being seduced in college by Berger's reading of the "birth of Venus" passage in Spenser's *Faerie Queene,* in which Berger, in effect, contends the passage is really about the reader experiencing the "birth of Venus," i.e., lust, while *reading* about the birth of Venus.

And then there was Stanley Fish, before he became a crusading relativist, in his brilliant book on Milton, *Surpris'd by Sin.* In which Fish makes the surprisingly persuasive case that it is Milton's recurrent ploy in his poem to seduce the reader into an appreciation of beauty, particularly of landscape, flesh and classical literary allusions, and then to shame the reader for having succumbed—for having fallen into a trap, or trapdoor, just as Adam and Eve fell. Seduced by Satan's promise of knowledge and beauty: surprised by sin.

What I didn't realize, what will make this sound like a gaffe to those in the know, those who possess Booth's hard-to-find *Essay on Shakespeare's Sonnets,* is that Booth made his initial reputation as a scholar in that book with a fairly scathing critique of Empson's famous interpretation of Sonnet 94. I know, you didn't see it on the front pages of the tabs; it barely registered in the literary quarterlies, but in certain circles, which, alas, did not include me, this was *big news.*

In any case, it was something I only learned later when I got my hands on the elusive book, and so I thought I was complimenting Booth when I brought up Empson. We were having coffee and doughnuts one morning on the mezzanine level of the Blackfriars Playhouse between a couple of the ten-minute scholarly paper sessions and I asked him if he thought himself in a way an avatar of the Empsonian tradition.

"Well, I read and would very much admire Empson if only Empson would read Empson."

I thought I caught on to what he was suggesting, knowing how peremptory Empson could be in his judgment about things.

"You're saying that Empson says he's all for ambiguity but in fact he thinks he knows the one true or truer meaning."

Booth nodded assent.

Here is Sonnet 94, the issue over which Booth attacked Empson (and everybody else). It has long been one of the most elusive and enigmatic of all the 154 and that's saying something. Particularly hard to discover is the speaker's attitude toward the subject of the sonnet, the enigmatic, elusive sort "that have pow'r to hurt, and will do none."

They that have pow'r to hurt, and will do none,
That do not do the thing they most do show,
Who moving others, are themselves as stone,
Unmoved, cold, and to temptation slow,
They rightly do inherit heaven's graces,
And husband nature's riches from expense;
They are the lords and owners of their faces,
Others but stewards of their excellence.
The summer's flow'r is to the summer sweet,
Though to itself it only live and die,
But if that flow'r with base infection meet,
The basest weed outbraves his dignity:
For sweetest things turn sourest by their deeds;
Lilies that fester smell far worse than weeds.

"Recent interest in 94," Booth wrote, "got its start from a lengthy account of the sonnet by William Empson in 1933. All of Empson's comments on the poem are instructed by his assumption of not only the justice but the comprehensiveness of the following précis:

" 'The best people are indifferent to temptation and detached from the world; nor is this state selfish, because they do good by unconscious influence, like the flower. You must be like them; you are quite like them already. But even the best people must be continually on their guard, because they become the worst, just as the pure and detached lily smells worst, once they fall from their perfection.' "

Booth proceeds to describe and dismiss this and all the other major critics of Sonnet 94 for the past fifty years in his characteristic waspish style.

"These are remarkable paragraphs," he says of one critic (not Empson), "first for introducing the obvious relevance of the Sermon on the Mount into criticism of this sonnet, and secondly for being incoherent."

What he objects to in each reading, including Empson's, is its tendency to be reductive: to reduce the contradictory characterization of the subject of the sonnet—"They that have pow'r to hurt, and will do none"—to either/or, to a single synopsis or paraphrase. To decide whether to see the poem as either praising or damning the person in question.

Speaking of whom I thought it interesting that Booth should choose this particular sonnet, this particular enigmatic personality for the centerpiece of his analysis of how to read the Sonnets, considering how much like Booth the figure in Sonnet 94 is. Cool, detached, the figure in Sonnet 94 is one of the most enigmatic characters in all Shakespeare. If Booth is Empson minus the certainty, the figure in 94 is uncertainty personified. Uncertain as well is Shakespeare's attitude toward the character. He or she is beautiful enough to *harm* those vulnerable to physical beauty. And yet is praised at first for his or her unwillingness to use that beauty to its full dangerous effect. He or she withholds his or her self not out of altruism but out of coldness. Is this person cruel to be kind or just (inadvertently) kind because cold?

Biographers have focused on this contradictory treatment of the person in Sonnet 94—the way the Sonnet ranges from the serene compliment to the desperate warning about its object—as the closest thing we have to a portrait of the man or woman who comes closest to driving Shakespeare mad in "real life."

It is something we will probably never know, although it was fascinating to me to think of how much Booth resembled the figure in Sonnet 94. He had a certain serene aloofness to him that was intellectually appealing but he did have the power to hurt: he could have ridiculed my as yet untutored appreciation of his intellectual worth, and yet gracefully did not, except in the sense of a kind of wry irony: "I like that fellow: he thinks I'm smart." But such biographical speculations about Booth and Shakespeare and "They that have pow'r to hurt" are beyond proof or disproof and not the focus of Booth's concern in Sonnet 94. Booth doesn't even accept the need to believe it's about a lover:

"On no internal evidence whatever . . . Empson paraphrases the poem as a direct statement to and about the beloved. The assumption is unwarranted but it's entirely understandable."

To challenge Empson—and most previous readers of the poem—on such a basic point was daring for a Ph.D. student, and to bring such confidence to the assertion is surprising.

But when Booth looks at Sonnet 94 he sees something more fundamental going on than the question of Shakespeare's love life. Again it's not Shakespeare's heart, it is his *art* he's after, the "esthetic nuts and bolts" of these fourteen-line engines that produce dizzying pleasure and disorientation. The mechanics of Shakespeare's spell.

Here is how he describes the state the sonnet seeks to create and how it creates it:

" 'They that have pow'r to hurt' should not endear themselves to a reader first coming upon them," Booth begins. But 'They that have pow'r to hurt, and will do none' sounds like the stuff of heroes. Having the power to hurt makes them sound bad or at least dangerous; not using it sounds good.

"This first line describes a dichotomy in the nature of its subject. The only two qualities it presents for 'they' are *irrevocably connected and also antipathetic* [italics mine]. The line also begins a process of creating a state of mind in the reader in which *contrary but inseparable* reactions uneasily coexist."

This is worth repeating because I believe it may contain the skeleton key to Booth's vision of what the Sonnets are about and how they work:

"The line also begins a process of creating a state of mind in the reader in which contrary but inseparable reactions uneasily coexist."

Contrary but inseparable. The double cherry of discourse.

Here in a Shakespearean nutshell is the effect that Booth focuses on in the Sonnets. Particularly in his hard-to-find *Essay.* And I'm going to digress from my series of gaffes down in Staunton to the moment a couple of months later when I finally got my hands on a copy of Booth's *Essay on Shakespeare's Sonnets.* I found within it, at last, not just the heart of Booth's vision of the secret play within the Sonnets; I found what finally seemed to explain what happened to me in that long-ago moment at Yale when I found myself temporarily destabilized by one sonnet in particular.

What Booth is suggesting about Sonnet 94 is that it is not so much about love, although it may be about love, as it is about creating in the reader that state of "contrary but inseparable" feelings, the uncertainty of stance in the reader, the flickering forth and back, the destabilization that is characteristic of the state of *being* in love, while being uncertain about whether one *is* loved, one of the most exquisitely tortured, divided, ecstatic and maddening states known to man or woman. Or so I hear.

Again it's something he almost tosses off offhandedly: "the effect of this byplay on a series of poems [the Sonnets] concerned with unsteady relationships is worth some consideration." I love the offhand characterization of all love as "unsteady relationships."

Some consideration indeed: to read the Sonnets attentively is to feel implicated in the process of experiencing the dizzying instability of being in love, the particular delirious instability of the ground shifting under one's feet (the earth moving?). The ground of meaning, the ground of being, the ground of being oneself, the ground of being *one self.* Booth repeatedly argued to me that that's not what "all the fuss is about," the thematic connection between what effects reading the Sonnets have on you and what effect love has on you; he thinks the former—the state of being in the Sonnets, not the state of being in love—is what "all the fuss is about," but he doesn't dismiss the latter, merely characterizes love dismissively as an "unsteady relationship."

When I finally got hold of Booth's *Essay on Shakespeare's Sonnets* I slowly began to get the sense of just how infinitely resonant, on a microcrystalline level one might say, the Sonnets appear through his shifting lenses.

Even in the *sound,* in the "subliminal alliterations" he finds "the smallest scale in which the Sonnets exhibit the principle of simultaneous likeness and difference," the Wordsworthian sexual pleasure "in the apprehension of unity and division is phonetic [in the] pulsating alliteration as well. . . . Time after time in the Sonnets a pair of sounds will come together and pull apart."

"Coming together and pulling apart": yes, there is an obvious analogy, but on another level what's interesting is his invocation of "pulsation": the way the microcosm of each sonnet somehow partakes of some universal vision of cosmic pulsation that animates the universe of language—and the universe of love.

Pulsation: it's that sense of flickering from one-ness to two-ness, from being to nonbeing. From "to be" to "not to be." It partakes of something the director John Barton calls fundamental to Shakespearean language: antithesis. But a *pulsation;* not a static opposition but a mutually subversive ever-shifting pulsation between thesis and antithesis.

It crops up again a few pages later in his *Essay on Shakespeare's Sonnets* when Booth speaks of one of his favorite obscure Greek figures of speech, one he finds repeatedly in Shakespeare, particularly the Sonnets—*antanaclasis* (the rebound), a figure in which as Booth puts it "a repeated word shifts from one to another of its meanings as in 'to England will I steal and there I'll steal.' "

The use of *antanaclasis* in the Sonnets "is remarkable," says Booth, because Shakespeare uses it constantly. *Antanaclasis,* "like pulsating alliteration, evokes a sense of insecurity, of flux, of motion. . . ." There's that pulsing alliteration again.

Here's another line I found in the *Essay* that led me to an eye-opening revelation about what Booth was getting at:

"Like so many of his predecessors, Shakespeare compares the condition of a lover to that of a state in civil war. Unlike his predecessors Shakespeare evokes in his reader something very like the condition he talks about."

But a different kind of civil war: not the usual one in which one is constantly changing sides, not shifting loyalties but shifting identities. To extend the civil war metaphor one goes from blue to gray, say, without changing uniforms. Or as Russ McDonald's annotation on that page had it: "Not only do we learn about mutability, we participate in mutability." (It also makes one think of the whole sweep of Shakespeare's history plays, especially the ones about the internal civil war as being, if not a love story exactly, then having more in common with the Sonnets' internal dividedness than one imagined.)

Here are two final Boothian remarks from the *Essay on Shakespeare's Sonnets* which at last made me realize that what Booth was talking about was the cumulative effects of subtle disorientation and displacement or double-placement I felt at the blackboard at Yale:

"The style of the Sonnets recreates the experience of paradox, of coping with things in more than one frame of reference, not for, but *in* the reader."

In the reader. A name at last for what happened to me at the blackboard at Yale as the chalk rebounded from "absent" to "present." *Antanaclasis! Antanaclasis* in a classroom, no less. Somehow I felt a pulsing, shifting sensation as I was present-absent, absent-present, here-there, here *and* there simultaneously.

It was one of the first things I asked of Booth when I finally spoke to him: Was this strange experience of mine what the Sonnets were *about* in some way? That was the impression one got from reading the *Essay,* that it was the purpose, the design of the shifting subliminal pulsations, shifts of frameworks, of readings and of ambiguities, the harmonics and dissonances of sound patterns, the way the couplets were reframed by the quatrains, the quatrains by the sestets, the sestets by the octaves—each part by the remaining whole in a never-ending dance of possible (nonrandom) significations—that it was the purpose of all this to create the sudden surprising moment of ec-stasis, the experience I felt at the blackboard at Yale. It's wordplay beyond wordplay, it's something more complex, meta-wordplay, the *play* of wordplay, echoing intricately through the fourteen lines and the other 153 sonnets for that matter.

Samuel Johnson famously decreed Shakespearean wordplay and puns as Shakespeare's "fatal Cleopatra"—the love affair for which he abandons reason for rapture as Antony did for Cleopatra.

Booth doesn't see Shakespearean wordplay as a failing, a whoring after a linguistic temptress, but as being at the heart of the experience the Sonnets re-create within the reader. Even if he doesn't want to come out and call it love, I do.

The wordplay is designed to manipulate the mind of the reader, whipsaw it back and forth, "keep the mind in a constant motion" as Booth puts it, in a state of "rebound," *antanaclasis.* The way I felt when the chalk was rebounding off the blackboard at Yale and I found myself rebounding between two separate selves in effect, feeling an almost physical shift in state, in identity between self and the absent lover. A kind of exchange of being with another being that is at the heart of the experience of love. And sex. Or so I hear.

Booth remarks that "Sonnet 36 rests on the Neoplatonic commonplaces that the lover and the beloved are one, and that the lover *becomes* the beloved. . . ." (italics mine). It seemed to me he was being a bit too casually dismissive in calling them "commonplaces." I found it immensely uncommon to experience, through the reading of a fourteen-line poem, the kind of communion and separation the poem was purportedly about.

Booth says the sonnet "rests" on "Neoplatonic commonplaces," but in Booth's vision the Sonnets are never at rest; each sonnet is always pulsating in and out of phase with a haze of possible or rather multiple meanings. Something pulsating, pleasurable, sensual and sexual in a way—way beyond Wordsworth's polite metaphor of sexuality: "the pleasure the mind takes in similitude and dissimilitude."

Booth's "esthetic nuts and bolts" of the Sonnets are finely tuned to manipulate us with ever-so-subtle jolts into a state of exalted "athleticism," if not a state of grace, indeed often a state of *disgrace* ("When in disgrace with Fortune and men's eyes . . . ," Sonnet 29) in the reader, something pulsating, vacillating, pleasurable and frightening, something like love, something like sex. The Sonnets are meant to manipulate us like poetic geishas.

PLEASURE FROM DISPLEASURE

Or so I thought when I finally got to ask Booth whether what happened to me at Yale was what he was describing in the *Essay.* In order to get to that moment I had to read the *Essay on Shakespeare's Sonnets* thoroughly and then I read three other essays Booth sent me in addition to "The Witty Partition" paper, the better he said to represent the latest direction in his critical thinking.

But finally several months after the Shenandoah conference there we were on the phone—him in Berkeley, me in my New York apartment recording with his permission the conversation that I had prepared for for months since I met him in Virginia. I would also have lunch with him later that summer in New York. At first he had seemed as reluctant to talk as I had felt unprepared, but he mentioned reading my piece on *Hamlet* texts in *The New Yorker* and it may have convinced him my intentions were serious, that it was no shame necessarily that "that fellow thinks I'm smart." Still I felt the same trepidation and humility talking to him I'd felt with Peter Brook.

In any case at some point I described my experience at Yale to Booth.

"I think I understand what you mean," he said a bit gingerly. "But the thing that you need to remember is that this has only happened once, it happened with something that you presumably knew well just before you did this, and the big difference between what you experienced and what I'm talking about is that you became *conscious* of it and that in Shakespeare one is unconscious of it."

Unconscious? "And yet it has at least some kind of subconscious effect, no?" I asked him.

"What you had at the chalkboard and what the Sonnets would be like if one experiences them as I describe them in the notes, is the difference between a Shakespearean play and a Brecht play. In Brecht you become consciously aware of stuff in a way that you never will be again."

I'm not sure I agree the experience is unrepeatable, but the distinction Booth is making is an important one. He is, I believe, saying that all the super-subtle effects he elucidates from the shifting correspondences, echoes and resonances within the Sonnets primarily affect the mind at a kind of subliminal if not subconscious level. These wicked little engines of pleasure don't even disclose their effect to our conscious minds; it is in the cumulative unconscious tickling of the brain that we feel ourselves elevated to some new level of extremely refined and subtle pleasure, although we're not quite aware (or conscious) of why or how. What happened to me at Yale, Booth was saying, was that I became suddenly aware of the mechanics of flight in the midst of being transported. The way a cartoon character who dashes mistakenly off a cliff keeps rotating his legs until he realizes he's "running" on thin air.

Again I'm not sure if I entirely agree here with this "unheard melodies are the sweetest" argument. I'm not sure either that it has only happened once to me; it is my suspicion that these things break through into the conscious realm more often than not, the more one reads Shakespeare, and that it is these moments of apprehension—moments on the threshold of comprehension—that define what makes Shakespeare exceptional.

But is it a purely gymnastic, athletic exercise of the mind as Booth argues?

For want of a better metaphor, I'd say that Booth's is a balletomane's appreciation for Shakespeare. For the balletomane, the story, the theme, are of less significance than the balletic leaps, the pas de deux of words and phrases, the lightning-like leaps and shifts and relationships not just in the realm of the stage, but on the stage of the spectator's mind—the extent to which reading Shakespeare lifts the mind into a balletic realm.

He doesn't dismiss the importance of theme in Shakespeare, it's just not for Booth an explanation of what "all the fuss is about."

This emerged in our discussion of the *Henry IV, Part 2* paper, one of the three recent works he sent to me. Booth suggests in that paper that audiences are "likely to find themselves persistently trying to, failing to, and feeling somehow guilty in failing to, respond the way they did in Part One," the far more celebratory and joyful first Falstaff play.

Booth doesn't find this an esthetic fault so much as he feels that it embodies in some way the themes of disappointment and rejection that characterize the play. Again the trapdoor, the hole, makes for a greater *whole.*

"Shakespeare appears to have been fascinated by audiences' generically or locally derived expectations and assumptions and by the theatrical energy to be had from playing *his* play off against the one the audience manufactures and tries to see [italics mine]. . . . *Henry IV. Part 2* is merely the most perverse and vexing of Shakespeare's many experiments with perversity." Shakespeare loves to use "the rhetorical potential available in friction between what an audience wants and expects and what it gets"—the breaking of implicit dramatic promises.

Booth typically tosses off, almost as an aside, the thematic implications of this rhetorical and dramaturgic strategy: "the breaking of promises that were never quite made [i.e., Hal's promises to Falstaff] is also a topic of this play."

Just as love or "unsteady relationships" just happen to be a topic of the Sonnets.

I thought this was a remarkably astute, even eye-opening reading, one that linked the structural tics of the play to its deepest theme, a genuine achievement of close reading.

But Booth almost comically downplays it: it's "also a topic of this play."

Later in our phone conversation when I asked Booth why he tossed off this thematic connection between formal and emotional disappointments he told me, "I don't want to say that it's not worth paying attention to, but it doesn't relate to the question I'm always trying to answer: *what's all the fuss about.* Why do we care so much about Shakespeare. And I don't think an echo in the experience of the play *of* the experience of the characters has anything to do with why we value it, why we make such a fuss about it."

It was exhilarating finally talking to Booth at length all this time after meeting him. And after months of preparation, not round-the-clock, but reading and thinking about why his approach to Shakespeare resonated with me.

It was fascinating hearing his early experiences with Shakespeare—the cloud of cornstarch, etc.—and even more surprising when I asked him what was the genesis of his approach to the Sonnets and he told me it all had to do with reading a George Herbert poem "Love (3)" in his sophomore year at Harvard.

"Reading *The Temple* [the book of poems climaxed by "Love (3)"] made me feel the hair stand up on my neck," he told me. "I had been trained to argue the essence of a poem away—its effect."

At this point I raised the question that had always troubled me about the logic of New Criticism and close reading: Is there any limit to the polysemous effects one can find, in say the Sonnets?

He slightly evades the question by saying, "I'm usually not concerned with that—with meanings or multiple meanings, but with the experience, what reading does to you. I leave meaning to the man with the note at the foot of the page to tell you what it means."

"Okay, forget meaning," I say, "what about the 'ideational static' you spoke of in your 'Witty Partition' talk?" I read him the quote about this "ideational static": "substantively insignificant, substantively inadmissible, substantively accidental linguistic configurations . . . are exciting to the minds it *plays across* and probably brings those listening minds a sense of possessing and casually, effortlessly exercising an athleticism beyond that imaginable in human beings. . . . 'More than cool reason ever comprehends.' "

"Is *that* what you're talking about when you talk about 'what all the fuss is about' over Shakespeare?"

"Yes," he said. "You know I think I got everything important I ever said into that talk."

And here's where he introduced the pole-vaulting-on-the-moon metaphor.

"This athleticism you speak of, is it available to everyone who reads Shakespeare?"

"My guess," he said, "is that it's something like pole-vaulting on the moon. Pole-vaulting is something you can't imagine being able to do. Or at least I can't imagine being able to do. I once took a pole and ran toward that little pocket [where you're supposed to plant the pole] and ran right past the little pocket. While with Shakespeare you feel the ability to apprehend or comprehend what you can't possibly apprehend or comprehend otherwise."

His insistence that this experience is available to all, not just to superattentive readers like himself, raises an interesting philosophical question about close reading: If a tree—or an allusion, say—falls in the forest and no one notices, or no one notices it but the nearby superb close reader, can it be said to *be* a feature of the poem or of its ordinary reader? Aren't there certain kinds of violinists, certain kinds of listeners, who can hear things in Beethoven others might not?

In his passage on athleticism, Booth mentioned the mind reading Shakespeare being capable of attaining the graceful leaping pirouettes of Michael Jordan.

"But everybody's not Michael Jordan in that respect, right?" I asked Booth.

"I think that everybody *is* Michael Jordan."

But what about repeated rereading, rereading in cycles? Doesn't that result in your becoming a better athlete, so to speak?

"No," he says, stretching the metaphor: "it may make you a better *sports reporter.*" That is, better at articulating what has always been happening. Here he shifts metaphors to make an important distinction.

"It's important to me," he said, "to get you to understand the difference between audience experience and critical perception."

He chooses a startlingly homespun mechanical metaphor to illustrate this point.

"It's like the difference between riding in a car and being an automobile mechanic. The *experience* of riding in a car is not much different for someone who could take the engine apart and put it back together, from someone who didn't have any idea how the engine ran."

Before I could object he anticipated my objection:

"I get people a lot who will say, 'But automobile mechanics can *hear* what's going on.' But I don't think it's a great difference."

Of course he says that from the perspective of someone who has one of the most finely tuned ears for—to extend the mechanic metaphor—what's going on under the hood, beneath the surface of the lines.

I would say that here Booth is being not so much disingenuous as, I think, genuinely modest. He doesn't want to say that his intimate knowledge of the esthetic nuts and bolts that make the car (or verse) run makes his experience superior in any way. But I just don't think—not after hearing his tour de force disquisition on "The Witty Partition"—that this is true.

I'd pose against his automobile mechanic metaphor my violinist one. That the experience of an audience hearing Isaac Stern play Mozart is exalted, but not quite as exalted as the experience Isaac Stern has playing Mozart.

(Recently as I was writing this passage I ran into Brian Kulick, who was directing *Twelfth Night* at New York's Shakespeare-in-the-Park Delacorte Theatre. I told him about Booth's auto mechanic contention and what Kulick said, picking up on the surprisingly useful, if unpromising-sounding, metaphor, was that as a director what *he* found was that the nature of the *car* changed in the process of rehearsal and preview.)

LOVE (3)

At this point I sought to shift gears, so to speak, and see what Booth thought of my theory of Theory, my belief that close reading brought many too close to unbearable pleasure and led to the flight into Theory, which offered the comfort or the illusion of distance.

"I don't know," he began cautiously. "I certainly believe that about the distancing. . . ."

But, he said, he wasn't sure close reading brought people closer; close readers were really close interpreters, and he felt that where close reading went wrong was in its tendency to search for a single reductive interpretation: close reading that closes out rather than multiplying the possibilities. Because it was this multiplicity of possibilities that was responsible for the effect of, if not pleasure, the *physical response* great poetry gave him.

Here is where George Herbert's "Love (3)" comes in. Booth told me he'd had a transformative experience reading "Love (3)," a poem he then proceeded to recite for me from memory at a rapid-fire pace over the telephone line.

Herbert was one of those knotty seventeenth-century "Metaphysical poets" whose championing by T. S. Eliot brought him back from obscurity in the first half of the twentieth century. Herbert is the author of difficult, resonant, religious poems—piety that managed to be shocking, in the way Emily Dickinson can be shocking, in a brilliantly compressed, almost sneaky way. A poet of trapdoors if ever there was one.

"Love (3)" comes at the very close of a book of nearly two hundred short poems called *The Temple.* As is perhaps not necessary to say, it is the third poem with the name "Love" and because the experience became the basis for Booth's reading of Shakespeare, I want to reproduce it:

Love bade me welcome: yet my soul drew back,
    Guilty of dust and sin.
But quick-eyed Love, observing me grow slack
    From my first entrance in,
Drew nearer to me, sweetly questioning
    If I lacked anything.

A guest, I answered, worthy to be here:
    Love said: you shall be he.
I, the unkind, ungrateful? Ah, my dear,
    I cannot look on thee.
Love took my hand, and smiling did reply,
    Who made the eyes but I?

Truth, Lord; but I have marred them; let my shame
Go where it doth deserve.
And know you not, says Love, who bore the blame?
My dear, then I will serve.
You must sit down, says Love, and taste my meat:
So I did sit and eat.

"What *was* it about 'Love (3)'?" I asked Booth.

"It made the hairs on the back of my neck stand up," he repeated.

Not having "Love (3)" at hand, I did not press him about why this poem in particular should have shaped his approach to the Sonnets, but clearly his preoccupation with the physical response engendered by the Sonnets may well have grown out of the effect of reading "Love (3)." And when I had a chance to dig out my copy of George Herbert's collected poems I saw lines there that did it for me and might, I guessed, have done it for Booth.

In particular there was that exchange between the poet and personified Love that went:

I, the unkind, ungrateful? . . .
I cannot look on thee.
Love took my hand, and smiling did reply,
Who made the eyes but I?

Who made the eyes but I? It's Sonnet-like wordplay endowed with a higher Love.

A couple of weeks after our first interview I e-mailed Booth asking him if he could tell me more about his response to "Love (3)." He came back with the demurral that it would take "two hours of fast typing" to even approach his feelings about "Love (3)." He did recall that that year as a college sophomore "I was initiated into a remarkably non-exclusive club for bookish boys [at Harvard] and got drunk for the first time in my life, and that the next day a junior who was newly my fellow member met me at lunch and said, 'You know, Booth, the reason we elected you was because we wanted someone who could talk about George Herbert for two hours without pausing for breath.' "

Is Booth drunk on the Sonnets the way he was drunk on Herbert? I'm not sure; "intoxicated" might be a better word. What's interesting about

Herbert is that his are love poems, like the Sonnets yes, but love poems to a far more reliable, welcoming and dependable lover, namely God. But I saw something else in "Love (3)" I had not seen before—something that seemed to bear upon Booth's critical method: a focus on that which appears *marred,* that which appears strenuously impertinent if not impenitent. And the revelation that that which appears marred can be mended in a transformative way. One that makes for instance an apparently marred passage in Shakespeare, a trapdoor, a hole, the key to its transcendent wholeness.

It perhaps helps elucidate, that difference, what at times is, if not my *problem* with the Sonnets, then my resistance: their ambiguities are so destabilizing that there is no center. No one irritant to become a pearl, but rather a sickly, slippery iridescence. With Herbert, like the fluctuation and nutations in the orbit and spin of the planets, there is a kind of universal gravity at least, at the dependably Newtonian calculable level, prevailing—God's Love—while with the Sonnets, with few exceptions there is an unstable, even fickle, sometimes cold Sun at the center of a haze of probabilities.

But Booth's recollection of drunken ecstasy over "Love (3)" was one I found touching, first because it suggested a side of Booth that is not immediately evident in his reserved, aloof persona. It suggests that he is not the cool sardonic customer of "They that have pow'r to hurt, and will do none."

Another thing that struck me also about Booth's later work can be found in the abstract of his paper on *The Winter's Tale,* when he talks about the way "I've spent a lot of time and ink in the last few years on particular elements in Shakespeare plays that displease us. . . ." On elements that seem unworthy, but looked at through the eyes of Love, or of "Love (3)," one might say, become far more worthy than one could have imagined. "Who made the eyes but I?" Booth, it could be said, is now the one who makes the eyes—envisions the way *we* see—the purported faults and sins of Shakespeare, and how they are "redeemed" by closer reading.

But to return to the question of close reading, Booth takes pains to separate a true love for the text from what has become in his eyes a caricature of true close reading, one that seeks simply to decode a single hidden meaning: creates cosmic mystery only to solve it as if it were an Agatha Christie.

He opposes this search for meaning as "trying to squeeze the juice out and then maybe squeezing the vitamins out of the juice."

Boothian reading is—he doesn't put it this way—but in retrospect after thinking about his love for "Love (3)," I would say Boothian reading is about loving all the "nonsignifying, even insignificant meanings." Especially the insignificant meanings. A redemptive love for the conspicuous irrelevances and the strenuous impertinences of linguistic transgression.

When I read him the passage from his "Witty Partition" paper, his ten-minute summa, the passage about the attraction he has to the "ideational static" in Shakespeare's plays generated by "substantively insignificant configurations," he interrupted me to say, "Did I say insignificant or nonsignifying?" I repeated the quote emphasizing "insignificant."

"Well, I'm glad," he said. (I sensed he thought I got it wrong, which indeed, I may have. But with characteristic charity he turned something marred—my memory—into something stronger.) In some ways one could add to the balletomane metaphor for Boothian reading another analogy: that in his most extreme formulation Booth sees Shakespeare as Moorish art—infinitely filigreed and gracefully echoic, full of intricate beauty but *signifying* nothing—nothing beyond the infinite beyond-signifying beauty of the Cosmos. In a sense *that* signification is at least part of "what the fuss is all about."

To some, even among Booth's most fervent admirers, this can be too extreme. Consider one of the most thoughtful critiques of Booth as expressed by Russ McDonald, whose underlined copy of Booth's *Essay on the Sonnets* I had been reading. In *Shakespeare and the Arts of Language* McDonald writes:

> Stephen Booth argues that "clarification" or "epiphany" or whatever spiritually charged term we choose has little to do with the real value of Shakespeare's use of language. This argument resembles the position taken in his later years by the philosopher Ludwig Wittgenstein: in the *Principia* he called it "the language game"; he proposed that the virtue of language resides chiefly in its power to amuse, and insisted that we should not attempt to overstate its explanatory capacities. For Booth, it is the *experience* of the clarification that matters, the pleasure of making the discovery [the threshold of comprehension!], not the content of the revelation. Process is all. Speaking of the first scene of *Twelfth Night* he contends "that to experience that scene is to be given a small but metaphysically glorious holiday from the limitation of ordinary logic . . . an effectively real holiday from the inherent limitations of the human mind. The artifice of the dramatic language ensures that we never entirely lose ourselves. That we recognize, even as we watch, that we are on holiday, and this double-vision gives the spectator an immense sense of pleasure."

I think Booth would disagree mainly with McDonald's suggestion that Booth completely dismisses "significance." I think for Booth significance is there, significance is *significant;* it's just that significance is just not "what all the fuss is about" in Shakespeare. Or not the only thing.

The fact that Booth could call the end of *Lear* "the most terrifying five minutes in literature" is a response to more than its nonsignifying patterning. It's a deeply humanistic response. But not the only response for Booth. Or even the deepest, most bottomless one.

PORNOGRAPHY AND PEARLS

I dwell on these questions because to me and to others Booth's reading of Shakespeare is often revelatory in the way Peter Brook's direction is. (Indeed Booth told me that he too saw, and he too was electrified by, Brook's *Dream* when he was doing graduate study at Cambridge.) And still influential.

We had a funny exchange on the question of Booth's influence when I pressed Booth on what he'd call what he does.

"If you don't like 'close reading,' what would you call Boothian reading, or is it sui generis?"

"Apparently, yeah," he said laughing, implying the literal meaning of "sui generis"—that he alone did it.

"But it's very influential, isn't it, among smart people?" (Okay: I wince at the question, preserve it only because it evoked a very funny Boothian response.)

"Well, that brings the number of smart people to around three, and I'm married to one," he said, typically self-deprecating and yet simultaneously (both/and) twitting me for including myself in the circle of smart people.

"Well," I said, "there are many others. I just had dinner with Kenneth Gross"—one of the most consistently thoughtful and provocative of a younger generation of scholars—"he'd been down in Staunton and spoke in the same tones as me at how dazzling he thought 'The Witty Partition' talk was. He spoke of the way Booth had the deep focus of one of the great scholars of our age."

"Well," Booth said, "I've got more than my share of admiration and applause but that's different from being influential. You take Jesus," he said dryly. So dryly I broke into laughter, which I think was the intent. "He was widely praised and admired. But *influential*? No." (Great line, no?)

We proceeded to the question of his latest work, his focus on "strenuous impertinence." I asked him if he'd heard the term I'd been using, "conspicuous irrelevance," or who coined it and whether it seemed analogous in some way to his "strenuous impertinence." Booth told me it must have been the coinage of one of my professors; he was unfamiliar with it but "I certainly like it, my recent work has often been about what gives displeasure in Shakespeare and how that somehow makes for, if not greater pleasure, then greater wholeness."

Again, as he puts it in the "Abstract" of his *Winter's Tale* piece:

> I've spent a lot of time and ink in the last few years on particular elements in Shakespeare plays that displease us, and on arguing that, although whatever element it is I fix on is undeniably unpleasant, it increases its play's power, and power to please. The present paper is much more of the same. Most of it is taken up with a catalogue of the various "wrongnesses" with which *The Winter's Tale* is crammed, elements so numerous as to seem calculated, as inviting challenges to audience credulity. . . .

Specifically he speaks of the bear (as in the famously silly stage direction in *The Winter's Tale:* "Exit, pursued by a bear"), he speaks of the wrongheaded geography of *The Winter's Tale*'s famous "sea-coast of Bohemia," and the fact that the name of a real sculptor, Julio Romano, is used in the play; he's said to have created the statue that comes to life (the use of the real name and the fact that Julio Romano was purportedly better known for his pornographic drawings than his sculptures is the "strenuous impertinence" here).* "The fact that Bohemia has no seacoast except in *The Winter's Tale* is not a mistake or inattention on Shakespeare's part but a *deliberate* reversal of the geography in the source material," Booth points out. (The source tale opens in Bohemia and the little baby is set down on the seacoast of Sicily, of which there actually is one.)

* Subsequent to our conversation a fascinating controversy broke out over whether Shakespeare's Julio Romano was in fact infamous for pornography. A scholar on the SHAKSPER listserv had discovered the existence of another Julio Romano, contemporary with Shakespeare and evidently not known for pornographic images, a fact that if established would invalidate much published speculation about the repression/emergence of the sexual in *The Winter's Tale.* Although that might depend on *which* Julio Romano was in the mind of the playgoer.

Booth characteristically sees this and other dramatic improbabilities in the play as challenges to the audience's *faith.* Challenges that, surmounted, lead to greater faith in the dramatic illusion of the play.

Again he insists, in conclusion, that Shakespeare gives us a "muddle" that is "muted but aesthetically thrilling to minds that never bring its existence to consciousness."

This is one of those paradoxical contentions where one doubt about Boothian reading again arises in my mind: the insistence that the effects he writes about are never brought to consciousness.

But then by *bringing* them to consciousness (in writing about them), isn't he in effect doing something transgressive, making it impossible for experiences that are thrilling because *not* quite conscious ever to thrill again because he's brought them to consciousness? Turning Shakespeare into Brecht, as he said of my Yale experience? Or is the potential for thrills in Shakespeare limitless, bottomless?

In any case I'd asked him whether his emphasis on non (thematic) significance, on "ideational static" over ideological clarity, has some relationship to "conspicuous irrelevance."

"In *The Winter's Tale* you're looking for holes that make a greater whole, right?"

"Well," he said, "that certainly is an elegant way of putting it, but the word 'looking' is bothersome." In the sense that he believes it should *emerge* from reading. "But now I see where you were applying the idea of 'conspicuous irrelevance.' I guess the business of my career has been with the things in great works that people *complain* about. And how does it happen there *are* such things in great works, when in high school all they'd ever tell us about was the things you were supposed to admire, and they spent all the time pointing out what that was."

Suddenly in a way the penny dropped and the relationship between "Love (3)" and his latest criticism became apparent:

"Love (3)" is about the ability for Love, God (Jesus to Herbert)—although he doesn't say the name Jesus, he just says "Love"—to embrace the unworthy speaker almost *for* his unworthiness. It's about someone who is theologically a hole being made whole, redeemed, even holy.

I thought it was interesting to think of Booth's preoccupation with what's "wrong" in Shakespeare in comparison with Frank Kermode's less redemptive vision of "wrongness." Kermode asks us to accept the fact of bad, apparently incoherent Shakespeare; he singles out late Shakespeare,

Coriolanus and *The Winter's Tale.* There are passages in these plays, Kermode says, that are often just bad or sloppy, irredeemably bad (not the kind of bad Booth makes whole) because Shakespeare's thoughts were racing too fast for his pen and the poetic embodiment of his thoughts to catch up, or because he didn't take the time to clarify some of his more knotted formulations.

Kermode believes it important that we allow ourselves the liberty of letting Shakespeare be bad at times because it gives credibility when we praise him for his being good: we are not then "bardolaters" who believe he is perfect in every way.

Booth's focus is on the way the things that seem bad are redemptively good, thrilling, create the pole-vault lift from hole to whole. I tried to get at the question behind this important distinction about *types* of badness when I asked Booth if he thought this was a conscious strategy on Shakespeare's part. Creating displeasures, disjunction.

"You call it a 'conscious strategy of genuine but constructive perversity.' Conscious on the part of Shakespeare?"

"Well," he says, "in this place, yes." He's speaking of the way, in *The Winter's Tale,* Shakespeare reverses Sicily and Bohemia to give us the famous impossible "seacoast of Bohemia" line.

"Because otherwise he's following the previous [source] play so closely," Booth said.

"You call it 'superhumanly perverse' . . . because it draws attention to the larger greatness?"

"No, because it *enhances* its greatness," Booth says. "Like the geography problem in *The Winter's Tale* all of these things are sort of irritants to understanding the play."

When he said that about "irritants" it made me think of the phrase "enraged affection" in *Much Ado.*

Booth's affection is anything but enraged, it's true. There is a serenity to it expressed in that pole-vaulting metaphor which he returns to once more by saying of those "irritants" and "displeasures," "I think they do contribute to the greatness of the play in the way that makes pole-vaulting more of a pleasure, more of a value to the pole vaulter, than taking a ladder, climbing over the bar, then climbing down the other side."

Booth then proceeds to pole-vault to a higher, more energized level of praise for this hole/whole, pole-vaulting quality:

"The fact that Shakespeare can hold the stuff in there and cause audiences to like it is astounding! The ability to feel the wholeness of a play like *The Winter's Tale* that is so busy cracking apart in so many ways. . . ."

"Are these 'irritants' you speak of like those in oysters that cause pearls to grow around them?" I asked, consciously linking to the line in *The Tempest* from the "Full Fathom Five" song: "Those are pearls that were his eyes: / Nothing of him that doth fade, / But doth suffer a sea-change / Into something rich and strange."

"No," he said flatly at first.

For some reason I refused to accept his no.

"Are you sure of that?"

"I'm not," he said, more generously than seriously at first. "I'm close to sure, in the sense the greater attention the irritant endows the point with . . . the trouble is the irritation is felt by the audience and is real and part of the experience. . . . I'm feeling the lure of this pearl metaphor," he finally said, laughing, "but I feel there's a hook in there somewhere. The audience's achievement is essentially in being able to feel mastery over an object in which their mastery is so aggressively challenged. By having to think about the seacoast of Bohemia, or a bear, or having the first character in *King Lear* you feel any sympathy for [Edmund] turning out to be a little Iago. . . ."

"DEATH ARROW" AND SHAKE-SPEARE

I returned to the question of intentionality which goes in and out of fashion in literary studies. When I was at Yale it was one of the three "Forbidden Fallacies," whose fallaciousness was not as self-evident as it was meant to sound: "The Intentional Fallacy," "The Affective Fallacy" and "The Fallacy of Imitative Form."* Under the rule of the Intentional Fallacy one is not to inquire about authorial intention. The poem is to be taken as a "verbal icon" that might as well be inscribed on a meteor that crashed from some distant galaxy whose author or intentions cannot be known. Only the isolated verbal icon itself counts. The Affective Fallacy, which Booth has made his métier, says that one must not pay attention to the effect the poem has on the reader, since we are neither able to recover the author's intended effects, nor will the effects be the same on every reader. The Fallacy of Imitative Form argues against a lesser Boothian sin which is that certain *formal* configurations should not be given *thematic* significance. As when Booth, in an

* All decreed, or named, by Prof. W. K. Wimsatt.

offhand way, related the instability produced by the Sonnets about Love to the instability produced by Love itself. (I tend to think the Fallacy of Imitative Form is not a fallacy in that, while "imitative form" can be abused—as it is in those who argue that their disordered art is an inevitable product and portrait of a disordered universe—nonetheless it is a technique that is used to great effect by almost all great literature.)

Booth has forged a critical realm of his own that goes beyond New Critical Close Reading, but only to get closer, not to distance himself from the experience of Shakespeare the way the Theorists who supplanted the Close Readers do.

"I'm really indifferent to the whole issue of intent," Booth told me.

"It's effect you're concerned with?"

"One can certainly guess what an author intends but in the end it doesn't matter."

He draws on his decidedly arcane knowledge of popular culture history to give me an example.

"There was the rumor that the silent-film actress Theda Bara chose her name because it was a close anagram of 'death arrow.' That had nothing to do with it, it was simply that she was Theodosia Goodman and needed a new name and chose Theda Bara. But even if she didn't have the slightest *intention* for it, the 'death arrow' rumor affected the way audiences saw her." (I couldn't help wondering if there was an intentional or inadvertent linkage between "death arrow" and "Shake-speare.")

To bring things full circle I asked Booth a question about infinitude, I quoted to him, actually, from Peter Brook's Berlin lecture, that line about splitting open a word, a phrase, a line from Shakespeare and how it was like splitting the atom, it releases infinite energies.

"Oh," Booth said, "one has to believe in the feel of something like infinity but presumably you would come to the last one."

Typically Boothian in that the question of Shakespeare's bottomlessness is answered in a commonsense way that doesn't deny its essence. The feeling, the affect, the glimpse, the imagined brush with infinitude is more important than any actual number. And one doesn't feel that *Booth* feels he has "come to the last one."

To return to Edgar's description of the endless plummet from the illusory lip of the Cliffs of Dover in *King Lear,* which conjures up endless depths for his blind father: what's important is not whether the fathomless cliff drop is *there,* but whether the blind father believes it is. When it comes to infinitude we're all blind fathers (which makes more sense to me than that we're all Michael Jordans).

"There's a big difference between what feels infinite and what is," Booth says, "but that feeling is there, even if it's pretty clear the valuable readings don't go on forever. The feeling is real and invaluable." An important remark for Booth's critics: "the valuable readings don't go on forever." They just feel like they do, and given our limited lifespans they are rarely exhausted.

He shifts into a discussion of the kind of "ideational static" that has been occupying his mind recently. With a kind of self-deprecating precision he says, "I have known for almost two weeks that *hair* is a theme in *The Tempest.* You know Shakespeare likes to take body parts and build plays around them."

"I didn't know that."

"Oh, yes. Arms in *Troilus,* ears in *Hamlet,* feet in *Lear,* hands in *Twelfth Night,* trunks in *Cymbeline.*"

"Hair," he goes on, "that is pronounced *'air'* in *The Tempest* is an 'air' in the musical sense, you've got the air that things vanish into, the air that Ariel is, you've got heirs to things that people will be, and then there are a couple of perfectly unnecessary references to 'hair' in the play. Now, did I mention the difference between 'theme' and 'meaning'? Hair's a theme, not a meaning. Just not ideationally interesting or dignified. While 'father and children' in *Lear* and *The Winter's Tale*—that's a topic of *meaning.*"

OUR CONVERSATION ENDED ON A SOMEWHAT DRAMATIC NOTE. Just two days before my phone call with Booth, Donald Foster had dropped a bombshell on SHAKSPER, the electronic discussion list. Foster conceded that he'd been wrong all this time in believing the "Funeral Elegy" to be by Shakespeare. One scholar on another list said, "This is seismic!"

I knew that Booth had gone on record with qualified belief in the Elegy. On a panel at UCLA shortly after Foster's initial claim made headlines and in a paper based on his talk there that later became incorporated into a *Shakespeare Quarterly* forum on the question, Booth had called the Elegy "A long boring poem, probably by William Shakespeare." His imprimatur, however qualified, had done much for Foster's credibility.

It turned out I was the first to tell him of Foster's retraction.

Booth's first reaction was "No kidding!" Then he put his finger on the real question: "Can you define what is 'Shakespearean' with a computer? Presumably if Foster took *Merry Wives of Windsor* through the computer he would find it to be by Shakespeare, but that would not make it 'Shakespearean.' Not very, not the bulk of it."

I was about to disagree with him a bit on *Merry Wives,* which I see as self-conscious Shakespearean self-parody. But Booth seemed a bit shaken by the disclosure of Foster's retraction. And he had put the focus on the essence of the great Elegy fiasco: the search for a way to define what is or isn't "Shakespearean."

"So he took it back . . ." he said, almost disbelievingly.

I DON'T WANT TO END ABRUPTLY ON THIS NOTE OF BOOTH'S FALlibility, although perhaps it's useful to balance the genuine awe I feel at his engagement with Shakespeare with at least a suggestion that even for Booth, someone so finely attuned to Shakespearean complexity, the question of how to define what is "Shakespearean" can still be elusive.

It's true that I have a temperamental preference for the fine-textured attentiveness to the play of language in Booth over the overblown thematic invocations of Bloom. Booth's work doesn't reduce Shakespeare to "themes" and I have sought to offer an appreciation, however inadequate, of Booth's complexity as a corrective to the imbalance that exalts Bloom as our High Priest of Shakespeare, and marginalizes Booth because he doesn't just bat around Big Themes. Because his Shakespeare is difficult, demanding, subtle, however—ultimately—pleasurable. Bloom's Shakespeare is so much easier and undemanding, certainly of subtlety. It's Shakespeare Made Simple on a Grand Scale.

But this does not mean that Booth's approach is and Bloom's isn't an aspect of Shakespeare. Bloom and Booth—all-theme and anti-theme—might indeed be said to be the "double cherry" of Shakespearean exegesis.

One half of that double has nonetheless suffered from neglect. Booth's Shakespeare requires a lifetime of closer and closer and closer attention, the virtual dissolution or at least humble submission of the self to the language; Bloom's vaunting oracular pronouncements require not close reading but virtually no reading at all.

As I was revising this chapter I came across an essay I'd saved from the Summer 1998 issue of the quarterly *Raritan* in which Frank Kermode first published in essay form his "Explorations in Shakespeare's Language" with its tour de force close reading of the phrase "prone and speechless language" in *Measure for Meaure.* A line which Kermode, as Peter Brook put it, split open to release infinite energies.

He starts off with a reading of William Empson's reading of that phrase (an example of Empson's "seventh type" of ambiguity, one in which the mind is divided against itself, a "compaction" to be observed, Kermode says, reading Empson, only in "the *deepest* poetry, what Empson called, with only a little irony, 'the secret places of the Muses' "). Empson, Kermode quotes Jonathan Bate saying, was "the first man to see the literature of the past through quantum's altered notion of reality." He is "modernism's Einstein."

"We need new terms to praise the early Empson," Kermode says, distancing himself from quantum theory and modernism, but asserting with great conviction, "it is a return to that body of work [the early Empson], to the spirit of that work, wherever he got it from that offers us our best hope of restoring and invigorating the process of critical analysis."

I feel something similar could be said about Stephen Booth's work on Shakespeare, and indeed it was one of the great pleasures to find (as I shall relate in the following chapter), in the beauty of Bermuda, even in the rain, a Shakespeare scholarly convention that may be remembered as having marked the return to that spirit.

VI

Love, Beauty, Pleasure and Bad Weather in Bermuda

Looking for Love in *As You Like It*; Looking for an Orgasm in *Romeo and Juliet*

THE FIRE THIS TIME

I wanted to write about love, but somehow I found myself sidetracked by pleasure.

I wanted to write about love in Shakespeare after I had another theater-fire experience. You'll recall (I hope) the one I had when the theater caught fire during a performance of Peter Brook's *Dream* on Broadway. The fire I came to think of as a kind of metaphor for the incandescence of the production.

Well, it happened again. Not quite the same thing. But that won't stop me from making a metaphor out of it. It was not clear whether an actual fire broke out, or it was a false alarm triggered by smoke and an oversensitive alarm system. In any case there were notable similarities: a Shakespearean production on stage, a fire alarm, a halt in the proceedings that left one wondering whether to flee the theater or sit and reflect on the incandescent performance we were seeing: an incandescent incarnation of Shakespearean love.

The fire alarm began clanging shortly after the intermission in Sir Peter Hall's 2005 production of *As You Like It* starring his daughter, Rebecca Hall.

Yes, the ultra-demanding Peter Hall had cast his twenty-two-year-old daughter in one of the most notoriously difficult roles in all Shakespeare—and she was a revelation in the part!

Incandescent does not begin to capture it. Rapturous begins at least. She changed my mind, not only about the play, *As You Like It,* but about love in Shakespeare.

Perhaps I had been spending a *bit* too much time with textual scholars on the variant endings of devastating tragedies, and so I was particularly vulnerable to an experience like this. Not *Shakespeare in Love,* but Love in Shakespeare. But I don't think it was just that. I think she was just *that good.* Her Rosalind would have set off fire alarms of some sort no matter what I'd been doing.

Fascinating: this was the second Peter Hall progeny production I'd seen within a year that had that unexpected effect on me. His son Edward Hall, artistic director of the Propeller Theater, had put on a remarkable all-male production of *A Midsummer Night's Dream* the previous year. It was part of an Originalist trend in performances initiated by the London Globe, a return to the all-male casts that had originally performed Shakespeare's plays (although not quite Originalist: the female parts in Shakespeare's theater had been played by young boys; here it was grown men). I'm not sure what I feel about the trend itself, but I found this *Dream* one of the best since Peter Brook's (James Lapine's Central Park production in the early eighties its only rival in my experience). Maybe there was something to Peter Hall's pause, after all. Some gentle generational translation of its delicacy and insisture.

The Halls' *As You Like It* had opened first in the United Kingdom and I was fortunate to catch it at the Brooklyn Academy of Music. I almost didn't go because—I know this is heresy—*As You Like It* is the one Shakespeare play I've never really liked.

I know it's said by many to be among Shakespeare's greatest works, many scholars and theater people rhapsodize about it. But it is the one play of Shakespeare's major phase that had always—certainly on stage—left me cold.

It is possible, I believe, to love Shakespeare and not love *As You Like It.* When I uttered these sentiments to a scholar I admired, Russ McDonald, he asked me, with wonder in his voice, how I could hold such a view.

I recall my saying that I found the "witty jests" and "spirited raillery" everyone likes to talk about "leaden and strained."

And Rosalind herself, preening in her self-congratulatory verbal gymnastics, often seemed a manufactured wit machine, rather than the appealing spirit so often, so reverently spoken of.

The conventionality of its satire on love and the lack of any sense that there was something real about love worth satirizing left me cold. For a play about love it seemed remarkably loveless, however much Harold Bloom would rhapsodize about Rosalind as the only Being, the only woman, worthy of the exalted company of Hamlet and Falstaff. I had even contemplated a chapter to be entitled "Why I *Don't* Like *As You Like It.*"

But then I saw Rebecca Hall's Rosalind. Now, I'll admit I haven't seen many Rosalinds and I've heard people rave about ones I haven't seen. But the ones I have seen didn't prepare me for this one.

So many previous Rosalinds were simply unable to handle the overly complicated language, much less the wit. They bogged down in verbiage that was meant to be skipped through. It's just hard for even the most gifted to make such sallies work today. For instance when Rosalind finds Orlando has been hanging poems to her on trees, she tells Touchstone, the allegedly witty clown,

"I'll graff it with you, and then I shall graff it with a medlar. Then it will be the earliest fruit i' th' country; for you'll be rotten ere you be half ripe, and that's the right virtue of the medlar."

Even if everyone in a modern audience knows a medlar is "an apple-like fruit that is not ready to eat until it is on the verge of decay," as *The Riverside Shakespeare* glosses it, it's hard to communicate the complexity of the conceptual wordplay in an appealingly offhanded, teasing, spirited manner.

Or consider Rosalind's greeting to her friend Celia, showing her the poems Orlando has hung on trees for her: "I was seven of the nine days out of the wonder before you came; for look here what I found on a palm tree. I was never so berhym'd since Pythagoras' time, that I was an Irish rat, which I can hardly remember."

Or if some Rosalinds did (barely) master the complicated verbiage, they focused on the mockery of love and rarely convincingly evoked its real presence. They rarely made you believe that there was anything worth mocking.

In her father's production what Rebecca Hall offered was, to me, a sense that there is more to love than the weight of the play's mockery of love would have you believe. That there are places in the play where love flares up despite all attempts to mock it. Flares up and catches fire.

(And before going any further, I think I ought to say how deeply I was touched by the kind of father-daughter love on display in the production: for Peter Hall to risk his own reputation, and to subject his daughter to the potential cruelty of critics on the lookout for nepotism, betokened an enormous confidence and courage on the part of both of them. But it worked beautifully; the director gave his daughter a setting that was so perfect for her indubitable talent to flourish, to flare up, it was something lovely to behold.)

In any case, the moment the fire alarm began clanging at the Brooklyn Academy—the moment the five players on stage first tried to shout their lines over it, then stopped to gaze out into the darkness for the cause of the alarm—I was hurled back to that moment when the fire broke out in Peter Brook's *Dream.*

This time there may not have been a fire at all, in the sense of an out-of-control blaze, it may have been an oversensitive alarm system, not the fire, that was out of control. This might define the difference in my reactions to the two moments. The Brook fire was transformative, the BAM fire less life-changing (my life had already been changed), but nonetheless deeply illuminating.

It started with Hall's decision to make the forest of Arden cold. In the text of course there's no suggestion of a chill. As one character puts it of Duke Senior, leader of the Arden outcasts, "They say he is already in the forest of Arden, and a many merry men with him; and there they live like the old Robin Hood of England. They say many young gentlemen flock to him every day, and fleet the time carelessly, as they did in the golden world."

While the description doesn't specify a temperature, fleeting the time "as they did in the golden world" suggests the pastoral meadows of classical Greece. Not the bleak chilly hardship of Peter Hall's forest of Arden in this production.

Hall's forest scene looks like a homeless or hobo encampment with shivering outcasts clutching ratty blankets around themselves as they cluster about a smoky fire for warmth.

I didn't quite understand the point of it at first until it occurred to me one could defend the choice as a manifestation of the subtextual chilliness of this supposed "pastoral comedy." A chilliness perhaps reflecting the coldness of human nature that all the labored frolicking couldn't conceal. "Shakespeare's Bitter Arcadia" is the title the critic Jan Kott gave to his chapter on *As You Like It* and the other pastoral comedies.

I think I understood that Hall ("Shakespeare hated sex") didn't necessarily share Kott's bleak, contrarian view of the world of those plays, but that he wanted to acknowledge it and to use it as a setting for the potential blazing and redemptive warmth that could be found in the part of Rosalind by an actress who was right for it. One like Rebecca Hall.

But, in any case, the chill Arden he created and the fire it required sent plumes of smoke ascending to the rafters of the theater, where apparently the fire-sensors, not attuned to the *contextual importance* of the fire, saw it as a threat and began setting off a noisily noxious clanging.

After trying to compete, the actors just sat down on their various forest perches and a voice came over the public address system announcing that there was "trouble with the alarm system" and asked the actors to leave the stage.

At first there was an incipient revolt. The actors refused to leave the stage. Perhaps there was some thought of creating a "moment" with the audience, which was remaining hesitantly in its seats. A moment of communion in the face of a shared threat. Was there a theatrical equivalent of "going down with the ship"?

But the alarm kept ringing and after a brief interval the actors quietly filed out stage left. Before too long the alarm stopped and they filed back and resumed.

For most of those in the theater things returned to normal. But if you're someone with my history you pay attention to deeper resonances when you hear a fire alarm on stage during a Shakespearean play.

And I had been paying attention. I remember the moment that did it for me. Early in act 1, Rosalind, who has fallen for Orlando as she watches him triumph in the wrestling match, approaches the victorious warrior to give him a token to wear. In this production it's a necklace she's been wearing which she drapes around his neck.

She's already been won over before speaking to him. It's another instance of the Marlowe line that Shakespeare actually quotes in *As You Like It:* "Whoever lov'd that lov'd not at first sight?"

Rebecca Hall played that moment in a way that was both balletic and goofy, leaning her slender body like a swan's neck into Orlando when they first meet and then collapsing in laughter at her infatuation. Expressive and resistant, responsive as if to magnetism, and then exaggerating her response in a swoony way that embarrasses and caricatures herself.

It is almost as if she were, with extreme subtlety in gesture and body language, turning that single moment into a compression of the entire two-millennia-long debate over love in Western culture.

Speaking of which, that fire alarm, false or not, was a kind of wake-up call for me because I had up till then failed to look more deeply into the argument about Love and Beauty (and Sex and Pleasure) in Shakespeare studies.

Or the puzzling recent absence of such argument.

One of the best summaries I've come across of the conflict in the literature that led up to Shakespeare can be found in a 1985 Cambridge University Press study, *The Metaphysics of Love,* by the British philosopher A. J. Smith.

Smith tells us that "a prolonged debate about the spiritual worth of love looms large, so large in spiritual regard from the twelfth century to the twentieth century, because it challenged man's rage for fulfillment beyond change, brings home to us human creatures our thralldom to time and circumstance, the incongruity of our designs with the universe we encounter. Is love strong as death? Or does it betray us to corruption? . . . The attempt to find spiritual value in sexual love becomes urgent when the love of a fellow human being is taken to redeem our nature in a corrupted world, or when sexual experience is felt to give meaning to life."

We're probably all familiar with that argument and with the conflict—not that anyone's resolved it—but then Smith raises a fascinating question. He refers to a certain "momentous" assumption in those writing about love in literature—the assumption "that human love in some way rehearses a universal condition. This conceit seized the European metaphysicians in a debate that haunted English love poetry in the seventeenth century."

What an understated way of posing an utterly unexpected question. Which is: Are we all talking about the same thing when we talk about the experience of love? Or as Raymond Carver might put it, "What do we talk about when we talk about love?"

It's an unanswerable but philosophically troubling question. On one level it's not entirely different from asking whether we all experience the taste of chocolate or the color blue in the same way. (Could your chocolate be my vanilla, your blue my red?)

But this is, as Smith put it, more "momentous." In a way, it occurred to me the question is implicitly there in the title—"As You Like It." Implying that some may like the same thing but in a different way. No judgments on what you like, or nothing to found them on. As the epilogue suggests, "ladies" may like it ("it" being, ostensibly, the play) in a different way from men. But "it" also recalls the mythological account of Tiresias, the seer whom the gods asked to settle the question whether men or women get more pleasure from sex. (He metamorphosed into a woman so he could make a valid comparison. FYI: he said women had it better.)

Is there some universal "love" that touches us all in different degrees regardless of love object or gender identity?

It was after seeing Rebecca Hall's Rosalind and contemplating A. J. Smith's question about love's universality, the possibility that shared language conceals radically different experiences, that I thought I would find some provocative scholarly contentions about love.

It was, after all, a scandalizing question about love that drove me from graduate school and put me in the path of Peter Brook's life-changing *Dream.* That apparently deeply inappropriate question I'd asked about Chaucer's attitude toward love, the question that a brilliant but condescending graduate student had dismissed because, he sniffed, the really *interesting* question in Chaucer (and implicitly in all literature) was not about such things as the nature of love, but about "the making of poetry."

And it was love of a different, but not entirely unrelated sort, that drove me back to writing about Shakespeare: love of the language, love of the pleasures that increase with recurrent reading. As Shakespeare wrote of Cleopatra: others

. . . cloy
The appetites they feed, but she makes hungry
Where most she satisfies . . .

What could be more exciting than finding the locus of scholarly contentions about love in Shakespeare and writing about those contentions? But there was one problem: there *were* no active contentions about love, at least that's what one of my most authorative scholarly sources informed me.

I'd sent an e-mail to Russ McDonald, someone whose work represented to me the very best of contemporary scholarship—let me recommend again his Oxford University Press study, *Shakespeare and the Arts of Language,* as an exemplary instance of how scholarly work on Shakespeare can be done with an illuminating clarity as well as intellectual complexity.

In reading McDonald I felt I was reading one of the few scholars with the acuity about the potential of language that Peter Brook displays, an instinctive sense of the secret play of language. Someone whose work would last, someone whose work I wanted to and intend to hold up as an example that scholars still, after four hundred years, can have fresh and illuminating things to say to us about Shakespeare.

Indeed McDonald's remarkable essay "Late Shakespeare: Style and the

Sexes" may be the single most illuminating scholarly essay I'd read in the course of writing this book. I'll return to it in some detail when I take up the contentious issue of Shakespeare's "late language," the argument over whether we must, with Frank Kermode, find the "late language" occasionally sloppy and opaque. Or, with Stephen Booth, construe apparent holes in the linguistic fabric as greater wholes. Or is there, McDonald suggests, a "third way" of looking at it?

But at the time I e-mailed him I hadn't read the essay or talked to him about the "late language" question. I was focused on finding the debate over love in Shakespeare studies.

McDonald certainly seemed like the person to ask. Since I had last seen him at the Shenandoah Shakespeare Blackfriars conference, he had edited a nine-hundred-page volume called *Shakespeare: An Anthology of Criticism and Theory 1945–2000*. He seemed in close touch with the trends and tendencies of Shakespeare studies.

So I e-mailed to ask him if he could tell me what the locus of the debate over love was now, what "the smart current contentions" were.

Frankly no, he said in reply. "Nobody has written much about love in the past three decades or so. Poststructuralism, even though its harshest, most skeptical strains didn't have a very powerful effect on Shakespeareans, still manages to set the tone for much criticism, and poststructuralists aren't much interested in the representation of ideals or in the positive side of such topics.

"That's a crude but not inaccurate explanation of why we've had so much about sex and the body and other physical matters for the past few years. In other words there aren't any 'smart current contentions' [about love] at the moment."

Could it be true? I knew of one exception: *Shakespeare on Love and Lust* by Maurice Charney, the scholar who—perhaps not coincidentally—coined the phrase "O-groans." But as McDonald suggested, even discussion of the Sonnets focused not on love but on sex, the body, the gaze. He did, however, hold out some hope that a change might be in the wind.

"We are moving back to the possibility of discussion of such things to be sure: the plenary session of the Shakespeare Association of America conference in Bermuda next month—we've finally caught up with the dentists on choice of conference venue—is 'Beauty' and I'm in a seminar on 'Pleasure.' "

Beauty and Pleasure! In Bermuda! The island that was (by most accounts) the inspiration for the magical island in *The Tempest,* perhaps Shakespeare's final solo work.

The focus on such concepts as beauty and pleasure represented a new development, McDonald told me. "The profession," he said, of Shakespeare studies, and literary studies in general, is returning to the discussion of "ideals" and these were two harbingers of that turn.

This was remarkable news and I wondered if something hopeful I'd written five years earlier about the direction of Shakespearean scholarship in *The New York Times Book Review* (in August 2000)—something I'd come to think of, in subsequent years, as somewhat wishful thinking—might at last be coming true.

Back then, writing about some signs and hints I saw at the Shakespeare Association of America conference in Montreal (including Linda Charnes's Bloom paper), I'd suggested that the reign of Theory in literary studies was coming to an end and that the smarter scholars, recognizing the exhaustion if not meretriciousness of Theory, were searching for a post-Theory, post-postmodernist perspective.

There was a plenary session in Montreal entitled "Before Theory," paying renewed attention and respect to three great literary minds—William Empson, T. S. Eliot and Oscar Wilde—who responded to Shakespeare as if there was some special reason to value his work (that notion—literary value—long dismissed by the more stringent of the Theorists). One of the session's participants, Columbia's David Scott Kastan, had just published a book called *After Theory.*

The way I read the SAA's collective mindset then, Theory still remained the central event in the history of literary studies, the divide between the B.C. and the A.D. of thinking about Shakespeare. But the interest these days was in what lay on both sides of the divide, especially what might lie ahead. With all the speculation about Before Theory and After Theory, that which might be called "mere Theory" seemed suddenly retro.

Of course in speaking so hopefully, I had underestimated the inertial drag that tenure tracks clogged with Theorists would exert (in practical terms it meant tenure track aspirants had to adopt the jargon of the faculty thesis adviser to get ahead and so younger intellects had to wait 'til they got tenure to be free to express a view that, nonetheless, would still prevent them from advancing to a position at a more prestigious institution).

But now in 2005, some of the smartest young faculty had established posts from which they could abandon the intellectual aridity, if not outright sterility, of Theory and explore notions such as "ideals"—Beauty, Pleasure, etc.—that had long been abandoned as meaningless terms, empty abstractions at best, at worst tools of the oppressive hegemonic authority. McDonald himself was a partisan of a revived, "reconceived close reading," as he put it.

And by 2005 a number of developments all seemed to converge. In addition to the return to "ideals" McDonald spoke of, I would soon discover there had been a parallel post-Theory rehabilitation of "formalism" (as close attention to the internal resonances of a poem is somewhat misleadingly called) which McDonald was influential in advancing. A "neo-formalism" that reinstated close reading (with lip service paid to the "incorporation of the insights of Theory").

A scholarly tendency that involved, as I would learn, to my great pleasure, the revaluation, one might almost say rehabilitation, of Stephen Booth's work.

Beauty! Pleasure! Vindication! Bermuda! I made reservations immediately.

THE ANATOMY OF PLEASURE

What could be more pleasurable in a certain way than savoring the irony of intense discussions of Beauty and Pleasure in hotel conference rooms shut off from the natural beauty and pleasure of the island outside the hotel (the Southampton Princess no less, Southampton of course having been one of Shakespeare's first patrons).

I had been thinking about pleasure in Shakespeare, the pleasures *of* Shakespeare and the arguments over it for some time. Unbearable pleasure is, after all, at the heart of my theory of the rise of Theory in literary studies: close reading brought some too close to a core meltdown, so to speak, too close to pleasures whose destabilizing intensity threatens the dissolution of the self. After all, look at the way pleasure is often described: "giving in to the pleasure," "giving one's self up to pleasure." Giving up the self: never a light matter.

One thing all the diverse theorizing methodologies that took over literary studies like a cult with pretensions to science did was distance, protect one's self from having to "give in" to pleasure, absorption, immersion, contemplation of the bottomless abyss of the text. Rather the text must be made to "give in" to us, to submit itself to our theoretical constructs, dance (or rather collapse) to our tune. If as the critic Louis Menand once put it, the New Criticism made things cohere too readily, deconstruction made them fall apart too perfectly and predictably.

And, one could speculate, the peculiar preference for reading Shakespearean biographies, shuffling and reshuffling the same old anecdotes, is another way of avoiding the destabilizing pleasures of reading and rereading the work. Frankly, the little we know about Shakespeare is far less threatening than "the Shakespearean" with its dizzying plentitude.

Pleasure is at the heart of Stephen Booth's argument about what "all the fuss is about" in Shakespeare, the exhilarating pleasures the mind discovers itself capable of when reading Shakespeare, the pleasures of "pole-vaulting on the moon."

And the more I thought about the subject of pleasure the more I realized there is an argument about pleasure in just about every play in Shakespeare, and in the poems as well, of course. An argument about pleasure and the dangers of pleasure that is laid out in the simplest, starkest terms at the close of *Love's Labor's Lost* in the "debate" between the songs of Spring and Winter.

THE SONG OF SPRING (OR "VER")

When daisies pied, and violets blue,
And lady-smocks all silver-white,
And cuckoo-buds of yellow hue
Do paint the meadows with delight,
The cuckoo then on every tree
Mocks married men; for thus sings he,
"Cuckoo;
Cuckoo, cuckoo"—O word of fear,
Unpleasing to a married ear!

It's impossible not to notice the way the initial "delight" and painted pleasures of spring swiftly slide to words of "fear." From pleasure to the "unpleasing," destabilizing hint of jealousy, betrayal, mockery, deceit.

Sometimes pleasure is seen to contain the seed of its own destruction: the amorous delight of the spring licensing the call of the cuckoo signaling, instigating sexual treachery, cuckoldry and Shakespeare's virtual obsession with venereal diseases as the consequence of "venery," veneration of Venus, a savage goddess dangerous to those she loves and those she's beloved by.

In some plays the argument is divided into clear-cut personifications of pleasure and anti-pleasure: in *Twelfth Night* it's Sir Toby and his relish for a realm of "cakes and ale" counterposed to Malvolio and his penchant for restrictions.

Sometimes it is embodied in one conflicted body as it is in Falstaff and Cleopatra, both conflicted icons of pleasure and indulgence. Actually *they* are not conflicted about their pleasures—they regret nothing—but they bear the burden of their indulgences. In Falstaff the punishment for pleasure is written, embellished, em-bellied on his body—the burden is physical: fat and age, alcohol and sexual diseases have made him pay for the pleasures of the flesh.

If there is a defining moment in Shakespearean pleasure, it may be found in Enobarbus's recollection in *Antony and Cleopatra* of Cleopatra's first appearance to Mark Antony in Alexandria. Here art and nature incite each other to "o'er-picture" the other in the spectacle of Cleopatra resplendent in a golden barge sailing forth to dazzle Mark Antony for the first time.

We are fortunate to have the original description from the Greek historian Plutarch, the source Shakespeare relied upon (in a translation by Thomas North), and I'll quote it in a moment, but this is Shakespeare writing about pleasure in perhaps his most sensually pleasurable mode. And I'd prefer to begin with the final refinement:

The barge she sat in, like a burnish'd throne,
Burnt on the water. The poop was beaten gold,
Purple the sails, and so perfumed that
The winds were love-sick with them; the oars were silver,
Which to the tune of flutes kept stroke, and made
The water which they beat to follow faster,
As amorous of their strokes. For her own person,
It beggar'd all description: she did lie
In her pavilion—cloth of gold, of tissue—
O'er-picturing that Venus where we see
The fancy outwork nature.
. . . At the helm
A seeming mermaid steers; the silken tackle
Swell with the touches of those flower-soft hands,

That yarely frame the office. From the barge
A strange invisible perfume hits the sense
Of the adjacent wharfs. The city cast
Her people out upon her; and Antony
Enthron'd i' th' market-place, did sit alone,
Whistling to th' air, which, but for vacancy,
Had gone to gaze on Cleopatra too,
And made a gap in nature.

That's pleasure. Now, this has been done before, notably by Jonathan Bate, but I want to do it my way, and it can't be done enough: comparing those lines above to Shakespeare's source in Plutarch.

Here's the Plutarch version of that same scene:

> She disdained to set forward otherwise, but to take her barge in the river of Cydnus, the poope whereof was of gold, the sailes of purple and owers [oars] of silver which kept stroke in rowing after the sound of the music of the flutes, howboyes [oboes], citherns, violls, and such other instruments that they played upon in the barge.

[Sorry to interrupt, but I can't help noting at this point how Plutarch just completely loses focus in this pointless *enumeration* of the musical instruments. Compare the way Shakespeare's oars "to the tune of flutes kept stroke, and made / The water which they beat to follow faster, / As amorous of their strokes." He doesn't *list* the musical instruments, but rather, lets us hear the flutes and their bewitching power to transform the rhythm of the oars in the water into an erotic engagement. Back to Plutarch.]

> And now for the person of her self she was layed under a pavillion of cloth of gold of tissue, apparelled and attired like the goddesse Venus, commonly drawn in picture

[Note that "commonly drawn"—one almost thinks Plutarch is consciously resisting the seductiveness of this uncommon Venus.]

> and hard by her, on either hand of her, pretie faire boyes apparelled as painters doe set forth god Cupide, with little fans in their hands, with the which they fanned wind upon her. Her ladies and gentlewomen

> also, the fairest of them were apparelled like the nymphs Nereides (which are the mermaides of the waters) and like the Graces, some stearing the helme, others tending the tackle and ropes of the barge,

[Look at the way this focus on nautical technique becomes a focus on another kind of technique in Shakespeare: "the silken tackle / Swell with the touches of those flower-soft hands, / That yarely frame the office." Perhaps the most erotic line in all Shakespeare. "Flower-soft hands"! Back to Plutarch's barge . . .]

> out of the which there came a wonderful passing sweete savor of perfumes, that perfumed the wharfes side, pestered with innumerable numbers of people . . .

Enough! "Pestered" indeed. (Yes, it's North's word, but still . . .) But we must be grateful to Plutarch for the plodding template that gave birth, like Venus from the foam, to Shakespeare's lush, louche, amorous, seductive, near-pornographic excursus on pleasure. Evoking in words alone the sensual manifestations of eros, it is perhaps the most purely sensual passage in all Shakespeare, perhaps the most intense and exhilarating in the language. (The "hounds and echo" passage in the *Dream,* while lovely esthetically and even sensually, is not necessarily erotic, or if erotic, only in a more distanced estheticized way, although the sound and echoes could prefigure the way the oars and "The water which they beat . . . follow faster, / As amorous of their strokes." Echoes are, in a way, amorous followers of the sounds they respond to.)

The Plutarch passage is often compared with Shakespeare's to demonstrate how often, how blatantly Shakespeare "copied" from his sources. But the difference between Plutarch and *Antony and Cleopatra* is all the difference in the world. All the difference we identify as Shakespearean.

The things being described and the actions being taken are exactly the same in each passage and we get to see how Shakespeare turned the plodding Plutarch's reporting into sublimely pleasurable poetry. And while much of this is infusing, transubstantiating Plutarch's prose into sensual beauty, barely on the "threshold of comprehension," there is one addition that is most purely Shakespearean. While Plutarch has the "Cupids" fanning Cleopatra, Shakespeare had "Cupids, / With divers-color'd fans, whose wind did seem / To glow the delicate cheeks which they did cool, / And what they undid did." Glowing the cheeks they cooled, doing and undoing is Shakespeare alone.

"What they undid did." That "undid did"—the literal pressing together of doing and undoing, being and not-being, the suggestiveness of the verbal sexual coupling, is remarkable. Echoed, embodied in the image of the way the fans heat to a flushed "glow the delicate cheeks which they did cool." It's an endlessly, bottomlessly reciprocating process of inflaming, fulfilling and regenerating desire. Amazing the pleasure that passage gives.

It is here one can't help, no matter how one distrusts biographical opportunism, to stop and wonder at what the moment of writing this passage was like for Shakespeare. The decision to give himself up to pleasurable excess in language, in the attempt to embody the power of Cleopatra's spell, in the way it bewitches the winds and waves around her. It is no accident that, when Samuel Johnson sought to find words to condemn Shakespeare for taking too much pleasure in puns and wordplay, he called them Shakespeare's "fatal Cleopatra," the embodiment of pleasure taken to illicit excess, pleasure as self-destructive seductiveness.

A SEA CHANGE IN BERMUDA

It was more than island breezes that had me anticipating the convention of Shakespeare scholars in Bermuda. I was looking forward to a lunch during the conference (after the Beauty Plenary, before the Pleasure Seminar) with Russ McDonald. Especially so after I had discovered his essay on Shakespeare's "late language," which I thought was a crucial document in the debate over the evolution of what we think of as "Shakespearean" language.

It was raining outside during the Beauty Plenary. A chill wind was whipping the palm trees. Not exactly a tempest, but the easy irony of pedants ignoring the beauty of a glorious island day to discourse on the *theory* of beauty was unavailable. In fact it rained three out of the four days of the "beauty and pleasure convention," as I came to think of that year's Shakespeare Association of America conference.

The star of the Beauty Plenary was Stephen Greenblatt. There were two other papers on beauty delivered to the five hundred or so scholars packed into the main conference room, but neither of them addressed the subject of Shakespearean beauty directly. (One spent the time examining Renaissance printers' use of random blocks of print type as design motifs.)

One has to give Greenblatt credit: riding the crest of publicity and sales from *Will in the World* (and scholarly suspicion of popular success), he was nonetheless prepared to take on one of the long-scorned "ideals"—Beauty!—that the profession had assiduously avoided for fear of the taint of "bardolatry" or "essentialism."

Indeed I wondered what was going through the minds of the large audience of scholars, many of whom had learned to look at Shakespeare through the lens of Greenblatt's New Historicism with its skepticism about such things as "beauty" and "literary value" or at least the value of talking about them when there was so much historicizing to be done.

And even though he'd been jettisoning theoretical baggage in his recent work, the fact that Greenblatt was willing to address an ideal, an ideal as eternally contentious as Beauty, was almost shocking.

And in fact there was something even *more* shocking in the very last sentence of his talk. For most of his forty minutes Greenblatt delivered what I thought was a modest, impressively well-illustrated (many slides of architectural façades) talk about the Renaissance conception of beauty. The conception of beauty prevalent in the culture that was the historical context for Shakespeare, yes, but then he ended up describing the way Shakespeare's concept of beauty *differed*—resisted historicist determinism—to achieve and celebrate a different kind of beauty from that which might be dictated by the zeitgeist.

He argued that the ideal of beauty as it was commonly described and produced in the Renaissance involved a kind of "featurelessness," an abstractedness from individuality, a proportionality, a harmony that subsisted in the relationship of perfectly formed, virtually interchangeable parts rather than in the particular features themselves.

And that for Shakespeare, beauty involved something different: singularity.

He chose to illustrate this with a single image: the "cinque-spotted mole" in *Cymbeline*.

You might recall in that play that the malicious schemer Iachimo has wagered he can seduce Posthumus's wife Innogen while they're apart. (Innogen was long spelled "Imogen" but most scholars now believe it was the former.) Iachimo hides himself in Innogen's bedroom and gets a glimpse of her body while she sleeps unawares. And then tells Posthumus that he has proof of his success at seduction. The "evidence" Iachimo gives to bolster the lie is "On her left breast / A mole cinque-spotted, like the crimson drops / I' th' bottom of a cowslip."

"It is something deeply *individuated,*" Greenblatt pointed out at the Beauty Plenary. "Imogen is beautiful, but she is not a featureless beauty. Her mole is not a part of any total perfection, but it is also not an adornment [like the artificial beauty marks women affixed to their cheeks at the time], or if it is a mark, it is a mark of all that Shakespeare found indelibly beautiful in singularity. And a mark of all that we find indelibly beautiful in his work." End of talk.

But did you catch that? It was in a quiet way a sensational moment. Greenblatt, the avatar of a historicism that rejected "essentialist" concepts, ideals like "beauty," had spoken of what we find "indelibly beautiful" in Shakespeare.

The phrase "sea change" has been so often misused as if it were an overnight transformation, mistakenly used as if it were merely a synonym for "a big change," when in fact in the context of the beautiful "full fathom five" song in *The Tempest,* one of the indubitable if not indelible beauties of Shakespeare, it refers to the redemptiveness of slow evolutionary epochal-scaled change in transforming death into beauty:

Full fathom five thy father lies,
Of his bones are coral made:
Those are pearls that were his eyes:
Nothing of him that doth fade,
But doth suffer a sea-change
Into something rich and strange.

So a sea change is a very slow process, bones being made into coral through a long, long process of being transubstantiated from remains of the dead to emblems of undersea life, infiltrated by, then transformed to, living coral.

But nonetheless one could almost say that, in terms of scholarly theory-epochs, which proceed somewhat faster than coralization of bones, Stephen Greenblatt had shown evidence of having undergone, yes, a sea change.

And, one wondered if it might signal a process that had been going on throughout "the profession" of Shakespeare scholarship, the dry bones of Theory infused with new intellectual life. An inevitable consequence of immersion in the ocean of Shakespearean language? All the attempts to escape the effects of immersion in vain before the richness and strangeness of the spell cast by Beauty and Pleasure?

I was struck in particular by the way Greenblatt chose to evoke his vision of beauty and individuality in Shakespeare.

That Greenblatt chose a phrase—"mole cinque-spotted"—that seemed to conjure up (for me at least) the five-spotted, cinque-stressed syllables of the pentameter line, made it seem as if he had hit upon an image of Shakespearean self-disclosure, each line a blossom founded upon five inky marks, spotting the syllabic petals, so to speak, a fully fathomed five, you might say.

Also not without interest (to me, anyway): he chose a phrase as the virtual signature of Shakespearean beauty that contains "bottom" within it. The "bottom of a cowslip." And with bottom in Shakespeare there is always the suggestion of bottomlessness. Beauty and identity, the five spots, like the five fathoms, mark the threshold of bottomlessness.

"All that we find indelibly beautiful in his work." Those not all too closely familiar with trends in lit-crit theory may not appreciate the courage it took to utter that phrase in that setting. Not just "beautiful," but "indelibly beautiful."

"Beautiful" alone suggests the possibility of subjectivity. "Indelibly beautiful," yes, it's something "we find," but there is the suggestion of an absolute here. Beauty that is indelible is not beauty that can be reduced, contextualized, subjectivized, historicized, conceptually *erased.*

And beauty whose signature is "individuation" does not sound like the "beauty" "produced," as the cultural materialists like to say, by the "hegemonic discourse," but the product of an individual author, not some mouthpiece for the zeitgeist.

I thought this, in a certain sense, was *news*! Greenblatt had challenged "the profession" to accept or reject the idea that Shakespeare offered timeless beauties. Not beauty as beauty was seen in a particular socio-historical context, but "indelible" beauties that would by definition transcend history's erasure.

It remains to be seen how many if any will take up the challenge of further examining what we talk about when we talk about beauty in Shakespeare. I'd merely like to look a little more closely at "indelible."

It seemed to me to be a carefully chosen word. I mean if you were at the apex of the academic study of Shakespeare and were contemplating a single word to describe the "beauty" of Shakespeare, when the very word "beauty" had been virtual anathema to much of your profession, what word, what adjective would you modify beauty with?

Indelible: it suggests, in non-Shakespearean contexts, ink that cannot be erased. In a Shakespearean context it conjures up the recurrent image in the Sonnets of inked "lines"—lines of verse written in ink—lines giving an immortality to perishable human beauty by capturing it in lines on the page ineradicably and everlastingly. Indelibly.

"The indelible beauties of Shakespeare": Greenblatt was going further than I'd ever heard him go, further than I imagined he ever would, further, even, than I'd be willing to go, in the absolutism of his phrase. Because isn't "indelible" a way of saying both "immortal" and "absolute"? "Indelible" doesn't say these beauties are going to be with us a long time. It says these beauties will *never* disappear; their future is bottomless. I applaud the daring but lack the confidence, I guess, to say anything will last forever. I'm not opposed to it lasting forever. But for another millennium? Perhaps, like Homer, in translation, but is that the same?

I'm just grateful this beauty has been legible long enough for me to take pleasure in it, indelible or not.

Still it's interesting, it's not easy when you challenge yourself to come up with a better way to describe the "beauties" of Shakespeare in a single word or phrase. I would actually go with "rich and strange" if I had to choose three words or less. If I had to choose one word: Bottomless? Unbearable?

And is "beauty" itself the right word, or the most important word, to use when describing Shakespeare? When we say the tragedies are "beautiful," do we mean because they are executed with great beauty, meaning with great art or artfulness, despite the horror that is being executed?

I'd accept the idea that Lear's fifth-act *never*s are or can be made to be something of great beauty, however devastating each successive restatement of negation: "Never, never, never, never, never." And by the way, are those five "nevers" of the Folio version 67 percent more beautiful than the three nevers of the Quarto? Would another "never" make it 20 percent more beautiful? There is alas a reductio ad absurdum in making beauty an absolute.

But has Greenblatt committed himself to the idea that one can confidently and absolutely claim to define beauty objectively and assign it to Shakespeare without any cavil, caveats, or "I don't know how to define it, but I know it when I see it" type concessions to subjectivity?

"The indelible beauties of Shakespeare." It seemed a bit of a shame that he *ended* his talk with that line, since, in a way, it's where a number of fascinating discussions might begin. Does the indelibility of Shakespeare's beauties have something to do with this "individuation" that Greenblatt ascribes to him? Do other great writers offer beauties as indelible or individuated, or is Shakespeare alone capable of it? Is he, then, not on the same continuum as other great writers, but capable of beauties singularly indelible? Is this an "exceptionalist" argument: Shakespeare indelible, others, well, "delible"?

If not, how many other indelibly beautiful writers are there, and how does one distinguish the indelible from the non-indelible from the limited perspective of the present? Does everything indelible, like everything that rises, converge? To a single summit of impossible-to-surpass-or-erase singularity of beauty? With his final words Greenblatt had in a way almost given permission to his listeners to throw off the shackles of Theory and consider such questions again. I wonder if they will.

At the very least what we may have been witnessing was Greenblatt himself at last casting off his own shackles, finally able to declare a love, a love that transcends historicizing, for that indelible beauty.

TERROR AT THE PLEASURE SEMINAR

The Pleasure Seminar took place on the afternoon of the day following the Beauty Plenary. And it took the obverse approach from Greenblatt's embrace of Beauty. It took the form in many instances of wrestling with the pleasure not within Shakespeare but the corresponding pleasure Shakespeare arouses within ourselves. This is not as self-involved as it sounds at first; it goes to the heart of the question of why we value what we value in literature. It is, as well, Stephen Booth's territory.

It was only in his extremely provocative final sentence that Greenblatt had addressed the question of the beauty *of* Shakespeare, and its uniqueness. Most of the talk had been about what was defined as beauty *in* Shakespeare.

By contrast almost all the scholarly discussants in the seminar officially titled "The Pleasure Principle" focused their attention less on the conception of pleasure *in* Shakespeare (as in the debate over Falstaff), more on the pleasure *of* Shakespeare. How pleasure affected readers, spectators. What is regarded, defined *as* pleasure.

I'd been to such seminars before and this was one of the better ones. There was something venturesome about the discussion on this, again, long-dismissed or deconstructed "ideal" (Pleasure) and the way Shakespearean experiences translate themselves into physical, emotional, intellectual and even sexual pleasure.

Well, a verbal simulacrum of sexual pleasure, according to one of the participants, who—sounding as if he were basing his speculation on personal experience—made a remarkable conjecture about the most intense and visionary representation of an orgasm in Shakespeare.

It took me a while to absorb the significance of this conjecture which I will explore further in the context of the other pleasure papers, but first I feel it is incumbent upon me to issue a warning.

I must suggest that this section is not for the faint of heart. Raise your terror alert level, because we are about to talk about pleasure and you know of course how dangerous that is.

If you don't, you haven't been reading the lit-crit "discourse on pleasure" and noticed the way that it has been entwined with the discourse of terror, of "the abyss," of the disintegration of the self, the loss of identity. Pleasure in academic discourse is strong stuff, threatening, you're taking your life, or your self, into your hands.

AND NOT FIVE MINUTES HAD PASSED IN THE BERMUDA PLEASURE Seminar before the word "terror" entered into the discussion. Let me set the scene: a smaller hotel conference room than for the Beauty Plenary, a room with a view of those rain-whipped palms outside. (The trees of pleasure being lashed with a fury, and even seeming to bend in terror, or, who knows, pleasure. This is what's known as "the pathetic fallacy," reading one's own pathos in the tempestuous state of the world or the weather outside.)

Anyway in the middle of the room there was a long seminar table for the fifteen or so discussants who had exchanged papers on aspects of pleasure over the past few months and were now about to spend three hours trying to engage in productive discussion of pleasure. And along the periphery of the room there were folding chairs for auditors such as myself.

It was not five minutes into the pleasure discussion that the word "terror" was uttered. One discussant, perhaps reacting to Greenblatt's "indelible beauty," raised the notion of "the terror of beauty." An analogue to what I've been calling the sometimes "unbearable pleasure" of Shakespeare.

Nor was it long before another seductive but threatening word, popularized by Roland Barthes, was invoked: *jouissance,* a word Frank Kermode renders as "a response [to pleasure] so intense that it shatters identity."

Evidence of the way that terror, or fear of *jouissance,* has become central to the discussion of pleasure could be found outside that seminar room, of course. Take for example another kind of pleasure seminar. A slim volume of essays I'd discovered shortly before the Bermuda conference. A book called *Pleasure and Change: The Aesthetics of Canon.*

It consisted of Frank Kermode's 2001 Tanner Lecture at Berkeley and an introductory essay by noted literary scholar Robert Alter followed by commentaries and responses by other equally prominent esthetic theorists: Geoffrey Hartman, John Guillory and Carey Perloff, all of which were followed by a response to their responses by Kermode. It's fascinating testimony to the pervasive linkage of terror and pleasure.

Before we are ten pages into *Pleasure and Change* Robert Alter tells us that "Geoffrey Hartman worries that the term and concept of pleasure 'glides over the abyss.' "

He suggests Hartman's "horror of the abyss that is opened up through the concept of pleasure" may be "reacting to a discussion by Kermode of Roland Barthes' notions of *'jouissance'* with a suggestion of a response so intense that it shatters identity."

Kermode himself goes on to explain that "Barthes distinguished between the pleasures of reading and what he called *'jouissance,'* a term associated in French with, among other things, orgasm, and connoting an experience not simply pleasant but mixed with something perhaps best described as dismay."

And then after Kermode finishes linking pleasure and dismay, Hartman makes things sound even worse: "the word, pleasure, is problematic—I am tempted to say 'abysmal'—for several reasons." One being the derivation of "abysmal" from *abyss.* And it is here that he tells us pleasure "glides over the abyss." Which abyss he doesn't specify. But it makes me feel he's thinking of the abyss of bottomlessness. The fear of the endless fall into soul-dissolving pleasure.

And then a warning from Hartman: although Kermode has evoked orgasm, "any sexualization of pleasure runs a double danger. The first is the danger of making it appear as if the pleasure linked to art were the by-product of a repression, a successful repression, Freud surmised, but still a sublimated or cerebral derivative." The second "danger" is that Ol' Devil *jouissance.* Disintegration from too much or rather too *intense* a pleasure. *Jouissance* represents the "destructive rather than constructive side of Eros," Hartman tells us, and thus "*jouissance* jeopardizes . . . all identity constructs."

Hartman then goes further than Kermode's rather mild (in comparison) linkage of *jouissance* with "dismay," which has connotations of *tristesse,* postcoital or noncoital. Hartman is talking not about sadness or dismay but about self-destruction.

In other words, abandon all hope ye who seek pleasure from pleasure. You can't handle the destabilizing truth of beauty. The price is too high, the abyss too terrifyingly bottomless.

Kermode's response to Hartman and the other responders contains one of the driest, wittiest remarks I've seen in recent critical literature, and it relates to what I've talked about as the kind of "scaffolding" that Theory has erected to distance us from the dangers of pleasure:

"Neutralizing pleasure," Kermode says, "is a task that may be carried on in various ways, but it seems odd to regard it as a good thing."

Odd to regard it as a good thing! How perfectly stated.

Still the rhetoric of pleasure among Kermode's discussants was terrifying, "gliding over the abyss" and all that. It made me look upon the efforts of the Pleasure Principle seminar I attended in Bermuda with respect: they were braving dangerous territory, this realm of "abysmal," "destructive" pleasure and terror and shattered identity.

But all kidding aside, I was struck by how daring, and provocative, some of the Pleasure Principle papers were.

WHO WAS IT FOR YOU, DEAR?

I'm looking over my notes and tapes and some of the papers and paper summaries from the Pleasure Seminar. And in addition to "the terrors of beauty" two high points stand out: the orgasm and "accidence" arguments. The orgasm conjecture was presented by Alexander Leggatt, whose exegesis of the last words of Lear I've spoken of. At the Pleasure Seminar he offered a novel orgasmic interpretation of a famous passage in *Romeo and Juliet.* It emerged from a contention about what distinguishes Shakespearean from non-Shakespearean language:

"In the act two storm in *Pericles* [the act the current consensus asserts was written not by Shakespeare but by George Wilkins] both Pericles and Gower comment on the chaos of the elements in a flat, moralizing way," Leggatt observes. "In the act three storm [Shakespeare at the helm] we suddenly hear the roar of the water, feel the rocking of the boat, and sense the dreadful otherness of the natural world."

And then he compares this heightening of the tempestuousness of the storm to the heightened representation of sex in Shakespeare: "Sex in the early scenes of *Romeo and Juliet,* in the jokes of the servants and Mercutio, is a matter of standing and thrusting, putting things into other things: weaponry and plumbing. But when Juliet anticipates her wedding—and though she has never had sex, she knows what she wants—she evokes the feeling of a shared orgasm that wipes out consciousness and identity. The pleasure created in these moments of surprise is the pleasure of discovering there is more in this character, more in language, more in our own experience than we thought possible five minutes ago."

Needless to say, I sought to recall that "shared orgasm that wipes out consciousness" moment in *Romeo and Juliet,* wondering if it had wiped out *my* consciousness of it. But fortunately Leggatt supplies the citation, takes note of a debate over it and goes on to make a surprisingly more persuasive case for his conjecture than I had imagined.

He cites the line in the third act when Juliet cries out, "Give me my Romeo, and, when I shall die / Take him and cut him out in little stars" (3.2.21–22). And, Leggatt tells us, "the collapsing of Romeo's death into hers (editors used to find this illogical and emended accordingly) is the wiping out of consciousness and individual identity in a moment of love-making after which the lovers could ask, 'Which of us came just now?' "

What was that last bit again? Let's proceed slowly through this, beginning with Leggatt's passing but crucial remark about editors' emendations of "when I shall die."

He did not spell out the "emendation" debate, assuming, I'd guess, that the scholars around the table were all familiar with it, although this auditor on the periphery was not. But it becomes apparent that the emendation he says editors employed was to follow the Fourth Quarto and have Juliet say, "Give me my Romeo, and, when *he* shall die . . . cut him out in little stars," rather than "when *I* shall die," which appears in the earlier printed texts.

The emended version "when he shall die" makes more obvious sense, why cut him up into stars when he's still alive?

But Leggatt seems to suggest something more sexual than astronomical is being referred to here. Leggatt's interpretation depends on construing Juliet's "to die" as a synonym for "to have an orgasm," a common sexual connotation at the time. This is plausible; Shakespeare and Donne are tireless in making recurrent plays upon this duality.

So, if I'm reading Leggatt right, he's saying that when Juliet talks about dying and cutting Romeo out in stars to make the night shine, she's imagining an orgasm (without having had sex, he concedes, but "knowing what she wants"). And not just any orgasm, but one where she'll, in effect, "see stars," Romeo making "the face of heaven so fine" for her. A kind of orgasmic light show, accompanied by loss of consciousness, of identity of the sort that has the lovers wondering, as Leggatt puts it, "Which of us came just now?"

Not "*How* was it for you, dear?", but "*Who* was it for you, dear?"

I admired the daring of Leggatt's conjecture, so unashamedly confessional as well as exegetical. Almost like Greenblatt declaring his love. A thought crossed my mind: On this tempest-tossed weekend in Bermuda, was some *Tempest*-like spell causing ordinarily reserved scholars to *declare* themselves in ways rarely heard before?

Greenblatt coming out frankly praising Shakespeare's "indelible beauties," Leggatt locating in Juliet's lines a peak of sexual pleasure in Shakespeare, a moment of orgasmic identity loss, one that Leggatt seemed willing to declare he shared with his Juliet.

I suppose I've tended to wishful thinking about signs such as these, but there were, I suspect, more than these two signs. It felt a bit like the fabled "Prague Spring" in academia here in Bermuda, with the old orthodoxies of Theory open to question, and a return to (a revised, contextualized, historicized, heavily theorized) version of close reading once again.

But I don't want to scant Leggatt's close reading of that "cut him out in little stars" passage, I don't want to do a disservice if I characterize his conjecture as merely confessional. It was exegetical as well and I'd like to look more closely at his exegesis of the "cut him out in little stars" passage. It had always struck me as one of those moments of wild Shakespearean beauty, exquisitely excessive, and, yes, once heard, indelible. A uniquely Shakespearean moment of pleasure.

And I thought it interesting that Leggatt spoke of it in terms of identity exchange. I'd been struck in recent cycles of rereading by the recurrent moments of identity exchange (not just gender change) in Shakespeare—there's one in virtually every single play. The theme of exchange of eyes, the exchange of "I's," the exchange of selves in Shakespeare.

I've spoken of the experience of dissociation of identity that a single sonnet had on me (granted, in a nonsexual context, the Yale classroom). I got the feeling that Leggatt had had that experience in *some other* context, let's say, one that he nonetheless related to what he believes to be an otherwise cryptic passage in Shakespeare.

Let me put the moment in more context since it could be said to be the very fulcrum of the play, the very threshold of the tragedy, the moment when the tragic end has already been triggered, but the news has not yet reached Juliet, who is ardently awaiting Romeo's visit so they can consummate their surreptitious marriage. It is the moment just before she learns that Romeo has killed her cousin Tybalt, initiating a concatenation of events that will lead to their deaths in the Capulets' tomb.

But for the moment she is expressing impatience with the night for not hurrying and bringing Romeo and consummation with him. Here it is again. Read it through Leggatt's lens and see if *you* feel there's an orgasm in there, see if Leggatt's reading makes sense to you.

Come, gentle night, come, loving, black-brow'd night,
Give me my Romeo, and, when I shall die,
Take him and cut him out in little stars,
And he will make the face of heaven so fine
That all the world will be in love with night,
And pay no worship to the garish sun.

Where is the orgasmic identity exchange? Leggatt locates it vaguely and obscurely in "the collapsing of Romeo's death into hers." Something he points to as happening in the conspicuously unusual original version that has Juliet saying "when *I* shall die" rather than "when *he* shall die." Making it about her sexuality, rather than his death . . . And the collapsing? Perhaps in the traces of the death—Romeo's—we expected her to speak of? The result of Juliet somehow collapsing her death into the expected death of Romeo? Or conjuring up another kind of death, a sexual "death," a *petite mort* for herself? I think that's what he's saying.

But what about "the wiping out of consciousness and individual identity in a moment of love-making"? Is this Leggatt getting into a fond reverie, or is he persuasive in reading into the text a moment of imagined (very special) orgasm?

In Leggatt's defense I could cite a markedly similar moment of identity change later in the same speech of Juliet.

When she speaks of having been married, but not having consummated the marriage, Juliet says:

O, I have bought the mansion of a love,
But not possess'd it, and though I am sold,
Not yet enjoy'd.

There is that same identity switch—confusion, dissociation, doubleness, whatever you want to call it—in these lines. She is both buyer and object bought: she bought the mansion, then she *is* the mansion bought. So, metaphorically, she's possessor of Romeo's body but also the body to be possessed, arguably both at the same time. Both, simultaneously, the same mansion. A collapsing of identity, or rather perhaps a *cohabiting* of identity.

Russ McDonald perceptively pointed out, in a 1994 introduction to an essay on the revival of close reading, that the term "undecidability" had replaced "ambiguity" in Shakespeare studies, in literary studies in general. I'm not sure I'm happy with the replacement.

"Undecidable" carries more than a trace of the failed imperative *to* decide, as if deciding should be the goal, as if decidability were preferable to undecidability. As opposed to "both/and" ambiguity, entertaining both possibilities without deciding. Entertaining in the sense of both giving and taking pleasure in the possibilities. Allowing both to exist simultaneously, changing each other's identity in a pulsating fashion if you follow Stephen Booth's recurrent metaphor.

All of which is to say I think Leggatt's conjecture probably should remain in the new realm of "undecidability," textual purgatory for a while. I'd like to see other responses to it.

Despite some reservations I might have about his specific readings, Leggatt is the kind of scholar I admire, one with an instinct for particularly resonant passages. Who causes us to look closer at moments like Lear's last words, and Juliet's . . . whatever happened to her in that passage.

Another thing I liked about Leggatt's paper was the emphasis he put on "surprise." In fact he called his paper "The Pleasure of Surprise," and the element of surprise figures prominently in his account of Shakespearean pleasure. It's akin to Kermode's evocation of the experience of being on the "threshold of comprehension" of something new. The brink of surprise and the brink of surmise. The brink of amazement. The brink of a maze.

And Leggatt's conclusion was a frank challenge: "A good deal of Shakespeare criticism makes us feel we have had the meaning but missed the experience; we need to start recovering the experience." Recovering: John Andrews seeks to recover the original spelling for the deeper experience of the Shakespearean spell, Steven Berkoff the original emotional spell. I thought of Berkoff doing the Garrick gesture, that signature gesture of Shakespearean surprise: Hamlet's seeing his father's ghost. What I find over and over in Shakespeare is that, on one level or another, I'm throwing up my hands in surprise, on the brink of comprehension, seeing, if not a ghost, then an unexpected specter emerging from the text. Trying to recover such moments—and recover from them.

O HAPPY ACCIDENCE

If there is an element of surprise peculiar to Shakespearean pleasure it is often the surprise of continually exceeded expectations. A passage that seems familiar, one you've read a dozen times, suddenly surprises you with an entirely new dimension. Perhaps because until one has reread all of Shakespeare a dozen times and other passages have successively yielded up new dimensions, only then does *this one* suddenly become available, apparent when it hadn't been before. Only the cumulative experience, the critical mass of previous rereadings, can propel it over the threshold of comprehension.

In Bermuda at the Pleasure Seminar, in Joseph Porter's talk I found a word I liked for the kind of thing one discovers in such circumstances: "accidence." A word that sounds like but does not exactly mean "accidents" but which *does* have an element of suddenness, surprise and even shock to it, the shock at the discovery of some unexpected coherence, correlation between a phrase in one play and a phrase in the same or another play, that gives one a deeper sense of the vibrancy of the whole.

The somewhat obscure title of Porter's talk, "Pangs of Scriptive Transparency," referred to what I found to be a thoughtful and earnest attempt by the Duke professor and literary novelist to capture just what is unique to Shakespearean pleasure. Something we feel, but somehow find hard to put into words that do justice to it.

Porter begins by defending the idea of seeking to elucidate the nature of Shakespearean pleasure against what he calls the "puritanical renunciation of the pleasures of the text in Shakespeare study of recent decades."

Then he tries to describe something he calls Shakespeare's "distinctively, transparently scriptive pleasures," how Shakespeare provides distinctive pleasure through "his pervasive and transparent writtenness . . . and it is a pleasure *Shakespeare himself* seems to take from his work" (my italics).

"Writtenness"? "Scriptiveness"? Yes, we all know Shakespeare was initially written, scripted with a pen and all that. No, I think he's referring to certain passages where Shakespeare seems carried away with the power of words, with his own power over words, and conjures them into a localized tour de force, sometimes excessive seeming, sometimes almost *about* the fructifying excess of language, about reveling in the pleasure of it when under its spell. The hounds-and-echo passage. The double-cherry passage.

Porter cites an example from an essay by the poet and critic John Crowe Ransom. Ransom singled out a three-line phrase from *Macbeth:*

> *. . . No; this my hand will rather*
> *The multitudinous seas incarnadine,*
> *Making the green one red.*

It's Macbeth speaking of the way he can't wash the blood off his hands; implicitly if he dips them in the ocean it will turn the ocean itself red with blood.

I'm always struck by the use of "incarnadine" as a transitive verb, for "turn red." Porter calls the passage "a jewel . . . that serves as a lexical lens or synopsis of the whole body of Shakespeare's language. Its pleasures are partly metrical—the striking hypermetrical 'multitudinous' enacting itself in a surf-like wash, and the metrically striking 'green one red' concentrating the tripartite structure of the entire preceding line."

What is it about such passages that gives pleasure?

For Porter the passage "opens vantages into Shakespeare's pervasive scriptiveness, present even in performance which reveals itself transparently in the features noted and also in the scriptive and readerly movement from 'hand' through 'seas' (to 'sees') to 'red' ('read'). Such pleasures furthermore do not occlude Macbeth's character and extremity. Rather the lines let us peer into the unprecedented fear of the warrior never before disturbed by blood even as the lines also *in their transparent writtenness evince something like an attendant imaginative bloodying of the writer's hand*" (my italics).

There's an appealing combination of attentive close reading and winging it (does "red" really evoke "read"?) all balanced on the very threshold of comprehension. He's circling around something real but hard to define explicitly in his almost ritual incantation of "writerliness" and "scriptiveness." I think he's talking about the same thing Stephen Booth was talking about when he hailed the hounds-and-echo passage in the *Dream* for what, with Boothian faux naïveté, he called "inspired dog talk." We love the moments of "thick description" as anthropologists call it in Shakespeare's work, when the hounds of his verbal imagination are loosed from the leash of dramatic economy.

But Porter's final attempt at getting at the question was the most illuminating, I thought.

He concluded by citing Hal in *Henry IV*: "nothing pleaseth but rare accidents." And makes another daring but more persuasive leap (than "red"/ "read") by summoning up the secondary meaning of "accidents" at the time Shakespeare wrote: "accidence," a secondary meaning which the *OED* says was current from 1589 to 1612 and which describes what we might call *resonances* between phenomena, and, here especially, words. In a way "accidence" is the opposite of "accidents." (It's coherent instances of things that *co-incide,* rather than *coincidence.*) Resonances that once again are apprehended on the "threshold of comprehension."

Porter concluded his paper by praising Shakespeare's "characteristic acumen about the rarity, the enabling and poignant transience of all pleasure."

A beautiful, pleasurable sentence about pleasure. "Enabling and poignant transience" is an almost Shakespearean hendiadys,* and I'd suspect an intentional attempt to approximate one. "Enabling transience"—the vitalizing charge that the inevitability of death and change give to life. Poignant because a consequence of mortality. Again a Bermuda effect? Porter, self-described in his paper as "a literary novelist" as well as scholar, making a daring raid on Shakespearean language.

But I liked an "accidence" because it seemed another way of expressing what I've been groping toward saying when I speak of the dizzying pleasure of bottomlessness, the thrill of unending, ever-deepening and echoing resonances of accidence. Bottom's Dream and "The Bay of Portugal that hath no bottom" in *As You Like It.*

THE PLEASURES AND DISPLEASURES OF THE LATE LANGUAGE

I had been looking forward to my Bermuda lunch with Russ McDonald before I'd read his essay on the "late language" issue. An essay which I would like somehow to enshrine as a model of scholarly erudition and extraordinarily sensitive engagement with language.

* "Hendiadys" is the figure of speech for a phrase that exhibits simultaneous division and fusion. "The book and volume of my brain" in *Hamlet,* for instance. Frank Kermode and George T. Wright here in the United States wrote famous analyses of hendiadys in *Hamlet,* a play where it occurs more than in any other Shakespearean drama. Reflecting perhaps the dividedness of its hero.

The "late language." When it comes to "undecidability" there may be no more seductive yet irresolvable question than the one that has been posed, most recently by Frank Kermode, about the pleasures and displeasures of Shakespeare's "late language."

I want to consider it under the aspect of pleasure because I believe the question of what we find displeasing and how we define our displeasure can tell us something about pleasure.

For too long, Kermode argues in his continually provocative *Shakespeare's Language,* scholars and exegetes have sought to rescue Shakespeare from himself, sought to find—as Stephen Booth does—that passages that appear to give displeasure, passages that seem opaque, needlessly, even carelessly, tangled rather than merely knotted—subsequently turn out to yield a higher pleasure when what *appears* opaque is rendered transparent (or translucent). When what *appears* tangled is unknotted by close reading. Holes become wholes.

Kermode argued, on the contrary, that not only is it true that Shakespeare *could* write badly, but that in places, especially in the later plays such as *Coriolanus* and *The Winter's Tale,* he did seem to write in a fashion that was sloppily or hastily opaque. Opaque in a way that could not be made transparent by the most gifted exegete.

It is also true and important, Kermode said, to acknowledge Shakespeare's responsibility, his occasional limitations, if, in effect, we want to credit him with the kind of greatness some find "indelible."

The distinctiveness of Kermode's approach, in fact the genesis of his new book, he told me in a phone call from his office at Cambridge University, was his willingness to argue that some of Shakespeare, particularly some of the later, deeply knotted, compacted verse, simply failed to make sense. "There's lots of what has to be called bad writing," Kermode said.

Around 1600, in works like *Hamlet* and *Measure for Measure,* Kermode believes Shakespeare found a new way of representing the mind in the process of thinking. (This is not the same as Bloom's great claim that Shakespeare "invented the human" or created self-consciousness—Kermode told me he regards such claims by Bloom as "incense burning.") But Kermode also believes that by 1608, beginning with *Coriolanus,* Shakespeare's language often becomes too fraught, too overwrought to bear the weight of the meaning he wants to load into it: "He doesn't take the time to make it work."

OF COURSE THE PROBLEM IS THAT READERS, EXEGETES, OFTEN DO give up too soon, and there are times one can render what *seems* opaque, if not transparent, at least translucent (trans-lucid? trance lucid?). So we always have to ask ourselves: Is it him or is it we who are not making sense? Is it we because we have not reread the plays in their entirety enough times to be able to make a lucid conjecture about the apparent opacity?

And it takes a kind of critical daring, if not hubris, to say with any finality that it's Shakespeare who failed or failed to try (as Kermode has it) to make himself clear. And then of course we have to question how high a value we place on clarity when obscurity can give off a dark glow that can transcend transparency. Shakespearean translucence.

Kermode believes *Coriolanus* is a kind of test of this question. It was perhaps the last tragedy Shakespeare wrote and represents an endpoint of Shakespeare's testing the limits of language, "probably the most difficult play in the canon. . . . It has passages that continue to defeat modern editors." One such passage he cites is this from the first act:

When steel grows soft as the parasite's silk,
Let him be made an overture for th' wars.
No more, I say! For that I have not wash'd
My nose that bled, or foil'd some debile wretch—
Which, without note, here's many else have done—
You [shout] me forth
In acclamations hyperbolical,
As if I lov'd my little should be dieted
In praises sauc'd with lies.

For Kermode such passages in *Coriolanus* are not without virtues despite their confusion. He believes that *Coriolanus* represents the endpoint of an evolution of Shakespearean language that began with his earliest (1594) tragedy, *Titus Andronicus,* and culminated nearly fifteen years later in *Coriolanus,* a play in which we "register the pace of the speech, its sudden turns, its backtrackings, its metaphors flashing before us and disappearing before we can consider them. This is new: the representation of excited anxious thought; the weighing of confused possibilities and dubious motives; the proposing of a theory or explanation followed at once by its abandonment or qualification as in the meditation of a person under stress. . . ."

At times, he implies, under too *much* stress to maintain coherency. To return to that passage above, about the "parasite's silk." The general sense of it isn't that hard to get, is it? Corrupt and luxurious times breed weakness. In the absence of steel-minded men the parasite thrives, a situation which is overture, prelude to a war invited by weakness.

But when you try to make the sentence make some kind of literal sense, there's a problem. Beginning with who's "him" in the first two lines? The parasite or the softened men of steel?

And look at the three-word judgment that appears in the footnote on "overture" in the respected *Riverside Shakespeare:* "Hard to explain."

That's it? "Hard to explain"? Well, there are a few stabs at it cited by the *Riverside:* "Sisson takes [overture] to mean 'herald'—let the parasite summon men to war. Many editors adopt Tyrwhitt's emendation *coverture*—let silk supersede armor as martial garb. Moore Smith conjectures [that 'overture' is actually] *officer*—let the parasite become a soldier."

Don't you love centuries-long disputes like this? Well, I do. And here is the great dilemma of close reading. Must we join Moore Smith and conjecture that this is just an *error*—that Shakespeare wouldn't have written or meant "overture"? That it was "coverture"? Or should we join Sisson and Tyrwhitt in tying ourselves into knots to make "overture" work? Or Kermode in saying there's no knot but an impossible tangle? Are the possibilities of making this passage "work" bottomless, or is there a point at which we should give up, having exhausted even the conspicuously irrelevant possibilities, and find we're digging a grave rather than "gliding over an abyss"?

Kermode believes that late Shakespeare sometimes didn't quite hone the inking of what he was thinking to the point of making mere semantic sense, because he was capturing the way a disordered mind races ahead of its words—or because a hurried playwright raced over something too trying, or too time-consuming, to stop, return and regularize.

Nobody has a very persuasive answer really, although I tend to side with those, like Booth, whose instinct is to feel it's *us,* in most cases—that we've just so far failed to see the coherence in the *apparent* incoherence. Because I've had the repeated experience on rereading something for the tenth or twelfth time and suddenly seeing it in a new light entirely, seeing it as an echo of some other passage that struck me three rereadings ago, seeing something beneath the surface that was invisible before.

Would we want the "parasite's silk" passage to read differently? "Parasite's silk": it hisses in a sinister way as it rustles past us surreptitiously, conjuring up the worm in the cocoon, the serpentine origin of beautiful lines, casting enough of a malign spell to convince us we've grasped its meaning. Shakespeare, one imagines, came up with the phrase and there were so many things he could do with it, he left it in a somewhat flawed setting, perhaps bewildered himself about the richness, pleasure and potential of the phrase. Not wishing to pin down the pupa within that silk cocoon before it can become a butterfly.

There are moments in Shakespeare's late language when one could say with Kermode that Shakespeare's mind is racing too fast for his "scriptiveness" to completely catch up. And then there are moments like this when we might rather have it that way—have the hint of something so intense or complex even Shakespeare can't completely capture it in words. And so he leaves us with a less than perfectly articulate record of something *having* happened, leaves us a gesture of surprise, with the writer as well as the reader on the threshold of comprehension. A clue to the landscape where words fail even Shakespeare. Eliot called poetry "a raid on the inarticulate." We should be grateful when even Shakespeare's raids bring back barely articulable fragments.

It's as if Shakespeare was reaching a limit to how much *accidence* could be loaded into a line or passage without it collapsing on itself.

THE ULTIMATE FLOATING SIGNIFIER

I had been thinking about the question, and by happy accidence had come upon, in the booksellers' room at the Bermuda convention, a Cambridge University Press volume, *Shakespeare and Language,* edited by Catherine Alexander.

It contained a number of essays by scholars I'd found illuminating in the past. There was Stephen Booth's essay "Shakespeare's Language and the Language of Shakespeare's Time" that begins with a memorable one-liner, an inimitable Boothian witticism at the beginning, droll yet profound: "Shakespeare," his essay opens, "is our most underrated poet."

It's joking, but it's a serious argument in its own way. Contained within that opening sentence is really the polar opposite position to that of Kermode. Kermode says Shakespeare occasionally has not slowed down sufficiently to make complete sense. And that we tend to overrate his words at times. Booth is saying *we* are not (yet) worthy, we have not given Shakespeare enough credit. That when we feel he's failed, it may be our failure because we continue to vastly underestimate the beauties of his accidence.

Nor may we ever be able to plumb the depths. Shakespeare may not be bottomless "objectively," but he may be bottomless in practice, bottomless to us, given the limited time on the planet we have to reread and reread Shakespeare. The works will exhaust us, outlive us before we reach bottom. Not only are there too many ways we can read a line but too many ways we can speak it and too many ways we can act it, and too many combinations and permutations of commentaries in each of these categories we can apprehend. That may be the problem with Shakespearean obscurity: it's not necessarily "undecidable," there's just not enough time to decide. Not "evidentiary despair" but *exegetical* despair. Life is too short to really plumb the depths.

And then, in that same volume as the Booth essay, another perspective entirely on the "late language": Russ McDonald's essay, which I hadn't read before: "Late Shakespeare: Style and the Sexes." Published in 1994, some six years or more before Kermode's book, it nonetheless suggested a way of looking at the whole "late language" dispute in a new context: the debate between Ciceronian and Senecan rhetorical principles and the gendered connotations of each.

Wait! Please don't all rush for the exits! This is a truly important piece of thinking about Shakespearean language—it addresses directly the question Kermode raises about the almost willful difficulty of the late language, and I don't want to do it a disservice with that summary by making it seem too arcanely academic. In fact, it gave me great pleasure to read, there are so many felicities of thought and feeling. And one very profound conjecture.

It sets itself apart from conventional academic thinking with its opening announcement of its methodological assumption.

His method, McDonald says, of comparing complex verse patterns in the late plays "assumes artistic agency, an author in whose dramatic productions we may observe both a distinctive style and distinct mutations in that style. In this respect it resists the claims of much recent discursive criticism which behaves as if a play were author of itself and 'knew no other kin' " (a phrase from *Coriolanus*).

Artistic agency! It's the postmodern way of saying that an artist has some autonomy and personal responsibility, for better or worse, for his or her work. At the time McDonald wrote, the concept was in much disrepute in mainstream lit-crit Theory.

You can see McDonald treading carefully, with such an explosive notion to convey: he takes pains to say he's not denying "external [historical, cultural] influences" but he believes in the existence of an author whose choices can in some sense be said to be the result of his own deliberations.

He speaks of doing so, "the currently low repute of formalist criticism notwithstanding." And makes a politic plea that he is not seeking to reinstate pre-Theory formalism (looking only at the "internal" rather than "external" contexts and aspects of the poem). Good God, not that! Instead he defers to respected scholar Patricia Parker's contention that " 'to pay attention to the structural force of rhetorical figures' " or characteristics of artistic technique is to " 'suggest that the impasse of a now apparently outworn formalism and a new competing emphasis on politics and history might be breached [that is, the "impasse" might be bridged] by questions which fall in between and hence remain unasked by both.' "

It's remarkable that in the decade or so since this was written with its reference to "the currently low repute of formalist criticism," the "low repute" would morph into what was coming increasingly to be called "neo-formalism," a resurgence of close reading under the guise of having "incorporated the insights of Theory."

It would be a mistake to underestimate the influence of Russ McDonald on this salutary development. In particular the influence of another book on close reading (*Shakespeare Re-read*), a collection of essays he edited, and the subtle but powerful force of his argument for rereading close reading in the Introduction to that book.

In it he contended it was time to get past "a phase in which context supplanted text, history dominated poetry." He called for "a rapprochement between the intrinsic and external" but made clear that what he really hoped for was "reconceiving the possibilities of close reading."

If there is a figure in Shakespeare studies whose work gives me the most hope for "the profession," it's Russ McDonald and the evident influence his careful brilliant scholarship has had in leading others to a return to the study of the language, a "reconceived" close reading. Indeed next to my iBook as I write are a stack of books and Shakespearean quarterlies which attest to a genuine sea change in "the profession" (one of the better ones: *Renaissance Literature and Its Formal Engagements,* edited by Mark David Rasmussen).

I have a feeling that McDonald's own work was the best advertisement for his position. He had found a way to bring something, if not new, then newly reconsidered, to the study of Shakespeare's language: an attentiveness to the rich literature on figurative speech that saturated the bookstalls of London during Shakespeare's time. Guides to figures of speech, metaphors, tropes taken from classical and medieval handbooks, manuals of rhetorical devices. George Puttenham's *Arte of English Poesie* and Henry Peacham's *Garden of Eloquence* for instance.

McDonald identified the way the excited debate about language in the Elizabethan age, the ferment over figurative and rhetorical style and technique, shaped—and was reshaped by—Shakespeare, and the thematic implications of the formal effects to be found embedded in the language.

I met McDonald for lunch in the bar lounge of Bermuda's Southampton Princess. He's a soft-spoken Southerner; his father, he tells me, was a mill worker in Houston. As a student he too had a transformative experience of Peter Brook's *Dream.* He became one of those scholars of Shakespearean language who are enthusiasts for stage productions as well. In fact, as I've had occasion to mention earlier, one of his most recent books is *Look to the Lady,* a study of three great Shakespearean actresses over the past three centuries: Sarah Siddons, Ellen Terry and Judi Dench.

And his essay on the "late language" that I'd found so illuminating might be said to look to the lady as well. Nonetheless I sensed McDonald wince slightly when I brought it up because, he said, it had been misunderstood in some quarters. It was, in part, a careful study of the misogynist Elizabethan caricature of femininity and the way it had crept into the debates over linguistic style at the time. But some, I gathered he feared, might have thought he was *advocating* the position on the sexual typology of language he was *examining.*

He summarizes his argument this way at the opening of the essay (which first appeared in *Shakespeare Survey,* a respected annual):

That the difficult "complex verse patterns in the late plays are intimately related to Shakespeare's imaginative recovery of the feminine, and that the origins of the conflict between masculine and feminine rhetoric emerge in the late classical tragedies and that the romances constitute a kind of conditional resolution of these concerns."

He argues that this "recovery of the feminine" can be found even in the way the metrics of the pentameter line shift "from what has been called the end-stopped form of tragedy" to "the more open form of the romance."

The essay offers a beautiful example of McDonald's method, which combines erudite scholarship and close reading. For instance, he agrees with Kermode about the difficulty of the language in *Coriolanus:* ". . . there are almost no conjunctions, Martius's [Coriolanus's] speeches lack connectives both within and between sentences and such withholding creates a disjunctivity. . . ."

But where Kermode finds this "disjunctivity" a careless, unfinished, not fully thought-out quality, at least in some places, McDonald draws on his extensive knowledge of Elizabethan rhetorical literature—those "gardens of eloquence" and handbooks of classical Latin and Greek figures of speech popular during Shakespeare's time—and tells us, "The pertinent rhetorical figure here is *asyndeton,* the omission of conjunctions between words, phrases or clauses."

In other words, one may dislike Shakespeare's rhetorical style in *Coriolanus* but it is not necessarily the result of carelessness; it has a formal and classical precedent that may have been a matter of choice rather than laziness.

He argues that there's a thematic significance to the choice of rhetorical trope, to the use of asyndeton:

"It is not difficult to see how Shakespeare's most habitually isolated hero [Coriolanus] should speak a language in which the interdependence of sentences is suppressed, in which clauses do not touch. . . . His speech constitutes the grammatical equivalent of his famous desire for freedom from familial or other types of relations, his desire to 'stand / As if a man were author of himself / and knew no other kin.' "

It is only now that McDonald puts his risky rhetorical strategy into play. Puts the difficulty of the late language in the perspective of the debate over language and gender that swirled throughout the amazing burst of eloquence that was the Elizabethan age.

In particular the debate between the Senecan and the Ciceronian style, between Seneca's and Cicero's opposed philosophies of word and world, between "masculine" and "feminine" language.

The debate between the highly embellished Ciceronian style and the comparatively Spartan Senecan style, McDonald writes, "is grounded in conceptions of sexual difference and is related to the figuration of language as feminine, and action as masculine in early modern language theory. The misogynist tradition inherited from the Middle Ages propagated the notion that language resembles women in being treacherous and unreliable, subject to extravagance, malleability and error."

In other words, he adds, "the attack on women familiar to medieval literature was often a simultaneous attack on language. Commentators reached as far back as Eden to connect the female with the decorative, the artificial, the inessential. . . . As Tertullian [the early church theologian] put it, 'with the word, the garment entered.' " Just as garments "entered" after the Fall. Cloaking naked truth with verbal ambiguity and potential deceptiveness.

McDonald puts *Coriolanus* in the context of this dispute over the allegedly treacherous femininity of language. He speaks of the way "*Coriolanus* . . . presents a contest of styles with each side sexually marked. The Baconian, phallic position informs the laconic speech of Coriolanus, who flees from words. Volumnia [his mother] on the other hand represents Ciceronian loquacity and indirection."

And then he turns from the last pure tragedy to that mixture of tragedy and romance, *Antony and Cleopatra,* where the "contest" has shifted in favor of, or at least in thematic attentiveness to, Cleopatra as "the embodiment of those [language] values for which Volumnia so eloquently and lengthily pleads—multiplicity, equivocation. . . . Enshrined on the barge through the medium of Enobarbus' encomium [the description quoted earlier] she is the ultimate floating signifier, the play's main figure (like her ancestor, Falstaff) of verbal prowess and ambiguity."

"The ultimate floating signifier"! It is, among other things, a great lit-crit in-joke, "floating signifier" being a favorite postmodernist term for the waywardness of language's signification. McDonald has in effect *re-constructed* the deconstructionist idea of a floating signifier and embodied it in Cleopatra floating, shimmering on her barge. It's a remarkably smart and funny line that makes "floating signifier" far more persuasive a concept than I've ever found it before.

That description of Cleopatra on the barge becomes for McDonald the locus of a momentous shift in late Shakespeare language from masculine to feminine, from Senecan to Ciceronian. A shift not unaccompanied by ambiguity, or as McDonald puts it: "the playwright's ambiguous attitude toward ambiguity" becomes evident as well as his inability to resist it and its potential treachery. (Love the "ambiguous attitude toward ambiguity"!)

It is for McDonald the pivotal, fulcrum-like moment when Shakespeare embraces baroque embellishment, not just of plot, but of language, without renouncing his mistrust. The way one can embrace a woman despite one's mistrust. (Or so I've heard.) The moment when Shakespeare becomes, in effect, Mark Antony, and language his "fatal Cleopatra." Loved madly, a Cleopatra to whom he gives himself over, however self-destructively. Even at times, at the expense of sense.

McDonald proposes a comparison so insightful, it made me envious: "If we were to read Shakespeare's professional development allegorically as I have proposed, then Antony becomes the central figure for the dramatist poised stylistically between the masculine and feminine, the Attic [classical Greek] and the [stereotypically more wild and baroque] Asiatic."

Antony's "dissolute behavior is censured by Octavius in language of dissolution ('the ebb'd man') and Antony himself adopts such terms in the celebrated passage from the suicide scene that begins with the image of the shifting cloud, continues with the liquid metaphor of lost difference ('as indistinct / As water is in water') [the lost drop of water from *Comedy of Errors* wanders, or trickles, back into the picture!] and ends with 'Here I am Antony, / Yet cannot hold this visible shape . . .' As the rhythms and syntax of *Antony and Cleopatra* indicate, the contours of Shakespeare's verse tend to melt in the heat of the Egyptian sun."

I guess some of this—Shakespeare as Antony—might have been implicit in Samuel Johnson's rather dire condemnation of Shakespeare's inability to resist the seduction of strained puns and wordplay as his "fatal Cleopatra."

But in Johnson's pejorative metaphor Shakespeare is Antony whoring after *unworthy* temptresses. After the kind of forced punning that Alexander Leggatt dismisses when he describes the sexual puns at the opening of *Romeo and Juliet* as about plumbing, what part goes where, crude and sexual. McDonald is saying something more here.

When he's talking about Shakespeare as Antony (and Cleopatra as language), he's not just talking about the punning language Johnson objected to, but about *all* the beauties and pleasures, the extravagance and treacheries, the fluidity, liquidity, slipperiness of language, as his Cleopatra. Not his fatal Cleopatra, but his *final* Cleopatra. Not someone he whores after, but someone he falls madly in love with.

At last: here was the kind of contention about love in Shakespeare I'd been looking for.

McDonald is careful to support his contention through close reading particularly attentive to the metrical style of the "late language." He cites

George T. Wright, the superb analyst of Shakespearean metrics, who "points out about the late style in general, 'the sense runs over . . . into the next line, a tendency facilitated by Shakespeare's radically increased use of weak and light line-endings,' or what used to be called feminine endings. . . .

"Rhythmically," McDonald continues, "the sense o'er flows the measure of the line [like the Nile and its banks]. In its syntax *Antony and Cleopatra* depends heavily on the figure known as *hyperbaton,* or as Puttenham [the sixteenth-century author of the guide to figures of speech *Arte of English Poesie*] Englishes it, 'the trespasser.' "

The trespasser! According to McDonald, Puttenham defines "the trespasser" in Book III of the *Arte of English Poesie,* "Of Ornament," in which he calls the "trespasser" a class of figures and literary devices that disrupt the classical formalities of verse. As McDonald catalogs its manifestations, they include: "Inverted word orders and disrupted sentences . . . inserted episodes, digressive scenes and disordered geography . . . increasingly metrical irregularity and syntactic disorder . . . frequent ellipsis and a reliance on verbless constructions."

Let us take a moment here to give McDonald credit for giving us an example of the values of actual scholarship: how many Shakespeareans have actually read Book III of the *Arte of English Poesie*? And how many would emerge from it with a breathtaking conjectural leap about love and language as McDonald does?

> The final movement, from Antony's suicide to the end of the play, constitutes the bridge between the tragedies and the romances because it attests to Shakespeare's developing attitude toward fictional language . . . this final episode depends upon an imaginative scrambling of gender, a recombination of the masculine and feminine. Cleopatra, a boy actor, neither man nor woman, talks her way into the male role of tragic hero, using women's weapons [extravagant language] . . . this imaginative union of the masculine and the feminine helps to account for Shakespeare's reconceived attitude towards words, verse style, dramatic mode, and the theatrical enterprise itself.

I have quoted at length from McDonald because his essay represents to me a different kind of Shakespearean pleasure one comes across all too infrequently: the pleasures of genuine scholarship combined with the pleasures of the scholar's own style. Locating in an obscure sixteenth-century rhetorical text a vocabulary that helps us speak about some deeply mysterious change in the DNA of Shakespearean language.

What struck me as well about McDonald's essay was its reticence. That phrase of his, "Shakespeare's recovery of the feminine," has an academic air about it that belies what he seems to be speaking about.

"Recovery of the feminine"? Yes, in part it's a way of referring to Shakespeare recovering "feminine" language from the disapprobation of the anti-Ciceronians.

It's the recovery of the feminine within the writer, within his language, within the way he plays with words, the pleasure he takes in extravagance and display. But it's also the "recovery of the feminine" in the sense that he abandons the mockery of love we find in *As You Like It,* say, and the recurrently cruel and unfaithful women that populate the tragedies.

The recovery of the feminine is also the recovery of love in Shakespeare. I think in "recovery of the feminine" McDonald is alluding as well to Shakespeare's increasingly tempestuous, yet forgiving, relationship, his love affair, with language.

Chapter Fifteen

"No Cause": The Unexpected Pleasures of Forgiveness

I WOULD LIKE TO MAKE A SUGGESTION ABOUT FORGIVENESS AND pleasure in Shakespeare, about forgiveness as perhaps the ultimate pleasure.

It's not a familiar way to think about it—forgiveness as pleasure. Pleasure being associated so often with the sensual, the carnal, the esthetic, and forgiveness with the ascetic and spiritual. And yet, forgiveness: perhaps it's not merely an ideal, it is, in a certain sense, on another level, a pleasure as well. It's not often defined as a pleasure, it's rarely mentioned as one of those numinous "pleasures of Shakespeare," but I've come to think a case can be made that the pleasures of forgiveness are, in some way, more central to the Shakespearean experience than often recognized.

Forgiveness, both for the forgiver and the forgiven: if it's not a pleasure of the senses, nor a pleasure (solely) of the intellect, it still can feel at some level deeply pleasurable. It's a different kind of pleasure, but it's felt as a pleasure of some kind nonetheless, isn't it?

Perhaps the experience of the "sea change" in the profession in Bermuda had something to do with my focus on forgiveness. I was able to give up some of my anger at academia as the tide and tyranny of Theory receded. But I must give credit to my friend Helen Whitney, the documentary filmmaker with whom I'd once worked (PBS's *Faith and Doubt at Ground Zero*). Helen is a rare phenomenon: a subtle intellect not afraid to take on big topics—"ideals"—that many less audacious intellects shy away from. Shortly after I came back from Bermuda, she told me over coffee that she'd been approached to make a documentary on the theme of "forgiveness."

I think that's when I began to start thinking consciously, systematically, about forgiveness in Shakespeare—although it hadn't been absent from my thinking about Shakespeare before then. When doing an essay on a production of *Henry V* for *The Shakespeare Newsletter* I was surprised when I found myself focusing on forgiveness as the neglected subtextual drama of the play.

I was fascinated by the recurrent staging and restaging of moments of forgiveness in *Henry V*: pleas for forgiveness, hypocritical forgiveness, debates about mercy, displays of what you might call "meretricious mercifulness" in that play. I argued, "*Henry V* is as much a play about mercy as *Merchant of Venice.*"

So much so that I gave the essay the somewhat perverse title "The Quality of Mercy in *Henry V*," after the line in Portia's famous speech on the subject in *The Merchant.*

What I began to realize, as I focused further on it, was that in almost every Shakespearean play one could find an examination of "the quality of mercy," the pleasure of forgiveness, or the conspicuous absence of it.

And thinking about forgiveness in Shakespeare I suddenly found myself coming full circle in a way. My initiation, my induction into Shakespeare had climaxed with a powerfully memorable moment of forgiveness at the close of Peter Brook's *Dream.*

I found myself thinking what a *shock* of pleasure that moment had been, with an emphasis on the somatic impact in "shock." It still gives me chills when I think of it. It reminded me what a primal function theater can serve, that Shakespeare can serve, moving us physically, shaking us with laughter or sobs, shocking us, leaving us pierced, shaken, Shake-speared with pleasure.

It was that moment at the climax of the *Dream* when Puck makes the traditional epilogue plea for forgiveness from the audience. That moment after the action of the play (Puck's final blessing on the three newlywed couples) comes to an end. The moment when Puck steps to the front of the stage, breaks the fourth wall to address the audience directly and begins to ask for forgiveness on behalf of the players and (implicitly) the playwright:

"If we shadows have offended, / Think but this, and all is mended . . ."

And concludes: "Give me your hands, if we be friends, / And Robin shall restore amends."

Forgive us and let us make amends: It is an almost literally crowd-pleasing moment. Especially in that case, when so many in the crowd had been given so much pleasure, we had so little to forgive and yet were being asked for forgiveness.

It was beautiful, it was pleasurable, and it became more than abstract when Brook's cast literalized "give me your hands" and Puck and the other actors came crawling over the lip of the stage to stretch out their hands, grasp ours and crawl into our world, almost as if out of the womb of fantasy.

An act reciprocated by the audience by grabbing their hands and pulling them off the stage into the pit. The power of that moment is what's remarkable to me. It felt extraordinary then, but I was young. Perhaps, I thought, life would be filled with moment after moment like this. Maybe it is for some, but not for me. I'm still grateful for that one.

Only later did I realize that, in a sense, they *did* have something to ask our forgiveness for. I realized this from talking to a wide range of people who'd seen Brook's *Dream.* Almost all of them said something similar to what I felt: it made virtually every later experience of Shakespeare on stage a disappointment to some degree. Left us feeling something was missing. Left us longing for that unique exhilaration we'd felt once and failed to recapture. So Brook and company have a lot to answer for.

I keep coming back to that "shock of pleasure." It was a shock that almost redefined pleasure for me. It was neither sensual nor strictly intellectual. I hesitate to say it was a spiritual pleasure, but it was not unlike a spiritual experience.

What was it? It was as if they were asking forgiveness for the inevitable separation from us, one that the clasped hands would only postpone. For the inevitable separation of reality and dream, reality and the realm of higher reality they'd briefly ascended to like Bottom. Taking us with them and then waking us and forcing us to abandon the dream.

And then—come on!—to find this experience repeated again when the theater caught fire as it did the second time I saw Brook's *Dream.* I'm not saying there's anything supernatural about it, but I do feel grateful for the conjuncture of those experiences. It felt like fate, and, in important ways, my fate *was* being shaped by seeing that play.

The fire, it seemed, and the response to it by actors and audience, was a kind of spontaneous combustion that validated a sense of primal communal experience embedded in this "insubstantial pageant." Something Brook, like Prospero, conjured up. A pleasure until then unknown to me.

A remarkable moment in my life, and certainly in my thinking about Shakespeare. And the more I began to think about it, the more I thought about other striking moments of forgiveness in Shakespeare and the way they are, so often, the final dramatic fulcrum in the plays. Often, in a way, the *real* denouement.

What I mean by this is that we know comedies will end in marriage, and tragedies will end in death. But underneath the familiar dramatic arcs defined by genre there are often other dramatic arcs whose resolution is less predictable: Who will be forgiven, who will be refused forgiveness?

A play beneath the play, often more suspenseful and unpredictable in denouement than that of the larger play. A play beneath the play whose arc and terminus are sometimes in harmony, sometimes out of synch with the arc and terminus of the play as a whole. A play beneath the play that climaxes when the possibility of forgiveness is fulfilled or not.

It suddenly occurred to me to wonder, is this the secret play, or at least *one* secret play, beneath all the plays?

Obviously the final plays of Shakespeare's career, if they are "about" anything, are explicitly about the possibility of forgiveness. But this shouldn't blind us to the preoccupation with the question of forgiveness in the earlier plays. Indeed, thinking about the epilogue of Brook's *Dream* made me realize how often moments of forgiveness within the other plays are echoed in the often overlooked (by me) epilogues to the plays.

I feel I owe the epilogues a debt of forgiveness: all too often I'd looked upon the epilogues as the remnant of a stale theatrical convention. They are often spoken in doggerel verse, not even pentameter. Not "Shakespearean" it sometimes seemed, in the grandest sense of the term, but rather Shakespeare deliberately diminishing himself and his powers to make the expected but pro forma plea for forgiveness.

But there he or she is, in play after play, the epilogue awkwardly appended at times, with a convoluted and de-familiarizing naked plea for forgiveness, which cumulatively make it impossible not to think there is something "Shakespearean" about them that deserves more attention and respect. Perhaps the plea for forgiveness is not pro forma at all.

And it occurred to me how many moments in the plays that are touchstones for me, are those moments of suspense on the "threshold of comprehension" (or perhaps "the threshold of compassion") when forgiveness is—often unexpectedly and dramatically—granted.

What is it about that moment in Lear's reunion with Cordelia that has such power? The moment when he tells her:

If you have poison for me, I will drink it.
I know you do not love me, for your sisters

Have (as I do remember) done me wrong:
You have some cause, they have not.

And Cordelia merely murmurs:

No cause, no cause.

Every time I hear that exchange, specifically every time I hear "No cause, no cause," I feel something akin to that same sweet shock I felt at the forgiveness epilogue of Brook's *Dream.*

There's Lear still unforgiving of his other daughters, but telling Cordelia *she* has cause to be unforgiving to him, he knows he has done wrong to her. And all she says is "No cause, no cause."

Of course there is cause, but nothing he's done is unforgivable, nothing he has done is "cause" enough, is cause anymore.

No cause, no cause. There seems to be no cause indeed—if one just gazes at the words on the page—why "no cause" should be the cause of such a powerful effect. One almost needs to see and hear a great actress murmur, "No cause, no cause."

No cause: forgiveness suspends the old laws of cause and effect. Cause has been uncaused. Causality, the entire weight of the past, the way we got to *here,* here with all our regrets and regrettable acts, has been abolished.

No cause: you hear inverse echoes of it in Othello who, on his way to murder Desdemona, speaks obsessively to himself: "It is the cause. It is the cause." The obscurity and impersonality of "it": almost a declaration of the dehumanized deadliness of causality.

No cause, no cause: one of the few moments that come close to having that impact on me is from the *Dream,* when the aristocratic couples are all mocking the plebeian players and their mangled version of *Pyramus and Thisby,* and Theseus tells them to stop their railing and forgive: "The best in this kind are but shadows . . ."

I ALWAYS GET A CHILL WHEN I HEAR THAT. WHAT IS IT BUT A BLESSing that forgives *us,* the shadows in the audience, for the private sense of insubstantiality we (well, some of us) sense about ourselves. For our own clumsy attempts to "personate" ourselves. Something we feel—okay, I feel—about the provisional nature of our selves. The self we're all pretending to be, or not to be. None of us has cause to feel shame at our insubstantiality, the line forgivingly assures us.

And then there is that moment I'd never thought deeply about before until reading Peter Brook's Berlin lecture, the one where he talks about splitting open any line of Shakespeare and in doing so, releasing infinite energies.

The line he chose to split open was a line about forgiveness. The one at the close of *The Tempest.* This is what Brook said about that particular line in that lecture (reprinted as *Evoking Shakespeare*):

"These are the last words of *The Tempest,* maybe the last words Shakespeare ever wrote." (Yes, there are plays perhaps written later, but *Henry VIII* and *The Two Noble Kinsmen* were written with coauthors, so it is fair to say, with one quibble as we'll see, that "these are the last words Shakespeare ever wrote.")

Those "last words" are Prospero's remarkably violent plea to the playgoers for forgiveness:

And my ending is despair,
Unless I be reliev'd by prayer,
Which pierces so, that it assaults
Mercy itself, and frees all faults.

Listen to what Brook says, delivering with offhand authority a stunning conjecture about the physicality of Shakespeare's writing process, especially as it relates to the phrase "assaults mercy":

". . . you can always see in Shakespeare's writing that as he writes, when his hand comes back to the beginning of a new line there is always a special force. You feel it in the actual texture of the writing, that the end of the phrase is like an upbeat in music that's leading to—what?—suspense."

It's Peter Hall's pause, Kermode's "threshold of comprehension," Peter Brook's "suspense."

"And the word that follows 'assaults,' " Brook adds, "is 'mercy.' "

Perhaps that is at least part of what distinguishes the pleasures of forgiveness: the suspense over whether pardon will be given, mercy shown, faults forgotten, penance accepted, sins remitted, flaws mended, ill deeds undone, repentance rewarded. . . .

And the welcome relief from suspense, from suspension, when it is. Especially when it becomes more than forgiving a debt, but giving a blessing, a benediction: "No cause, no cause." The highest degree of forgiveness, but not the only one. Forgiveness comes in many forms and degrees, and that relationship—between the forgiver and the forgiven—turns out to be as important a dyadic relationship in Shakespeare as lover and beloved, ruler and ruled, father and daughter.

Curiously—this is the quibble I mentioned—Brook makes a minor omission when he says the lines he quotes might have been the "last lines" Shakespeare wrote. He omits the last two lines that follow the ones he quotes, the true, literal "last lines" of the play. They too are part of Prospero's plea for forgiveness, but they turn attention back from the forgiven to the forgiver:

As you from crimes would pardon'd be,
Let your indulgence set me free.

Perhaps Brook omits this two-line tag because, for Brook, this makes forgiveness not unmerited mercy, not something that is given with "no cause," but rather because it invokes a cause, a logic. A rationale for forgiveness that is less humble and selfless. Perhaps Brook's omission reflects a trace of the Socinian heresy. An antipathy to a tit-for-tat doctrine of salvation: God demanding a price to forgive man.

Forgive us, because we too would want to be forgiven. It's the difference between "love thy neighbor as thyself" and love thy neighbor, no matter what, love thine enemy, with "no cause" but love itself. Coleridge spoke of Iago's "motiveless malignity," Cordelia offers causeless forgiveness, motiveless magnanimity.

Or perhaps Prospero's last two lines are *not* less selfless, perhaps he's generous in welcoming the forgiver into the circle of those who will come to value, to experience the pleasure of being forgiven. Something akin to the doctrine of "the happy Fall": that it was better that Adam and Eve sinned and fell and were punished, because it made their forgiveness, their redemption sweeter, the God who granted it more full of grace.

IT'S ALSO CURIOUS HOW OFTEN AND HOW AWKWARDLY THE MOment of forgiveness can seem forced into the play. The moment for instance near the close of *As You Like It* when we're told the bad brother of

Duke Senior happens to come upon an "Old Religious Man" and after a little conversation, gives up his bad behavior (and his kingdom) to his brother, in order to devote himself to a life of prayer. Shakespeare doesn't even make a gesture at giving us some realistic "explanation," some moral evolution on the part of the evil brother, that would make him so vulnerable to the power of a little talk with the "Old Religious Man."

It's as if Shakespeare is *signaling* us that this is a gratuitous act on his part, injecting forgiveness almost like a "trespasser" into the play, emphasizing its unpredictability. The absence of a gesture at explanation is itself a gesture that suggests the arbitrariness of forgiveness, which can suddenly show up anywhere, in almost anyone.

Yes, forgiveness is one of those "ideals," but one of the most complex and contentious for all its ostensibly gentle demeanor.

Just as there was often an argument over pleasure, the fact that there was tension, even suspense over forgiveness in so many Shakespearean plays didn't seem an accident. Think of the multilayered complexity of the moment of suspense and suspended forgiveness in *Hamlet*—the moment when Hamlet comes upon Claudius kneeling in prayer.

For Claudius it's a moment when he tries but fails to find forgiveness, or as he puts it, "My words fly up, my thoughts remain below." Is this a genuine attempt to ask forgiveness (if his thoughts remain below), genuine regret, or does it suggest the hollowness of mere words?

Hamlet, who has come to kill Claudius, spies surreptitiously on this moment, sees only Claudius on his knees praying, dreads the idea that Claudius might have asked and received forgiveness, absolution, decides not to kill him with the flower of repentance on him, thereby sending him to heaven, rather than hell.

One of the great moments of moral complexity in literature, another moment of *suspension* in fact. One that reflects and deflects the memory of Pyrrhus's sword suspended over doomed Priam's head. And perhaps the biblical memory of Abraham's knife suspended over Isaac. (A Socinian moment, you might say, in the Old Testament.)

The dilemma of forgiveness is transposed to Hamlet's mind and soul. And in a strict sense Hamlet fails the forgiveness test. He seeks to spare Claudius's life and (ultimately) send him to hell rather than kill him and send his (apparently) repentant soul to heaven. Do we condemn Hamlet for knowingly sending to hell a soul he might—or feared he might—have saved by killing the body?

The complexities of forgiveness: it seemed a Shakespearean obsession that I wanted to examine further.

First, just to see whether my sense of its prevalence was an illusion, I checked the words "forgive," "forgiven" and "forgiveness" in *The Harvard Concordance to Shakespeare.* "Forgive" appears in one of those three guises 95 times in 32 out of 37 plays by my count. But then there are 220 instances of "mercy" or "merciful." Forms of the word "pardon" appear more than 300 times. Of course the raw numbers tell us nothing of context or distinction or degree, but they indicate a presence.

The complexity of the question is suggested by contrasting Peter Brook's attention to Prospero's final lines, his epilogue plea to us, with the kind of forgiveness, if you can call it that, Prospero offers the treacherous brother who deposed him and cast him adrift at sea to die. Toward the end of the fifth act Prospero tells his brother:

For you, most wicked sir, whom to call brother
Would even infect my mouth, I do forgive
Thy rankest fault—all of them; and require
My dukedom of thee, which perforce, I know
Thou must restore.

If there were a spectrum of forgiveness, this would fall at the extreme end, wouldn't it? Just as vengeance can be a double-edged sword, forgiveness can be a double-edged word. Here it's a grudging forgiveness, but one that reminds us forgiveness can be dyadic, the forgiven and the forgiver in an unstable relationship where at times (as here) the forgiver lacks—seems to need—forgiveness himself for his failure to offer true mercy.

Contrast this with the complex, self-aware forgiveness that Prospero offers to Caliban, who tried to rape his daughter and led a rebellion to depose him. "This thing of darkness I acknowledge mine," he says of Caliban. Forgiveness as a kind of "acknowledgment" of one's own defect, Caliban as an aspect of Prospero's own self he gives recognition to. Forgiveness as self-recognition. That's where the drama in the recognition scenes such as the ones in *Pericles* and *Lear* comes from: the dawning recognition that forgiveness is possible.

I wondered if there could be said to be an evolution in the complexity of forgiveness in the course of the plays.

Shakespeare's first comedy, perhaps his first play, *The Comedy of Errors,* closes with the almost too simple moment of forgiveness between the slave-twins:

We came into the world like brother and brother;
And now let's go hand in hand, not one before another.

Simple, but from the beginning, something deeply affecting about it.

On the other hand, at the end of *Love's Labor's Lost* we find a kind of *punitive* forgiveness. The frivolous, mendacious behavior, the oath-breaking wooing the four lords have engaged in, can be forgiven, but only after they spend a year redeeming themselves. Rosalind tells Berowne that to earn redemption he must work with "the speechless sick" and dying: ". . . your task shall be, / With all the fierce endeavor of your wit, / To enforce the pained impotent to smile."

To which Berowne replies, in one of those suddenly intense lines so characteristic of forgiveness moments: "To move wild laughter in the throat of death? / It cannot be, it is impossible."

"To move wild laughter in the throat of death": what a line! Impossible, perhaps. That's the point, says Rosalind, his "idle scorns" are likely to fail and when they do, "throw away that spirit, / And I shall find you empty of that fault, / Right joyful of your reformation."

His forgiveness is dependent on performance of a kind of community service—actually his recognition of his failure and subsequent humility—and his "reformation" shall be her joy, part of the joy being the anticipation of the pleasure of bestowing forgiveness.

If it is found in the comedies, although often in a harsher key for the most part than I imagined, it's found in the tragedies as knowledge that comes too late if at all.

Forgive me if you feel I'm going on too much about forgiveness, but there's something pleasurable about the evident pleasure Shakespeare takes in bestowing and withholding it.

EDMUND IS BELOVED!

Consider one obscure and one famous—or notorious—moment of forgiveness.

The obscure moment was brought to my attention by Brian Kulick, the talented American Shakespearean director. I was talking to him about the two-endings-of-*Lear* problem when he brought up a surprising moment near the close of *Lear* that had struck him recently.

It's the moment in the chaos of the fifth act when the villainous Edmund, defeated in battle, lies dying and then, as the stage direction has it, "The bodies of Goneril and Regan are brought in."

Both women have, of course, in addition to cutting off their father, Lear, and casting him out into the storm, connived to cheat on their husbands with Edmund. Goneril has poisoned her sister and rival for Edmund, Regan, and then killed herself after learning Edmund was dying.

Brian Kulick said he was struck by the first line of Edmund's reaction to the spectacle of the bodies of the two women being carried in, the bodies of the two dead women who committed murder and suicide out of love for him.

Facing his own doom as well, Edmund looks upon them and says, "Yet Edmund was belov'd!"

It's one of those lines I'd overlooked, but when looked over closely can be taken in a number of different ways. I'd always seen it as a moment of black humor, Edmund able somehow to make a sarcastic joke at the spectacle of death he's responsible for. An actor can play it with sneering cynicism. Edmund unrelenting in his nihilism. Especially if one reads it with the two lines that follow:

Yet Edmund was belov'd!
The one the other poison'd for my sake,
And after slew herself.

A kind of perverse satisfaction at the dire consequences of his manipulations. That's how I'd seen it when I'd paid attention to it, which I rarely did. And yet, Brian Kulick said, it struck him that it could also be read with a sense of wonder: "Yet Edmund was *belov'd*!", spoken with a slow, meditative, dawning sense of wonder that even a self-confessed blackhearted creature such as himself, with nothing but contempt for ideals such as love, is somehow deeply *affected* by the idea that he, of all people, was "belov'd."

It sounded unlikely at first, but I've found that directors like Kulick often come up with remarkable, unpredictable close readings. And in Kulick's favor it may be said that within a few lines Edmund undergoes one of those miraculous conversions such as the one in *As You Like It,* effected by the sudden materialization of "the Old Religious Man."

"I pant for life," the dying Edmund says, but "Some good I mean to do, / Despite of mine own nature."

And he proceeds to disclose what he has withheld before: what he has done with Cordelia and Lear and the fact that he's given orders for Cordelia to be executed, her death, in one final Machiavellian twist, to be made to look like suicide.

Suddenly he wants to help save her life from his own fatal command. He gives his sword to be taken to her place of captivity as his "token of reprieve" to those he ordered to carry out the execution, and urges haste.

And so with his dying words and act he seeks—too late—to save Cordelia's life. Again, an all-too-miraculous conversion, conspicuous irrelevance, or if not irrelevant, conspicuous in its unlikelihood.

"Yet Edmund was belov'd!" Beloved by whom exactly? Yes, by the two dead women he connived with. But beloved, perhaps, by his creator, by Shakespeare. (He is one of his great eloquent schemer-characters.) Beloved enough perhaps to be given a line that at least ambiguously shows the possibility that even someone as professedly anti-sentimental as Edmund could be moved by love. Moved to redeem himself and attempt to "reprieve" Cordelia from her fate. It recalls Peter Brook extolling Shakespeare's "generosity" to his characters.

In giving Edmund that line, Brian Kulick contended, Shakespeare was giving a character one thought one knew an utterly surprising, deeper dimension. He is, if not forgiven, endowed with an unexpected touch of humanity "despite [his] own nature."

Despite his own nature, but it then *becomes* his own nature, doesn't it? And so we find ourselves spiraling into the self-contradictory but more complex vision of Edmund this act of authorial forgiveness provokes. It's another one of those lines that split open, releases infinite energies.

GRACE AT LAST

And then there is the one most obvious moment of forgiveness in Shakespeare, one that for some reason I'd always resisted. Perhaps because it was so obvious, or so it seemed. That moment in *The Winter's Tale* when the statue of Hermione, supposedly driven to death twenty years earlier by her jealous husband Leontes, comes to life. And forgives him.

I had resisted it because it had become such an icon of theatrical Shakespeare. The staging of that moment, a statue come to life, was often the centerpiece of a director's career, the triumphal flourish of a Shakespearean actress, always written about as if we must be spellbound by its beautiful mystery.

I'd long resisted this allegedly miraculous moment of forgiveness because of what I thought of as the generic imperative that made it less miraculous, more expected. When I say "generic imperative" I'm talking about the way *The Winter's Tale* is one of the Late Romances, and Shakespeare's Late Romances, from *Pericles* through *Cymbeline, The Winter's Tale* and *The Tempest,* all end with miraculous redemptions and moments of reunion and forgiveness.

The forgiveness devices in the Late Romances seem to grow gradually more obtrusive. While the close of *Pericles* is a miraculous reunion, it is also beautifully human. *Cymbeline*'s end is facilitated by the hard-not-to-seem-ridiculous descent of the Roman eagle, a Big Bird ex machina. It's all magic in *The Tempest,* beautiful but often strenuous magic.

And *The Winter's Tale*? That statue coming to life? It's hard to know how to react. I've found myself rationalizing it: well, it *is* a Late Romance and as one of my professors at Yale Graduate School, Howard Felperin, liked to emphasize, a Tragedy is an uncompleted Romance, a Romance a completed Tragedy. A miraculous ending was not "unnatural" in a Romance, it was part of the groundwork of its being.

Still I've resisted it on the stage and on the page. A statue coming alive. It's too . . . blatantly symbolic I guess. The transformation of art into life. Art redeeming life. All that. It never gave me the pleasure, nothing like the shock that "No cause, no cause" does even now, tapping it onto my keyboard.

By contrast, the statue coming to life almost seemed to me as if it were the Emperor's New Clothes of the Shakespeare appreciators, the graven image of the bardolaters. Everyone acclaimed it, yet did they really love it, or did they think they were *supposed to*?

And so this moment, this epitome of Shakespearean forgiveness, somehow had always left me stone cold—like a statue I guess. Gave me no pleasure. But I was prompted to revisit it by conversation with the scholar Grace Tiffany.

Most will know the story: deluded by a fit of Othello-like jealousy, with no Iago but his inner demons to prompt him, King Leontes of Sicily has driven his wife Hermione to her death, which leads his son to die of grief, while he sends his newborn girl to be exposed to the elements and (presumably) death. But sixteen years later, when the long-lost daughter returns to the court of the grieving Leontes (who has found, to his sorrow, how unjust his suspicions of Hermione were), the daughter, called Perdita, asks to see the statue of her mother Hermione in the home of her loyal attendant, Paulina.

The whole court accompanies Perdita to see the statue, which, we are told by a "Third Gentleman," was created "by that rare Italian master, Julio Romano, who, had he himself eternity and could put breath into his work, would beguile Nature of her custom, so perfectly he is her ape. He so near to Hermione hath done Hermione that they say one would speak to her and stand in hope of answer."

It's hard not to see in this sculptor, "Julio Romano," Shakespeare's evocation of an artist not unlike himself, one who sees himself as both Nature's rival and Nature's "ape." But, in any case, the statue is unveiled, Leontes the guilty husband is "so far transported that / He'll think anon it lives."

Paulina, the former queen's attendant and keeper of the statue, tells Leontes that she can make the statue move, indeed "descend and take you by the hand."

When Leontes expresses doubt, Paulina tells those assembled, "It is requir'd / You do awake your faith," which they apparently do to a satisfactory degree, because when Paulina commands music to "strike," then it happens. The statue of Hermione steps down from the pedestal, comes to life, embraces Leontes, gives her blessing to her daughter:

"You gods, look down / And from your sacred vials pour your graces / Upon my daughter's head!"

I've found Hermione's forgiveness of her husband—who in effect killed their first child—almost less convincing than her transformation from statue to living being. (The transformation is never really explained. Was Paulina hiding her alive, is this just a simulation of a miracle—because the "statue" reflects her having aged sixteen years—or is this some genuine miracle of art awakening to life? No certain indication one way or another in the text. Undecidable.)

And it's such a conspicuous dea ex machina that it skews every reading or staging of the play after the first time you've seen it. No matter what happens in the early acts you know the statue's going to come alive, forgive and redeem (all but the dead boy).

Why have I resisted? Perhaps because it lacked the surprise of transformation in human nature that affects me deeply in other forgiveness moments. There was no unexpectedness, it didn't seem to partake of what I found most appealing in other forgiveness moments: the surprise of seeing people act better than they might be expected to. Why is this a pleasure? I can't speak for others, but perhaps it holds out a hope that some day, in some way, *we* may act better than might be expected of us. Forgiveness will transform us from a kind of statuelike lifelessness to a higher plane of life.

Then I had an e-mail exchange with Grace Tiffany; she's a Shakespearean scholar who specializes in religious aspects of the works, and who writes deliciously witty reviews of hopelessly jargonic scholarly articles for *The Shakespeare Newsletter,* in addition to being author of one of the smarter Shakespearean novels, *Will.*

I'd asked her if she had any thoughts on the idea of forgiveness as pleasure in Shakespeare and what moments she found most exemplary.

She agreed that almost nothing surpasses "No cause, no cause." But she made a case that there was more than dea ex machina miracle-work going on in Hermione's descent from the pedestal and her forgiveness of Leontes.

"When Hermione comes down from her pedestal and wordlessly embraces her husband," Professor Tiffany wrote me, "Shakespeare gives her nothing to say. It seems that he understood that the best expressions of forgiveness were wordless and tending toward silent expressions. Even 'No cause, no cause' is as minimal and simple as it is because of the action of Cordelia; she is kneeling to him; her father tries to kneel to her."

And then she added something I thought particularly perceptive: "And of course the eloquence of *doing* and the potential rottenness of *saying* is a major theme in *Lear.*"

Only someone who knows the potential of speech so well as Shakespeare knows all too well the potential rottenness of speech.

"In *The Winter's Tale* he omitted the speech of forgiveness entirely," Ms. Tiffany added, "it all has to be done by gesture. There's a poem I've always liked by Edwin Morgan wherein Shakespeare gives instructions to a boy actor on how to play Hermione coming down from the pedestal. He concentrates on the action:

" 'You move a foot, slow, steady, down, you guard your balance in case you're stiff / You move, you step, slow, down from the pedestal / Control your start with one hand, the other hand / you now hold out / to your husband who wronged you long ago . . . / finally he embraces you, and there's nothing / I can give you to say boy, but you must *show* that you have forgiven him.'

"In the end," Ms. Tiffany concludes, "Shakespeare chose silence to represent such a moment."

From "No cause, no cause," to "No words, no words."

I was won over. I have a new appreciation of this moment of forgiveness, and the silent pleasure it offers. One given to me by someone—I can't resist saying this—named Grace.

Her emphasis on silence (was this Peter Brook's vibrant silence?) made me think of a line in Frank Kermode's book *Shakespeare's Language:*

"Shakespeare's later language, and so his theatre, does not lose all contact with the eloquence of his early work, but moves deliberately in the direction of a kind of reticence that . . . might be close to silence."

The always astute Shakespearean critic Anne Barton once said something similiar in her essay "Shakespeare and the Limitations of Language." She argued that in Shakespeare's last solo play, *The Tempest,* "he had reached a point in his investigation of the capabilities of words beyond which he found it difficult to proceed."

A fascinating conjecture which, I think, can be taken two ways, not necessarily contradictory: Shakespeare had reached and recognized the limits of his *own* linguistic powers. Or, more radically, he had reached and recognized the limits of language itself.

Here I must acknowledge my own limits in not feeling able to decide between these final contending conjectures in the Shakespeare wars.

And so, dear reader, perhaps this is the time, epilogue-like, for me to ask your forgiveness. For all I've left out of this book, especially all the scholars, actors and directors with so much worthy to say whom I have not been able to include. You know who you are; I hope you'll understand. I ask your forgiveness for all I've left out of the book, and yes, for what's in: for my necessarily limited perspective on a limitless subject.

The rest is silence. A vibrant one, I hope.

And, oh yes: I forgive *you,* Peter Brook.

Bibliographic Notes

I don't pretend to plumb the bottomless depths of Shakespearean scholarship here but rather have a more specific purpose.

One thing I've attempted to do throughout this book is highlight the contributions of Shakespearean scholars I most admire, many of whom have written with clarity and insight but whose works are often out of print, or available in limited, expensive, academic press editions not readily accessible to the reading public.

Nonetheless things are changing in the online world, and in various ways (Google Scholar, JSTOR, Project Muse, etc.) many of these works have a chance at a second life. One of the most satisfying things that resulted from my column writing for *The New York Observer* has been the reissue of the out-of-print novels of Charles Portis, including his classic, *The Dog of the South*—which, by the way, contains within it one of the single funniest lines involving Shakespeare I've ever read. (It would require too much space here to give it the context that it requires; just take my word for it and read the novel.)

If this book somehow similarly encourages some smart publisher to reissue or make accessible Stephen Booth's *Essay on Shakespeare's Sonnets* so that it's no longer scholarly samizdat, I will feel it has served a purpose.

The notes that follow are designed to be more personal and selective than any comprehensive attempt to survey all Shakespeare controversies, much less all Shakespeare studies. I just want to call attention to some of the works that have meant the most to me in writing this book, works that demonstrate that there is much exciting thinking out there overshadowed lately by the fad for books that beat the dead horse of dubious biographical speculation. And by the emphasis in the academy on running all Shakespeare through the jargonic milling machine of the latest Theory fashion.

Here's another example of the kind of works I'd like to see made more accessible: I know one of the most valuable experiences for me in the course of writing this book was compiling an almost complete set of *Shakespeare Survey,* the journal published annually by the Stratford-on-Avon–based Shakespeare Institute and Cambridge University Press since 1947. Going through those volumes sequentially was an invaluable way of tracing a half century's evolution of the most sophisticated—and accessible—Shakespearean scholars' thinking, along with reports on publications and—particularly—memorable performances over that span. It would be wonderful if back issues of journals such as *Shakespeare Studies* and *Shakespeare Quarterly* as well as the *Survey* could be made available online, scanned and archived on the Web in some form so that "outsiders" could get a sense of what scholars have been arguing about.

But before proceeding on a chapter-by-chapter basis let me venture a personal favorite. If one had to have a *single* Shakespearean reference work, while there are so many I admire—Russ McDonald's *Bedford Companion to Shakespeare* (Bedford Books, 1996), for instance—the one I would never wish to be without is Marvin Spevack's *Harvard Concordance to Shakespeare* (Belknap Press, 1974), an indispensable, inexhaustible delight. This huge 1600-page volume essentially does nothing but list, alphabetically, all the words in Shakespeare, and—play by play—compiles every instance in which that word is used, usually in a ten-word contextual excerpt.

So one can turn to the entry for "sweet," for instance, and read that the word is used 873 times (out of some 884,000 words in the complete works, according to Spevack's count), and then one can plunge into the sweetness. One can trace the flavors of sweetness, and the nuances, the combinations and permutations of sweetness. Or one can follow the word "deep" through the plays and see how the contexts inflect its deepness. One can hear the way *sweet* and *deep* echoed in Shakespeare's mind as he wrote. One gets closer to Shakespeare's language in a unique way.

Having said that, let me begin with some chapter-by-chapter suggestions and digressions, along with, in some instances, more specific citations.

Preface: Why?

The limits of Shakespearean biographical raw material and the lengths to which biographers will stretch and elaborate upon the apocrypha are demonstrated in two invaluable books by the late Samuel Schoenbaum: *William Shakespeare: A Compact Documentary Life* (Oxford University Press, 1987), which exhibits the paltry undisputed records available, and *Shakespeare's Lives* (Oxford University Press, 1970), which exhibits the centuries of biographical fantasies projected upon those records, fantasies that tell us more in most cases about the biographers than about Shakespeare. One of the few attempts to paint a detailed portrait of Shakespeare's youth, for instance, *Shakespeare in Warwickshire* by Mark Eccles (University of Wisconsin Press, 1961), has the courage to admit, as most biographers will not, that "the picture of Shakespeare's life in Warwickshire is a mosaic with most of the pieces missing." The mosaic, however, is one worth viewing at the very least for context.

Again going against the grain of my animus toward biography, Katherine Duncan-Jones's *Ungentle Shakespeare* (Arden, 2001) offers a detailed contextualized portrait of the unceasing rivalries between Shakespeare and his playwright contemporaries. Jonathan Bate's *The Genius of Shakespeare* (Oxford University Press, 1998) seeks more successfully than most to explain why Shakespeare's work rose above and survived the scrum of his rivals. In addition Bate offers one of the most exciting conjectures about the intellectual history of Shakespearean criticism, one which, as I've sought to adumbrate in a previous chapter, explains the importance of William Empson's notion of ambiguity.

The line about biographers being like cardsharps at their worst is adapted from a review of Peter Ackroyd's biography in *Publishers Weekly* (July 11, 2005) by yours truly.

The quote from Daniel Swift's critique of Shakespeare biography on leaving "a space for wonder" appears in his essay in *The Nation* (March 13, 2006).

Recently John Updike wryly observed that most biographies are "novels with indexes." If you *must* rake over the worn fragments no one reinvigorates them more than Anthony Burgess's visionary novel *Nothing Like the Sun* (rpt. Norton, 1996). Russell Fraser calls his unconventional, frankly novel-like two-volume series, *Young Shakespeare* and *Shakespeare: The Later Years* (rpt. Columbia University Press, 1992, 1993), a "biography." But I like his elliptically compressed prose style and his book has the feel, the spirit if not the letter, of the life. As does Grace Tiffany's recent *Will* (Berkley Hardcover, 2004), which is filled with smart offhand observations about the work as well.

And I must admit a weakness for two novels about two largely imaginary figures: Robert Nye's *The Late Mr. Shakespeare* (Arcade, 1999) and Leon Rooke's (don't laugh) *Shakespeare's Dog* (Ecco Press, 1986).

Of all the recent books that take on Shakespeare as a whole, I'd recommend Frank Kermode's *Shakespeare's Language* (Farrar, Straus and Giroux, 2001) for its focus on what counts. I once witnessed Kermode and Harold Bloom speak at the 92nd Street Y in New York City. It wasn't a debate but as they say at the fights Kermode—ever so politely—wiped the floor with Bloom, leaving Bloom to mutter audibly to Kermode as he left the stage at intermission, "You should have been a lawyer." As if it were only lawyers' tricks that made Bloom's overblown vision of Shakespeare seem so impoverished by contrast with Kermode's rich immersion in the language.

I discuss Edward Pechter's notion of "Shakespeare the Writer" in my essay, "Shakespeare & Company" in the Winter 2005 edition of *The Wilson Quarterly*. Pechter's original essay appeared in *Textual Practice* (2003).

When I speak of circularity in biographical studies I'm referring to what's become known as "Dowdenism," named after Edward Dowden, the editor of the first Arden *Hamlet*. In his nineteenth-century biography of Shakespeare, Dowden adopted the soon-to-be-popular four-part periodization of Shakespeare's life: early comical historical years; mature *Hamlet, Henry IV* and *Henry V* period; then the alleged dark years, the 1606–1608 period, which included *Lear, Troilus and Cressida, Coriolanus, Timon of Athens;* and then the final fourth period: the Born Again Romantic spiritual period of the Late Romances. Nice if there were any biographical as opposed to conjectural evidence for the link between the life and the work. In fact, the contrary seems more true when you consider that the supposedly spiritualized Shakespeare of the Late Romances was involved in less than exalted, petty tax-farming transactions and moneylending in Stratford (not that there's anything wrong with that).

Dowdenism comes in for particular circular misuse when it comes to the Dark Years, where the darkness of the plays is said to betoken either a spiritual breakdown or the brain-damaging effects of syphilis, and the allegedly organic brain disease is then said to be the source of the embittered darkness.

I frankly didn't want to waste much space in the text of the book itself explaining why I don't care, for the purposes of this book, whether Shakespeare's work was written by one of the anti-Stratfordian candidates such as the Earl of Oxford, although I do refer to such fantasies as "the Family Romance of the Shakespeare explainers." Nonetheless for those who want to waste their time discovering what a waste of time the "anti-Stratfordian" arguments are, I recommend *Shakespeare, in Fact* (Continuum International Publishing Group, 1999) by Irvin Matus, or *The Case for Shakespeare: The End of the Authorship Question* by Scott McCrea (Praeger, 2005).

Chapter One: The Dream *Induction*

Since this is a chapter about the profound effect of a single brilliant production, a production that has left no visual recording behind, the first thing I'd like to do is urge some publisher to bring David Selbourne's *The Making of "A Midsummer Night's Dream"* (rpt. Routledge, 1984) back into circulation. It's the kind of book that's come to be known as a "rehearsal diary," but it's an important document in theater history, the only complete eyewitness account of how Peter Brook made his *Dream* so transformative.

I've found that I've often gotten to deeper levels of a play when I've had the privilege of watching rehearsals, especially when choices have to be made that are not explicitly called for in the text. The director Brian Kulick once allowed me to watch him rehearse the comic scenes in the fourth act of his *Winter's Tale* and I saw three gifted comic actors, Bill Buell as the Old Shepherd, Michael Stuhlbarg as his clownish son and Bronson Pinchot as the con man Autolycus, seek the various ways of evoking what they called "the invisible schtick"—the comic business Shakespeare had built into the text without spelling out in so many words, the comic business gifted clowns over centuries have tuned in to like dog whistles and turned into roars of laughter. All the implicit but unspoken physical actions, the double takes, the winking asides, and the like that made the comedy on the page come to life on the stage.

Tiffany Stern's *Rehearsal from Shakespeare to Sheridan* (Oxford University Press, 2001) is an illuminating account of the evolution of the practice of rehearsing, quite revelatory about the use of "cue scripts" during Shakespeare's time—most actors never saw the play as a whole before production; instead, they saw just a list of cue lines that immediately preceded *their* lines.

There's a long history of "rehearsal diaries" of memorable Shakespeare productions; they rarely sell well but I recommend that those who browse secondhand bookstores pick them up, as they're often the best way to learn the plays from the inside out.

My account of the fire in the theater during the Broadway run of the *Dream* that became so metaphorically important to me can be found reprinted in my collection *The Secret Parts of Fortune* (Random House, 2000; HarperPerennial, 2001), which is a good thing because otherwise I'd think it was a dream. There's a growing number of Peter Brook biographies and autobiographies and Peter Brook theoretical works, some of which I'll discuss in notes on the chapter devoted to him.

Still, the Peter Brook book I've quoted from at the end of this chapter, the thinnest of them all, his Berlin lecture, is, I'd argue, the most indispensable guide to Brook's own sensibility and his sense of Shakespeare. *Evoking Shakespeare* (Theatre Communications Group, 1999), it should be pointed out now, consists of *two* editions, starting with the original thirty-six-page translation of the lecture containing the quotes I refer to about assaulting mercy.

But there is a revised edition retitled *Evoking (and Forgetting!) Shakespeare* (Theatre Communications Group, 2003) that contains a full nine further pages, including a critique of naturalistic acting, of the conventional artifice of "Shakespeare voice" in acting and of the "reductionism to contemporary relevance" of much staging, and concludes: "Shakespeare never intended anyone to study Shakespeare, it is only when we forget Shakespeare that we begin to find him." Forget who?

When I speak of Peter Holland's footnote in his Oxford Edition of *A Midsummer Night's Dream* (Oxford University Press, 1994), it prompts me to say that some of the best, most accessible writing about Shakespeare by academics can be found in the introductions and footnotes to single-play editions, where some of the best scholars bring a welcome clarity to centuries of commentary and argument and reach out to the nonspecialist reader with their own and other perspectives on the play on the page and, more recently, the play in performance. Russ McDonald's Penguin edition of the *Dream* is another example of a graceful introductory essay prompted by that remarkable play.

Since the footnote on Bottom's dream explores the engagement of the rhetoric and images in the Bible, it's worth noting that such encounters are nowhere better explored than by Steven Marx in *Shakespeare and the Bible* (Oxford University Press, 2000), another of the excellent Oxford Shakespeare topic series.

Chapter Two: One Hamlet *or Three?*

Although I speak, in the epilogue to this chapter, of my admiration for Ann Thompson and Neil Taylor's third Arden edition of *Hamlet* (Thomson Learning, 2006), I would urge two things of Arden: first, to make the second volume (Q1 and the Folio) available in affordable paperback as opposed to the current expensive hardcover-only form; and second, keep Harold Jenkins's labor of love, the second Arden, the last Grand Unification *Hamlet,* in print. Setting aside the issue of conflation itself (I can see the intellectual, textual arguments against it), there is so much judicious scholarly commentary and so many valuable annotations and discussions, and so much of Jenkins's fine attentiveness to *Hamlet,* that if the culture is to have at least *one* unitary conflated *Hamlet* it should have this one.

One book I'd also like to see returned to contemporary appreciation is J. Dover Wilson's wonderfully obsessively eccentric *What Happens in Hamlet* (Cambridge University Press, 1935)—the source of the story I relate of Wilson's descent into *Hamlet* madness. Wilson's title in its faux-naïveté captures the terrible, wonderful truth that after four centuries, nobody really *knows* the answer to such questions as what "dozen or sixteen lines" Hamlet added to *The Murder of Gonzago,* whether and when he was feigning madness, what Gertrude's relationship to Claudius was before the murder of her husband, etc.—all questions that are not merely pedantic quibbles but that bear upon theme and meaning. (For an engaging novelistic examination of *Hamlet* questions through the lenses of its source-texts, John Updike's *Gertrude and Claudius* [Knopf, 2000] is irresistible.)

The self-deprecatory irony in Wilson's title says in effect: Millions of words have been written about what *Hamlet* means: Can we at least admit we still don't even know what *happens* in the play?

For those who want the full flavor of the 1603 First Quarto without committing to the Arden 3 or one of the other three-text editions I've mentioned, the New Cambridge Shakespeare offers *The First Quarto of Hamlet,* edited by Kathleen O. Irace (Cambridge University Press, 1998).

Spirited discussion of Q1's origins, vices and virtues can be found in *The Hamlet First Published,* edited by Thomas Clayton (University of Delaware Press, 1992). I particularly recommend the essay by Alan C. Dessen, one of my favorite scholars, for its clarification of the issues and willingness to reserve judgment.

Gary Taylor's impassioned contrarian look at bardolatry over the years, *Re-Inventing Shakespeare* (rpt. Oxford University Press, 1991), is worth reading for its perspective on all the *wrong* reasons Shakespeare has been idolized, although Taylor can sometimes, in the heat of his polemic, give one the impression that there is *no* special reason to admire Shakespeare.

I've long been an admirer of John Jones's *Shakespeare at Work* (Oxford University Press, 1995) for its nuanced close reading of the variations in *Hamlet* and *Lear,* even though I'm not as convinced as he is that we can be certain the changes he analyzes can be ascribed with certainty to Shakespeare.

By contrast, in his introduction to the New Cambridge *Hamlet* (Cambridge University Press, 1985), Philip Edwards makes one of the earliest, strongest counterarguments to the Revisers' case.

I feel sadness that Eric Sams died before completing the second volume of his powerfully argued if controversial book, *The Real Shakespeare: Retrieving the Early Years, 1564–1594* (Yale University Press, 1995). His son has donated his research materials to the Stratford Shakespeare Birthplace archives. I doubt Sams's certainty about the early draft theory of the Bad Quartos but I found his brio and urgency on these matters bracing and provocative. If I might be permitted a personal aside, I liked the old curmudgeon.

The best general introduction to the First Folio can be found in a pamphlet by Peter W. M. Blayney, *The First Folio of Shakespeare* (Folger Library Productions, 1991).

My *New Yorker* story, much of which was adapted from this chapter, appeared in the May 13, 2002, issue as "Shakespeare in Rewrite."

Chapter Three: A Digressive Comic Interlude Featuring Shakespeare's Ambiguously Revised Testimony in the Wigmakers' Lawsuit

Shortly after this chapter went into bound galleys an essay by Anne Barton in *The New York Review of Books,* highly critical of the biographical impulse, even called for some kind of "moratorium" to be imposed on further biographical studies. What I found most important about her essay was her refutation of the most commonly advanced defense of the continued biographical impulse.

"Shakespeare's biographers," she writes, in the May 11, 2006, issue, "have a way of justifying their endeavors by informing readers that more, in fact, is known about his life than about that of any other literary figure in the period, with the exception of Ben Jonson."

But, she points out, Jonson's highly, almost overdocumented life is a skewed exception: we know lots about him but that doesn't mean we know slightly-less-than-lots about Shakespeare. Nonetheless "the prying," as she puts it, "continues. . . . All the plays become documents to be ransacked for biographical clues—clues that turn out, unsurprisingly, to be both tendentious and conflicting."

E.A.J. Honigmann's *Shakespeare: The Lost Years* (Manchester University Press, 1999) presents the strongest if not the first argument for the "Shakeshafte theory." The first to make the case, though, was Father Peter Milward in his *Shakespeare's Religious Background* (rpt. Loyola Press, 1986).

The most influential and detailed dissent from the Shakeshafte theory can be found in Robert Bearman's " 'Was William Shakespeare William Shakeshafte?' Revisited," in *Shakespeare Quarterly,* vol. 53 (2002). Bearman is refuting Honigmann's refutation of a 1970 article ("Was William Shakespeare William Shakeshafte?") by Douglas Hamer, if that is not immediately apparent.

Honigmann's refutation of Bearman's refutation of Honigmann's refutation of Hamer's refutation can be found in "The Shakespeare/Shakeshafte Question Continues," *Shakespeare Quarterly,* vol. 54 (2003).

I haven't been convinced by this latest refutation of the refutation of the refutation of the refutation myself. I think it is too late to prove dispositively whether Shakeshafte was Shakespeare, and therefore larger conclusions founded upon the identity of the two have too shaky a foundation.

The Shakeshafte theory is but the latest to claim Shakespeare for some particular religious vision. A very popular book, blurbed by Prince Charles no less ("hard to put down"), called *The Secret of Shakespeare* (Inner Traditions, 1984) by Martin Lings, former Keeper of Oriental Manuscripts of the British Museum, maintains that all Shakespeare is a Christian allegory. Ted Hughes (yes, that Ted Hughes) in *Shakespeare and the Goddess of Complete Being* (Faber & Faber, Ltd., 1992) offers a mega-meta theory of All Shakespeare as a pagan allegory of the devouring female nature goddess, a theory Hughes first finds exemplified in *Venus and Adonis.*

And then in 1991 in a little-noticed essay in a short anthology, *The Essential Shakespeare* (Ecco Press), Hughes essentially changed his mind about Shakespeare's mind and expounded a very different version of Shakespeare's mystical transformation: a shift to a belief that all Shakespeare's greatest work was a product of a Higher Consciousness stimulated by an initiation into the mystical system of the magus of meditative memory systems, Giordano Bruno, the heretical disciple of Galileo eventually burned at the stake in Rome.

Bruno spent a period in England contemporaneous with Shakespeare's youth, and Hughes maintained, in his latest theory, that Shakespeare received some occult initiation into Bruno's system and that lines in the Sonnets like "When to the sessions of sweet silent thought / I summon remembrance of things past" were *really* about Brunovian meditation "sessions." Everyone wants to recruit Shakespeare to their System or reduce him to a cryptogram or code, a solvable algorithm.

Chapter Four: "Look There, Look There . . .": The Scandal of Lear's Last Words

I'd like to dedicate this chapter's notes to Peter W. M. Blayney, whose monumental *The Texts of King Lear and Their Origins,* Volume I, *Nicholas Okes and the First Quarto* (Cambridge University Press, 1982)—a heroic, destabilizing-to-read (and probably to research and write) exercise in textual scholarship—both revolutionized the study of *Lear* texts, and in its incompletion (Blayney claims, after twenty years' work on the second volume to have "no interest" in *Lear* or Shakespeare anymore), embodies the tragic situation of the greatest, most obsessed Shakespearean textual scholars: "Sole judge of truth, in endless error hurled,—/ The glory, jest and riddle of the world." As I understand the situation, the long-awaited Volume II, in which Blayney was to treat of the Folio version and its relationship to the 1608 First Quarto (revision? by Shakespeare?), has been abandoned. It is my hope that somehow Blayney will not let the perfect be the enemy of the good and try somehow to summarize his thoughts, however inconclusive, in a manageable form before they are lost to the world.

If I were forced to choose a single edition of *Lear* to recommend it would probably be the Third Arden version edited by R. A. Foakes. It's the closest thing to an Enfolded *Hamlet* in that it uses an initially off-putting but ultimately ingenious and illuminating method to conflate and yet distinguish the Folio and the Quarto.

Essentially Foakes uses superscript Q's and F's in the way Bernice Kliman uses curly and pointed brackets for Quarto-only and Folio-only words and passages. Consider this example:

> GLOUCESTER ^{F}*O,*^{F} *strange and fastened villain,*
> *Would he deny his letter,* ^{F}*said he?*^{F} ^{Q}*I never got him.*^{Q}

The passages between the ^{F} superscripts appear only in the Folio and those between the ^{Q} superscripts appear only in the Quarto. It has come in for some criticism, but I think it's worth doing.

More traditional ways of reading the two versions can be found in parallel text editions such as that by Rene Weis (Longman Group, 1993); a beautiful facsimile version of the original texts' typography aligned is *The Parallel King Lear* prepared by Michael Warren (University of California Press, 1989).

The arc of the debate over dividing *Lear* can be traced in the shift from *The Division of the Kingdoms: Shakespeare's Two Versions of King Lear,* edited by Gary Taylor and Michael Warren (Clarendon Press, 1983)—which takes as a given the belief that the two versions are two distinct works of art, or distinct *stages* of the same work of art—to *Lear from Study to Stage,* edited by James Ogden and Arthur H. Scouten (Fairleigh Dickinson University Press, 1997), in which opinion is far more divided. There one may find Richard Knowles's "Two *Lears*? By Shakespeare?" which aggressively attacks the Reviser evidence, and T. H. Howard-Hill's useful clarification of the question at stake in his notion of "considered second thoughts"—which variants are Shakespeare's own reconsiderations and which are the result of others' mistakes, accidents and interventions?

The maddening difficulties editing *Lear* presents are limned in *Berryman's Shakespeare,* edited and introduced by John Haffenden (Farrar, Straus and Giroux, 1999), which recounts the poet John Berryman's struggle with the *Lear* textual mystery. Haffenden is the devoted biographer of William Empson as well.

Steven Urkowitz, *Shakespeare's Revision of King Lear* (Princeton University Press, 1980), offers perhaps the best close-reading exegesis of the variations in the two texts and deserves to be returned to print.

Chapter Five: The Great Shakespeare "Funeral Elegy" Fiasco

I shouldn't neglect to mention that at the luncheon for Stephen Greenblatt I describe in chapter 4, Julia Reidhead of Norton's American complete works of Shakespeare, edited by Greenblatt, informed me that Norton was dropping the "Funeral Elegy" and Don Foster's introduction to it from the forthcoming revised edition.

To further clarify the matter of Don Foster, me, "Wanda Tinasky" and Thomas Pynchon, my original essay on the question has been reprinted in *The Secret Parts of Fortune;* I gave him credit in print for his solution in *The New York Observer,* September 10, 2001. His misrepresentation of my position appears in his *Author Unknown: On the Trail of Anonymous* (Henry Holt, 2000). My expression of agnosticism in fuller form—"I can't make up my mind. But I do know that if Wanda is not Mr. Pynchon, she or he, . . . ought to step forward to be honored for capturing . . . the spirit of Mr. Pynchon in her prose"—clearly does not imply I jumped on the Pynchon attribution bandwagon in a Fosterian way.

Foster's attempt to make this read as an endorsement of the Pynchon authorship theory is strained, to say the least.

The best, most comprehensive account of "the politics of attribution" in this affair can be found in Brian Vickers's *"Counterfeiting" Shakespeare: Evidence, Authorship, and John Ford's "Funerall Elegye"* (Cambridge University Press, 2002), which also deals with Gary Taylor's attribution of "Shall I Die?" to Shakespeare.

But when speaking of Professor Vickers I can't miss the opportunity to recommend his devastating critique of Theory sophistry, *Appropriating Shakespeare: Contemporary Critical Quarrels* (rpt. Yale University Press, 1994), which offers a thorough deconstruction of deconstruction and other Theory fashions, the best of its kind—although Graham Bradshaw's *Misrepresentations: Shakespeare and the Materialists* (Cornell University Press, 1993) is also powerful in a similar skeptical way.

The scholar Bruce Young felt I was being unfair to American academics in my initial *New York Observer* pieces criticizing the acceptance of the "Funeral Elegy." In a letter to the paper he argued that they didn't accept the attribution "en masse," that many—most, he believes—didn't buy it, the way J. J. Tobin doesn't in the Riverside introduction to it I quote.

It's perhaps true that many American academics didn't accept it, but few spoke out against this gross distortion of Shakespeare the writer—few published any critiques of the acceptance of a poem that would inevitably distort how Shakespeare's evolution as an artist and a person was understood, if the attribution were accepted. Yes there was vociferous discussion on the restricted SHAKSPER list, and as I mentioned a SHAKSPER post from John Kennedy first identified Ford, not Shakespeare, as the Elegy's author. But I still believe that more American academics should have cared more about what was—and wasn't—Shakespearean and why they believed this to be so. Cared enough to be appalled at the Elegy attribution and to come out and say so publicly in print. Few did, a phenomenon I can't help attributing to the "death"—or irrelevance—of the author in postmodern theory.

Chapter Six: The Indian, the Judean and Hand D

I should note that the play text in which Hand D appears is often referred to as *The Booke of "Sir Thomas More"* since the play never was, so far as we know, actually printed, and thus exists as a kind of handwritten "prompt book," thus "booke of the play."

Editions of the whole play, not just the 147-line scene and the 21-line soliloquy (which are to be found in most contemporary Complete Works editions), have been hard to find, but recently Oxford University Press announced it would bring out an edition of the entire play, certainly a worthy project since it juxtaposes the array and differential degree of playwrighting talent among Shakespeare's contemporaries within the framework of a single play.

The key texts containing the arguments about Hand D include *Shakespeare's Hand in the Play of Sir Thomas More,* edited by A. W. Pollard, first published in 1923, reprinted in 1976 by Folcroft Editions, though not readily available. R. W. Chambers's perceptive essay on the thematic similarities, such as "self devouring" and appetite as a "universal wolf," was called "Some Sequences of Thought in Shakespeare and in 147 Lines of 'Thomas More,' " and first appeared in the *Modern Language Review,* January 1, 1931. By the way, I should have added to my catalog of such images Othello's famous evocation of "the cannibals that each other eat / The Anthropophagi."

A different, more postmodern but smart examination of the theme of authority, power and human nature can be found in Hugh Grady's *Shakespeare's Universal Wolf* (Clarendon Press, 1996). And *Shakespeare and "Sir Thomas More": Essays on the Play and Its Shakespearean Interest,* edited by T. H. Howard-Hill, (Cambridge University Press, 1989), set the stage for the current near-canonization of the play.

Paul Werstine's dissent, "Shakespeare More or Less: A. W. Pollard and Twentieth Century Shakespeare Editing," appeared in *Florilegium* 16 (1999), Carleton University, Ottawa.

Edward Pechter's critique of Werstine's critique of textual editing can be found in "Crisis in Editing," *Shakespeare Survey* (2006). The most recent of Pechter's valuable and accessible (if challenging) assessments of leading tendencies in Shakespeare scholarship is *What Was Shakespeare? Renaissance Plays and Changing Critical Practice* (Cornell University Press, 1995).

Chapter Seven: The Search for the Shakespearean in a Delicate Pause

I strongly recommend John Barton's *Playing Shakespeare* (Anchor, 2001), which offers Sir Peter Hall's longtime collaborator and RSC cofounder's highly influential, antithesis-based method of speaking the speech.

And of course the entire *Players of Shakespeare* series—now six successive volumes from Cambridge University Press, edited variously by Philip Brockbank, Robert Smallwood, and Russell Jackson—makes for wonderful reading with its essays by actors and actresses on their Shakespearean roles, how they approached them and what they made of them.

As for Sir Peter himself, *Shakespeare's Advice to the Players* (Theatre Communications Group, 2003) and *Exposed by the Mask* (Theatre Communications Group, 2000) compress his years of experience and heartfelt, hard-won insights into acting and staging into vigorously and forcefully argued form.

An entertaining if sometimes tormented portrayal of the struggle between Hall and Laurence Olivier over the direction of the Royal National Theatre and the direction of staged Shakespeare can be found in *Peter Hall's Diaries: The Story of a Dramatic Battle* (Harper & Row, 1984), one of the best books of backstage Shakespearean intrigue one can find.

Cic Berry's most well-known work is *The Actor and the Text* (Applause Acting Series, 2000).

Patsy Rodenburg's *Speaking Shakespeare* (Palgrave Macmillan, 2002) is an admirable companion for those who want to pursue Shakespearean speech further.

Kristin Linklater's *Freeing Shakespeare's Voice* (Theatre Communications Group, 1992) is spoken of highly by many working actors and actresses, although a bit too New Agey for some.

But as counterpoint to these, Sarah Werner's critique of their unintended consequences, *Shakespeare and Feminist Performance* (Routledge, 2001), is worth paying attention to.

Chapter Eight: The Spell of the Shakespearean in "Original Spelling"

I'd recommend the Everyman editions as a gentle way of easing back into the unmodernized realm. They offer skillfully conflated modernized *typography* (but generally *unmodernized* spelling), single-volume paperback editions of the plays. John Andrews calls them "hybrid" editions incorporating as many features of the early printings as he could. Of course there are at least two relatively accessible unmodernized editions of the First Folio, the Routledge facsimile version (London, 1998) with the original typeface and the Applause First Folio "in modern type." There is also the expensive but authoritative Norton facsimile. It remains for some enterprising soul to offer unmodernized editions of, at least, the generally recognized "Good" Quartos.

As to the "shrewdly" and "shroudly" question, the newly available text of Ann Thompson and Neil Taylor's Third Arden *Hamlet* (Thomson Learning, 2006) changes "shroudly" to "shrewdly" in its 1604 Quarto text version, and explains in a footnote that "Q2's spelling, 'shroudly,' is attractive for its (fortuitous) association with 'shroud,' but it does not occur elsewhere, whereas 'shrodly' is recorded as an obsolete spelling of *shrewdly.*" In other words they imply there's no intentionality behind the use of "shroudly" or none that necessarily—as opposed to "fortuitously"—evokes a ghostly *shroud.* This may be true of the text on the page; a lot, however, depends on how it was pronounced to an audience's ear when played on stage. I like preserving "shroudly," or "enfolding" both versions. Otherwise "shroudly" disappears like the Ghost, survives only in the "band of terror" collations, a kind of textual purgatory, not unlike that occupied by Hamlet's father's enshrouded spirit.

The obverse of John Andrews's argument for unmodernization can be found in Stanley Wells's essay in *Modernizing Shakespeare's Spelling* (Clarendon Press, 1979). First it should be noted that Wells is not an *opponent* of unmodernized Shakespeare and that in their New Oxford Shakespeare project of the mid-eighties Wells and Gary Taylor produced an entire edition of all Shakespeare in (mostly) pure unmodernized form which was a major step in advancing the unmodernizing cause.

But in his Clarendon Press essay Wells argues that the exploration of how to modernize "may be seen, not as some would have it, as a work of popularization, even vulgarization, but a means of exploring Shakespeare's text that can make a real contribution to scholarship." In other words, he's saying that traveling the same road, but in an opposite direction from John Andrews, from unmodernized to modernized, encourages a close attentiveness to the language that often discloses nuances otherwise not spelled out, so to speak.

An illuminating debate about the implications of modernizing a single name—whether to call Pistol in *Henry V* "Ancient Pistol" as the unmodernized version has it—or "Ensign Pistol" as even the Oxford *Henry V* edited by unmodernized advocate Gary Taylor modernizes it, can be found in the winter 1985 edition of *Shakespeare Quarterly,* vol. 36, no. 4. It's an "Exchange" that begins with Jennifer Kraus's "Name Calling and the New Oxford *Henry V*" (p. 523) and continues with Gary Taylor's response, "Ancients and Moderns."

In her persuasive essay Kraus calls into question the Oxford decision to substitute "Ensign" for "Ancient" as the rank of the braggart soldier Pistol is rendered in the original unmodernized texts. She argues that "the 'modernization' of Pistol's title from Ancient to Ensign . . . alter[s] our critical interpretation of Pistol, and even, I submit, our view of the play as a whole."

Her essay even scores some points with the often unswayable Gary Taylor, who concedes in his reply that while "Shakespeare did sometimes use 'ancient' to mean 'ensign,' without any intimation of antiquity . . . and no immediate juxtaposition of 'old' and 'ancient' is demanded," nonetheless, as Peter Alexander put it, "Ensign . . . introduces inappropriate notions of youthful Victorian chivalry and it spoils Shakespeare's joke." In other words, unmodernized "Ancient Pistol" has comic, thematic resonances with Pistol's over-the-top, over-the-hill, rusty gallantry that "ensign" does not signify.

For those who wish to venture beyond mere spelling and go deeper into the profundities that can be found in the minutiae of Shakespearean punctuation, I'd suggest *Punctuation and Its Dramatic Value in Shakespearean Drama* (Associated University Presses, London, 1995) by Anthony Graham-White.

And while it doesn't fall precisely into the category of this chapter I wouldn't want to miss the opportunity to recommend George T. Wright on metrics. *Shakespeare's Metrical Art* (rpt. University of California Press, 1991) pushes to the very limits the expressive weight that can be imputed to metrical anomalies in Shakespeare. Its attentiveness is a pleasure, but inevitably (to me) raises the question of how much intentionality, how much is being read (often brilliantly) into said anomalies that may pass by all but the most gifted readers such as Wright. But reading Wright (reading right?) is a remedy for this.

Chapter Nine: Dueling Shylocks

On the question of acting and "original" emotion, one of the best ways of capturing the multiplicity of potential ways of playing Shakespeare is to pick up one of Marvin Rosenberg's *Masks* series. The late Rosenberg deserves more recognition as an exhaustive and intelligent chronicler of how roles were played, or reported to have been played, in some of the greatest Shakespearean productions over the centuries

In *The Masks of Hamlet* (University of Delaware Press, 1992) he fills 971 pages with eyewitness descriptions of how each scene, sometimes each line, was played individually and ensemble. Cumulatively it's dazzling and prodigious in the range of tone and subtleties it evokes. His works, which include *The Masks of Lear,* of *Othello,* of *Macbeth* (and the posthumously published *Antony and Cleopatra*), are the equivalent of the variorum of the stage. I recommend as well his *Adventures of a Shakespeare Scholar* (University of Delaware Press, 1997), his engaging autobiography.

The Garrick gesture and other moments in the history of the gesture on the Shakespearean stage are assessed in David Bevington's valuable study, *Action Is Eloquence: Shakespeare's Language of Gesture* (Harvard University Press, 1984).

John Gross's *Shylock: A Legend and Its Legacy* (Simon & Schuster, 1992) is the most intelligent account of the ugly history that I've come upon.

A surprisingly valuable (especially considering its nonstandard title for an academic book) look at the concept of "bonds" as manifested in *The Merchant of Venice* and the rest of Shakespeare can be found in Frederick Turner's *Shakespeare's Twenty-first Century Economics: The Morality of Love and Money* (Oxford University Press, 1999).

This is to be radically distinguished from such How to Succeed in Business by Reading Shakespeare books as Norman Augustine and Kenneth Adelman's *Shakespeare in Charge* (Miramax, 1999), which I reviewed in *Salon* in 1999.

I also found Stephen Orgel's "Imagining Shylock" chapter in his beautiful book on the history of Shakespearean images—*Imagining Shakespeare* (Palgrave Macmillan, 2003)—to be of great value.

And a recent collection of essays on the play, *The Merchant of Venice: New Critical Essays,* edited by John W. Mahon and Ellen Macleod Mahon (Routledge, 2002), demonstrates the wide range of differing contemporary perspectives.

Nor should I neglect—since I devote so much consideration to the "turquoise ring" device in the Pacino *Merchant,* Grace Tiffany's new novel by that name, *The Turquoise Ring* (Berkley Hardcover, 2005).

Finding William Empson's *Milton's God* (Chatto & Windus, 1961) was difficult and rewarding. As more of Empson's works are being brought back into print with the revival of his reputation and the publication of the first volume of John Haffenden's biography, *William Empson: Volume I: Among the Mandarins* (Oxford University Press, 2005), someone should bring *Milton's God,* this brilliant subversive book, back. It amounts to Empson's last testament.

Chapter Ten: Shakespeare on Film: A Contrarian Argument

Errol Morris drew my attention to George Orwell's valuable 1947 essay "Lear, Tolstoy and the Fool" (widely available on the Web), which anticipates Mailer's speculations about Tolstoy's hostility to Shakespeare's cinematic elision of closely observed psychological evolution—and helps explain Tolstoy's failure to understand Shakespeare in general.

For those skeptical of recent Luhrmann-like experiments in Shakespeare, I should like to recommend the less operatic, more minimalist and playfully intellectual *Hamlet* of Michael Almereyda. The one popularly known as the "Ethan Hawke Hamlet," or, as I think of it—considering Hawke's take on the Prince—"the Holden Caulfield *Hamlet.*" It demonstrates that filmed Shakespeare can be a witty riff on the full-blown play. I recall being stunned attending a preview of it at a Shakespeare Association of America annual convention in Montreal. A hall filled with three hundred or more serious-minded scholars watched, genuinely entertained by the film, applauded it vociferously and engaged in an enthusiastic dialogue with the director, who I thought showed great (justified) courage in showing his film to that kind of audience first. See if you agree.

There's a book-length account called *John Gielgud Directs Richard Burton in "Hamlet"* (Random House, 1967) a rehearsal diary by an actor who played the minor role of the Gentleman in that production and who took notes and smuggled in a tape recorder in a briefcase to tape Gielgud and Burton's dialogues. Not very Gentlemanly, but I'm glad he did, because he preserves for our guilty souls the intimate conversation of two of the greatest Shakespearean actors of the century as they prepare for the production.

I wish I had more space to praise more film and television productions. I'm one of the few people who really *enjoyed* Peter Brook's long-lost seventy-minute 1953 television version of *Lear* starring Orson Welles in a ridiculously horned helmet. Brook gave me the impression he hated it, did not like to be reminded that it still existed. But it's out there (go to the Poor Yorick website for such rarities). And then Julie Taymor's *Titus,* BBC TV's *Troilus and Cressida,* Michael Hordern as BBC TV's Lear and Prospero, John Gielgud voicing all the roles in Peter Greenaway's *Prospero's Books,* Ian McKellen's *Richard III.* There's a lot to like, much to love.

But there has been a valuable development in Shakespearean film studies, the development of an eloquent language of praise, represented by any and all the works of Herbert Coursen, Samuel Crowl and Kenneth Rothwell, for instance (although needless to say they have their problems with some works as well). Crowl's *Shakespeare at the Cineplex: The Kenneth Branagh Era* (Ohio University Press, 2003) is a good example. Coursen pioneered Shakespearean television criticism with *Watching Shakespeare on Television* (Fairleigh Dickinson University Press, 1993). I also admire Anthony Davies's work, including *Filming Shakespeare's Plays* (Cambridge, 1988).

Chapter Eleven: Peter Brook: The Search for the Secret Play

Most readers will be familiar with the reason I used a quote from Patrick Stewart as a semi-demi-epigraph to this chapter, but for those not: before his *Star Trek* fame eclipsed everything else, Patrick Stewart was—still is—one of the most widely admired Shakespearean actors of his generation in the United Kingdom. I was thrilled just watching a videotape of his Prospero in the New York Shakespeare Festival's Central Park *Tempest.*

When Peter Brook spoke of Shakespeare's generosity in emptying himself out, becoming, in both senses of the phrase, "no one," I recalled something Jorge Luis Borges said about Shakespeare in a short story whose name I'd forgotten. Fortunately, the key Borges quote appeared in the essay by Anne Barton in the May 11, 2006, *New York Review of Books.* She quotes the passage (from the story "Everything and Nothing") in which God speaks to a Shakespeare haunted by being "no one": "I too," Borges has God say, "am not I; I dreamed the world as you, Shakespeare, dreamed your own work, and among the forms of my dream are you, who like me are many, yet no one."

Interesting, in the Peter Brook connection, how Borges's God "dreamed the world." A dream again. We are living in His dream. The way we live in Shakespeare's dream in effect. Alexandre Dumas said, "After God, Shakespeare has created most." But what if, in a certain way, Shakespeare created *more* (that is, more than God could have dreamed up Himself, more than Darwin dreamed), something utterly unnecessary to existence or survival, something unimaginable by the spiritually inclined, nondetermined by the laws of science, an entity not "necessary" in the strictest Ockham's razor sense of necessity?

Brook's *Hamlet,* it should be noted, began as *Qui est là?* ("Who's there?"), originally done in a French translation which Brook claimed gave it a new kind of energy. Andy Lavender's study *Hamlet in Pieces* (Continuum, 2003) offers three idiosyncratic versions of the play including Brook's, Robert Lepage's and Robert Wilson's.

I've already mentioned Brook's *Evoking Shakespeare,* but his immensely influential book on theater in general, *The Empty Space* (MacGibbon & Kee, 1968), speaks to the genesis of his vision of emptiness, the vibrant silence. Brook's autobiography, *Threads of Time* (Methuen, 1998), may seem a bit reticent but two books by Brook followers, my colleague John Heilpern's *Conference of the Birds: The Story of Peter Brook in Africa* (Faber & Faber, 1977) and Margaret Croyden's *Conversations with Peter Brook: 1970–2000* (Faber & Faber, 2003), supply valuable observations and insight into his work. As does Michael Kustow's *Peter Brook: A Biography* (St. Martin's Press, 2005).

Chapter Twelve: "You Can't Have Him, Harold!": The Battle over Bloom and Bloom's Falstaff

The most consistently illuminating study I've found of the intersection of directors and textual editors, and directors *as* textual editors, is Alan C. Dessen's *Rescripting Shakespeare: The Text, the Director, and Modern Productions* (Cambridge University Press, 2002). Dessen is one of the most profoundly rewarding scholars of Shakespeare on stage.

It's unfortunate, the price structure of academic books being what it is, that *Harold Bloom's Shakespeare,* edited by Christy Desmet and Robert J. Sawyer (Palgrave Macmillan, 2002), essentially a collection of papers written for the Shakespeare Association seminar I mentioned as the stage on which Linda Charnes did her tour de force turn, lists for $79.95. (Charnes's essay is entitled "The 2% Solution: What Harold Bloom Forgot," and the book also offers the essay she cited by Sharon O'Dair, "On the Value of Being a Cartoon in Literature and Life," in addition to reflections by the always stimulating thinker Edward Pechter, and William Kerrigan's essay which offers the best defense of Bloom I've seen: "The Case for Bardolatry: Harold Bloom Rescues Shakespeare from His Critics."

I think everyone who's read Bloom, and those who have felt the Bloomian impact on Shakespeare studies, ought to have more easy access to some of these valuable reflections on Bloom—someone who might be called one of the great Shakespearean actors of our time.

And I should call attention to an essay that appeared just as I was to hand in these chapter notes, James Woods's "What Harold Bloom Can Teach God" (in the May 1, 2006, issue of *The New Republic*), on Bloom's pretentious but incoherent vision of the Old and New Testaments, testament to Bloom's preference for hectoring generalities over close reading.

Chapter Thirteen: Stephen Booth: 777 Types of Ambiguity

I've already made my plea for someone to bring Booth's *Essay on Shakespeare's Sonnets* back into print. I've just learned that another of his influential works, *King Lear, Macbeth, Indefinition, and Tragedy,* originally published in 1983 and long unavailable, has been reprinted in revised form by Cyber Editions. Time to bring back the *Essay*!

Devotees of the Sonnets will find different and valuable perspectives on them in both Helen Vendler's *The Art of Shakespeare's Sonnets* (Harvard University Press, 1997) and Katherine Duncan-Jones's Arden edition of the poems, and a survey of contemporary criticism in Paul Edmundson and Stanley Wells's *Shakespeare's Sonnets* (Oxford, 2004).

The questions raised by reconstructions such as the Globe and the Blackfriars remind me to point out the indispensibility of Andrew Gurr's work, especially *Playgoing in Shakespeare's London* (Cambridge University Press, rev. 2004).

The best place to begin reading Empson is his *Essays on Shakespeare* (Cambridge University Press, 1986) supplemented by a second volume of essays edited by John Haffenden, *The Strength of Shakespeare's Shrew* (Sheffield Academic Press, 1996). I still have a fondness for *Some Versions of Pastoral* (rpt. New Directions, 1960) and *Seven Types of Ambiguity* (rpt. New Directions, 1966). And for the true hard core, there is *The Structure of Complex Words* (Harvard University Press, 1989).

One of the most valuable discussions of the question of coherence, organic unity and the drawbacks of the search for it can be found in *Shakespearean Iconoclasm* by James R. Siemon (University of California Press, 1985). Perhaps *the* classic study of both/and ambiguity on the thematic level (as opposed to Booth's more purely esthetic focus) is Norman Rabkin's *Shakespeare and the Problem of Meaning* (University of Chicago Press, 1981). One of the best of Booth's fellow reader-reception types is Harry Berger, Jr., at the University of Santa Cruz, whose *Making Trifles of Terrors: Redistributing Complicities in Shakespeare* (Stanford University Press, 1997) is vital and challenging, and whose *Imaginary Audition: Shakespeare on Stage and Page* (University of California Press, 1989) was one of the first to make the case against what he calls "the New Histrionicism," the vogue for seeing Shakespeare as primarily, teleologically, a man of the stage rather than a man of the page. A case for the meditative contemplative rehearsing of the language (and reflection upon the reactions it provokes that are possible only in reading) is championed over the fleeting sounds of the words in performance, which rarely offer such opportunity.

I'm not sure there's an either/or argument here, as opposed to both/and; both reading and seeing the plays can afford complementary excitements.

Chapter Fourteen: Looking for Love in As You Like It; *Looking for an Orgasm in* Romeo and Juliet

Dreams of Love and Power by Joseph H. Summers (Oxford University Press, 1984) is not necessarily an exception to Russ McDonald's observation about the absence of *contemporary* contentions about Love in Shakespeare, since it was published two decades before he made the statement. But it is worth reading (it was recommended to me by Prof. Grace Tiffany) especially because of its beautiful chapter on *The Winter's Tale.*

For those with a taste for an intelligent postmodern struggle to admit the legitimacy of beauty, a struggle which is a symptom of both beauty's exile from and return to critical thought, I'd recommend *Beauty and the Contemporary Sublime* by Jeremy Gilbert-Rolfe (Allworth Press, 1999).

And for an examination of the aftermath of the fading of Theory there is of course *Theory's Empire: An Anthology of Dissent,* edited by Daphne Patai and Will H. Corral (Columbia University Press, 2005), a heavyweight series of essays that has had a great impact, or the more lighthearted *life.after.theory,* edited by Michael Payne and John Schad and featuring conversations with Frank Kermode, the late Jacques Derrida, Toril Moi and Christopher Norris (Continuum, 2003).

On the question of the "late language" and more generally how we regard Shakespeare when he's not at his best, *"Bad" Shakespeare: Revaluations of the Shakespeare Canon,* edited by Maurice Charney (Associated University Presses, 1988), has many provocative essays.

The essay by Russ McDonald, "Late Shakespeare: Style and the Sexes," which I dwell on, can be found in a valuable collection of essays called *Shakespeare and Language,* edited by Catherine M. S. Alexander (Cambridge University Press, 2004).

Bruce Young noted in a SHAKSPER post another possible symptom of what I've called in this chapter the "Bermuda effect" at the 2005 Shakespeare Association of America convention: a talk I had the misfortune to miss by Michael Bristol on the rediscovery of "character" as a legitimate subject worthy of investigating.

Chapter Fifteen: "No Cause": The Unexpected Pleasures of Forgiveness

Anne Barton's essay "Shakespeare and the Limits of Language" appears in her *Essays, Mainly Shakespearean* (Cambridge University Press, 1994). My essay on "The Quality of Mercy" in *Henry V* appeared in *The Shakespeare Newsletter* (Summer 2003) and is reprinted in *Shakespearean Criticism* (Thomson Gale, 2006).

Forgive me for digressing to mention a delightful (for me anyway) exchange that grew out of the latter essay and continued in the Winter 2003/2004 and Spring 2004 issues of *SNL* with legendary textual scholar George Walton Williams, who very politely raised the question (in the Winter 2003/2004 issue) of whether I had correctly attributed a pun to Pistol in his line "Be merciful, great duke, to men of mould."

I had asserted a belief that when Pistol calls himself a man of "mould" he was making a pun on "mould" that "fuses fashion and decomposition." Professor Williams argued—on the basis of a nineteenth-century *OED* notation—that "mould was not yet in general use as a word for 'mold' or mode (as in fashion) when Pistol used it." Of course this depends on whether one means when Pistol uses it as a historical (fifteenth-century) character or as a sixteenth- or seventeenth-century Elizabethan stage character. Especially since we have Ophelia, in a play written probably a year or so later, referring to Hamlet as "the glass of fashion and the mold of form."

I agreed with Professor Williams's general point that it is problematic to find "retroactive puns" as I called them—puns based on the later usage of a word not then in fashion, probably not "available" to the writer, when the writer wrote. ("Prospero's cell," for instance, cannot refer doubly to a mobile phone.) But I argued (at great length) that there was evidence that "mould" *was* in fashion as a word for ideal form at the time it was written (witness Ophelia) and was thus available to Shakespeare's punning imagination.

Of course there was no definitive way of knowing whether at the very moment Shakespeare wrote Pistol's words he *was* in fact aware of both potential connotations of the word, or whether indeed he might have at that very moment *created* another meaning for the word. Or whether we were witnessing in the transition from Pistol to Ophelia the evanescent period in which mould became à la mode as well as decay, so to speak.

In any case it was one of those moments for me in which I was able to enjoy the sheer delight of scholarly disputation, of *attempting* to match wits with a legendary textual scholar and feeling myself part of the continuing community of academics and independent scholars and obsessives who felt the value in worrying over Shakespeare's words. Because in a way we were worrying over the way Shakespeare's mind worked when it was engaged at play in the field of words. In that most touchy of questions—whether puns were indeed his "fatal Cleopatra."

Since these are notes to a chapter about pleasure and forgiveness, I hope you will extend to me forgiveness for not attempting an impossibly exhaustive survey of Shakespearean commentary and exegesis (the World Shakespeare Bibliography online will do that for you). And in return I'll leave you with a guaranteed pleasurable recommendation: the aptly titled *After Shakespeare,* the British critic John Gross's compilation of "Writing Inspired by the World's Greatest Author" (Oxford University Press, 2003).

In addition to a treasury of provocative Shakespearean reflections by centuries of great writers, it includes two excerpts from Vladimir Nabokov, for me the only contemporary writer whose genius is analogous to Shakespeare's. Mr. Gross's first excerpt was the comic misprision of *Hamlet* in Nabokov's *Bend Sinister,* in which two professors in a northern European dictatorship argue over whether *Hamlet* is a political allegory and *Fortinbras* is the real hero (and whether Fortinbras's father impersonated the ghost of Hamlet's father to trick him into killing Claudius).

In Gross's excerpt from *Bend Sinister,* Nabokov tells of an American filmmaker who wants to make a film about all the parts *left out* of the play, including "Hamlet at Wittenberg, always late, missing G. Bruno's lectures." Giordano Bruno again! Shakespeare's contemporary and fellow theoretician of the infinite, on the faculty of Hamlet's college, the Hamlet who celebrates man's "infinite faculties" and has dreams (or nightmares) of being "king of infinite space."

And then Gross devotes a section to Shakespeare as "a presiding presence" in *Pale Fire,* my favorite modern novel, one named for a Shakespearean passage of course ("The moon's an arrant thief, / And her pale fire she snatches from the sun"), the passage from *Timon of Athens* about the ambiguity of artistic "originality."

And to my great delight Gross quotes one of my favorite passages in *Pale Fire.* From the poem called "Pale Fire," in which Nabokov's poet character John Shade writes of the possibility of the dead persisting in this world in the form of electricity. I'll leave you with it:

The dead, the gentle dead—who knows?—
In tungsten filaments abide,
And on my bedside glows
Another man's departed bride.

And maybe Shakespeare floods a whole
Town with innumerable lights. . . .

Acknowledgments

First I want to thank—well, *no,* I want to *acknowledge the role of*—Adolf Hitler. (Got your attention, you non-Acknowledgment-reader types, right?) Seriously, had it not been for the deep despair I spiraled into after I completed *Explaining Hitler* it's unlikely I would have undertaken *this* book. Spending ten years writing a book seeking an adequate explanation for Hitler's evil was depressing enough, but after I'd had to let go of the galleys of that book—largely a critique of the *failure* of most attempts at Hitler explanation—I found myself in a state far more bleak than my customary gloomy outlook on life. One that persisted even after the gratifying reception of that book. It was a state perhaps not unconnected with the dissatisfaction the *lack* of an explanation left behind. As it turned out the only thing that helped was to start walking around the city listening to Shakespeare tapes on a Walkman.

Without overstraining the symmetry, I think I found that immersing myself in the genius for creation Shakespeare represented was a powerful antidote to Hitler's hideous genius for destruction. Shakespeare's work embodied the obverse side of human nature from Hitler's. And then the bridge to this book occurred to me: the so-called exceptionalist question about the uniqueness of Hitler's evil. Was he on the extreme end of the continuum of other evildoers or was he off the grid, in a realm of radical evil all his own? Similarly with Shakespeare: Was he on the continuum of other great writers or did he represent a uniquely exceptional realm of imaginative creation? Like many of the other issues in the Shakespeare wars, a provocative but perhaps unresolvable question.

So let me acknowledge and thank all the Shakespeare audiotape makers: there's an unusually high standard among the various series I've found, and listening on audiotape turns the mind into a stage without audience distractions or often disappointing visuals.

And, of course, although it seems radically presumptuous, how could I pen an Acknowledgments that didn't acknowledge my lifelong, life-changing debt to the "onlie begetter," W.S.?

Nonetheless, in addition to Hitler-induced depression and Shakespeare-induced exhilaration, this book owes its existence to many more people and influences. I guess I'll begin with a couple of inciting incidents, the chief one being my astonishing good fortune at being present at Peter Brook's *Midsummer Night's Dream* at Stratford-on-Avon. I've dedicated the book to Peter Brook and his cast but I also want to thank him for his patience with me during both interviews and the Embarrassing Incident I relate in chapter 11.

Another important incident was my lunch with Nicholas Hytner, who, among many encouraging comments, suddenly made the issue of verse-speaking and the fracture within the

Royal Shakespeare Company over a delicate pause in the pentameter line seem like a kind of template for writing about other fractious issues, in other chapters.

Then there were the three Davids. First David Scott Kastan, professor at Columbia and one of the general editors of the Arden Shakespeare, who told me about the scholarly and human situation involved in the transition from Harold Jenkins's second Arden edition of *Hamlet* (the last Grand Unification *Hamlet*) to Ann Thompson's radically divided three-text third Arden edition. David encouraged me to pursue the controversy that became a nucleus of the future book. I don't wish to make him responsible for any of my more opinionated judgments, just to thank him for getting me started.

The second David is D. Remnick of *The New Yorker,* who is himself quite knowledgeable about *Hamlet* questions and who understood why apparently arcane new textual arguments about the play mattered enough to underwrite my original travels among textual scholars and skillfully (with the help of Amy Tubke-Davidson and Dorothy Wickenden, among others at *The New Yorker*) turn a thirty-thousand-word manuscript on textual scholar issues into a manageable magazine story.

And then, preeminent in the development of this book, among distinguished Davids, David Ebershoff, who became my editor from almost the beginning. Which shouldn't take away credit from the estimable Jonathan Karp, my editor for *Explaining Hitler,* and the sagacious Ann Godoff, then head of Random House, under whose auspices the book began its life. I owe them both thanks for their belief in the concept and for not being fazed by my original sixty-chapter outline.

And after they left, their gifted successors, Daniel Menaker and Gina Centrello (president and publisher of the Random House Publishing Group, respectively), who both became valuable supporters who made me and my book feel more than welcome—for which I'm deeply grateful. As I am to so many others at Random House, including legal eagle Amelia Zalcman, managing editor Benjamin Dreyer, production editor Steve Messina, both wise and patient, the astute copy editor Michael Burke, and proofreaders Allison Merrill, Carol Shookhoff, Adrian James and Maralee Youngs. I don't want to neglect an editor, Judy Sternlight, who brought me into the Royal Shakespeare Company publication process; its editor Jonathan Bate, who had long been one of my favorite Shakespearean writers; Barbara Fillon; and Paul Taunton and Kate Hamill, David Ebershoff's able assistants.

I also want to add special thanks to Gabrielle Bordwin, who designed the book jacket, and to Karen Lau, who helped get it just right.

But to return to the third David . . . Since writers' praise of their editors inevitably labors under the shadow of mere obligation I will instead report what I almost invariably hear from the smartest writers, editors and publishing people when I tell them David Ebershoff is my editor: some variation on: "Oh you are *so* lucky!" And it's true I am. To have an editor so smart, who also has a gifted novelist's sensitivity to language and who also is able to say ever so diplomatically, when he reads an eighty-page draft of a chapter, "I have some problems with the middle forty pages" (and of course be right about it), is a rare blessing.

Another blessing of equal magnitude: Kathy Robbins, a literary agent who possesses one of the sharpest editorial minds, one of the sharpest senses of humor and one of the kindest hearts I know. She has always gone the extra mile for me when it comes to reading and rereading chapters and giving me invaluable advice about literary and not strictly literary matters. Kathy, I hope you know how much you mean to me.

Nor should I neglect the talented people with whom Kathy surrounds herself. So many have been snatched away in the seven years I've worked on this book, but let me pay tribute to the current crew, notably the distinguished agent and poker shark David Halpern and the cast of talented associates including: Coralie Hunter, Yaniv Soha, Kate Rizzo, Rachelle Bergstein, and Carol Choi, among others.

I want to thank the people at *The New York Observer.* The paper's inspired editor, Peter Kaplan, has given me an unparalleled opportunity to write about the clash of ideas in its pages, including a number of Shakespearean obsessions, such as my campaign against the misattributed "Funeral Elegy." I also want to thank my *Observer* editors over the years, including Maria Russo, Petra Bartosiewicz, Lizzy Ratner, Suzy Hansen and I-Huei Go. In addition, longtime colleagues including Tom McGeveran, Jake Brooks, Alexander Jacobs, Choire Sicha, Brian Kempner, Rick Syzmanski and Matt Grace, and éminence grise Peter Stevenson, as well as the too-many-to-name-them-all, ever-changing cast of talented people who have passed through the place. And Arthur Carter, who has created and supported a unique paper that became a unique voice of the city—and a home for me.

I'd like to thank the Shakespearean professors I studied with at Yale, Alvin Kernan and Howard Felperin, and the Chaucer and seventeenth-century specialists Henry Schroeder and M.J.K. O'Loughlin, respectively, for encouraging my affinity for close reading.

Much gratitude as well to Adriana Mnuchin and Nancy Becker, cofounders of the Shakespeare Society, a wonderful institution that has provided many important evenings of Shakespearean experiences, introductions to actors such as Keith Baxter (who memorably played Prince Hal in Orson Welles's *Chimes at Midnight* among many other Shakespearean roles) and Roger Rees (who's played with distinction just about every leading role in Shakespeare). The Shakespeare Society also allowed me to present an evening of film and panel discussion in which I could work out my thoughts on the differing merits of Shakespearean film and stage. And I owe thanks to the panelists who helped me: critic John Simon, directors Michael Kahn and Michael Almereyda and actor Liev Schreiber.

John Andrews and his Shakespeare Guild have been responsible for an equal number of provocative evenings and encounters with Shakespearean actors and directors as readers may have noted throughout the text. And Andrews himself has been a valuable source of thinking not just on the "unmodernized spelling" question but on the Shakespearean experience in all its incarnations.

Thanks as well to the New York Shakespeare Festival for giving me so many romantic evenings at the Central Park stage and for permitting me to write the program notes for the outdoor *Twelfth Night* and the indoor *Pericles* directed by Brian Kulick.

And to Brian Kulick, heartfelt thanks: I feel I probably learned more about how Shakespeare is staged—and how to think about Shakespeare in a more theatrical way—from my conversations over the years with Brian, who is not only one of the most talented at staging Shakespeare, but someone who offered some of the most profound ways of thinking about the plays I'd come upon. As is evident in the text, my conversations with directors Barry Edelstein and Jeffrey Horowitz have been similarly valuable.

I'd also like to thank Harry Keyishian and Fairleigh Dickinson University for inviting me to participate in their valuable colloquia.

Alex Star and Emily Eakin saw their magazine (*Lingua Franca*) fold before I could finish my assignments for them, but they enabled me to have an important conversation with Christopher Ricks, who himself merits thanks for his valuable insights and for being forbearing about the actual interview's evanescence.

My conversations with Dan Kornstein over the years about Shakespeare and literature (he is the author of the valuable study of Shakespeare and legal thematics *Kill All the Lawyers?: Shakespeare's Legal Appeal*) have been helpful as has been his wise counsel in matters legal.

The all-knowing Thomas Pendleton, coeditor of *The Shakespeare Newsletter,* has been a valuable interlocutor and discussant, has published my speculations in his pages and was kind enough to give an early stage of the manuscript a once-over to help me eliminate major errors. Any that remain have almost certainly been introduced later by me.

Thanks as well to Stephen Bates of the *Wilson Quarterly* for inviting me to do a review essay on Shakespearean staging, to Jodi Kantor at *The New York Times* for encouraging me to write about both *Henry IV* and *Henry V* and to Julie Just at *The New York Times Book Review* for encouraging my essay on the state of Theory, which led me to explore the future direction of Shakespeare studies.

My debt to Professor Russ McDonald is great both for the inspiring and challenging quality of his work and for his kindness and patience with my questions. The same could be said of just about everyone interviewed herein. And I've had valuable conversations with Barbara Mowat, Ed Pechter, Grace Tiffany, Tiffany Stern and Ralph Alan Cohen. Thomas Berger, A. R. Braunmuller and George Walton Williams were generous in admitting me into their company at a couple of scholarly conferences, as was John Meagher, author of the valuable work of dramaturgy *Shakespeare's Shakespeare.*

I'd like to tip my hat as well to the collective membership of the SHAKSPER electronic discussion list for the numerous provocative questions, suggestions, discussions and arguments that made its posts something to look forward to.

Errol Morris, Jonathan Rosen, Steven Weisman and Helen Whitney are friends who over the years have also been valuable sounding boards for testing out my ideas on this subject, although they bear no responsibility for my conjectures.

Two gifted editors and writers, Naomi Wax and Tara McKelvey, were kind enough to read drafts of several chapters and make helpful suggestions about them.

Noah Kimerling is a wise protective figure for many writers and I'm lucky to have found shelter under his umbrella. Dr. Joseph Fetto, Dr. Paul Belsky, Dr. George Dolger, Dr. Joyce Gerdis: thank you for keeping me going.

Turning to the more personal or the personal and professional, I'd like to thank a special group of friends, and people I've been close to or relied upon in various ways through the years I was writing his book. None rivals the contribution of my sister, the brilliant psychotherapist Ruth Rosenbaum, whose kindness, support and insight and wisdom have meant the world to me.

I feel nobody could have stronger or more supportive friends than Betsy Carter and Gary Hoenig. I've relied for years on the kindness and good humor of Helen Rogan and Alfred Gingold, and Alfred was responsible for the rediscovery of the vinyl recording of Olivier's amazing *Othello,* whose existence I only learned about at a party given by my friends Fred Kaplan and Brooke Gladstone during a conversation with Brooke's sisters Stacey and Lisa.

Special thanks to the talented Nina Roberts for the jacket photo and for having Nina Roberts's unique sense of humor.

Special thanks to Susan Kamil for her friendship and advice.

Special thanks to Liz Groden, whose word processing and research skills made writing this book possible.

Special thanks to Cynthia Ozick and Billy Collins for their generous early response to my manuscript.

Also important to my getting the book done: David Livingston, who did his best to keep order among my cluttered and collapsing stacks of Shakespeare books, the late Faye Beckerman, who cared for my cats, along with Dr. George Korin, Christine Sarkissian and Rachael Koeson. Special thanks to my high school classmate Holly Stavers, tireless sparkplug of the wonderful cat-rescue group City Critters, who was a source of great solace in finding me a successor to my orange cat Stumpy—my new orange cat, Bruno, who's been a valuable comic companion during long sessions of reading Shakespeare commentary.

My apologies to John Kennedy for inadvertently identifying him on page 187 in the first and second printings of the hardcover edition of this book as the first to name John Ford as the author of the "Funeral Elegy." This reference should have read, and now does, "Richard Kennedy."

And now a more amorphous but no less highly prized list of friends who have been helpful to me in Shakespearean and non-Shakespearean ways, including some who have sat through some bad Shakespeare for my sake:

So, thanks to Stanley Mieses, Jesse Sheidlower and Elizabeth Bogner, Nancy Donahoe, Chris Schoemer, Rachel Donadio and Daniel Kunitz. And to David Hirshey and other companions of the alas, now rarely reconvened Game (including David Blum, Gil Schwartz, Gene Stone, Robert Asahina, Richard Ben Cramer, Peter Herbst, Tom Jencks, and Michael Hirschorn, to name a few I've lost poker money to). To Liz Hecht, Kenneth Gross, Herbert Weil, Caroline Marshall, Terry Karten, Amy Gutman, Laura Frost, Zoe Rosenfeld, Virginia Heffernan, David Samuels, Michael Drosnin, Jeffrey Goldberg, Craig and Allison Karpel, Kathryn Paulsen, Petra Bartosiewicz, Larry Rosenblatt, the Slymans, Sarah Kernochan, Judith Shulevitz, Lisa Singh, Robert Vare, Antonia Cedrone, Natalie Standiford, the Greenberg family, Deb Friedman, Lauren Thierry, Jim Watkins, Sarah Alcorn, Eve Babitz, Dora Steinberg, Mark Steinberg, Tom Disch, David Yezzi, John Roche, Rebecca Wright, Michael Yogg, Gil Roth, Richard Molyneux and Julia Sheehan.

Profound gratitude to Tara McKelvey for helping me understand the meaning of love in the Sonnets.

Much appreciation to Diana Fox at Random House for her valuable work in preparing this paperback edition.

And to the many whom my poor memory—but not lack of gratitude—has caused me to neglect, let me "assault mercy" and ask your forgiveness.

Index

A

D

G

J

K

N

O

P

Q

Y

Z

PHOTO: NINA ROBERTS

RON ROSENBAUM studied literature at Yale, and briefly at Yale Graduate School, before leaving to write. His work has appeared in *Harper's, The New York Times Magazine, The New Yorker, The Atlantic, The New York Observer,* and *Slate,* among other publications. His book *Explaining Hitler,* a *New York Times* Notable Book of the Year in 1998, has been translated into ten languages. Random House published a collection of his essays and journalism, *The Secret Parts of Fortune,* in 2000 and an anthology he edited, *Those Who Forget the Past: The Question of Anti-Semitism,* in 2004. He has been a member of the advisory board of the Royal Shakespeare Company's publications project. He lives in New York City.